MONEY, BANK CREDIT, AND ECONOMIC CYCLES

SECOND EDITION

MONEY, BANK CREDIT, AND ECONOMIC CYCLES

SECOND EDITION

JESÚS HUERTA DE SOTO

TRANSLATED BY MELINDA A. STROUP

Ludwig
von Mises
Institute
AUBURN, ALABAMA

First Spanish edition 1998, *Dinero, Crédito Bancario y Ciclos Económicos*, Unión Editorial, Madrid
Copyright © 1998 Jesús Huerta de Soto

Second Spanish edition 2002, Unión Editorial, Madrid
Third Spanish edition 2006, Unión Editorial, Madrid

Copyright © 2006, 2009 Jesús Huerta de Soto
Money, Bank Credit, and Economic Cycles
Translated from Spanish by Melinda A. Stroup
First English edition 2006
Second English edition 2009

Cover design: Photograph by Guillaume Dubé of a series of arches in a cloister in Salamanca, Spain.

Ludwig von Mises Institute
518 West Magnolia Avenue
Auburn, Alabama 63832-4528

ISBN: 978-1-933550-39-8

CONTENTS

PREFACE TO THE
SECOND ENGLISH EDITION

I am happy to present the second English edition of *Money, Bank Credit, and Economic Cycles*. Its appearance is particularly timely, given that the severe financial crisis and resulting worldwide economic recession I have been forecasting, since the first edition of this book came out ten years ago, are now unleashing their fury.

The policy of artificial credit expansion central banks have permitted and orchestrated over the last fifteen years could not have ended in any other way. The expansionary cycle which has now come to a close began gathering momentum when the American economy emerged from its last recession (fleeting and repressed though it was) in 2001 and the Federal Reserve reembarked on the major artificial expansion of credit and investment initiated in 1992. This credit expansion was not backed by a parallel increase in voluntary household saving. For many years, the money supply in the form of bank notes and deposits has grown at an average rate of over 10 percent per year (which means that every seven years the total volume of money circulating in the world has doubled). The media of exchange originating from this severe fiduciary inflation have been placed on the market by the banking system as newly-created loans granted at very low (and even negative in real terms) interest rates. The above fueled a speculative bubble in the shape of a substantial rise in the prices of capital goods, real-estate assets and the securities which represent them, and are exchanged on the stock market, where indexes soared.

Curiously, like in the "roaring" years prior to the Great Depression of 1929, the shock of monetary growth has not significantly influenced the prices of the subset of consumer goods and services (approximately only one third of all goods). The last decade, like the 1920s, has seen a remarkable increase in productivity as a result of the introduction on a massive scale of new technologies and significant entrepreneurial innovations which, were it not for the injection of money and credit, would have given rise to a healthy and sustained reduction in the unit price of consumer goods and services. Moreover, the full incorporation of the economies of China and India into the globalized market has boosted the real productivity of consumer goods and services even further. The absence of a healthy "deflation" in the prices of consumer goods in a stage of such considerable growth in productivity as that of recent years provides the main evidence that the monetary shock has seriously disturbed the economic process. I analyze this phenomenon in detail in chapter 6, section 9.

As I explain in the book, artificial credit expansion and the (fiduciary) inflation of media of exchange offer no short cut to stable and sustained economic development, no way of avoiding the necessary sacrifice and discipline behind all high rates of voluntary saving. (In fact, particularly in the United States, voluntary saving has not only failed to increase in recent years, but at times has even fallen to a negative rate.) Indeed, the artificial expansion of credit and money is never more than a short-term solution, and that at best. In fact, today there is no doubt about the recessionary quality the monetary shock always has in the long run: newly-created loans (of money citizens have not first saved) immediately provide entrepreneurs with purchasing power they use in overly ambitious investment projects (in recent years, especially in the building sector and real estate development). In other words, entrepreneurs act as if citizens had increased their saving, when they have not actually done so. Widespread discoordination in the economic system results: the financial bubble ("irrational exuberance") exerts a harmful effect on the real economy, and sooner or later the process reverses in the form of an economic recession, which marks the beginning of the painful and necessary readjustment. This readjustment invariably requires the reconversion of every real productive structure inflation has distorted. The specific triggers of the end of the euphoric monetary "binge" and the beginning of the recessionary "hangover" are many, and they can vary from one cycle to another. In the current circumstances, the most obvious triggers have been the rise in the price of raw materials, particularly oil, the subprime mortgage crisis in the United States, and finally, the failure of important banking institutions when it became clear in the market that the value of their liabilities exceeded that of their assets (mortgage loans granted).

At present, numerous self-interested voices are demanding further reductions in interest rates and new injections of money which permit those who desire it to complete their investment projects without suffering losses. Nevertheless, this escape forward would only temporarily postpone problems at the cost of making them far more serious later. The crisis has hit because the profits of capital-goods companies (especially in the building sector and in real-estate development) have disappeared due to the entrepreneurial errors provoked by cheap credit, and because the prices of consumer goods have begun to perform relatively less poorly than those of capital goods. At this point, a painful, inevitable readjustment begins, and in addition to a decrease in production and an increase in unemployment, we are now still seeing a harmful rise in the prices of consumer goods (stagflation).

The most rigorous economic analysis and the coolest, most balanced interpretation of recent economic and financial events support the conclusion that central banks (which are true financial central-planning agencies) cannot possibly succeed in finding the most advantageous monetary policy at every moment. This is exactly what became clear in the case of the failed attempts to plan the former Soviet economy from above. To put it another way, the theorem of the economic impossibility of socialism, which the Austrian economists

Ludwig von Mises and Friedrich A. Hayek discovered, is fully applicable to central banks in general, and to the Federal Reserve—(at one time) Alan Greenspan and (currently) Ben Bernanke—in particular. According to this theorem, it is impossible to organize society, in terms of economics, based on coercive commands issued by a planning agency, since such a body can never obtain the information it needs to infuse its commands with a coordinating nature. Indeed, nothing is more dangerous than to indulge in the "fatal conceit"—to use Hayek's useful expression—of believing oneself omniscient or at least wise and powerful enough to be able to keep the most suitable monetary policy fine tuned at all times. Hence, rather than soften the most violent ups and downs of the economic cycle, the Federal Reserve and, to some lesser extent, the European Central Bank, have most likely been their main architects and the culprits in their worsening. Therefore, the dilemma facing Ben Bernanke and his Federal Reserve Board, as well as the other central banks (beginning with the European Central Bank), is not at all comfortable. For years they have shirked their monetary responsibility, and now they find themselves in a blind alley. They can either allow the recessionary process to begin now, and with it the healthy and painful readjustment, or they can escape forward toward a "hair of the dog" cure. With the latter, the chances of even more severe stagflation in the not-too-distant future increase exponentially. (This was precisely the error committed following the stock market crash of 1987, an error which led to the inflation at the end of the 1980s and concluded with the sharp recession of 1990–1992.) Furthermore, the reintroduction of a cheap-credit policy at this stage could only hinder the necessary liquidation of unprofitable investments and company reconversion. It could even wind up prolonging the recession indefinitely, as has occurred in Japan in recent years: though all possible interventions have been tried, the Japanese economy has ceased to respond to any monietarist stimulus involving credit expansion or Keynesian methods. It is in this context of "financial schizophrenia" that we must interpret the latest "shots in the dark" fired by the monetary authorities (who have two totally contradictory responsibilities: both to control inflation and to inject all the liquidity necessary into the financial system to prevent its collapse). Thus, one day the Federal Reserve rescues Bear Stearns, AIG, Fannie Mae, and Freddie Mac or Citigroup, and the next it allows Lehman Brothers to fail, under the amply justified pretext of "teaching a lesson" and refusing to fuel moral hazard. Then, in light of the way events were unfolding, a 700-billion-dollar plan to purchase the euphemistically named "toxic" or "illiquid" (i.e., worthless) assets from the banking system was approved. If the plan is financed by taxes (and not more inflation), it will mean a heavy tax burden on households, precisely when they are least able to bear it. Finally, in view of doubts about whether such a plan could have any effect, the choice was made to inject public money directly into banks, and even to "guarantee" the total amount of their deposits, decreasing interest rates to almost zero percent.

In comparison, the economies of the European Union are in a somewhat less poor state (if we do not consider the expansionary effect of the policy of deliberately depreciating the dollar, and the relatively greater European rigidities, particularly in the labor market, which tend to make recessions in Europe longer and more painful). The expansionary policy of the European Central Bank, though not free of grave errors, has been somewhat less irresponsible than that of the Federal Reserve. Furthermore, fulfillment of the convergence criteria involved at the time a healthy and significant rehabilitation of the chief European economies. Only the countries on the periphery, like Ireland and particularly Spain, were immersed in considerable credit expansion from the time they initiated their processes of convergence. The case of Spain is paradigmatic. The Spanish economy underwent an economic boom which, in part, was due to real causes (liberalizing structural reforms which originated with José María Aznar's administration in 1996). Nevertheless, the boom was also largely fueled by an artificial expansion of money and credit, which grew at a rate nearly three times that of the corresponding rates in France and Germany. Spanish economic agents essentially interpreted the decrease in interest rates which resulted from the convergence process in the easy-money terms traditional in Spain: a greater availability of easy money and mass requests for loans from Spanish banks (mainly to finance real-estate speculation), loans which these banks have granted by creating the money *ex nihilo* while European central bankers looked on unperturbed. When faced with the rise in prices, the European Central Bank has remained faithful to its mandate and has tried to maintain interest rates as long as possible, despite the difficulties of those members of the Monetary Union which, like Spain, are now discovering that much of their investment in real estate was in error and are heading for a lengthy and painful reorganization of their real economy.

Under these circumstances, the most appropriate policy would be to liberalize the economy at all levels (especially in the labor market) to permit the rapid reallocation of productive factors (particularly labor) to profitable sectors. Likewise, it is essential to reduce public spending and taxes, in order to increase the available income of heavily-indebted economic agents who need to repay their loans as soon as possible. Economic agents in general and companies in particular can only rehabilitate their finances by cutting costs (especially labor costs) and paying off loans. Essential to this aim are a very flexible labor market and a much more austere public sector. These factors are fundamental if the market is to reveal as quickly as possible the real value of the investment goods produced in error and thus lay the foundation for a healthy, sustained economic recovery in a future which, for the good of all, I hope is not long in coming.

We must not forget that a central feature of the recent period of artificial expansion was a gradual corruption, on the American continent as well as in Europe, of the traditional principles of accounting as practiced globally for centuries. To be specific, acceptance of the International Accounting Standards (IAS) and their incorporation into law in different countries (in Spain via the new General Accounting Plan, in effect as of January 1, 2008) have meant the abandonment of the traditional principle of prudence and its replacement by the principle of fair value in the assessment of the value of balance sheet assets, particularly financial assets. In this abandonment of the traditional principle of prudence, a highly influential role has been played by brokerages, investment banks (which are now on their way to extinction), and in general, all parties interested in "inflating" book values in order to bring them closer to supposedly more "objective" stockmarket values, which in the past rose continually in an economic process of financial euphoria. In fact, during the years of the "speculative bubble," this process was characterized by a feedback loop: rising stock-market values were immediately entered into the books, and then such accounting entries were sought as justification for further artificial increases in the prices of financial assets listed on the stock market.

In this wild race to abandon traditional accounting principles and replace them with others more "in line with the times," it became common to evaluate companies based on unorthodox suppositions and purely subjective criteria which in the new standards replace the only truly objective criterion (that of historical cost). Now, the collapse of financial markets and economic agents' widespread loss of faith in banks and their accounting practices have revealed the serious error involved in yielding to the IAS and their abandonment of traditional accounting principles based on prudence, the error of indulging in the vices of creative, fair-value accounting.

It is in this context that we must view the recent measures taken in the United States and the European Union to "soften" (i.e., to partially reverse) the impact of fair-value accounting for financial institutions. This is a step in the right direction, but it falls short and is taken for the wrong reasons. Indeed, those in charge at financial institutions are attempting to "shut the barn door when the horse is bolting"; that is, when the dramatic fall in the value of "toxic" or "illiquid" assets has endangered the solvency of their institutions. However, these people were delighted with the new IAS during the preceding years of "irrational exuberance," in which increasing and excessive values in the stock and financial markets graced their balance sheets with staggering figures corresponding to their own profits and net worth, figures which in turn encouraged them to run risks (or better, uncertainties) with practically no thought of danger. Hence, we see that the IAS act in a pro-cyclic manner by heightening volatility and erroneously biasing business management: in times of prosperity, they create a false "wealth effect" which prompts people to take disproportionate risks; when, from one day to the next, the errors committed come to light, the loss in the value of assets immediately decapitalizes companies, which are obliged to sell assets and attempt to recapitalize at the worst moment, i.e., when assets are worth the least and financial markets dry up. Clearly, accounting principles which, like those of the IAS, have proven so disturbing must be abandoned as soon as possible, and all of the accounting reforms recently enacted, specifically the Spanish one, which came into effect January 1, 2008, must be reversed. This is so not only because these reforms mean a dead end in a period of financial crisis and recession, but especially because it is vital that in periods of prosperity we stick to the principle of prudence in valuation, a principle which has shaped all accounting systems from the time of Luca Pacioli at the beginning of the fifteenth century to the adoption of the false idol of the IAS.

In short, the greatest error of the accounting reform recently introduced worldwide is that it scraps centuries of accounting experience and business management when it replaces the prudence principle, as the highest ranking among all traditional accounting principles, with the "fair value" principle, which is simply the introduction of the volatile market value for an entire set of assets, particularly financial assets. This Copernican turn is extremely harmful and threatens the very foundations of the market economy for several reasons. First, to violate the traditional principle of prudence and require that accounting entries reflect market values is to provoke, depending upon the conditions of the economic cycle, an inflation of book values with surpluses which have not materialized and which, in many cases, may never materialize. The artificial "wealth effect" this can produce, especially during the boom phase of each economic cycle, leads to the allocation of paper (or merely temporary) profits, the

acceptance of disproportionate risks, and in short, the commission of systematic entrepreneurial errors and the consumption of the nation's capital, to the detriment of its healthy productive structure and its capacity for long-term growth.
Second, I must emphasize that the purpose of accounting is
not to reflect supposed "real" values (which in any case are
subjective and which are determined and vary daily in the
corresponding markets) under the pretext of attaining a
(poorly understood) "accounting transparency." Instead, the
purpose of accounting is to permit the prudent management
of each company and to prevent capital consumption,[1] by
applying strict standards of accounting conservatism (based
on the prudence principle and the recording of either historical cost or market value, whichever is less), standards which
ensure at all times that distributable profits come from a safe
surplus which can be distributed without in any way endangering the future viability and capitalization of the company.
Third, we must bear in mind that in the market there are no
equilibrium prices a third party can objectively determine.
Quite the opposite is true; market values arise from subjective
assessments and fluctuate sharply, and hence their use in
accounting eliminates much of the clarity, certainty, and information balance sheets contained in the past. Today, balance
sheets have become largely unintelligible and useless to economic agents. Furthermore, the volatility inherent in market
values, particularly over the economic cycle, robs accounting
based on the "new principles" of much of its potential as a
guide for action for company managers and leads them to systematically commit major errors in management, errors which
have been on the verge of provoking the severest financial crisis to ravage the world since 1929.

---

[1]See especially F. A. Hayek, "The Maintenance of Capital," *Economica* 2
(August 1934), reprinted in *Profits, Interest and Investment and Other Essays on
the Theory of Industrial Fluctuations* (Clifton, N.J.: Augustus M. Kelley, 1979;
first edition London: George Routledge & Sons, 1939). See especially section
9, "Capital Accounting and Monetary Policy," pp. 130–32.

In chapter 9 of this book (pages 789–803), I design a process of transition toward the only world financial order which, being fully compatible with the free-enterprise system, can eliminate the financial crises and economic recessions which cyclically affect the world's economies. The proposal the book contains for international financial reform has acquired extreme relevance at the present time (November 2008), in which the disconcerted governments of Europe and America have organized a world conference to reform the international monetary system in order to avoid in the future such severe financial and banking crises as the one that currently grips the entire western world. As is explained in detail over the nine chapters of this book, any future reform will fail as miserably as past reforms unless it strikes at the very root of the present problems and rests on the following principles: (1) the reestablishment of a 100-percent reserve requirement on all bank demand deposits and equivalents; (2) the elimination of central banks as lenders of last resort (which will be unnecessary if the preceding principle is applied, and harmful if they continue to act as financial central-planning agencies); and (3) the privatization of the current, monopolistic, and fiduciary state-issued money and its replacement with a classic pure gold standard. This radical, definitive reform would essentially mark the culmination of the 1989 fall of the Berlin Wall and real socialism, since the reform would mean the application of the same principles of liberalization and private property to the only sphere, that of finance and banking, which has until now remained mired in central planning (by "central" banks), extreme interventionism (the fixing of interest rates, the tangled web of government regulations), and state monopoly (legal tender laws which require the acceptance of the current, state-issued fiduciary money), circumstances with very negative and dramatic consequences, as we have seen.

I should point out that the transition process designed in the last chapter of this book could also permit from the outset the bailing out of the current banking system, thus preventing its rapid collapse, and with it the sudden monetary squeeze which would be inevitable if, in an environment of widespread broken trust among depositors, a significant volume of bank deposits were to disappear. This short-term goal, which at present, western governments are desperately striving for with the most varied plans (the massive purchases of "toxic" bank assets, the *ad hominem* guarantee of all deposits, or simply the partial or total nationalization of the private banking system), could be reached much faster and more effectively, and in a manner much less harmful to the market economy, if the first step in the proposed reform (pages 791–98) were immediately taken: to back the total amount of current bank deposits (demand deposits and equivalents) with cash, bills to be turned over to banks, which from then on would maintain a 100-percent reserve with respect to deposits. As illustrated in chart IX-2 of chapter 9, which shows the consolidated balance sheet for the banking system following this step, the issuance of these banknotes would in no way be inflationary (since the new money would be "sterilized," so to speak, by its purpose as backing to satisfy any sudden deposit withdrawals). Furthermore, this step would free up all banking assets ("toxic" or not) which currently appear as backing for demand deposits (and equivalents) on the balance sheets of private banks. On the assumption that the transition to the new financial system would take place under "normal" circumstances, and not in the midst of a financial crisis as acute as the current one, I proposed in chapter 9 that the "freed" assets be transferred to a set of mutual funds created *ad hoc* and managed by the banking system, and that the shares in these funds be exchanged for outstanding treasury bonds and for the implicit liabilities connected with the public social-security system (pp. 796–97). Nevertheless, in the current climate of severe financial and economic crisis, we have another alternative: apart from canceling "toxic" assets with these funds, we could devote a portion of the rest, if desired, to enabling savers (not depositors, since their deposits would already be backed 100 percent) to recover a large part of the value lost in their investments (particularly in loans to commercial banks, investment banks, and holding companies). These measures would immediately restore confidence and would leave a significant remainder to be exchanged, once and for all and at no cost, for a sizeable portion of the national debt, our initial aim. In any case, an important warning must be given: naturally, and I must never tire of repeating it, the solution proposed is only valid in the context of an irrevocable decision to reestablish a free-banking system subject to a 100-percent reserve requirement on demand deposits. Any of the reforms noted above, if adopted in the absence of a prior, firm conviction and decision to change the international financial and banking system as indicated, would be simply disastrous: a private banking system which continued to operate with a fractional reserve (orchestrated by the corresponding central banks), would generate, in a cascading effect, and based on the cash created to back deposits, an inflationary expansion like none other in history, one which would eventually finish off our entire economic system.

The above considerations are crucially important and reveal how very relevant this treatise has now become in light of the critical state of the international financial system (though I would definitely have preferred to write the preface to this new edition under very different economic circumstances). Nevertheless, while it is tragic that we have arrived at the current situation, it is even more tragic, if possible, that there exists a widespread lack of understanding regarding the causes of the phenomena that plague us, and especially an atmosphere of confusion and uncertainty prevalent among experts, analysts, and most economic theorists. In this area at least, I can hope the successive editions of this book which are being published all over the world[2] may contribute to the theoretical

---

[2]Since the appearance of the first English-language edition, the third and fourth Spanish editions have been published in 2006 and 2009. Moreover, Tatjana Danilova and Grigory Sapov have completed a Russian translation,

training of readers, to the intellectual rearmament of new generations, and eventually, to the sorely needed institutional redesign of the entire monetary and financial system of current market economies. If this hope is fulfilled, I will not only view the effort made as worthwhile, but will also deem it a great honor to have contributed, even in a very small way, to movement in the right direction.

Jesús Huerta de Soto
Madrid
November 13, 2008

---

which has been published as *Dengi, Bankovskiy Kredit i Ekonomicheskie Tsikly* (Moscow: Sotsium Publishing House, 2008). Three thousand copies have been printed initially, and I had the satisfaction of presenting the book October 30, 2008 at the Higher School of Economics at Moscow State University. In addition, Professor Rosine Létinier has produced the French translation, which is now pending publication. Grzegorz Luczkiewicz has completed the Polish translation, and translation into the following languages is at an advanced stage: German, Czech, Italian, Romanian, Dutch, Chinese, Japanese, and Arabic. God willing, may they soon be published.

PREFACE TO THE FIRST ENGLISH-LANGUAGE EDITION

It is a genuine pleasure for me to see this handsomely-printed English edition of my book, *Dinero, Crédito Bancario y Ciclos Económicos*, which first appeared in Spain in 1998. This translation incorporates the small number of corrections included in the second Spanish edition of January 2002, and it is the result of the great effort of Melinda A. Stroup, who wrote the first English manuscript of the entire book.

This English version was thoroughly examined by Dr. Jörg Guido Hülsmann, whose comments on several important points improved the manuscript significantly. I would also like to acknowledge the work of my research assistant, Dr. Gabriel Calzada, who searched for various English editions of rare books unavailable in Spain and looked up certain quotations and references. Last, I personally inspected the final version in its entirety to ensure the accuracy of its content.

I am grateful to the Ludwig von Mises Institute, and especially to its president, Lewellyn H. Rockwell, Jr., for bringing the project to its culmination with such high standards.

Jesús Huerta de Soto
Señorío de Sarría
May 2005

Note: The author welcomes any comments on this English-language edition and requests they be sent to huertadesoto@dimasoft.es.

PREFACE TO
THE THIRD
SPANISH EDITION

In this, the third edition of *Dinero, Crédito Bancario y Ciclos Económicos*, an attempt has been made to preserve as far as possible the contents, structure, and page numbering of the two previous editions. However, changes have been necessary in certain cases, as I have taken this new opportunity to raise some additional arguments and points, both in the main text and in several footnotes. Also, the bibliography has been updated with the new editions and Spanish translations which have appeared in the four years since the previous edition, and with a few new books and articles which have a particular bearing on the topics covered in the book.[1] Finally, the editor of the English version, *Money, Bank Credit, and Economic Cycles*,[2] Judith Thommesen, very patiently and painstakingly

---

[1]One such book is Roger W. Garrison's *Time and Money: The Macroeconomics of Capital Structure*, published by Routledge in London and New York in 2001, three years after the appearance of the first Spanish edition of *Money, Bank Credit, and Economic Cycles*. Garrison's text can be viewed as complementary to this one. His book is especially noteworthy, because in it he develops the Austrian analysis of capital and economic cycles in the context of the different paradigms of modern macroeconomics, and the approach and language he uses to do so are fully consistent with those used by the mainstream in our discipline. Hence, Garrison's book will undoubtedly help build awareness among economists in general of the need to consider the Austrian perspective and its comparative advantages. I do feel that Garrison's explanations are too mechanistic

verified hundreds of quotations in English and other languages against their original sources. A significant number of small misprints had been detected and have now been rectified, and thus her efforts have helped to make this third edition even more polished. I am deeply grateful to her, as well as to Dr. Gabriel Calzada, Associate Professor at the Universidad Rey Juan Carlos, for his assistance in reviewing and correcting certain bibliographic references.

In the interval since the publication of the previous edition, economic trends have been marked by the high fiduciary inflation and the sharp increase in public deficits necessary to finance the war in Iraq and to meet the rising costs which the "welfare state," plagued by severe and insoluble problems, generates in most western countries. The money supply and the interest rate have been subject to further manipulation. In fact, the United States Federal Reserve lowered the rate to a historical minimum of 1 percent, thus preventing the necessary correction of the investment errors committed prior to the 2001 recession. The above circumstances have triggered a new speculative bubble in real estate markets, along with a dramatic rise in the price of the energy products and raw materials which are the object of almost unlimited demand on a worldwide scale, due to new investment projects undertaken mainly in the Asiatic basin, and particularly in China. Thus, we seem to be approaching the typical turning-point phase of

---

and that he falls short of providing sufficient justification for his analysis from the juridical-institutional standpoint. Nonetheless, I thought it advisable to promote the book's translation into Spanish by a team of professors and disciples from my department at the Universidad Rey Juan Carlos. Dr. Miguel Ángel Alonso Neira led the team, and the translation has already been published in Spain under the title *Tiempo y dinero: la macroeconomía en la estructura del capital* (Madrid: Unión Editorial, 2005).

[2]The English edition was beautifully published in 2006 as *Money, Bank Credit, and Economic Cycles* under the auspices of the Ludwig von Mises Institute in Auburn, Alabama, thanks to the support of the Institute's president, Llewellyn H. Rockwell.

the cycle, the phase which precedes every economic recession. Moreover, the very recent 180-degree turn in the monetary policy of the Federal Reserve, which has jacked up interest rates to 4 percent in only a few months, confirms the trend even further.

It is my hope that this new edition will help readers and scholars to better understand the economic phenomena of the world that surrounds them. May it also serve to convince specialists and framers of current economic policy that we must abandon social engineering in the monetary and financial sphere as soon as possible. The attainment of these goals will mean the complete fulfilment of one of my primary objectives.

Jesús Huerta de Soto
Formentor
August 28, 2005

PREFACE TO THE SECOND SPANISH EDITION

Following the success of the first edition of *Dinero, Crédito Bancario y Ciclos Económicos*, which sold out rapidly, I am pleased to present the second edition to Spanish-speaking readers. To avoid confusion and facilitate the work of scholars and researchers, the contents, structure, and page numbering of the first edition have been maintained in the second, though the book has been thoroughly examined and all misprints detected have been eliminated.

In the wake of a decade marked by great credit expansion and the development of a large financial bubble, the course of economic events in the world from 1999 through 2001 was characterized by the collapse of stock-market values and the emergence of a recession which now simultaneously grips the United States, Europe, and Japan. These circumstances have left the analysis presented in this book even more clearly and fully illustrated than when it was first published, at the end of 1998. While governments and central banks have reacted to the terrorist attack on New York's World Trade Center by manipulating interest rates, reducing them to historically low levels (1 percent in the United States, 0.15 percent in Japan and 2 percent in Europe), the massive expansion of fiduciary media injected into the system will not only prolong and hinder the necessary streamlining of the real productive structure, but may also lead to dangerous stagflation. In light of these worrisome economic conditions, which have repeated themselves since the emergence of the current banking system, I fervently hope the analysis this book contains will help the reader to understand and interpret the phenomena which surround him and will exert a positive influence on public opinion, my university colleagues and economic-policy authorities in government and central banks.

Various reviews of this book's first edition have appeared, and I am grateful to the eminent authors of them for their many positive comments.[1] A common denominator among all has been to urge the translation of this book into English, a task now complete. It is my hope that, God willing, the first English edition of this book will soon be published in the United States and will thus become available to some of the most influential academic and political circles.

Finally, since 1998 this manual has been employed successfully as a textbook during the semester devoted to the theory of money, banking, and business cycles in courses on Political Economy and in Introduction to Economics, first at the law school of Madrid's Universidad Complutense and later at the school of law and social sciences of the Universidad Rey Juan Carlos, also in Madrid. This educational experience has been based on an institutional and decidedly multidisciplinary approach to economic theory, and I believe this method can be easily and successfully applied to any other course connected with banking theory (Economic Policy, Macroeconomics, Monetary and Financial Theory, etc.). This experience would not have been possible without the keen interest and enthusiasm hundreds of students have expressed each academic year as they studied and discussed the teachings contained in the present volume. This book, to

---

[1] I am particularly grateful to Leland Yeager (*Review of Austrian Economics* 14 no. 4 [2001]: 255) and Jörg Guido Hülsmann (*Quarterly Journal of Austrian Economics* 3, no. 2 [2000]: 85–88) for their remarks.

which they have dedicated their efforts, is chiefly aimed at them, and I thank all of them. May they continue to cultivate their critical spirit and intellectual curiosity as they progress to higher and increasingly enriching stages in their formative journey.[2]

Jesús Huerta de Soto
Madrid
December 6, 2001

---

[2]Comments on this second edition are welcome and may be sent to huertadesoto@dimasoft.es.

INTRODUCTION

The economic analysis of juridical institutions has come to the fore in recent years and promises to become one of the most fruitful spheres of economics. Much of the work completed thus far has been strongly influenced by traditional neoclassical assumptions, namely by the concept of strict maximization in contexts of equilibrium. Still, economic analyses of law reveal the shortcomings of the traditional approach and do so perhaps better than any other branch of economics. In fact, juridical institutions are so intimately involved in daily life that it is notoriously difficult to apply the traditional assumptions of economic analysis to them. I have already attempted elsewhere to expose the dangers the neoclassical perspective brings to the analysis of juridical institutions.[1] Economic analyses of law are certainly necessary, but they call for a less restrictive methodology than has generally been used to date, one more suited to this particular field of research. The subjectivist view is a more fitting approach. Developed by the Austrian School, it is based on their concept of creative human action or entrepreneurial activity and implies a dynamic analysis of the general processes of social interaction. This perspective promises to make great contributions to the future development of the economic analysis of juridical institutions.

In addition, most studies of juridical institutions carried out so far have had exclusively *microeconomic* implications because, among other reasons, theorists have simply borrowed the traditional analytical tools of neoclassical microeconomics

---

[1]See Jesús Huerta de Soto, "The Ongoing Methodenstreit of the Austrian School," *Journal des Économistes et des Études Humaines* 8, no. 1 (March 1998): 75–113.

and applied them to the analysis of law. This has been the case, for example, with respect to the economic analysis of contracts and civil liability, bankruptcy law, the family, and even criminal law and justice. Very few economic analyses of law have had mainly *macroeconomic* implications, and this reflects the harmful decades-long separation between these two sides of economics. However, this need not be the case. It is necessary to recognize economics as a unified whole, where macroeconomic elements are firmly rooted in their microeconomic foundations. In addition, I will attempt to demonstrate that the economic analysis of some juridical institutions yields critical implications and conclusions that are essentially macroeconomic. Or, in other words, even when the basic analysis is microeconomic, the conclusions drawn and primary outcomes resulting from it are macroeconomic. By closing the profound artificial gap between micro and macroeconomics, we arrive at a unified theoretical treatment of legal issues in the economic analysis of law.

This is my primary goal as I undertake an economic analysis of the monetary *irregular-deposit* contract, in its different facets. Furthermore, I intend my examination to cast light on one of the most obscure and complex spheres of economics: the theory of money, bank credit, and economic cycles. Now that the issue of socialism has been resolved,[2] at least from a theoretical standpoint, and it has been empirically illustrated to be impracticable, the main theoretical challenge facing economists at the dawn of the twenty-first century lies most likely in the field of money, credit, and financial institutions. The highly abstract nature of social relationships involving money in its various forms makes these relationships remarkably difficult to understand and the corresponding theoretical treatment of them particularly complex. In addition, in the financial and monetary spheres of western countries, a series of institutions has been developed and imposed; namely central banks, bank legislation, a monopoly on the issue of currency,

---

[2]Jesús Huerta de Soto, *Socialismo, cálculo económico y función empresarial* (Madrid: Unión Editorial, 1992; 2nd ed., 2001).

and foreign exchange controls. These institutions thoroughly regulate every country's financial sector, rendering it much more similar to the socialist system of central planning than is appropriate to a true market economy. Hence, as I will attempt to demonstrate, the arguments which establish the impracticability of socialist economic calculation are fully applicable to the financial sphere. Supporters of the Austrian School of economics originally developed these arguments when they showed it was impossible to organize society in a coordinated fashion via dictatorial commands. If my thesis is correct, the impracticability of socialism will also be established in the financial sector. Furthermore, the inevitable discoordination to which all state intervention gives rise will be vividly revealed in the cyclical phases of boom and recession which traditionally affect the mixed economies of the developed world.

Any theoretical study today which attempts to identify the causes, stages, remedies for, and chances of preventing economic cycles is guaranteed to be front-page material. As a matter of fact, as I write these lines (November 1997), a serious financial and banking crisis grips Asian markets and threatens to spread to Latin America and the rest of the western world. This crisis comes in the wake of the period of apparent economic prosperity which in turn followed the severe financial crises and economic recessions that shook the world at the beginning of the nineties and particularly the end of the seventies. Furthermore, in the eyes of ordinary people, politicians, and the majority of economic theorists themselves, an understanding has not yet been reached as to the true causes of these phenomena, the successive and recurrent appearances of which are constantly used by politicians, philosophers, and interventionist theorists alike as a pretext for rejecting a market economy and justifying an increasing level of dictatorial state intervention in the economy and society.

For this reason, from the point of view of classical liberal doctrine, it is of great theoretical interest to scientifically analyze the origin of economic cycles, and in particular, to determine the ideal model for the financial system of a truly free society. Libertarian theorists themselves still disagree in this

area, and there are great differences of opinion as to whether
it is necessary to maintain the central bank or whether it
would be better to exchange it for a system of free banking,
and in the latter case, as to what concrete rules economic
agents participating in a completely free financial system
should have to follow. The central bank originally appeared as
the result of a series of dictatorial government interventions,
though these were mainly urged by various agents of the
financial sector (specifically by private banks themselves),
who on many occasions have considered it necessary to
demand state support to guarantee the stability of their business activities during stages of economic crisis. Does this
mean the central bank is an inevitable evolutionary outcome
of a free-market economy? Or rather, that the way private
bankers have characteristically done business, which at a certain point became corrupt from a legal point of view, has
brought about financial practices unsustainable without backing from a lender of last resort? These and other issues are of
utmost theoretical interest and should be the object of the
most careful analysis. In short, my main objective is to
develop a research plan to determine which financial and
banking system is appropriate for a free society.

I intend this research to be multidisciplinary. It will have to
rest not only on the study of juridical science and the history of
law, but also on economic theory and specifically on the theory
of money, capital, and economic cycles. Furthermore, my analysis will shed new light on some historical economic events
related to the financial realm, and will better illustrate the evolution of certain trends in the history of economic thought itself,
as well as the development of various accounting and banking
techniques. A proper understanding of finance requires the
integration of various disciplines and branches of knowledge,
and we will consider these from the three perspectives I deem
necessary to correctly comprehend any social phenomenon:
historical-evolutionary, theoretical, and ethical.[3]

---

[3]I have presented the theory of the three-tiered approach to studying
social issues in Jesús Huerta de Soto, "Conjectural History and Beyond,"
Humane Studies Review 6, no. 2 (Winter, 1988–1989): 10.

This book comprises nine chapters. In the first I describe the legal essence of the monetary irregular-deposit contract, paying special attention to the main characteristics distinguishing it from a loan contract, or mutuum. In addition, Chapter 1 deals with the different legal logic inherent in these two institutions, their mutual incompatibility at a fundamental level, and how the unique ways each is regulated embody traditional, universal legal principles identified and developed from the time of Roman classical law.

Chapter 2 is a historical study of economic events. There I examine ways in which the traditional legal principle governing the irregular-deposit contract has been corrupted over time, mainly due to the temptation felt by the first bankers to use their depositors' money to their own benefit. The intervention of the political establishment has also played an important role in this process. Always eager to secure new financial resources, political authorities have turned to bankers entrusted with others' deposits and have attempted to exploit these funds, granting the bankers all sorts of privileges, chiefly authorization to use their depositors' money for their own benefit (of course on condition that a significant part of such funds be loaned to the politicians themselves). This chapter offers three different examples (classical Greece and Rome, the resurgence of banking in medieval Italian cities, and the revival of banking in modern times) to illustrate the process by which the traditional legal principles governing the monetary irregular-deposit bank contract have become corrupted and to outline the resulting economic effects.

In chapter 3 I adopt a legal viewpoint to consider different theoretical attempts to come up with a new contractual framework in which to classify the monetary bank-deposit contract. Such attempts are aimed at justifying banks' lending of demand-deposit funds to third parties. I intend to show that these attempts at justification are riddled with an insoluble logical contradiction and therefore doomed to failure. I will also explain how the effects of privileged banking practices (see chapter 2) expose profound contradictions and weaknesses in the formulation of a new legal, theoretical basis for the monetary irregular-deposit contract. The attempt to establish such a foundation dates back to the Middle Ages and has continued until practically the present day. We will take a detailed look at different efforts to formulate an unorthodox legal principle capable of governing present-day monetary bank deposits in a logical, coherent manner. I conclude that such attempts could not possibly have been successful, because current banking practices are based precisely on the violation of traditional principles inherent in property rights, which cannot be violated without serious harmful effects on the processes of social interaction.

Chapters 4, 5, 6, and 7 comprise the heart of my economic analysis of the bank-deposit contract as it has developed over time; that is, using a fractional-reserve ratio in violation of traditional legal principles. I will explain why Hayek's insightful rule rings true in the banking field as well. This rule states that whenever a traditional legal principle is violated, sooner or later there are serious harmful effects on society. From a theoretical viewpoint, I will analyze the effects the current banking practice of disregarding traditional legal principles in the monetary-deposit contract has on the creation of money, intra- and intertemporal market coordination, entrepreneurship, and economic cycles. My conclusion is that the successive stages of boom, crisis, and economic recession recurring in the market result from the violation of the traditional legal principle on which the monetary bank-deposit contract should be based. They stem from the privilege bankers have come to enjoy and have been granted in the past by governments for reasons of mutual interest. We will study the theory of economic cycles in depth and critically analyze the alternative explanations offered by the monetarist and Keynesian schools for this type of phenomena.

Chapter 8 focuses on the central bank as a lender of last resort. The creation of this institution resulted inevitably from certain events. When the principles which should govern the irregular-deposit contract are violated, such acute and inescapable effects appear that private bankers soon realized they needed to turn to the government for an institution to act on their behalf as lender of last resort and provide support during stages of crisis, which experience demonstrated to be a recurrent phenomenon. I will endeavor to show that the central bank did not emerge spontaneously as the result of market institutions, but was forcibly imposed by the government and responds to the demands of powerful pressure groups. I will also examine the current financial system, which is based on a central bank, and apply to it the analytical economic theory of the impracticability of socialism. Indeed, the current financial system rests on a monopoly one government agency holds on the chief decisions regarding the type and quantity of money and credit to be created and injected into the economic system. Thus it constitutes a financial market system of "central planning" and therefore involves a high level of intervention and is to a great extent "socialist." Sooner or later the system will inevitably run up against the impossibility of socialist economic calculation, the theorem of which maintains it is impossible to coordinate any sphere of society, especially the financial sphere, via dictatorial mandates, given that the governing body (in this case the central bank) is incapable of obtaining the necessary and relevant information required to do so. The chapter concludes with a review of the recent central-banking/free-banking controversy. We will see that most current free-banking theorists have failed to realize that their plan loses much of its potential and theoretical weight if not accompanied by a call to return to traditional legal principles; that is, to banking with a 100-percent reserve requirement. Freedom must go hand-in-hand with responsibility and strict observance of traditional legal principles.

The ninth and last chapter presents an ideal, coherent model for a financial system which respects traditional legal principles and is thus based on the adoption of a 100-percent reserve requirement in banking. Also considered are the different arguments made against my proposal. I criticize them and explain how the transition from the current system to the proposed ideal system could be carried out with a minimum of tension. A summary of main conclusions wraps up the book, along with some additional considerations on the advantages of the proposed financial system. The principles studied here are also applied to certain urgent practical issues, such as the construction of a new European monetary system and of a modern financial system in the former socialist economies.

A summarized version of this book's essential thesis was first presented in a paper before the Mont Pèlerin Society in Rio de Janeiro in September 1993 and received the support of James M. Buchanan, to whom I am very grateful. A written, Spanish version has been partially published in the "Introducción Crítica" of the first Spanish edition of Vera C. Smith's book, *The Rationale of Central Banking and the Free Banking Alternative*.[4] It was later published in French as an article entitled "Banque centrale ou banque libre: le débat théorique sur les réserves fractionnaires."[5]

I express my gratitude to my colleague at the law school of Madrid's Universidad Complutense, Professor Mercedes López Amor, for her help in the search for sources and a bibliography regarding the treatment under Roman law of the irregular deposit of money. Also, my former professor, Pablo Martín Aceña, from the University of Alcalá de Henares (Madrid), offered direction in my study of the evolution of banking throughout the Middle Ages. Luis Reig, Rafael Manzanares, José Antonio de Aguirre, José Luis Feito, Richard Adamiak of Chicago, the late Professor Murray N. Rothbard,

---

[4]Vera C. Smith, *Fundamentos de la banca central y de la libertad bancaria* (Madrid: Unión Editorial/Ediciones Aosta, 1993), pp. 27–42. (*The Rationale of Central Banking and the Free Banking Alternative* [Indianapolis: Liberty Press, 1990].)

[5]Jesús Huerta de Soto, "Banque centrale ou banque libre: le débat théorique sur les réserves fractionnaires," in the *Journal des Économistes et des Études Humaines* 5, no. 2/3 (June-September 1994): 379–91. This paper later appeared in Spanish with the title "La teoría del banco central y de la banca libre" in my book, *Estudios de economía política*, chap. 11, pp. 129–43. Two other versions of this article were also later published: one in English, entitled "A Critical Analysis of Central Banks and Fractional Reserve Free Banking from the Austrian School Perspective," in *The Review of Austrian Economics* 8, no. 2 (1995): 117–30; the other in Romanian, thanks to Octavian Vasilescu, "Banci centrale si sistemul de free-banking cu rezerve fractionare: o analizá criticá din perspectiva Scolii Austriece," *Polis: Revista de stiinte politice* 4, no. 1 (Bucharest, 1997): 145–57.

and Professors Hans-Hermann Hoppe from Las Vegas University in Nevada, Manuel Gurdiel from the Universidad Complutense in Madrid, Pablo Vázquez from the University of Cantabria (Spain), Enrique Menéndez Ureña from the Universidad Comillas (Madrid), James Sadowsky from Fordham University, Pedro Tenorio from the U.N.E.D. (Spain), Rafael Termes from the I.E.S.E. (Madrid), Raimondo Cubeddu from the University of Pisa, Rafael Rubio de Urquía from the Universidad Autónoma in Madrid, José Antonio García Durán from the Universidad Central de Barcelona (Spain), and the learned José Antonio Linage Conde from the University of San Pablo-C.E.U. in Madrid have been a great help with their suggestions and provision of books, articles, and rare bibliographic references on banking and monetary issues. My students in doctorate courses at the law school of Madrid's Universidad Complutense, especially Elena Sousmatzian, Xavier Sampedro, Luis Alfonso López García, Rubén Manso, Ángel Luis Rodríguez, César Martínez Meseguer, Juan Ignacio Funes, Alberto Recarte and Esteban Gándara, along with Assistant Professors Óscar Vara, Javier Aranzadi, and Ángel Rodríguez, have provided innumerable suggestions and worked hard to correct typing errors in several previous versions of the manuscript. I express my gratitude to all of them and free them, as is logical, of all responsibility for the book's final contents.

Finally, I would like to thank Sandra Moyano, Ann Lewis, and Yolanda Moyano for their great help and patience in typing and correcting the different versions of the manuscript. Above all, I am grateful, as always, to my wife, Sonsoles, for her help, understanding, and continual encouragement and support throughout this entire project. This book is dedicated to her.

Jesús Huerta de Soto
Formentor
August 15, 1997

1

THE LEGAL NATURE OF THE MONETARY IRREGULAR-DEPOSIT CONTRACT

1
A PRELIMINARY CLARIFICATION OF TERMS: LOAN CONTRACTS (MUTUUM AND COMMODATUM) AND DEPOSIT CONTRACTS

According to the *Shorter Oxford English Dictionary*, a *loan* is "a thing lent; *esp.* a sum of money lent for a time, to be returned in money or money's worth, and usually at interest."[1] Traditionally there have been two types of loans: the loan *for use*, in which case only the use of the lent item is transferred and the borrower is obliged to return it once it has been used; and the loan *for consumption*, where the property of the lent item is transferred. In the latter case, the article is handed over to be consumed, and the borrower is obliged to return something of the same quantity and quality as the thing initially received and consumed.[2]

---

[1]*The Shorter Oxford English Dictionary*, 3rd ed. (Oxford: Oxford University Press, 1973), vol. 1, p. 1227.

[2]Manuel Albaladejo, *Derecho civil II, Derecho de obligaciones*, vol. 2: *Los contratos en particular y las obligaciones no contractuales* (Barcelona: Librería Bosch, 1975), p. 304.

THE COMMODATUM CONTRACT

Commodatum (from Latin) refers to a real contract made in good faith, by which one person—the lender—entrusts to another—the borrower or commodatary—a specific item to be used for free for a certain period of time, at the end of which the item must be restored to its owner; that is, the very thing that was loaned must be returned.[3] The contract is called "real" because the article must be given over. An example would be the loan of a car to a friend so he can take a trip. It is clear that in this case the lender continues to own the lent item, and the person receiving it is obliged to use it appropriately and return it (the car) at the end of the arranged period (when the trip is over). The obligations of the friend, the borrower, are to remain in possession of the article (the car or vehicle), to use it properly (following traffic rules and taking care of it as if it were his own), and to return it when the commodatum is finished (the trip is over).

THE MUTUUM CONTRACT

Though the commodatum contract is of some practical importance, of greater economic significance is the lending of *fungible*[4] and consumable goods, such as oil, wheat, and especially, money. *Mutuum* (also from Latin) refers to the contract by which one person—the lender—entrusts to another—the borrower or mutuary—a certain quantity of fungible goods, and the borrower is obliged, at the end of a specified term, to return an equal quantity of goods of the same type and quality (*tantundem* in Latin). A typical example of a mutuum contract is the monetary loan contract, money being the quintessential

---

[3]Juan Iglesias, *Derecho romano: Instituciones de derecho privado*, 6th rev. updated ed. (Barcelona: Ediciones Ariel, 1972), pp. 408–09.

[4]*Fungible* goods are those for which others of the same sort may be substituted. In other words, they are goods which are not treated separately, but rather in terms of quantity, weight, or measure. The Romans said that things *quae in genere suo functionem in solutione recipiunt* were fungible; that is, things *quae pondere numero mensurave constant*. Consumables are often fungible.

fungible good. By this contract, a certain quantity of monetary units are handed over today from one person to another and the ownership and availability of the money are transferred from the one granting the loan to the one receiving it. The person who receives the loan is authorized to use the money as his own, while promising to return, at the end of a set *term*, the same number of monetary units lent. The mutuum contract, since it constitutes a loan of fungible goods, entails an *exchange of "present" goods for "future" goods.* Hence, unlike the commodatum contract, in the case of the mutuum contract the establishment of an *interest agreement* is normal, since, by virtue of the time preference (according to which, under equal circumstances, present goods are always preferable to future goods), human beings are only willing to relinquish a set quantity of units of a fungible good in exchange for a greater number of units of a fungible good in the future (at the end of the term). Thus, the difference between the number of units initially delivered and the number received from the borrower at the end of the term is, precisely, the interest. To sum up, in the case of the mutuum contract, the lender assumes the obligation to hand over the predetermined units to the borrower or mutuary. The borrower or mutuary who receives the loan assumes the obligation to return the same number of units of the same sort and quality as those received (*tantundem*) at the end of the term set for the contract. Plus, he is obliged to pay interest, as long as an agreement has been made to that effect, as is usually the case. The essential obligation involved in a mutuum contract, or loan of a fungible good, is to return at the end of the specified term the same number of units of the same type and quality as those received, even if the good undergoes a change in price. This means that since the borrower only has to return the *tantundem* once the predetermined time period has ended, he receives the benefit of temporary *ownership* of the thing and therefore enjoys its complete availability. In addition, a *fixed term* is an essential element in the loan or mutuum contract, since it establishes the time period during which the availability and ownership of the good corresponds to the borrower, as well as the moment at which he is obliged to return the *tantundem. Without the explicit or implicit establishment of a fixed term, the mutuum contract or loan cannot exist.*

THE DEPOSIT CONTRACT

Whereas loan contracts (commodatum and mutuum) entail the transfer of the availability of the good, which shifts from the lender to the borrower for the duration of the term, another type of contract, the deposit contract, requires that *the availability of the good not be transferred.* Indeed, the contract of deposit (*depositum* in Latin) is a contract made in good faith by which one person—the depositor—entrusts to another—the depositary—a movable good for that person to guard, protect, and return at any moment the depositor should ask for it. Consequently, the deposit is always carried out in the interest of the depositor. Its fundamental purpose is the *custody* or *safekeeping* of the good and it implies, for the duration of the contract, that the complete availability of the good remain in favor of the depositor, who may request its return *at any moment.* The obligation of the depositor, apart from delivering the good, is to compensate the depositary for the costs of the deposit (if such compensation has been agreed upon; if not, the deposit is free of charge). The obligation of the depositary is to guard and protect the good with the extreme diligence typical of a good parent, and to return it *immediately* to the depositor as soon as he asks for it. It is clear that, while each loan has a term of duration during which the availability of the good is transferred, in the case of a deposit this is not so. Rather a deposit is always held and available to the depositor, and it terminates as soon as he demands the return of the good from the depositary.

THE DEPOSIT OF FUNGIBLE GOODS
OR "IRREGULAR" DEPOSIT CONTRACT

Many times in life we wish to deposit not specific things (such as a painting, a piece of jewelry, or a sealed chest full of coins), but fungible goods (like barrels of oil, cubic meters of gas, bushels of wheat, or thousands of dollars). The deposit of fungible goods is definitely also a deposit, inasmuch as its main element is the complete availability of the deposited goods in favor of the depositor, as well as the obligation on the part of the depositary to conscientiously guard and protect the goods. The only difference between the deposit of fungible goods and the regular deposit, or deposit of specific goods, is that when the former takes place, the goods deposited become indiscernibly mixed with others of the same type and quality (as is the case, for example, in a warehouse holding grain or wheat, in an oil tank or oil refinery, or in the banker's safe). Due to this indistinguishable mixture of different deposited units of the same type and quality, one might consider that the "ownership" of the deposited good is transferred in the case of the deposit of fungible goods. Indeed, when the depositor goes to withdraw his deposit, he will have to settle, as is logical, for receiving the exact equivalent in terms of quantity and quality of what he originally deposited. In no case will he receive the same specific units he handed over, since the goods' fungible nature makes them impossible to treat individually, because they have become indistinguishably mixed with the rest of the goods held by the depositary. The deposit of fungible goods, which possesses the fundamental ingredients of the deposit contract, is called an "irregular deposit,"[5] as one of its characteristic elements is different. (In the case of the contract of regular deposit, or deposit of a specific good,

---

[5]Our student César Martínez Meseguer argues convincingly that another adequate solution to our problem is to consider that in the irregular deposit there is no true transference of ownership, but rather that the concept of ownership refers abstractly to the *tantundem* or quantity of goods deposited and as such always remains in favor of the depositor and is not transferred. This solution is the one offered, for example, in the case of commixture covered in article 381 of the Spanish Civil Code, which admits that "each owner will acquire rights in proportion to the part corresponding to him." Though the irregular deposit has traditionally been viewed differently (as involving the actual transfer of ownership of physical units), it appears more correct to define ownership in the more abstract terms of article 381 of the Spanish Civil Code, in which case we may consider there to be no transference of ownership in an irregular deposit. Moreover, this seems to be the view of Luis Díez-Picazo and Antonio Gullón, *Sistema de derecho civil*, 6th ed. (Madrid: Editorial Tecnos, 1989), vol. 2, pp. 469–70.

ownership is not transferred, but rather the depositor continues to own the good, while in the case of the deposit of fungible goods, one might suppose that ownership is transferred to
the depositary). Nevertheless, we must emphasize that the
essence of the deposit remains unchanged and that the *irregular deposit* fully shares the same fundamental nature of all
deposits: the *custody and safekeeping* obligation. Indeed, in the
irregular deposit there is always an *immediate availability* in
favor of the depositor, who at any moment can go to the grain
warehouse, oil tank, or bank safe and withdraw the equivalent of the units he originally turned over. The goods withdrawn will be the exact equivalent, in terms of quantity and
quality, of the ones handed over; or, as the Romans said, the
tantundem iusdem generis, qualitatis et bonetatis.

2

THE ECONOMIC AND SOCIAL
FUNCTION OF IRREGULAR DEPOSITS

Deposits of fungible goods (like money), also called irregular deposits, perform an important social function which
cannot be fulfilled by regular deposits, understood as deposits
of specific goods. It would be senseless and very costly to
deposit oil in separate, numbered containers (that is, as sealed
deposits in which ownership is not transferred), or to place
bills in an individually-numbered, sealed envelope. Though
these extreme cases would constitute regular deposits in
which ownership is not transferred, they would mean a loss of
the extraordinary efficiency and cost reduction which result
from treating individual deposits jointly and indistinctly from
one another[6] at no cost nor loss of availability to the depositor,
who is just as happy if, when he requests it, he receives a *tantundem* equal in quantity and quality, but not identical in
terms of specific content, to that which he originally handed
over. The irregular deposit has other advantages as well. In

---

[6]In the specific case of the monetary irregular deposit, the occasional use
of cashier services offered by banks is an additional advantage.

the regular deposit, or deposit of specific goods, the depositary is not responsible for the loss of a good due to an inevitable accident or act of God, while in the irregular deposit, the depositary is responsible even in the case of an act of God. Therefore, in addition to the traditional advantages of immediate availability and safekeeping of the entire deposit, the irregular deposit acts as a type of *insurance* against the possibility of loss due to inevitable accidents.[7]

THE FUNDAMENTAL ELEMENT IN THE MONETARY IRREGULAR DEPOSIT

In the irregular deposit, the obligation to guard and protect the goods deposited, which is the fundamental element in all deposits, takes the form of an obligation to always maintain complete availability of the *tantundem* in favor of the depositor. In other words, whereas in the regular deposit the specific good deposited must be continually guarded conscientiously and *in individuo*, in the deposit of fungible goods, what must be continually guarded, protected and kept available to the depositor is the *tantundem*; that is, the equivalent in quantity and quality to the goods originally handed over. This means that *in the irregular deposit, custody consists of the obligation to always keep available to the depositor goods of the same quantity and quality as those received*. This availability, though the goods be continually replaced by others, is the equivalent in the case of fungible goods of keeping the *in individuo* good in the case of non-fungibles. In other words, the owner of the grain warehouse or oil tank can use the specific oil or grain he receives, either for his own use or to return to

---

[7]As Pasquale Coppa-Zuccari wisely points out,

> a differenza del deposito regolare, l'irregolare gli garantisce la restituzione del *tantundem* nella stessa specie e qualità, sempre ed in ogni caso. . . . Il deponente irregolare è garantito contro il caso fortuito, contro il quale il depositario regolare non lo garantisce; trovasi anzi in una condizione economicamente ben più fortunata che se fosse assicurato. (See Pasquale Coppa-Zuccari, *Il deposito irregolare* [Modena: Biblioteca dell' Archivio Giuridico Filippo Serafini, 1901], vol. 6, pp. 109–10)

another depositor, *as long as he maintains available to the original depositor oil or grain of the same quantity and quality as those deposited.* In the deposit of money the same rule applies. If a friend gives you a twenty-dollar bill in deposit, we may consider that he transfers to you the ownership of the specific bill, and that you may use it for your own expenses or for any other use, as long as you keep the equivalent amount (in the form of another bill or two ten-dollar bills), so that the moment he requests you repay him, you can do so immediately with no problem and no need for excuses.[8]

---

[8]Coppa-Zuccari may have expressed this essential principle of the irregular deposit better than anyone when he said that the depositary

> risponde della diligenza di un buon padre di famiglia indipendentemente da quella che esplica nel giro ordinario della sua vita economica e giuridica. Il depositario invece, nella custodia delle cose ricevute in deposito, deve spiegare la diligenza, *quam suis rebus adhibere solet.* E questa diligenza diretta alla conservazione delle cose propie, il depositario esplica: in rapporto alle cose infungibili, con l'impedire che esse si perdano o si deteriorino; il rapporto alle fungibili, col curare di averne sempre a disposizione la medesima quantità e qualità. Questo *tenere a disposizione* una eguale quantità è qualità di cose determinate, si rinnovellino pur di continuo e si sostituiscano, equivale per le fungibili a ciò che per le infungibili è l'esistenza della cosa *in individuo.* (Coppa-Zuccari, *Il deposito irregolare,* p. 95)

Joaquín Garrigues states the same opinion in *Contratos bancarios* (Madrid, 1975), p. 365, and Juan Roca Juan also expresses it in his article on the deposit of money (*Comentarios al Código Civil y Compilaciones Forales,* under the direction of Manuel Albaladejo, tome 22, vol. 1, *Editorial Revista del Derecho Privado EDERSA* [Madrid, 1982], pp. 246–55), in which he arrives at the conclusion that in the irregular deposit the safe-keeping obligation means precisely that the depositary

> must keep the quantity deposited available to the depositor at all times, and therefore must keep the number of units of the sort deposited necessary to return the amount *when it is requested of him.* (p. 251)

In other words, in the case of the monetary irregular deposit, the safe-keeping obligation means the demand for a continuous 100-percent cash reserve.

To sum up, the logic behind the institution of irregular deposit is based on universal legal principles and suggests that the essential element of custody or safekeeping necessitates the continuous availability to the depositor of a *tantundem* equal to the original deposit. In the specific case of money, the quintessential fungible good, this means the safekeeping obligation requires the continuous availability to the depositor of a 100-percent cash reserve.

RESULTING EFFECTS OF THE FAILURE TO COMPLY WITH THE ESSENTIAL OBLIGATION IN THE IRREGULAR DEPOSIT

When there is a failure to comply with the obligation of safekeeping in a deposit, as is logical, it becomes necessary to indemnify the depositor, and if the depositary has acted fraudulently and has employed the deposited good for his own personal use, he has committed the offense of misappropriation. Therefore, in the regular deposit, if someone receives the deposit of a painting, for example, and sells it to earn money, he is committing the offense of misappropriation. The same offense is committed in the irregular deposit of fungible goods by the depositary who uses deposited goods for his own profit without maintaining the equivalent *tantundem* available to the depositor at all times. This would be the case of the oil depositary who does not keep in his tanks a quantity equal to the total deposited with him, or a depositary who receives money on deposit and uses it in any way for his own benefit (spending it himself or loaning it), but does not maintain a 100-percent cash reserve at all times.[9] The criminal law

---

[9]Other related offenses are committed when a depositary *falsifies* the number of deposit slips or vouchers. This would be the case of the oil depositary who issues false deposit vouchers to be traded by third parties, and in general, of any depositary of a fungible good (including money) who issues slips or vouchers for a larger amount than that actually deposited. It is clear that in this case we are dealing with the offenses of *document forgery* (the issue of the false voucher) and *fraud* (if in issuing the voucher there is an intention to deceive third parties and obtain a specific profit). Later on we will confirm that the historical development of banking was based on the perpetration of such criminal acts in relation to the "business" of issuing banknotes.

expert Antonio Ferrer Sama has explained that if the deposit consists of an amount of money and the obligation to return the same amount (irregular deposit), and the depositary takes the money and uses it for his own profit, we will have to

> determine which of the following situations is the correct one in order to determine his criminal liability: at the time he takes the money the depositary has sufficient financial stability to return at any moment the amount received in deposit; or, on the contrary, at the time he takes the money he *does not have enough cash of his own with which to meet his obligation to return the depositor's money at any moment he requests it.* In the first case the offense of misappropriation has not been committed. However, if at the time the depositary takes the deposited amount he does not have enough cash in his power to fulfill his obligations to the depositor, he is guilty of misappropriation

from the very moment he takes the goods deposited for his own use and ceases to possess a *tantundem* equivalent to the original deposit.[10]

---

[10]Antonio Ferrer Sama, *El delito de apropiación indebida* (Murcia: Publicaciones del Seminario de Derecho Penal de la Universidad de Murcia, Editorial Sucesores de Nogués, 1945), pp. 26–27. As we indicated in the text and Eugenio Cuello Calón also explains (*Derecho penal*, Barcelona: Editorial Bosch, 1972, tome 2, special section, 13th ed, vol. 2, pp. 952–53), the crime is committed the moment it is established that appropriation or embezzlement has occurred, and the offense actually derives from the intention of committing the appropriation. Due to their private nature, these intentions must be perceived by the result of external acts (like the alienation, consumption or lending of the good). These deeds generally take place long before the discovery is made by the depositor who, when he tries to withdraw his deposit, is surprised to find that the depositary is not able to immediately hand over to him the corresponding *tantundem*. Miguel Bajo Fernández, Mercedes Pérez Manzano, and Carlos Suárez González (*Manual de derecho penal*, special section, "Delitos patrimoniales y económicos" [Madrid: Editorial Centro de Estudios Ramón Areces, 1993]) also conclude that the offense is committed the very moment the act of disposal takes place, no matter what the subsequent effects are, and continues to be a crime even when the object is recovered or the perpetrator fails to profit from the appropriation, *regardless of whether the depositary is able to return the tantundem the*

COURT DECISIONS ACKNOWLEDGING THE FUNDAMENTAL LEGAL
PRINCIPLES WHICH GOVERN THE MONETARY IRREGULAR-DEPOSIT
CONTRACT (100-PERCENT RESERVE REQUIREMENT)

As late as the twentieth century, court decisions in Europe have upheld the demand for a 100-percent reserve requirement, the embodiment of the essential element of custody and safekeeping in the monetary irregular deposit. On June 12, 1927, the Court of Paris convicted a banker for the crime of misappropriation for having used, as was the common practice in banking, funds deposited with him by a client. On January 4, 1934, another ruling of the same court maintained the same position.[11] In addition, when the Bank of Barcelona failed in

---

moment it is required (p. 421). The same authors contend that there exists an unacceptable legal loophole in Spanish criminal law, compared to other legal systems containing

> specific provisions for corporate crimes and breach of trust, under which it would be possible to include the unlawful behaviors of banks with respect to the irregular deposit of checking accounts. (p. 429)

In Spanish criminal law, the article governing misappropriation is article 252 (mentioned by Antonio Ferrer Sama) of the new 1996 Penal Code (article 528 of the former), which states:

> The penalties specified in article 249 or 250 will be applied to anyone who, to the detriment of another, appropriates or embezzles money, goods, securities or any other movable property or patrimonial asset which he has received on deposit, on consignment or in trust, or by way of another claim carrying the obligation to deliver or return the property, or who denies having received it, when the amount appropriated exceeds 300 euros. These penalties will be increased by 50 percent in the case of a necessary deposit.

Finally, the most thorough work on the criminal aspects of the misappropriation of money, which covers *in extenso* the position of Professors Ferrer Sama, Bajo Fernández, and others, is by Norberto J. de la Mata Barranco, *Tutela penal de la propiedad y delitos de apropiación: el dinero como objeto material de los delitos de hurto y apropiación indebida* (Barcelona: Promociones y Publicaciones Universitarias [PPU, Inc.], 1994), esp. pp. 407–08 and 512.

[11]These judicial rulings appear in Jean Escarra's *Principes de droit commercial*, p. 256; Garrigues also refers to them in *Contratos bancarios*, pp. 367–68.

Spain, Barcelona's northern court of original jurisdiction, in response to protests of checking-account holders demanding recognition as depositors, pronounced a judgment acknowledging them as such and identifying their consequent preferential status as creditors of a bankruptcy claiming title to some of the assets. The decision was based on the fact that the right of banks to use cash from checking accounts is necessarily restricted by the obligation to maintain the uninterrupted availability of these account funds to the checking-account holder. As a result, this legal restriction on availability ruled out the possibility that the bank could consider itself exclusive owner of funds deposited in a checking account.[12] Though the Spanish Supreme Court did not have the opportunity to rule on the failure of the Bank of Barcelona, a decision pronounced by it on June 21, 1928 led to a very similar conclusion:

> According to the commercial practices and customs recognized by jurisprudence, the monetary deposit contract consists of the deposit of money with a person who, though he does not contract the obligation to retain for the depositor the same cash or assets handed over, *must maintain possession of the amount deposited, with the purpose of returning it, partially or in its entirety, the moment the depositor should claim it; the depositary does not acquire the right to use the deposit for his own purposes, since, as he is obliged to return the deposit the moment it is requested of him, he must maintain constant possession of sufficient cash to do so.*[13]

---

[12]"Dictamen de Antonio Goicoechea," in *La Cuenta corriente de efectos o valores de un sector de la banca catalana y el mercado libre de valores de Barcelona* (Madrid: Imprenta Delgado Sáez, 1936), pp. 233–89, esp. pp. 263–64. Garrigues also refers to this ruling in *Contratos bancarios*, p. 368.

[13]José Luis García-Pita y Lastres cites this decision in his paper, "Los depósitos bancarios de dinero y su documentación," which appeared in *La revista de derecho bancario y bursátil* (Centro de Documentación Bancaria y Bursátil, October–December 1993), pp. 919–1008, esp. p. 991. Garrigues also makes reference to this ruling in *Contratos bancarios*, p. 387.

3

THE ESSENTIAL DIFFERENCES BETWEEN THE IRREGULAR DEPOSIT CONTRACT AND THE MONETARY LOAN CONTRACT

It is now important to review and stress the fundamental differences between the irregular deposit contract and the loan contract, both with respect to money. As we will see later in different contexts, much of the confusion and many of the legal and economic errors surrounding our topic derive from a lack of understanding of the essential differences between these two contracts.

THE EXTENT TO WHICH PROPERTY RIGHTS ARE TRANSFERRED IN EACH CONTRACT

To begin with, it is necessary to point out that the inability to clearly distinguish between the irregular deposit and the loan arises from the excessive and undue importance given to the fact that, as we already know, in the irregular deposit of money or of any other fungible good we may consider that the ownership of the deposited good is transferred to the depositary, "just as" in the loan or mutuum contract. This is the only similarity between the two types of contract and it has led many scholars to confuse them without reason.

We have already seen that in the irregular deposit the transfer of "ownership" is a secondary requirement arising from the fact that the object of the deposit is a fungible good which cannot be handled individually. We also know there are many advantages to putting a deposit together with other sets of the same fungible good and treating the individual units indistinctly. Indeed, as one may not, in strictly legal terms, demand the return of the specific items deposited, since this is a physical impossibility, it may appear necessary to consider that a "transfer" of ownership occurs *with regard to the individual, specific units* deposited, as these are indistinguishable from one another. So the depositary becomes the "owner," but only in the sense that, for as long as he continues to hold the *tantundem*, he is free to allocate the particular, indistinguishable units as he chooses. This is the full extent to which property rights are transferred in the irregular deposit, unlike the loan contract, where complete availability of the loaned good is transferred for the duration of the contract's term. Therefore, even given the one feasible "similarity" between the irregular deposit and the monetary loan (the supposed "transfer" of ownership), it is important to understand that this transfer of ownership has a very different economic and legal meaning in each contract. Perhaps, as we explained in footnote number five, it would even be wisest to hold that in the irregular deposit there is no transfer of ownership, but rather that the depositor at all times maintains ownership over the *tantundem* in an abstract sense.

FUNDAMENTAL ECONOMIC DIFFERENCES BETWEEN THE TWO CONTRACTS

This variation in legal content stems from the essential difference between the two contracts, which in turn derives from the distinct *economic foundation* on which each is based. Thus, Ludwig von Mises, with his habitual clarity, points out that if the loan

> in the economic sense means the exchange of a present good or a present service against a future good or a future service, then it is hardly possible to include the transactions in question [irregular deposits] under the conception of credit. A depositor of a sum of money who acquires in exchange for it a claim convertible into money at any time which will perform exactly the same service for him as the sum it refers to, has exchanged no present good for a future good. The claim that he has acquired by his deposit is also a present good for him. The depositing of the money in no way means that he has renounced immediate disposal over the utility that it commands.

He concludes that the deposit "is not a credit transaction, because the essential element, the exchange of present goods for future goods, is absent."[14]

---

[14]Ludwig von Mises, *The Theory of Money and Credit* (Indianapolis, Ind.: Liberty Classics, 1980), pp. 300–01. This is the best English edition of H.E. Batson's translation of the second German edition (published in 1924) of

Therefore, in the monetary irregular deposit there is no relinquishment of present goods in favor of a larger quantity of future goods at the end of a time period, but rather simply a change in the manner of possessing present goods. This change occurs because under many circumstances the depositor finds it more advantageous from a subjective standpoint (that is, more conducive to his goals) to make a monetary irregular deposit in which the actual good deposited is mixed with others of the same sort and treated indistinguishably from them. Among other advantages, we have already mentioned an insurance against the risk of loss due to inevitable accident and the opportunity to use the cashier services provided by banks to customers with a checking account. In contrast, the essence of the loan contract is radically dissimilar. The aim of the loan contract is precisely to *cede* today the availability of present goods to the borrower for his use, in order to obtain in the future a generally larger quantity of goods in exchange at the end of the term set in the contract. We say "generally larger" because, given the logical time preference inherent in all human actions, which indicates that, other things being equal, present goods are always preferable to future goods, it is necessary to add to the future goods a differential amount in the form of interest. Otherwise, it would be difficult to find anyone willing to give up the availability of present goods, which is a requirement of every loan.

Hence, from an economic viewpoint the difference between the two contracts is quite clear: the irregular deposit contract does not entail the exchange of present goods for future goods, while the loan contract does. As a result, in the irregular deposit the availability of the good is not transferred, but rather the good remains continuously available to the depositor (despite the fact that in a sense "ownership" has been shifted from a legal standpoint), while in the loan contract there is always a transfer of availability from the lender to the borrower. Furthermore, the loan contract usually includes an interest agreement, whereas in the monetary

---

Theorie des Geldes und der Umlaufsmittel, published by Duncker and Humblot in Munich and Leipzig. The first edition was published in 1912.

irregular-deposit contract, interest agreements are *contra natu-ram* and absurd. Coppa-Zuccari, with his customary insight, explains that the absolute impossibility of including an inter-est agreement in the irregular deposit contract is, from a legal viewpoint, a direct result of the right granted the depositor to withdraw the deposit *at any time*, and the depositary's corre-sponding obligation to maintain the associated *tantundem* con-stantly available to the depositor.[15] Ludwig von Mises also indicates that it is possible for the depositor to make deposits without demanding any type of interest precisely because

> the claim obtained in exchange for the sum of money is equally valuable to him whether he converts it sooner or later, or even not at all; and because of this it is possible for him, without damaging his economic interests, to acquire such claims in return for the surrender of money without demanding compensation for any difference in value arising from the difference in time between payment and repay-ment, such, of course, as does not in fact exist.[16]

Given the economic foundation of the monetary irregular-deposit contract, which does not imply the exchange of pres-ent goods for future goods, the uninterrupted availability in favor of the depositor and the incompatibility with an interest agreement arise logically and directly from the legal essence

---

[15]   Conseguenza immediata del diritto concesso al deponente di ritirare in ogni tempo il deposito e del correlativo obbligo del depositario di renderlo alla prima richiesta e di tenere sempre a disposizione del deponente il suo *tantundem* nel deposito irregolare, è l'impossibilità assoluta per il depositario di cor-rispondere interessi al deponente. (Coppa-Zuccari, *Il deposito irregolare*, p. 292)

Coppa-Zuccari also points out that this incompatibility between the irregular deposit and the payment of interest does not apply, as is logi-cal, to the completely separate case where interest is awarded because the depositary fails to return the money upon request, thus becoming a defaulter. As a result, the concept of *depositum confessatum* was, as we shall see, systematically used throughout the Middle Ages as a legal ploy to bypass the canonical prohibition on the charging of interest on loans.

[16]Mises, *The Theory of Money and Credit*, p. 301.

of the irregular deposit contract, which contrasts sharply with the legal essence of the loan contract.[17]

FUNDAMENTAL LEGAL DIFFERENCES BETWEEN THE TWO CONTRACTS

The essential legal element in the irregular deposit contract is the custody or safekeeping of the money deposited. To the parties deciding to make or receive an irregular deposit, this is the most important aim or *purpose of the contract*,[18] and it varies greatly from the essential purpose of the loan contract, which is the transfer of the availability of the loaned good to the borrower so he can use it for a period of time. Two other important legal differences arise from this essential dissimilarity in purpose between the two types of contract. First, the irregular deposit contract lacks a *term*, the essential element identifying a loan contract. Indeed, while it is impossible to

---

[17]The fact that interest agreements are incompatible with the monetary irregular-deposit contract does not mean the latter should be free of charge. Indeed, in keeping with its very nature, the irregular deposit usually includes the stipulation of payment by the depositor to the depositary of a certain amount for the costs of guarding the deposit or maintaining the account. The payment of interest is a reasonable indication that the essential obligation of safekeeping in the irregular deposit contract is almost certainly being violated and that the depositary is using the money of his depositors for his own benefit, misappropriating part of the *tantundem* which he should keep available at all times to the depositors.

[18]J. Dabin, *La teoría de la causa: estudio histórico y jurisprudencial*, translated by Francisco de Pelsmaeker and adapted by Francisco Bonet Ramón, 2nd ed. (Madrid: Editorial Revista de Derecho Privado, 1955), pp. 24 and on. That the purpose of the irregular deposit contract is custody or safekeeping and is different from the object of the loan contract is recognized even by authors who, like García-Pita or Ozcáriz-Marco, still do not accept that the unavoidable, logical consequence of its purpose of safekeeping is a 100-percent reserve requirement for bank demand deposits. See José Luis García-Pita y Lastres, "Depósitos bancarios y protección del depositante," *Contratos bancarios* (Madrid: Colegios Notariales de España, 1996), pp. 119–266, and esp. 167–91; and Florencio Ozcáriz Marco, *El contrato de depósito: estudio de la obligación de guarda* (Barcelona: J.M. Bosch Editor, 1997), pp. 37 and 47.

imagine a monetary loan contract without a fixed term (during
which not only is ownership transferred, but availability is lost
to the lender as well), at the end of which it is necessary to
return the *tantundem* of money originally loaned plus interest,
in the irregular deposit contract *there is no term whatsoever*, but
rather there is continuous availability in favor of the depositor,
who may withdraw his *tantundem* at any time.[19] The second
essential legal difference refers to the obligations of the two parties: in the irregular deposit contract the legal obligation
implied by the nature of the contract consists, as we know, of
the conscientious *custody or safekeeping* (as would be expected of
a good parent) of the *tantundem*, which is kept continually available to the depositor.[20] In the loan contract this obligation does
not exist, and the borrower may use the loaned amount with
total freedom. Indeed, when we speak of the legal "transfer of
ownership" in the two contracts, we allude to two very dissimilar concepts. Whereas the "transfer" of ownership in the

---

[19]Civil law experts unanimously agree that a term is *essential* to a loan
contract, unlike an irregular deposit contract, which *has no term*. Manuel
Albaladejo emphasizes that the mutuum contract concludes and the
loan must be given back at the end of the term (for example, see article
1125 of the Spanish Civil Code). He even indicates that if a term has not
been explicitly designated, then the intention to set one for the debtor
must always be assumed, since *a term is required by the essential nature of
the loan contract.* In this case a third party (the courts) must be allowed
to stipulate the corresponding term (this is the solution adopted in article 1128 of the Spanish Civil Code). See Albaladejo, *Derecho civil II, Derecho de obligaciones*, vol. 2, p. 317.

[20]Clearly, it is the *tantundem* which is kept continually available to the
depositor, and not the same specific units deposited. In other words,
even though ownership of the concrete physical units deposited is
transferred and they may be used, the *depositary does not gain any real
availability*, since what he gains with respect to the specific units
received is exactly compensated by the necessary loss of the equivalent
availability regarding other specific units already in his power, and this
necessity stems from the obligation to keep the *tantundem* constantly
available to the depositor. In the monetary deposit contract, this constant availability to the depositor is usually referred to by the expression
"on demand," which illustrates the essential, unmistakable purpose of
the checking account or "demand" deposit contract: to keep the *tantundem* continually available to the depositor.

TABLE 1-1

ESSENTIAL DIFFERENCES BETWEEN TWO RADICALLY DISTINCT CONTRACTS

Monetary Irregular Deposit	*Monetary Loan*

Economic Differences

1. Present goods are not exchanged for future goods.	1. Present goods are exchanged for future goods.
2. There is complete, continuous availability in favor of the depositor.	2. Full availability is transferred from lender to borrower.
3. There is no interest, since present goods are not exchanged for future goods.	3. There is interest, since present goods are exchanged for future goods.

Legal Differences

1. The essential element (and the depositor's main motivation) is the *custody* or safekeeping of the *tantundem*.	1. The essential element is the transfer of availability of the present goods to the borrower.
2. There is no term for returning the money, but rather the contract is "on demand."	2. The contract requires the establishment of a *term* for the return of the loan and calculation and payment of interest.
3. The depositary's obligation is to keep the *tantundem* available to the depositor at all times (100-percent cash reserve).	3. The borrower's obligation is to return the *tantundem* at the end of the term and to pay the agreed-upon interest.

irregular deposit contract (which could be considered a
requirement of the fungible nature of the deposited goods)
does not imply a simultaneous transfer of availability of the
tantundem, in the loan contract there is a *complete* transfer of
ownership and availability of the *tantundem* from lender to
borrower.[21] The differences covered in this section are outlined in Table 1-1.

4

THE DISCOVERY BY ROMAN LEGAL EXPERTS OF THE GENERAL LEGAL PRINCIPLES GOVERNING THE MONETARY IRREGULAR-DEPOSIT CONTRACT

THE EMERGENCE OF TRADITIONAL LEGAL PRINCIPLES ACCORDING TO MENGER, HAYEK, AND LEONI

The traditional, universal legal principles we dealt with in
the last section in relation to the irregular deposit contract
have not emerged in a vacuum, nor are they the result of *a priori* knowledge. The concept of law as a series of rules and
institutions to which people constantly, perpetually and customarily adapt their behavior has been developed and refined

---

[21]At this point it is important to draw attention to the "time deposit"
contract, which possesses the economic and legal characteristics of a
true loan, not those of a deposit. We must emphasize that this use of terminology is misleading and conceals a true loan contract, in which present goods are exchanged for future goods, the availability of money is
transferred for the duration of a fixed *term* and the client has the right to
receive the corresponding interest. This confusing terminology makes it
even more complicated and difficult for citizens to distinguish between
a true (demand) deposit and a loan contract (involving a term). Certain
economic agents have repeatedly and selfishly employed these terms to
take advantage of the existent confusion. The situation degenerates further when, as quite often occurs, banks offer time "deposits" (which
should be true loans) that become *de facto* "demand" deposits, as the
banks provide the possibility of withdrawing the funds at any time
without penalty.

through a repetitive, evolutionary process. Perhaps one of Carl Menger's most important contributions was the development of a complete economic theory of social institutions. According to his theory, social institutions arise as the result of an evolutionary process in which innumerable human beings interact, each one equipped with his own small personal heritage of subjective knowledge, practical experiences, desires, concerns, goals, doubts, feelings, etc. By means of this spontaneous evolutionary process, a series of behavior patterns or *institutions* emerges in the realms of economics and language, as well as law, and these behaviors make life in society possible. Menger discovered that institutions appear through a social process composed of a multiplicity of human actions, which is always led by a relatively small group of individuals who, in their particular historical and geographical circumstances, are the first ones to discover that certain patterns of behavior help them attain their goals more efficiently. This discovery initiates a decentralized trial and error process encompassing many generations, in which the most effective behavior patterns gradually become more widespread as they successfully counter social maladjustments. Thus there is an unconscious social process of learning by imitation which explains how the pioneering behavior of these most successful and creative individuals catches on and eventually extends to the rest of society. Also, due to this evolutionary process, those societies which first adopt successful principles and institutions tend to spread and prevail over other social groups. Although Menger developed his theory in relation to the origin and evolution of *money*, he also mentions that the same essential theoretical framework can be easily applied to the study of the origins and development of *language*, as well as to our present topic, *juridical institutions*. Hence the paradoxical fact that the moral, juridical, economic and linguistic institutions which are most important and essential to man's life in society are not of his own creation, because he lacks the necessary intellectual might to assimilate the vast body of random information that these institutions generate. On the contrary, these institutions inevitably and spontaneously emanate from the social processes of human

interaction which Menger believes should be the main subject
of research in economics.[22]

Menger's ideas were later developed by F.A. Hayek in
various works on the fundamentals of law and juridical institutions,[23] and especially by the Italian professor of political
science, Bruno Leoni, who was the first to incorporate the following in a synoptic theory on the philosophy of law: the economic theory of social processes developed by Menger and
the Austrian School, the most time-honored Roman legal tradition, and the Anglo-Saxon tradition of rule of law. Indeed,
Bruno Leoni's great contribution is having shown that the
Austrian theory on the emergence and evolution of social
institutions is perfectly illustrated by the phenomenon of common law and that it was already known and had been formulated by the Roman classical school of law.[24] Leoni, citing

----

[22]Carl Menger, *Untersuchungen über die Methode der Socialwissenschaften
und der Politischen Ökonomie insbesondere* (Leipzig: Duncker and Humblot, 1883), esp. p. 182. (*Investigations into the Method of the Social Sciences
with Special Reference to Economics* [New York: New York University
Press, 1985]). Menger himself eloquently formulates this new question
which his proposed scientific research program for economics is
designed to answer:

> How is it possible that the institutions which are most signif-
> icant to and best serve the common good have emerged with-
> out the intervention of a deliberate common will to create
> them? (pp. 163–65)

The best and perhaps the most brilliant synopsis of Menger's theory on
the evolutionary origin of money appears in his article, "On the Origin
of Money," *Economic Journal* (June 1892): 239–55. This article has been
reprinted by Israel M. Kirzner in his *Classics in Austrian Economics: A
Sampling in the History of a Tradition* (London: William Pickering, 1994),
vol. 1, pp. 91–106.

[23]F.A. Hayek, *The Constitution of Liberty* (London: Routledge, 1st edition
[1960] 1990); *Law, Legislation and Liberty* (Chicago: University of Chicago
Press, 1978); and *The Fatal Conceit: The Errors of Socialism* (Chicago: University of Chicago Press, 1989).

[24]See Jesús Huerta de Soto, *Estudios de economía política* (Madrid: Unión
Editorial, 1994), chap. 10, pp. 121–28, and Bruno Leoni, *Freedom and the
Law* (Princeton, N.J.: D. Van Nostrand Company, 1961), essential reading
for all jurists and economists.

Cicero's rendering of Cato's words, specifically points out that Roman jurists knew Roman law was not the personal invention of one man, but rather the creation of many over generations and centuries, given that

> there never was in the world a man so clever as to foresee everything and that even if we could concentrate all brains into the head of one man, it would be impossible for him to provide for everything at one time without having the experience that comes from practice through a long period of history.[25]

In short, it was Leoni's opinion that law emerges as the result of a continuous trial-and-error process, in which each

---

[25] Nostra autem res publica non unius esset ingenio, sed multorum, nec una hominis vita, sed aliquod constitutum saeculis et aetatibus, nam neque ullum ingenium tantum extitisse dicebat, ut, quem res nulla fugeret, quisquam aliquando fuisset, neque cuncta ingenia conlata in unum tantum posse uno tempore providere, ut omnia complecterentur sine rerum usu ac vetustate. (Marcus Tullius Cicero, *De re publica*, 2, 1–2 [Cambridge, Mass.: The Loeb Classical Library, 1961], pp. 111–12. See Leoni, *Freedom and the Law*, p. 89)

Leoni's book is by all accounts exceptional. Not only does he reveal the parallelism between the market and common law on the one hand, and socialism and legislation on the other, but he is also the first jurist to recognize Ludwig von Mises's argument on the impossibility of socialist economic calculation as an illustration of

> a more general realization that no legislator would be able to establish by himself, without some kind of continuous collaboration on the part of all the people concerned, the rules governing the actual behavior of everybody in the endless relationships that each has with everybody else. (pp. 18–19)

For information on the work of Bruno Leoni, founder of the prestigious journal *Il Politico* in 1950, see *Omaggio a Bruno Leoni*, Pasquale Scaramozzino, ed. (Milan: Ed. A. Guiffrè, 1969), and the article "Bruno Leoni in Retrospect" by Peter H. Aranson, *Harvard Journal of Law and Public Policy* (Summer, 1988). Leoni was multifaceted and extremely active in the fields of university teaching, law, business, architecture, music, and linguistics. He was tragically murdered by one of his tenants while trying to collect the rent on the night of November 21, 1967. He was fifty-four years old.

individual takes into account his own circumstances and the behavior of others and the law is perfected through a selective evolutionary process.[26]

ROMAN JURISPRUDENCE

The greatness of classical Roman jurisprudence stems precisely from the realization of this important truth on the part of legal experts and the continual efforts they dedicated to study, interpretation of legal customs, exegesis, logical analysis, the tightening of loopholes and the correction of flaws; all of which they carried out with the necessary standards of prudence and equanimity.[27] The occupation of classical jurist was a true *art*, of which the constant aim was to identify and define the essence of the juridical institutions that have developed throughout society's evolutionary process. Furthermore, classical jurists never entertained pretensions of being "original" or "clever," but rather were "the servants of certain *fundamental principles*, and as Savigny pointed out, herein lies their greatness."[28] Their fundamental objective was to discover the universal principles of law, which are unchanging and inherent in the logic of human relationships. It is true, however, that social evolution itself often necessitates the

---

[26]In the words of Bruno Leoni, law is shaped by

> una continua serie de tentativi, che gli individui compiono quando pretendono un comportamento altrui, e si affidano al propio potere di determinare quel comportamento, qualora esso non si determini in modo spontaneo. (Bruno Leoni, "Diritto e politica," in his book *Scritti di scienza politica e teoria del diritto* [Milan: A. Giuffrè, 1980], p. 240)

[27]In fact, the interpreter of the *ius* was the *prudens*, that is, the legal expert or *iuris prudens*. It was his job to *reveal* the law. Jurists provided advice and assistance to individuals and instructed them in business practices and types of contracts, offered answers to their questions and informed judges and magistrates. See Juan Iglesias, *Derecho romano: Instituciones de derecho privado*, 6th rev. ed. (Barcelona: Ediciones Ariel, 1972), pp. 54–55.

[28]Iglesias, *Derecho romano: Instituciones de derecho privado*, p. 56. And esp. Rudolf von Ihering, *El espíritu del derecho romano, Clásicos del Pensamiento Jurídico* (Madrid: Marcial Pons, 1997), esp. pp. 196–202 and 251–53.

application of these unchanging universal principles to new situations and problems arising continually from this evolutionary process.[29] In addition, Roman jurists worked independently and were not civil servants. Despite multiple attempts by official legal experts in Roman times, they were never able to do away with the free practice of jurisprudence, nor did the latter lose its enormous prestige and independence.

Jurisprudence, or the science of law, became an independent profession in the third century B.C. The most important jurists prior to our era were Marcus Porcius Cato and his son Cato Licianus, the consul Mucius Scaevola, and the jurists Quintus Mucius Scaevola, Servius Surpicius Rufus, and Alfenus Varus. Later, in the second century A.D., the classical era began and the most important jurists during that time were Gaius, Pomponius, Africanus, and Marcellus. In the third century their example was followed by Papinian, Paul, Ulpian, and Modestinus, among other jurists. From this time onward, the solutions offered by these independent jurists received such great prestige that the force of law was attached to them; and to prevent the possibility of difficulties arising from differences of opinion in the jurists' legal writings, the force of law was given to the works of Papinian, Paul, Ulpian, Gaius, and Modestinus, and to the doctrines of jurists cited by them, as long as these references could be confirmed upon comparison with original writings. If these authors were in disagreement, the judge was compelled to follow the doctrine defended by the majority; and in the case of a tie, the opinion of Papinian was to prevail. If he had not communicated his opinion on an issue, the judge was free to decide.[30]

---

[29]   The occupation of *interpretatio* was intimately related to the role of advisor to individuals, magistrates, and judges, and consisted of applying time-honored principles to new needs; this meant an expansion of the *ius civile*, even when no new institutions were formally created. (Francisco Hernández-Tejero Jorge, *Lecciones de derecho romano* [Madrid: Ediciones Darro, 1972], p. 30)

[30]This force of law was first acquired in a constitution from the year 426, known as the Citation Law of Theodosius and Valentinianus III. See Hernández-Tejero Jorge, *Lecciones de derecho romano*, p. 3.

Roman classical jurists deserve the credit for first discovering, interpreting, and perfecting the most important juridical institutions that make life in society possible, and as we will see, they had already recognized the irregular deposit contract, understood the essential principles governing it, and outlined its content and essence as explained earlier in this chapter. The irregular deposit contract is not an intellectual, abstract creation. It is a logical outcome of human nature as expressed in multiple acts of social interaction and cooperation, and it manifests itself in a set of principles which cannot be violated without grave consequences to the network of human relationships. The great importance of law in this evolutionary sense, distilled and rid of its logical flaws through the science of legal experts, lies in the guidance it provides people in their daily lives; though in most cases, due to its abstract nature, people may not be able to identify or understand the complete specific function of each juridical institution. Only recently in the historical evolution of human thought has it been possible to understand the laws of social processes and gain a meager grasp on the role of the different juridical institutions in society, and the contributions of economics have been mostly responsible for these realizations. One of our most important objectives is to carry out an economic analysis of social consequences resulting from the violation of the universal legal principles regulating the monetary irregular-deposit contract. In chapter 4 we will begin this theoretical economic analysis of a juridical institution (the monetary bank-deposit contract).

The knowledge we have today of universal legal principles as they were discovered by Roman jurists comes to us through the work of the emperor Justinian, who in the years 528–533 A.D. made an enormous effort to compile the main contributions of classical Roman jurists and recorded them in three books (the *Institutiones*, the *Digest*, and the *Codex Constitutionum*, later completed by a fourth book, the *Novellae*), which, since the edition of Dionysius Gottfried,[31] are known as the *Corpus Juris Civilis*. The *Institutiones* is an essential work

---

[31]*Corpus Juris Civilis* (Geneva: Dionysius Gottfried, 1583).

directed at students and based on Gaius's *Institutiones*. The *Digest* or *Pandecta* is a compilation of classical legal texts which includes over nine thousand excerpts from the works of different prestigious jurists. Passages taken from the works of Ulpian, which comprise a third of the *Digest*, together with excerpts from Paul, Papinian, and Julianus, fill more of the book than the writings of all of the rest of the jurists as a group. In all, contributions appear from thirty-nine specialists in Roman classical law. The *Codex Constitutionum* consists of a chronologically-ordered collection of imperial laws and constitutions (the equivalent of the present-day concept of legislation), and *Novellae*, the last work in the *Corpus*, contains the last imperial constitutions subsequent to the *Codex Constitutionum*.[32]

Now let us follow up this brief introduction by turning to the Roman classical jurists and their treatment of the institution of monetary irregular deposit. It is clear they understood it, considered it a special type of deposit possessing the essential deposit characteristics and differentiated it from other contracts of a radically different nature and essence, such as the mutuum contract or loan.

THE IRREGULAR DEPOSIT CONTRACT UNDER ROMAN LAW

The deposit contract in general is covered in section 3 of book 16 of the *Digest*, entitled "On Depositing and Withdrawing" (*Depositi vel contra*). Ulpian begins with the following definition:

> A deposit is something given another for safekeeping. It is so called because a good is *posited* [or placed]. The preposition *de*

---

[32]Justinian stipulated that the necessary changes be made in the compiled materials so that the law would be appropriate to the historical circumstances and as close to perfect as possible. These modifications, corrections and omissions are called *interpolations* and also *emblemata Triboniani*, after Tribonian, who was in charge of the compilation. There is an entire discipline dedicated to the study of these interpolations, to determining their content through comparison, logical analysis, the study of anachronisms in language, etc., since it has been discovered that a substantial number of them were made after the Justinian era. See Hernández-Tejero Jorge, *Lecciones de derecho romano*, pp. 50–51.

intensifies the meaning, which reflects that all obligations corresponding to the *custody* of the good belong to that person.[33]

A deposit can be either regular, in the case of a specific
good; or irregular, in the case of a fungible good.[34] In fact, in
number 31, title 2, book 19 of the *Digest*, Paul explains the difference between the loan contract or mutuum and the deposit
contract of a fungible good, arriving at the conclusion that

> if a person deposits a certain amount of loose money, which
> he counts and does not hand over sealed or enclosed in
> something, then the only duty of the person receiving it is to
> return the same amount.[35]

---

[33]Ulpian, a native of Tyre (Phoenicia), was advisor to another great
jurist, Papinian, and together with Paul, he was an advising member of
the *concilium principis* and *praefectus praetorio* under Alexander Severus.
He was murdered in the year 228 by the Praetorians. He was a very pro-
lific writer who was better known for his knowledge of juridical literature than for his creative work. He wrote clearly and was a good com-
piler and his writings are regarded with special favor in Justinian's
Digest, where they comprise the main part. On this topic see Iglesias,
Derecho romano: Instituciones de derecho privado, p. 58. The passage cited
in the text is as follows in Latin:

> Depositum est, quod custodiendum alicui datum est, dictum
> ex eo, quod ponitur, praepositio enim de auget depositum, ut
> ostendat totum fidei eius commissum, quod ad custodiam rei
> pertinet. (See Ildefonso L. García del Corral, ed., *Cuerpo de
> derecho civil romano*, 6 vols. [Valladolid: Editorial Lex Nova,
> 1988], vol. 1, p. 831)

[34]However, as Pasquale Coppa-Zuccari astutely points out, the expression *depositum irregolare* did not appear until it was first used by Jason
de Maino, a fifteenth century annotator of earlier works, whose writings were published in Venice in the year 1513. See Coppa-Zuccari, *Il
deposito irregolare*, p. 41. Also, the entire first chapter of this important
work deals with the treatment under Roman law of the irregular
deposit, pp. 2–32. For an excellent, current treatment in Spanish of bibliographic sources on the irregular deposit in Rome, see Mercedes
López-Amor y García's article, "Observaciones sobre el depósito irregular romano," in the *Revista de la Facultad de Derecho de la Universidad
Complutense* 74 (1988–1989): 341–59; and also Alicia Valmaña Ochaita, *El
depósito irregular en la jurisprudencia romana* (Madrid: Edisofer, 1996).

[35]This is actually a summary by Paul of Alfenus Varus's *Digest*. Alfenus
Varus was consul in the year 39 A.D. and the author of forty books of the
Digest. Paul, in turn, was a disciple of Scaevola and an advisor to Papinian

In other words, Paul clearly indicates that in the monetary irregular deposit the depositary's only obligation is to return the *tantundem*: the equivalent in quantity and quality of the original deposit. Moreover, whenever anyone made an irregular deposit of money, he received a written *certificate* or *deposit slip*. We know this because Papinian, in paragraph 24, title 3, book 16 of the *Digest*, says in reference to a monetary irregular deposit,

> *I write this letter by hand* to inform you, so that you will know, that the one hundred coins you have entrusted to me today through Sticho, the slave and administrator, are in my possession and I will return them to you immediately, whenever and wherever you wish.

This passage reveals the immediate availability of the money to the depositor and the custom of giving him a deposit slip or receipt certifying a monetary irregular deposit, which not only established ownership, but also had to be presented upon withdrawal.[36]

---

during the time Papinian was a member of the imperial council under Severus and Caracalla. He was a very ingenious, learned figure and the author of numerous writings. The passage cited in the text is as follows in Latin:

> Idem iuris esse in deposito; nam si quis pecuniam numeratam ita deposuisset ut neque clausam, neque obsignatam traderet, sed adnumeraret, nihil aliud eum debere, apud quem deposita esset, nisi *tantundem* pecuniae solvere. (See Ildefonso L. García del Corral, ed., *Cuerpo de derecho civil romano*, 6 vols. [Valladolid: Editorial Lex Nova, 1988], vol. 1, p. 963)

[36]Papinian, a native of Syria, was *Praefectus Praetorio* beginning in the year 203 A.D. and was sentenced to death by the emperor Caracalla in the year 212 for refusing to justify the murder of his brother, Geta. He shared with Julianus the reputation for being the most notable of Roman jurists, and according to Juan Iglesias, "His writings are remarkable for their astuteness and pragmatism, as well as for their sober style" (*Derecho romano: Instituciones de derecho privado*, p. 58). The passage cited in the text is as follows in Latin:

> centum numos, quos hac die commendasti mihi annumerante servo Sticho actore, esse apud me, ut notum haberes, hac epitistola manu mea scripta tibi notum facio; quae quando volis, et ubi voles, confestim tibi numerabo. (García del Corral, ed., *Cuerpo de derecho civil romano*, vol. 1, p. 840)

The essential obligation of depositaries is to maintain the *tantundem* constantly available to depositors. If for some reason the depositary goes bankrupt, the depositors have absolute privilege over any other claimants, as Ulpian skillfully explains (paragraph 2, number 7, title 3, book 16 of the *Digest*):

> Whenever bankers are declared bankrupt, usually addressed first are the concerns of the depositors; that is, those with money on deposit, not those earning interest on money left with the bankers. So, once the goods have been sold, the depositors have priority over those with privileges, and those who received interest are not taken into account— it is as if they had relinquished the deposit.[37]

Here Ulpian indicates as well that interest was considered incompatible with the monetary irregular deposit and that when bankers paid interest, it was in connection with a totally different contract (in this case, a mutuum contract or loan to a banker, which is better known today as a time "deposit" contract).

As for the depositary's obligations, it is expressly stated in the *Digest* (book 47, title 2, number 78) that he who receives a good on deposit and uses it for a purpose other than that for which it was received is guilty of theft. Celsus also tells us in the same title (book 47, title 2, number 67) that taking a deposit with an intent to deceive constitutes theft. Paul defines theft as "the fraudulent appropriation of a good to gain a profit, either from the good itself or from its use or possession; this is forbidden by *natural law*."[38] As we see, what

---

37   Quoties foro cedunt numularii, solet primo loco ratio haberi depositariorum, hoc est eorum, qui depositas pecunias habuerunt, non quas foenore apud numularios, vel cum numulariis, vel per ipsos exercebant; et ante privilegia igitur, si bona venierint, depositariorum ratio habetur, dummodo eorum, qui vel postea usuras acceperunt, ratio non habeatur, quasi renuntiaverint deposito. (García del Corral, ed., *Cuerpo de derecho civil romano*, vol. 1, p. 837)

38   Furtum est contrectatio rei fraudulosa, lucri faciendi gratia, vel ipsius rei, vel etiam usus eius possessionisve; quod lege naturali prohibitum est admittere. (Ibid., vol. 3, p. 645)

is today called the crime of misappropriation was included under the definition of theft in Roman law. Ulpian, in reference to Julianus, also concluded:

> if someone receives money from me to pay a creditor of mine, and, himself owing the same amount to the creditor, pays him in his own name, he commits theft. (*Digest*, book 47, title 2, number 52, paragraph 16)[39]

In number 3, title 34 (on "the act of deposit"), book 4 of the *Codex Constitutionum* of the *Corpus Juris Civilis*, which includes the constitution established under the consulship of Gordianus and Aviola in the year 239, the obligation to maintain the total availability of the *tantundem* is even clearer, as is the commission of theft when the *tantundem* is not kept available. In this constitution, the emperor Gordianus indicates to Austerus,

> if you make a deposit, you will with reason ask to be paid interest, *since the depositary should thank you for not holding him responsible for theft, because he who knowingly and willingly uses a deposited good for his own benefit, against the will of the owner, also commits the crime of theft.*[40]

Section 8 of the same source deals expressly with depositaries who loan money received on deposit, thus using it for their own benefit. It is emphasized that such an action violates the principle of safekeeping, obligates depositaries to pay interest, and makes them guilty of theft, as we have just seen in the constitution of Gordianus. In this section we read:

> If a person who has received money from you on deposit loans it in his own name, or in the name of any other person,

---

[39] Ibid., p. 663.

[40] Si depositi experiaris, non immerito etiam usuras tibi restitui flagitabis, quum tibi debeat gratulari, quod furti eum actione non facias obnoxium, siquidem qui rem depositam invito domino sciens prudensque in usus suus converterit, etiam furti delicto succedit. (Ibid., vol. 4, p. 490)

he and his successors are most certainly obliged to carry out the task accepted and to fulfill the trust placed in them.[41]

It is recognized, in short, that those who receive money on deposit are often tempted to use it for themselves. This is explicitly acknowledged elsewhere in the *Corpus Juris Civilis* (*Novellae, Constitution LXXXVIII*, at the end of chapter 1), along with the importance of properly penalizing these actions, not only by charging the depositary with theft, but also by holding him responsible for payment of interest on arrears "so that, in fear of these penalties, men will cease to make evil, foolish and perverse use of deposits."[42]

Roman jurists established that when a depositary failed to comply with the obligation to immediately return the *tantundem* upon request, not only was he clearly guilty of the *prior* crime of theft, but he was also liable for payment of interest on arrears. Accordingly, Papinian states:

> He who receives the deposit of an unsealed package of money and agrees to return the same amount, yet uses this money for his own profit, must pay interest for the delay in returning the deposit.[43]

This perfectly just principle is behind the so-called *depositum confessatum*, which we will consider in greater detail in the next chapter and refers to the evasion of the canonical prohibition on interest by disguising actual loan or mutuum contracts

---

[41]   Si is, qui depositam a te pecuniam accepit, eam suo nomine vel cuiuslibet alterius mutuo dedit, tam ipsum de implenda suscepta fide, quan eius successores teneri tibi, certissimum. est. (Ibid., p. 491)

[42]"Ut hoc timore stultorum simul et perversorum maligne versandi cursum in depositionibus homines cessent." As is clear and we will later expand upon, it had already been demonstrated that depositaries made perverse use of money entrusted to them by their depositors. See ibid., vol. 6, pp. 310–11.

[43]   Qui pecuniam apud se non obsignatam, ut tantundem redderet, depositam ad usus propios convertit, post moram in usuras quoque iudicio depositi condemnandus est. (Ibid., vol. 1, p. 841)

as irregular deposits and then deliberately delaying repayment, thus authorizing the charging of interest. If these contracts had from the beginning been openly regarded as loan or mutuum contracts they would not have been permitted by canon law.

Finally, we find evidence in the following extracts (among others) that Roman jurists understood the essential difference between the loan or mutuum contract and the monetary irregular-deposit contract: number 26, title 3, book 16 (passage by Paul); number 9, point 9, title 1, book 12 of the *Digest* (excerpts by Ulpian); and number 10 of the same title and book. However, the clearest and most specific statements to this effect were made by Ulpian in section 2, number 24, title 5, book 42 of the *Digest*, in which he expressly concludes that "To loan is one thing and to deposit is another," and establishes

> that once a banker's goods have been sold and the concerns of the privileged attended to, preference should be given people who, according to attested documents, deposited money in the bank. Nevertheless, those who have received interest from the bankers on money deposited will not be dealt with separately from the rest of the creditors; and with good reason, since to loan is one thing and to deposit is another.[44]

---

[44]   In bonis mensularii vendundis post privilegia potiorem eorum causam esse placuit, qui pecunias apud mensam fidem publicam secuti deposuerunt. Set enim qui depositis numis usuras a mensulariis accepurunt, a ceteris creditoribus non seperantur; et merito, aliud est enim credere, aliud deponere. (Ibid., vol. 3, p. 386)

Papinian, for his part, states that if a depositary fails to comply with his responsibilities, money to return deposits can be taken not only from deposited funds found among the banker's assets, but from all the defrauder's assets. The depositors'

> privilege extends not only to deposited funds still among the banker's assets, but to all of the defrauder's assets; and this is for the public good, given that banking services are necessary. However, necessary expenses always come first, since the calculation of assets usually takes place after discounting them. (The principle reflected here of bankers' unlimited liability appears in point 8, title 3, book 16 of the *Digest*.)

It is therefore clear from Ulpian's writings in this section that bankers carried out two different types of operations. On one hand, they accepted deposits, which involved no right to interest and obliged the depositary to maintain the full, continuous availability of the *tantundem* in favor of the depositors, who had absolute privilege in the case of bankruptcy. And, on the other hand, they received loans (mutuum contracts), which did obligate the banker to pay interest to the lenders, who lacked all privileges in the case of bankrupcy. Ulpian could show no greater clarity in his distinction between the two contracts nor greater fairness in his solutions.

Roman classical jurists discovered and analyzed the universal legal principles governing the monetary irregular-deposit contract, and this analysis coincided naturally with the development of a significant business and trade economy, in which bankers had come to play a very important role. In addition, these principles later appeared in the medieval legal codes of various European countries, including Spain, despite the serious economic and business recession resulting from the fall of the Roman Empire and the advent of the Middle Ages. In *Las Partidas* (law 2, title 3, item 5) it is established that a person who agrees to hold the commodities of another takes part in an irregular deposit in which control over the goods is transferred to him. Nevertheless, he is obliged, depending upon agreements in the corresponding document, to return the goods or the value indicated in the contract for each good removed from the deposit, either because it is sold with the authorization of the original owner, or is removed for other, unexpected reasons.[45] Moreover, in 1255 the *Fuero Real* (law 5,

---

[45]In *Las Partidas* (c. 1312) deposits are called *condesijos* [hidden deposits], and in law 2 of this work we read that

> Control over the possession of goods given another for safe-keeping is not transferred to the receiver of the goods, except when the deposit can be counted, weighed or measured when handed over; and if it is given the receiver in terms of quantity, weight or measure, then control is transferred to him. However, he must return the good or the same amount of another equal to that given him for safekeeping.

title 15, book 3) the distinction is made between the deposit "of some counted money or raw silver or gold," received from "another, by weight," in which case "the goods may be used and goods of the same quantity and quality as those received may be returned;" and the deposit "which is sealed and not counted or measured by weight," in which case "it is not to be used, but if it is used, it must be paid back double."[46] These medieval codes contain a clear distinction between the regular deposit of a specific good and the irregular deposit of money, and they indicate that in the latter case ownership is transferred. However, the codes do not include the important clarifications made in the *Corpus Juris Civilis* to the effect that, though ownership is "transferred," the safekeeping obligation remains, along with the responsibility to keep continually available to the depositor the equivalent in quantity and quality (*tantundem*) of the original deposit. Perhaps the reason for this omission lies in the increasing prevalence of the *depositum confessatum*.

In conclusion, Roman legal tradition correctly defined the institution of monetary irregular deposit and the principles governing it, along with the essential differences between this contract and other legal institutions or contracts, such as the loan or mutuum. In chapter 2 we will consider ways in which the essential principles regulating human interactions in the monetary irregular deposit (and more specifically, the rights of availability and ownership implied by the contract) were gradually corrupted over the centuries as a result of the combined actions of bankers and politicians. We will analyze the circumstances which made these events possible, as well as the reasons behind them. In chapter 3 we will study the different attempts made by the legal profession to justify contracts

---

This topic is covered with the utmost eloquence and clarity in *Las Partidas*. See *Las Siete Partidas*, annotated by the university graduate Gregorio López; facsimile edition published by the *Boletín Oficial del Estado* [official gazette] (Madrid, 1985), vol. 3, 5th Partida, title 3, law 2, pp. 7–8.

[46]See the reference made by Juan Roca Juan to the *Fuero Real* in his article on "El depósito de dinero," in *Comentarios al Código Civil y Compilaciones Forales*, vol. 1, tome 22, p. 249.

which, against traditional legal principles, gradually gained acceptance. Then in chapter 4 we will begin to consider the economic consequences of these events.

2

HISTORICAL VIOLATIONS OF THE LEGAL PRINCIPLES GOVERNING THE MONETARY IRREGULAR-DEPOSIT CONTRACT

In this chapter we will present various examples to show how bankers have throughout history violated traditional legal principles in the irregular deposit, and we will consider the reasons behind the failure of society's regulatory mechanisms to put a stop to these abuses. We will also contemplate the role of governments in this process. Far from endeavoring to scrupulously defend property rights, they supported bankers' improper activity almost from the beginning and granted exemptions and privileges in order to take advantage of this activity for their own uses. Thus the intimate complicity and solidarity traditionally present (and still existent) in relations between state and bank institutions. To understand why the different attempts to legally justify abuses have failed, we must first properly understand the legally corrupt origin of fractional reserves in monetary bank deposits. We will examine attempts at justification in chapter 3.

1
INTRODUCTION

In the last chapter we presented the clear, coherent legal nature of the monetary irregular-deposit contract. Undoubtedly,

those who from the beginning received money from their fellow citizens for safekeeping knew the obligations they were
taking on, specifically, to guard the *tantundem* like a good parent, to keep it constantly available to the depositor. This is precisely the meaning of safekeeping in a deposit contract of a
fungible good. However, while the legal nature of the irregular deposit contract is clear and easy to understand, human
nature is imperfect and weak. Therefore it is comprehensible
that those receiving monetary deposits were tempted to violate the safekeeping obligation and use for themselves money
that should have been kept available to others. The *temptation*
was very strong: without depositors realizing it, bankers
could handle large amounts of money; and if they used it well,
it could generate substantial profit or interest, which bankers
could keep without openly harming anyone.[1] Given the weakness of human nature and the almost irresistible temptation
felt by bankers, it is comprehensible that the traditional principles of safekeeping on which the monetary irregular-deposit
contract is based were violated from the very beginning in a
concealed manner. In addition, given the abstract, confusing
nature of monetary relations, most citizens and the majority of
authorities in charge of enforcing moral and legal principles
failed to notice this phenomenon, except in rare instances.
And once abuses and cases of fraud began to surface and
became better understood, the institution of banking had

---

[1]We are referring to the most obvious source of profit, which initially
motivated bankers to misappropriate depositors' money. In chapter 4
we will examine a source of much greater earnings: the power of
bankers to issue money or create loans and deposits out of nowhere. The
resulting profit is immensely larger; however, as it arises from an
abstract process, it is certain not even bankers were fully aware of it
until very late in the evolution of finance. Nevertheless, the fact that
they did not understand, but only intuited, this second type of profit
does not mean they failed to take advantage of it completely. In chapter
4 we will explain how bankers' violation of traditional legal principles
through fractional-reserve banking makes it possible to create loans out
of nowhere, the return of which is then demanded in hard cash (with
interest to boot!). In short, we are dealing with a constant, privileged
source of funding in the shape of deposits bankers create out of nothing
and constantly employ for their own uses.

already been in operation so long and had acquired such power that it was practically impossible to effectively curb corruption. Moreover, the gradual discovery authorities made of banks' immense power to create money explains why, in most instances, governments ended up becoming accomplices to banking fraud, granting privileges to bankers and legalizing their improper activity, in exchange for the opportunity to participate, directly or indirectly, in their enormous profits. In this way they established an important alternative source of state funding. Furthermore, this corruption of the state's traditional duty to define and defend property rights was encouraged by governments' enormous, recurrent need for resources, due to their historical irresponsibility and lack of financial control. Thus, a more and more perfect symbiosis or community of interests was formed between governments and bankers, a relationship which to a great extent still exists today.

However, despite the complexity of the above situation, certain shrewd thinkers long ago began to understand it. Doctor Saravia de la Calle, in his book, *Instrucción de mercaderes*, attributes the destructive effects of banking to the fact that

> man's insatiable greed has so thoroughly banished his fear
> of God and sense of shame, and I even believe it is due to the
> neglect of the republic's spiritual and temporal leaders.[2]

If Saravia de la Calle shows any weakness, it is an excess of charity toward the leaders. He correctly attributes fraud in the irregular deposit to men's frailty or greed, but he only holds the leaders responsible for their "neglect" in not being able to end abuses. Historical events reveal that, apart from demonstrating undeniable neglect, on many occasions governments have clearly and explicitly taken advantage of the large profits of the banking "business." In addition, we will see that, in other instances, authorities have not only granted

---

[2]Luis Saravia de la Calle, *Instrucción de mercaderes* (Medina del Campo: Pedro de Castro, 1544; Madrid: Colección de Joyas Bibliográficas, 1949), chap. 8, p. 179.

the bankers privileges so they could carry out their activities with impunity in exchange for specific favors, but they have even created government banks in order to *directly* take advantage of the corresponding profits.

Although banking activities developed long ago and practically coincided with the appearance of money, the dawn of trade, and the first steps in the division of labor[3], we will present and illustrate the violation of traditional legal principles in

---

[3]The archeologist Lenor Mant discovered among the ruins of Babylon a clay tablet with an inscription attesting to intercity trading and the use of commercial and financial means of payment. The tablet mentions an Ardu-Nama (the drawer, of the city of Ur) ordering a Marduk-Bal-at-Irib (the drawee) of the city of Orkoe to pay in Ardu-Nama's name the sum of four minas and fifteen shekels of silver to Bel-Abal-Iddin within a set time period. This document is dated the 14th of Arakhsamna, year 2 of the reign of Nabonaid. For his part, the researcher Hilprecht discovered in the ruins of the city of Nippur a total of 730 baked clay tablets with inscriptions, thought to have belonged to the archives of a bank existing in the city in 400 B.C., called Nurashu and Sons (see "Origen y desenvolvimiento histórico de los bancos," in the *Enciclopedia universal ilustrada europeo-americana* [Madrid: Editorial Espasa-Calpe, 1979], vol. 7, p. 477). In turn, Joaquín Trigo, apart from offering us the above information, reports that around the year 3300 B.C. the temple of Uruk owned the land it exploited, received offerings and deposits and granted loans to farmers and merchants of livestock and grain, becoming the first bank in history. In the British Museum we also find tablets recording the financial operations of the bank Sons of Egibi. The sequence of the tablets demonstrates that from the time of the Assyrians, and for more than 180 years, the institution was controlled by a true financial dynasty. The Code of Hammurabi facilitated the transfer of property and strictly regulated the rights associated with it, as well as commercial activity, limiting interest rates and even establishing public loans at 12.5 percent. Partnership agreements were also regulated, as was the keeping of accounts of operations. The Manu Smriti of India also makes reference to banking and financial operations. In short, remaining records indicate that financial operations occurred between 2300 and 2100 B.C., though the spread of the "banking" business began between 730 and 540 B.C., when Assyrian and New Babylonian dynasties ensured safe trade, which gave rise to specialized banks. This activity also spread to Egypt, and later from there to the Ancient Greek world (Joaquín Trigo Portela, "Historia de la banca," chapter 3 of the *Enciclopedia práctica de la banca* (Barcelona: Editorial Planeta, 1989), vol. 6, esp. pp. 234–37).

the irregular deposit by bankers and authorities in three different historical instances: the Greco-Roman world; the Mediterranean trading cities of the late Middle Ages and the beginning of the Renaissance; and finally, the emergence of the first
important government banks beginning in the seventeenth
century. Moreover, the evolution of banking in these three separate historical instances produced to a large extent the same
characteristic results. Indeed, in each case we observe that as
people began to violate traditional legal principles, harmful
effects followed, not only in the shape of bank failures, but
also profound financial and economic crises. In the following
historical examples the same frauds are committed, followed
by the same typical stages and results, and the same failed
attempts to enforce traditional principles of safekeeping. The
same damaging effects then inexorably follow, and this process
is repeated again and again, up to the present day. Let us now
examine the violation of legal principles and authorities' complicity in banking frauds and abuses throughout history.

2

BANKING IN GREECE AND ROME

In ancient Greece temples acted as banks, loaning money
to individuals and monarchs. For religious reasons temples
were considered inviolable and became a relatively safe
refuge for money. In addition, they had their own militias to
defend them and their wealth inspired confidence in depositors. From a financial standpoint the following were among
the most important Greek temples: Apollo in Delphi, Artemis
in Ephesus, and Hera in Samos.

TRAPEZITEI OR GREEK BANKERS

Fortunately certain documentary sources on banking in
Greece are available to us. The first and perhaps most important is *Trapezitica*,[4] written by Isocrates around the year 393

---

[4]Raymond de Roover points out that the current term banker originated
in Florence, where bankers were called either *banchieri* or *tavolieri*,
because they worked sitting behind a bench (*banco*) or table (*tavola*). The

B.C.[5] It is a forensic speech in which Isocrates defends the interests of the son of a favorite of Satyrus, king of Bosphorus. The son accuses Passio, an Athenian banker, of misappropriating a deposit of money entrusted to him. Passio was an ex-slave of other bankers (Antisthenes and Archetratos), whose trust he had obtained and whose success he even surpassed, for which he was awarded Athenian citizenship. Isocrates's forensic speech describes an attempt by Passio to appropriate

---

same logic was behind terminology used in ancient Greece as well, where bankers were called *trapezitei* because they worked at a *trapeza*, or table. This is why Isocrates's speech "On a Matter of Banking" is traditionally known as Trapezitica. See Raymond de Roover, *The Rise and Decline of the Medici Bank, 1397–1494* (Cambridge, Mass.: Harvard University Press, 1963), p. 15. The great Diego de Covarrubias y Leyva, for his part, indicates that

> the remuneration paid to money changers for the exchange of money was called collybus by the Greeks, and therefore money changers were called collybists. They were also called nummularii and argentarii, as well as trapezitei, mensularii or bankers, because apart from changing money, they carried out a much more profitable business activity: they received money for safekeeping and loaned at interest their own money and that of others.

See chapter 7 of *Veterum collatio numismatum*, published in *Omnium operum* in Salamanca in 1577.

[5]Isocrates was one of the ancient *macróbioi*, and he lived to be almost 100 years old (436–338 B.C.). His life began during the last years of peaceful Athenian dominance over Persia and lasted through the Peloponnesian War, Spartan and Theban supremacy and the Macedonian expansion, which ended in the battle of Chaeronea (Chaironeia), in which Philip II defeated the Delian League the same year Isocrates died. Isocrates's father, Theodorus, was a middle-class citizen whose flute factory had earned him considerable wealth, permitting him to give his children an excellent education. Isocrates's direct teachers appear to have included Theramines, Gorgias, and especially Socrates (there is a passage in Phaedrus where Plato, using Socrates as a mouthpiece, praises the young Isocrates, apparently ironically, predicting his great future). Isocrates was a logographer; that is, he wrote legal speeches for others (people suing or defending their rights) and later he opened a school of rhetoric in Athens. For information on Isocrates, see Juan Manuel Guzmán Hermida's "Introducción General" to *Discursos* (Madrid: Biblioteca Clásica Gredos, 1979), vol. 1, pp. 7–43.

deposits entrusted to his bank by taking advantage of his depositor's difficulties, for which he did not hesitate to deceive, forge, and steal contracts, bribe, etc. In any case, this speech is so important to our topic that it is worth our effort to consider some of its passages in detail.

Isocrates begins his arguments by pointing out how hazardous it is to sue a banker, because

> deals with bankers are made without witnesses and the injured parties must put themselves in jeopardy before such people, *who have many friends, handle large amounts of money and appear trustworthy due to their profession.*[6]

It is interesting to consider the use bankers have always made of all of their social influence and power (which is enormous, given the number and status of figures receiving loans from them or owing them favors) to defend their privileges and continue their fraudulent activity.[7]

----

[6]Isocrates, "Sobre un asunto bancario," in *Discursos* I, p. 112.

[7]More than 2200 years after Isocrates, the Pennsylvanian senator Condy Raguet also recognized the great power of bankers and their use of it to intimidate their enemies and to in any way possible discourage depositors from withdrawing their deposits and hinder these withdrawals, with the vain hope, among others, of avoiding crises. Condy Raguet concluded that the pressure was almost unbearable and that

> an independent man, who was neither a stockholder or a debtor who would have ventured to compel the banks to do justice, would have been persecuted as an enemy of society.

See the letter from Raguet to Ricardo dated April 18, 1821, published in David Ricardo, *Minor Papers on the Currency Question 1805–1823*, Jacob Hollander, ed. (Baltimore: The Johns Hopkins University Press, 1932), pp. 199–201. This same idea had already been expressed almost three centuries earlier by Saravia de la Calle, who, indicating obstacles created by bankers to keep depositors from withdrawing their money, obstacles few dared to protest, mentioned the

> other thousands of humiliations you inflict upon those who go to withdraw their money from you; you detain them and make them waste money waiting and threaten to pay them in weak currency. In this way you coerce them to give you all you want. You have found this way to steal, because when

Isocrates explains that his client, who was planning a trip, deposited a very large amount of money in Passio's bank. After a series of adventures, when Isocrates's client went to withdraw his money, the banker claimed he "was without funds at the moment and could not return it." However, the banker, instead of admitting his situation, publicly denied the existence of any deposit or debt in favor of Isocrates's client. When the client, greatly surprised by the banker's behavior, again claimed payment from Passio, he said the banker,

> after covering his head, cried and said he had been forced by economic difficulties to deny my deposit but would soon try to return the money to me; he asked me to take pity on him and to keep his poor situation *a secret* so it would not be discovered he had committed fraud.[8]

It is therefore clear that in Greek banking, as Isocrates indicates in his speech, bankers who received money for safekeeping and custody were obliged to safeguard it by keeping it available to their clients. For this reason, it was considered fraud to employ that money for their own uses. Furthermore, the attempt to keep this type of fraud *a secret* so people would conserve their trust in bankers and the latter could continue

---

> they go to withdraw their money they do not dare ask for cash, but leave the money with you in order to collect much larger and more infernal profits. (*Instrucción de mercaderes*, p. 183)

Richard Cantillon mentions a list of tricks used by bankers to delay the payment of deposits in his *Essai sur la nature du commerce en général* (London: Fletcher Gyles, 1775), pp. 425–26. Finally, Marx also mentions the fear and reverence bankers inspire in everyone. He cites the following ironic words of G.M. Bell:

> The knit brow of the banker has more influence over him than the moral preaching of his friends; does he not tremble to be suspected of being guilty of fraud or of the least false statement, for fear of causing suspicion, in consequence of which his banking accommodation might be restricted or cancelled? The advice of the banker is more important to him than that of the clergyman. (Karl Marx, *Capital*, vol. 3: *The Process of Capitalist Production as a Whole*, Friedrich Engels, ed., Ernest Untermann, trans. [Chicago: Charles H. Kerr and Company, 1909], p. 641)

[8]Isocrates, "Sobre un asunto bancario," pp. 114 and 117.

their fraudulent activity is very significant. Also, we may deduce from Isocrates's speech that for Passio this was not an isolated case of fraud, an attempt to appropriate the money of a client under favorable circumstances, but that he had difficulty returning the money because he had not maintained a 100-percent reserve ratio and had used the deposited money in private business deals, and he was left with no other "escape" than to publicly deny the initial existence of the deposit.

Isocrates continues his speech with more words from his client, who states:

> Since I thought he regretted the incident, I compromised and told him to find a way to return my money while saving face himself. Three days later we met and both promised to keep what had happened a secret; (he broke his promise, as you will find later in my speech). He agreed to sail with me to Pontus and to return the gold to me there, in order to cancel the contract as far from this city as possible; that way, no one from here would find out the details of the cancellation, and upon sailing back, he could say whatever he chose.

Nevertheless, Passio denies this agreement, causes the disappearance of the slaves who had been witnesses to it and forges and steals the documents necessary to try to demonstrate that the client had a debt with him instead of a deposit. Given the secrecy in which bankers performed most of their activities, and the secret nature of most deposits,[9] witnesses were not used, and Isocrates was forced to present indirect witnesses who knew the depositor had taken a large amount of money and had used Passio's bank. In addition, the witnesses knew that at the time the deposit was made the depositor had changed more than one thousand staters into gold.

---

[9]The Greeks distinguished between monetary demand deposits (phanerà ousía) and invisible deposits (aphanés ousía). The distinction, rather than denote whether or not the money was continually available to the depositor (in both cases it should have been), appears to have referred to whether or not the deposit and its amount were publicly known. If they were, the money could be seized or confiscated, mostly for tax reasons.

Furthermore, Isocrates claims that the point most likely to convince the judges of the deposit's existence and of the fact that Passio tried to appropriate it was that Passio always refused to

> turn over the slave who knew of the deposit, for interroga-
> tion under torture. What stronger evidence exists in con-
> tracts with bankers? We do not use witnesses with them.[10]

Though we have no documentary evidence of the trial's verdict, it is certain that Passio was either convicted or arrived at a compromise with his accuser. In any case, it appears that afterward he behaved properly and again earned the trust of the city. His house was inherited by an old slave of his, Phormio, who successfully took over his business.

More interesting information on the activity of bankers in Greece comes from a forensic speech written by Demosthenes in favor of Phormio. Demosthenes indicates that, at the time of Passio's death, Passio had given fifty talents in loans still out-standing, and of that amount, "eleven talents came from bank deposits." Though it is unclear whether these were time or demand deposits, Demosthenes adds that the banker's profits were "insecure and came from the money of others." Demos-thenes concludes that "among men who work with money, it is admirable for a person known as a hard worker to also be honest," because "credit belongs to everyone and is the most important business capital." In short, banking was based on depositors' trust, bankers' honesty, on the fact that bankers should always keep available to depositors money placed in demand deposits, and on the fact that money loaned to bankers for profit should be used as prudently and sensibly as possible. In any case, there are many indications that Greek bankers did not always follow these guidelines, and that they used for themselves money on demand deposit, as described by Isocrates in *Trapezitica* and as Demosthenes reports of other bankers (who went bankrupt as the result of this type of activity) in his speech in favor of Phormio. This is true of

---

[10]Isocrates, "Sobre un asunto bancario," p. 116.

Aristolochus, who owned a field "he bought while owing money to many people," as well as of Sosynomus, Timodemus, and others who went bankrupt, and "when it was necessary to pay those to whom they owed money, *they all suspended payments* and surrendered their assets to creditors."[11]

Demosthenes wrote other speeches providing important information on banking in Greece. For example, in "Against Olympiodorus, for Damages,"[12] he expressly states that a certain Como

> placed some money on demand deposit in the bank of Heraclides, and the money was spent on the burial and other ritual ceremonies and on the building of the funerary monument.

In this case, the deceased made a demand deposit which was withdrawn by his heirs as soon as he died, to cover the costs of burial. Still more information on banking practices is offered in the speech "Against Timothy, for a Debt," in which Demosthenes affirms that

> bankers have the custom of making entries for the amounts they hand over, for the purpose of these funds, and for deposits people make, so that the amounts given out and those deposited are recorded for use when balancing the books.[13]

---

[11]Demosthenes, *Discursos privados I, Biblioteca Clásica Gredos* (Madrid: Editorial Gredos, 1983), pp. 157–80. The passages from the text are found on pp. 162, 164 and 176, respectively, of the above edition. For information on the failure of Greek banks, see Edward E. Cohen, *Athenian Economy and Society: A Banking Perspective* (Princeton, N.J.: Princeton University Press, 1992), pp. 215–24. Nevertheless, Cohen does not seem to understand the way in which bank credit expansions caused the economic crises affecting the solvency of banks.

[12]Demosthenes, *Discursos privados II, Biblioteca Clásica Gredos* (Madrid: Editorial Gredos, 1983), pp. 79–98. The passage mentioned in the main text is found on p. 86.

[13]Ibid., pp. 99–120. The passage cited is found on p. 102.

This speech, delivered in 362 B.C., is the first to document that bankers made book entries of their clients' deposits and withdrawals of money.[14] Demosthenes also explains how checking accounts worked. In this type of account, banks made payments to third parties, following depositors' instructions.[15] As legal evidence in this specific case, Demosthenes

> adduced the bank books, demanded copies be made, and after showing them to Phrasierides, I allowed him to inspect the books and make note of the amount owed by this individual.[16]

Finally, Demosthenes finishes his speech by expressing his concern at how common bank failures were and the people's great indignation against bankers who went bankrupt. Demosthenes mistakenly attributes bank failures to men who

> in difficult situations request loans and believe that credit should be granted them based on their reputation; however, once they recover economically, they do not repay the money, but instead try to defraud.[17]

We must interpret Demosthenes's comment within the context of the legal speech in which he presents his arguments. The purpose of the speech was precisely to sue Timothy for not returning a bank loan. It would be asking too much to expect Demosthenes to have mentioned that most bank failures occurred because bankers violated their obligation to safeguard demand deposits, and they used the money for themselves and put it into private business deals up to the point when, for some reason, the public lost trust in them and tried to withdraw their deposits, finding with great indignation that the money was not available.

---

[14]G.J. Costouros, "Development of Banking and Related Book-Keeping Techniques in Ancient Greece," *International Journal of Accounting* 7, no. 2 (1973): 75–81.

[15]Demosthenes, *Discursos privados II*, p. 119.

[16]Ibid., p. 112.

[17]Ibid., p. 120.

On various occasions research has suggested Greek
bankers usually knew they should maintain a 100-percent
reserve ratio on demand deposits. This would explain the lack
of evidence of interest payments on these deposits, as well as
the proven fact that in Athens banks were usually not considered sources of credit.[18] Clients made deposits for reasons of
safety and expected bankers to provide custody and safekeeping, along with the additional benefits of easily-documented
cashier services and payments to third parties. Nevertheless,
the fact that these were the basic principles of legitimate banking did not prevent a large group of bankers from yielding to
the temptation to (quite profitably) appropriate deposits, a
fraudulent activity which was relatively safe as long as people
retained their trust in bankers, but in the long run it was destined to end in bankruptcy. Moreover, as we will illustrate
with various historical examples, networks of fraudulent

---

[18]Stephen C. Todd, in reference to Athenian banking, affirms that

> banks were not seen as obvious sources of credit . . . it is strik-
> ing that out of hundreds of attested loans in the sources only
> eleven are borrowed from bankers; and there is indeed no evi-
> dence that a depositor could normally expect to receive inter-
> est from his bank. (S.C. Todd, *The Shape of Athenian Law*
> (Oxford: Clarendon Press, 1993), p. 251)

Bogaert, for his part, confirms that bankers paid no interest on demand
deposits and even charged a commission for their custody and safekeeping:

> Les dépôts de paiement pouvaient donc avoir différentes
> formes. Ce qu'ils ont en commun est l'absence d'intérêts.
> Dans aucun des cas précités nous n'en avons trouvé des
> traces. Il est même possible que certains banquiers aient
> demandé une commission pour la tenue de comptes de dépôt
> ou pour "l'exécution des mandats." (Raymond Bogaert, *Ban-
> ques et banquiers dans les cités grecques* [Leyden, Holland: A.W.
> Sijthoff, 1968], p. 336)

Bogaert also mentions the absence of any indication that bankers in
Athens maintained a certain fractional-reserve ratio ("Nous ne possé-
dons malheureusement aucune indication concernant l'encaisse d'une
banque antique," p. 364), though we know that various bankers, including Pison, acted fraudulently and did not maintain a 100-percent reserve
ratio. As a result, on many occasions they could not pay and went bankrupt.

bankers operating, against general legal principles, with a fractional-reserve ratio bring about credit expansion[19] unbacked by real savings, leading to artificial, inflationary economic booms, which finally revert in the shape of crises and economic recessions, in which banks inexorably tend to fail.

Raymond Bogaert has mentioned the periodic crises affecting banking in ancient Greece, specifically the economic and financial recessions of 377–376 B.C. and 371 B.C., during which the banks of Timodemus, Sosynomus and Aristolochus (among others) failed. Though these recessions were triggered by the attack of Sparta and the victory of Thebes, they emerged following a clear process of inflationary expansion in which fraudulent banks played a central part.[20] Records also reflect the serious banking crisis which took place in Ephesus following the revolt against Mithridates. This crisis motivated authorities to grant the banking industry its first express, historically-documented privilege, which established a ten-year deferment on the return of deposits.[21]

In any case, the bankers' fraudulent activity was extremely "profitable" as long as it was not discovered and banks did not fail. We know, for example, that the income of Passio reached 100 minas, or a talent and two-thirds. Professor Trigo Portela has estimated that this figure in kilograms of gold would be equivalent today to almost two million dollars a year. This does not seem an extremely large amount, though it was really quite spectacular, considering most people lived at mere subsistence level, ate only once a day and had a diet of cereals and vegetables. Upon his death, Passio's fortune

---

[19]   The money supply at Athens can thus be seen to consist of bank liabilities ("deposits") and cash in circulation. The amount of increase in the bank portion of this money supply will depend on the volume and velocity of bank loans, the percentage of these loan funds immediately or ultimately redeposited in the trapezai, and the time period and volatility of deposits. (Cohen, *Athenian Economy and Society*, p. 13)

[20]Bogaert, *Banques et banquiers dans les cités grecques*, pp. 391–93.

[21]Ibid., p. 391.

amounted to sixty talents; given a constant value for gold, this would add up to nearly forty-four million dollars.[22]

BANKING IN THE HELLENISTIC WORLD

The Hellenistic period, especially Ptolemaic Egypt, was a turning point in the history of banking because it marked the creation of the first government bank. The Ptolemies soon realized how profitable private banks were, and instead of monitoring and cracking down on bankers' fraudulent activities, decided to cash in on the overall situation by starting a government-run bank which would conduct business with the "prestige" of the state.

Although there was never a true government monopoly on banking, and private banks (mostly run by Greeks) continued to operate, Egypt's prosperity secured a predominant role for the state bank. Rostovtzeff observes that the Ptolemaic bank also developed a sophisticated accounting system:

> Refined accounting, based on a well-defined professional terminology, replaced the rather primitive accounting of fourth-century Athens.[23]

Several archaeological studies show how widespread banking was during the Hellenistic period in Egypt. An incomplete document found in Tebtunis containing daily account records of a rural bank in the province of Heracleopolis shows the unexpectedly high number of villagers

---

[22]Trigo Portela, "Historia de la banca," p. 238. Raymond Bogaert, in contrast, estimates Passio's annual income before his death at nine talents, several times larger:

> Cela donne en tout pour environ 9 talents de revenus annuels. On comprend que le banquier ait pu constituer en peu d'années un important patrimonie, faire des dons généreux à la cité et faire les frais de cinq triérchies. (Bogaert, *Banques et banquiers dans les cités grecques*, p. 367 and also Cohen, *Athenian Economy and Society*, p. 67)

[23]Michael Rostovtzeff, *The Social and Economic History of the Hellenistic World* (Oxford: Oxford University Press, 1953), vol. 1, p. 405.

who, whether farmers or not, did business through banks and made payments out of their deposits and bank accounts. Relatively wealthy people were few, and most of the bank's customers were retailers and indigenous craftspeople, linen merchants, textile workers, tailors, silversmiths and a tinker. Also, debts were often paid in gold and raw silver, following the ancient Egyptian tradition. Grain, oil and cattle dealers, as well as a butcher and many innkeepers were documented as clients of the bank. The Ptolemaic government bank, private banks, and temples alike kept custody of different kinds of deposits. According to Rostovtzeff, bankers accepted both demand deposits and interest-paying time deposits. The latter were, in theory, invested in

> credit operations of various sorts—loans on collateral security, pledges, and mortgages, and a special very popular type—bottomry loans.[24]

Private banks kept custody of their clients' deposits while at the same time placing their own money in the government bank.

The main innovation of Egyptian banking was centralization: the creation of a government central bank in Alexandria, with branches in the most important towns and cities, so that private banks, when available, played a secondary role in the country's economy. According to Rostovtzeff, this bank held custody of tax revenues and also took in private funds and deposits from ordinary clients, investing remaining funds in benefit of the state. Thus, it is almost certain that a fractional-reserve system was used and that the bank's huge profits were appropriated by the Ptolemies. Zeno's letters provide ample information on how banks received money from their clients and kept it on deposit. They also tell us that Apollonius, the director of the central bank in Alexandria, made personal deposits in different branches of the royal bank. All of these sources show how frequently individuals used the bank for

---

[24]Michael Rostovtzeff, *The Social and Economic History of the Hellenistic World* (Oxford: Oxford University Press, 1957), vol. 2, p. 1279.

making deposits as well as payments. In addition, due to their highly-developed accounting system, paying debts through banks became extremely convenient, as there was an official record of transactions—an important piece of evidence in case of litigation.

The Hellenistic banking system outlived the Ptolemaic dynasty and was preserved during Roman rule with minor changes. In fact, Ptolemaic centralized banking had some influence on the Roman Empire: a curious fact is that Dio Cassius, in his well-known Maecenas speech, advocates the creation of a Roman government bank which would offer loans to everyone (especially landowners) at reasonable interest rates. The bank would draw its capital from earnings on all state-owned property.[25] Dio Cassius's proposal was never put into practice.

BANKING IN ROME

Since there are no Latin equivalents of the speeches by Isocrates and Demosthenes, Roman banks are not documented in as much detail as their Greek counterparts. However, we know from Roman law that banking and the monetary irregular deposit were highly developed, and we have already considered (in chapter 1) the regulations classical Roman jurists provided in this area. Indeed, Roman *argentarii* were not considered free to use the *tantundem* of deposits as they pleased, but were obliged to safeguard it with the utmost diligence. This is precisely why money deposits did not pay interest and in theory were not to be lent, although the depositor could authorize the bank to use the money for making payments in his name. Likewise, bankers took in time "deposits," which were actually loans to the bank or *mutuum* contracts. These paid interest and conferred upon bankers the right to use the funds as they thought fit for the duration of the agreed-upon term. References to these practices appear as early as 350 B.C. in comedies such as Plautus's *Captivi, Asinaria* and *Mostellaria*, and Terence's *Phormio*, where we find

---

[25]Ibid., p. 623.

delightful dialogues describing financial operations, clearings, account balances, the use of checks and so on.[26] In any case, it appears the work done by professional jurists better regulated Roman banking and provided at least a clearer idea of what was and was not legitimate. However, this is no guarantee that bankers behaved honestly and refrained from using money from demand deposits to their own benefit. In fact, there is a rescript by Hadrianus to the merchants in Pergamum who complained about the illegal exactions and general dishonesty of their bankers. Also, a written document from the city of Mylasa to the emperor Septimius Severus contains a decree by the city council and the people aimed at regulating the activities of local bankers.[27] All this suggests that, while perhaps less frequently than was common in the Hellenic world, there were in fact unscrupulous bankers who misappropriated their depositors' funds and eventually went bankrupt.

THE FAILURE OF THE CHRISTIAN CALLISTUS'S BANK

A curious example of fraudulent banking is that of Callistus I, pope and saint (217–222 A.D.), who, while the slave of the Christian Carpophorus, acted as a banker in his name and took in deposits from other Christians. However, he went bankrupt and was caught by his master while trying to escape. He was finally pardoned at the request of the same Christians he had defrauded.[28]

---

[26]In Plautus's *Captivi*, for example, we read: "Subducam ratunculam quantillum argenti mihi apud trapezitam sied" (i.e., "I go inside because I need to calculate how much money I have in my bank") cited by Knut Wicksell in his *Lectures on Political Economy* (London: Routledge and-Kegan Paul, 1935), vol. 2, p. 73.

[27]Trigo Portela, "Historia de la banca," p. 239.

[28]The extraordinary fact that someone in the banking profession actually became Pope and later a saint would seem to make Callistus I a good choice for a patron saint. Unfortunately, he set a bad example as a failed banker who abused the good faith of his fellow Christians. Instead, the patron saint of bankers is St. Charles Borromeo (1538–1584), Archbishop of Milan. He was the nephew and administrator of Giovanni Angelo Medici (Pope Pius IV) and his feast day is November 4.

Refutatio omnium haeresium, a work attributed to Hippolytus and found in a convent on Mount Athos in 1844, reports
Callistus's bankruptcy in detail.[29] Like the recurring crises
which plagued Greece, the bankruptcy of Callistus occurred
after a pronounced inflationary boom followed by a serious
confidence crisis, a drop in the value of money and the failure
of multiple financial and commercial firms. These events took
place between 185 and 190 A.D. under the rule of the Emperor
Commodus.

Hippolytus relates how Callistus, at the time a slave to his
fellow Christian Carpophorus, started a banking business in
his name and took in deposits mainly from widows and
Christians (a group that was already increasing in influence
and membership). Nevertheless, Callistus deceitfully appropriated the money, and, as he was unable to return it upon
demand, tried to escape by sea and even attempted suicide.
After a series of adventures, he was flogged and sentenced to
hard labor in the mines of Sardinia. Finally, he was miracu-
lously released when Marcia, concubine of the Emperor Commodus and a Christian herself, used her influence. Thirty years
later, a freedman, he was chosen the seventeenth Pope in the
year 217 and eventually died a martyr when thrown into a well
by pagans during a public riot on October 14, 222 A.D.[30]

We can now understand why even the Holy Fathers in
their Apostolic Constitutions have admonished bankers to be
honest and to resist their many temptations.[31] These moral
exhortations warning bankers against temptation and remind-
ing them of their duties were used constantly among early
Christians, and some have even tried to trace them back to the
Holy Scriptures.

---

[29]Hippolytus, *Hippolytus Wercke*, vol. 2: *Refutatio omnium haeresium*
(Leipzig: P. Wendland), 1916.

[30]Juan de Churruca, "La quiebra de la banca del cristiano Calisto (c.a.
185–190)," *Seminarios complutenses de derecho romano*, February–May 1991
(Madrid, 1992), pp. 61–86.

[31]"Ginesthe trapezitai dókimoi" ("bankers, you must be honest!"). See
"Orígenes y movimiento histórico de los bancos," in *Enciclopedia universal
ilustrada europeo-americana* (Madrid: Espasa Calpe, 1973), vol. 7, p. 478.

THE SOCIETATES ARGENTARIAE

Banker associations or *societates argentariae* were a peculiarity of banking in the Roman world. Financial contributions from members supplied the capital to form them, and this capital was relied upon to pay debts. However, as banks were of particular public interest, Roman law established that members of the *societates argentariae* must guarantee deposits with all of their assets.[32] Hence, members' joint, unlimited liability was a general principle of Roman law, intended to minimize the effects of fraud and abuse by bankers and to protect depositors' right to recover their money at any time.[33]

---

[32]See Manuel J. García-Garrido, "La sociedad de los banqueros (societas argentaria)," in *Studi in honore di Arnaldo Biscardi* (Milan 1988), vol. 3, esp. pp. 380–83. The unlimited liability of banker association members under Roman law was established, among other places, in the aforementioned text by Ulpian (*Digest*, 16, 3, 7, 2–3) and also in a passage by Papinian (*Digest*, 16, 3, 8), where he dictates that money to repay the debts of fraudulent bankers be drawn not only from "deposited funds found among the banker's assets, but from all the defrauder's assets" (*Cuerpo de derecho civil romano*, vol. 1, p. 837). Some present-day authors have also proposed a return to the principle of unlimited liability for bankers, as an incentive for them to manage money prudently. However, this requirement is not necessary to achieve a solvent banking system, nor would it be a sufficient measure. It is not necessary, since a 100-percent reserve requirement would eliminate banking crises and economic recessions more effectively. It is not sufficient, because even if banks' stockholders had unlimited liability, bank crises and economic recessions would still inevitably recur when a fractional reserve is used.

[33]Under the Roman Empire, some large, influential temples continued to double as banks. Among these were the temples at Delos, Delphi, Sardis (Artemis), and most importantly, Jerusalem, where Hebrews, rich and poor, traditionally deposited their money. This is the context in which we must interpret Jesus's expulsion of the money changers from the temple in Jerusalem, as described in the New Testament. In Matthew 21:12–16 we read that Jesus, entering the temple,

> overturned the tables of the money changers and the benches of those selling doves. "It is written," he said to them, "My house will be called a house of prayer," but you are making it a "den of robbers."

Mark 11:15–17 offers an almost identical text. John 2:14–16 is a bit more explicit and tells us how, after entering the temple courts,

The *argentarii* conducted their business in a special place called a *taverna*. Their books reflected the debits and credits made to their clients' checking accounts. Roman bankers' books qualified as evidence in court and had to be kept as set down in the *editio rationum*, which stipulated the way accounts were to be dated and managed.[34] Bankers were also

---

> he found men selling cattle, sheep and doves, and *others sitting at tables exchanging money*. So he made a whip out of cords, and drove all from the temple area, both sheep and cattle; *he scattered the coins of the money changers and overturned their tables*.

(New International Version). The translation of these biblical passages is not very accurate, and the same mistake is found in García del Corral's translation of the *Digest*. Instead of "money changers," it should read "bankers," which is more in accordance with the literal sense of the Vulgate edition of the Bible in Latin, in which Matthew's account reads as follows:

> Et intravit Iesus in templum et eiiciebat omnes vendentes et ementes in templo, et *mensas numulariorum*, et cathedras vendentium columbas evertit: et dicit eis: Scriptum est: Domus mea domus orationis vocabitur: vos autem fecistis illam speluncam latronum. (*Biblia Sacra iuxta Vulgatam Clementinam*, Alberto Colunga and Laurencio Turrado, eds. (Madrid: Biblioteca de Autores Cristianos, 1994), Mateo 21:12–13, p. 982)

These evangelical texts confirm that the temple at Jerusalem acted as a true bank where the general public, rich or poor, made deposits. Jesus's clearing of the temple can be interpreted as a protest against abuses stemming from an illicit activity (as we know, these abuses consisted of the use of money on deposit). In addition, these biblical references illustrate the symbiosis already present between bankers and public officials, since both the chief priests and the teachers of the law were outraged by Jesus's behavior (all italics have, of course, been added). On the importance of the Jerusalem temple as a deposit bank for Hebrews, see Rostovtzeff, *The Social and Economic History of the Roman Empire*, vol. 2, p. 622.

[34]Jean Imbert, in his book, *Historia económica (de los orígenes a 1789)*, Spanish translation by Armando Sáez (Barcelona: Editorial Vicens-Vives, 1971), p. 58, points out that

> the praescriptio was an equivalent of today's checks. When a capitalist instructed a banker to make a loan payment in his name, the banker would do so upon presentation of a bank draft called a praescriptio.

called *mensarii*, after the *mensa* or counter where they originally carried out their money-changing activities. Much like
today's banking licenses, the *mensa* could be transferred. In
Rome, however, as the state owned the premises where banking took place, it was the right to operate (granted by the state)
that was transmitted. A transfer could include all furniture
and implements of the *taverna*, as well as financial assets and
liabilities. In addition, bankers formed a guild to defend their
common interests and obtained significant privileges from
emperors, especially Justinian. Some of these privileges
appear in the *Corpus Juris Civilis*.[35]

The economic and social disintegration of the Roman
Empire resulted from inflationary government policies which
devalued the currency, and from the establishment of maximum prices for essential goods, which in turn caused a general shortage of these goods, the financial ruin of merchants
and the disappearance of trade between different areas of the
Empire. This was also the end for banking. Most banks failed
during the successive economic crises of the third and fourth
centuries A.D. In an attempt to contain the social and economic decay of the Empire, additional coercive, interventionist measures were taken, further accelerating the process of
disintegration and enabling the barbarians (whom Roman
legions had defeated repeatedly and kept at bay for years) to
devastate and conquer the remains of the ancient, thriving
Roman Empire. The fall of the classical Roman world began
the long medieval period, and it was nearly eight hundred
years later that banking was rediscovered in the Italian cities
of the late Middle Ages.[36]

---

[35]See, for instance, *New Constitution 126* on "Bank Contracts," edict 7
("Decree and Regulation Governing Bank Contracts") and edict 9, "On
Bank Contracts," all by Justinian and included in the *Novellae* (see *Cuerpo
de derecho civil romano*, vol. 6, pp. 479–83, 539–44 and 547–51).

[36]A superb overview of the causes of the fall of the Roman Empire
appears in Ludwig von Mises's work, *Human Action: A Treatise on Economics*, Scholar's Edition (Auburn, Ala.: Ludwig von Mises Institute,
1998), pp. 161–63. We will also quote Mises's *Human Action* by the more
widespread third edition (Chicago: Henry Regnery, 1966), pp. 767–69.

3

BANKERS IN THE LATE MIDDLE AGES

The fall of the Roman Empire meant the disappearance of most of its trade and the feudalization of economic and social relationships. The enormous reduction in trade and in the division of labor dealt a definitive blow to financial activities, especially banking. The effects of this reduction lasted several centuries. Only monasteries, secure centers of economic and social development, could serve as guardians of economic resources. It is important to mention the activity in this field of the Templars, whose order was founded in 1119 in Jerusalem to protect pilgrims. The Templars possessed significant financial resources obtained as plunder from their military campaigns and as bequests from feudal princes and lords. As they were active internationally (they had more than nine thousand centers and two headquarters) and were a military and religious order, the Templars were safe custodians for deposits and had great moral authority, earning them the trust of the people. Understandably, they began to receive both regular and irregular deposits from individuals, to whom they charged a fee for safekeeping. The Templars also carried out transfers of funds, charging a set amount for transportation and protection. Moreover, they made loans of their own resources and did not violate the safekeeping principle on demand deposits. The order acquired a growing prosperity which aroused the fear and envy of many people, until Philip the Fair, the King of France, decided to dissolve it. He condemned those in charge to be burned at the stake (including Jacques de Molay, the *Grand Maître*), with the prime objective of appropriating all of the order's riches.[37]

---

[37]See, for example, Jules Piquet's book, *Des banquiers au Moyen Age: Les Templiers, Étude de leurs opérations financièrs* (Paris, 1939), cited by Henri Pirenne in his work, *Histoire Économique et Sociale Du Moyen Age* (Paris: Presses Universitaires de France, 1969), pp. 116 and 219. Piquet believes he sees the beginnings of double-entry bookkeeping and even a primitive form of check in the records kept by the Templars. However, it appears the Templars' accounting practices were, at most, mere direct predecessors of double-entry bookkeeping, later formalized in

The end of the eleventh century and beginning of the twelfth brought a moderate resurgence of business and trade, mainly among the Italian cities on the Adriatic (especially Venice), Pisa, and later, Florence. These cities specialized in trade with Constantinople and the Orient. Significant financial growth in these cities led to the revival of banking, and the pattern we observed in the classical world was reproduced. Indeed, bankers at first respected the juridical principles passed down from Rome and conducted their business lawfully, avoiding illicit use of demand deposits (i.e., irregular deposits of money). Only money received as loans (i.e., *time* "deposits") was used or lent by bankers, and only during the agreed-upon term.[38] Nevertheless, bankers again became tempted to take advantage of money from demand deposits. This was a gradual process which led to abuses and the resumption of fractional-reserve banking. The authorities were generally unable to enforce legal principles and on many occasions even granted privileges and licenses to encourage bankers' improper activity and derive benefits from it, in the shape of loans and tax revenues. They even created government banks (such as

---

1494 by Luca Pacioli, the great Venetian monk and friend of Leonardo da Vinci. A bank in Pisa used double-entry bookkeeping as early as 1336, as did the Masari family (tax collectors in Genoa) in 1340. The oldest European account book we have evidence of came from a Florentine bank and dates back to 1211. See G.A. Lee, "The Oldest European Account Book: A Florentine Bank Ledger of 1211," in *Accounting History: Some British Contributions*, R.H. Parker and B.S. Yamey, eds. (Oxford: Clarendon Press, 1994), pp. 160–96.

[38] In theory at least, early banks of deposit were not discount or lending banks. They did not create money but served a system of 100 percent reserves, such as some monetarists today would like to see established. Overdrafts were forbidden. In practice, the standards proved difficult to maintain, especially in face of public emergency. The Taula de Valencia was on the verge of using its deposited treasure to buy wheat for the city in 1567. Illegal advances were made to city officials in 1590 and illegal loans to the city itself on a number of occasions. (Charles P. Kindleberger, *A Financial History of Western Europe*, 2nd ed. [Oxford: Oxford University Press, 1993], p. 49)

Barcelona's Bank of Deposit, or *Taula de Canvi*, and others we
will consider later).[39]

THE REVIVAL OF DEPOSIT BANKING IN MEDITERRANEAN EUROPE

Abbott Payson Usher, in his monumental work, *The Early
History of Deposit Banking in Mediterranean Europe*,[40] studies the
gradual emergence of fractional-reserve banking during the
late Middle ages, a process founded on the violation of this
general legal principle: full availability of the *tantundem* must
be preserved in favor of the depositor. According to Usher, it
is not until the thirteenth century that some private bankers
begin to use the money of their depositors to their own advantage, giving rise to fractional-reserve banking and the opportunities for credit expansion it entails. Moreover, and contrary
to a widely-held opinion, Usher believes this to be the most
significant event in the history of banking, rather than the
appearance of banks of issue (which in any case did not occur
until much later, in the late seventeenth century). As we will
see in chapter 4, although exactly the same economic effects
result from the issuance of bank notes without financial backing and the loaning of funds from demand deposits, banking
was historically shaped more by the latter of these practices

---

[39]Islamic law also banned bankers' personal use of irregular deposits
throughout the medieval period, especially on the Iberian Peninsula.
See, for instance, the *Compendio de derecho islámico* (Risála, Fí-l-Fiqh), by
the tenth-century Hispano-Arabic jurist Ibn Abí Zayd, called Al-
Qayrawání, published with the support of Jesús Riosalido (Madrid: Editorial Trotta, 1993). On p. 130 we find the following statement of a juridical principle: "he who uses a money deposit to do business commits a
reprehensible act, but if he uses his own money, he may keep the profit."
(See also pp. 214–15, where it is stipulated that, in the case of a true loan
or mutuum, the lender may not withdraw the money at will, but only at
the end of the agreed-upon term; the Islamic legal concept of money
deposit closely parallels that of the Roman irregular deposit.)

[40]Abbott Payson Usher taught economics at Harvard University and
authored the celebrated work, *The Early History of Deposit Banking in
Mediterranean Europe* (Cambridge, Mass.: Harvard University Press,
1943).

than by the former. Usher states that: "the history of banks of issue has, until lately, obscured the importance of due deposit banking in all its forms, whether primitive or modern." In an ironic reference to the undue importance given by economists to the problems of banks of issue versus the older but equally harmful activities of deposit banks, he concludes that:

> the demand for currency, and the theoretical interests cre-
> ated by the problem, did much to foster misconceptions on
> the relative importance of notes and deposits. Just as French
> diplomats "discovered" the Pyrenees in the diplomatic cri-
> sis of the eighteenth century, so banking theorists "discov-
> ered" deposits in the mid-nineteenth century.[41]

Again and again, Usher shows that the modern banking system arose from fractional-reserve banking (itself the result of fraud and government complicity, as Usher illustrates in detail via the example of the late medieval Catalonian banking system), and not from banks of issue, which appeared much later.

Usher points out that the first banks in twelfth-century Genoa made a clear distinction in their books between demand deposits and "time" deposits, and recorded the latter as loans or *mutuum* contracts.[42] However, bankers later began gradually to make self-interested use of demand deposits, giving rise to expansionary capabilities present in the banking system; more specifically, the power to create deposits and grant credits out of nowhere. Barcelona's Bank of Deposit is a case in point. Usher estimates that the bank's cash reserves amounted to 29 percent of total deposits. This meant their capacity for credit expansion was 3.3 times their cash reserves.[43]

---

[41]Ibid., pp. 9 and 192.

[42]"In all these Genoese registers there is also a series of instruments in which the money received is explicitly described as a loan (mutuum)." Ibid., p. 63.

[43]   Against these liabilities, the Bank of Deposit held reserves in specie amounting to 29 percent of the total. Using the phrase-ology of the present time, the bank was capable of extending credit in the ratio of 3.3 times the reserves on hand. (Ibid., p. 181)

Usher also highlights the failure of public officials at different levels to enforce sound banking practices, particularly a 100-percent reserve requirement on demand deposits. Moreover, the authorities ended up granting banks a government license (a privilege—*ius privilegium*) to operate with a fractional reserve. Banks were nevertheless required to guarantee deposits.[44] At any rate, rulers were usually the first to take advantage of fraudulent banking, finding loans an easy source of public financing. It is as if bankers were granted the privilege of making gainful use of their depositors' money in return for their unspoken agreement that most of such use be in the shape of loans to public officials and funding for the government. On various occasions, rulers went so far as to create government banks, in order to *directly* reap the considerable profits available in banking. As we will see, Barcelona's Bank of Deposit, the *Taula de Canvi*, was created with this main objective.

However, we cannot agree with the statement Usher makes immediately afterward; he contends that private banks also operating in Barcelona at the time must have had a much lower reserve ratio. Quite the opposite must have been true. As private banks were smaller, they would not have inspired as much confidence in the public as the municipal bank did, and as they operated in a strictly competitive environment, their cash reserves must have been higher (see pp. 181–82 of Usher's book). In any case, Usher concludes that

> there was considerable centralization of clearance in the early
> period and extensive credit creation. In the absence of com-
> prehensive statistical records, we have scarcely any basis for
> an estimate of the quantitative importance of credit in the
> medieval and early modern periods, though the implications
> of our material suggest an extensive use of credit purchasing
> power. (Ibid., pp. 8–9)

We will later cite works by C. Cipolla, which fully confirm Usher's main thesis. In chapter 4 we will examine bank multipliers in depth.

[44]In fifteenth-century Catalonia, guarantees were not required, though only bankers who offered them were allowed to spread tablecloths over their counters. By this system, the public could easily identify the more solvent businesses. Ibid., p. 17.

The Canonical Ban on Usury and the "Depositum Confessatum"

The ban on usury by the three major monotheistic religions (Judaism, Islam and Christianity) did much to complicate and obscure medieval financial practices. Marjorie Grice-Hutchinson has carefully studied the medieval prohibition of interest and its implications.[45] She points out that Jews were not forbidden to loan money at interest to Gentiles, which explains why, at least during the first half of the medieval period, most bankers and financiers in the Christian world were Jewish.[46]

This canonical ban on interest added greatly to the intricacies of medieval banking, though not (as many theorists have insisted) because bankers, in their attempt to offer a useful, necessary service, were forced to constantly search for new ways to disguise the necessary payment of interest on loans. When bankers loaned money received from clients as a loan (or "time" deposit), they were acting as true financial intermediaries and were certainly doing a legitimate business and significantly contributing to the productive economy of their time. Still, the belated recognition by the Church of the legitimacy of interest should not be regarded as overall approval of the banking business, but only as authorization for banks to loan money lent to them by third parties. In other words, to

---

[45]Marjorie Grice-Hutchinson, *Early Economic Thought in Spain 1177–1740* (London: George Allen and Unwin, 1978). See "In Concealment of Usury," chap. 1, pp. 13–60.

[46]   Until the thirteenth century, the greater part of financial activity was in the hands of Jews and other non-Christians, usually from the Near East. For such unbelievers from the Christian point of view there could be no salvation in any event, and the economic prohibitions of the Church did not apply to them. . . . Hatred for the Jews arose on the part of the people who resented such interest rates, while monarchs and princes, if less resentful, scented profits from expropriation of this more or less helpless group. (Harry Elmer Barnes, *An Economic History of the Western World* [New York: Harcourt, Brace and Company, 1940], pp. 192–93)

act as mere financial intermediaries. The evolution of Church doctrine on interest in no way implies a sanction of fractional-reserve banking, i.e., bankers' self-interested use (which usually means granting loans) of demand deposits.[47]

To a great extent, the conceptual confusion we are dealing with arose in the Middle Ages as a result of the canonical ban on interest. One of the main artifices[48] devised by economic agents to conceal actual interest-paying loans was to disguise them as demand deposits. Let us see how they did it. First, we must think back to our discussion of the monetary irregular-deposit contract in chapter 1. One of the most notable guidelines found for this contract in the *Corpus Juris Civilis* stipulated that, if the depositary were unable to return the deposit on demand, not only was he guilty of theft for misappropriation, but he was also obliged to pay interest to the depositor for his delay in repayment (*Digest*, 16, 3, 25, 1). Hence, it should come as no surprise that throughout the Middle Ages,

---

[47]This is precisely the opinion held by Father Bernard W. Dempsey S.J., who concludes in his remarkable book *Interest and Usury* (Washington, D.C.: American Council of Public Affairs, 1943) that even if we accept interest as legitimate, fractional-reserve banking amounts to "institutional usury" and is especially harmful to society, since it repeatedly generates artificial booms, bank crises and economic recessions (p. 228).

[48]A clear, concise list of the tricks used to systematically disguise loans and interest can be found in Imbert's book, *Historia económica (de los orígenes a 1789)*, pp. 157–58. Imbert mentions the following methods of concealing interest-bearing loans: (a) bogus contracts (such as repurchase agreements or real estate guarantees); (b) penalty clauses (disguising interest as economic sanctions); (c) lying about the amount of the loan (the borrower agreed to repay a sum higher than the actual loan); (d) foreign exchange transactions (which included the interest as an additional charge); and (e) income or annuities (life annuities including a portion of both the interest and the repayment of the principal). Jean Imbert makes no express mention of the *depositum confessatum*, one of the most popular ways of justifying interest. It fits well into the "penalty clauses" category. See also the reference Henri Pirenne makes to the "utmost ingenuity" used to conceal "dangerous interest." *Economic and Social History of Medieval Europe* (London: Kegan Paul, Trench, Trubner and Company, 1947), p. 140.

in order to circumvent the canonical ban on interest, many bankers and "depositors" *expressly declared* that they had taken part in a monetary irregular-deposit contract, when they had actually formalized a true loan or *mutuum* contract. The method of concealment to which this declaration belonged was aptly named *depositum confessatum*. It was a simulated deposit which, despite the declarations of the two parties, was not a true deposit at all, but rather a mere loan or *mutuum* contract. At the end of the agreed-upon term, the supposed depositor claimed his money. When the professed depositary failed to return it, he was forced to pay a "penalty" in the shape of interest on his presumed "delay," which had nothing to do with the actual reason for the "penalty" (the fact that the operation was a loan). Disguising loans as deposits became an effective way to get around the canonical ban on interest and escape severe sanctions, both secular and spiritual.

The *depositum confessatum* eventually perverted juridical doctrine on the monetary irregular deposit, robbing these tenets of the clarity and purity they received in classical Rome and adding confusion that has persisted almost to the present day. In fact, regardless of experts' doctrinal stand (either strictly against, or "in favor" within reasonable limits) on interest-bearing loans, the different approaches to the *depositum confessatum* led theorists to stop distinguishing clearly between the monetary irregular deposit and the mutuum contract. On one hand, over-zealous canonists, determined to expose all hidden loans and condemn the corresponding interest, tended to automatically equate deposit contracts with mutuum contracts. They believed that by exposing the loan they assumed was behind *every* deposit they would put an end to the pretense of the *depositum confessatum*. This is precisely where their error lay: they regarded all deposits, even actual ones (made with the essential purpose of safeguarding the *tantundem* and keeping it always available to the depositor) as *deposita confessata*. On the other hand, those experts who were relatively more supportive of loans and interest and searched for ways to make them acceptable to the Church, defended the *depositum confessatum* as a kind of precarious loan which, according to the principles embodied in the *Digest*, justified the payment of interest.

As a result of both doctrinal stances, scholars came to believe that the "irregularity" in the monetary irregular deposit referred not to the deposit of a certain quantity of a fungible good (the units of which were indistinguishable from others of the same type and the *tantundem* of which was to be kept continually available to the depositor), but rather to the irregularity of *always* disguising loans as deposits.[49] Furthermore, bankers, who had used the *depositum confessatum* to disguise loans as deposits and to justify the illegal payment of interest, eventually realized that the doctrine which held that deposits always concealed loans could also be extremely profitable to them, because they could employ it to defend even the misappropriation of money which had actually been placed into demand deposits and had not been loaned. Thus,

---

[49]Canonists' equation of the monetary irregular deposit with the mutuum or loan contract led experts to search for a common juridical feature between the two contracts. They soon realized that in the deposit of a fungible good, "ownership" of the individual units deposited is "transferred," since the depositary is only obliged to safeguard, maintain, and return upon demand the *tantundem*. This transfer of ownership appears to coincide with that of the loan or mutuum contract, so it was natural for scholars to automatically assume that all monetary irregular deposits were loans, since both include a "transfer" of "ownership" from the depositor to the depositary. Hence, theorists overlooked the essential difference (see chapter 1) between the monetary irregular deposit and the mutuum or loan: the main purpose of the irregular deposit is the custody and safekeeping of the good, and while "ownership" is in a sense "transferred," availability is not, and the *tantundem* must be kept continually available to the depositor. In contrast, a loan entails the transfer of full availability, apart from ownership (in fact, present goods are exchanged for future goods) and involves this fundamental element: a term during which the goods cease to be available to the lender. Irregular deposits do not include such a term. In short, since the canonical prohibition of interest gave rise to the fraudulent and spurious institution of the *depositum confessatum*, it was indirectly responsible for the loss of clarity in the distinction between the monetary irregular deposit and the mutuum. This confusion is clearly behind the wrong 1342 final court decision on the *Isabetta Querini vs. The Bank of Marino Vendelino* case, mentioned by Reinhold C. Mueller in *The Venetian Money Market: Banks, Panics, and the Public Debt, 1200–1500* (Baltimore: Johns Hopkins University Press, 1997), pp. 12–13.

the canonical ban on interest had the unexpected effect of obscuring Roman jurists' clear, legal definition of the monetary irregular-deposit contract. Many capitalized on the ensuing confusion in an attempt to legally justify fraudulent banking and the misappropriation of demand deposits. Experts failed to clear up the resulting legal chaos until the end of the nineteenth century.[50]

Let us now examine three particular cases which together illustrate the development of medieval banking: Florentine banks in the fourteenth century; Barcelona's Bank of Deposit, the *Taula de Canvi*, in the fifteenth century and later; and the Medici Bank. These banks, like all of the most important banks in the late Middle Ages, consistently displayed the pattern we saw in Greece and Rome: banks initially respected the traditional legal principles found in the *Corpus Juris Civilis*, i.e., they operated with a 100-percent reserve ratio which guaranteed the safekeeping of the *tantundem* and its constant availability to the depositor. Then, gradually, due to bankers' greed and rulers' complicity, these principles began to be violated, and bankers started to loan money from demand

---

[50]In fact, Pasquale Coppa-Zuccari, whose work we have already cited, was the first to begin to reconstruct the complete legal theory of the monetary irregular deposit, starting from the same premise as the classical Roman scholars and again revealing the illegitimacy of banks' misappropriation of demand deposits. Regarding the effects of the *depositum confessatum* on the theoretical treatment of the juridical institution of irregular deposit, Coppa-Zuccari concludes that

> le condizioni legislative dei tempi rendevano fertile il terreno in cui il seme della discordia dottrinale cadeva. Il divieto degli interessi nel *mutuo* non valeva pel *deposito irregolare*. Qual meraviglia dunque se chi aveva denaro da impiegare fruttuosamente lo desse a deposito irregolare, *confessatum* se occorreva, e non a mutuo? Quel divieto degli interessi, che tanto addestrò il commercio a frodare la legge e la cui efficacia era nulla di fronte ad un mutuo dissimulato, conservò in vita questo ibrido instituto, e fece sì che il nome di *deposito* venisse imposto al mutuo, che non poteva chiamarsi col proprio nome, perchè esso avrebbe importato la nullità del patto relativo agli interessi. (Coppa-Zuccari, *Il deposito irregolare*, pp. 59–60)

deposits, often, in fact, to rulers. This gave rise to fractional-reserve banking and artificial credit expansion, which in the first stage appeared to spur strong economic growth. The whole process ended in a general economic crisis and the failure of banks that could not return deposits on demand once the recession hit and they had lost the trust of the public. Whenever loans were systematically made from demand deposits, the historical constant in banking appears to have been eventual failure.[51] Furthermore, bank failures were accompanied by a strong contraction in the money supply (specifically, a shortage of loans and deposits) and by the resulting inevitable economic recession. As we will see in the following chapters, it took economic scholars nearly five centuries to understand the theoretical causes of all of these processes.[52]

---

[51]For example, Raymond Bogaert mentions that of the 163 known banks in Venice, documentary evidence exists to show that at least 93 of them failed. Bogaert, *Banques et banquiers dans les cités grecques*, note 513, p. 392. A detailed list of 46 failures of deposit banks in Venice can also be seen in Mueller, *The Venetian Money Market*, pp. 585–86. This same fate of failures affected all banks in Seville in the 15th century. Hence, the systematic failure of fractional-reserve private banks not supported by a central bank (or equivalent) is a fact of history. Pascal Salin overlooks this fact in his article "In Defense of Fractional Monetary Reserves," presented at the Austrian Scholars Conference, March 30–31, 2001.

[52]As is logical, bankers always carried out their violations of general legal principles and their misappropriations of money on demand deposit in a secretive, disgraceful way. Indeed, they were fully aware of the wrongful nature of their actions and furthermore, knew that if their clients found out about their activities they would immediately lose confidence in the bank and it would surely fail. This explains the excessive secrecy traditionally present in banking. Together with the confusing, abstract nature of financial transactions, this lack of openness largely protects bankers from public accountability even today. It also keeps most of the public in the dark as to the actual nature of banks. While they are usually presented as true financial intermediaries, it would be more accurate to see banks as mere creators of loans and deposits which come out of nowhere and have an expansionary effect on the economy. The disgraceful, and therefore secretive, nature of these banking practices was skillfully revealed by Knut Wicksell in the following words:

BANKING IN FLORENCE IN THE FOURTEENTH CENTURY

Around the end of the twelfth and beginning of the thirteenth centuries, Florence was the site of an incipient banking
industry which gained great importance in the fourteenth century. The following families owned many of the most important banks: The Acciaiuolis, the Bonaccorsis, the Cocchis, the
Antellesis, the Corsinis, the Uzzanos, the Perendolis, the
Peruzzis, and the Bardis. Evidence shows that from the beginning of the fourteenth century bankers gradually began to
make fraudulent use of a portion of the money on demand
deposit, creating out of nowhere a significant amount of
expansionary credit.[53] Therefore, it is not surprising that an
increase in the money supply (in the form of credit expansion)
caused an artificial economic boom followed by a profound,
inevitable recession. This recession was triggered not only by
Neapolitan princes' massive withdrawal of funds, but also by
England's inability to repay its loans and the drastic fall in the

> in effect, and contrary to the original plan, the banks became
> credit institutions, instruments for increasing the supplies of
> a medium of exchange, or for imparting to the total stock of
> money, an increased velocity of circulation, physical or vir-
> tual. Giro banking continued as before, though no actual
> stock of money existed to correspond with the total of deposit
> certificates. So long, however, as people continued to believe
> that the existence of money in the banks was a necessary con-
> dition of the convertibility of the deposit certificates, these
> loans had to remain a profound secret. If they were discov-
> ered the bank lost the confidence of the public and was
> ruined, especially if the discovery was made at a time when
> the Government was not in a position to repay the advances.
> (Wicksell, *Lectures on Political Economy*, vol. 2, pp. 74–75)

[53]Various articles have been written on this topic. See the interesting one
by Reinhold C. Mueller, "The Role of Bank Money in Venice,
1300–1500," in *Studi Veneziani* n.s. 3 (1979): 47–96, and chapter 5 of his
book, *The Venetian Money Market*. Carlo M. Cipolla, in his notable publication, *The Monetary Policy of Fourteenth-Century Florence* (Berkeley: University of California Press, 1982), p. 13, also affirms: "The banks of that
time had already developed to the point of creating money besides
increasing its velocity of circulation."

price of Florentine government bonds. In Florence, public debt had been financed by speculative new loans created out of nowhere by Florentine banks. A general crisis of confidence occurred, causing all of the above banks to fail between 1341 and 1346. As could be expected, these bank failures were detrimental to all deposit-holders, who, after a prolonged period, received half, a third, or even a fifth of their deposits at most.[54] Fortunately, Villani recorded the economic and financial events of this period in a chronicle that Carlo M. Cipolla has resurrected. According to Villani, the recession was accompanied by a tremendous tightening of credit (referred to descriptively as a *mancamento della credenza*, or "credit shortage"), which further worsened economic conditions and brought about a deluge of industry, workshop, and business failures. Cipolla has studied this economic recession in depth and graphically describes the transition from economic boom to crisis and recession in this way: "The age of 'The Canticle of the Sun' gave way to the age of the *Danse macabre*."[55] In fact, according to Cipolla, the recession lasted until, "thanks" to the devastating effects of the plague, which radically diminished the population, the supply of cash and credit money per capita approached its pre-crisis level and laid the foundation for a subsequent recovery.[56]

---

[54]Cipolla, *The Monetary Policy of Fourteenth-Century Florence*, p. 9.

[55]Ibid., p. 1. See also Boccaccio's commentary on the economic effects of the plague, cited by John Hicks in *Capital and Time: A Neo-Austrian Theory* (Oxford: Clarendon Press, 1973), pp. 12–13; see footnote 60, chap. 5.

[56]Carlo M. Cipolla's interpretive analysis of historical events reveals a greater knowledge and application of economic theory than other authors have displayed (such as A.P. Usher and Raymond de Roover, who both express surprise at medieval economic recessions, the origins of which are often "mysterious and inexplicable" to them). Still, his analysis, monetarist in nature, focuses on the stages of recession, which he attributes to a shortage of the money supply, resulting in turn from an overall tightening of credit. Remarkably, he ignores the prior economic boom, unconsciously lapsing into a "monetarist" interpretation of history and thus failing to recognize the artificial boom caused by credit expansion as the true source of the ensuing, inevitable recessions. Cipolla's thesis that it was the Black Death that eventually resolved the

THE MEDICI BANK

The history of the Medici Bank has come to light through the research and determination of Raymond de Roover, whose work was in turn advanced by the 1950 discovery of the Medici Bank's confidential ledgers (*libri segreti*) in Florence's *Archivio di Stato*.[57] The secrecy of these ledgers again betrays the hidden, shameful nature of bankers' activities (see footnote 52), as well as the desire of many customers of Italian banks (nobles, princes, and even the Pope) to deposit their money in secret accounts. The discovery of these bank books was indeed fortunate, as they provide us with an in-depth understanding of how the Medici Bank operated in the fifteenth century.

We must stress that the Medici Bank did not initially accept demand deposits. At first it only took time deposits, which were actually true loans from the customer to the bank. These mutuum contracts were called *depositi a discrezione*. The words *a discrezione* indicated that, as these supposed "deposits" were really loans, the bank could make full use of them and invest them freely, at least for the length of the stipulated term.[58] *Discrezione* also referred to the interest the

---

"shortage" of money is highly debatable, since money shortages tend to correct themselves spontaneously through a general drop in prices (via a corresponding increase in the value of money) which makes it unnecessary for individuals to maintain such high cash balances. There is no need for a war or plague to decimate the population. Even if there had been no plague, once the investment errors made during the boom had been corrected, the process of economic decline would have ended sooner or later, due to an increase in the value of money and a subsequent reduction in cash balances. This process undoubtedly coincided with, yet occurred independently of the Black Death's effects. Hence, even the most educated and insightful historians, like Cipolla, clearly make partial judgement errors in their interpretations when they do not use the appropriate theoretical tools. At any rate, it is still very significant that these defenders of an inflationary interpretation of history continue to point out the "positive effects" of wars and plagues and consider them the key to recovery from economic crises.

[57]De Roover, *The Rise and Decline of the Medici Bank, 1397–1494*.

[58] The Medici Bank and its subsidiaries also accepted deposits from outsiders, especially great nobles, church dignitaries,

bank paid clients who loaned it money in the form of time "deposits."

In his book, Raymond de Roover performs a thorough, detailed study of the development and vicissitudes of the Medici Bank through the century of its existence. For our purposes, it is only necessary to emphasize that at some point the bank began to accept demand deposits and to use a portion of them inappropriately as loans. The *libri segreti* document this fact. The accounts for March 1442 accompany each demand deposit entry with a note in the margin indicating the likelihood that each depositor would claim his money.[59]

A balance sheet from the London branch of the Medici Bank, dated November 12, 1477, shows that a significant number of the bank's debts corresponded to demand deposits. Raymond de Roover himself estimates that at one point, the bank's primary reserves were down to 50 percent of total demand liabilities.[60] If we apply the standard criterion used by A.P. Usher, this implies a credit expansion ratio of twice the demand deposits received by the bank. There is evidence, however, that this ratio gradually worsened over the bank's life span, especially after 1464, a year that marked the beginning of growing difficulties for the bank. The roots of the general economic and bank crisis that ruined the Medici Bank resemble those Carlo M. Cipolla identifies in his study of fourteenth-century Florence. As a matter of fact, credit expansion resulting from bankers' misappropriation of demand deposits gave rise to an artificial boom fed by the increase in the money supply and its seemingly "beneficial" short-term effects. Nevertheless, since this process sprang from an increase in the money supply, namely credit

---

condottieri, and political figures, such as Philippe de Com-
mines and Ymbert de Batarnay. Such deposits were not usually payable on demand but were either explicitly or implicitly time deposits on which interest, or rather *discrezione*,
was paid. (De Roover, *The Rise and Decline of the Medici Bank
1397–1494*, p. 101)

[59]Ibid., p. 213.

[60]Ibid., p. 245.

unbacked by growth in real savings, the reversal of the process was inevitable, as chapters 4 and following will explain in detail. This is exactly what happened in Italy's large business centers in the second half of the fifteenth century. In terms of economic analysis, Raymond de Roover's grasp of the historical process is unfortunately even shallower than Cipolla's, and he even goes so far as to state, "what caused these general crises remains a mystery."[61] However, it is not surprising that the Medici Bank eventually failed, as did the other banks that depended on fractional-reserve banking for a large part of their business. Though Raymond de Roover claims he does not understand what caused the general crisis at the end of the fifteenth century, his blow-by-blow historical account of the final stage of the Medici Bank reflects all of the typical indications of an inescapable recession and credit squeeze following a process of great artificial credit expansion. De Roover explains that the Medicis were forced to adopt a policy of credit restriction. They demanded the repayment of loans and attempted to increase the bank's liquidity. Moreover, it has been demonstrated that in its final stage the Medici Bank was operating with a very low reserve ratio, which even dropped below 10 percent of total assets and was therefore inadequate to meet the bank's obligations during the recession period.[62] The Medici Bank eventually failed and all

---

[61]Ibid., p. 239.

[62]Hence, over the bank's lifespan, its owners gradually increased their violations of the traditional legal principle requiring them to maintain possession of 100 percent of demand deposits, and their reserve ratio continuously decreased:

> A perusal of the extant balance sheets reveals another significant fact: the Medici Bank operated with tenuous cash reserves which were usually well below 10 percent of total assets. It is true that this is a common feature in the financial statements of medieval merchant-bankers, such as Francesco Datini and the Borromei of Milan. The extent to which they made use of money substitutes is always a surprise to modern historians. Nevertheless, one may raise the question whether cash reserves were adequate and whether the Medici Bank was not suffering from lack of liquidity. (Ibid., p. 371)

of its assets fell into the hands of its creditors. The bank's competitors failed for the same reasons: the unavoidable effects of the artificial expansion and subsequent economic recession invariably generated by the violation of the traditional legal principles governing the monetary irregular deposit.

BANKING IN CATALONIA IN THE FOURTEENTH AND FIFTEENTH CENTURIES: THE *TAULA DE CANVI*

The emergence of private banks in Barcelona coincided with the development of private banking in large Italian business centers. During the reign of Jaime I, the Conqueror, (1213–1276), the Gothic and Roman laws governing business were repealed and replaced by the *Usos de Barcelona*. In addition, a thorough, detailed set of regulations to control banking was established by the Cortes of 1300–1301. It set down the powers, rights, and responsibilities of bankers, and stipulated requirements with respect to guarantors. Some of the rules adopted are quite relevant to our topic.

For example, on February 13, 1300 it was established that any banker who went bankrupt would be vilified throughout Barcelona by a public spokesman and forced to live on a strict diet of bread and water until he returned to his creditors the full amount of their deposits.[63] Furthermore, on May 16, 1301, one year later, it was decided that bankers would be obliged to obtain collateral or guarantees from third parties in order to operate, and those who did not would not be allowed to spread a tablecloth over their work counter. The purpose was to make clear to everyone that these bankers were not as solvent as those using tablecloths, who were backed by collateral. Any banker who broke this rule (i.e., operated with a tablecloth but without collateral) would be found guilty of fraud.[64] In view of these regulations, Barcelona's banking system must initially have been quite solvent and banks must have largely respected the essential legal principles governing the monetary bank deposit.

---

[63]Usher, *The Early History of Deposit Banking in Mediterranean Europe*, p. 239.

[64]Ibid., p. 239.

Nevertheless, there are indications to show that, in spite of everything, private bankers soon began to deceive their clients, and on August 14, 1321 the regulations pertaining to bank failures were modified. It was established that those bankers who did not immediately fulfill their commitments would be declared bankrupt, and if they did not pay their debts within one year, they would fall into public disgrace, which would be proclaimed throughout Catalonia by a town crier. Immediately afterward, the banker would be *beheaded* directly in front of his counter, and his property sold locally to pay his creditors. In fact, this is one of the few historical instances in which public authorities have bothered to effectively defend the general principles of property rights with respect to the monetary bank-deposit contract. While it is likely that most Catalonian bankers who went bankrupt tried to escape or pay their debts within a year, documentary evidence shows that at least one banker, a certain Francesch Castello, was beheaded directly in front of his counter in 1360, in strict accordance with the law.[65]

Despite these sanctions, banks' liquid funds did not match the amount received on demand deposit. As a result, they eventually failed en masse in the fourteenth century, during the same economic and credit recession that ravaged the Italian financial world and was studied by Carlo M. Cipolla. Though there are signs that Catalonian banks held out a bit longer than Italian ones (the terrible penalties for fraud undoubtedly raised reserve ratios), documents show that in the end, Catalonian banks also generally failed to meet their obligations. In March 1397, further regulations were introduced when the public began to complain that bankers were reluctant to return money deposited, offered their clients all

---

[65]Ibid., pp. 240 and 242. In light of recent scandals and bank crises in Spain, one could jokingly wonder if it might not be a good idea to again punish fraudulent bankers as severely as in fourteenth-century Catalonia. A student of ours, Elena Sousmatzian, says that in the recent bank crisis that devastated Venezuela, a senator from the Social-Christian Party Copei even "seriously" suggested such measures in a statement to the press. Incidentally, her remarks were quite well-received among depositors affected by the crisis.

sorts of excuses, told them to "come back later" and would pay them (in the end, if the clients were lucky) only in small coins of little value and never in the gold which had originally been deposited.[66]

The bank crisis of the fourteenth century did not lead to increased monitoring and protection of the property rights of depositors. Instead, it resulted in the creation of a municipal government bank, the *Taula de Canvi*, Barcelona's Bank of Deposit. This bank was formed with the purpose of taking in deposits and using them to finance city expenditures and the issuance of government bond certificates for the city of Barcelona. Hence, the *Taula de Canvi* fits the traditional model of a bank created by public authorities to take direct advantage of the dishonest profits of banking. A.P. Usher studied the life of this bank in detail. Predictably, it ended up suspending payments (in February 1468), because a large portion of its reserves had been channeled into loans to the city of Barcelona and the bank was unable to satisfy depositors' demands for cash withdrawals.[67] From that point on, the bank was reorganized and gradually given more and more privileges, such as a monopoly on all deposits deriving from judicial attachments and seizures. This was an almost guaranteed source of continuous income and acted as collateral for loans to finance the city's projects. The *Taula* was also granted a monopoly on resources from all administrative deposits, guardianships and testate proceedings. These funds were deposited and fixed in the bank.[68]

---

[66]Ibid., p. 244.

[67] In February 1468, after a long period of strain, the Bank of Deposit was obliged to suspend specie payments completely. For all balances on the books at that date, annuities bearing interest at 5 percent were issued to depositors willing to accept them. Those unwilling to accept annuities remained creditors of the bank, but they were not allowed to withdraw funds in cash. (Ibid., p. 278)

[68]Documents show that in 1433, at least 28 percent of deposits in Barcelona's Taula de Canvi came from compulsory judicial seizures and were very stable. See Usher, *The Early History of Deposit Banking in Mediterranean Europe*, p. 339, and Kindleberger, *A Financial History of*

4

Banking During the Reign of Charles V and the Doctrine of the School of Salamanca[69]

Banking during the reign of Charles V is a good example of the scenario we have been describing. First, the massive influx of precious metals from the Americas shifted the economic focus, at least temporarily, from the Northern Italian trading cities to Spain; specifically, Seville and the other Spanish business centers. Second, due to his imperial policy, Charles V was in constant need of funds, and he turned to the banking system for a continual source of financing. In this way, he unscrupulously took advantage of the liquidity it provided him and powerfully reinforced the traditional complicity between authorities and bankers. A more disguised collaboration between the two was already the norm at that time. Furthermore, Charles V was unable to keep the royal treasury from going bankrupt, which, as could be expected, had very negative effects on the Spanish economy and on the bankers who had financed his projects. All of these events motivated the most brilliant minds of the time, the scholars of the School of Salamanca, to reflect on the financial and banking activities they witnessed. These theorists left us with some very valuable analyses worthy of being studied in detail. We will now examine each of the historical events in order.

Western Europe, p. 49. At any rate, the reserve ratio progressively worsened until the suspension of payments in 1468. Following its reorganization at that time, Barcelona's Bank of Deposit managed a fragile financial existence for the next 300 years, due to the privileges it enjoyed with respect to judicial deposits and the limits established on loans to the city. Shortly after Barcelona was captured by the Bourbons on September 14, 1714, the bank was taken over by a new institution with statutes drafted by the Count of Montemar on January 14, 1723. These statutes were the bank's backbone until its final liquidation in the year 1853.

[69]Another English version of this section appeared in Jesús Huerta de Soto, "New Light on the Prehistory of the Theory of Banking and the School of Salamanca," *Review of Austrian Economics* 9, no. 2 (1996): 59–81.

THE DEVELOPMENT OF BANKING IN SEVILLE

Ramon Carande deserves credit for uncovering in some detail the development of private banking in Seville during the reign of Charles V.[70] According to Carande, his research was aided by the discovery of a list of bankers compiled prior to the confiscation of precious metals by Seville's *Casa de Contratación* (Trading House) in 1545. An impoverished treasury prompted Charles V to disregard the most basic legal principles and seize funds where he could find them: i.e., deposited in the vaults of Seville's bankers. Granted, these bankers also violated the basic legal principles governing the monetary irregular deposit and employed in their own private dealings a large share of the money deposited. However, the emperor's policy of directly confiscating whatever funds remained in their vaults incited bankers to routinely loan to third parties most money on deposit. If there was ultimately no guarantee that public authorities would respect bank reserves (and bankers' own experience taught them that, when short of money, the emperor had no qualms about forcibly appropriating those funds in the form of compulsory loans to the Crown), it seemed wiser to invest most deposited money in loans to private industry and commerce, thus evading expropriation and earning higher profits.

The practice of confiscating deposits is perhaps the most extreme example of public authorities' traditional tendency to capitalize on banking profits by expropriating the assets of those who have a legal duty to better guard the deposits of others. It is therefore understandable that rulers, being the main beneficiaries of bankers' dubious activities, ended up justifying them and granting bankers all kinds of privileges to allow them to continue operating with a fractional reserve, on the fringes of legality.

In his chief work, *Carlos V y sus banqueros*, Ramón Carande lists the most important bankers in the Seville of Charles V, namely the Espinosas, Domingo de Lizarrazas, and Pedro de

---

[70]Ramón Carande, *Carlos V y sus banqueros,* 3 vols. (Barcelona and Madrid: Editorial Crítica, 1987).

Morga, along with the less prominent Cristóbal Francisquín, Diego Martínez, Juan Íñiguez, and Octavio de Negrón. All of them inexorably went bankrupt, for the most part due to a lack of liquidity with which to satisfy depositors' withdrawals of demand deposits. This demonstrates they were operating with a fractional reserve, aided by a license or privilege obtained from the city of Seville and from Charles V himself.[71] We do not have information on their exact reserve ratio, but we do know that on many occasions they made personal investments in the fleet used for trading with the Americas, in the collection of taxes, etc. Such risky ventures were always tremendously tempting, because when they went reasonably well they yielded enormous profits. Moreover, as mentioned above, the repeated confiscation of bank deposits of precious metals only further encouraged bankers to carry on their illegitimate activities. Consequently, the Espinosas' bank failed in 1579 and the senior partners were imprisoned. The bank of Domingo de Lizarrazas failed on March 11, 1553, when he was unable to make a payment of more than six and a half million maravedis, while the bank of Pedro de Morga, who began his operations in 1553, failed in 1575, during the second bankruptcy of Philip II. The less prominent banks suffered the same fate. Thomas Gresham made an interesting comment on this issue. He had traveled to Seville with instructions to withdraw three hundred twenty thousand ducats in cash, for which he had obtained the necessary license from the emperor and Queen Mary. Gresham marveled that in the very city that received the treasures of the Indies money could be so extremely scarce. The same was true for the markets, and Gresham feared that all the city's banks would suspend payments

---

[71]Spanish banks of the seventeenth century had no better luck:

> At the beginning of the seventeenth century there were banks in the court, Seville, Toledo and Granada. Shortly after 1622, Alejandro Lindo complained that not one still existed, the last one (owned by Jacome Matedo) having failed in Seville. (M. Colmeiro, *Historia de la economía política española* [1863; Madrid: Fundación Banco Exterior, 1988], vol. 2, p. 342)

as soon as his withdrawal was completed.[72] It is unfortunate that Ramón Carande uses such inadequate analytical tools and that his interpretation of these bank failures derives mainly from anecdotal information, such as the greed for metals, which constantly threatened banks' solvency; bankers' daring personal business ventures (their involvement in the chartering of vessels, overseas merchant shipping, insurance, various types of speculation, etc.), which continually placed them in serious predicaments; and the royal treasury's repeated confiscation of valuables and its want of liquidity. He never once mentions the following chain of events: Fractional-reserve banking led to an artificial credit expansion unsupported by sufficient real savings; this, along with the inflation of precious metals from the Americas, generated an artificial boom; the boom, in turn, produced an economic crisis and inevitable recession; and this was the true cause of the bank failures.

Fortunately, Ramón Carande's omission of theory has been at least partially compensated for by Carlo M. Cipolla's interpretative study of the economic and bank crisis of the second half of the sixteenth century. Though this analysis refers strictly to Italian banks, it is also directly applicable to the Spanish financial system, due to the intimate relationship existent at the time between the financial and trade routes of the two countries.[73] Cipolla explains that in the second half of the sixteenth century, the money supply (what we refer to today as M1 or M2) included a large amount of "bank money," or deposits created out of nowhere by bankers who did not maintain possession of 100 percent of the cash on demand deposit. This gave rise to a period of artificial economic growth, which began to

---

[72]Eventually, after much effort, he was able to obtain around 200,000 ducats, writing at the time, "I am afraid I will cause the failure of all the banks in Seville." See Carande, *Carlos V y sus banqueros*, vol. 1, pp. 299–323, esp. pp. 315–16, which refer to Gresham's visit to Seville.

[73]See Cipolla's *Money in Sixteenth-Century Florence* (Berkeley: University of California Press, 1989), esp. pp. 101ff. The intimate financial and trade relationship between Spain and Italy in the sixteenth century is very well documented in Felipe Ruiz Martín's book, *Pequeño capitalismo, gran capitalismo: Simón Ruiz y sus negocios en Florencia* (Barcelona: Editorial Crítica, 1990).

reverse in the second half of the sixteenth century, when depositors nervously started to experience economic difficulties and the most important Florentine banks began to fail.

According to Cipolla, this phase of expansion was set in motion in Italy by the directors of the Ricci Bank, who used a very large share of their deposits to buy government securities and grant loans. The other private banks were obliged to adopt the same policy of credit expansion if their managers wanted to be competitive and conserve their profits and market share. This process gave rise to a credit boom which led to a phase of great artificial expansion that soon began to reverse. In 1574, a proclamation accused bankers of refusing to return deposits in cash and denounced the fact that they only "paid with ink." It became increasingly more difficult for them to return deposits in ready cash, and Venetian cities began to experience a significant money scarcity. Craftsmen could not withdraw their deposits nor pay their debts and a severe credit squeeze (i.e., deflation) followed, along with a serious economic crisis analyzed in detail by Cipolla in his interesting work. From a theoretical standpoint, Cipolla's analysis is stronger than Ramón Carande's, although it is not completely adequate either, as it places more emphasis on the crisis and credit squeeze than on the prior stage of artificial credit expansion, wherein lies the true root of the evil. The credit expansion phase, in turn, is rooted in the failure of bankers to comply with the obligation to safeguard and maintain intact 100 percent of the *tantundem*.[74]

---

[74]Cipolla indicates that in the 1570s, the Ricci Bank could no longer meet demands for cash withdrawals and actually suspended payments, only paying "in ink" or with bank policies. Florentine authorities focused on just the symptoms of this worrisome situation and made the typical attempt to resolve it with mere ordinances. They imposed upon bankers the obligation to pay their creditors immediately in cash, but they did not diagnose nor attack the fundamental source of the problem (the misappropriation of deposits and channeling of them into loans and the failure to maintain a 100-percent cash reserve). Consequently, the decrees which followed failed to have the desired effect and the crisis gradually worsened until it exploded violently in the mid-1570s. See Cipolla, *Money in Sixteenth-Century Florence*, p. 107.

Of international relevance were the long-standing relations between Charles V and members of the prominent Fugger banking family (known in Spain as the *Fúcares*). The Fuggers of Augsburg started out as wool and silver merchants and also traded spices between their city and Venice. Later they concentrated on banking, and in their heyday they operated eighteen branches in different parts of Europe. They granted loans to help finance the election of Charles V as emperor and later funded his exploits on many occasions, receiving as collateral both the silver shipments from the Americas and the authorization to collect taxes. Their business came to a standstill and barely escaped bankruptcy in 1557 when Philip II *de facto* suspended payments, and in fact they continued to lease the lands belonging to military orders until 1634.[75]

THE SCHOOL OF SALAMANCA AND THE BANKING BUSINESS

These financial and banking phenomena did not go unnoticed by the illustrious minds of members of the School of Salamanca who, according to the most reliable research, paved the way for the modern subjectivist theory of value, developed by the Austrian School of economics.[76]

---

[75]The best source on the relations between the Fugger Bank and Charles V is arguably Ramón Carande's *Carlos V y sus banqueros*. Also deserving mention is a study by Rafael Termes Carreró, entitled *Carlos V y uno de sus banqueros: Jacobo Fugger* (Madrid: Asociación de Caballeros del Monasterio de Yuste, 1993). Rafael Termes makes an interesting observation about the Fuggers' dominance in Spain, pointing out that

> there is a street in Madrid named after the Fuggers. Calle de Fúcar, between Atocha and Moratín streets, bears the hispanized version of their last name. In addition, the word fúcar is listed even today as meaning "rich and wealthy person" in the *Diccionario* of the Spanish Royal Academy. (p. 25)

[76]The following authors, among others, have recently examined the contributions of Spanish scholastics to economic theory: Murray N. Rothbard, "New Light on the Prehistory of the Austrian School," in *The Foundations of Modern Austrian Economics*, Edwin G. Dolan, ed. (Kansas City, Mo.: Sheed and Ward, 1976), pp. 52–74, and *Economic Thought Before Adam Smith*, chap. 4, pp. 97–133; Lucas Beltrán, "Sobre los orígenes hispanos de la economía de mercado," in *Ensayos de economía*

Chronologically speaking, the first work to consider, and perhaps the most relevant to our thesis, is *Instrucción de mercaderes* (Instruction to merchants), written by Doctor Luis

---

política (Madrid: Unión Editorial, 1996), pp. 234–54; Marjorie Grice-Hutchinson, *The School of Salamanca: Readings in Spanish Monetary Theory 1544–1605* (Oxford: Clarendon Press, 1952), *Early Economic Thought in Spain 1177–1740* (London: George Allen and Unwin, 1978), and *Economic Thought in Spain: Selected Essays of Marjorie Grice-Hutchinson*, Laurence S. Moss and Christopher K. Ryan, eds. (Aldershot, England: Edward Elgar, 1993); Alejandro A. Chafuen, *Christians for Freedom: Late-Scholastic Economics* (San Francisco: Ignatius Press, 1986); and Huerta de Soto, "New Light on the Prehistory of the Theory of Banking and the School of Salamanca," pp. 59–81. The intellectual influence of the School of Salamanca on the Austrian School is not a mere coincidence or quirk of history, but a consequence of the close historical, political and cultural connections established between Spain and Austria during the time of Charles V and his brother Ferdinand I. These ties lasted for several centuries, and Italy played a crucial role in them, acting as a true cultural, economic and financial link between the two furthermost tips of the Empire (Spain and Vienna). (On this subject, we recommend Jean Bérenger's interesting book, *A History of the Habsburg Empire, 1273–1700*, C.A. Simpson, trans. [London: Longman, 1994, pp. 133–35]). Nevertheless, the scholastics' doctrine on banking has been largely overlooked in the above writings. Marjorie Grice-Hutchinson does touch upon the topic with a near verbatim reproduction of Ramón Carande's brief contribution to the matter (see *The School of Salamanca*, pp. 7–8). Ramón Carande, in turn, simply cites (on pp. 297–98 of volume 1 of his book, *Carlos V y sus banqueros*) Tomás de Mercado's reflections on banking. A more profound examination is made by Alejandro A. Chafuen, who at least reports Luis de Molina's views on banking and considers the extent to which the School of Salamanca approved or disapproved of fractional-reserve banking. Another relevant source is Restituto Sierra Bravo's work, *El pensamiento social y económico de la Escolástica desde sus orígenes al comienzo del catolicismo social* (Madrid: Consejo Superior de Investigaciones Científicas, Instituto de Sociología "Balmes," 1975). Volume 1, pp. 214–37 includes a rather biased interpretation of the views of members of the School of Salamanca on the banking business. According to Sierra Bravo, some among the School's theorists (including Domingo de Soto, Luis de Molina, and even Tomás de Mercado) tended to accept fractional-reserve banking. However, he ignores the writings of other members of the School who, on firmer theoretical grounds, held a radically opposing view. The same criticism can be applied to references Francisco G. Camacho makes in his prefaces to the Spanish translations of Molina's works, particularly his "Introduction" to *La teoría del justo precio*

Saravia de la Calle and published in Medina del Campo in 1544. Saravia de la Calle criticizes bankers harshly, calling them "voracious gluttons who swallow everything, destroy everything, confuse everything, steal and soil everything, like the harpies of Phineus."[77] He says bankers "go out into the street and square with their table and chair and cash-box and book, like harlots to the brothel with their chair," and having obtained the necessary license and guarantee required by the laws of the kingdom, they set about acquiring deposits from clients, to whom they offer bookkeeping and cashier services, making payments from clients' accounts as ordered and even paying interest on such deposits.

With sound legal reasoning, Saravia de la Calle indicates that interest is incompatible with the nature of the monetary deposit, and that in any case, the banker should receive a fee for the custody and safekeeping of the money. He even severely rebukes customers who enter into such deals with bankers, and states:

> And if you say, merchant, that you do not lend the money, but that you deposit it, that is a greater mockery; for who ever saw the depositary pay? He is usually paid for the trouble of safeguarding the deposit. Furthermore, if you now entrust your money to the profiteer as a loan or deposit, just as you receive a part of the profit , you also earn a portion of guilt, even a greater portion.[78]

In chapter 12 of his book, Saravia de la Calle makes a neat distinction between the two radically different operations

---

(Madrid: Editora Nacional, 1981), esp. pp. 33–34. This version of the doctrine, according to which some members of the School of Salamanca accepted fractional-reserve banking, has been greatly influenced by an article by Francisco Belda, S.J., entitled "Ética de la creación de créditos según la doctrina de Molina, Lessio y Lugo," published in *Pensamiento* 19 (1963): 53–89. For the reasons indicated in the text, we disagree with the interpretation these authors make of the doctrine of the School of Salamanca with respect to banking. We will consider these objections in greater detail in section 1 of chapter 8.

[77]Saravia de la Calle, *Instrucción de mercaderes*, p. 180.

[78]Ibid., p. 181.

bankers carry out: demand deposits and time "deposits." In the first case, customers entrust their money interest-free to bankers

> so the money will be safer, and more accessible for making payments, and to avoid the hassle and trouble of counting and guarding it, and also because, in gratitude for this good deed they do the moneylender in giving him their money, if it so happens they have no money left under his charge, he will also accept some overdrafts without interest.[79]

The second operation, the time "deposit," is very different from the first and is in fact a true loan or mutuum which is granted the banker for a fixed term and yields interest. Saravia de la Calle, in compliance with the traditional canonical doctrine on usury, condemns these transactions. Furthermore, he clearly states that in the case of the demand-deposit contract, customers should pay the banker

> for if they deposit money, they should pay for the safekeeping and should not derive as much profit as the laws permit when depositing money or property that requires safeguarding.[80]

Saravia de la Calle goes on to censure those clients who selfishly try to capitalize on the illicit activity of bankers, making deposits and expecting bankers to pay interest. As he vividly puts it,

> He who deposits his money with someone he knows will not guard it, but will spend it, is not free from sin, at least venial sin. He acts as one who turns over a virgin to a lecher or a delicacy to a glutton.[81]

Moreover, the depositor cannot ease his conscience by thinking the banker will loan or use other people's money but not his own.

---

[79]Ibid., p. 195.

[80]Ibid., p. 196.

[81]Ibid., p. 197.

He believes the banker will probably guard the money he deposits and not do business with it, when this cannot be expected of any of these profiteers. On the contrary, the banker will soon invest the deposit for profit and try to earn money with it. How could bankers who pay 7 and 10 percent interest to those who provide them with money to do business with possibly refrain from using deposits? Even if it had been clearly demonstrated that you do not sin (which is not the case, quite the opposite), the moneylender very certainly sins when he does business with your money and he definitely uses your money to steal the property of your neighbors.[82]

Saravia de la Calle's doctrine is very coherent, inasmuch as the self-interested use (via the granting of loans) of money placed on demand deposit with bankers is illegitimate and implies a grave sin. This doctrine coincides with the one originally established by the classical authors of Roman law, a doctrine which derives naturally from the very essence, purpose, and legal nature of the monetary irregular-deposit contract, which we studied in chapter 1.

Saravia de la Calle also vividly describes the disproportionate profits bankers obtain through their illegitimate practice of appropriating deposits instead of being satisfied with the more modest earnings they would receive for the simple custody or safekeeping of deposits. His explanation is quite descriptive:

> If you receive a wage, it should be moderate and adequate for your support, not the excessive loot with which you build superb houses, buy lavish estates, pay servants and provide extravagant luxuries for your families, and you give great feasts and dress so splendidly, especially when you were poor before you began your dealings, and you left humble trades.[83]

In addition, Saravia de la Calle explains that bankers are quite prone to bankruptcy, and he even carries out a cursory

---

[82]Ibid.

[83]Ibid., p. 186.

theoretical analysis which demonstrates that the expansionary phase brought on by the artificial expansion of credit granted by these "profiteers" is inevitably followed by a period of recession, during which the non-payment of debts produces a chain of bank failures. He adds that

> the merchant does not pay the profiteer, he causes him to go bankrupt, and he suspends payments and all is lost. As is common knowledge, these moneylenders are the beginning, occasion and even the cause of all this, *because if they did not exist, each person would use his money to the extent he could and no more, and things would cost what they are worth and more than a fair cash price would not be charged.* Therefore it would be very worthwhile for princes to stop tolerating these profiteers in Spain, since no other nation in the world tolerates them, and to banish this pestilence from their court and kingdom.[84]

As we know, it is not true that the authorities of other nations had controlled the activity of bankers more successfully than Spanish authorities. Instead, the same thing happened more or less everywhere, and rulers eventually granted bankers privileges to allow them to make self-interested use of their depositors' money, in exchange for the ability to capitalize on a banking system which provided much faster and easier financing than taxes.

To conclude his analysis, Saravia de la Calle affirms that

> a Christian should under no circumstances give his money to these profiteers, because if he sins in doing so, as is always the case, he should refrain from it to avoid sinning; and if he does not sin, he should refrain to avoid causing the moneylender to sin.

Furthermore, he adds that if bankers' services are not used, the following additional advantage will result: the depositors

> will not be shocked if the moneylender suspends payments; if he goes bankrupt, as we see so often and Our Lord God permits, let him and his masters be lost like dishonest gains.[85]

---

[84]Ibid., p. 190; italics added.

[85]Ibid., p. 198.

As we see, Saravia de la Calle's analysis, along with his cleverness and humor, is impeccable and free from contradictions. However, in his criticism of bankers, he perhaps places too much emphasis on the fact that they charged and paid interest in violation of the canonical prohibition of usury, instead of emphasizing that they misappropriated demand deposits.

Another writer who examines the monetary irregular-deposit contract is Martín de Azpilcueta, better known as "Doctor Navarro." In his book, *Comentario resolutorio de cambios* (Resolutory commentary on exchanges), first published in Salamanca at the end of 1556, Martín de Azpilcueta expressly refers to "banking for safekeeping," which consists of the bank contract of monetary demand-deposit. For Martín de Azpilcueta, banking for safekeeping, or the irregular deposit contract, is fully just and means that the banker is

> guardian, depositary and guarantor of the money given him or exchanged for whatever purpose by those who give or send him money, and that he is obliged to make payments to merchants or persons to whom depositors want payments made in such and such a way, [for which] he may legitimately charge a fair fee to the republic or the depositors, as this trade and responsibility are useful to the republic and free from iniquity; for it is fair for a worker to earn his wages. And it is the moneychanger's job to receive, safeguard and keep the money of so many merchants ready, and to write and keep their accounts, with great difficulty and at times risk of error in their records and in other things. This arrangement could be formalized in a contract by which a person commits himself to hold other people's money in deposit, make payments and keep records as arranged by them, etc., since this is an agreement to hire a person for a job, which is a well-known, just and blessed contract.[86]

---

[86]Martín de Azpilcueta, *Comentario resolutorio de cambios* (Madrid: Consejo Superior de Investigaciones Científicas, 1965), pp. 57–58. In our study of Dr. Navarro's doctrines we have used the first Spanish edition,

As we see, Martín de Azpilcueta regards the monetary irregular-deposit contract as a completely legitimate contract by which people entrust the custody of their money to a professional (the banker), who must safeguard it like a good parent and keep it constantly available to the depositors, providing whatever cashier services they ask of him; and he has a right to charge the depositors a fee for his services. As a matter of fact, Martín de Azpilcueta feels it is the depositors who must pay the depositary or banker and never the *reverse*, so depositors "pay in compensation for the trouble and worries the moneychanger has in receiving and safeguarding their money," and bankers must conduct

> their business honestly and be satisfied with a fair wage, receiving it from those who owe it to them and whose money they safeguard and whose accounts they keep, and not from those who are not indebted to them.[87]

Moreover, in an effort to clarify matters and avoid confusion, Martín de Azpilcueta (using the same reasoning as Doctor Saravia de la Calle) expressly condemns clients who wish to pay nothing for the custody of their deposits and try to even earn interest on them. Doctor Navarro concludes that

> in this sort of exchange, not only the moneychangers sin, but also . . . those who entrust their money to them for safekeeping as above. They later refuse to pay a fee, claiming the profits earned with their money and received from those they pay in cash is enough of a wage. And if the moneychangers request a fee, the customers leave them and take their business elsewhere. So, to keep these clients, the bankers renounce their fee and instead take money from those who owe them nothing.[88]

---

published by Andrés de Portanarijs in Salamanca in 1556, as well as the Portuguese edition, published by Ioam de Barreyra in Coimbra in 1560 and entitled *Comentario resolutorio de onzenas*. In this edition, the text corresponding to the above quotes appears on pp. 77–80.

[87]Azpilcueta, *Comentario resolutorio de cambios*, pp. 60–61.

[88]Ibid., p. 61.

In his book, *Suma de tratos y contratos* (Compilation of deals and contracts) (Seville 1571), Tomás de Mercado performs an analysis of the banking business very much in the same line as the studies by the preceding authors. He begins by correctly stating that depositors should pay bankers for the work of safeguarding their monetary deposits, concluding that

> it is a common, general rule among all bankers to be able to take wages from those who deposit money in their bank, a certain amount each year or for each thousand, because bankers serve depositors and safeguard their assets.[89]

Nevertheless, Tomás de Mercado ironically points out that bankers in Seville are so "generous" they charge nothing for guarding deposits: "those of this city, it is true, are so regal and noble they ask for and take no wage."[90] Tomás de Mercado observes that these bankers have no need to charge anything, since the large amount of currency they obtain from deposits earns them substantial profits in personal business deals. We must emphasize that, in our opinion, Tomás de Mercado simply verifies a fact here and does not imply that he considers these actions in any way legitimate, as various modern authors (among others, Restituto Sierra Bravo and Francisco G. Camacho) appear to suggest.[91] Quite the opposite is true. From the standpoint of the purest Roman doctrine and the essential legal nature of the monetary irregular-deposit contract analyzed in chapter 1, Tomás de Mercado is the scholastic writer who most clearly demonstrates that the transfer of property in the irregular deposit does not imply a concomitant

---

[89]We quote the Instituto de Estudios Fiscales edition published in Madrid in 1977, edited and prefaced by Nicolás Sánchez Albornoz, vol. 2, p. 479. Restituto Sierra Bravo has another edition, published by the Editora Nacional in 1975. The above excerpt appears on page 401 of this edition. The original edition was published in Seville in 1571 "en casa de Hernando Díaz Impresor de Libros, en la calle de la Sierpe."

[90]Mercado, *Suma de tratos y contratos*, vol. 2, p. 480 of the Instituto de Estudios Fiscales edition and p. 401 of the Restituto Sierra Bravo edition.

[91]See the writings by Restituto Sierra Bravo, Francisco Belda, and Francisco García Camacho cited in footnote 76.

transfer of availability of the *tantundem* and therefore, for all practical purposes, there is no *full* transfer of property. He expresses himself quite well: "they [bankers] must understand that the money is not theirs, but belongs to others; and it is not fair that by using it, they cease to serve its owner." Tomás de Mercado adds that bankers should obey two fundamental principles. First: they should

> not strip the bank so bare they cannot then cover the drafts they receive, because if they become unable to pay them because they have spent and invested the money in shady business and other deals, they certainly sin. . . . Second: they should not become involved in risky business deals, for they sin even if the deals turn out successfully, because the bankers chance not being able to fulfill their responsibilities and doing serious harm to those who have trusted them.[92]

Though one could take these recommendations as an indication that Tomás de Mercado resigns to accept a certain fractional reserve, it is important to keep in mind that he is very emphatic in expressing his legal opinion that deposited money does not ultimately belong to bankers but to depositors, and in stating, furthermore, that none of the bankers complies with his two recommendations:

> however, since when business goes well, in affluent circumstances, it is very difficult to bridle greed, none of them takes heed of these warnings nor meets these conditions.[93]

For this reason, he considers the regulations enacted by the Emperor Charles V in this respect to be very beneficial. They prohibited bankers from carrying out personal business deals and were aimed at eliminating the temptation to finance such dealings indefinitely with money obtained from depositors.[94]

---

[92]Mercado, *Suma de tratos y contratos*, vol. 2, p. 480 of the Instituto de Estudios Fiscales edition and p. 401 of the Restituto Sierra Bravo edition.

[93]Ibid.

[94]*Nueva Recopilación*, law 12, title 18, book 5, enacted in Zamora on June 6, 1554 by Charles V, Queen Juana, and Prince Philip; it reads:

Also, at the end of chapter 4 of *Suma de tratos y contratos*, Tomás de Mercado states that the bankers of Seville hold deposits of money and precious metals belonging to merchants who traded with the New World, and that with such considerable deposits they "make great investments," obtaining hefty profits. Here he does not openly condemn these practices, but we must remember that the passage in question is, again, more a description of a state of affairs than a judgment on its legitimacy. However, he does consider the issue of legitimacy in greater depth in chapter 14, which we have already covered. Tomás de Mercado concludes as well that bankers

> are also involved in exchanging and charging; bankers in this republic engage in an extremely wide range of activities, wider than the ocean, but sometimes they spread themselves too thin and all is lost.[95]

The scholastics most misguided in their doctrinal treatment of the monetary irregular-deposit contract are Domingo de Soto and (especially) Luis de Molina and Juan de Lugo. Indeed, these theorists allowed themselves to be influenced

---

> Because the public banks in the markets of Medina del Campo, Rioseco and Villalón, and in the cities, towns and villages of these kingdoms . . . [have engaged in business other than their specific task concerning money], they have as a result suspended payments and failed; [in order to] avoid the above-mentioned events, we decree that, *from now on, they confine themselves to their specific duty*, and that not just one person but at least two be required to establish these public banks . . . and that before they . . . [can practice their profession], they must provide sufficient guarantees. (italics added)

Note that "public banks" refers here not to government banks but to private banks which may receive deposits from the public under certain conditions (at least two owners, sufficient guarantees, etc.). See José Antonio Rubio Sacristán, "La fundación del Banco de Amsterdam (1609) y la banca de Sevilla," *Moneda y crédito* (March 1948).

[95]This is the quotation of Mercado which Ramón Carande includes in vol. 1 of *Carlos V y sus banqueros*, in the introduction to his treatment of bankers in Seville and the crisis that led them all to fail. See Mercado, *Suma de tratos y contratos*, vol. 2, pp. 381–82 of the 1977 edition of the Instituto de Estudios Fiscales and p. 321 of the Sierra Bravo edition.

by the medieval tradition of the glossators, which we covered in section 2 of this chapter, and especially by the doctrinal con-fusion resulting from the *depositum confessatum*. De Soto and especially Molina view the irregular deposit as a loan in which both the ownership and full availability of the *tantundem* are transferred to the banker. Therefore, they believe the practice of loaning deposited funds to third parties is legitimate, as long as bankers act in a "prudent" manner. Domingo de Soto could be considered the first to maintain this thesis, though he did so very indirectly. In fact, in book 6, topic 11 of his work, *La justicia y el derecho* (On justice and law) (1556), we read that bankers have the

> custom, it is said, of being liable for a greater amount of money than that deposited if a merchant makes his deposit in cash. I gave the moneychanger ten thousand; so he will be liable to me for twelve, perhaps fifteen; because having cash is very profitable for the moneychanger. Neither is any evil seen in it.[96]

Another typical example of credit creation which Domingo de Soto appears to accept is a loan in the form of the discount of bills, financed using clients' deposits.

Nevertheless, the Jesuit Luis de Molina is the scholar who has most clearly maintained an erroneous doctrine on the bank contract of monetary irregular deposit.[97] Indeed, in

---

[96]   Habet autem praeterea istorum usus, ut fertur si mercatorum quispiam in cambio numeratam pecuniam deponat, campsor pro maio ri illius gratia respondeat. Numeravi campsori dece milia: fide habebo apud ipsum & creditu pro duodecim, & for-fam pro quim decim: qui capsori habere numerata pecuniam bonum est lucrum. Neq, vero quicq vitij in hoc foedere apparet. (Domingo de Soto, *De iustitia et iure* [Salamanca: Andreas Portonarijs, 1556], book 6, topic 11, the only article, p. 591. Instituto de Estudios Políticos edition [Madrid, 1968], vol. 3, p. 591)

Sierra Bravo (*El pensamiento social y económico de la Escolástica*, p. 215) is of the opinion that these words by Domingo de Soto imply his accept-ance of fractional-reserve banking.

[97]It is very significant that various authors, including Marjorie Grice-Hutchinson, hesitate to place Luis de Molina among the theorists of the

Tratado sobre los cambios (Treatise on exchanges) (1597), he upholds the medieval doctrine that the irregular deposit is a loan or mutuum contract in favor of the banker, a contract in which not only ownership is transferred, but full availability of the *tantundem* as well, which means the banker can legitimately use the money in his own interest, in the form of loans or in any other manner. Let us see how he presents his argument:

> Because these bankers, like all the others, are true owners of the money deposited in their banks, and they differ greatly in this way from other depositaries . . . so they receive the money as a precarious loan and hence, at their own risk.

Further on he indicates even more clearly that

> such a deposit is really a loan, as has been said, and ownership of the money deposited is transferred to the banker, so if it is lost it is lost to the banker.[98]

This position conflicts with the doctrine Luis de Molina himself upholds in *Tratado sobre los préstamos y la usura* (Treatise on loans and usury), where he indicates that a *term* is an essential element of all loan contracts, and that if the duration of a loan has not been expressly stipulated and a date for its return set, "it will be necessary to accept the decision of the judge as to the loan's duration."[99] Moreover, Luis de Molina ignores all of the arguments presented in chapter 1 to demonstrate that the irregular deposit contract has nothing in common, in

---

School of Salamanca: "The inclusion of Molina in the School seems to me now to be more dubious." Marjorie Grice-Hutchinson, "The Concept of the School of Salamanca: Its Origins and Development," chapter 2 of *Economic Thought in Spain: Selected Essays of Marjorie Grice-Hutchinson*, p. 25. It seems clear that the core members of the School of Salamanca were Dominican, and at least on banking matters it is necessary to separate them from Jesuit theologians, a deviationist and much less rigorous group.

[98]Luis de Molina, *Tratado sobre los cambios*, edited and introduced by Francisco Gómez Camacho (Madrid: Instituto de Estudios Fiscales, 1991), pp. 137–40. The original edition was published in Cuenca in 1597.

[99]Luis de Molina, *Tratado sobre los préstamos y la usura*, edited and introduced by Francisco Gómez Camacho (Madrid: Instituto de Estudios Fiscales, 1989), p. 13. The original edition was published in Cuenca in 1597.

terms of legal nature and essence, with the loan or mutuum contract. Therefore, his doctrinal attempt to identify the two contracts with each other is a clear step backward, not only in relation to the much more coherent views of Saravia de la Calle and Martin de Azpilcueta, but also with respect to the true legal nature of the contract as it had already been developed by Roman juridical science. Therefore, it is strange that a mind as bright and penetrating as Luis de Molina did not realize the extreme danger of accepting the violation of the general legal principles governing the irregular deposit, and that he claimed,

> it never occurs that all the depositors need their money in such a way that they do not leave many thousands of ducats deposited, with which the bankers can do business and either earn a profit or suffer a loss.[100]

Molina does not recognize that in this way not only is the objective or essential purpose of the contract (custody and safekeeping) violated, but also that an incentive is provided for all sorts of illicit dealings and abuses which inexorably generate an economic recession and bank failures. When the traditional legal principle requiring the continual safekeeping of the *tantundem* in favor of the depositor is not respected, there is no clear guide to avoiding bank failures. Furthermore, it is obvious that such vague, superficial suggestions as "try to act prudently" and "do not become involved in risky business deals" are not sufficient help in preventing the very harmful economic and social effects of fractional-reserve banking. At any rate, Luis de Molina does at least bother to state,

> It is important to warn that [bankers] commit mortal sin if they use in their own business dealings so much of the money they hold on deposit that they are later unable, at the right time, to hand over the quantities the depositors request or order to be paid against their deposited funds. . . . In addition, they commit mortal sin if they become involved in business dealings entailing a risk of not being able to return deposits. For example, if they send so much merchandise

---

[100]Molina, *Tratado sobre los cambios*, p. 137.

overseas that, should the ship sink or be captured by pirates, they would not be able to repay deposits even after selling all of their assets. *And they are not guilty of mortal sin only when the deal turns out poorly, but also when it turns out well. This is due to the chance they take of hurting depositors and the guarantors they themselves supply for the deposits.*[101]

We find this warning of Luis de Molina admirable, but at the same time we are astonished at his failure to recognize the profound contradiction that ultimately exists between his warning and his explicit acceptance of "prudent" fractional-reserve banking. The fact is, regardless of how prudent bankers are, the only surefire way to avoid risks and ensure that deposits are permanently available to depositors is to maintain a 100-percent reserve ratio at all times.[102]

---

[101]Ibid., pp. 138–39; italics added.

[102]After Molina, the leading scholar with a similar viewpoint on banking issues is Juan de Lugo, also a Jesuit. This suggests that, with regard to banking, the School of Salamanca comprised two currents of thought: one which was sound, doctrinally well-supported, close to the future Currency School, and represented by Saravia de la Calle, Martín de Azpilcueta, and Tomás de Mercado; and another, one more prone to the follies of inflationism and to fractional-reserve banking, and close to the future Banking School. Luis de Molina, Juan de Lugo, and to a much lesser extent, Domingo de Soto exemplified this current. In chapter 8 we will set out this thesis in greater detail. For now we would just like to point out that Juan de Lugo followed in Molina's footsteps and gave an especially clear warning to bankers:

> Qui bene advertit, eivsmodi bancarios depositarios peccare graviter, & damno subsequuto, cum obligatione restituendi pro damno, quoties ex pecuniis apud se depositis tantam summam ad suas negotiationes exponunt, ut inhabiles maneant ad solvendum deposentibus, quando suo tempore exigent. Et idem est, si negotiationes tales aggrediantur, ex quibus periculum sit, ne postea ad paupertatem redacti pecunias acceptas reddere non possint, v.g. si euenrus ex navigatione periculosa dependeat, in qua navis hostium, vel naufragij periculo exposita sit, qua iactura sequunta, ne ex propio quidem patrimonio solvere possint, sed in creditorum, vel fideiussorum damnum cedere debet. (R.P. Joannis de Lugo Hispalensis, S.I., *Disputationum de iustitia et iure tomus secundus*, Disp. 28, section 5 [Lyon: Sumptibus Petri Prost, 1642], pp. 406–07)

5

A New Attempt at Legitimate Banking: The Bank of Amsterdam. Banking in the Seventeenth and Eighteenth Centuries

The Bank of Amsterdam

The last serious attempt to establish a bank based on the general legal principles governing the monetary irregular deposit and to set up an efficient system of government control to adequately define and defend depositors' property rights took place with the creation of the Municipal Bank of Amsterdam in 1609. It was founded after a period of great monetary chaos and fraudulent (fractional-reserve) private banking. Intended to put an end to this state of affairs and restore order to financial relations, the Bank of Amsterdam began operating on January 31, 1609 and was called the Bank of Exchange.[103] The hallmark of the Bank of Amsterdam was its commitment, from the time of its creation, to the universal legal principles governing the monetary irregular deposit. More specifically, it was founded upon the principle that the obligation of the depository bank in the monetary irregular-deposit contract consists of maintaining the constant availability of the *tantundem* in favor of the depositor; that is, maintaining at all times a 100-percent reserve ratio with respect to "demand" deposits. This measure was intended to ensure legitimate banking and prevent the abuses and bank failures which had historically occurred in all countries where the state had not only not bothered to prohibit and declare illegal the misappropriation of money on demand deposit in banks, but on the contrary, had usually ended up granting bankers all sorts of privileges and licenses to allow their fraudulent operations, in exchange for the opportunity to take fiscal advantage of them.

---

[103]As for the curious reference to the public banks of Seville (and Venice) as models (!) for the Bank of Amsterdam, included in a petition from leading Dutch merchants to the Council of Amsterdam, see José Antonio Rubio Sacristán, "La fundación del Banco de Amsterdam (1609) y la banca de Sevilla."

For a very long time, over one hundred fifty years, the Bank of Amsterdam scrupulously fulfilled the commitment upon which it was founded. Evidence reflects that during the first years of its existence, between 1610 and 1616, both the bank's deposits and its cash reserves came very close to one million florins. From 1619 to 1635, deposits amounted to nearly four million florins and cash reserves exceeded three million, five hundred thousand. After this slight imbalance, equilibrium was restored in 1645, when deposits equaled eleven million, two hundred eighty-eight thousand florins and cash reserves added up to eleven million, eight hundred thousand florins. Equilibrium and growth were more or less stable, and in the eighteenth century, between 1721 and 1722, the bank's deposits totaled twenty-eight million florins and its stock of cash reached nearly that amount, twenty-seven million. This great increase in the deposits of the Bank of Amsterdam stemmed, among other causes, from its role as a refuge for capital fleeing the crazy inflationist speculation that the system of John Law produced in France in the 1720s. We will deal with this more in depth later. This continued until 1772, in which both deposits and cash reserves totaled twenty-eight to twenty-nine million florins. As is evident, during this entire period, to all intents and purposes *the Bank of Amsterdam maintained a 100-percent cash reserve*. This allowed it, in all crises, to satisfy each and every request for cash withdrawal of deposited florins. Such was true in 1672, when panic caused by the French threat gave rise to a massive withdrawal of money from Dutch banks, most of which were forced to suspend payments (as occurred with the Rotterdam and Middelburg banks). The Bank of Amsterdam was the exception, and it logically had no trouble returning deposits. Increasing and lasting confidence in its soundness resulted, and the Bank of Amsterdam became an object of admiration for the civilized economic world of the time. Pierre Vilar indicates that in 1699 the French ambassador wrote in a report to his king:

> Of all the towns of the United Provinces, Amsterdam is without any doubt the foremost in greatness, wealth and the extent of her trade. There are few cities even in Europe to equal her in the two latter respects; her commerce stretches

over both halves of the globe, and her wealth is so great that
during the war she supplied as much as fifty millions a year
if not more.[104]

In 1802, when, as we will now see, the Bank of Amsterdam
started to become corrupt and violate the principles on which
it was founded, the bank still enjoyed enormous prestige, to
the point that the French consul in Amsterdam noted:

> At the end of a maritime war which has kept the treasures
> of the mines pent up in the Spanish and Portuguese
> colonies, Europe is suddenly inundated with gold and silver
> in quantities far above what is needed, so that they would
> decline in value if they were put into circulation all at once.
> In such an eventuality, the people of Amsterdam deposited
> the metal in ingots in the Bank, where it was kept for them
> at a very low cost, and they took it out a little at a time to
> send to different countries as the increase in the rate war-
> rants it. This money, then, which if allowed to flood in too
> rapidly would have driven up the prices of everything
> exceedingly, to the great loss of all who live on fixed and
> limited incomes, was gradually distributed through many
> channels, giving life to industry and encouraging trade. The
> Bank of Amsterdam, then, did not act only according to the
> special interests of the traders of this city; but the whole of
> Europe is in its debt for the greater stability of prices, equi-
> librium of exchange and a more constant ratio between the
> two metals of which coin is made; and if the bank is not re-
> established, it could be said that the great system of the
> trade and political economy of the civilised world will be
> without an essential part of its machinery.[105]

---

[104]Pierre Vilar, *A History of Gold and Money, 1450–1920*, Judith White,
trans. (London: NLB, 1976), p. 207. The deposit and reserve figures we
have cited in the text are also found here on pp. 208–09. Two other European banks modeled after the Bank of Amsterdam were the Bank of
Venice and the Bank of Hamburg. They were both founded in 1619.
Although the first eventually violated the strict safekeeping obligation
and disappeared in 1797, the Bank of Hamburg operated in a more consistent manner and survived until merging with the Reichsbank in 1873.
J.K. Ingram, "Banks, Early European," in *Palgrave's Dictionary of Political
Economy*, Henry Higgs, ed. (London: Macmillan, 1926), vol. 1, pp. 103–06.

[105]Vilar, *A History of Gold and Money, 1450–1920*, p. 209.

Therefore, we see that the Bank of Amsterdam did not try to attain disproportionate profits through the fraudulent use of deposits. Instead, in keeping with the dictates of Saravia de la Calle and others we have mentioned, it contented itself with the modest benefits derived from fees for safeguarding deposits and with the small income obtained though the exchange of money and the sale of bars of stamped metal. Nevertheless, this income was more than sufficient to satisfy the bank's operating and administration costs, to generate some profit and to maintain an honest institution that fulfilled all of its commitments.

The great prestige of the Bank of Amsterdam is also evidenced by a reference to it found in the incorporation charter of the Spanish Banco de San Carlos in 1782. Although this bank, from its very inception, lacked the guarantees of the Bank of Amsterdam, and it was created with the intention of using its deposits, authority, and clout to help finance the Treasury, it could not escape the immense influence of the Dutch bank. Thus, its article XLIV establishes that private individuals may hold deposits or

> equivalent funds in cash in the bank itself, and whoever wishes to make deposits shall be allowed to do so, either in order to draw bills on the money or to withdraw it gradually, and in this way they will be exempt from having to make payments themselves, their bills being accepted as payable at the bank. In their first meeting, the stockholders will determine the amount per thousand which merchants must pay the bank in relation to their deposits, *as they do in Holland*, and will establish all other provisions concerning the best dispatch of discounts and reductions.[106]

---

[106]We quote directly from a copy of the *Real Cédula de S. M. y Señores del Consejo, por la qual se crea, erige y autoriza un Banco nacional y general para facilitar las operaciones del Comercio y el beneficio público de estos Reynos y los de Indias, con la denominación de Banco de San Carlos baxo las reglas que se expresan* (Royal Charter of H.M. and Members of the Council, by which a universal, national bank is created, erected and authorized, to promote trade and the common good of these kingdoms and the New World), printed by Pedro Marín (Madrid, 1782), pp. 31–32; italics added. There is an excellent profile on the history of the Banco de San Carlos by

DAVID HUME AND THE BANK OF AMSTERDAM

A sign of the enormous prestige of the Bank of Amsterdam among scholars and intellectuals, as well as merchants, is the express mention David Hume makes of it in his essay *Of Money*. This essay first appeared, with others, in a book called *Political Discourses*, published in Edinburgh in 1752. In it David Hume voices his opposition to paper currency and argues that the only solvent financial policy is that which forces banks to maintain a 100-percent reserve ratio, in accordance with traditional legal principles governing the irregular deposit of money. David Hume concludes that

> to endeavour artificially to encrease such a credit, can never be the interest of any trading nation; but must lay them under disadvantages, by encreasing money beyond its natural proportion to labour and commodities, and thereby heightening their price to the merchant manufacturer. And in this view, it must be allowed, *that no bank could be more advantageous, than such a one as locked up all the money it received, and never augmented the circulating coin, as is usual, by returning part of its treasure into commerce. A public bank, by this expedient, might cut off much of the dealings of private bankers and money-jobbers; and though the state bore the charge of salaries to the directors and tellers of this bank (for, according to the preceding supposition, it would have no profit from its dealings), the national advantage, resulting from the low price of labour and the destruction of paper credit, would be a sufficient compensation.*[107]

Hume is not completely correct when he claims the bank would not earn a profit, since its safekeeping fees would be sufficient to cover operating costs, and it might even generate modest profits, as in fact the Bank of Amsterdam did. However his analysis is categorical and reveals that, in defending

---

Pedro Tedde de Lorca, entitled *El banco de San Carlos, 1782–1829* (Madrid: Banco de España and Alianza Editorial, 1988).

[107]We quote from pp. 284–85 of the excellent reissue of David Hume's work, *Essays: Moral, Political and Literary*, edited by Eugene F. Miller and published by Liberty Fund, Indianapolis 1985; italics added.

the creation of a public bank with these characteristics, he had in mind the success of the Bank of Amsterdam and the example it had already set for over one hundred years. Furthermore the third edition of his *Essays and Treatises on Several Subjects,* published in four volumes in London and Edinburgh, 1753–1754, includes a note by Hume in reference to the phrase, "no bank could be more advantageous, than such a one as locked up all the money it received." Footnote number four contains the following words: "This is the case with the Bank of Amsterdam." It appears that Hume wrote this footnote with the intention of more clearly emphasizing his view that the Bank of Amsterdam was the ideal model for a bank. Hume was not the very first to propose a 100-percent reserve requirement in banking. He was preceded by Jacob Vanderlint (1734) and especially by the director of the Royal mint, Joseph Harris, for whom banks were useful as long as they "issued no bills without an equivalent in real treasure."[108]

SIR JAMES STEUART, ADAM SMITH, AND THE BANK OF AMSTERDAM

Sir James Steuart offers us an important contemporary study of the Bank of Amsterdam's operation in his treatise published in 1767 entitled, *An Enquiry into the Principles of Political Oeconomy: Being an Essay on the Science of Domestic Policy in Free Nations.* In chapter 39 of volume 2, Steuart presents an analysis of the "circulation of coin through the Bank of Amsterdam." He maintains that "every shilling written in the books of the bank is actually locked up, in coin, in the bank repositories." Still, he states,

> Although, by the regulations of the bank, no coin can be issued to any person who demands it in consequence of his credit in bank; yet I have not the least doubt, but that *both the credit written in the books of the bank, and the cash in the repositories which balances it, may suffer alternate augmentations and*

---

[108]Quoted by Rothbard, *Economic Thought Before Adam Smith,* pp. 332–35 and 462.

diminutions, according to the greater or less demand for bank money.[109]

At any rate, Steuart indicates that the bank's activities "are conducted with the greatest secrecy," in keeping with the traditional lack of openness in banking and especially significant in the case of the Bank of Amsterdam, whose statutes and operation demanded the maintenance of a continuous 100-percent reserve ratio. If Steuart is correct and this ratio was at times violated, it is logical that at the time the Bank of Amsterdam tried to hide the fact at all costs.

Although there are signs that at the end of the 1770s the Bank of Amsterdam began to violate the principles upon which it had been founded, in 1776 Adam Smith still affirmed in his book, *An Inquiry into the Nature and Causes of the Wealth of Nations*, that

> The Bank of Amsterdam professes to lend out no part of what is deposited with it, but, for every guilder for which it gives credit in its books, to keep in its repositories the value of a guilder either in money or bullion. That it keeps in its repositories all the money or bullion for which there are receipts in force, for which it is at all times liable to be called upon, and which, in reality, is continually going from it and returning to it again, cannot well be doubted. . . . At Amsterdam no point of faith is better established than that for every guilder, circulated as bank money, there is a correspondant guilder in gold or silver to be found in the treasure of the bank.[110]

Adam Smith goes on to say that the city itself guaranteed the operation of the Bank of Amsterdam as described above

---

[109]We quote from the original edition, published by A. Miller and T. Cadell in the Strand (London, 1767), vol. 2, p. 301; italics added. Prior to Steuart's analysis, we find a more superficial study of the Bank of Amsterdam's operation in the Abbot Ferdinando Galiani's famous book, *Della moneta*. The original edition was published by Giuseppe Raimondi (Naples, 1750), pp. 326–28.

[110]We quote directly from the original edition of Adam Smith, *An Inquiry into the Nature and Causes of the Wealth of Nations* (London: W. Strahan and T. Cadell in the Strand, 1776), vol. 2, pp. 72–73.

and that it was under the direction of four burgomasters who changed each year. Each burgomaster visited the vaults, compared their content in cash with deposit entries in the books and with great solemnity declared under oath that the two coincided. Adam Smith remarks, tongue-in-cheek, that "in that sober and religious country oaths are not yet disregarded."[111] He ends his commentary by adding that all of these practices were sufficient to guarantee the absolute safety of deposits in the bank, a fact which was demonstrated in various Dutch political revolutions. No political party was ever able to accuse the prior of disloyalty in the management of the bank. By way of example, Adam Smith mentions that even in 1672, when the king of France marched into Utrecht and Holland was in danger of being conquered by a foreign power, the Bank of Amsterdam satisfied every last request for repayment of demand deposits. As we stated before, this acted as an even more impressive reinforcement of the public's confidence in the absolute solvency of the bank.

As additional evidence that the Bank of Amsterdam maintained a 100-percent reserve ratio, Adam Smith offers the anecdote that some coins removed from the bank appeared to have been damaged in the building fire that struck the bank soon after its creation in 1609, which shows those coins had been kept in the bank for over one hundred fifty years. Finally, Adam Smith, in strict keeping with the true legal nature of the irregular-deposit contract, which requires that it be the depositors who pay the bank, indicates that the bank's income stemmed from safekeeping fees:

> The City of Amsterdam derives a considerable revenue from the bank, besides what may be called the warehouse-rent above mentioned, each person, upon first opening an account with the bank, pays a fee of ten guilders, and for every new account three guilders three stivers; for every transfer two stivers; and if the transfer is for less than three hundred guilders, six stivers, in order to discourage the multiplicity of small transactions.[112]

---

[111]Ibid., p. 73.

[112]Ibid., p. 74.

In addition, Adam Smith refers to other sources of income we have already mentioned, such as the exchange of money and the sale of gold and silver bars.

Unfortunately, in the 1780s the Bank of Amsterdam began to systematically violate the legal principles on which it had been founded, and evidence shows that from the time of the fourth Anglo-Dutch war, the reserve ratio decreased drastically, because the city of Amsterdam demanded the bank loan it a large portion of its deposits to cover growing public expenditures. Hence, deposits at that time amounted to twenty million florins, while there were only four million florins' worth of precious metals in the vaults; which indicates that, not only did the bank violate the essential principle of safekeeping on which it had been founded and its existence based for over one hundred seventy years, but the reserve ratio had been cut from 100 percent to less than 25 percent. This meant the final loss of the Bank of Amsterdam's long-standing reputation: deposits began to gradually decrease at that point, and in 1820 they had dwindled to less than one hundred forty thousand florins.[113] The Bank of Amsterdam was the last bank in history to maintain a 100-percent reserve ratio, and its disappearance marked the end of the last attempts to found banks upon general legal principles. The financial predominance of Amsterdam was replaced by the financial system of the United Kingdom, a much less stable and less solvent system based on the expansion of credit, deposits and paper currency.

THE BANKS OF SWEDEN AND ENGLAND

The Bank of Amsterdam was a forerunner of the Bank of Stockholm (Riksbank), which began operating in 1656 and was divided into two departments: one responsible for the safekeeping of deposits (using a 100-percent reserve ratio) and modeled after the Bank of Amsterdam; and another devoted to loans. Although the departments supposedly functioned

---

[113]Vilar, *A History of Gold and Money, 1450–1920*, p. 208. On the operation of the Bank of Amsterdam see also Wicksell, *Lectures on Political Economy* vol. 2, pp. 75–76.

separately from one another, in practice they were separate only on paper, and the Bank of Stockholm soon abandoned the standards set by the Dutch bank.[114] The Swedish authorities nationalized it in 1668, making it the first government bank of the modern world.[115] Not only did it violate the traditional principles which guided the Bank of Amsterdam, but it also initiated a new fraudulent and systematic practice: the issuance of banknotes or deposit receipts for a sum higher than actual deposits received in cash. This is how banknotes were born, along with the lucrative practice of issuing them for a higher amount than the total of deposits. Over time, this activity would become the banking practice *par excellence*, especially in the centuries that followed, during which it deceived scholars, who failed to realize that the issuance of banknotes had the same repercussions as artificial credit expansion and deposit creation, two practices which, as A.P. Usher has noted, had been at the core of the banking business from its origins.

The Bank of England was created in 1694 and was also patterned after the Bank of Amsterdam, due to the considerable influence Holland exerted on England following the accession of the House of Orange to the English throne. However, the bank was not constituted with the same legal guarantees of safekeeping as the Bank of Amsterdam. Instead, one of its main aims from the outset was to help finance public expenditures. For this reason, although the Bank of England was intended to stop the commonplace, systematic abuses committed by private bankers and the government,[116] in practice this goal was

---

[114]In this sense, as Kindleberger perceptively points out in *A Financial History of Western Europe*, pp. 52–53, the Riksbank's system of organization was a precursor to the structure which two centuries later the Peel Act (Bank Charter Act) of 1844 assigned the Bank of England.

[115]In celebration of the tercentenary of the Bank of Stockholm in 1968, an endowment was made to fund a yearly Nobel Prize in economics.

[116]For instance, in 1640, Charles I, echoing the policies pursued in Spain a hundred years earlier by his namesake the emperor Charles V, seized the gold and valuables deposited for safekeeping in the Tower of London and in the process completely ruined the reputation of the mint as a safe place for valuables. Thirty-two years later, Charles II also failed in his duty, causing the royal treasury to suspend payments and precipitating

never achieved. In short, the Bank of England eventually failed, despite its privileged role as the government's banker, its monopoly on limited liability in England and its exclusive authorization to issue banknotes. As a result of its systematic neglect of the safekeeping obligation and its practice of granting loans and advances to the Treasury against the bank's deposits, the Bank of England eventually suspended payments in 1797 after various colorful vicissitudes, including the South Sea Bubble.[117] Also in 1797, the same year the Bank of England was forbidden to return deposits in cash, it was declared that taxes and debts were to be paid in bills issued by

---

the bankruptcy of many private banks that had extended loans to the crown or had directly bought treasury bonds with funds from demand deposits. See Kindleberger, *A Financial History of Western Europe*, pp. 53–54.

[117]In 1720 the South Sea Company devised an ambitious plan to take over Britain's national debt for a sum of money. This company emerged from the Tory party, just like the Bank of England, and was intended to help finance the war. In return, the government granted privileges to certain corporations. The actual aim of South Sea Company promoters was to speculate with company stock, to the extent that government debt obligations were accepted in payment for new stocks. During that year the Bank of England extended loans on its own securities to facilitate their acquisition, just as the South Sea Company had done. This set off an inflationary process in which the price of company and bank stock was driven to great heights, generating huge profits. Speculators, including many company officials, took advantage of these benefits. A portion of profits was invested in land, the price of which also rose significantly. All of this speculative and inflationist mania came to an abrupt halt during the summer of 1720, at the same time John Law's network of speculation began to deteriorate in Paris. Once prices began to fall it became virtually impossible to stop their plunge. South Sea Company stock prices plummeted from 775 points in September to 170 in mid-October and Bank of England stocks dropped from 225 points to 135 in just one month. Parliament responded by passing the Bubble Act, which from that time on severely limited the establishment of corporations. However, it was not until 1722, and after much difficult negotiation, that the financial problem was alleviated. That year Parliament approved an agreement between the Bank of England and the South Sea Company, stipulating that the former was to receive four million pounds of the latter's capital through yearly payments of 5 percent, guaranteed by the Treasury. See also the end of footnote 43 of chapter 7.

the bank, and an attempt was made to limit advances and loans to the government.[118] This was the dawn of the modern banking system, based on a fractional-reserve ratio and a central bank as lender of last resort. In chapter 8 we will analyze in detail the reasons central banks were created, their role and theoretical incapability of fulfilling it, as well as the central banking vs. free banking controversy and its influence on the different theories of money, banking and economic cycles. The current chapter would not be complete, however, without a brief reference to the development of banking and paper money in eighteenth-century France.

John Law and Eighteenth-Century Banking in France

The history of money and banking in eighteenth-century France is closely linked to the Scottish financier John Law and the "system" he concocted and put into practice there. Law persuaded the French regent, Philippe d'Orleans, that the ideal bank was one that made use of the deposits it received, since this increased the amount of money in circulation and "stimulated" economic growth. Law's system, like economic

---

[118]From this point on many theorists, especially in the United States, proclaimed the great threat posed to individual liberty by an implicit or explicit alliance between bankers and governments. This type of pact was expressed through the continual, systematic granting of privileges to allow banks to violate their legal commitments by suspending the cash repayment of deposits. For example, John Taylor, an American senator from the second half of the eighteenth century, classified this practice as true fraud, stating that "under our mild policy the banks' crimes may possibly be numbered, but no figures can record their punishments, because they are never punished." See John Taylor, *Construction Construed and Constitutions Vindicated* (Richmond, Va.: Shepherd and Polland, 1820; New York: Da Capa Press, 1970), pp. 182–83. Another very interesting piece on this topic is James P. Philbin's article entitled "An Austrian Perspective on Some Leading Jacksonian Monetary Theorists," published in *Journal of Libertarian Studies* 10, no. 1 (Fall, 1991): 83–95, esp. 89. Murray N. Rothbard wrote a magnificent summary of the emergence of fractional-reserve banking in the early United States: "Inflation and the Creation of Paper Money," chapter 26 of *Conceived in Liberty*, vol. 2: "Salutary Neglect": *The American Colonies in the First Half of the 18th Century* (New York: Arlington House, 1975), pp. 123–40; 2nd ed. (Auburn, Ala.: Ludwig von Mises Institute, 1999).

interventionism in general, arose from three different, though interconnected factors. First, disregard for traditional legal and moral principles, particularly the requirement for continual safekeeping of 100 percent of deposited money. Second, a reasoning error that appears to justify violating legal principles to attain seemingly beneficial goals quickly. Third, the fact that there will always be certain agents who view in proposed reforms an opportunity to make huge profits. The combination of these three factors allowed a political dreamer like Law to launch his "banking system" in France at the beginning of the eighteenth century. In fact, once the bank had earned people's trust, it began to issue banknotes far exceeding deposits on hand and to extend loans against deposits. The quantity of bills in circulation increased very rapidly, and as is logical, a significant artificial economic boom resulted. In 1718 the bank was nationalized (becoming the royal bank) and began churning out even more bills and granting more loans. This encouraged stock market speculation in general, and in particular speculative buying and selling of shares of Law's *Compagnie de la Lousiane ou d'Occident* or Mississippi Trading Company, aimed at fostering trade and advancing colonization of this French territory in America. By 1720 the absurd proportions of the financial bubble had become clear. Law tried desperately to stabilize the price of the company's stock and the value of his bank's paper money: the bank and trading company were merged, company stock was declared legal tender, coins lost part of their weight in an attempt to restore their relationship to bills, etc. However, all was in vain and the inflationary bubble burst, bringing financial ruin not only to the bank but also to many French investors who had placed their trust in it and in the trading company. The losses were so heavy and the suffering so immense that for over a hundred years it was even considered a faux pas in France to utter the word "bank," a term which for a time was synonymous with "fraud."[119] The ravages of inflation plagued France again a

---

[119]A detailed account of Law's notorious bank failure in France by a scholar with first-hand knowledge of the events can be found in the book *Della moneta* by Ferdinando Galiani, pp. 329–34; and in chapter 23 through 35 of volume 2 of *An Enquiry into the Principles of Political*

few decades later, as evidenced by the serious monetary chaos during the revolutionary period and the uncontrolled issuance of *assignats* at that time. All these phenomena made a permanent impression on the collective psyche of the French, who are still aware today of the grave dangers of paper money inflation and preserve the custom of storing considerable amounts of gold coins and ingots. In fact, France, together with India, is one of the countries whose people hold the largest stock of gold on a private basis.

All of the above notwithstanding, and in spite of his ill-fated banking experiment, John Law made some contributions to monetary theory. Although we cannot accept his inflationist and proto-Keynesian views, we must acknowledge, as Carl Menger did, that Law was the first to formulate a sound theory on the spontaneous, evolutionary origins of money.

RICHARD CANTILLON AND THE FRAUDULENT VIOLATION OF THE IRREGULAR-DEPOSIT CONTRACT

It is a remarkable fact that three of the most noted monetary theorists of the eighteenth and early nineteenth centuries were bankers: John Law, Richard Cantillon,[120] and Henry

---

Oeconomy, by Sir James Steuart (pp. 235–91). An enlightening and theoretically solid analysis of the financial, monetary, and banking systems in eighteenth-century France is found in F.A. Hayek's article "First Paper Money in Eighteenth Century France," first published as chapter 10 in the book, *The Trend of Economic Thinking: Essays on Political Economists and Economic History*, vol. 3 of *The Collected Works of F.A. Hayek*, W.W. Bartley III and Stephen Kresge, eds. (London and New York: Routledge, 1991), pp. 155–76. The best biography of John Law is by Antoin E. Murphy, *John Law: Economic Theorist and Policy Maker* (Oxford: Clarendon Press, 1997).

[120]Richard Cantillon was the first to maintain that "safe" banking could be conducted with only a 10 percent reserve ratio: "Dans ce premier exemple la caisse d'un Banquier ne fait que la dixième partie de son commerce." See p. 400 of the original edition of *Essai sur la nature du commerce en général*, published anonymously (and falsely) in London, Fletcher Gyles in Holborn, 1755. Incredibly, Murray Rothbard does not mention this in his brilliant study on Cantillon. See Rothbard, *Economic Thought Before Adam Smith*, pp. 345–62.

Thornton. Their banks all failed.[121] Cantillon alone escaped relatively unscathed, not only because he stopped his risky speculation in time, but also (and most importantly) because of the large profits he fraudulently obtained by violating the obligation to safeguard his customers' assets.

Indeed, Cantillon clearly violated the contract of irregular deposit, however in this case the deposit was not of money, but shares of stock in the Mississippi Trading Company, founded by John Law. Cantillon's fraudulent scheme was as follows: he loaned large amounts of money to his customers to allow them to buy shares in the company, on the condition that the stocks act as collateral and remain at Cantillon's bank as an irregular deposit, in this case of fungible and indistinguishable shares. Later Cantillon, *unbeknownst to his clients,* misappropriated the deposited securities, selling them when he thought their market price was high and keeping the money from the sale. Once the shares had lost practically all of their value, Cantillon bought them back for a fraction of their old price and restored deposits, securing a hefty profit. Finally, he demanded repayment of the loans he had initially made to his clients, who were unable to return the money, since the collateral they had at the bank was worth close to nothing. These fraudulent operations led to multiple criminal charges and civil suits against Cantillon, who, upon being arrested and briefly incarcerated, was forced to leave France in a hurry and flee to England.

Cantillon, in defense, put forward the same argument so often used throughout the Middle Ages by writers determined to confuse the irregular deposit with the loan. In fact,

---

[121] Admittedly, Thornton's bank did not fail until after his death, in December 1825. See pp. 34–36 of F. A. Hayek's "Introduction" to Henry Thornton's book *An Inquiry into the Nature and Effects of the Paper Credit of Great Britain*, originally published in 1802 and reissued by Augustus M. Kelley, 1978. A.E. Murphy also notes that Law and Cantillon share the unhappy "distinction" of being the only economists, apart from Antoine de Montchrétien, who were accused of murder and other crimes. See A.E. Murphy, *Richard Cantillon: Entrepreneur and Economist* (Oxford: Clarendon Press, 1986), p. 237. Thornton's religious and puritanical reputation at least protected him from being charged with such atrocities.

Cantillon tried to defend himself by claiming that the stocks deposited with him as unnumbered fungible goods had not actually constituted a true deposit, but a loan implying the full transference of ownership and availability to the banker. Thus, Cantillon considered his operations perfectly "legitimate." Nevertheless, we know his legal argument was unsound and even though the deposit of securities was considered an irregular deposit of fungible goods, the obligation to safeguard the shares and maintain continual possession of all of them remained. Therefore, when Cantillon sold the shares to the detriment of his customers he clearly committed the criminal act of misappropriation. F.A. Hayek explains Cantillon's attempt to justify his fraudulent actions:

> His point of view was, as he later explained, that the shares given to him, since their numbers had not been registered, were not a genuine deposit, but rather—as one would say today—a block deposit so that none of his customers had claim to specific securities. The firm actually made an extraordinary profit in this way, since it could buy back at reduced prices the shares sold at high prices, and meanwhile the capital, for which they were charging high interest, lost nothing at all but rather was saved and invested in pounds. When Cantillon, who had partially made these advances in his own name, asked for repayments of the loans from the speculators, who had suffered great losses, and finally took them to court, the latter demanded that the profits obtained by Cantillon and the firm from their shares be credited against these advances. They in turn took Cantillon to court in London and Paris, charging fraud and usury. By presenting to the courts correspondence between Cantillon and the firm, they averred that the entire transaction was carried out under Cantillon's immediate direction and that he therefore bore personal responsibility.[122]

In the next chapter we will explain that the violation of the irregular deposit of securities is just as corrupt from a legal standpoint as the violation of the irregular deposit of money and gives rise to very similar economic and social evils. A perfect example in the twentieth century was the failure of the

---

[122]See Hayek, "Richard Cantillon (1680–1734)," chapter 13 of *The Trend of Economic Thinking*, pp. 245–93, esp. p. 284. And also the report by

Bank of Barcelona and of other Catalonian banks that systematically accepted the irregular deposit of securities without keeping full custody of them.[123] Instead, to attain a profit, they used them in all sorts of speculative operations to the detriment of their true owners, just as Cantillon had done two hundred years earlier. Richard Cantillon was brutally murdered at his London home in 1734, after twelve years of litigation, two arrests, and the constant threat of imprisonment. Although the official version was that he was murdered and his body burned beyond recognition by an ex-cook who killed him to rob him, it is also plausible that one of his many creditors instigated the murder, or even, as suggested by A.E. Murphy, his most recent biographer, that Cantillon staged his own death to escape and to avoid more years of lawsuits and legal action against him.[124]

Cantillon's lawyer Henry Cochin, *Memoire pour Richard Cantillon, intimé & apellant* (Paris: Andre Knapen, 1730).

[123]On the irregular deposit of securities and the type of misappropriation committed by Cantillon and later Catalonian bankers until the start of the twentieth century, see *La cuenta corriente de efectos o valores de un sector de la banca catalana: su repercusión en el crédito y en la economía, su calificación jurídica en el ámbito del derecho penal, civil y mercantil positivos españoles según los dictámenes emitidos por los letrados señores Rodríguez Sastre, Garrigues, Sánchez Román, Goicoechea, Miñana y Clemente de Diego, seguidos de un estudio sobre la cuenta de efectos y el mercado libre de valores de Barcelona por D. Agustín Peláez, Síndico Presidente de la Bolsa de Madrid* (Madrid: Delgado Sáez, 1936).

[124]Antoin E. Murphy, *Richard Cantillon: Entrepreneur and Economist* (Oxford: Clarendon Press, 1986), pp. 209 and 291–97. Murphy mentions the following facts in support of this last thesis: (1) Cantillon liquidated a substantial part of his assets the day prior to his murder; (2) The body was burned beyond recognition; (3) His family displayed a mysterious indifference following the murder; and (4) The accused behaved strangely, never acting like the typical murderer.

3

ATTEMPTS TO
LEGALLY JUSTIFY
FRACTIONAL-RESERVE
BANKING

T his chapter contains a critical examination of the different theoretical attempts to legally justify fractional-reserve banking. We will consider the proposed arguments intended to legally support a monetary irregular deposit contract in which the depositary can make self-interested use of money on demand deposit. In light of the legal doctrine presented in chapter 1 and the economic analysis to be performed in the following chapters, we will critique two main lines of defense.

1
INTRODUCTION

The legal doctrines aimed at justifying fractional-reserve banking have been formulated *ex post facto*. They have not been based on preexisting legal principles that have given rise to certain legal acts. On the contrary, as we explained in the previous chapter, banking practices have long infringed upon basic, universal legal principles and have done so in response to specific circumstances which have conspired to make these violations possible (human avarice; inadequate regulation; governments' financial needs; systematic intervention of the authorities and confusion arising from the *depositum confessa-tum*, a product of the canonical ban on interest). As is logical, the lack of a legal basis for such a widespread practice soon prompted bankers and theorists alike to search for a fitting legal justification. Moreover, this urge was reinforced by the fact that, on almost all occasions, the government or public authorities ended up being the main beneficiary of fraudulent banking practices. Therefore it is not surprising, given the traditional symbiosis between political authorities and the intelligentsia, that the latter was driven by the former to search for legal grounds to support the practices it permitted and encouraged.[1]

Finding adequate legal grounds was essential to the survival of the whole network of vested interests which fractional-reserve banking generates. It was clear to any educated person that these practices should be based on something sounder than a mere *de facto* situation. It is not enough to realize and affirm, as Shepard B. Clough does, that

> In fact, [goldsmiths] even lent money given them for safe-keeping on the theory and experience that they needed to have on hand only enough to meet the expected, current demand of depositors. This practice led them, at least by the seventeenth century, to the issuing of "promises to pay," that is, "goldsmiths' notes," which, like modern banknotes, circulated from person to person. These "promises to pay," which could be paid by using the deposits of customers, came actually to exceed the amount of money on deposit. When this happened credit had been actually created by issuing paper—*a very major discovery.*[2]

Nevertheless, no matter how "major" one considers the "discovery" that it is possible to make fraudulent use of depositors' money or issue deposit receipts for a greater

---

[1]See Bertrand de Jouvenel, "The European Intellectuals and Capitalism," in Friedrich A. Hayek, ed., *Capitalism and the Historians* (Chicago: University of Chicago Press, 1954).

[2]Shepard B. Clough, *The Economic Development of Western Civilization* (New York: McGraw-Hill, 1959), p. 109; italics added.

amount than is actually deposited, it is clear that these acts share the same characteristic present in all other criminal acts of misappropriation which have always been the object of doctrinal analysis by criminal law experts. The similarity between the two sets of actions is therefore so obvious that theorists could not remain impassive in the face of a legal irregularity such as this in the economy.

Hence it is not surprising that great efforts have been made to justify what appears completely unjustifiable: that it is legitimate, from the standpoint of general legal principles, to misappropriate funds deposited for safekeeping and to issue deposit receipts for more money than is actually deposited. However, the interested parties (bankers and governments, mostly) have found it so important to find an adequate theoretical justification beyond the easy solution of simply declaring legal a corrupt, criminal practice (which is what has ultimately happened, despite all the doctrinal façades and constructions), that many jurists are still at work trying to confer legal respectability on a procedure that is commonplace even now.

Doctrinal attempts to justify the use of a fractional reserve in the irregular deposit can be classified into two large groups. The first group of doctrines was intended to settle the issue by equating the irregular deposit contract with the loan contract. We will analyze this group of theories in detail and show that, from a legal point of view, it is impossible to equate these two contracts. Writers of the second and more recent set of doctrines start by acknowledging that there are fundamental differences between the loan and irregular deposit contract. These theorists have focused their efforts on the construction of a new legal concept of "availability" and hold that this notion should be taken "loosely," meaning bankers should only be required to carry out their investments "prudently" and to comply with regulations and bank legislation at all times. A detailed study of this second set of theories will demonstrate that they ultimately entail a return to the failed attempt of the first group, i.e., to justify the use of a fractional reserve in the irregular deposit by equating the deposit contract with the loan contract. Thus, the doctrines of the second set fall into the same errors and legal contradictions we will see in those of the first. In addition, in the next chapter we will explain why the doctrinal essence of the new interpretation of availability (based on the "law of large numbers") is inadmissible from the standpoint of economic theory.

We therefore conclude that past attempts to legally justify fractional-reserve banking with respect to demand deposits have failed. This explains the ambiguity constantly present in doctrines on this type of bank practice, the desperate efforts to avoid clarity and openness in its treatment, the generalized lack of accountability and ultimately (since fractional-reserve banking cannot possibly survive economically on its own), the fact that it has been provided with the support of a central bank which institutes the regulations and supplies the liquidity necessary at all times to prevent the whole set-up from collapsing. In chapter 8 we will discuss central banking and show, through a theoretical analysis, that the nationalization of money and the central bank's regulation of the banking system and its laws governing it have been incapable of maintaining a stable financial system that avoids economic cycles and averts bank crises. Thus, we may conclude that the fractional-reserve banking system has failed as well, even though it is backed and protected by a central bank.

At the end of this chapter we will examine several new types of financial contracts, some of which closely resemble those bankers employ in connection with bank deposits. In particular, we will consider the different financial operations involving a "repurchase agreement." We will show that these entail an evasion of the law; whenever payment of a previously-established price is guaranteed regardless of the secondary-market price at the time the agreement is implemented, such operations conceal a true deposit contract. Finally, we will take a look at the profound, essential differences between the financial operations related to banking and those connected with life insurance. The latter represents a perfected form of true saving, where present goods are exchanged for future goods. It is an exchange with especially appealing features, but they in no way involve appropriation of demand deposits, credit creation, nor issuance of receipts without backing. We will also discuss the corrupting influence exerted on the insurance business by the recent trend (most apparent in government legislation) toward clouding and obscuring the traditional legal and technical boundaries between the two types of institutions (life insurance and banking).

2
WHY IT IS IMPOSSIBLE TO EQUATE THE IRREGULAR DEPOSIT WITH THE LOAN OR MUTUUM CONTRACT

THE ROOTS OF THE CONFUSION

The attempts to legally equate the monetary irregular-deposit contract with the loan or mutuum contract are particularly attractive to those who most benefit from banking practices (bankers and authorities). Indeed, in chapter 1, which contained an explanation of the legal nature of both institutions, we indicated that a loan implies the transfer not only of ownership of the lent item, but of its full availability as well, and therefore the borrower can make full use of it, by investing it, spending it, etc. Considering that this is ultimately what a banker does when appropriating demand deposit funds, the ideal legal solution for him is clearly to equate the irregular deposit contract with the loan contract. Moreover, a worn-out legal pretext has persistently been used to reinforce the argument for equating the two. Lax and superficial, it is as follows: Since the irregular deposit contract consists of the deposit of fungible goods, the very essence of which implies the inevitable transfer of ownership of individual items deposited (because they are indistinguishable from one another), the deposit and the loan *are naturally one and the same,* as both institutions entail the transfer of ownership.

In chapter 1 we saw that this line of reasoning is fallacious, superficial, and abstruse. In fact, even if ownership is transferred in both cases, the two contracts still differ *radically* concerning the availability of the item (an essential feature of the contracts). Indeed, whereas in the loan contract full availability of the item is transferred along with ownership, the very essence of the irregular deposit contract demands that *the purpose of safekeeping or custody predominate.* Accordingly, although we might in theory consider that ownership is transferred, in practice such a transference is negligible, since the safekeeping or custody of the fungible good requires the constant availability of the *tantundem* to the depositor. Therefore, even if ownership were transferred in the same sense in both institutions, an essential legal difference would still exist between them: the contrast in availability.

It may come as a surprise that the jurists who have chosen to equate the deposit contract with the mutuum or loan contract have overlooked such an obvious difference. The association between the contracts is so forced and the arguments so weak that it is amazing that a certain group of theorists have tried to defend them. However, their attempt has a historical, theoretical explanation: the *depositum confessatum*, a legal artifice which arose in the Middle Ages from attempts to avoid the canonical ban on interest. Although we have already shown that the canonical prohibition on interest and the development of fractional-reserve banking shared very little direct connection, the *depositum confessatum* acted as a strong, indirect link between them. We already know that from the time of Roman law, if a depositary violated the essence of the deposit contract, based on safekeeping, and appropriated deposits and was not able to immediately return the funds when the depositor demanded them, then the depositary was obliged to pay interest. Then, irrespective of any other foreseeable civil or criminal actions (the *actio depositi* and the *actio furti*), as is logical, an additional suit was filed to obtain interest for late payment and the loss of availability to the depositor up to the point when the depositary returned his funds.[3] Thus, it is easy to understand how convenient it was in the Middle Ages

---

[3]As we know, the fact that the monetary irregular deposit is a deposit contract means the *actio depositi directa* applies to it. Roman jurists developed this concept, which leaves it to the depositor to decide at any moment when his deposit is to be returned to him. This availability is so pronounced that the depositor's claim is considered equivalent to the ownership of the money deposited (since the *tantundem* of the deposit is fully and immediately available to him).

to disguise a loan as a deposit in order to make the payment of interest legal, legitimate and socially acceptable. For this reason, bankers started to systematically engage in operations in which the parties openly declared they were entering into a deposit contract and not a loan contract. However, as the Latin saying goes, *excusatio non petita, accusatio manifesta* (an unsolicited excuse is tantamount to a self-accusation). Indeed, with a true deposit it was not necessary to make any express declaration, and such a declaration, when made, only revealed an attempt to conceal a loan or mutuum contract. The purpose of disguising a loan as a deposit was to evade the strict canonical prohibitions on interest-bearing loans and to permit many true credit transactions highly necessary, both economically and socially.

The *depositum confessatum* clouded the decidedly clear legal boundaries between the irregular deposit contract and the loan or mutuum contract. Whatever a scholar's stance on the canonical prohibition of usury, the *depositum confessatum* almost inevitably led to the "natural" identification of deposit contracts with mutuum contracts. To a theorist who wished to discover and expose all violations of the canonical prohibition and each case of concealment of interest, anything that sounded like a "deposit" was sure to appear suspicious from the start, and the most obvious and efficient solution from this point of view was to automatically equate deposits with loans and condemn the payment of interest in all cases, regardless of the operation's outer legal appearance. Paradoxically, the more "liberal" moralists did not stop at defending the legal existence of deposits and the consequent legitimacy of interest for late payment; they went on to indicate that such deposits were ultimately loans, and hence the banker could use or invest the money. These authors sought not only to justify the payment of interest, but also to legitimize an institution that permitted the same acts of investment, or exchange of present goods for future goods, that the loan contract had traditionally made possible. Furthermore, this type of exchange was quite necessary to industry and trade. Throughout the Middle Ages, most jurists who commented on law texts held this position. As we saw in the last chapter, it was also the opinion of several members of the School of Salamanca, such as Luis de Molina, who believed the monetary irregular-deposit contract to be a "precarious loan" in which ownership of the money is transferred to the banker (which we have seen is admissible in the case of a deposit of fungible money), as well as full availability (which we know is impossible and contrary to the very essence of the deposit).[4]

Moreover, as we have already seen, the Irish banker and economist Richard Cantillon, in the civil and criminal suits brought against him for misappropriating securities deposited with him as fungible goods through an irregular deposit contract during the wave of speculation generated in France by John Law's system, tried to defend himself using the only doctrinal justification that had at that point been developed in favor of his position: that because the contract was for an "irregular" deposit (i.e., the securities were considered fungible goods), a complete transfer of both ownership and availability took place. Thus, he could legitimately appropriate the shares, sell them, and use them to speculate on the market without committing any crime nor harming his depositors.[5]

The same legal line of argument used by Richard Cantillon's defense had been developed by scholars with respect to the monetary irregular deposit (and not the irregular deposit of securities). Consequently, if it is considered legally appropriate and justified to equate the monetary deposit contract with the mutuum contract, the same would certainly be applicable,

---

[4]See Luis de Molina, *Tratado sobre los cambios*, edited and prefaced by Francisco Gómez Camacho, *Disputation* 408, 1022 d., p. 138. As we have seen, Juan de Lugo shares Molina's viewpoint, and Domingo de Soto does also, though to a much lesser degree. All other members of the School of Salamanca, particularly Dr. Saravia de la Calle, being wise jurists true to Roman tradition, were against fractional-reserve banking despite the pressures they were subjected to and the practices they witnessed.

[5]See F.A. Hayek, "Richard Cantillon (1680–1734)," in *The Collected Works of F.A. Hayek*, vol. 3: *The Trend of Economic Thinking: Essays on Political Economists and Economic History*, p. 159. See also the classic article by Henry Higgs, "Richard Cantillon," in *The Economic Journal* 1 (June 1891): 276–84. Finally, A.E. Murphy, *Richard Cantillon: Entrepreneur and Economist*; and the report by Cantillon's lawyer Henri Cochin, *Memoire pour Richard Cantillan*.

mutatis mutandis, to all other deposits of fungible goods; and in particular, to deposits of securities as goods indistinguishable from one another. Hence we must emphasize that any possible doctrinal analysis against the legality of a complete transfer of ownership *and availability* in an irregular deposit of securities also ultimately constitutes a powerful case against the use of a fractional reserve in the monetary irregular deposit. The great Spanish mercantilist Joaquín Garrigues has recognized this fact. He states:

> The reasoning thus far leads us to the affirmation that when a customer entrusts his shares to the bank he intends to contract a bank deposit; however, immediately after making this assertion, we become aware of another contract with a similar financial purpose. This contract also involves the entrusting to the bank of a fungible good (money) and cashier services are provided by the bank. This—defenders of the checking account will say—is another unique contract which is not called a loan nor a deposit in bank documents and which has the same legal effects as the securities current account; namely, the transference of ownership to the bank and the bank's return of the *tantundem.*[6]

Despite Garrigues's forced and unconvincing attempt to persuade us that these two deposits are different, it is obvious that both contracts of irregular deposits of fungible goods (of money and of securities) are essentially identical, and therefore if we accept the transfer of full availability of the good in one case (the deposit of money), we must also accept it in the other. Consequently, there is no denying the legality of one (the deposit of securities) without denying the

---

[6]On this topic see pp. 194ff. in the "Dictamen de Joaquín Garrigues," included in the book, *La cuenta corriente de efectos o valores de un sector de la banca catalana y el mercado libre de valores de Barcelona,* pp. 159–209. In this remarkable book, many of the arguments against the thesis that full availability is transferred in the irregular deposit of securities as fungible goods are therefore also directly applicable to criticism of the same theory with respect to the irregular deposit of money as a fungible good. We will incorporate these arguments into our study whenever appropriate.

legality of the other (the deposit of money).[7] In conclusion, the legal arguments used by Cantillon in his defense were derived from theories regarding the monetary irregular-deposit contract, and if we consider them valid, then they also justify Cantillon's obvious swindling of his customers and the host of irregular and fraudulent activities later performed in connection with irregular deposits of securities in the other countries, especially Spain. Catalonian bankers carried out such fraud well into the twentieth century, and Spanish scholars have correctly and unanimously recognized the dishonest, criminal nature of their behavior.[8]

THE MISTAKEN DOCTRINE OF COMMON LAW

The doctrine equating the monetary irregular-deposit contract with the loan or mutuum contract has also prevailed in Anglo-Saxon common law, via the creation of law in the binding case system. At the end of the eighteenth century and throughout the first half of the nineteenth, various lawsuits were filed by which depositors, upon finding they could not secure the repayment of their deposits, sued their bankers for misappropriation and fraud in the exercise of their safekeeping obligations. Unfortunately, however, British case-law judgments fell prey to pressures exerted by bankers, banking

---

[7]The opposite would be an inadmissible logical contradiction; Florencio Oscáriz Marco, however, makes such an error. He maintains that deposits of bulk goods are not irregular deposits "because there is no power to use them and even less to take them at will, only power to mix them," while in the case of deposits of another fungible good (money), he mysteriously does consider there to be a transfer of power over use and availability, a transfer converting deposits into "loans." In addition to this conceptual error, Oscáriz makes an error in terminology: he cites the decision of the Spanish Supreme Court regarding a deposit of oil made by some olive dealers (Spanish Supreme Court decision of July 2, 1948) in an analysis of the "unique case" of deposits of bulk goods. In actuality the bulk goods deposit is the best model example imaginable of a deposit of fungible goods or irregular deposit. See Oscáriz Marco, *El contrato de depósito: estudio de la obligación de guarda*, pp. 110–12.

[8]See *La cuenta corriente de efectos o valores de un sector de la banca catalana y el mercado libre de valores de Barcelona*.

customs, and even the government, and it was ruled that the monetary irregular-deposit contract was no different from the loan contract, and therefore that bankers making self-interested use of their depositors' money did not commit misappropriation.[9] Of all of these court rulings, it is worthwhile to consider Judge Lord Cottenham's decision in *Foley v. Hill* and others in 1848. Here the judge arrives at the erroneous conclusion that

> the money placed in the custody of a banker is, to all intents and purposes, the money of the banker, to do with it as he pleases. He is guilty of no breach of trust in employing it. He is not answerable to the principal if he puts it into jeopardy, if he engages in a haphazardous speculation; he is not bound to keep it or deal with it as the property of his principal, but he is, of course, answerable for the amount, because he has contracted, having received that money, to repay to the principal, when demanded, a sum equivalent to that paid into his hands.[10]

---

[9]This type of ruling contrasts with the trend of sound judgments established by the declaration that American grain depositaries acted fraudulently in the 1860s when they appropriated a portion of the grain deposits they were to safeguard and speculated with it on the Chicago market. In response to this disconcerting event, Rothbard wonders:

> [W]hy did grain warehouse law, where the conditions—of depositing fungible goods—are exactly the same . . . develop in precisely the opposite direction? . . . Could it be that the bankers conducted a more effective lobbying operation than did the grain men?

See Murray N. Rothbard, *The Case Against the Fed* (Auburn, Ala.: Ludwig von Mises Institute, 1994), p. 43. The same valid legal doctrine has been evident in Spanish court decisions regarding bulk deposits of oil in olive oil mills. (See the Spanish Supreme Court decision of July 2, 1948.)

[10]See the note on p. 73 of the book by E.T. Powell, *Evolution of Money Markets* (London: Cass, 1966), and Mark Skousen's comments on this decision in his book, *The Economics of a Pure Gold Standard* (Auburn, Ala.: Ludwig von Mises Institute, 1977), pp. 22–24. Two precedents of Lord Cottenham's decision were Sir William Grant's ruling of 1811 in *Carr v. Carr* and the judgment delivered five years later in *Devaynes v. Noble*. See J. Milnes Holden, *The Law and Practice of Banking*, vol. 1: *Banker and Customer* (London: Pitman Publishing, 1970), pp. 31–32 and 52–55.

Considering this type of ruling, it is not surprising that Richard Cantillon fled from France to England, where financial practices were much more lax, and as we have seen, court rulings ended up defending the same line of argument he used in his defense. In continental Europe, in contrast, the Roman legal tradition still exerted great influence. Roman jurists had impeccably formulated the nature of the monetary irregular deposit, basing it on the safekeeping obligation and the unlawfulness of banks' appropriation of deposited funds. Hence Richard Cantillon's fear is understandable. He fled continental Europe at a time when the Bank of Amsterdam was still operating with its full prestige and a 100-percent reserve ratio.[11] Also, the concept of irregular deposit began to return to its classical legal roots (which outlawed fractional-reserve banking). It had already become clear that all banking systems which had been based on a fractional reserve had failed (i.e., the systematic failure of European banks of the late Middle Ages, of banks in Seville and Italy in the sixteenth and seventeenth centuries and the system of Law in eighteenth-century France), and judges had regularly pronounced rulings against bankers' appropriation of funds on deposit (and as we know, such decisions have even been made well into the twentieth century in France and Spain).

We must emphasize that, at least with respect to the institution that concerns us (the irregular deposit), clearly the Anglo-Saxon common law system has less effectively guaranteed the defense of property rights and the correct regulation of social interaction than the legal system of continental Europe. We do not mean that the continental system in its latest version, Kelsenian and positivist, is superior to the common law system, only that the latter has often been inferior to Roman law. By "Roman law" we refer to the evolutionary, customary system based on the logical, exegetic, and doctrinal analysis of jurists of the Roman classical school. To put it another way, in the Anglo-Saxon common law system, past decisions are too binding,

---

[11]Incredibly, Cantillon does not mention in his *Essai* this then well-known fact under the pretext that "he could not get the exact information about . . . *cash* kept in the vaults to pay all deposits" (p. 407). It must be assumed that the *Essai* was mainly written to facilitate Cantillon's defense in his lawsuits against his claimants.

judges being often more influenced by the specific details of each case and by ostensible business activity than by the dispassionate, logical, and exegetic analysis which should be carried out based on essential legal principles. In short the Anglo-Saxon legal system depends excessively on precedents, while the continental system, based on Roman law, rests on precedents, sound doctrine, and juridical theory.

The Doctrine of Spanish Civil and Commercial Codes

A group of Spanish theorists has also tried to equate the monetary irregular-deposit contract and the loan contract. Citing several articles in the Spanish Civil and Commercial Codes, they claim the irregular deposit is not recognized as a separate concept in Spanish legislation and therefore is no more than a simple loan or mutuum contract. Nevertheless, not even Spanish positive law guarantees the association between the irregular deposit contract and the loan contract. On the contrary, such a connection is very doubtful and uncertain, and in fact, the majority of modern Spanish theorists have concluded, in keeping with the classical construction, that even from the standpoint of current Spanish positive law, the loan contract is one thing and the irregular deposit contract quite another.

To justify equating the two types of contracts, theorists have frequently referred to Article 1768 of the Spanish Civil Code. This article states that

> when the depositary has permission to use the good deposited, the contract ceases to be a deposit and becomes a loan or commodatum. Permission is not assumed, but must be proven.

According to this article, if we were to understand *use* in its most general and lax sense, then as all irregular deposit contracts imply a transfer of ownership of the individual items deposited and hence of the indistinct "use" of the fungible good, the irregular deposit contract would always *ipso facto* become a loan or mutuum. Although later we will examine the different instances in which it could be considered that a "transfer of use" takes place, for now it is enough to remember that, as we saw in chapter 1, a general transfer of ownership and use is one thing, but in light of whether or not the *tantundem* is constantly kept fully available to the depositor, it is quite another. To the extent that Article 1768 is only intended to distinguish whether or not the *tantundem* is kept continuously available to the depositor, it would be perfectly possible under Spanish positive law to recognize the existence of an irregular deposit contract that is radically distinct from the loan contract. In fact Article 1770 of the very Civil Code seems to suggest this second interpretation. Indeed, this article stipulates that

> the deposited good shall be returned along with all of its proceeds and accessions. Should the deposit consist of money, the same provisions established in Article 1724 regarding the representative apply to the depositary.

In other words, it seems the Civil Code itself allows for a type of monetary deposit which is not a loan. As José Luis Albácar and Jaime Santos Briz correctly point out,

> When faced with such a discrepancy—we may even call it an antinomy—between conflicting statutory provisions [the "classical" and the "modern"], we should note that nowadays the more common idea seems to be that the mutuum and the irregular deposit are different, to the extent that some people believe that in these cases we are dealing with a type of deposit, an atypical and complex concept: the irregular deposit.[12]

The treatment the monetary irregular deposit receives in the Spanish Commercial Code could also appear contradictory and lend itself to both interpretations. In fact Article 309 stipulates that

---

[12]José Luis Albácar López and Jaime Santos Briz, *Código Civil: doctrina y jurisprudencia* (Madrid: Editorial Trivium, 1991), vol. 6, p. 1770. Navarra's civil code, in law 554 at the end of title 12, also makes reference to the irregular deposit:

> When in the deposit of a fungible good the depositary is either expressly or tacitly granted the power to use the good, the provisions established for the monetary loan in laws 532, 534 and 535 shall be applied.

As we see, the content of Article 1768 of the Spanish Civil Code is repeated here almost literally.

whenever the depositary, with the consent of the depositor, uses the goods deposited, either for himself or his business activities, or in operations ordered by the depositor, the rights and obligations of depositor and depositary shall cease, in favor of the rules and provisions applicable to the commercial loan, the commission or the contract carried out instead of the deposit.

It seems, therefore, that some parallels exist between Article 309 of the Spanish Commercial Code and Article 1768 of the Civil Code. However, Article 307 of the Commercial Code, which regulates cash deposits, states that

when cash deposits are made in unmarked currency or in an open, unsealed package, the depositary shall be responsible for their preservation and safety according to the terms established in paragraph 2 of Article 306.

And Article 306, paragraph 2 reads as follows:

in the safekeeping of deposits, the depositary shall be accountable for any damage to the deposited goods resulting from malice or negligence, as well as from the nature of the goods or defects in them, if in such cases he fails to take necessary measures to avoid or repair the damage, *notifying the depositor as soon as the damage becomes obvious.* (Italics added)

Thus, if we consider the last paragraph of Article 307 together with the second paragraph of Article 306, the Spanish Commercial Code itself fully allows for the concept of the monetary irregular deposit contract and imposes a very clear safekeeping obligation on the depositary in the depositor's favor, and even requires that, should any damage occur to the fungible money deposited, the depositary immediately notify the depositor. Nevertheless, Article 310 of the Commercial Code grants bankers a statutory privilege which legalizes the appropriation of funds deposited with them. This article specifies that

regardless of the provisions laid down in the preceding articles, deposits made in banks, public warehouses, credit associations or any other company shall be governed first by that

company's statutes, then by the prescriptions of this code
and last by common law rules applicable to all deposits.

The nature of the "odious" privilege enjoyed by banks and
other similar associations is obvious. Even from the standpoint of Spanish positive law, it could be argued that, according to Article 306 (cited above) of the Commercial Code, any
person who is not a banker or similar professional and uses
the money entrusted to him through an irregular deposit
would violate the safekeeping obligation and therefore commit the crime of misappropriation. Bankers, however, are
exempt from this possibility if their company's statutes determine that they may use and appropriate depositors' funds for
their own business activities. Nevertheless bank statutes and
contracts are not at all easy to understand. On the contrary,
documents of this type are usually ambiguous and confusing,[13] which explains court decisions stating that Spanish

---

[13]Curiously Spanish banks, when specifying the general conditions for
their different checking account contracts, avoid using the word
"deposit" for fear of the legal repercussions of such a contract (especially charges of misappropriation). They also avoid the words "loan"
and "credit" because, although they would be legally covered if they
called monetary irregular deposits "loans," it is obvious that business-
wise, it would be much harder to attract deposits from customers if
they were generally aware that in opening a checking account they
are actually loaning money to the bank rather than making a deposit.
Consequently, bankers prefer to maintain the current ambiguity and
confusion, since the existing contractual obscurity benefits them as long
as they enjoy the privilege of using a fractional-reserve ratio and are
backed by the central bank in the event of a liquidity crisis. However,
bankers' own legal classifications of their operations sometimes give
them away. For example, the sixth general condition established by the
Banco Bilbao-Vizcaya for draft discounting reads as follows:

> Regardless of the different accounts and operations of the
> assignor, whether in cash, securities, collateral, guarantees or
> another type of document representing them, and notwith-
> standing the manner in which they are itemized . . . the bank is
> authorized to offset them by the loans it chooses to contract for
> any entitlement, including any type of deposit . . . this condi-
> tion shall apply even to operations and loans which the
> assignor holds against the bank prior to the current transaction.

positive law requires bankers to maintain continuously available to depositors the entire amount of their deposits (*tantundem*); that is, to maintain a 100-percent reserve ratio. These judgments (such as the Spanish Supreme Court decision of June 21, 1928 and others cited in chapter 1) have been based on case-law interpretations of Spanish positive law and have been pronounced well into the twentieth century.

Finally we must mention Articles 7 and 8 of the Bank of Spain's bylaws, which concern deposits. The first two paragraphs of Article 7 establish that "authorized offices may receive deposits of local currency or of notes from the bank itself." Article 8 states that "the responsibility of the bank as a depositary is to return the same amount in local currency as is deposited in cash." Article 10, which relates to checking accounts, has more or less the same content:

Moreover, whereas the Banco Bilbao-Vizcaya, in reference to the demand deposit represented by the so-called "savings passbook," classified the latter as "the justificatory claim representing the right of the holder to request and obtain full or partial repayment of the balance in his favor," the Banco Hispano-Americano went even further, establishing that the passbook "constitutes the nominative and non-negotiable document which is evidence of the holder's ownership." As we see, in the latter case, the bank, without realizing it, attributes ownership status to the deposit contract; incidentally, this classification is much closer to the true legal nature of the institution (given the continuous availability in favor of the depositor) than that of a mere loan claim on the deposited sum. On this subject, see Garrigues, *Contratos bancarios*, pp. 368–79, footnotes 31 and 36. Garrigues notes that private bankers do not refer directly to monetary deposit contracts by name, but instead usually call demand deposits checking accounts, as revealed by an examination of deposit slips and general terms of accounts, as well as by bank statements, balance notices, etc. Moreover, this reluctance to speak of "monetary deposits" is evident even on bank balance sheets where there is never any mention of such a heading and where monetary irregular deposits are instead entered under "Checking Accounts" in the corresponding liabilities column under "Creditors." Thus from a legal and contractual standpoint, with the consent of financial authorities, bankers purposefully contrive to conceal the true legal nature of their activities, especially from third parties and clients. The effects of the confusion created by banks are studied by Jörg Guido Hülsmann in his article, "Has Fractional-Reserve Banking Really Passed the Market Test?" *The Independent Review* 7, no. 3 (Winter, 2003): 399–422.

the bank may open and manage checking accounts of cash
or securities for individuals or legal entities and duly represented corporations or organizations whose application is
confidentially reviewed by the institution and accepted. The
following may be deposited in ordinary cash accounts: legal
banknotes and coins, checks and other documents related to
other checking accounts . . . for each type of checking
account the bank will provide the checkbooks needed by the
account holder; and via the duly authorized checks, it will
pay the sums and return the securities to the debit of the corresponding balances. Against cash checking accounts the
following are also admissible: bearer, order, personal and
crossed checks.

As we see, these articles of the Bank of Spain's bylaws, and
in general the statutes of all other banks, only regulate the
operation of monetary irregular-deposit accounts and checking accounts from the standpoint of depositors, and they
always maintain the confusion and ambiguity regarding
whether such money is continuously safeguarded and kept
available by the bank or whether the bank is expressly
authorized by the depositor to appropriate funds and invest
them in personal business deals. We must turn to Article 180
of the Commercial Code to see the true original meaning of
Spanish commercial legislation on this point. Indeed, Article
180 specifies that "banks will keep cash in their vaults equivalent to at least one fourth the sum of deposits and checking
accounts in cash and bills in circulation." This ratio, which has
traditionally been used by the Spanish central bank as an
instrument of monetary policy and has been reduced to a current 2 percent, is the culmination of the statutory privilege
enjoyed by the banking industry. Banking is the only institution expressly authorized by Spanish positive law to violate
the safekeeping obligations of the monetary irregular-deposit
contract, thus receiving permission to appropriate depositors'
money for bankers' own use in investments and personal
business activities. Although the reserve requirement alone
*keeps bankers from being criminals under the positive law in force in
Spain*, it does not in the least compensate for the lack of legal
justification for the bank-deposit contract in its current form,
nor, as is logical, for the damaging economic effects on society

of the violation of traditional principles of property rights with respect to the monetary irregular deposit. In the following chapters we will examine these effects (the distortion of the productive structure; the generation of successive, recurrent stages of economic boom and recession; the promotion of widespread malinvestment; the creation of massive unemployment and the perpetuation of a privileged financial system incapable of guaranteeing smooth economic development).

CRITICISM OF THE ATTEMPT TO EQUATE THE MONETARY IRREGULAR-DEPOSIT CONTRACT WITH THE LOAN OR MUTUUM CONTRACT

Even though the doctrinal association between irregular deposits and monetary loan or mutuum contracts is the perfect tool for justifying fractional-reserve banking, this association is so awkward that the most prestigious experts in commercial law have failed to accept it. Joaquín Garrigues, though he seems to want to unreservedly defend the doctrine of association, ultimately realizes that it is not justifiable, and he concludes that, despite the possible positive-law arguments (Article 1768 of the Spanish Civil Code and Article 309 of the Spanish Commercial Code, both cited earlier) that could be used to justify the association between the loan or mutuum contract and the irregular deposit contract,

> there are still *some factors* which lead one to continue considering the contract a deposit and not a loan (for example, the free availability to the depositor, the fact that the depositor initiates the contract, the limited interest, etc.).[14]

Curiously, Joaquín Garrigues does not expound on these factors, mentioning them only in passing. Instead he immediately tries to construct the theory based on the reinterpretation of the concept of availability, which we will study in the next section. Nevertheless, considering what we covered in chapter

---

[14]Garrigues, *Contratos bancarios*, p. 363; italics added.

1, it would have been very interesting to know what Garrigues could and should have said about the arguments against equating the two contracts, a matter we will now consider in greater depth.[15]

THE DISTINCT CAUSE OR PURPOSE OF EACH CONTRACT

The most significant and definitive argument in favor of a distinction between the irregular deposit contract and the loan or mutuum contract lies in the essential difference between the *cause* or *purpose* of each. These terms refer to a fundamental,

---

[15]Strangely, our top commercial law scholar rushes into an attempted justification of fractional-reserve banking while preserving the concept of the irregular deposit through the artifice of a redefinition of availability, without pausing first to examine the factors that make it impossible to equate the irregular deposit contract and the loan contract. It is as if Garrigues were ultimately aware that his redefinition implicitly entails equating deposits and loan contracts—at least from the banker's (the recipient's) perspective. For this reason it does not behoove him to advance a detailed argument against equating deposits and loans, because such an argument would backfire on the doctrine he later defends. This attitude is quite understandable in a famed scholar whose chief customers were the country's banks and bankers and who would therefore think twice before jeopardizing his prestige and academic standing by questioning the legitimacy of such an influential institution as fractional-reserve banking, which was rooted in practice and government-endorsed. In addition, during the years when Garrigues was developing his theories, he could only depend for support on an economic theory which, paralyzed by Keynesian doctrines (see footnote 20 in ibid.), justified any system of credit expansion, no matter how expedient, on the mistaken assumption that this would benefit "economic activity." During those years of doctrinal poverty in economics, the only possible defense for the processes of social interaction against banking practices would have been strict observance of the basic principles governing the irregular deposit, which unfortunately received very weak support from mainstream theorists and were quickly abandoned. Despite all of these adverse circumstances, the writings of Garrigues and others who concentrate on the same topic, an unmistakable impression persists: that in order to justify the unjustifiable, theorists carry out the most forced legal reasoning and maneuverings to disguise as legal an activity that results from an unseemly, unlawful privilege granted by the government.

legal motive (related to the so-called *cause*[16] of contracts) which is closely connected with the parties' distinct subjective reason[17] for deciding to enter into one contract or another. *Therefore a perfect symbiosis exists between the subjectivist conception on which modern economic theory is based[18] and the legal point of view that mainly takes into account the different subjective goals of the parties in entering into one type of contract or another.*

In chapter 1 we studied the essential, irreconcilable differences between the monetary irregular-deposit contract and the monetary loan or mutuum contract. All of those differences could ultimately be traced to the distinct cause or purpose of each contract. On one hand, the loan contract always implies an exchange of present goods, the availability of which is lost to the lender, for future goods, which the borrower must return along with an added amount in the form of interest, in payment for the inexorable loss of availability of the present goods when they are transferred from lender to borrower. On the other hand, in the monetary irregular

---

[16]See, for example, the legal treatment Jean Dabin gives the cause of contracts in *La teoría de la causa*.

[17]For Antonio Gullón,

> *the equating of the irregular deposit with the mutuum is still an artifice that conflicts with the true will of the parties.* The depositor of money, for example, does not intend to grant a loan to the depositary. Just as in the regular deposit, he desires the safekeeping of the good and to always have it available. He happens to achieve these objectives more easily with the irregular deposit than with the regular deposit, since with the latter he risks the loss of his deposit in the event of an unavoidable accident, and he would bear the loss instead of the depositary. Meanwhile, in the irregular deposit, the depositary is the debtor of a type of good, which as such is never lost. (Italics added)

Cited by José Luis Lacruz Berdejo, *Elementos de derecho civil*, 3rd ed. (Barcelona: José María Bosch, 1995), vol. 2, p. 270.

[18]This subjectivist conception is the basis of the logic of action on which all economic theory is constructed, according to the Austrian School of economics, founded by Carl Menger. On this topic, see our article, "Génesis, esencia y evolución de la Escuela Austriaca de Economía," published in Huerta de Soto, *Estudios de economía política*, pp. 17–55.

deposit, the objective or cause of the contract is radically different. In this case there is no exchange of present goods for future goods, nor does the depositor have the faintest desire to lose the immediate availability of the good deposited. Hence the essential element in the irregular deposit contract is not, as in the loan contract, the transfer of availability, but rather the custody and safekeeping of the *tantundem*, which constitutes the legal cause or fundamental purpose motivating the depositor to enter into the contract. For this reason, there is no term, and the funds are deposited "on demand;" that is, they can be withdrawn at any time. If the depositor were informed that the contract he plans to sign is a loan contract by which he will grant a loan to the bank, and that therefore the money will no longer be available to him, he would certainly not go through with the contract as if it were a deposit, and he very well might decide to keep his money. Thus, there is absolutely no doubt that the cause or legal purpose of each contract is radically different from that of the other, and that attempting to mix them is like trying to mix oil and water, given the essential difference between them.

Theorists who attempt to equate the irregular deposit contract with the loan contract fail to realize that their doctrinal stance ignores the true cause or purpose motivating the contracting parties to enter into a contract. And no matter how many relatively empty statements they make about the equivalence of the two contracts, they inevitably come up against the same legal wall: the radical, essential difference between the legal *cause* behind each contract. Therefore, they can go no further than to state that each of the parties to the monetary bank-deposit contract *thinks* it is entering into a "different" contract. In other words, *depositors hand over money as if making a deposit, and bankers receive it as if it were a loan.* Yet, what kind of contract has two essentially distinct legal causes? Or to put it another way: How is it possible that both parties to the same contract simultaneously intend to retain the availability of the same sum?[19] Indeed, depositors clearly turn

---

[19]Francisco Belda, following the example of Luis de Molina and Juan de Lugo, believes he resolves this contradiction with the facile, superficial

over their money with the desire to retain full availability of the good turned over (monetary deposit "on demand"),[20] while banks accept deposits not with the aim of keeping 100 percent of the *tantundem* in their possession at all times, but rather with the intention of using most of what they receive on deposit to make personal loans and investments. This "dual availability" could not possibly be ignored by Garrigues, who logically finds it very disquieting and confusing with respect to legality.[21] As a matter of fact, for Garrigues the most outstanding feature of monetary bank deposits in their current version (which does not require a 100-percent reserve) is dual availability: the deposited goods are *simultaneously* available to both the bank and the customer. He adds that

---

assertion that "each of the two has the perfect right to view the operation from the angle which most behooves him." However, Belda fails to realize that, as there is an essential difference and a contradiction between the causes motivating the parties to enter into the contract, the problem is quite another: it is not that each party views the contract as most behooves him, but rather that the fulfillment of the aim or cause of one party (the investment of funds by the banker) prevents the successful fulfillment of the aim or cause of the other (the custody, safekeeping and continual availability of the money). See Belda, S.J., "Ética de la creación de créditos según la doctrina de Molina, Lesio y Lugo," pp. 64–87. See also Oscáriz Marco, *El contrato de depósito: estudio de la obligación de guarda*, footnote 83, p. 48.

[20]The fact that depositors sometimes receive interest in no way detracts from the essential purpose of the deposit (the safekeeping of money). Since interest is attractive, the unsuspecting depositor will jump at the offer of it if he still trusts the banker. But in the case of a true deposit, the depositor would enter the contract even if he were not to receive any interest and had to pay a safekeeping fee. The essential nature of the contract is not altered by the unnatural payment of interest to depositors, and only indicates that bankers are making undue use of the money placed with them.

[21]Significantly, the only theoretical reference cited by Garrigues in his book, *Contratos bancarios,* is Keynes's *Treatise on Money,* which he expressly mentions at least twice in the main text (pp. 357 and 358) and twice in the footnotes (pp. 352 and 357, footnotes 1 and 11, respectively). With such a theoretical basis, the confusion evident in Garrigues's entire discussion of the irregular deposit is hardly surprising. It seems as if his remarkable legal instinct were pointing him in the right direction, while the economic treatises he was reading on banking were leading him astray.

this *dual availability* is precisely the reason it is difficult to formulate a legal description of the contract, because availability in favor of the depositor, a key feature of deposits, *harmonizes poorly* with availability in favor of the bank.[22]

Rather than to say it is difficult to formulate a legal description of the contract, it would be more accurate to say such a description is *legally impossible*, given the radical difference between the cause or purpose of the two types of legal transactions. Therefore, it is not that one instance of availability "harmonizes poorly" with the other, but that the two instances are mutually exclusive on a fundamental level.[23] Joaquín Garrigues's uncertainty is even more obvious when in a footnote[24] he cites the rulings of the Court of Paris which we covered in chapter 1. These court decisions support a strict safekeeping obligation and a 100-percent reserve ratio for banks, which Garrigues calls "surprising assertions." What is surprising is that Garrigues does not realize that *his own analysis* leads inevitably to the conclusion that the two contracts are different and that it is therefore impossible to equate in any

---

[22]Garrigues, *Contratos bancarios*, p. 367; italics added. It is surprising that Garrigues has not realized that in economic terms, dual availability means "it becomes possible to create a fictitious supply of a commodity, that is, to make people believe that a supply exists which does not exist." See William Stanley Jevons, *Money and the Mechanism of Exchange* (New York: D. Appleton, 1875 and London: Kegan Paul, 1905), p. 210. Convincing the public of the existence of a fictitious stock of fungible goods is definitive proof of the illegitimacy of all irregular deposits (of fungible goods) in which a fractional-reserve ratio (any ratio under 100 percent) is allowed.

[23]Garrigues, demonstrating his characteristic gift of expression, concludes that in this contract "the banker counts on the money as if it were his, and the customer counts on the money even though it is not his." The solution to this apparent paradox is very simple, because although the customer has ceased to own the money, he retains the right to demand the custody and safekeeping of the *tantundem* by the banker at all times; that is, a 100-percent reserve ratio, in keeping with the essential, ontological legal nature of the monetary irregular-deposit contract, which we covered in chapter 1. See Garrigues, *Contratos bancarios*, p. 368.

[24]Ibid., footnote 31 on pp. 367–68.

way the irregular deposit contract with the loan contract. Upon reading Garrigues's treatment of monetary bank-deposit contracts, one inevitably gets the impression that Garrigues himself suffers from a rather "guilty conscience" for carrying out such a forced legal analysis to try to justify the unjustifiable: the supposed existence of a monetary irregular-deposit contract which legally, and in accordance with legal principles and logic, permits the banker to freely use the goods deposited; in other words, fractional-reserve banking.

THE NOTION OF THE UNSPOKEN OR IMPLICIT AGREEMENT

Also inadmissible is the argument that Article 1768 of the Spanish Civil Code suggests that in irregular deposit contracts a type of "implicit or unspoken agreement" exists by which depositors authorize bankers to use money on deposit. This course of reasoning is unacceptable mainly because Article 1768 speaks of permission "to use the good deposited," and we know that it is not the power to use the good that makes the monetary-deposit contract an irregular deposit contract. This authorization is inherent in all deposits of fungible goods, the very nature of which prevents them from being handled individually. In a sense, a transfer of ownership results, which in turn implies authorization for the depositary to use the goods. Nevertheless, we have already seen that this transfer of ownership and of power to use the deposited goods should be understood in a *general sense*. If it is not possible to track the individual units deposited, then we may certainly consider there to be a transfer of ownership and of power to use the specific items deposited. However, as is logical, this is perfectly compatible with a continuous 100-percent reserve requirement; that is, the custody and safekeeping of the *tantundem* and its availability to the depositor. This constitutes the banker's essential obligation and is the foundation of the deposit contract's essential purpose. To put it another way, the characteristic, essential nature of the irregular deposit contract is not determined by the transfer of authority to use the goods, but by the fungible nature of the items deposited and by the contract's purpose. A transfer of authority to use deposited goods may occur independently of an irregular deposit, and this is indeed what happens, for example, in the

mutuum or loan contract. As we know, the legal cause or purpose of this contract is radically different (it entails not only
the transfer of ownership and power to use the goods, but also
the transfer of the availability of the goods, which is simultaneously lost to the lender). Therefore, and according to Coppa-
Zuccari, the claim that supposed authorization (express or
tacit) from the depositor converts the irregular deposit contract
into a loan or mutuum is both unnecessary and inaccurate. It is
unnecessary in the sense that all irregular deposit contracts,
due to their very nature, involve the transfer of ownership
and of the power to use the good (which is compatible, as is
logical, with the fundamental obligation to maintain 100 percent of the *tantundem* in reserve). And it is inaccurate, since even
though the power to use the deposited good is transferred, in
no way does this alter the original purpose of the contract,
which is none other than the custody and safekeeping of the
tantundem.[25] In fact, three logical possibilities exist with respect
to the supposed authorization (express or tacit) to use the
deposited good. Let us consider each one separately.

First, we may suppose that the vast majority of depositors
are not aware that by depositing their money in a bank, they at
the same time authorize the banker to use the money for his
own profit in private business deals. It is certain that when the
overwhelming majority of depositors make a demand
deposit, they are under the honest impression that they are in
fact doing just that: entering into an irregular deposit contract,
the essential purpose of which is to transfer the custody or
safekeeping of their money to the banker. In all cases, the
banker simultaneously receives the money as if it were a loan
or mutuum; that is, he considers that the full availability of the
good is transferred to him and that he is therefore authorized
to use it in his own business deals. It is obvious that the cause
or purpose of each party's participation in the contract does
not coincide with the objective of the other party: one enters
into the contract believing it to be a deposit and hands over
the money based on that assumption, and the other receives
the money as if it were a loan or mutuum and based on that

---

[25]Coppa-Zuccari, *Il deposito irregolare*, p. 132.

idea invests it. Hence, this is a clear case of *error in negotio*, which is an error concerning the nature of the transaction and renders it completely void.[26] To many this conclusion may appear extreme or disproportionate, but it is difficult to arrive at any other if we base our analysis on the legal arguments and principles inherent in the contracts we are studying.[27]

Second, let us now assume that a certain group of bank customers (or for the sake of argument, all of them) enter into a deposit contract aware and fully accepting that banks will invest (or loan, etc.) a large portion of the money they deposit. Even so, this knowledge and hypothetical authorization does not in any way detract from the essential cause or purpose of the contract for these customers, whose intention is still to entrust their money to the banker for safekeeping; that is, to carry out a monetary irregular-deposit contract. In this case, the contract the depositors believe they have finalized is *impossible* from a technical and legal standpoint. If they allow the banker to use the money, then it can no longer be available to them, which is precisely the essential cause or purpose of the contract. Moreover, in chapter 5 we will see from the perspective of economic theory that in a fractional-reserve banking system the massive signing of contracts and the "law of large numbers" cannot *possibly* ensure the fulfillment of all depositor requests for full repayment of deposits. At this time, we will delay going into detail on our thesis, except to say that it rests on the acknowledgment that the current banking system generates loans without the backing of real savings. These loans in turn foster the foolish investment of resources and give rise to unwisely-invested business assets which are either

---

[26]See Hernández-Tejero Jorge, *Lecciones de derecho romano*, pp. 107–08. Hernández-Tejero himself provides the following example, which is perfectly applicable to the case we are dealing with: "If one person entrusts to another a good on deposit, and the person receiving the good believes the transaction to be a mutuum or loan, then neither a deposit nor a mutuum exists."

[27]Furthermore, it is obvious that permission or authorization to use the good cannot be assumed but must be proven in each case. It seems unlikely that in most demand deposit contracts entered into by individuals such proof would be possible.

worthless or of limited value and therefore incapable of balancing the corresponding deposit accounts on bank balance sheets. Consequently, bank insolvency tends to recur, banks being repeatedly unable to meet their obligations (without the external support of the central bank).

In addition, if for the sake of argument we assume that the law of large numbers is applicable to banking, then in the presence of a fractional reserve the deposit contract clearly becomes an *aleatory* contract.[28] In such a contract, delivery of services by the bank is in any case an uncertain event which depends upon circumstances particular to each case. The contract's uncertainty stems precisely from the possibility that depositors of a percentage of deposits exceeding the reserve ratio will attempt to withdraw their deposits and hence be unable to do so. The first to arrive would be able to retrieve their money, but those arriving after a certain point would not. Surely not even the depositors of this second hypothesis intend to enter into an aleatory contract subject to the risk we have just described. Therefore, the most logical conclusion in this second case is either that the contract does not exist, since its purpose is impossible (without a 100-percent reserve ratio, it is impossible to insure that the banker will always be able to meet his obligations), or that the supposed authorization from the depositors lacks legal validity, because the essential objective is still the safekeeping of the good, and this inevitably and obligatorily requires the custody of 100 percent of the *tantundem*.[29]

---

[28]On aleatory contracts see Albaladejo, *Derecho civil II, Derecho de obligaciones*, vol. 1: *La obligación y el contrato en general*, pp. 350–52. It is important to emphasize that the fact that there is an aleatory nature to the monetary irregular-deposit contract with a fractional reserve in which the law of large numbers is fulfilled (in fact impossible) is only secondary to the other points we raise against such a contract.

[29]The popular reaction of Argentinian citizens against the banking crisis of 2001 and the subsequent blockade of all their demand deposits (known as *corralito*) is a perfect empirical illustration of the true safekeeping purpose of bank deposit contracts and of the impossibility of fractional-reserve banking (without a lender of last resort).

A natural incompatibility exists between the legitimate irregular deposit contract, the purpose of which is the custody or safekeeping of the deposited goods, and the authorization for depositaries to use for their own profit the money they receive. These depositaries (bankers) take in funds they agree to return as soon as requested by checking-account holders, but once the bankers have received the money, they make investments, grant loans and enter into business deals that tie it up and under various circumstances actually prevent its immediate return. The supposed authorization, either express or tacit, for bankers to use money on deposit is of little importance if the essential purpose of the contract, the deposit of money for safekeeping, continues intact. In this case the supposed authorization would be irrelevant, due to its incompatibility with the contract's purpose, and it would thus be *as legally null and void as any contract in which one of the parties authorizes the other to deceive him or accepts in writing self-deception to his own detriment.* As the great Spanish expert in civil law, Felipe Clemente de Diego, so appropriately states, an irregular deposit contract in which the depositary is allowed to maintain a fractional-reserve ratio and hence can make self-interested use of a portion of deposited funds is a legal aberration, since at a fundamental level it conflicts with universal legal principles. For Felipe Clemente de Diego, there is no doubt that this contract

> has the disadvantage of leading us to the discovery of a *monster* which, by its very nature, lacks legal viability, like humans with devastating malformations (*monstrua prodigia*), whom Roman law did not grant legal status. Article 30 of the Spanish Civil Code expresses a more moderate version of the same concept: "For civil purposes, only fetuses with a *human figure* will be reported as *born*. . . . " For every being has its own nature, and when this is not found in the being itself, but is drawn from others more or less similar to it, the being's true nature appears to flee and vanish and ceases to envelop it, reducing it to a monstrous hybrid bordering on a non-being.[30]

---

[30]"Dictamen del señor de Diego (Felipe Clemente)" in *La cuenta corriente de efectos o valores de un sector de la banca catalana y el mercado libre de*

It would be difficult to express more accurately and suc-
cinctly the fundamental incompatibility and the insoluble
logical contradiction between the monetary irregular-deposit
contract and the loan contract. Clemente de Diego concludes
by criticizing

> attempts to convert that radical opposition (between the
> irregular-deposit contract and the loan contract) into a sin-
> gle unit that would make up a new contract, which would
> neither be one nor the other, but instead would be both at
> the same time; this is impossible, as its terms are mutually
> exclusive.

Such a contract is simply ontologically impossible.

To conclude our comments on this second possibility, we
must add that the contradiction is so obvious that bankers, in
their contracts, general conditions, and forms, are always
reluctant to specify the precise nature of the agreement and of
the safekeeping obligation they acquire, and whether or not
they have been authorized by the depositor to invest
deposited funds for their own profit. Everything is expressed
in a vague and confusing manner, and therefore it would not
be rash to claim that depositors' complete and perfect consent
is missing, because the ambiguity, complexity and obscurity
of the contract undoubtedly deceive customers, who in good
faith believe they are entering into a true deposit contract. If

---

valores de Barcelona, pp. 370–71. It is true that Felipe Clemente de Diego
makes this comment in response to the argument of bankers who
wished to defend the validity of the contract of irregular deposit of securities, with a fractional-reserve ratio, in which the depositary would be
permitted to freely use the deposited goods, like in the monetary irregular-deposit contract. Yet as we have already mentioned, the arguments
for and against either institution are identical, as both are contracts of
the irregular deposit of fungible goods, whose legal nature, cause, purpose and circumstances are the same. Pasquale Coppa-Zuccari also
highlights the contradictory nature of the monetary bank-deposit contract which, in the form in which it has been "legalized" by governments, is neither a deposit nor a loan, "La natura giuridica del deposito
bancario," *Archivio giuridico "Filippo Serafini,"* Modena n.s. 9 (1902):
441–72.

the value and efficacy of surrendering a good depend on the procedure or document accompanying the action, then it is clearly important that the procedure or contract be well-defined and appropriately named, that its conditions be well-regulated and that both parties be aware of the legal consequences of these conditions. To fail to clarify or fully specify these details indicates a remarkable ambiguity on the part of bankers, and in the event that adverse legal consequences result, their weight should fall on the bankers' shoulders and not on those of the contracting party, who with good faith enters into the contract believing its essential purpose or cause to be the simple custody or safekeeping of the money deposited.

Third and last, we may suppose that, if this is the depositors' real desire, they could change their original plan to make an irregular deposit of money and instead enter into a mutuum or loan contract in which they agree to the loss of availability of the good and to its transfer to the banker for a set term in exchange for interest. This would constitute a true *novation* of the contract, which would change from an irregular deposit to a loan. The novation would be subject to general legal regulations regarding this type of contractual modification. This is a fully legitimate legal possibility which is little used in practice. Moreover, paradoxically, when novations take place in banking their purpose is usually the opposite. In other words, what undoubtedly begins as a mutuum or loan contract, although it is called a "time" deposit because it involves the real transfer of availability of the good to the banker for a set term or time period, on many occasions becomes an irregular deposit contract via the corresponding novation. This is what happens when bankers, in order to maintain their resources or attract more, either publicly or privately, and either verbally or in writing, offer the holder of a "time" deposit account the possibility of withdrawing his money *at any time* with very little or no financial penalty. To the extent that account holders make these "time" deposits (which are clearly loans) with the subjective and primary goal of depositing the money for safekeeping, then a monetary irregular deposit clearly takes place, regardless of its external appearance. Furthermore, insofar as the contract's fundamental cause or purpose is the exchange of present goods for future goods plus interest, a true time "deposit" takes place. From a legal standpoint, this is unquestionably a mutuum or loan which can later be changed to or substituted for by a monetary irregular deposit through an express agreement between the parties.[31]

In short, whichever way you look at it, the monetary irregular-deposit contract cannot be equated with the mutuum or loan contract. The two are essentially incompatible, and the existence of the demand deposit in fractional-reserve banking, despite its being a "monster" or "legal aberration," can only be accounted for insofar as it was initially tolerated and later deliberately legalized by those exercising political power.[32] Nevertheless, the fact that such a "monstrous" (according to Clemente de Diego) legal institution plays a role in the course of human interaction inevitably produces damaging economic and social consequences. In the following chapters we will explain why fractional-reserve banking is responsible for the crises and recessions that repetitively grip the economy, and this will constitute an additional argument against the legitimacy of the bank-deposit contract, even when both parties are in perfect agreement. Furthermore, this explains the impossibility of at all times guaranteeing the repayment of these deposits without the creation of a whole government superstructure called the central bank. Once this organization has

---

[31]We do not support the doctrine that time "deposits" are not loan or mutuum contracts from the legal perspective, since both their economic and legal natures reflect all the fundamental requirements we studied in chapter 1 for a loan or mutuum. Among the scholars who attempt to justify the theory that time "deposits" are not loans, José Luis García-Pita y Lastres stands out with his paper, "Los depósitos bancarios de dinero y su documentación," esp. pp. 991ff. The arguments García-Pita y Lastres offers here on this topic fail to convince us.

[32]That is, fractional-reserve banking conflicts with traditional legal principles and only survives as a result of an act of coercive intervention found in a mandate or governmental statutory privilege, something that other economic agents cannot take advantage of and which expressly states that it is legal for bankers to maintain a fractional-reserve ratio (Article 180 of the Spanish Commercial Code).

established a monopoly on the issue of paper money and declared it legal tender, it has the function of ensuring the creation of all the liquid assets necessary to satisfy any immediate need private banks may have for funds. In chapter 8 we will study the resulting emergence of a centralized monetary policy, which like all attempts to coordinate society through coercive measures (socialism and interventionism), and for the same reasons, is ultimately doomed to failure. Indeed, central banks and governmental monetary policy are the main culprits in the chronic inflation which in varying degrees affects western economies, as well as in the successive and recurrent stages of artificial boom and economic recession which cause so many social upheavals. But first, let us continue with our legal analysis.

3

AN INADEQUATE SOLUTION:
THE REDEFINITION OF THE CONCEPT OF AVAILABILITY

The belief, held by the most qualified theorists, that it is impossible to reconcile two contracts as incompatible as the monetary irregular deposit and the loan contract, along with the fact that the majority of contracts sustaining present-day banking are demand deposits (monetary irregular-deposit contracts) have led scholars to try to formulate alternative juridical constructions to harmonize the irregular deposit contract with "traditional" banking, i.e., fractional-reserve banking. Some have tried to solve this contradiction by "redefining" availability. In fact, for subscribers to this line of thought, availability need not be understood in a strict sense (100-percent reserve ratio or keeping the *tantundem* available to the depositor at all times), but could be interpreted in a "lax" one: for example, the "general" solvency of the bank by which it meets its obligations; "prudent" investing; avoidance of high-risk speculation and the corresponding losses; maintenance of appropriate liquidity and investment ratios; and in short, compliance with an entire body of rigorous banking laws, which together with the hypothetical operation of the "law of large numbers" in the opening of deposit accounts and withdrawal of demand deposits, could ultimately guarantee the bank's ability to return deposits whenever requested by a depositor.

Thus, to Garrigues the obligation to maintain deposits available to depositors "becomes a duty to work diligently, to make prudent and sensible use of deposits, so the bank is always capable of returning them on demand."[33] Following Lalumia's example, Garrigues adds that the depositary is not "obliged to keep the *tantundem*, but only to invest it wisely and keep it liquid so he is always in a position to return it if necessary."[34] The bank would only have to keep in its vaults enough money to satisfy the "probable" demands of its clients. Garrigues therefore concludes that

> in bank deposits, the element of custody is replaced by the technical element of calculating the probability of deposit withdrawals. In turn, this calculation depends on the fact that bank deposits are made on a large-scale.[35]

---

[33]Garrigues, *Contratos bancarios*, p. 375.

[34]Ibid., p. 365.

[35]Ibid., p. 367. García-Pita y Lastres defends the same theory in his paper "Los depósitos bancarios de dinero y su documentación," where he concludes that

> under the circumstances, instead of regarding "availability" as the simple right to claim immediate repayment, we should consider it a combination of behaviors and economic and financial activities aimed at making repayment possible. (p. 990)

He continues in the same vein in his paper "Depósitos bancarios y protección del depositante," pp. 119–226. Also espousing this view, Eduardo María Valpuesta Gastaminza argues that

> the bank is under no obligation to hold the deposited good, but rather custody becomes a responsibility to prudently manage both the customers' and the bank's resources, and to keep these available, which is also ensured by legitimate governmental regulations (which set the reserve requirement, limits to risk-taking, etc.). (pp. 122–23)

See "Depósitos bancarios de dinero: libretas de ahorro" in *Contratos bancarios*, Enrique de la Torre Saavedra, Rafael García Villaverde, and Rafael Bonardell Lenzano, eds. (Madrid: Editorial Civitas, 1992). The same doctrine has been endorsed in Italy by Angela Principe in her

Quite significantly, Garrigues himself acknowledges that all of this doctrine involves "the unavoidable replacement of the traditional concept of custody by an *ad hoc* concept, the plausibility of which is highly doubtful."[36] Garrigues is right in considering this reinterpretation by theorists of the concept of availability "forced" (even though he eventually accepts it). The theory that in the irregular deposit contract the safekeeping obligation merely consists of using resources "prudently" so the bank retains the solvency necessary to pay its debts is actually untenable. The prudent use of resources is advisable in all human actions; for instance, in *all loan* (not deposit) contracts which specify that certain resources are to be used and then returned following a set term. That is, it is advisable if there is a desire to comply with this obligation (the very meaning of *solvency*).[37] However, as we know, the purpose of the irregular deposit contract is different from that of the loan contract and requires something markedly different: the custody or safekeeping of the good at all times. So if the depositors try to withdraw their deposits and the bank cannot pay them, regardless of whether it is solvent overall and can pay once it converts its investments into cash, the essential obligation in the deposit contract is clearly violated. This is due to the fact that some contracting parties (depositors) who have entered into the contract believing its fundamental purpose to be the custody and safekeeping of the good and its continuous availability are compelled to become something radically different: *forced lenders*. As such, they lose the immediate availability of their goods and are obliged to wait for a prolonged

---

book *La responsabilità della banca nei contratti di custodia* (Milan: Editorial Giuffrè, 1983).

[36]Garrigues, *Contratos bancarios*, p. 365.

[37]Furthermore, the standard criterion of "prudence" is not applicable in this case: an imprudent bank may be successful in its speculations and preserve its solvency. By the same token, a very "prudent" banker may be seriously affected by the crises of confidence that inevitably follow artificial booms, which are generated by the fractional-reserve banking system itself. Hence, prudence is of little use when there is a violation of the only condition capable of guaranteeing the fulfillment of the bank's commitments at all times (a 100-percent reserve ratio).

period of time until the bank has, in a more or less orderly fashion, converted its assets into cash and can pay.

Though the concepts of solvency and the prudent use of resources are not sufficient to modify the essential meaning of availability in the irregular deposit contract, one might at least think the problem could be resolved by the calculation of probabilities and the "law of large numbers," to which Garrigues refers. Nevertheless, as we argued above, even if it were statistically possible to calculate probabilities in this field (which is certainly not the case, as will be shown in the following chapters), the contract would at any rate cease to be a deposit and become an aleatory contract in which the possibility of obtaining the immediate repayment of the deposited good would depend on the greater or lesser probability that a certain number of depositors would not simultaneously go to the same bank to withdraw their deposits.

In any case, in chapter 5 we will argue that we cannot apply the *objective calculation* of probabilities to human acts in general, and in particular to those related to the irregular deposit. This is because the very institution of irregular deposit with no safekeeping obligation (i.e., with a fractional reserve), a legally paradoxical contract, triggers economic processes leading banks to make, on a large scale, unwise loans and investments with the deposits they appropriate or create. This is the case because these loans and investments are ultimately financed by credit expansion which has not been preceded by an increase in real savings. Economic crises inevitably result, along with a decrease in banks' solvency and depositors' confidence in them, which in turn sets off a massive withdrawal of deposits. Every actuary knows that if the consequences of an event are not completely independent of the existence of the insurance policy itself, these consequences are not technically insurable, due to moral hazard. In the following chapters we will show that the fractional-reserve banking system (i.e., a system based on the monetary irregular deposit in which 100 percent of the *tantundem* is not kept in reserve and available to depositors) *endogenously*, inevitably and repeatedly generates economic recessions, making it regularly necessary to liquidate investment projects, return loans and withdraw deposits on a massive scale. Therefore, the banking system based on the irregular deposit with a fractional reserve, the institution Clemente de Diego called an "aberration" or "legal monster," invariably and ultimately (and this is one of the main contributions made by economic analysis to this field of law) leads bankers to become insolvent and unable to honor their commitment to return deposits on demand, even if they maintain a sufficiently elevated reserve ratio. This is precisely the reason the overwhelming majority of private banks that did not fully comply with the safekeeping obligation eventually failed. This state of affairs existed until bankers demanded the creation of a central bank[38] and their demands were met. The central bank was to act as a lender of last resort, ready to grant bankers all the liquidity they needed during the recurrent stages of crisis caused by the instability of the fractional-reserve system itself.

Hence, the redefinition of the concept of availability is a leap into the void. First, banks continue to accept deposits as if they were loans and accordingly invest them in private business deals, and depositors still make deposits with the main intention of transferring the custody and safekeeping of their money while retaining its full availability. In other words, the forced attempt to redefine the concept of availability has not lessened the contradiction in legal logic. Second, from the strict viewpoint of private law and in keeping with the teachings of economic theory, the general guideline of a "prudent" use of resources and the application of the "calculation of probabilities" not only is not sufficient to guarantee that when

---

[38]Rothbard, *The Case Against the Fed*, pp. 90–106. This is how Rothbard explains the leading role private bankers, especially J.P. Morgan, played in the creation of the American Federal Reserve:

> J.P. Morgan's fondness for a central bank was heightened by the memory of the fact that the bank of which his father Junius was junior partner—the London firm of George Peabody and Company—was saved from bankruptcy in the Panic of 1857 by an emergency credit from the Bank of England. The elder Morgan took over the firm upon Peabody's retirement, and its name changed to J.S. Morgan and Company. (p. 93 footnote 22)

a fractional reserve is used the bank will always be able to honor all repayment requests, but it also infallibly starts a process which, at least every certain number of years, results in the inevitable loss of confidence in banks and the massive unforeseen withdrawal of deposits. *Conclusive proof of all of the above is offered by the fact that fractional-reserve banking (i.e., banking without a strict safekeeping obligation) has not been able to survive without a government-created central bank, which by imposing legal-tender regulations and compelling the acceptance of paper money, could produce out of nowhere the liquidity necessary in emergencies.* Only an institution in conformity with general legal principles can survive in the marketplace without the need of privileges and government support, but solely by virtue of citizens' voluntary use of its services within the framework of general and abstract civil-law rules.

Availability has also been defined as private banks' compliance with the whole structure of government banking legislation in exchange for the backing of the central bank as lender of last resort. However, this requirement is also artificial and shifts the issue of the impossibility of legally defining the fractional-reserve bank deposit contract from the field of private law (where the two cannot be reconciled) to the field of public law; that is, administrative law and pure voluntarism *by which the authorities can legalize any institution, no matter how legally monstrous it may seem.* It is an odd paradox that the entire financial system is made to depend on the supervision of the state (which historically has been the first to benefit from profits obtained through the non-fulfillment of the safekeeping obligation in the monetary-deposit contract), and, as F.A. Hayek wisely indicates,

> The history of government management of money has . . . been one of incessant fraud and deception. In this respect, governments have proved far more immoral than any private agency supplying distinct kinds of money in competition possibly could have been.[39]

---

[39]Hayek, *The Fatal Conceit*, pp. 103–04.

Hayek means that today's banking structure may appear sustainable despite its juridical inconsistency, due to the support it currently receives from the state and to an official central-banking institution which generates the liquidity necessary to bail out banks in trouble (in exchange for their compliance with a tangled web of administrative legislation comprising endless, cryptic and *ad hoc* directives and memoranda). Nevertheless, the violation of the traditional legal principles governing property rights inescapably results in negative social consequences. For instance, the return of deposits may be thus "guaranteed" at least theoretically (even using a fractional-reserve ratio, assuming the central bank lends its support). *However, what cannot be guaranteed is that the purchasing power of the monetary units will not vary greatly* with respect to the original deposit. In fact, ever since the creation of modern monetary systems, each year with slight differences in degree, we have been plagued by serious chronic inflation which has significantly decreased the purchasing power of the monetary units returned to depositors. We must also consider the effects of the intra- and inter-temporal social discoordination inflicted on modern economies by the current financial system, based on a fractional reserve for private banks and the conducting of monetary policy by the central bank. These effects consist of recurrent, successive phases of artificial boom and economic recession involving high unemployment rates, which do great harm to the harmonious, stable development of our societies.

As a result, in the banking and monetary fields we again observe the validity of Hayek's seminal idea that whenever a traditional rule of conduct is broken, either through direct governmental coercion or the granting of special governmental privileges to certain people or organizations, or a combination of both (as occurs in the monetary irregular deposit with a fractional reserve), sooner or later damaging, undesired consequences follow, to the great detriment of the spontaneous social processes of cooperation. The traditional rule of conduct broken in banking, as we have studied in detail in these first three chapters, is the general legal principle that in the monetary irregular-deposit contract, *custody and safekeeping* (the essential element or purpose of all deposits) should always

take the form of a continuous 100-percent reserve requirement. Consequently, any use of this money, particularly to
make loans, entails a violation of this principle and an act of
misappropriation. Throughout history, bankers have been
quick to violate this traditional rule of conduct, making self-
interested use of their depositors' money, as demonstrated by
various examples in chapter 2. At first the bankers did this
guiltily and in secret, since they were still aware of the wrongful nature of their actions. Only later, when they obtained the
government *privilege* of making personal use of their depositors' money (generally in the form of loans, which at first were
often granted to the government itself), did they gain permission to openly and legally violate the principle. The legal
orchestration of the privilege is clumsy and usually takes the
form of a simple administrative provision authorizing only
bankers to maintain a reduced reserve ratio.

This marks the beginning of a now traditional relationship
of complicity and symbiosis between governments and banks.
This relationship explains the intimate "comprehension" and
close "cooperation" which is still present today between the
two types of institutions and has almost always existed, with
slight variations, in all western countries. Bankers and authorities soon realized that by sacrificing traditional legal principles in the deposit they could take part in an extremely lucrative financial activity, though a lender of last resort, or central
bank, was required to provide the necessary liquidity in times
of difficulty, and experience showed that sooner or later these
times always returned. However, the damaging social consequences of this *privilege* granted only to bankers were not fully
understood until the theory of money and capital theory
made sufficient progress in economics and were able to
explain the recurrent emergence of economic cycles. The Austrian School in particular has taught us that the contradictory
(from a legal-contractual as well as a technical-economic
standpoint) objective of offering a contract comprising essentially incompatible elements and aimed at combining the
advantages of loans (especially the possibility of earning interest on "deposits") with those of the traditional monetary
irregular deposit (which by definition must allow the depositor to withdraw his funds at any time) is sooner or later bound

to cause inevitable spontaneous adjustments. At first these adjustments manifest themselves as expansions in the money supply (via the creation of loans which do not correspond to an actual increase in voluntary saving), inflation, a generalized poor allocation of society's scarce productive resources at a microeconomic level, and ultimately, recession, the rectification of errors caused in the productive structure by credit expansion, and widespread unemployment. The next chapters will be devoted to examining all these issues from the standpoint of economic theory. Nevertheless, first we should wrap up our legal study with the analysis of some other juridical institutions related to bank deposits.

To conclude this section, the following table displays seven possible ways to legally classify the bank-deposit contract from the perspective of the logic inherent in the institution (and naturally, not from the viewpoint of positive law, which as we know, can give legal force to anything).

4

THE MONETARY IRREGULAR DEPOSIT, TRANSACTIONS WITH A REPURCHASE AGREEMENT AND LIFE INSURANCE CONTRACTS

In these first three chapters we have undertaken an analysis of the legal nature of the irregular deposit contract, and this analysis could serve, among other uses, as a reliable guide to identifying (from among the rich variety of legal contracts in the fast-changing real world) true loan contracts, irregular deposits in which the safekeeping obligation is met and contracts of a contradictory or even fraudulent nature. This is an important guide, as human ingenuity knows no bounds when it comes to attempting to fraudulently circumvent traditional legal principles for one's own benefit and to the detriment of others.

Moreover, this danger is especially acute when legal principles are not adequately defined nor defended by public authorities, especially in a field, like that of finance, which is very abstract and difficult to understand for most citizens.

TABLE 1
SEVEN POSSIBLE LEGAL CLASSIFICATIONS OF THE
BANK-DEPOSIT CONTRACT WITH A FRACTIONAL RESERVE

1. There is *deception* or *fraud:* the crime of misappropriation is committed and the contract is null and void (the historically corrupt origin of fractional-reserve banking).

2. There is no deception, but there is an *error in negotio*: contract null and void.

3. There is no *error in negotio*, but each party pursues his typical cause in the contract: contract null and void due to essentially incompatible causes.

4. Even if the incompatible causes are considered compatible, the contract is null and void because it is impossible to carry out (without a central bank).

5. Subsidiary argument: even if the "law of large numbers" were valid (which is not the case), the contract would still be an *aleatory contract* (it would be neither a deposit nor a loan contract).

6. The implementation of the contract depends on a government mandate (*privilege*) and the support of a *central bank* that nationalizes money, imposes legal-tender regulations and creates liquidity.

7. In any case, the contract is null and void because it does serious *harm to third parties* (economic crises aggravated by the central bank), much greater harm than that caused by a counterfeiter of money.

Transactions with a Repurchase Agreement

Whenever we observe, as in the monetary deposit, that the immediate availability of the good is offered to customers in order to attract their funds[40] and then invest their money or employ it in private transactions, etc., we should be on our guard, irrespective of the legal appearance of the transaction. For example, in certain *contracts with a repurchase agreement*, one of the parties commits to repurchase from the other, whenever requested by the second party, a security, right or financial asset at a prefixed price at least equal to that originally paid for the good. The intention in these cases, against legal principles, is to conceal a true monetary irregular-deposit contract, in which one of the contracting parties pursues the essential objective of guaranteeing the immediate availability of the good, and the other pursues the familiar, contradictory purpose or cause of gathering monetary resources to invest them in different business deals. In short, these are often even fraudulent transactions, in which the professional deposit "gatherer" tries to convince his "customers" to turn over their available assets easily and without a heavy commitment, in exchange for the fundamental promise that their money will remain available to them and be returned to them whenever they desire (via the "repurchase agreement").

We observe a similar case when, as often happens more or less explicitly in practice, an institution (for example, a bank) attempts to systematically maintain or "conserve" the market value of its stocks by carrying out a series of financial operations to indicate to the market that the sale of the stocks is "guaranteed" at a set price. If this is true, and to the extent that the general public believes it, we witness another transaction in which a monetary irregular-deposit contract is ultimately orchestrated via investment in securities, stocks or bonds

---

[40]Many "irregular" transactions are accompanied by the "guarantee" of continuous availability to persuade the customer that there is no need to relinquish it nor make the sacrifice required by lending. This practice makes attracting funds much easier, especially when the customer is naïve and can be tempted (as in any sham or swindle) with the possibility of obtaining high profits with no sacrifice nor risk.

whose liquidity on the market is implicitly "guaranteed" at all times by a trustworthy institution.[41] Therefore, it is not surprising that many bank crises have arisen more from the massive sale of bank stocks than from a widespread withdrawal of deposits. These stocks were supposed to constitute a safe refuge for money while nearly guaranteeing its immediate availability. When the bank's solvency comes into question, its securities are the first to be sold on a massive scale, rendering the bank unable to continue honoring its implicit commitment to maintain the market value of the stocks. At least in the past, these massive sales have resulted from the fact that the indiscriminate assistance supplied by central banks to private banks in times of need has not reached the point of *continual* preservation of shares' current market price. The most recent bank crises in Spain and other countries have demonstrated that ultimately, the only "depositors" to lose out have been the stockholders themselves.

There are many other "borderline" cases. For example, some finance and holding companies, to encourage the subscription of their stocks, "commit" to repurchase them at the original price whenever requested by the shareholder. In general, we should be suspicious of any transaction with a repurchase agreement in which the price of the repurchase is fixed and *is not the current price of the item on the corresponding secondary market*.[42] Hence, it falls to the jurist and the economist to

---

[41]If we carry this line of reasoning to extremes, the entire stock market could be viewed as an orchestrator of true deposits if the state were to at all times guarantee the creation of the liquidity necessary to maintain stock market indexes. For reasons of public image, governments and central banks have insisted on pursuing this objective and policy at least occasionally, during many stock market crises.

[42]Another example of a simulated deposit is a temporary assignment with an agreement of repurchase on demand. This transaction is conducted as a loan from customer to bank: Collateral is offered in the form of securities, normally national bond certificates, in case of noncompliance by the depositary. The loan bears interest at an agreed-upon rate up until a specified date and is repayable at the simple request of the "lender" prior to that date. If he exercises this option of early cancellation, the resulting amount to be paid him is calculated by compounding

employ their analytical judgment in the study of this economic-financial transaction and to decide exactly what type of
operation it is, its true nature and its consequences, in light of
the legal principles examined in these first three chapters and
the economic implications we will now consider.[43] Furthermore, this analysis would acquire vital importance if one day
in the future the existent financial system based on the
monopoly of a public central bank were ever completely privatized and a free-banking system subject to general legal
principles were established. In this case, the current tangled
web of administrative banking regulations would be replaced

---

the interest on the original amount at the agreed-upon rate up until the
date he exercises the option. For the client, this operation is identical to
a loan backed by securities, combined with an American option. An
option is an agreement conferring the right, not the obligation, to buy or
sell a certain quantity of an asset on a particular date or up until a particular date. An option to purchase is a call option, and an option to sell,
a put option. If the right granted lasts until a specified date, the option
is called an "American" option; if it refers to a particular date, a "European" option. The acquirer of the right compensates the other party via
the payment of a premium at the moment the contract is finalized. The
client will exercise his option only if the interest rates paid on new time
deposits maturing at the same time as his exceed the rate he originally
negotiated. He will not exercise the option if interest rates fall, even if he
needs the liquidity, because he will normally be able to take out a loan for
the remainder of the term at a lower rate of interest and provide the bond
certificates as collateral. Some institutions even offer these contracts
accompanied by the cashier services typical of checking accounts, so the
customer can issue checks and pay bills by direct debiting. Banks use this
contract as a way to speculate with securities, since the public finances
them and banks keep the profits. We are grateful to Professor Ruben
Manso for providing us with some details of this type of operation.

[43]Another interesting question is how to determine in practice when
time "deposits" (loans) with a very short term become true deposits.
Although the general rule is clear (the subjective intention of the parties
must prevail, and upon maturity all loans become deposits requiring a
100-percent reserve until withdrawn), for practical purposes a temporary limit is often needed (a month? a week? a day?), under which loans
granted to the bank should be regarded as actual deposits. As for the so-
called secondary medium of exchange, which are not money but can be
converted into cash very easily, meriting an additional premium for
their purchase on the market, see Mises, *Human Action*, pp. 464–67.

by a few clear, simple rules included in the Civil, Commercial and Penal Codes. The main purpose of these rules would be to guarantee adherence to the strict safekeeping principle (100-percent reserve requirement) regarding not only monetary demand-deposit contracts, but also any other economic-financial transaction in which the chief goal of the participants is to obtain custody and safekeeping for their deposits. In this (for now) hypothetical situation, the analysis we are proposing would greatly assist judges and jurists in making sense of the rich, extremely complex variety of contracts and transactions constantly emerging in the economic-financial world and would allow them to determine when to classify these transactions as null and void and/or criminal according to general civil and penal provisions.[44]

At any rate, we should avoid a selfishly defeatist attitude common in the financial sector. It is based on the belief that human ingenuity will be capable of finding ever more sophisticated means of fraudulently evading universal legal principles and that therefore in practice they will never be obeyed and defended. We should avoid this defeatist posture, because the proliferation of ingenious ways to violate these principles stems precisely from the fact that public authorities have always defined and defended them in an extremely confusing, ambiguous and contradictory manner, and as a result there is no general awareness of the importance of respecting them. Quite the opposite is true. The prevailing values and ideas have over time become so corrupted that now people consider the irregular deposit contract with a fractional reserve to be legitimate. If general legal principles were again understood and respected, the number of irregular behaviors would decrease significantly (especially if public authorities really took care to preserve and defend the corresponding property rights). At the same time, the proven fact that human ingenuity continually searches for

---

[44]In the model we propose (and which we will consider in greater detail in the last chapter), the control exerted in the financial sphere by the central bank and its officials would be replaced by that of judges, who would recover their full authority and central role in the application of general legal principles in the financial area as well.

new ways to break the law and defraud others does not in the least detract from the fundamental importance of a set of clear principles to guide citizens and direct authorities in their duty to define and defend property rights.

THE CASE OF LIFE INSURANCE CONTRACTS

Life insurance is a typical time-honored legal institution, one that has been very well-formulated with respect to its essence and legal content and well-supported by actuarial, economic and financial practices. Nevertheless, lately some have tried to use it to conduct transactions which are very similar to the monetary irregular deposit with a fractional reserve. These attempts have been very detrimental to the development and traditional solvency of life insurance as an institution and have involved deceiving supposed "policy-holders-depositors."

Indeed, above all it is important to understand that the contract of life insurance bears no relation to the monetary irregular-deposit contract. Life insurance is an *aleatory* contract by which one of the parties, the contracting party or policy-holder, commits to the payment of the *premium* or price of the operation, and in return the other party, the insurance company, agrees to pay certain benefits in the event that the policyholder dies or survives at the end of a *term* specified in the contract. Therefore, *the premiums paid by the policyholder completely cease to be available to him*, and availability is fully transferred to the insurer.[45] Hence, all life insurance contracts involve an exchange of present, certain goods for future, uncertain goods (since their payment depends on an uncertain

---

[45]As life insurance entails disciplined saving over a period of many years, it is much more difficult to sell than other financial products sold with the guarantee that the customer's money will remain continuously available to him (deposits). For this reason life insurance is sold through a costly network of salespeople, while the public goes willingly and without prompting to make bank deposits. Life insurance companies foster and encourage voluntary, long-term saving, whereas banks produce loans and deposits from nothing and require no one to make the prior sacrifice of saving.

event, such as the death or survival of the policyholder). The
life insurance contract is therefore equivalent to a savings
transaction (in which the ownership and availability of present goods are relinquished in exchange for the ownership
and availability of future goods), but it is a form of *perfected
savings*, because it makes it possible to receive a considerable
sum from the very moment the contract takes effect, given the
anticipated, uncertain event takes place (for example, the policyholder dies). Any other traditional savings method (traditional mutuum or loan operation) would require a prolonged
period of many years of saving to accumulate the capital paid
by an insurance company in case of death. In other words, life
insurance contracts, the calculation of probabilities based on
mortality and survival tables, and the principle of mutualism
or dividing loss among all policyholders sustaining an institution *make it possible from the first moment to receive, should the
anticipated event occur, a significant sum of money which, using
other methods, could only be accumulated after a period of many
years.*

Moreover life insurance is a long-term contract which
incorporates complex financial and actuarial components and
requires the prudent investment of significant resources. The
availability of these resources is transferred to the mutual or
life insurance company, which must collect and invest the
mathematically-calculated reserves necessary to make the
future payments it will be obliged to make. These amounts are
called "mathematical," because they result from the calculation of probabilities of death and survival according to mortality tables, which are extremely reliable and highly constant
for most western populations. It is possible to calculate, with
as small a probability of ruin as is desired, the amount of
money necessary to pay all guaranteed benefits. Later we will
examine the radical differences which from an economic-
financial standpoint exist between life insurance and the irregular deposit contract with a fractional reserve. As opposed to
life insurance, the irregular deposit contract does not permit
the calculation of probabilities, since the institution (fractional-reserve banking) does not exist completely independently of the recurrent massive withdrawal of deposits.

An added complexity emerges because some types of life insurance include the right of *surrender*. This means policy-holders can cancel their contract and obtain in cash the math-ematical liquidation value of their policy. Some theorists have defended the position that insurance policies which include this "surrender value" are very similar to monetary irregular-deposit contracts with fractional reserves.[46] Against this view, it is important to point out that whether or not a covert irreg-ular deposit exists depends ultimately on the true motive, purpose or subjective cause with which the contract is carried out. If, as is usual with *traditional* life insurance policies, the client intends to keep the policy until the end of its term and is not aware that he can redeem the funds at any time, then the transaction is clearly not an irregular deposit but a traditional life insurance contract. This type of insurance is sold with the idea that surrender is a "last resort," a solution to be applied only in situations of pressing need when a family is com-pletely unable to continue making payments on a policy which is so necessary for the peace of mind of all of its mem-bers.[47]

However, we must acknowledge that (for the most part) recently banks and other financial institutions have exerted constant pressure to erase the fundamental, traditional dis-tinctions and blur the boundaries between life insurance and bank-deposit contracts.[48]

---

[46]Murray N. Rothbard, "Austrian Definitions of the Supply of Money," in *New Directions in Austrian Economics*, Louis M. Spadaro, ed. (Kansas City: Sheed Andrews and McMeel, 1978), pp. 143–56, esp. pp. 150–51. Rothbard's position is fully justified, however, with respect to all the new "life insurance" operations conceived to simulate deposit contracts.

[47]Furthermore the surrender of the insurance policy traditionally entails a significant financial penalty for the policyholder. This penalty results from the company's need to amortize the high acquisition costs it incurs during the first year of the contract. The tendency to reduce these penal-ties is a clear indication that the operation has ceased to be a traditional life insurance policy and has become a simulated bank deposit.

[48]As we will see at the end of chapter 7, from 1921 to 1938, while chair-man of the National Mutual Life Assurance Society, a leading British life

True monetary-deposit operations have begun to appear
on the market disguised as life insurance policies. The main
selling point presented to customers is that with these transactions they need not commit to a long-term savings operation involving regular payments, since the funds handed over
to the insurance company may be recovered at any time with
no penalty and no expense whatsoever (and may even include
interest). One reason companies disguise these operations as
life insurance policies is to take advantage of the customary
tax incentives almost every government in the developed
world grants insurance companies in recognition of their beneficial influence on society at all levels as promoters of *voluntary* saving and foresight, and hence on the sustained, non-
inflationary economic growth and development of the nation.
Thus, bogus "life insurance" operations have been negotiated
en masse and have really been nothing but camouflaged
deposits made effortlessly by the public, who have held the
idea that at any time their money could be recovered penalty-
free if they needed it or simply wished to place it in another
financial institution. This has generated a good deal of confusion. For instance, figures corresponding to bank deposits

-----

insurance firm, John Maynard Keynes played a key role in the corruption of traditional principles governing life insurance. During his chair-
manship, he not only promoted an "active" investment policy strongly
oriented toward variable-yield securities (abandoning the tradition of
investing in bonds), but he also defended unorthodox criteria for the
valuation of assets (at market value) and even the distribution of profits
to policyholders through bonuses financed by unrealized stock market
"earnings." All these typical Keynesian assaults on traditional insurance
principles put his company in desperate straits when the stock market
crashed in 1929 and the Great Depression hit. As a result, Keynes's colleagues on the Board of Directors began to question his strategy and
decisions. Disagreements arose between them and led to Keynes's res-
ignation in 1938, since, as he put it, he did not think "it lies in my power
to cure the faults of the management and I am reluctant to continue to
take responsibility for them." See John Maynard Keynes, *The Collected
Writings* (London: Macmillan, 1983), vol. 12, pp. 47 and 114–54. See also
Nicholas Davenport, "Keynes in the City," in *Essays on John Maynard
Keynes*, Milo Keynes, ed. (Cambridge: Cambridge University Press,
1975), pp. 224–25. See also footnote 108 of chapter 7.

(operations completely unrelated to life insurance) have been included in the official statistics of life insurance premiums, and in the midst of the great confusion in the market, traditional life insurance policies have become discredited and their definition blurred.[49]

Fortunately, normality is being restored, and both traditional private insurers and public authorities are beginning to realize that nothing hurts life insurance more than blurring the distinctions between it and bank deposits. This confusion has been detrimental to everyone: traditional life insurance, which has lost many of its tax incentives and faced increasing intervention and control by the central bank and monetary authorities; clients, who have taken out life insurance thinking they were making bank deposits and *vice versa*; banks, which on many occasions have attracted funds from true deposits (disguised as life insurance) and tried to make long-term investments with them, endangering their solvency; and finally, supervising public authorities, who have gradually lost control over the institution of life insurance, which has become blurred in its definition and to a great extent taken over by another institution (the central bank). Banks are a completely separate type of institution, whose financial and legal foundations leave much to be desired, as we are seeing.

---

[49]In short, the apparent boom in life insurance sales was an illusion, since the figures actually corresponded to radically different operations, i.e., fractional-reserve bank deposits. These figures completely lose their splendor if, instead of contrasting them with traditional life insurance sales (much more modest, since abnegation and a long-term commitment to saving and foresight are required), we compare them to the total of a country's bank deposits, of which they make up only a small percentage. When only genuine life insurance sales are included in sector statistics, the situation is put back in perspective, and the mirage everyone (especially the government) strained to see vanishes.

4

THE CREDIT
EXPANSION PROCESS

T his chapter and the following five comprise an analysis of the *economic* consequences of violating the general legal principles inherent in the irregular deposit contract. We examined the legal and historical consequences of such violations in chapters 1, 2, and 3 and will now focus on the process by which banks create loans and deposits from nothing and on the different implications this process has for society. The most serious consequence of banks' creation of loans is the following: to the extent loans are granted without the corresponding backing of voluntary saving, the real productive structure is inevitably distorted and recurrent economic crises and recessions result. We will explain the circulation credit theory of the business cycle and then critically analyze the macroeconomic theories of monetarism and Keynesian economics. In addition we will carry out a brief review of the recurring economic crises which have thus far assailed the world. The first of the two final chapters contains a theoretical study of central banking and free banking, and the second consists of an examination of the proposal of a 100-percent reserve requirement for banking.

1
INTRODUCTION

The economic theory of money, banking, and business cycles is a relatively recent development in the history of economic thought. This body of economic knowledge has followed the relevant events (the development of fractional-reserve banking and the recurring cycles of boom and recession) and corresponding legal formulations with *great delay*. As we have seen, the study of legal principles, the analysis of their loopholes and contradictions, the search for and correction of their logical defects, etc. took place much earlier in history and can even be traced back to classical Roman legal doctrine. In any case, in keeping with the evolutionary theory of institutions (legal, linguistic, and economic), according to which institutions emerge through a lengthy historical process and incorporate a huge amount of information, knowledge, and experience, the conclusions we will reach through our economic analysis of the monetary bank-deposit contract in its current form are hardly surprising. They largely coincide with and support inferences the reader may have already drawn (from a purely legal standpoint) in preceding chapters.

Our analysis of banking will be limited to the study of the monetary deposit contract, which in practice applies to so-called demand checking accounts, savings accounts and time deposits, whenever the last two permit the *de facto* withdrawal of the balance by the customer at any time. Hence, our study excludes numerous activities private banks presently engage in which are in no way related to the monetary irregular-deposit contract. For example, modern banks offer their customers *bookkeeping* and *cashier services*. They also buy and sell foreign currencies, following a *money-changing* tradition that dates back to the appearance of the first monetary units. In addition, banks accept *deposits of securities* and on behalf of their clients collect dividends and interest from the issuers, informing customers of increases in owner's equity, stockholders' meetings, etc. Moreover, banks *buy and sell securities* for their clients through discount houses and offer *safe deposit box* services at their branches. Likewise, on many occasions banks act as *true financial intermediaries*, attracting loans from their customers (that is, when customers are aware they are providing a loan to the bank, as holders of bonds, certificates, or true time "deposits") and then lending those funds to third parties. In this way, banks derive a profit from the *interest rate differential* between the rate they receive on loans they grant and the one they agree to pay to customers who initially give loans to them. None of these operations constitutes a monetary bank-deposit, a transaction we will examine in the following sections. As we will see, this contract undoubtedly represents the most significant operation banks carry out today and the most important from an economic and social standpoint.

As we have already pointed out, an economic analysis of the monetary bank-deposit contract provides one more illustration of Hayek's profound insight: whenever a universal legal principle is violated, either through systematic state coercion or governmental privileges or advantages conferred on certain groups or individuals, the spontaneous process of social interaction is inevitably and seriously obstructed. This idea was refined in parallel with the theory of the impossibility of socialism and has spread. Whereas at one point it was only applied to systems of so-called real socialism, it has now also come to be associated with all parts or sectors of mixed economies in which systematic state coercion or the "odious" granting of privileges prevails.

Although the economic analysis of interventionism appears to pertain more to coercive governmental measures, it is no less relevant and illuminating with respect to those areas in which traditional legal principles are infringed via the granting of favors or privileges to certain pressure groups. In modern economies there are two main areas where this occurs. Labor legislation, which thoroughly regulates employment contracts and labor relations, is the first. Not only are these laws the basis for coercive measures (preventing parties from negotiating the terms of an employment contract as they see fit), they also confer important privileges upon pressure groups, in many ways allowing them to act on the fringes of traditional legal principles (as unions do, for instance). The second area in which both privileges and institutional coercion are preponderant is the general field of money, banking, and finance, which constitutes the main focus of this book. Although both areas are very important, and thus it is urgent that both be theoretically examined in order to introduce and carry through the necessary reforms, the theoretical analysis of institutional coercion and the granting of privileges in the labor field is clearly less complex. As a result, the awareness it arouses has spread faster and penetrated deeper at all levels of society. Related theories have been significantly developed and broad social consensus has even been reached regarding the need for reforms and the direction they should take. In contrast, *the sphere of money, bank credit and financial markets remains a formidable challenge to theorists and a mystery to most citizens.* Social relationships in which money is directly or indirectly involved are by far the most abstract and difficult to understand, and as a result the related knowledge is the most vast, complex, and elusive. For this reason, systematic coercion in this area by governments and central banks is by far the most harmful and pernicious.[1] Furthermore, the insufficient formulation of monetary and banking theory adversely affects the development of the world economy. This is evidenced by the fact that, despite theoretical advances and government efforts, modern economies have yet to be freed of recurring booms and recessions. Only a few years ago, despite all the sacrifices made to stabilize western economies following the crisis of the 1970s, the financial, banking and monetary field was invariably again plagued by the same reckless errors. As a result, the beginning of the 1990s marked the inevitable appearance of a new worldwide economic recession of considerable severity, and the western economic world has only

---

[1]   The operation of the money and credit structure has, . . . with language and morals, been one of the spontaneous orders most resistant to efforts at adequate theoretical explanation, and it remains the object of serious disagreement among specialists. . . . [S]elective processes are interfered with here more than anywhere else: selection by evolution is prevented by government monopolies that make competitive experimentation impossible. . . . The history of government management of money has . . . been one of incessant fraud and deception. In this respect, governments have proved far more immoral than any private agency supplying distinct kinds of money in competition possibly could have been. (Hayek, *The Fatal Conceit*, pp. 102–04)

recently managed to recover from it.[2] And once again, more recently (in the summer of 1997), an acute financial crisis devastated the chief Asian markets, threatening to spread to the rest of the world. A few years later (since 2001) the three main economic areas of the world (the United States, Europe, and Japan) have simultaneously entered into a recession.

The purpose of the economic analysis of law and legal regulations is to examine the role the latter play in the spontaneous processes of social interaction. Our economic analysis of the monetary bank-deposit contract will reveal the results of applying traditional legal principles (including a 100-percent reserve requirement) to the monetary irregular-deposit contract. At the same time, it will bring to light the damaging, unforeseen consequences that follow from the fact that, in violation of these principles, bankers have been permitted to make self-interested use of demand deposits. Until now these effects have gone mainly unnoticed.

We will now see how bankers' use of demand deposits enables them to *create* bank deposits (that is, money) and in turn, loans (purchasing power transferred to borrowers, whether businessmen or consumers) *from nothing*. These deposits and loans do not result from any real increase in voluntary saving by social agents. In this chapter we will concentrate

---

[2]It is also interesting to note that the monetary and financial excesses which provoked this crisis stemmed mainly from the policies applied in the latter 1980s by the supposedly neoliberal administrations of the United States and the United Kingdom. For example, Margaret Thatcher recently acknowledged that the key economic problem of her term in office originated "on the 'demand side' as money and credit expanded too rapidly and sent the prices of assets soaring." See Margaret Thatcher, *The Downing Street Years* (New York: HarperCollins, 1993), p. 668. In addition, in the field of money and credit, the United Kingdom merely followed the process of irresponsibility that had been initiated in the United States during the second Reagan administration. If possible, these events indicate even more plainly the importance of advancing theory to prevent other political authorities (even those with pro free-market views) from committing the same errors as Reagan and Thatcher and to allow them to clearly identify the type of monetary and banking system appropriate for a free society, something many people with a laissez-faire stance remain distinctly unsure about.

on substantiating this assertion and some of its implications and in subsequent chapters will undertake the study of the economic effects of credit expansion (the analysis of economic crises and recessions).

To continue the pattern set in the first chapters, we will first consider the effects from an economic and accounting perspective in the case of the loan or mutuum contract. In this way, by comparison, we will be better able to understand the economic effects of the essentially distinct monetary bank-deposit contract.

2
THE BANK'S ROLE AS A TRUE
INTERMEDIARY IN THE LOAN CONTRACT

Let us begin by supposing a banker receives a loan of 1,000,000 monetary units (m.u.) from a customer. A true legal loan contract exists, stipulating that the customer is to give up the availability of 1,000,000 m.u. in the form of present goods (money) he could have spent or keep it for himself, and that he is to do so for a period of time or term (the essential element of any loan contract) lasting one year. In exchange for these present goods, the banker agrees to return after one year a larger quantity than that originally received. If the agreed-upon interest rate is 10 percent, at the end of one year the banker will have to return 1,100,000 monetary units. The following book entry is made when the loan is received:

(1)   Bank A

Debit	Credit
1,000,000 m.u. Cash (Input in the bank's cash asset account)	Loan received 1,000,000 m.u. (Increase in liabilities)

Economically speaking, this contract clearly involves a simple exchange of present goods (the availability of which is transferred from the lender to the bank) for future goods (which Bank A agrees to turn over to the lender at the end of one year). *Therefore, from a monetary standpoint there is no change.* A certain number of monetary units simply cease to be available to the lender and become available to the bank (for a predetermined period of time). A mere transfer of 1,000,000 m.u. takes place, without any resulting variation in the total number of preexisting monetary units.

We could view entry (1) as the journal entry made the day the contract is signed and 1,000,000 m.u. are handed over to the bank by the lender. We could also see it as Bank A's balance sheet, drawn up immediately following the transaction and registering on the left side (the asset side) 1,000,000 m.u. in the cash account and on the right side (the liability side) the debt of 1,000,000 m.u. contracted with the lender.

Let us also suppose that Bank A carries out this operation because its managers plan in turn to loan 1,000,000 m.u. to Business Z, which urgently needs the money to finance its operations and is willing to pay 15 percent interest per year for the loan of 1,000,000 m.u. from Bank A.[3]

When Bank A loans the money to Business Z, an entry in Bank A's journal is made to reflect the output of 1,000,000 m.u. from the cash account and Business Z's debt to the bank, replacing the original cash asset. The entry is as follows:

(2)   Bank A

Debit	Credit
1,000,000 Loan granted (Accounts receivable)	Cash 1,000,000 (Output from cash account)

---

[3]We could likewise have assumed that Bank A used the money to grant consumer loans or short-term loans to trade, as occurs when bills are discounted three, six, nine and twelve months before maturity. The consideration of these uses is irrelevant to our analysis, however.

In this case Bank A clearly acts as a *true financial intermediary*. Its managers recognize and take advantage of a business opportunity.[4] Indeed, they see a chance to make a profit, since at one place in the market there is a lender willing to loan them money at 10 percent interest, and at another Business Z is willing to take out a loan at 15 percent, leaving a profit differential of 5 percent. Therefore, the bank acts as intermediary between the original lender and Business Z, and *its social function consists precisely of recognizing the existing disparity or lack of coordination* (the original lender wished to loan his money but could not find a creditworthy borrower willing to take it, while Business Z urgently needed a loan of 1,000,000 m.u. and its managers did not know where to find a suitable lender). The bank, by obtaining a loan from one and granting a loan to the other, satisfies the subjective needs of both and derives a *sheer entrepreneurial profit* in the form of the interest differential of 5 percent.

At the end of a year, Business Z will return the 1,000,000 m.u. to Bank A, together with the agreed-upon 15 percent interest. The entries are as follows:

(3)   Bank A

Debit		Credit	
1,000,000	Cash	Loan granted (Repayment)	1,000,000
150,000	Cash	Interest received from Business Z (Revenue for the year)	150,000

---

[4]On the essence of entrepreneurship, consisting of discovering and taking advantage of opportunities for profit, and on the sheer entrepreneurial profit that results, see chapter 2 of Huerta de Soto, *Socialismo, cálculo económico y función empresarial*, pp. 41–86.

Soon afterward, Bank A must in turn honor the contract it entered into with the original lender, returning to him the 1,000,000 m.u. its managers had committed to pay at the end of one year, along with 10 percent interest. The entries are as follows:

(4)   Bank A

Debit		Credit	
1,000,000	Loan received (Repayment)	Cash	$1,000,000
100,000	Interest payment (Expenses for the year)	Cash	$100,000

In other words, the bank repays the loan, records the output from its cash account of the 1,000,000 m.u. received from Business Z and adds to that sum the 100,000 m.u. (also charged to the cash account) in agreed-upon interest it pays the original lender. On the bank's income statement, this interest is registered as a charge in the form of interest payments made during the year.

After these entries, at the end of the year, the bank's income statement would appear as follows:

(5)   Bank A
                          Income Statement
                          (During the Year)

Expenses		Revenues	
Interest paid	100,000	Interest Received	150,000
Net income	50,000		
Total Debit	150,000	Total Credit	150,000

This income statement reflects an entrepreneurial profit for the year of 50,000 m.u., a net income derived from the difference between the year's revenue (150,000 m.u. in interest received) and the year's expenses (100,000 m.u. in interest paid).

At the end of the year, Bank A's balance sheet would appear as follows:

(6)

Bank A
Balance Sheet
(End of the year)

Assets		Liabilities	
Cash	50,000	Owner's equity (Profit for the year)	50,000
Total Assets	50,000	Total Liabilities	50,000

If we look at the balance sheet drawn up at the very end of the year, we see that the bank's assets include 50,000 m.u. available in the cash account that correspond to the year's profit, which has been placed in the corresponding owner's equity account (capital and retained earnings) under Liabilities.

The following points recapitulate our description in accounting terms of a banking activity based on receiving and granting a loan or mutuum: *one,* for one year the original lender relinquished the availability of 1,000,000 m.u, present goods; *two,* the availability of this money was transferred to Bank A for exactly the same time period; *three,* Bank A discovered an opportunity to make a profit, since its managers knew of a borrower, Business Z, which was willing to pay a higher interest rate than the one the bank had agreed to pay; *four,* the bank granted a loan to Business Z, relinquishing in turn the availability of 1,000,000 m.u. for one year; *five,* Business Z obtained the availability of the 1,000,000 m.u. for one year in order to expand its activities; *six,* therefore, for the period of one year, the number of m.u. did not vary, as they were simply transferred from the original lender to Business Z via the intermediary—Bank A—; *seven*, in the course of its activities, Business Z brought in a profit enabling it to make the interest payment of 150,000 m.u. (these 150,000 m.u. do not represent any money creation, but are simply obtained by Business Z as the result of its sales and purchases); *eight*, at the end of one year, Business Z returned 1,000,000 m.u. to Bank A, and Bank A paid the same amount back to the original lender, along with 100,000 m.u. in interest; *nine*, as a result, Bank A obtained an entrepreneurial profit of 50,000 m.u. (the difference between the interest it paid the original lender and the interest it received from Business Z), a sheer entrepreneurial profit resulting from its legitimate business activity as intermediary.

As is logical, Bank A could have been mistaken in its choice of Business Z. It could have miscalculated the risk involved, or the ability of Business Z to return the loan and pay the interest. Therefore, the success of the bank's activity in this case depends not only upon its bringing the operation with Business Z to a successful conclusion, but also on its own obligation (to return to the original lender 1,000,000 m.u. plus 10-percent interest) falling due *after* Business Z repays the loan to the bank, along with 15-percent interest. In this way the bank can maintain its solvency and avoid any unfortunate incidents. Nevertheless, like any other business, banks are subject to possible entrepreneurial error. For example, Business Z could be unable to return on time the amount it owes the bank, or it could even suspend payments or go bankrupt, which would render Bank A insolvent as well, since it would be unable to in turn pay back the loan it received from the original lender. However, this risk is no different from that inherent in any other business activity and can be easily reduced through the use of prudence and deliberation by the bank in its business activities. Moreover, for the length of the operation (throughout the year), the bank remains fully solvent and faces no liquidity problems, *since it has no obligation to make any cash payments for as long as its loan contract with the original lender remains in force.*[5]

---

[5]Murray N. Rothbard, in reference to banks' role as true intermediaries between original lenders and final borrowers, states:

3
THE BANK'S ROLE
IN THE MONETARY
BANK-DEPOSIT CONTRACT

The economic events and accounting procedures involved in the monetary bank-deposit contract are substantially different from those examined in the preceding section, on the loan or mutuum. (We covered the loan contract first in order to better illustrate by comparison the essential differences between the two contracts.)

In the case of a *regular* (or sealed) deposit of a certain number of perfectly and individually marked monetary units, the person receiving the deposit need not record anything under Assets or Liabilities, because no transfer of ownership occurs. However, as revealed by our study of the legal essence of the *irregular* (or open) deposit contract, this second contract represents a deposit of fungible goods, in which it is impossible to distinguish between the individual units deposited, and therefore a certain transfer of "ownership" does take place. This occurs in the strict sense that the depositary is not obliged to return the very same units received (which would be impossible, given the difficulty of specifically identifying the units of a fungible good received), but others of equal quantity and quality (the *tantundem*). Nevertheless, even though a

---

[t]he bank is expert on where its loans should be made and to whom, and reaps the reward of this service. Note that there has still been no inflationary action by the loan bank. No matter how large it grows, it is still only tapping savings from the existing money stock and lending that money to others. If the bank makes unsound loans and goes bankrupt, then, as in *any* kind of insolvency, its shareholders and creditors will suffer losses. This sort of bankruptcy is little different from any other: unwise management or poor entrepreneurship will have caused harm to owners and creditors. Factors, investment banks, finance companies, and money-lenders are just some of the institutions that have engaged in loan banking. (Murray N. Rothbard, *The Mystery of Banking* [New York: Richardson and Snyder, 1983], pp. 84–85)

transfer of ownership may be established, *availability* is not transferred to the depositary, because in the irregular deposit contract he is obliged to continuously safeguard the *tantundem* of the deposit and therefore must always maintain available to the depositor units of an equal quantity and quality as those originally received (though they may not be the same specific units). Hence, the only justification a depositary has for entering a deposit contract in his account books lies precisely in the transfer of ownership entailed by the irregular deposit; however, it is important to point out that given the extremely limited sense in which this transfer of ownership occurs (it is not at all equal to a transfer of availability), at most the information should be recorded in mere "memorandum accounts" with purely informative purposes. Let us imagine that we have traveled back in time to the dawn of fractional-reserve banking and that a depositor, Mr. X, decides to deposit 1,000,000 m.u. in Bank A (or if you prefer, any person today decides to open a checking account in a bank and deposit 1,000,000 m.u.). This second case involves a true deposit contract, though an irregular one, given the fungible nature of money. In other words, the essential cause or purpose of the deposit contract is the desire of Depositor X that Bank A *safeguard* the 1,000,000 m.u. for him. Mr. X believes that, despite having opened the checking account, he retains the *immediate availability* of 1,000,000 m.u. and can withdraw them at any time for whatever use he pleases, since he has made a "demand" deposit. *From an economic standpoint, for Mr. X the 1,000,000 m.u. are fully available to him at all times and therefore contribute to his cash balances*: that is, even though the monetary units were deposited in Bank A, from a subjective viewpoint they remain as available to Mr. X as if he carried them in his pocket. The entry corresponding to this irregular deposit is as follows:

Bank A

(7)	Debit		Credit	
1,000,000	Cash		Demand deposit (made by Mr. X)	1,000,000

(This should be a mere memorandum entry.)

We see that, although Bank A is justified in making this book entry, since it becomes owner of the monetary units and stores them in its safe without distinguishing them from others, the reference entries should only affect information or memorandum accounts. This is due to the fact that, though the ownership of the monetary units has been transferred to the bank, *it has not been completely transferred*, but remains totally restricted, in the sense that Depositor X still possesses the full availability of the monetary units.

Apart from this last observation, nothing unusual has yet happened from an economic or accounting standpoint. A Mr. X has made an irregular deposit of money in Bank A. *Up to now* this contract has not resulted in any modification of the quantity of money in existence, which continues to be 1,000,000 m.u. and remains available to Mr. X who, for his own convenience, has deposited it in Bank A. Perhaps depositing the money is convenient for Mr. X because he wishes to better safeguard his money, avoiding the dangers that await it in his own home (theft and losses), and to receive cashier and payment services from the bank. In this way Mr. X avoids having to carry money in his pocket and can make payments by simply writing a sum down on a check and instructing the bank to send him a summary each month of all the operations carried out. These banking services are all very valuable and warrant the decision of Mr. X to deposit his money in Bank A. Furthermore, Bank A is fully justified in charging the depositor for these services. Let us suppose the agreed-upon price for the services is 3 percent per year of the quantity deposited (the bank could also charge a flat rate unrelated to the amount deposited, but for the purpose of illustration we will assume the cost of the services depends on the entire amount deposited), a sum with which the bank can cover its operating costs and also achieve a small profit margin. If we suppose the operating costs are equivalent to 2 percent of the amount deposited, the bank will obtain a profit of 1 percent per year, or 10,000 m.u. If Mr. X pays this annual fee (30,000 m.u.) in cash, the following book entries would result from the rendering of the above-mentioned services:

Bank A

(8)	Debit		Credit	
30,000	Cash		Income from Client X in payment for services	30,000
20,000	Operating expenses paid by the bank in order to offer its services		Cash	20,000

At the end of the year, Bank A's income statement and balance sheet would be as follows:

(9)

Bank A
Income Statement
(During the year)

Expenses		Revenues	
Operating costs	20,000	Income from services rendered	30,000
Net Income	10,000		
Total Debit	30,000	Total Credit	30,000

Balance Sheet
(End of the year)

Assets		Liabilities	
Cash	1,010,000	Owner's equity (Profit for the year) Demand deposit	10,000 1,000,000
Total Assets	1,010,000	Total Liabilities	1,010,000

As we see, up to now there has been nothing unusual or surprising about the economic events or accounting processes resulting from the monetary irregular-deposit contract. The bank has made a small legitimate profit, derived from its role as a renderer of services valued by its customer at 30,000 m.u. Moreover, there has been no change in the quantity of money, and after all of the transactions, the bank's cash account has only increased by 10,000 m.u. This sum corresponds to the pure entrepreneurial profit derived by the bank from the difference between the price paid by the client for services (30,000 m.u.) and the operating cost of providing them (20,000 m.u.).

Finally, given that the depositor believes the money he deposited in Bank A remains constantly available to him, a situation equal to or even better than his keeping the money in his own pocket or at home, he need not demand any additional compensation, as in the case of the loan contract, which is radically different. The loan contract required the lender to relinquish the availability of 1,000,000 m.u. of present goods (in other words, to *lend*) and to transfer the availability to the borrower in exchange for the corresponding interest and the repayment of the principal one year later.[6]

4

THE EFFECTS PRODUCED BY
BANKERS' USE OF DEMAND DEPOSITS:
THE CASE OF AN INDIVIDUAL BANK

Nevertheless, as we saw in chapter 2, bankers were soon tempted to violate the traditional rule of conduct requiring

---

[6]Mises, *The Theory of Money and Credit* offers this explanation:

> Therefore the claim obtained in exchange for the sum of money is equally valuable to him whether he converts it sooner or later, or even not at all; and because of this it is possible for him, without damaging his economic interests, to acquire such claims in return for the surrender of money *without demanding compensation for any difference in value arising from the difference in time between payment and repayment, such, of course, as does not in fact exist.* (p. 301; italics added)

them to maintain the *tantundem* of monetary irregular deposits continuously available to depositors, and they ended up using at least a portion of demand deposits for their own benefit. In chapter 3 we covered the comments of Saravia de la Calle with respect to this human temptation. Now we must stress how overwhelming and nearly irresistible it is, given the *huge profits that result from yielding to it*. When bankers first began using their depositors' money, they did so shame-facedly and in secret, as shown by chapter 2's analysis of different historical cases. At this time bankers were still keenly aware of the wrongful nature of their actions. It was only later, after many centuries and vicissitudes, that bankers were successful in their aim to openly and legally violate the traditional legal principle, since they happily obtained the governmental privilege necessary to use their depositors' money (generally by granting loans, which initially were often given to the government itself.)[7] We will now consider the way

---

[7]Stephen Horwitz states that bankers' misappropriation of depositors' money began as "an act of true entrepreneurship as the imaginative powers of individual bankers recognized the gains to be made through financial intermediation." For reasons given in the main text, we find this assertion dangerously erroneous. Furthermore, as we will see, in the appropriation of demand deposits no financial intermediation takes place: only an awkward creation of new deposits from nothing. As for the supposedly "commendable" act of "entrepreneurial creativity," we do not see how it could possibly be distinguished from the "creative entrepreneurship" of any other criminal act, in which the criminal's powers of imagination lead him to the "entrepreneurial discovery" that he benefits from swindling others or forcibly taking their property. See Stephen Horwitz, *Monetary Evolution, Free Banking, and Economic Order* (Oxford and San Francisco: Westview Press, 1992), p. 117. See also Gerald P. O'Driscoll, "An Evolutionary Approach to Banking and Money," chap. 6 of *Hayek, Co-ordination and Evolution: His Legacy in Philosophy, Politics, Economics and the History of Ideas,* Jack Birner and Rudy van Zijp, eds. (London: Routledge, 1994), pp. 126–37. Perhaps Murray N. Rothbard has been the strongest, most articulate critic of Horwitz's idea. Rothbard states:

> [a]ll men are subject to the temptation to commit theft or fraud. . . . Short of this thievery, the warehouseman is subject to a more subtle form of the same temptation: to steal or "borrow" the valuables "temporarily" and to profit by speculation

bankers record the appropriation of demand deposits in their account books. Our study will begin with the case of an individual bank and will later extend to the banking system as a whole.

THE CONTINENTAL ACCOUNTING SYSTEM

Two accounting systems, the continental and the Anglo-Saxon, have traditionally been used to document the phenomenon we are studying. The continental system is based on the false notion that for the depositor, the irregular deposit contract is a true deposit contract, while for the banker it is a loan or mutuum contract. In this case, Mr. X makes a "demand" deposit of 1,000,000 m.u. in Bank A, and Bank A receives the money not as a deposit, but as a loan it can freely use, considering the depositor will not be aware of this use nor be affected by it. Moreover, while keeping only a portion of deposits on hand as a *security reserve*, the bank estimates it will be able to comply with depositors' withdrawal requests. These expectations are especially strong, given that under normal circumstances it is highly unlikely customers will attempt to withdraw an amount exceeding the security margin or reserve ratio. Experience appears to show this is true, and the trust the bank has earned through years of properly safeguarding clients' deposits contributes to the unlikelihood of such a predicament, as does the fact that many withdrawals are offset by new deposits. If we suppose the banker considers a 10-percent security reserve (also called a "reserve ratio") sufficient to satisfy possible demands for deposit withdrawals, then the other 90 percent of demand deposits, or 900,000 m.u., would be available to him to use to his own benefit. Using the

---

or whatever, returning the valuables before they are redeemed so that no one will be the wiser. This form of theft is known as *embezzlement*, which the dictionary defines as "appropriating fraudulently to one's own use, as money or property entrusted to one's care." (Rothbard, *The Mystery of Banking*, p. 90)

For more on why the above activity should be legally classified as a criminal act of misappropriation, see chapter 1.

European accounting system, this economic event would be represented in the following way:[8]

When Mr. X makes the demand deposit, a book entry identical to number (7) is made, though this time it is not considered a memorandum entry.

Bank A

(10) Debit		Credit	
1,000,000	Cash	Demand deposit (made by Mr. X)	1,000,000

Once the bank yields to the temptation to appropriate most of the *tantundem*, which it should keep on hand and available to the depositor, the following entry is made:

Bank A

(11) Debit		Credit	
900,000	Loan to Z	Cash	900,000

At the moment the banker appropriates the money and loans it to Z, an economic event of great significance occurs: 900,000 m.u. are created *ex nihilo,* or out of nothing. Indeed, Mr. X's essential motive for making a demand deposit of 1,000,000 m.u. was the custody and safekeeping of the money, and with good reason he subjectively believes he retains the complete availability of it, just as if he had it in his pocket, and in a sense better. To all intents and purposes, Mr. X still has 1,000,000 m.u.

---

[8]The description of the different accounting systems (the English and the continental) and how they ultimately bring about identical economic results is found in F.A. Hayek, *Monetary Theory and the Trade Cycle* (Clifton, N.J.: Augustus M. Kelley, [1933] 1975), pp. 154ff.

in cash as if the money were physically "in his possession," since according to his contract it remains fully available to him. From an economic standpoint, there is no doubt the 1,000,000 m.u. Mr. X deposited in Bank A continue to contribute to his cash balances. However, when the bank appropriates 900,000 m.u. from deposits and loans them to Z, it simultaneously generates additional purchasing power from nothing and transfers it to Z, the borrower, who receives 900,000 m.u. It is clear that, both subjectively and objectively, Z enjoys the full availability of 900,000 m.u. beginning at that point and that these monetary units are transferred to him.[9] Therefore, *there has been an increase in the amount of money in circulation in the market, due to beliefs held simultaneously and with good reason by two different economic agents: one thinks he has 1,000,000 m.u. at his disposal, and the other believes he has 900,000 m.u. at his disposal. In other words, the bank's appropriation of 900,000 m.u. from a demand deposit results in an increase equal to 900,000 m.u. in the aggregate balances of money existing in the market. In contrast, the loan or mutuum contract covered earlier involves no such occurrence.*

We should also consider the location of the existing money in the market from the time the banker appropriates the deposit. The number of monetary units in the market has clearly grown to 1,900,000, though these units exist in different forms. We say there are 1,900,000 m.u. because different economic agents subjectively believe they have at their disposal 1,900,000 m.u. to exchange in the market, and money consists of all generally-accepted mediums of exchange.

---

[9]Money is the only perfectly liquid asset. The bank's failure to comply with a 100-percent reserve ratio on demand deposits brings about a serious economic situation in which two people (the original depositor and the borrower) simultaneously believe they are free to use the same perfectly liquid sum of 900,000 m.u. It is logically impossible for two people to simultaneously own (or have fully available to them) the same perfectly liquid good (money). This is the fundamental economic argument behind the legal impracticability of the monetary irregular-deposit contract with fractional reserves. It also explains that when this "legal aberration" (in the words of Clemente de Diego) is imposed by the state (in the form of a privilege—*ius privilegium*—given to the bank), it entails the creation of new money (900,000 m.u.).

Nevertheless the form of the money varies: Borrower Z possesses it in a different form from Mr. X, who made the deposit. Indeed, Z has available to him 900,000 *physical* monetary units (which we could call *commodity money* or, nowadays, *paper money* or *fiat money*), while Depositor X has a checking account containing a deposit of 1,000,000 m.u. Considering the bank has kept 100,000 m.u. in its vault as a security reserve or reserve ratio, the difference between 1,900,000 m.u. and the 1,000,000 m.u. existing in physical form is equal to the amount of money the bank created from nothing. (A total money supply of 1,900,000 m.u. minus 900,000 physical m.u. in Z's possession and 100,000 physical m.u. in the bank's vault equals 900,000 m.u. which do not physically exist anywhere.) As this money lacks the corresponding backing and exists due to the confidence Depositor X has in Bank A, it is called *fiduciary money* (or, better, *fiduciary media*). It is important to emphasize that to all intents and purposes demand deposits are like *physical* units; that is, they are perfect *money substitutes*. The depositor can use them to make payments at any time by issuing a check on which he writes the sum he wishes to pay and giving instructions to the bank to make the payment. The portion of these perfect money substitutes, or demand deposits, which is not fully backed by physical monetary units in the bank's vault (the 900,000 m.u. not backed by reserves in the present example) is called *fiduciary media*.[10]

Demand deposits backed by cash reserves at the bank (100,000 m.u. in our example) are also called *primary deposits*, while the portion of demand deposits not backed by the

---

[10]"If the money reserve kept by the debtor against the money-substitutes issued is less than the total amount of such substitutes, we call that amount of substitutes which exceeds the reserve *fiduciary media*." Mises, *Human Action*, p. 430. Mises clarifies that it is not generally possible to declare whether a particular money substitute is or is not a fiduciary medium. When we write a check, we do not know (because the bank does not directly inform us) what portion of the check's sum is backed by physical monetary units. As a result, from an economic standpoint, we do not know what portion of the money we are paying is a fiduciary medium and what portion corresponds to physical monetary units.

bank's reserves (fiduciary media) is also called a *secondary deposit or derivative deposit.*[11]

Once banks had violated the legal principle that no one may appropriate a deposit made with them for safekeeping, and had ceased to guard 100 percent of the *tantundem*, it was natural for them to try to justify their activity and defend themselves with the argument that they had actually received the money *as if* it were a loan. In fact, if a banker considers the money received a loan, then there is nothing improper in his conduct, and from the economic and accounting viewpoint described in the previous section, he is only playing the legitimate, necessary role of intermediary between lenders and borrowers. Nonetheless, an essential difference arises here: the money is not handed over to the bank as a loan, but as a deposit. In other words, when Mr. X made his deposit, he did not have the slightest intention of relinquishing the availability of present goods in exchange for a somewhat higher figure (considering interest) of future goods. Instead, his only desire was to improve the custody and safekeeping of his money and to receive other peripheral services (cashier and bookkeeping services), while at all times retaining the full, unaltered availability of the *tantundem*. This absence of an exchange of present goods for future goods is precisely what

---

[11]This terminology has become the most widespread, as a result of Chester Arthur Phillips's now classic work. Phillips states:

> a primary deposit is one growing out of a lodgement of cash or its equivalent and not out of credit extended by the bank in question . . . derivative deposits have their origins in loans extended to depositors . . . they arise directly from a loan, or are accumulated by a borrower in anticipation of the repayment of a loan. (*Bank Credit: A Study of the Principles and Factors Underlying Advances Made by Banks to Borrowers* [New York: Macmillan, (1920) 1931], pp. 34 and 40)

Nonetheless, we have a small objection to Phillips's definition of "derivative deposits" as deposits originating from loans. Though loans are their most common source, derivative deposits are created the very moment the bank uses, either for granting loans or any other purpose, a portion of the deposits received, converting them *ipso facto* into fiduciary media or derivative deposits. On this topic, see Richard H. Timberlake, "A Reassessment of C.A. Phillips's Theory of Bank Credit," *History of Political Economy* 20 no. 2 (1988): 299–308.

indicates we are faced with a radically different economic event, one that involves the creation *ex nihilo* of 900,000 m.u. of fiduciary media or derivative deposits when the bank loans 90 percent of the money it has in its vault.

In addition it is important to understand clearly that if the bank uses the money to grant a loan to Z, as we have supposed in our example and is usually the case, this loan does entail the exchange of present goods for future goods, *though it is not backed anywhere in the market by a necessary, previous increase of 900,000 m.u. in voluntary saving*. Indeed, the bank creates from nothing money it loans to Z in the form of present goods, while no one has been first obliged to increase his savings by the amount of the loan. Mr. X, the original depositor, continues to subjectively believe he possesses the full availability of the 1,000,000 m.u. he deposited in the bank, that is, he thinks he has at his disposal 1,000,000 m.u. of a completely liquid asset (money). At the same time, Borrower Z receives for his investments 900,000 m.u. of new liquidity which has not come from anyone's savings. In short, two different people simultaneously believe they have at their full disposal the same liquid asset of 900,000 m.u., which correspond to the portion of the deposit of 1,000,000 m.u. which the bank loaned to Z (derivative deposit). At this point it is obvious banks generate liquidity which is invested without any prior saving. This phenomenon constitutes the main cause of recurring economic crises and recessions, and we will examine its crucial economic importance in the following chapters.

Once the bank has given the loan to Z, the bank's balance sheet appears as follows:

(12)

Bank A
Balance Sheet
(End of the year)

Assets		Liabilities	
Cash	100,000	Demand deposit	1,000,000
Loans granted	900,000		
Total Assets	1,000,000	Total Liabilities	1,000,000

Clearly, the banker will tend to deceive himself, thinking he has received his depositors' money as a loan. Furthermore, it will never occur to him that by granting the loan to Business Z he has created 900,000 m.u. *ex nihilo*, nor much less that he has granted a loan without the prior backing of an actual increase in saving by anyone. Moreover, the banker will consider the natural counteraction between withdrawals and new deposits, and in accordance with his "experience," he will deem his decision to maintain a cash or security reserve of 10 percent adequate and the resulting cash reserve of 100,000 m.u. more than sufficient to satisfy requests for *normal* deposit withdrawals by customers.[12] The whole structure is made possible by customers' faith that the bank will honor its future commitments. The bank must build up this faith through the impeccable custody and safekeeping of the money for an extended period of time, without any misappropriation.[13] It is understandable that a banker may not be familiar with economic theory and therefore not recognize the fundamental economic events we have just described. It is more difficult to excuse the fact that his misappropriation of deposits constitutes a violation of traditional legal principles which, in the absence of a theory to explain the social processes involved, serve as the only safe guide to follow in order to avoid severe social damage. However, any intelligent person, banker or not, would surely be able to see some *signs* of what is really happening. Why is it necessary for the banker to maintain *any* reserve ratio? Does he not realize that when he acts legitimately as true intermediary between lenders and borrowers he need not maintain any? Does he not understand, as Röpke states, that his bank is "an institution which, finding it possible to hold less cash than it promises to pay and living on the difference,

---

[12]Nevertheless we will demonstrate that the fractional-reserve banking system itself regularly generates abnormal (massive) withdrawals of deposits and cannot with a fractional-reserve ratio fulfill at all times depositors' demands for these withdrawals.

[13]We are, of course, referring to the different historical stages in which fractional-reserve banking emerged (prior to the existence of central banks); we covered these in chapter 2.

regularly promises more than it could actually pay should the worse come to the worst"?[14] In any case, these are simply indications which any practical person could understandably interpret in a wide variety of ways. Legal principles exist for precisely this reason. They act as an "automatic pilot" for behavior and facilitate cooperation between people, though given the abstract nature of these principles, we may not be able to identify their exact role in the processes of social interaction.

As Mises correctly indicates, as long as confidence in the bank is preserved, the bank will be able to continue using the majority of deposited funds, and customers will remain unaware that the bank lacks the necessary liquidity to meet all of its commitments. It is as if the bank had found a permanent source of financing in the creation of new money, a source it will continue to tap as long as the public retains its faith in the bank's ability to fulfill its commitments. In fact, as long as these circumstances last, the bank will even be able to use its newly created liquidity for covering its own expenses or for any other purpose besides granting loans. In short, the ability to create money *ex nihilo* generates wealth the banker can easily appropriate, provided customers do not doubt his good conduct. The generation of this wealth is detrimental to many third parties, each of whom suffers a share of the damage caused by the banker's activities. It is impossible to identify these individuals, and they are unlikely to recognize the harm they suffer or to discover the identity of the perpetrator.[15]

---

[14]Wilhelm Röpke, *Economics of the Free Society*, trans. Patrick M. Boarman (Grove City, Pa.: Libertarian Press, 1994), p. 97.

[15]We will examine the process of loan creation and the resulting transfer of wealth to bankers in our analysis of the effects fractional-reserve banking has from the perspective of the entire banking system. Regarding the fact that it is not necessary for fiduciary media to be lent (though in practice this is always or almost always the case), Ludwig von Mises states:

> [i]t is known that some deposit banks sometimes open deposit accounts without a money cover not only for the purpose of granting loans, but also for the purpose of directly procuring resources for production on their own behalf. More than one of the modern credit and commercial banks has

Though private bankers may often be unaware that their ability to create new money *ex nihilo* (by using customers' deposits to grant loans) constitutes a source of huge profits, and although they may naively believe they are merely loaning a part of what they receive, the majority of their profits still derive from a general process in which they are immersed and the implications of which they do not completely comprehend. We will see this point confirmed later when we study the effects of fractional-reserve banking in terms of the entire *banking system*. One thing bankers understand perfectly, however, is that by loaning most of the funds clients deposit, they make a *much larger* profit than they would if they acted only as legitimate intermediaries between lenders and borrowers—entries (1) to (6)—or as mere providers of bookkeeping and cashier services—entries (8) and (9). In fact on the loan made to Z, Bank A will earn an interest rate of 15 percent of the amount of the loan (900.000 m.u.); that is, 135,000 m.u. The entry is as follows:

Bank A

(13)	Debit		Credit	
135,000	Cash		Revenue from interest on loans	135,000

---

invested a part of its capital in this manner . . . the issuer of fiduciary media may, however, regard the value of the fiduciary media put into circulation *as an addition to his income or capital*. If he does this he will not take the trouble to cover the increase in his obligations due to the issue by setting aside a special credit fund out of his capital. He will pocket the profits of the issue, which in the case of token coinage is called seigniorage, as composedly as any other sort of income. (Mises, *The Theory of Money and Credit*, p. 312; italics added)

In light of these considerations, it is not surprising that of all economic institutions, banks generally display to the public the most spectacular, luxurious buildings and spend the most disproportionate amount on offices, payroll, etc. It is no less surprising that governments have been the first to take advantage of banks' great power to create money.

If we suppose the bank performs the cashier and book-keeping services described earlier, which are typical of checking accounts and generate an operating cost of 20,000 m.u. in our example, then by covering these costs with interest income it is even able to provide these services free of charge. The following entry is made to record the operating costs:

<table>
<tr><td colspan="4" align="center">Bank A</td></tr>
<tr><td>(14)</td><td>Debit</td><td>Credit</td><td></td></tr>
<tr><td>20,000</td><td>Operating costs
of services</td><td>Cash</td><td>20,000</td></tr>
</table>

Although the bank would be completely justified in continuing to charge 30,000 m.u. (3 percent of the amount deposited) for its services, and although it may offer these services free to its depositors to attract more deposits and to pursue the more or less covert objective of using these deposits to grant loans, it still makes a very large profit, equal to the 135,000 m.u. it receives in interest, minus the 20,000 m.u. it pays in operating costs.

In fact the bank's profit of 115,000 m.u. is more than *double* the legitimate profit it would make as a mere financial intermediary between lenders and borrowers and more than ten times what it would bring in by charging its customers for cashier and bookkeeping services.[16] The bank's income statement would hence appear as follows:

(15)

Bank A
Income Statement
(During the year)

<table>
<tr><td colspan="2">Expenses</td><td colspan="2">Revenues</td></tr>
<tr><td>Operating costs</td><td>20,000</td><td>Interest received</td><td>135,000</td></tr>
<tr><td>Net Income</td><td>115,000</td><td></td><td></td></tr>
<tr><td>Total Debit</td><td>135,000</td><td>Total Credit</td><td>135,000</td></tr>
</table>

---

[16]See footnote number 25.

After carrying out all of the operations, the bank's balance sheet would appear as follows:

(16)   Bank A

Balance Sheet
(End of the year)

Assets		Liabilities	
Cash	215,000	Owner's Equity (Profit for the year)	115,000
Loans granted	900,000	Demand deposits	1,000,000
Total Assets	1,115,000	Total Liabilities	1,115,000

ACCOUNTING PRACTICES IN THE ENGLISH-SPEAKING WORLD

English banking practices reflect fewer reservations about plainly recording in the accounts the creation *ex nihilo* of fiduciary media. Indeed, as Hayek states, "English banking practice credits the account of the customer with the amount borrowed before the latter is actually utilized."[17]

In English-speaking countries, when a customer makes a demand deposit of 1,000,000 m.u. at a bank, the first account entry made corresponds exactly to that made in the continental system:

Bank A

(17) Debit		Credit	
1,000,000 Cash		Demand deposits	1,000,000

---

[17]Hayek, *Monetary Theory and the Trade Cycle*, p. 154. Hayek goes on to say: "Granted this assumption, the process leading to an increase of circulating media is comparatively easy to survey and therefore hardly ever disputed."

The difference between the Anglo-Saxon and the continental system lies in the entry the English-speaking banker makes upon deciding to grant a loan to Z, and hence to make self-interested use of 900,000 m.u. the banker holds in his vault in excess of his security reserve. In Anglo-Saxon banking practices, an entry is made to record the loan under Assets, and at the same time a checking account in favor of the borrower is opened under Liabilities for the sum of the loan (900,000 m.u.). The entry looks like this:

Bank A

(18)	Debit	Credit	
900,000	Loans granted	Demand deposits	900,000

Thus, in this respect the English custom is much more straightforward and appropriate to the actual economic events than the continental custom. Anglo-Saxon accounting practices distinctly reflect the *ex nihilo* creation of 900,000 m.u. which results when demand deposit funds are loaned to Z. After the loan is granted, the bank's balance sheet appears as follows:

Bank A
Balance Sheet

(19)	Assets		Liabilities	
Cash	1,000,000		Demand deposits	1,900,000
Loans	900,000			
Total Assets	1,900,000		Total Liabilities	1,900,000

In keeping with the English custom, this balance sheet clearly reveals that the moment the bank grants a loan of

900,000 m.u., it simultaneously generates deposits *ex nihilo* for the sum of 900,000 m.u. In other words, the bank places at the disposal of the borrower up to 900,000 m.u., which raises the balance of demand deposits to 1,900,000 m.u. Of this amount, 1,000,000 m.u. correspond to physical monetary units; that is, to primary deposits. The other 900,000 m.u. reflect fiduciary media created from nothing; in other words, derivative or secondary deposits.

If we again suppose for the sake of argument that the banker regards as a *loan* the money placed with him on demand deposit, then because this loan derives from a monetary irregular-deposit contract, which by definition stipulates no term for the return of the money (as it is "on demand"), the "loan" in question would clearly have no term. Furthermore, if the depositors trust the bank, the banker will rightly expect them to withdraw only a small fraction of their deposits under normal conditions. As a result, even though the "loan" he has supposedly received from his depositors is "on demand," the banker may with good reason consider it a "loan" *he will never have to return*, since it ultimately lacks a term. Obviously if the banker receives a loan believing he will never have to return it (and in most cases he does not even have to pay interest on it, though this is not fundamental to our argument), then rather than a loan, we are dealing with a *de facto gift* the banker gives himself and charges to the funds of his depositors. This means that although for accounting purposes the bank recognizes a debt (parallel to the loan granted) in the form of "demand deposits" (derivative or secondary deposits for the sum of 900,000 m.u.), under ordinary circumstances what the bank actually does is to create from nothing a perennial source of financing which the banker supposes *he will never have to return*. Therefore, despite the impression the account books give, the banker ultimately appropriates these funds and considers them his property. In short, banks amass tremendous wealth, mainly by generating means of payment to the detriment of third parties. The harm done is very generalized and diluted, however, and takes the form of a gradual relative loss of purchasing power. This phenomenon occurs constantly and stems from the banking system's *ex nihilo* creation of means of payment. This continuous transfer of wealth to bankers persists as long as the banking business suffers no disruptions and assets keep increasing bankers' balances in the form of loans and investments backed by the corresponding deposits created from nothing. The full recognition of this never-ending source of financing and of the enormous wealth banks have accumulated to the detriment of other citizens (which still contribute to the banks' balances, disguised as active investments backed by "deposits") will prove very important in the last chapter, when we propose a model for changing and reforming the current banking system. Though these funds in fact only benefit banks and governments, and though from an economic and accounting standpoint they belong to alleged depositors, in all reality *they do not belong to anyone*, since these depositors view their deposits as perfect money substitutes. Therefore, as we will see when we study the process of banking reform, these resources could be used to pursue important goals in the public interest. Such goals might include eliminating the remaining public debt or even financing a process of social-security reform to accomplish a transition from a pay-as-you-go public system to an entirely private system based on investment.

Let us return now to our example. As Borrower Z gradually uses his money by writing checks on the account opened for him by the bank, the two banking systems, the Anglo-Saxon and the Continental, would begin to reflect the bank's account records in an increasingly similar way. Let us suppose the borrower withdraws his loan in two portions, one on each of two separate, consecutive occasions. On the first occasion (t_1) he withdraws 500,000 m.u., and on the second (t_2), 400,000 m.u. The accounting entries would appear as follows:

Bank A (t_1)

(20)	Debit	Credit	
500,000	Demand deposits (part of the loan withdrawn by Z)	Cash	500,000

Bank A (t₂)

(21) Debit		Credit	
400,000 Demand deposits (the remainder of the loan)		Cash	400,000

After the borrower withdraws the entire loan, the bank's balance sheet looks like this:

(22)

Bank A
Balance Sheet

Assets		Liabilities	
Cash	100,000	Demand deposits	1,000,000
Loans	900,000		
Total Assets	1,000,000	Total Liabilities	1,000,000

This balance sheet corresponds exactly with balance sheet (12), which we obtained using continental accounting methods and which comprises demand deposits of 1,000,000 m.u. made by customers and backed by 100,000 m.u. in cash (the reserve ratio or requirement) and 900,000 m.u. in loans granted to Z. Therefore once the borrower withdraws his entire loan, the accounting records of both systems are identical: 1,900,000 m.u. exist in the market, of which 900,000 m.u. correspond to fiduciary media (the portion of demand deposits which are not backed by cash balances at the bank, in this case 1,000,000 m.u. minus 100,000 m.u.) and 1,000,000 m.u. are physical monetary units (the 100,000 m.u. in the bank's vault and the 900,000 m.u. that have been handed over to Borrower Z and which he has already used for his own purposes).[18]

---

[18]The banking practices of the English-speaking world have been adopted in Spain as well, as evidenced, among other sources, by Pedro

The main advantage of the Anglo-Saxon accounting system is that it demonstrates, as Herbert J. Davenport pointed out in 1913, that banks "do not lend their deposits, but rather, by their own extensions of credit, *create* the deposits."[19] In other words, banks *do not act as financial intermediaries* when they loan money from demand deposits, since this activity does not constitute mediation between lenders and borrowers.

Pedraja García's book, *Contabilidad y análisis de balances de la banca*, vol. 1: *Principios generales y contabilización de operaciones* (Madrid: Centro de Formación del Banco de España, 1992), esp. pp. 116–209.

[19]Herbert J. Davenport, *The Economics of Enterprise* (New York: Augustus M. Kelley, [1913] 1968), p. 263. Fourteen years later, W.F. Crick expressed the same idea in his article, "The Genesis of Bank Deposits," *Economica* (June 1927): 191–202. Most of the public and even some scholars as distinguished as Joaquín Garrigues fail to understand that banks are mainly creators of loans and deposits, rather than mediators between lenders and borrowers. In his book *Contratos bancarios* (pp. 31–32 and 355), Garrigues continues to insist that banks are primarily credit mediators that "loan money which has been lent to them" (p. 355) and also that bankers

> loan what they are lent. They are credit mediators, businessmen who mediate between those who need money for business deals and those who wish to invest their money profitably. Banks, however, may engage in two different types of activities: they may act as mere mediators who bring together contracting parties (direct credit mediation) or they may carry out a double operation consisting of borrowing money in order to later lend it (indirect credit mediation). (p. 32)

Garrigues clearly does not realize that, with respect to banks' most important enterprise (accepting deposits while maintaining a fractional reserve), banks actually grant loans from nothing and back them with deposits they also create from nothing. Therefore, rather than credit mediators, they are *ex nihilo* creators of credit. Garrigues also subscribes to the popular misconception that "from an economic standpoint," the bank's profit consists of "the difference between the amount of interest it pays on the deposit operation and the amount it earns on the loan operation" (p. 31). Though banks appear to derive their profit mainly from an interest rate differential, we know that in practice the chief source of their profit is the *ex nihilo* creation of money, which provides banks with financing indefinitely. Banks appropriate these funds for their own benefit and charge interest on them to boot. In short, bankers create money from nothing, loan it and require that it be returned with interest.

Instead banks simply grant loans against deposits they create from nothing (*fiduciary media*) and which therefore have not first been entrusted to them by any third party as deposits of physical monetary units. Not even under the continental accounting system are banks financial intermediaries, since true original depositors turn their money over for custody and safekeeping, not as a loan to the bank. Furthermore we have already shown that by reducing to a fraction the number of monetary units they keep on hand (reserve ratio), banks create fiduciary media in proportion to the total sum of their unbacked deposits. Thus, by a somewhat more abstract analysis, the continental accounting system leads us to the same conclusion as the Anglo-Saxon system: rather than credit intermediaries, banks are creators of loans and deposits, or fiduciary media. Nevertheless, the process is much more obvious and easier to understand when evaluated according to Anglo-Saxon accounting criteria, because from the beginning this method reflects the fact that the bank creates deposits *ex nihilo* and grants loans against them. Therefore, no abstract intellectual exercise is required to understand the process.

From the perspective of economic theory, the chief disadvantage of both accounting systems is that they reflect a *much lower* volume of deposit creation and loan concession than truly exists. That is, they reveal only a fraction of the total volume of deposits and loans which the banking system *as a whole* is capable of creating. Only when we consider the effects of fractional-reserve banking from the standpoint of *the overall banking system* will this important fact be confirmed. However, first it is necessary to identify the limits to deposit creation and loan concession by an isolated bank.

AN ISOLATED BANK'S CAPACITY FOR CREDIT EXPANSION AND DEPOSIT CREATION

We will now consider the limits to an isolated bank's capacity to create loans and expand deposits from nothing. The following variables are involved:

d: the money originally deposited in the bank's vault;

d_1: the money or reserves which leave the bank as a result of loans it grants;

x: the bank's maximum possible credit expansion starting from d;

c: the cash or reserves ratio maintained by the bank, in keeping with the banker's experience and his careful judgment on how much money he needs to honor his commitments; and

k: the proportion of loans granted which, on average, remain unused by borrowers at any given time.

From the above definitions it is clear that the reserves which leave the bank, d_1, will be equal to the loans granted multiplied by the percentage of these loans which is used by borrowers; that is:

[1] $$d_1 = (1 - k)x$$

In addition, if we consider that the money which leaves the bank, d_1, is equal to the amount originally deposited, d, minus the minimum amount kept on reserve, cd, in relation to the money originally deposited, plus ckx, in relation to the percentage of loans which on average remains unused, then we have:

[2] $$d_1 = d - (cd + ckx)$$

If we now replace d_1 in formula [2] with the value of d_1 in [1], we have:

$$(1 - k)x = d - (cd + ckx)$$

Next we work to solve the equation, factor out common factors and isolate x:

$$(1 - k)x = d - cd - ckx$$

$$(1 - k)x + ckx = d - cd$$

$$x(1 - k + ck) = d(1 - c)$$

Therefore the maximum credit expansion, x, an isolated bank could bring about *ex nihilo* would be:[20]

$$x = \frac{d\,(1-c)}{1 - k(1-c)}$$

---

[20]Significantly, however, Ludwig von Mises, in his important theoretical treatises on money, credit and economic cycles, has always resisted basing his analysis on the study of the credit expansion multiplier we have just worked out in the text. These writings of Mises all focus on the disruptive effects of creating loans unbacked by an increase in actual saving, and the fractional-reserve banking system which carries out such loan creation by generating deposits or fiduciary media. Mises's resistance to the multiplier is perfectly understandable, considering the aversion the great Austrian economist felt to the use of mathematics in economics and more specifically to the application of concepts which, like the bank multiplier, may be justly labeled "mechanistic," often inexact and even deceptive, mainly because they do not take into account the process of entrepreneurial creativity and the evolution of subjective time. Furthermore, from the strict viewpoint of economic theory, it is unnecessary to work out the multiplier mathematically to grasp the basic concept of credit and deposit expansion and how this process inexorably provokes economic crises and recessions. (Ludwig von Mises's chief theoretical goal was to arrive at such an understanding.) Nevertheless the bank multiplier offers the advantage of simplifying and clarifying the explanation of the continual process of credit and deposit expansion. Therefore, for the purpose of illustration, the multiplier reinforces our theoretical argument. The first to employ the bank multiplier in a theoretical analysis of economic crises was Herbert J. Davenport in his book, *The Economics of Enterprise*, (esp. chap. 17, pp. 254–331) a work we have already cited. Nonetheless F.A. Hayek deserves recognition for incorporating the theory of the bank credit expansion multiplier to the Austrian theory of economic cycles (*Monetary Theory and the Trade Cycle*, pp. 152ff.). See also note 28, in which Marshall, in 1887, provides a detailed description of how to arrive at the most simplified version of the bank multiplier formula.

Or to put it another way:

$$[3] \qquad\qquad x = \frac{d\,(1-c)}{1 + k(c-1)}$$

As formula [3] makes clear, the reserve ratio, c, and the average percentage of loans which remain unused, k, have opposite effects on an isolated bank's capacity to create loans and deposits. That is, the lower c is and the higher k is, the higher x will be. The economic logic of formula [3] is therefore very plain: the higher the reserve ratio estimated necessary by the bank, the fewer the loans it will be able to grant; in contrast, if the reserve ratio or requirement remains unchanged, the fewer the loaned funds the bank believes, on average, will be withdrawn by borrowers, the more money it will have available for expanding loans.

Up until now we have assumed k to be the average percentage of loans unused by borrowers. However, according to C.A. Phillips, k can include other phenomena which have the same ultimate effect.[21] For instance, k can stand for the very great likelihood that, in a market where few banks operate, a borrower will make payments to some other customers of his own bank. It is assumed that when this happens, these customers will deposit their checks in their own accounts at the same bank, thus keeping money from leaving the bank. This phenomenon has the same ultimate effect as an increase in the average percentage of loans unused by borrowers. The fewer the banks operating in the market, the higher k will be; the higher k is, the less money will leave the bank; the less money leaves the bank, the greater the bank's capacity for expanding loans. One of the strongest motivations behind the trend toward bank mergers and acquisitions which has always been obvious in fractional-reserve banking systems is precisely the desire to increase k.[22] In fact, the more banks merge and the

---

[21]Phillips, *Bank Credit*, pp. 57–59.

[22]Other forces exist to explain the process of bank mergers. They all stem from banks' attempt to minimize the undesirable consequences

larger their subsequent market share, the greater the possibility that the citizens who receive the banks' fiduciary media will be their own customers. Therefore both k and the corresponding capacity to create loans and deposits from nothing will be increased and the resulting profit much greater. The value of k is also increased when monetary deposits are made in other banks, which in turn expand their loans, and their borrowers ultimately deposit in the original bank a significant portion of the new money they receive. This phenomenon also causes an increase in the bank's monetary reserves and therefore in its capacity for credit expansion.

For example, if we suppose that the reserve ratio or requirement, c, is 10 percent; that the proportion of loans which remain unused, k (which also includes the effects of a larger number of bank customers, as well as other factors), is

---

they suffer as a result of their violation, via the corresponding state privilege, of the essential principles behind the monetary irregular-deposit contract. One advantage banks gain from mergers and acquisitions is the ability to establish centralized cash reserves, which are kept available for fulfilling withdrawal requests at any location where a higher than average number of them may be made. In a market where many banks operate, this benefit is lost, since each bank is then obliged to maintain separate, relatively higher cash reserves. Public authorities also urge rapid mergers, because they hope it will make it easier for them to prevent liquidity crises, implement monetary policy and regulate the banking industry. We will later analyze bankers' persistent desire to increase the volume of their deposits, since as the formula shows, the sum of deposits forms the basis for the multiple expansion of loans and deposits, which banks create *ex nihilo* and from which they derive so many benefits. On bank mergers, see Costantino Bresciani-Turroni, *Curso de economía política*, vol. 2: *Problemas de economía política* (Mexico: Fondo de Cultura Económica, 1961), pp. 144–45. In any case, it is important to recognize that the irresistible bank-merger process results from state interventionism in the field of finance and banking, as well as from the privilege that allows banks to operate with fractional reserves on demand deposits, against traditional legal principles. In a free-market economy with no government intervention, where economic agents are subject to legal principles, this continual trend toward bank mergers would disappear, banks' size would be practically immaterial and there would be a tendency toward a very high number of entirely solvent banks.

20 percent; and that the sum of the original deposits, d, made in the bank is equal to 1,000,000 m.u.; then, by substituting these values into formula [3] we obtain:

$$[4] \quad x = \frac{1,000,000\,(1 - 0.1)}{1 + 0.2\,(0.1 - 1)} = 1,097,560 \text{ m.u.}$$

Therefore we see that a bank which accepts 1,000,000 m.u. in demand deposits, and which maintains a reserve ratio of 10 percent and a k of 20 percent will be able to grant loans not only for the sum of 900,000 m.u., as we assumed for the purpose of illustration in entries (18) and following, but for a considerably larger amount, 1,097,560 m.u. Hence, even in the case of an isolated bank, the capacity for credit expansion and *ex nihilo* deposit creation is 22 percent greater than we initially supposed in entries (18) and following.[23] As a result, we should modify our earlier accounting entries to reflect that, in keeping with the Anglo-Saxon accounting system, when $c=0.1$ and $k=0.2$, the bank will be able to expand its credit by 1,097,560 m.u., instead of the 900,000 we assumed before (that is, the bank's capacity for credit expansion is 22 percent greater). The modified journal entries and corresponding balance sheet would appear as follows (compare with initial entries 18 and 19):

----

[23]Even though, from the standpoint of an isolated bank, it appears as if the bank were loaning a portion of its deposits, the reality is that even an isolated bank creates loans *ex nihilo* for a sum larger than that originally deposited. This demonstrates that the principal source of deposits is not depositors, but rather loans banks create from nothing. (Deposits are a secondary result of these loans.) This will be even clearer when we study the overall banking system. C.A. Phillips expresses this fact by stating, "It follows that for the banking system, deposits are chiefly the offspring of loans." See Phillips, *Bank Credit*, p. 64, and the quotation from Taussig in note 63, chapter 5.

Bank A

(23) Debit	Credit
1,000,000 Cash	Demand deposits 1,000,000
	(checking accounts)
1,097,560 Loans granted	Demand deposits 1,097,560
	(newly-created deposits)

These entries correspond to an original deposit of 1,000,000 m.u. and an isolated bank's *ex nihilo* creation of loans and deposits for the sum of 1,097,560 m.u. The value of k (0.2) indicates that, on average, borrowers only withdraw 80 percent of the funds they are lent. When this withdrawal is made (and even if a greater amount is withdrawn, when some of the final recipients of the money are also customers of the original bank and deposit their money there), the following entry is recorded:[24]

---

[24]Former continental accounting methods are more complex. However, it is possible to arrive at balance sheet (25) by supposing that the statement $k=0.2$, instead of referring to the percentage of loan funds unused (which, as we know, this system does not reflect), represents the proportion of the public which does business regularly with the bank and therefore will deposit funds back into it. In this case, the entries would appear as follows:

Bank A

(26) Debit	Credit
1,000,000 Cash	Demand deposits 1,000,000

Upon loaning 900,000 m.u., the bank would make the following entry:

Bank A

Debit	Credit
900,000 Loans	Cash 900,000

Bank A

(24)	Debit		Credit	
878,048	Demand deposits (80% of 1,097,560)		Cash	878,048

The bank's balance sheet would appear as follows:

_____

If we suppose that 20 percent of the 900,000 m.u. which leave the bank's vault will again be deposited in the same bank, and that 90 percent of that amount will then be loaned, etc., the entries appear as follows:

(27)	Debit		Credit	
180,000	Cash		Demand deposits	180,000

When 90 percent of this amount is loaned:

Bank A

(28)	Debit		Credit	
162,000	Loans		Cash	162,000
32,400	Cash		Demand deposits	32,400
29,160	Loans		Cash	29,160
5,832	Cash		Demand deposits	5,832
5,248	Loans		Cash	5,248

We have supposed that 20 percent of each loan granted has returned to the bank's vault, given that the final recipients of that proportion of funds loaned are customers of the bank.

Therefore, a balance sheet drawn up according to the continental system would look like this:

(25)

Bank A
Balance Sheet
c=0.1 and *k=0.2*

Assets		Liabilities	
Cash	121,952	Demand deposits 1,219,512	
Loans	1,097,560		
Total Assets	1,219,512	Total Liabilities	1,219,512

THE CASE OF A VERY SMALL BANK

Let us now consider a particular type of isolated bank: a very small or "Lilliputian" bank; that is, one in which $k=0$.

(29)

Bank A
Balance Sheet
(By the continental system)
$c=0.1\ k=0.2$

Assets		Liabilities	
Cash	121,824	Demand deposits	1,218,232
Loans	1,096,408		
Total Assets	1,218,232	Total Liabilities	1,218,232

These figures are practically identical to those in balance sheet (25). They do not match exactly because our example stops at the third repetition of the loan-deposit process. If we had continued to follow the process, the numbers in balance sheet (29) would have become more and more similar to those in (25), and they eventually would have matched exactly.

This means borrowers immediately withdraw the entire amount of their loans, and those to whom they make payments are not customers of the same bank as the borrowers. If $k=0$, then by substituting this value into formula [3] we obtain formula [5]:

[5] $$x = d(1 - c)$$

And since in our example $d = 1,000,000$ m.u. and $c = 0.1$, then:

$x = 1,000,000(1 - 0.1) = 1,000,000 \cdot 0.9 = 900,000$ m.u.

This is precisely the sum of deposits or fiduciary media created *ex nihilo* which appears in entries (11) and (18). Nevertheless, we saw in the last section that in practice, even if k is only slightly larger than 0, an isolated bank can create a considerably larger amount of fiduciary media. (If $k=0.2$, it can create 22 percent more, or 1,097,560 m.u. instead of the 900,000 m.u. in the first example.) This is true whether the bank uses the continental accounting system or the Anglo-Saxon system, and the sum created may even exceed the total of original deposits in the isolated bank.

With this in mind, it is easy to understand why banks compete as fiercely as they do to attract the largest possible number of deposits and customers. Bankers try to obtain as much money as possible in the form of deposits, because they are capable of expanding credit for an even greater amount than the volume of their deposits. Thus, the greater the volume, the more the bank will be able to expand the corresponding credit. Bankers try to attract as many customers as they can, because the more customers they have, the larger k will be; and the larger k is, the greater their capacity to expand loans and generate deposits. Most importantly, bankers are technically unable to discern whether their growth policies lead to a broadening of their individual spheres of activity at the expense of other banks, or whether their policies ultimately result in a generalized increase in credit expansion involving the entire banking system, or whether both occur at once.

Banks expand credit and deposits on their own and also participate in processes which bring about even greater credit and deposit expansion in the banking system as a whole. Moreover, in this process banks strive to play an increasingly important role with respect to other banks, and as a result they continually provide fresh impetus to credit expansion on the level of individual banks and in the banking system as a whole. In any case, k is a crucial factor in determining a bank's earning power. Competition between banks keeps k significantly below 1, however each bank fights to continually raise the value of its k factor. To do so banks take advantage of their opportunities (with respect to geographic expansion, the ability to exclude or take over competitors and the development of competitive advantages).[25] Though a k factor equal to one is impossible for an isolated bank (except in the case of a monopolistic bank), k values significantly greater than zero are very common, and under almost all circumstances, banks make a supreme effort to increase k. Among other phenomena, this explains the constant pressure they face to merge with other banks.

For illustrative purposes, we have compiled the following table of different combinations of reserve ratios, c, and percentages of loans unused or customers banking with the same institution, k, which allow an isolated bank to alone double its money supply (by substituting these values into formula [3], we obtain $x=d$).

Reserve ratio "c"   Percentage of loans unused "k"

$$k = \frac{c}{1-c} \quad (x = d = 1)$$

---

[25]In some cases banks even pay interest to their checking-account holders in order to attract and keep new deposits. As a result, they ultimately reduce the large profit margins reflected in entry (15). This does not affect our essential argument nor banks' capacity to create deposits, their main source of profit. In the words of Mises, in this competitive process "some banks have gone too far and endangered their solvency." Mises, *Human Action*, p. 464.

2 percent	2.04 percent
5 percent	5.26 percent
7 percent	7.52 percent
13 percent	14.94 percent
15 percent	17.64 percent
17 percent	20.48 percent
20 percent	25.00 percent

CREDIT EXPANSION AND *EX NIHILO* DEPOSIT CREATION BY A SOLE, MONOPOLISTIC BANK

Let us now suppose that $k=1$. We are dealing either with a sole, monopolistic bank in which borrowers are obliged, because there is no other, to maintain as deposits all funds they are lent; or a situation exists in which all final recipients of payments made by borrowers of the bank are also clients of the bank. (This "ideal" goal would be reached at the merger of all remaining megabanks.) When we substitute the value $k=1$ into formula [3], we obtain:

$$[6] \qquad x = \frac{d\,(1-c)}{c}$$

Returning to our example in which $d=1,000,000$ m.u. and $c=0.1$, if we substitute these values into the formula, we obtain:

$$[7] \quad x = \frac{1,000,000\,(1-0.1)}{0.1} = \frac{1,000,000 \cdot 0.9}{0.1} = \frac{900,000}{0.1} = 9,000,000 \; m.u.$$

In this case, the bank could alone create *ex nihilo* loans and deposits or fiduciary media for the sum of 9,000,000 m.u., which means it could multiply its total money supply by ten (1,000,000 m.u. originally deposited, plus 9,000,000 m.u. in the form of fiduciary media or deposits created from nothing to back the loans granted by the bank).

Following the example of Bresciani-Turroni,[26] and assuming all payment transactions are carried out between customers of the same bank (given that it is monopolistic, or because certain circumstances exist which produce this situation), we will now use accounting records to show the process leading to this result.

We will now follow the traditional continental system (as opposed to the Anglo-Saxon) in which all payments are registered in the cash account. The following represents the journal at moments t_1, t_2, t_3, ... t_9, etc., and reflects the bank's practice of repetitively granting its own clients loans for an amount equal to 90 percent of the funds it receives in cash. The clients withdraw the full amount of the loan, but because they have no account in any other bank (or there is no other bank in society), they ultimately deposit the money they receive back into the same bank. This permits the bank, in turn, to grant new loans and generate new deposits, and the process is repeated again and again:

(30)

Bank A
(Journal of the year's operations)

Debit	Credit	
t_1 1,000,000 Cash	Demand deposits	
	made by Mr. X	1,000,000
t_2 900,000 Loans to U	Cash	900,000

Let us suppose that U withdraws the entire amount of his loan and pays his creditor, A. A is also a customer of U's bank and deposits the 900,000 m.u. he receives. The following entries result:

---

[26]Bresciani-Turroni, *Curso de economía*, vol. 2: *Problemas de economía política*, pp. 133–38.

t_3 900,000 Cash	Demand deposits made by A	900,000
t_4 810,000 Loans to V	Cash	810,000

We will assume that Borrower V withdraws his money and pays Creditor B, who is also a customer of the bank and deposits his money back into it. This repetitive process continues, producing the following journal entries:

t_5 810,000 Cash	Demand deposits made by B	810,000
t_6 729,000 Loans to Y	Cash	729,000
t_7 729,000 Cash	Demand deposits made by C	729,000
t_8 656,000 Loans to Z	Cash	656,000
t_9 656,000 Cash	Demand deposits made by D	656,000

This occurs again and again, until at the end of the year the bank's total deposits equal:

[8]

$$1,000,000 + 1,000,000 \times 0.9 + 1,000,000 \times 0.9^2 + 1,000,000 \times 0.9^3 + 1,000,000 \times 0.9^4 + ... = 1,000,000(1 + 0.9 + 0.9^2 + 0.9^3 + 0.9^4 + ...)$$

The above expression represents the sum of the terms in a geometrical progression. The terms increase and have a common ratio of 0.9.[27]

In our example, $r=0.9$ and $a=1,000,000$ m.u., and hence the sum of the terms would be equal to:

$$[13] \quad \frac{a}{1-r} = \frac{1,000,000}{1-0.9} = \frac{1,000,000}{0.1} = 10,000,000 \text{ m.u.}$$

---

[27]The sum of the sequence:

[9] $Sn = a + ar + ar^2 \ldots + ar^{n-1}$; if multiplied by the common ratio r, is:

[10] $rSn = ar + ar^2 + ar^3 \ldots + ar^{n-1} + ar^n$; by subtracting [10] from [9], we obtain:

$Sn - rSn = a - ar^n$; and factoring out the common factor on both sides:

$Sn(1-r) = a(1-r^n)$; then we isolate Sn:

$$[11] \quad Sn = \frac{a(1-r^n)}{1-r} \text{ ; and when } r < 1, \ r^n \text{ approaches } 0$$

$$\text{and the } \lim_{n \to \infty} Sn = \lim_{n \to \infty} \frac{a(1-r^n)}{1-r} = \frac{a}{1-r} \text{ ; if } |r| < 1.$$

Therefore we may conclude that:

$$[12] \quad Sn = \frac{a}{1-r} \text{ ; if } |r| < 1$$

The Greek sophist Zeno was the first to pose the problem of adding the terms in a sequence with a common ratio less than one. He addressed the problem in the fifth century B.C., posing the well-known question of whether or not the athlete Achilles would be able to catch the turtle. The problem was not satisfactorily solved, however, because Zeno failed to realize that infinite series with a common ratio less than one have a convergent sum (not a divergent sum, like he believed). See *The Concise Encyclopedia of Mathematics*, W. Gellert, H. Kustner, M. Hellwich and H. Kastner, eds. (New York: Van Nostrand, 1975), p. 388.

If we keep in mind that d represents the 1,000,000 m.u. originally deposited, and that $r=1-c$; that is, $r=1-0.1=0.9$, then clearly the sum of all the bank's deposits (original and secondary) would be:

[14] $$\frac{d}{1-(1-c)} = \frac{d}{c}$$

Thus, the total volume of deposits in a monopolistic bank (or in a bank where all those who receive money from the bank's borrowers also ultimately have their accounts) would be equal to the value of the original deposits, d, divided by the reserve ratio, c.

Formula [14] is the simplest version of the so-called *bank multiplier*, and it is identical to formula [27], which yields the same result for a banking system of multiple small banks and appears to have been worked out for the first time by Alfred Marshall in 1887.[28]

We could use the following formula to calculate the net credit expansion the bank brings about *ex nihilo* (in other

---

[28]This is how Marshall describes the procedure which led him to this formula:

> I should consider what part of its deposits a bank could lend, and then I should consider what part of its loans would be redeposited with it and with other banks and, vice versa, what part of the loans made by other banks would be received by it as deposits. Thus I should get a geometrical progression; the effect being that if each bank could lend two-thirds of its deposits, the total amount of loaning power got by the banks would amount to three times what it otherwise would be. If it could lend four-fifths, it will then be five times; and so on. The question how large a part of its deposits a bank can lend depends in a great measure on the extent on which the different banks directly or indirectly pool their reserves. But this reasoning, I think, has never been worked out in public, and it is very complex. (Alfred Marshall, "Memoranda and Evidence before the Gold and Silver Commission," December 19, 1887, in *Official Papers by Alfred Marshall* [London: Royal Economic Society, Macmillan, 1926], p. 37)

words, the deposits or fiduciary media generated from nothing to make the credit expansion possible):

[15] $x = \dfrac{d}{c} - d = \dfrac{d}{c} - \dfrac{dc}{c}$

Now we factor out common factors:

[16] $x = \dfrac{d(1-c)}{c}$

The above formula coincides with [6].

In fact, when $d=1,000,000$ m.u. and $c=0.1$, in the case of a monopolistic bank, the net credit expansion would be equal to:

[17] $x = \dfrac{1,000,000(1-0.1)}{0.1} = 9,000,000$ m.u.

Therefore the balance sheet of Bank A, a monopolistic bank, would ultimately appear as follows:

(31)

Bank A
(Monopolist)
Balance Sheet

Assets		Liabilities	
Cash	1,000,000	Demand deposits	
Loans to U	900,000	By X	1,000,000
Loans to V	810,000	By A	900,000
Loans to Y	729,000	By B	810,000
Loans to Z	656,000	By C	729,000
.	.	By D	656,000
.	.	.	.
.	.	.	.
Total Assets	10,000,000	Total Liabilities	10,000,000

With only 1,000,000 m.u. in original deposits safeguarded in its vault, Bank A, a monopolist, has expanded credit by granting loans for the sum of 9,000,000 m.u. and creating from nothing 9,000,000 m.u. in new deposits or fiduciary media to back these loans.[29]

5

CREDIT EXPANSION AND NEW DEPOSIT CREATION BY THE ENTIRE BANKING SYSTEM

We have already observed the great capacity isolated banks have for creating fiduciary loans and deposits. In fact, they are normally able to double their money supply on their own. We will now see how the fractional-reserve banking system as a whole generates *ex nihilo* a much larger volume of

---

[29]Also relevant is the formula for the maximum credit expansion an isolated bank can bring about based not on the money it receives in original deposits, but on the reserves it holds, r, in excess of the required amount, cd. In this case, the decrease in reserves which results from the new expansion $x(1 - k)$ must be equal to the excess reserves, r, minus the reserve ratio corresponding to the portion of loans unused, $k \cdot c \cdot x$. In other words:

[18] $(1 - k)x = r - k \cdot c \cdot x$

$k \cdot c \cdot x + (1 - k)x = r$

$x(kc + 1 - k) = r$

[19] $\quad x = \dfrac{r}{kc + 1 - k}$

If, as in our example, we suppose that an original deposit of 1,000,000 m.u. is made, $c=0.1$ and $k=0.2$, the excess of reserves is precisely $r=900,000$, and therefore:

[20] $\quad x = \dfrac{900,000}{0.2 \cdot 0.1 + 1 - 0.2} = \dfrac{900,000}{1.02 - 0.2} = \dfrac{900,000}{0.82} = 1,097,560 \; m.u.$

This, of course, is exactly the same result we obtained with formula [4].

deposits and brings about much greater credit expansion. Indeed, in this respect the fractional-reserve system produces effects resembling those of a monopolistic bank. We will base our demonstration on the most general case, a banking system comprised of a group of normal banks, each of which maintains cash reserves, c, of 10 percent. Also, on average, the customers of each fail to withdraw 20 percent of loans granted (or 20 percent of fiduciary media return to the bank because a significant number of the final recipients are also clients of the bank). Hence, $k=20$ percent.

Let us suppose that Mr. X deposits 1,000,000 m.u. in Bank A. The bank would then make the following entry in its journal:

Bank A

(32) Debit	Credit
1,000,000 Cash	Demand deposits 1,000,000 (made by X)

Bank A would then be able to create and grant loans to Z for a sum determined by the formula in [3]. The following entry would result:

Bank A

(33) Debit	Credit
1,097,560 Loans to Z	Demand deposits 1,097,560

And since $k=0.2$, 80 percent of loans granted would be withdrawn, resulting in the following entry:

Bank A

(34) Debit		Credit	
878,048	Demand deposits	Cash	878,048

The balance sheet of Bank A following these entries would look like this:

(35)

Bank A
Balance Sheet
c=0.1 and k=0.2

Assets		Liabilities	
Cash	121,952	Demand deposits	1,219,512
Loans	1,097,560		
Total Assets	1,219,512	Total Liabilities	1,219,512

Let us suppose that when Z withdraws his deposit he pays Y, who is a customer of Bank B and deposits the money there. Three entries parallel to the above three would result. Formula [3] would again be used to determine the amounts.

Bank B

(36) Debit		Credit	
878,048	Cash	Demand deposits (made by Y)	878,048
963,710	Loans to V	Demand deposits	963,710
770,969	Demand deposits	Cash	770,969

After these operations, Bank B's balance sheet would appear as follows:

(37)

Bank B
Balance Sheet
$c=0.1$ and $k=0.2$

Assets		Liabilities	
Cash	107,079	Demand deposits	1,070,789
Loans	963,710		
Total Assets	1,070,789	Total Liabilities	1,070,789

If we imagine that V pays his debts to U, who in turn deposits the money he receives in his bank, Bank C, then the following journal entries would result:

Bank C

(38) Debit		Credit	
770,969	Cash	Demand deposits (made by U)	770,969
846,185	Loans to R	Demand deposits	846,185
676,948	Demand deposits	Cash	676,948

The bank would make this last entry when R withdraws 80 percent ($k=0.2$) of his loan from Bank C to pay his creditors (T, for example).

Once these operations have been completed, Bank C's balance sheet would appear as follows:

(39)

Bank C
Balance Sheet
c=0.1 and *k=0.2*

Assets		Liabilities	
Cash	94,021	Demand deposits	940,206
Loans	846,185		
Total Assets	940,206	Total Liabilities	940,206

And if Creditor T, upon receiving the money he was owed, deposits it in his own bank, Bank D, these entries would result:

(40)

Bank D

Debit		Credit	
676,948	Cash	Demand deposits (made by T)	676,948
742,992	Loans to S	Demand deposits	742,992
594,393	Demand deposits	Cash	594,393

The bank would make this last entry in its journal when S pays his creditors.

At this point, Bank D's balance sheet would appear as follows:

(41)   Bank D
                                      Balance Sheet
                                      c=0.1 and k=0.2

Assets		Liabilities	
Cash	82,555	Demand deposits	825,547
Loans	742,992		
Total Assets	825,547	Total Liabilities	825,547

The process continues in this way, and the chain of deposits and loans extends to all banks in the system. Once the effects of the original deposit of 1,000,000 m.u. have completely disappeared, the total deposits created by the banking system would be the sum of the following sequence:

[21]

$1{,}219{,}512 + 1{,}219{,}512 \times 0.878 + 1{,}219{,}512 \times 0.878^2 + \dots$

$$= a + ar + ar^2 + \dots = \sum_{n=0}^{\infty} ar^n; \text{ where } a = 1{,}219{,}512$$

and the common ratio $r = (1 - k)\ \dfrac{(1 - c)}{1 + k(c - 1)}$

This is due to the fact that, in our example, r would be equal to 80 percent $(1 - k)$ of the proportion of deposits newly created by each bank at each stage. This proportion comes from formula [3] and is equal to:

$$\frac{(1 - c)}{1 + k(c - 1)}$$

Therefore: [22]

$$r = (1 - 0.2)\ \frac{1 - 0.1}{1 + 0.2(0.1 - 1)} = 0.8 \cdot \frac{0.9}{1 + 0.2(0.1 - 1)} = \frac{0.72}{1 - 0.18}$$

$$r = \frac{0.72}{0.82} = 0.87804878$$

And since $|r| < 1$, we apply formulas [11] and [12].

$$[23] \quad \sum_{n=0}^{\infty} ar^n = \frac{a}{1-r} = \frac{1{,}219{,}512}{0.1219512} = 10{,}000{,}000 \text{ m.u.}$$

Thus the sum of the deposits in the banking system, D, would be equal to:

$$[24] \quad D = \frac{ds_1}{1 - \dfrac{(1-k)(1-c)}{1 + k(c-1)}} = 10{,}000{,}000 \text{ m.u.}$$

In this example, ds_1 represents Bank A's secondary deposits and equals 1,219,512 m.u.

The net credit expansion, x, brought about by the entire banking system would equal:

$$[25] \quad x = D - d = 10{,}000{,}000 - 1{,}000{,}000 = 9{,}000{,}000$$

A summary of these results appears in Table IV-1 and Chart IV-1. Details are given for each member bank in the banking system.

CREATION OF LOANS IN A SYSTEM OF SMALL BANKS

Let us now suppose that all the banks in the system are very small. They each have a k equal to zero and a c equal to 0.1. If we follow the pattern of past entries, the journal entries for this banking system would look like this:

TABLE IV-1
SYSTEM OF "NORMAL"-SIZED BANKS
(k=0.2 and c=0.1)

	Money remaining in each bank's vault	Credit expansion (Loans created ex nihilo)	Deposits
Bank A	122,000	1,098,000	1,220,000
Bank B	107,100	964,000	1,071,000
Bank C	94,000	846,000	940,000
Bank D	82,600	743,000	826,000
Bank E	72,500	652,000	725,000
Bank F	63,700	573,000	637,000
Bank G	55,900	503,000	559,000
Bank H	49,100	442,000	491,000
Bank I	43,000	387,000	430,000
Bank J	37,800	340,000	378,000
· ·	·	·	·
· ·	·	·	·

Banking System totals $d=1,000,000$ $x=D-d=9,000,000$ $D=10,000,000$

Note: The last three digits have been rounded.

When a demand deposit of 1,000,000 m.u. is made at Bank A:

Bank A

(42) Debit	Credit
1,000,000 Cash	Demand deposits 1,000,000
900,000 Loans to Z	Demand deposits 900,000
900,000 Demand deposits	Cash 900,000

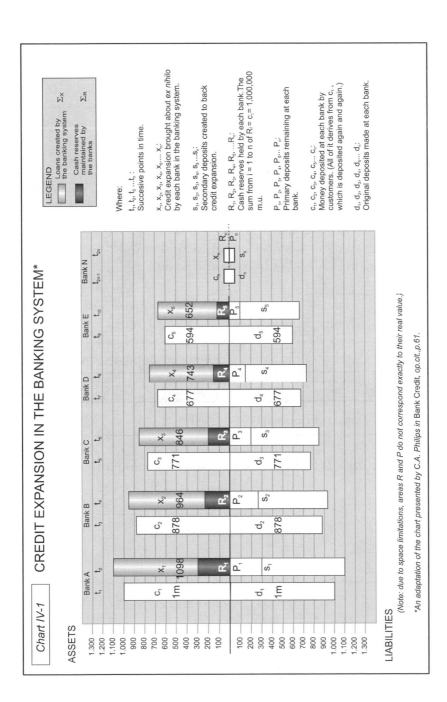

Chart IV-1   CREDIT EXPANSION IN THE BANKING SYSTEM*

LEGEND

☐ Loans created by the banking system Σ_x

■ Cash reserves maintained by the banks Σ_R

Where:

$t_1, t_2, t_3 \ldots t_n$:
Succesive points in time.

$x_1, x_2, x_3, x_4, x_5 \ldots x_n$:
Credit expansion brought about *ex nihilo* by each bank in the banking system.

$s_1, s_2, s_3, s_4, s_5 \ldots s_n$:
Secondary deposits created to back credit expansion.

$R_1, R_2, R_3, R_4, R_5 \ldots R_n$:
Cash reserves held by each bank. The sum from $i = 1$ to n of $R_i = c_i = 1,000,000$ m.u.

$P_1, P_2, P_3, P_4, P_5 \ldots P_n$:
Primary deposits remaining at each bank.

$c_1, c_2, c_3, c_4, c_5 \ldots c_n$:
Money deposited at each bank by customers. (All of it derives from c_1, which is deposited again and again.)

$d_1, d_2, d_3, d_4, d_5 \ldots d_n$:
Original deposits made at each bank.

(Note: due to space limitations, areas R and P do not correspond exactly to their real value.)

*An adaptation of the chart presented by C.A. Philips in Bank Credit, op.cit.,p.61.

When Z withdraws 900,000 m.u. to pay Y, Bank A's balance sheet would appear as follows:

(43)   Bank A
                                Balance Sheet
                                $c=0.1$ and $k=0$

Assets		Liabilities	
Cash	100,000	Demand deposits	1,000,000
Loans to Z	900,000		
Total Assets	1,000,000	Total Liabilities	1,000,000

If Y, in turn, deposits the 900,000 m.u. in his bank, Bank B, also a small bank with a k equal to zero and a c equal to 0.1, the following journal entries would result:

Bank B

(44) Debit	Credit	
900,000 Cash	Demand deposits	900,000
810,000 Loans to V	Demand deposits	810,000
810,000 Demand deposit	Cash	810,000

And Bank B's balance sheet would look like this:

(45)   Bank B
                                Balance Sheet
                                $c=0.1$ and $k=0$

Assets		Liabilities	
Cash	90,000	Demand deposits	900,000
Loans to V	810,000		
Total Assets	900,000	Total Liabilities	900,000

Now, if V withdraws the loan from his bank to pay U, and U deposits the money in his bank, Bank C, also a small bank with a k equal to zero and a c equal to 0.1, these would be Bank C's entries:

Bank C

(46)	Debit	Credit	
810,000 Cash		Demand deposits	810,000
729,000 Loans to T		Demand deposits	729,000
729,000 Demand deposits		Cash	729,000

And Bank C's balance sheet would look like this:

(47)

Bank C
Balance Sheet
$c=0.1$ and $k=0$

Assets		Liabilities	
Cash	81,000	Demand deposits	810,000
Loans to T	729,000		
Total Assets	810,000	Total Liabilities	810,000

When T pays his creditor, S, and S deposits the money in his bank, Bank D, also small, with a k equal to zero and a c equal to 0.1, the following entries would result:

Bank D

(48) Debit	Credit
729,000 Cash	Demand deposits 729,000
656,100 Loans	Demand deposits 656,100
656,100 Demand deposits	Cash 656,100

In turn, Bank D's balance sheet would appear as follows:

(49)

Bank D
Balance Sheet
c=0.1 and k=0

Assets		Liabilities	
Cash	72,900	Demand deposits	729,000
Loans to T	656,100		
Total Assets	729,000	Total Liabilities	729,000

The total deposits in a system of very small banks is equal to the sum of a sequence identical to the one in formula [8], which referred to a monopolistic bank:

[26] $1,000,000 + 1,000,000 \times 0.9 + 1,000,000 \times 0.9^2 +$

$$1,000,000 \times 0.9^3 + \ldots = \sum_{n=0}^{\infty} ar^n;$$

where $a=1,000,000$ and $r=0.9$.

As shown in footnote 27, this sum is in turn equal to:

$$\frac{a}{1-r} = \frac{a}{1-(1-c)} = \frac{a}{c} = \frac{1,000,000}{0.1} = 10,000,000 \text{ m.u.}$$

As $a=d=1,000,000$ m.u. originally deposited, the total deposits would be indicated by the formula:

[27] $$\frac{d}{1-(1-c)} = \frac{d}{c}$$

This formula is identical to the deposit multiplier in the case of a single, monopolistic bank [14].

Let us also remember that:

[28] $$r = (1-k) \frac{1-c}{1+k(c-1)}$$

In view of the fact that the banking system is in this case composed of small banks and $k=0$, if we substitute this value for k in formula [28], we obtain $r=1-c=0.9$, which we already knew.

Therefore, an entire banking system comprised of small banks brings about a volume of deposits (10,000,000 m.u.) and a net credit expansion (9,000,000 m.u.) identical to those of a monopolistic bank for which $k=1$. These results are summarized in Table IV-2.

A system of small banks (where $k=0$) is clearly an exception within the overall banking system (where k is less than 1 but greater than 0). However, it is an easy example to understand and therefore in textbooks is generally the model used to explain the creation of credit money by the financial system.[30]

---

[30]See, for example, Juan Torres López, *Introducción a la economía política* (Madrid: Editorial Cívitas, 1992), pp. 236–39; and José Casas Pardo, *Curso de economía*, 5th ed. (Madrid, 1985), pp. 864–66.

TABLE IV-2
SYSTEM OF SMALL BANKS
(k=0 and c=0.1)

	Money remaining in each bank's vault	Credit expansion (Loans created ex nihilo)	Deposits
Bank A	100,000	900,000	1,000,000
Bank B	90,000	810,000	900,000
Bank C	81,000	729,000	810,000
Bank D	72,900	656,000	729,000
Bank E	65,600	590,000	656,000
Bank F	59,000	531,000	590,000
Bank G	53,100	478,000	531,000
Bank H	47,800	430,000	478,000
Bank I	43,000	387,000	430,000
Bank J	38,700	348,000	387,000
· ·	·	·	·

Banking
System totals d=1,000,000 $x = \dfrac{d(1-c)}{c} = 9{,}000{,}000$ $\dfrac{d}{c} = 10{,}000{,}000$

Note: The last three digits have been rounded.

It is also true that a banking system composed of one monopolistic bank (when k=1) is a unique instance within the broader category of isolated banks which expand deposits and loans.

To conclude, two particular cases lead to identical results regarding new loans created (9,000,000 m.u.) and the total volume of deposits (10,000,000 m.u.). The first case is a banking system made up of tiny banks, each with a k equal to zero. The second is an isolated bank with a k equal to one. Given that both cases are easy to comprehend, they are generally chosen as examples in textbooks to explain the creation of loans and the volume of deposits generated by the banking system.

Depending upon the text, the author refers either to a system of tiny banks or to a single, monopolistic bank (or one whose customers are the final recipients of the loans it grants).[31]

6

A Few Additional Difficulties

When Expansion is Initiated Simultaneously by All Banks

In light of the fact that in this context we are forced to offer a simplified view of the processes of credit expansion, it is now necessary to make a few supplementary points and clarifications. To begin with, the expansion process we have described originates entirely from an increase in money deposited at the original bank (in our example, *d* represents 1,000,000 m.u. deposited in Bank A). Nevertheless, both historically, as banking developed, and currently, all processes of credit expansion have been characterized by the fact that the new money reaches the banking system not through one single bank, but through many (if not, to a larger or smaller extent, through all the banks in the system). As Richard G. Lipsey reveals,[32] credit expansion such as we have described, which takes place *ex nihilo* and is backed by the creation of the necessary bank deposits, *will recur as often as 1,000,000 m.u. are deposited in any of the different banks. Therefore, the widespread expansion process is, in practice, much more substantial and qualitatively more complicated, since it originates simultaneously at many banks and from many deposits.* In our example alone, which involved a reserve ratio of 10 percent, loans for the sum of 9,000,000 m.u. were ultimately created, an amount nine times larger than the original deposit, and as a result the total money supply was multiplied by ten. The main conclusion to be drawn is that if all banks simultaneously receive new deposits of money, they will be able to

---

[31]This is the example Bresciani-Turroni prefers to follow in his book, *Curso de economía*, vol. 2, pp. 133–38.

[32]Richard G. Lipsey, *An Introduction to Positive Economics*, 2nd ed. (London: Weidenfeld and Nicolson, 1966), pp. 682–83.

expand credit without having to decrease their cash reserves, because although they grant loans which could lead to a withdrawal of cash (as we have supposed up until now in the accounting entries), they simultaneously receive the deposit of a portion of the money loaned by other banks. Hence *in practice, significant decreases in each bank's reserves will not necessarily occur, and each bank, while maintaining its reserves practically intact, will be able to make loans and therefore create deposits without serious risk.*

This theoretical argument has prompted various authors, among them Murray N. Rothbard,[33] to write about the process of credit expansion in the banking system from the viewpoint that an isolated bank does not lose reserves when it grants new loans. Instead, while maintaining the volume of its reserves intact, it makes every attempt to make new loans for a multiple determined by the inverse of the reserve ratio. The argument for explaining the bank multiplier in this way, even in the case of an isolated bank, is that the bank will attempt to avoid reducing its reserves in the process of granting loans (i.e., the banker will not wish to keep 100,000 m.u. and loan 900,000). Instead, it is much more advantageous for the bank to maintain its reserve ratio by loaning a much larger amount of money and keeping the initial cash reserves unaltered (that is, by holding 1,000,000 m.u. in cash and creating *ex nihilo* 9,000,000 m.u. in new loans). In practice, the level of cash reserves can be ensured if the credit expansion process takes place *simultaneously* at all banks. This is because the decrease in cash a bank experiences upon granting loans will tend to be compensated for by the reception of new deposits originating in loans made by other banks.

When the expansion process is presented in this way, it is not often easily understood by nonspecialists, nor even by professionals in the banking sector, who are accustomed to considering their "business" mere intermediation between depositors and borrowers. However, clear evidence that the

---

[33]Rothbard, *The Mystery of Banking*, chap. 8, pp. 111–24.

approach of Rothbard and others is totally correct lies in the fact that for our purposes it makes no difference whether we study the case examined up to this point (an original deposit, extended throughout the banking system, of 1,000,000 m.u. in Bank A), or we consider a banking system comprised of ten banks, each of which simultaneously receives a deposit of 100,000 m.u. (i.e., a total of 1,000,000 m.u. divided among ten banks). In the latter case, each bank will keep unaltered 100,000 m.u. in cash, making it possible for the banks to expand their loans and create *ex nihilo* new fiduciary media for the sum of 900,000 m.u. Each bank will be able to maintain stable cash reserves of 100,000 m.u. if possible reductions in these reserves as the result of loans granted are offset by new deposits originating from loans made by other banks. Therefore if all of the banks bring about expansion simultaneously, each one is able to maintain its cash reserves unaltered, and with a reserve ratio of 0.1, create from nothing, in the form of loans backed by new fiduciary media, up to nine times its initial deposits. Let us examine this process of simultaneous expansion in terms of accounting entries.

We will assume that each of ten banks receives 1,000,000 m.u. in new, original deposits of money. The ten banks are all of the same size, and each has a reserve ratio, c, of 10 percent, and (to keep it simple) a k equal to zero. Let us also suppose that each bank has a market share of 10 percent. In other words, each bank receives the business of 10 percent of all the customers in the market in which it operates. Moreover, these customers are randomly distributed. If these banks simultaneously begin to expand credit according to the process described in entries (42) and following, it is obvious that any one of them, for example Bank A, will eventually receive deposits coming from loans granted by the other banks, as shown in Table IV-2. If all of the banks expand credit simultaneously, Bank A's journal entries would appear as follows:

(50)

Bank A

Debit	Credit
1,000,000 Cash	Demand deposits 1,000,000
900,000 Loans	Demand deposits 900,000
900,000 Demand deposits	Cash 900,000

This decrease in cash would be counteracted by a demand deposit from a final recipient of a loan granted, for example, by Bank B, resulting in the following entries:

(51)

Bank A

Debit	Credit
900,000 Cash	Demand deposits from loans granted by Bank B 900,000
810,000 Loans	Demand deposits 810,000
810,000 Demand deposits	Cash 810,000

Bank A would eventually recuperate these 810,000 m.u. in the form of a deposit originating from loans granted, for example, by Bank C. The journal entries would look like this:

(52)   Bank A

Debit	Credit
810,000 Cash	Demand deposits from loans granted by Bank C 810,000
729,000 Loans	Demand deposits 729,000
729,000 Demand deposits	Cash 729,000

As this process continues, Bank A would receive deposits from the recipients of loans granted by Banks D, E, F, G, H, I, and J. We have greatly simplified the process in our explanation. In reality, the bank receives, on average, 10 percent of the ten loans of 900,000 m.u. granted in the first stage by each bank in the system. It then receives 10 percent of the ten loans of 810,000 m.u. made by each of the banks in the second phase, 10 percent of the ten loans of 729,000 m.u. made by each in the third phase, etc.

Hence, if we suppose that each of ten banks receives 1,000,000 m.u. in original deposits, and the banks expand credit simultaneously, the balance sheet of any of them, Bank A, for instance, would appear as follows:

(53)   Bank A
                         Balance Sheet
                         $c=0.1$ and $k=0$

Assets		Liabilities	
Cash	1,000,000	Demand deposits (primary)	1,000,000
Loans	9,000,000	Demand deposits (secondary)	9,000,000
Total Assets	10,000,000	Total Liabilities	10,000,000

Therefore, the balance sheet of each bank would coincide with the one we discovered when we assumed k was equal to one (a monopolistic bank or one whose clients are the ultimate recipients of the loans it grants). This is due to the fact that although in this case there is no monopoly, the loss of cash each bank initially experiences upon expanding credit is eventually offset by deposits originating in loans expanded by the other banks.

We may conclude from balance sheet (53) that each banker need not reduce his cash reserves to expand his bank's credit; instead, if the rest of his colleagues expand their credit at the same time, he can maintain his level of cash reserves unaltered and proceed directly to grant loans for a sum equal to a multiple of his reserves. (In our case, each banker holds 1,000,000 m.u. in cash reserves and creates from nothing 9,000,000 m.u. in loans backed by 9,000,000 m.u. in secondary deposits.) Therefore Rothbard's interpretation of the process is correct even in the case of an isolated bank, when each of the other banks in the system also receive original deposits (that is, a proportional amount of the new money created in the system) and all expand their credit simultaneously. The cash each bank would theoretically lose by granting loans is counteracted by deposits received from recipients of loans expanded by the banker's colleagues. Thus each bank can alone expand its credit for the sum of 9,000,000 m.u. In turn, the system's total expansion would be equal to 90,000,000 m.u., and the amount of total deposits or the money supply would be 100,000,000 m.u.

We can achieve numerical results identical to those in Table IV-2 simply by supposing that an original deposit of 1,000,000 m.u. is made at Bank A and is divided equally among the ten banks in the system, each of which receives 100,000 m.u. Those 100,000 m.u. would remain unaltered in each bank's vault. Each bank could expand its credit by 900,000 m.u., and therefore the entire banking system could generate 9,000,000 m.u. in new loans and a total of 10,000,000 m.u. in primary and secondary deposits.

Obviously this last example, which wraps up our accounting analysis of the expansion of loans and deposits by isolated banks and banking systems, is the most realistic. In the current monetary system, increases in the money supply filter throughout the system and reach practically all banks, permitting them to expand their credit simultaneously according to the processes we have studied. In addition, there are clear historical indications that banks have never emerged alone, but in groups. Even Saravia de la Calle mentions that bankers established themselves in groups, offering "guarantors and acting as guarantors for each other."[34] This means that by the time of the sixteenth-century Castilian markets, bankers were already aware of the intimate relationship and strong community of interests uniting them in terms of the success or failure of their businesses, and they realized they needed to support one another mutually.

With respect to the gold standard and a money supply based on the discovery of new gold mines and on the development of extraction techniques, we can assume that new money originating from substantial, new discoveries would initially reach only a few bankers, and from there it would extend throughout the rest of the banking system. Therefore, it would not set off a process of simultaneous expansion, but a gradual process by which the money would filter throughout the entire system.

We can conclude that if there are many banks and many new deposits, and the banks expand their credit simultaneously following the processes we have studied, even an isolated bank will be able to maintain a stable level of reserves and by itself expand loans and deposits for a multiple of this level, an amount determined by the inverse of the reserve ratio (when $k=0$).[35] Therefore it is obviously only in the

---

[34]Saravia de la Calle, *Instrucción de mercaderes*, p. 180.

[35]Under these circumstances, which most closely resemble actual market conditions, Phillips's statement loses credibility. In his words (*Credit Banking*, p. 64), "It follows for the banking system that deposits are chiefly the offspring of loans. For an individual bank, loans are the offspring of deposits." This second affirmation is the incorrect one under true conditions. This is due to the fact that, given the existence of many

account books that deposits back the wealth bankers appropriate upon expanding their credit. From an accounting (but not a legal) standpoint, the formal ownership of these loans corresponds to the deposit-holders, since under normal circumstances they consider their deposits money (perfect money substitutes) they can use in their transactions without ever having to withdraw them in physical monetary units. Nonetheless, it is clear that the assets generated by the banking system do not actually belong to anyone. To a large extent, however, they could be considered the property of banks' shareholders, directors and administrators, the people who actually take advantage of many of the economic benefits of this wealth, with the additional advantage of not appearing as the owners, since the account books indicate that the depositors own the wealth.

In other words, under normal conditions, deposits come from loans and are merely a secondary result, reflected in the account books, of the wealth banks accumulate and retain indefinitely. We will return to this topic later in the book, in a discussion on banknotes and in the last chapter, where we present our proposal for a process of banking reform.

---

banks and many original deposits, and considering that these banks expand credit simultaneously, the deposits of each individual bank are also a result of the credit expansion carried out by all of the banks in unison. In chapter 8 we will examine the distinct possibility (denied by Selgin) that, even in a free-banking system, all banks might simultaneously initiate credit expansion, even when the volume of primary deposits does not increase in all of them (that is, through a generalized decrease in their cash or reserve ratio). In the same chapter, we will explain, as Mises has done, that in a free-banking system, any bank which unilaterally expands its credit by reducing its cash reserves beyond a prudent level will endanger its own solvency. These two phenomena account for the universal tendency of bankers to agree among themselves to jointly orchestrate (usually through the central bank) a uniform rate of credit expansion.

FILTERING OUT THE MONEY SUPPLY
FROM THE BANKING SYSTEM

Another complexity derives from the fact that in reality, each time loans are granted and deposits are created and withdrawn, a certain percentage of the money supply "filters" out of the system and is kept by individuals who do not wish to deposit it in a bank. The larger the percentage which physically "filters" into the pockets of individuals at each stage and remains outside the banking system, the smaller the bank's expansive capacity to generate new loans.

In a system of small banks (in which $k = 0$) with a reserve requirement of 10 percent ($c = 0.1$), if f refers to the proportion of the money supply that filters out of the banking system and $f = 0.15$, then when Bank A loans 900,000 m.u., the amount of money which would return to the banking system would be equal to $(1 - f)\ 900,000 = (1 - 0.15)\ 900,000 = 0.85 \times 900,000 = 765,000$ m.u. Therefore if we are dealing with a system of small banks and we assume that $k=0$, $c=0.1$ and $f=0.15$, we can use the following formulas:

If D_N refers to the total net deposits, which are comprised of gross deposits, D_G, minus the total sum of money, F, that filters out of the banking system, then:

[29] $$D_N = D_G - F$$

The total sum of money that filters out of the banking system will logically be equal to f times the total sum of gross deposits, D_G, where f is the percentage of money which filters out of the system. That is:

[30] $$F = fD_G$$

In turn, the amount of money initially deposited is equal to the sum of net deposits multiplied by the corresponding reserve ratio plus the total sum which has filtered out of the system:

[31] $$d = D_N \cdot c + F$$

If we substitute into this equation the value of D_N in formula [29] and the value of F in [30], we obtain:

[32] $\qquad d = (D_G - F) \cdot c + fD_G$

If we replace F in the equation with fD_G, we obtain:

[33] $\qquad d = (D_G - fD_G)c + fD_G$

Then we factor out D_G:

[34] $\qquad d = D_G (c - cf + f)$

And therefore:

[35] $\qquad D_G = \dfrac{d}{c - cf + f}$

As $D_N = D_G(1\text{-}f)$,

[36] $\quad D_N = D_G(1 - f) = \dfrac{d(1 - f)}{c - cf + f} = \dfrac{d(1 - f)}{c(1 - f) + f} = \dfrac{d}{c + \dfrac{f}{1 - f}}$

This would be the formula for the net deposits created by the banking system. The credit expansion brought about by a banking system out of which some money filters would be equal to:

[37] $\quad x = D_N - d = \dfrac{d}{c + \dfrac{f}{1 - f}} - d$

If we substitute a value of zero for f in the preceding formulas, we are left with the same equations we have used until now to determine the total volume of deposits and the total credit expansion:

[38] $\quad D_N = \dfrac{d}{c} = \dfrac{1{,}000{,}000}{0.1} = 10{,}000{,}000$

and

[39] $\quad x = \dfrac{d}{c} - d = \dfrac{d(1-c)}{c} = \dfrac{1{,}000{,}000(0.9)}{0.1} = 9{,}000{,}000$

Let us see to what value credit expansion is reduced if, as before, $d = 1{,}000{,}000$ m.u. and $c = 0.1$, while in addition 15 percent of the money supply filters out of the banking system ($f = 0.15$).

[40]

$$D_N = \frac{1{,}000{,}000}{0.1 + \dfrac{0.15}{1 - 0.15}} = \frac{1{,}000{,}000}{0.1 + \dfrac{0.15}{0.85}} = \frac{0.85 \times 1{,}000{,}000}{0.085 + 0.15}$$

$$= \frac{850{,}000}{0.235} = 3{,}617{,}021$$

Hence, in a banking system where 15 percent of the money supply filters out of the system, the total sum of deposits would be 3,617,021 m.u., instead of 10,000,000 m.u., as is the case when $f = 0$.

The net credit expansion would be equal to $x = 3{,}617{,}021$ - 1,000,000 = 2,617,021, instead of the 9,000,000 m.u. which are created when no money filters out of the system. Therefore, when the percentage of money which filters out is greater than zero, the capacity of the banking system to create loans and generate deposits *ex nihilo* decreases noticeably.[36]

---

[36]We have arrived at these formulas following the process described by Armen A. Alchian and William R. Allen in *University Economics* (Belmont, Ca.: Wadsworth Publishing, 1964), pp. 675–76. If the legal reserve requirement were reduced to zero, as is increasingly demanded, the total sum of net deposits, D_N, would be:

THE MAINTENANCE OF RESERVES EXCEEDING THE MINIMUM REQUIREMENT

Another complication which produces effects similar to those covered in the preceding section takes place when banks hold cash reserves exceeding the minimum requirement. This tends to occur at certain stages in the economic cycle in which banks behave relatively more prudently, or they are obliged to increase their reserves due to difficulties in finding enough creditworthy borrowers willing to request loans, or both. This occurs, for example, in the phases of economic recession that follow credit expansion. At any rate, the maintenance of cash reserves exceeding the necessary level reduces the system's capacity for credit expansion in the same way as f, a percentage of the money supply which filters out of the banking system.[37]

$$D_N = \frac{d}{\dfrac{f}{1-f}} = \frac{d(1-f)}{f} = \frac{1,000,000(0.85)}{0.15} = 5,666,667 \text{ m.u.}$$

And the net credit expansion, x:

$$x = D_N - d = 4,666,667 \ m.u.$$

Therefore we must conclude that if no portion of the money supply were to filter out of the system ($f = 0$), and the banking authorities were to eliminate the reserve requirement ($c = 0$), these authorities could drive the volume of credit expansion as high as they chose, since:

$$D_N = \frac{d}{0} = \infty$$

(This expansion would bring about numerous disruptive effects on the real productive structure, on which its impact would be severe. See chapter 5.)

[37]To illustrate how significantly the above factors can contribute to a decrease in the bank expansion multiplier, we must first note that in Spain, for instance, the total money supply consists of about 50 trillion pesetas (166.386 pesetas = 1 euro), which includes cash held by the

DIFFERENT RESERVE REQUIREMENTS FOR DIFFERENT TYPES OF DEPOSITS

Finally, another complication we could consider derives from the fact that in many countries the reserve requirement for demand deposits differs from the requirement for time deposits, even though as we know, in practice the latter are often true demand deposits. Although the formulas we have considered up until now could be worked out again for both deposit types, the degree of complexity involved would not be worth the slight additional value the analysis could afford, so we have chosen not to do so here.[38]

---

public, demand deposits, savings deposits and time deposits. (In the Spanish banking system, despite their name, time deposits are usually true demand deposits, because they can be withdrawn at any time without penalty or with a very small penalty). Of the total money supply, only about 6.6 trillion pesetas are in the form of cash in the hands of the public. This means that a little over 13.2 percent of the total corresponds to this cash held by the public, and therefore the bank expansion multiplier in Spain would be greater than 7.5 times (which would be equal to a reserve ratio of 13.2 percent). Since the current reserve requirement in Spain is 2 percent (from the Bank of Spain's monetary circular 1/1996, October 11, and confirmed afterward by European Central Bank regulations), the difference between that and 13.2 percent can be attributed to the influence of f, the percentage of money which filters out of the system and into the pockets of private citizens. Perhaps the past economic recession has played a role by increasing the volume of cash and deposits held by banks and temporarily reducing their potential for boosting credit expansion. Our comments are based on provisional data from June published in August 1994 in the *Boletín Estadístico del Banco de España*, kindly supplied by Luis Alfonso López García, an inspector from the Bank of Spain.

[38]Nevertheless, the relevant formulas are devised in Laurence S. Ritter and William L. Silber, *Principles of Money, Banking and Financial Markets*, 3rd rev., updated ed. (New York: Basic Books, 1980), pp. 44–46. Other writings which cover in detail the formulation of the bank multiplier theory are: John D. Boorman and Thomas M. Havrilesky, *Money Supply, Money Demand and Macroeconomic Models* (Boston: Allyn and Bacon, 1972), esp. pp. 10–41; Dorothy M. Nichols, *Modern Money Mechanics: A Workbook on Deposits, Currency and Bank Reserves*, published by the Federal Reserve Bank of Chicago, pp. 29–31; and the interesting book by

7

THE PARALLELS BETWEEN THE CREATION OF DEPOSITS
AND THE ISSUANCE OF UNBACKED BANKNOTES

The economic analysis of the issuance of unbacked banknotes, an operation which emerged long after the discovery of
fractional-reserve banking, is not one of the main purposes of
this book.[39] However it could be useful at this point to consider in some detail the accounting and legal aspects of the
issuance of unbacked banknotes, since as we will demonstrate, its effects are identical to those produced by banks' creation of loans and deposits from nothing.

Let us imagine that banking is just beginning to emerge, and
banks act as true depositaries of money as stipulated in an irregular deposit contract. As long as the general legal principles we
studied in chapters 1 through 3 are upheld, banks will accept
monetary units (usually gold or any other type of commodity
money) and keep them in their vaults, and in return they will
give depositors deposit certificates, receipts or banknotes for
the entire sum deposited. A bank which correctly honors its
commitments will make the following entry in its journal:

Bank A

(54)	Debit		Credit	
Cash	1,000,000	Deposit receipts or banknotes	1,000,000

Phillip Cagan, *Determinance and Effects of Changes in the Stock of Money,
1875–1960* (New York: Columbia University Press, 1965). Also, José
Miguel Andreu García has written extensively on the topic of bank multipliers and reserve requirements. For example, see his articles, "En
torno a la neutralidad del coeficiente de caja: el caso español," in *Revista
de Economía*, no. 9, and "El coeficiente de caja óptimo y su posible vinculación con el déficit público," *Boletín Económico de Información Comercial Española* (June 29–July 5, 1987): 2425ff.

[39]Usher, *The Early History of Deposit Banking in Mediterranean Europe*, pp.
9 and 192.

If the bank fulfills its commitments for a lengthy period of time and people completely trust it, it is certain that the public will gradually begin to use the banknotes (or the deposit slips or receipts the bank issues in exchange for monetary units deposited) as if they were the units of commodity money themselves, thus converting the banknotes into monetary units (perfect money substitutes, to use Mises's terminology). Given that money is a present good people need and use only as a medium of exchange and not for their own consumption, if depositors trust the bank, their use of banknotes as money could be prolonged indefinitely (they would not need to go to the bank and withdraw the monetary units they originally deposited). When this situation arises, bankers may start to feel tempted to issue deposit receipts for an amount exceeding the sum of monetary units actually deposited.

Clearly if bankers succumb to this temptation, they violate universal legal principles and commit not only the crime of counterfeiting (by issuing a false receipt unbacked by a corresponding deposit), but the crime of fraud as well, by presenting as a means of payment a document that in reality lacks all backing.[40] Nevertheless, if people place enough trust in the bank and the banker knows from experience that a reserve ratio, c, of 0.1 will permit him to honor his commitments under ordinary circumstances, he will be able to issue up to nine times more in new false deposit receipts or banknotes. His corresponding journal entry will appear as follows:

Bank A

(55)	Debit	Credit	
9,000,000	Loans	Banknotes	9,000,000

---

[40] He who has made a special promise to give definite parcels of goods in return for particular individual papers, cannot issue any such promissory papers without holding corresponding goods. If he does so, he will be continually liable to be convicted of fraud or default by the presentation of a particular document. (Jevons, *Money and the Mechanism of Exchange*, p. 209)

We have assumed the bank uses the counterfeit bills to grant loans, but it could use them for any purpose, for example to purchase any other asset (like lavish buildings) or simply to pay day-to-day expenses. If the bank uses the bills to grant loans, its balance sheet will appear as follows:

(56)

Bank A
Balance Sheet

Assets		Liabilities	
Cash	1,000,000	Banknotes	10,000,000
Loans	9,000,000		
Total Assets	10,000,000	Total Liabilities	10,000,000

If people trust the bank, borrowers will agree to receive their loans in bills, which will circulate as if they were money. Under these conditions the banker may even believe, with good reason, that no one will ever return these bills to the bank to withdraw the original money deposited. The moment the banker decides this is the case, his judgment may manifest itself as an accounting entry identifying the 9,000,000 false bills put into circulation by the bank as part of the year's profit, which the banker may freely appropriate. The following journal entries will be made:

Bank A

(57)	Debit	Credit	
1,000,000	Cash	Banknotes	1,000,000
9,000,000	Loans	Banknotes	9,000,000
9,000,000	Banknotes	Profit	9,000,000

These accounting entries reflect the fact that the banker is sure he will never have to return the sum of the bills, since his bills circulate as money. The bank's balance sheet will look like this:

(58)   Bank A
                           Balance Sheet

Assets		Liabilities	
Cash	1,000,000	Banknotes	1,000,000
Loans	9,000,000	Profit (equity)	9,000,000
Total Assets	10,000,000	Total Liabilities	10,000,000

From this balance sheet we can conclude that once the banknotes have acquired the nature of monetary units, no one will ever return them to the bank to withdraw the money deposited, since the bills circulate freely and are considered money themselves. Only 1,000,000 of the banknotes issued are recorded in the Liabilities column, because 10 percent is sufficient to comply with ordinary requests for conversion. Hence this balance sheet amounts to an acknowledgment of the fraud the bank commits when it issues bills for an amount exceeding the sum of money deposited. Bankers have never thus recorded in their account books the issuance of unbacked banknotes, as it would fully reveal the fraud they commit. By their deceitful actions they harm third parties, whose money drops in value due to the increase in the money supply, not to mention economic crises and recessions, an effect we will consider later. Nonetheless this last balance sheet is clearly more honest, in the sense that at least it demonstrates the banker's maneuver and the fact that the issuance of unbacked bills constitutes an endless source of financing which permits bankers to appropriate a very large volume of wealth.

The reader will surely have noticed that records (54) through (56) are identical to ones we studied with respect to deposits. In fact the nature of unbacked banknotes is identical to that of secondary deposits and both produce the same economic effects. They actually represent the same operation and result in identical accounting records.

Both activities generate considerable assets for banks, who gradually take this wealth from all economic agents in the market through a process the agents cannot understand or identify, one which leads to small decreases in the purchasing power of the monetary units all use in society. Credit expansion is backed by the creation of new deposits or bills, and since these are considered money in themselves, from the subjective point of view of the public, they will never be withdrawn under normal conditions. In this way banks appropriate a large volume of wealth, which from an accounting standpoint they guarantee with deposits or bills that permit them to disguise the fact that economically speaking they are the only beneficiaries who completely take advantage *de facto* of these assets. Thus they have found a perennial source of financing which will probably not be demanded from them, a "loan" they will never have to return (which is ultimately the same as a "gift"). From an economic point of view, bankers and other related economic agents are the ones who take advantage of these extraordinary circumstances. They possess the enormous power to create money, and they use this power continually to expand their assets, open new offices, hire new employees, etc. Furthermore they have managed to keep their activities relatively hidden from most of the public, including economists, by backing their created loans with liability accounts (deposit accounts or banknote accounts) that do not coincide with their actual equity. In short, bankers have discovered their *Philosopher's Stone* (much like the one sought-after in the Middle Ages), which enables them to create new monetary units from nothing, and thus to generate hidden wealth, harming and deceiving third parties in the process. In account books depositors are formally recognized as the owners of such wealth, but in practice it does not belong to anyone (however, economically speaking, it belongs to the bankers themselves). As we mentioned before, the recognition of this fact is fundamental to our arguments in the last chapter, where we propose a plan for reforming the banking system.

The wealth banks have gradually accumulated can and must be returned to the citizens. Through a process of privatization, it should become available for different uses of great importance to society (for example, to help pay off the national debt, or make a transition to a private Social Security system based on investment).

The parallels between the issuance of unbacked banknotes and credit expansion backed by secondary deposits created *ex nihilo* are now evident. Indeed all of the arguments offered in the preceding pages hold true for banknotes as well as for demand deposits. With that in mind, let us briefly consider a few entries. For example, when loans are granted against the issuance of banknotes:

Bank A

(59) Debit		Credit	
1,000,000	Cash	Banknotes	1,000,000
900,000	Loans	Banknotes	900,000

In this case the bank grants loans from nothing by simply issuing "false" bills and giving them to borrowers. In the worst of cases, if these borrowers return the bills to the bank to withdraw units of commodity money from the vault, the bank's balance sheet will look like this:

(60)

Bank A
Balance Sheet

Assets		Liabilities	
Cash	100,000	Banknotes	1,000,000
Loans	900,000		
Total Assets	1,000,000	Total Liabilities	1,000,000

If we suppose that the borrowers pay this money to other people, who eventually take it to another bank, for instance Bank B, which also issues banknotes without backing, Bank B would make the following journal entries:

Bank B

(61) Debit		Credit	
900,000 Cash		Banknotes	900,000
810,000 Loans		Banknotes	810,000

Bank B's balance sheet would appear as follows:

(62)

Bank B
Balance Sheet

Assets		Liabilities	
Cash	90,000	Banknotes	900,000
Loans	810,000		
Total Assets	900,000	Total Liabilities	900,000

The process continues in this manner and spreads throughout the system. If we suppose that the reserve ratio, c, for banknotes is equal to 0.1 and $k = 0$, we know the system will be able to create from nothing:

$$[41] \quad \frac{d(1-c)}{c} = \frac{1,000,000(0.9)}{0.1} = 9,000,000$$

monetary units in the form of bills unbacked by original money (gold or any other type of commodity money).

We would have obtained the same result in the case of a monopolistic bank, one that enjoys the trust and business of everyone, with a reserve ratio, c, of 0.1 and a k of 1. In this case the credit expansion, x, would be equal to:

$$[42] \quad x = \frac{d(1 - c)}{1 + k(c - 1)}$$

and when $k = 1$, x equals: $\dfrac{d(1 - c)}{c}$ banknotes created *ex nihilo*.

If we suppose that all the banks issue bills simultaneously and receive new original monetary units at the same rate, then by maintaining its cash reserves unaltered, a single bank will be able to generate banknotes equal to:

$$\frac{d(1 - c)}{c}$$

This is the same formula we applied to deposits. The following entries will be made:

Bank A

(63) Debit		Credit	
1,000,000	Cash	Banknotes	1,000,000
9,000,000	Loans and other uses	Unbacked banknotes	9,000,000

We could also reproduce all of the accounting entries for the more general case in which $k > 0$ (in our previous example $k = 0.2$). If $c = 0.1$, then for each 1,000,000 m.u. a bank receives, it will be able to create from nothing new banknotes for a sum equal to:

$$[43] \quad \frac{d(1 - c)}{1 + k(c - 1)}$$

That is, the bank will have the capacity to create 1,097,560 m.u. in the form of unbacked bills. One by one we could duplicate for banknotes all of the results we obtained for bank deposits, which shows that there is no economic difference between the issuance of unbacked bills and the *ex nihilo* expansion of bank-credit backed by deposits generated from nothing. The only substantial difference is of a legal nature, since according to universal legal principles, the issuance of unbacked bills implies counterfeiting and the crime of fraud, while the monetary bank-deposit contract only involves misappropriation.

Nonetheless there are some differences regarding the way the operation is carried out. Banknotes take the form of bearer bonds and each has a particular face value, allowing the notes to be transferred from one person to another without it being necessary for the bank to make any accounting entry in its books (and as a result the cost of bank transactions decreases). In contrast deposits offer customers the advantage of being able to write an exact figure on a check without needing to hand over a specific number of bills of a set value. However the fact that the banker must follow the transactions conducted and record them in his books constitutes a disadvantage.

Still, apart from these legal differences and differences in form, from an economic standpoint the two operations are essentially identical and produce the same effects. As we will see later, however, when the theory of money was first being developed, theorists only recognized the immorality of the creation of unbacked banknotes and the serious harm it causes. They did not initially realize nor respond to the fact that the expansive creation of loans backed by deposits generated from nothing has exactly the same effects. This explains why the Peel Act of July 19, 1844, the foundation of all modern banking systems, prohibited the issuance of unbacked bills yet failed miserably to achieve its objectives of monetary stability and an adequate definition and defense of citizens' property rights with respect to banking. Its failure was due to legislators' inability to comprehend that bank deposits with a fractional reserve have exactly the same nature and economic effects as unbacked banknotes. As a result, the Act did not outlaw fractional-reserve banking and allowed the age-old practice of "issuing" unbacked (secondary) deposits to continue. In reality secondary deposits predated the fiduciary issue of banknotes, but because the former proved much more complex, only the latter was (very belatedly) prohibited. The monetary bank-deposit contract with a fractional reserve is still legal today, even though it has exactly the same economic nature and produces the same damaging effects as the issuance of unbacked banknotes prohibited in 1844 by the Peel Act.[41]

---

[41]As chapter 8 will reveal in greater detail (pp. 605 ff. and 625 ff.), the first theorist to realize that bank deposits are money and that fractional-reserve banking increases the money supply was the Spanish scholastic Luis de Molina, *Tratado sobre los cambios*, edited and prefaced by Francisco Gómez Camacho (Madrid: Instituto de Estudios Fiscales, 1991; first edition was published in Cuenca in 1597). See esp. *Disputation* 409, pp. 145–56, esp. p. 147. Nevertheless, Luis de Molina did not observe the parallels between secondary deposits and unbacked bills, since in his time banks had still not begun to exploit the possibility of issuing banknotes. It would not be until 1797 that Henry Thornton would for the first time refer to the equivalence of bills and deposits (see his Response of March 30, 1797 in "Evidence given before the Lords' Committee of Secrecy appointed to inquire into the courses which produced the Order of Council of the 27th February 1797," reproduced in *An Inquiry into the Nature and Effects of the Paper Credit of Great Britain*, F. A. Hayek, ed. (Fairfield, N.J.: Augustus M. Kelley, 1978), p. 303. Several years later the same conclusion was reached by Walter Boyd, James Pennington, and the Pennsylvania senator Condy Raguet, who believed that deposits and banknotes both constituted part of the money supply and that any bank which failed to immediately and on demand pay the value of banknotes issued by it should lose its license to operate, as should any bank which failed to immediately and in cash honor requests for withdrawals of deposits the bank had issued [see the "Report on Bank Charters" by Condy Raguet, included in the *Journal of the Senate, 1820–1921*, Pennsylvania Legislature, pp. 252–68 and Murray N. Rothbard's related comments included in his book, *The Panic of 1819: Reactions and Policies* (New York and London: Columbia University Press, 1962), p. 148]. Quite significantly, Banking School theorists themselves were the first to rightly insist that it was very paradoxical to try to limit the issuance of unbacked bills while not advocating the same measure regarding deposits, given that bills and deposits had exactly the same economic nature. See, for example, James Wilson's book, *Capital, Currency and Banking* (London:

8

THE CREDIT TIGHTENING PROCESS

One of the central problems posed by the process of credit expansion and *ex nihilo* deposit creation, and thus by the bank deposit contract involving a fractional reserve, is that just as this process inevitably unleashes forces that *reverse* the effects of credit expansion on the real economy, it also looses forces which lead to a parallel process of *credit tightening or contraction. Ceteris paribus,* any of the following

---

The Economist, 1847), p. 282; see also Vera C. Smith's comments in her book, *The Rationale of Central Banking and the Free Banking Alternative,* p. 89. Smith makes a most perceptive observation when referring to Wilson and to the grave error of the Currency School, which was incapable of recognizing the economic parallels between bills and deposits. She states:

> The reason the currency school usually gave for this distinction was that bank notes increased the circulation and deposits did not. Such an argument was not, of course, acceptable to Wilson as a member of the banking school of thought which both denied that the issue of notes could be increased to any undesirable extent so long as convertibility was strictly maintained, and pointed out that the difference claimed between notes and deposit liabilities was invalid. But it was still denied in many quarters that demand deposits formed part of the circulation, and it was probably by no means generally admitted right up to the time of MacLeod. (p. 89)

Wilson was completely justified in pointing out this contradiction; given the economic equivalence of banknotes and deposits, the arguments in favor of regulating the issuance of one unbacked form are directly applicable, *mutatis mutandis,* to the other. Moreover this is the same inconsistency manifested nearly a century later by defenders of the contract of irregular deposit of securities in which the bank is allowed to make use of deposits. This controversy arose at the beginning of the twentieth century with respect to banking practices in Barcelona, and at that time the use of a fractional reserve in connection with irregular deposits of securities was called into question and harshly condemned. As defenders of this contract correctly argued at the time, the reasons put forward against this practice should also be applied to monetary bank deposits with a fractional reserve (see related observations in chapter 3).

events serve to establish that such a process has been set in motion: (a) a decrease in original deposits; (b) an increase in the desire of the public to hold monetary units outside the banking system (i.e., an increase in f); (c) a rise in banks' "prudence," leading them to boost their reserve ratio, c, in order to be able to comply with the higher average number of possible withdrawal requests; (d) a sudden rise in loan repayment not offset by an increase in loans granted; and (e) an escalation in the number of borrowers unable to return their loans, i.e., many more defaulters.

First, it is clear that if a certain sum in original deposits is withdrawn from a bank (for instance, the 1,000,000 m.u. deposited in past illustrations), all created loans and deposits such as we referred to in preceding examples would disappear in a chain reaction, resulting in fewer loans and deposits. If we suppose that $c = 0.1$ and $k = f = 0$, then the decrease in loans and deposits would equal 9,000,000 m.u., implying a significant *drop in the money supply*, which would fall to one-tenth of its prior sum. The result is severe *deflation*, or a decline in the amount of money in circulation, leading to a reduction in the prices of goods and services, which, in the short and medium term, further aggravates the recession ultimately caused in the market by all processes of credit expansion.

Second, a desire of the public to keep more money outside the banking system produces the same effects. It provokes an increase in f and a decline in banks' capacity for credit expansion, which in turn brings about a recession and a monetary squeeze.

Third, a decision by banks to be more "prudent" and to increase their reserve ratio leads to a contraction as well.

Fourth, the repayment of loans produces equally deflationary effects (when enough new loans are not granted to at least offset the ones returned). Let us consider this possibility in greater detail. We will begin by imagining a bank with $c = 0.1$, $k = 0$ and $f = 0$, whose borrowers pay back their loans. The accounting entries and balance sheet prepared when the loans are granted are as follows:

Bank A

(64) Debit	Credit
1,000,000 Cash	Demand deposits 1,000,000
900,000 Loans	Demand deposits 900,000
900,000 Demand deposits	Cash 900,000

(65)

Bank A
Balance Sheet
$c=0.1, k=0$ and $f=0$

Assets		Liabilities	
Cash	100,000	Demand deposits	1,000,000
Loans	900,000		
Total Assets	1,000,000	Total Liabilities	1,000,000

In previous examples we observed the creation through the banking system of new loans and deposits for the sum of 9,000,000 m.u. In this instance, when borrowers return the loans the last two accounting entries are canceled as follows:

Bank A

(66) Debit	Credit
900,000 Cash	Demand deposits 900,000
900,000 Demand deposits	Loans 900,000

The balance sheet of Bank A now looks like this:

(67)

Bank A
Balance Sheet
c=0.1, k=0 and *f=0*

Assets		Liabilities	
Cash	1,000,000	Demand deposits	1,000,000
Total Assets	1,000,000	Total Liabilities	1,000,000

Economically speaking, this means that from the point of view of an individual bank, there has been a 900,000 m.u. decrease in the money supply, which has gone from 1,900,000 m.u. at the time the loans were given (1,000,000 in deposits and 900,000 in money handed over to the borrowers) to 1,000,000 m.u., the only money left once the loans are repaid. Therefore from the standpoint of an isolated bank the money supply clearly contracts.

Given that all banks expand credit and receive original deposits simultaneously, we already know each bank is able to maintain its cash reserves constant and grant loans for a multiple of its reserves. Hence the balance sheet of any bank, Bank A for instance, would appear as follows:

(68)

Bank A
Balance Sheet
c=0.1, k=0 and *f=0*

Assets		Liabilities	
Cash	1,000,000	Demand deposits	10,000,000
Loans	9,000,000		
Total Assets	10,000,000	Total Liabilities	10,000,000

If all the bank's borrowers return their loans paying with checks, the bank's balance sheet will look like this:

(69)

Bank A
Balance Sheet
$c=0.1$, $k=0$ and $f=0$

Assets		Liabilities	
Cash	1,000,000	Demand deposits	1,000,000
Total Assets	1,000,000	Total Liabilities	1,000,000

This balance sheet clearly reflects the 9,000,000 m.u. reduction in the money supply or tightening of credit. An identical decline would result from the simultaneous repayment of loans in isolated banks, as in entries (66) and (67), through a process identical to the inverse of the one shown in Table IV-2.

Fifth, if the loans lose their value due to the failure of the economic activity for which they were employed, the corresponding bank must record this fact as a loss, as shown here:

Bank A

(70) Debit		Credit	
Losses due to defaulters (expenses)	9,000,000	Loans	9,000,000

The bank's balance sheet would then look like this:

(71)

Bank A
Balance Sheet
$c=0.1, k=0$ and $f=0$

Assets		Liabilities	
Cash	1,000,000	Deposits	10,000,000
Losses for the year	9,000,000		
Total Assets	10,000,000	Total Liabilities	10,000,000

If we compare this balance sheet with (69), we see the bank holds the same amount in cash reserves in each instance, yet a very significant difference exists: in (71) the Liabilities column reflects 10,000,000 m.u. in deposits, as opposed to 1,000,000 m.u. in (69). In other words, *the bank has technically failed*. Nevertheless as long as depositors continue to trust it, no decrease in the money supply will take place. In fact, since no one will claim the 9,000,000 m.u. of secondary deposits the bankers created from nothing, they may even consider this amount part of the year's profits, a sum to compensate for the 9,000,000 m.u. lost to defaulters, leaving the balance sheet as it appears in (69).[42] However in terms of deflation this situation is obviously even more dangerous than that following the repayment of a loan: before arriving at this situation, banks will heavily restrict new loans (they will be much more rigorous in their criteria for granting them), accelerating the deflationary process; and if the measures they take do not prove sufficient to avoid defaulters and the risk of failure, they will

---

[42]It is interesting to note how bankers involved in crises invariably complain that with just a little assistance from someone (the state or the central bank) in restoring their customers' confidence, they could continue to function with no problem and quickly reestablish their "solvency."

be one step away from losing the confidence of their depositors, who may force them to suspend payments and/or
declare bankruptcy, and in this case even the 1,000,000 m.u.
originally deposited in cash would be withdrawn, threatening
the existence of the entire banking system.

Under *ordinary conditions* the contraction or deflation we
are describing does not occur, because when a customer of one
bank returns a loan, the sum is compensated for by another
loan granted by another bank; in fact even within the same
bank the attempt is always made to replace the repaid loan
with a new one. In addition under normal circumstances the
bank may consider payment arrears just one more operating
cost. The crucial problem posed by credit tightening (as we
will examine in the following chapters) consists of the fact that
the very process of credit expansion based on a fractional
reserve inevitably triggers the granting of loans unsupported
by voluntary saving, resulting in a process of intertemporal
discoordination, which in turn stems from the distorted information the banking system imparts to businessmen who
receive loans generated *ex nihilo* by the system. Hence businessmen rush out to launch investment projects *as if society's
real saving had increased, when in fact this has not happened. The
result is artificial economic expansion or a "boom," which by
processes we will later study in detail, inevitably provokes an adjustment in the form of a crisis and economic recession.* This sums up
the negative effects exerted on the real economy by the financial practice of expanding credit through the issuance of fiduciary media (deposits).

The crisis and economic recession reveal that a highly significant number of investment projects financed under new
loans created by banks *are not profitable* because they do not
correspond to the true desires of consumers. Therefore many
investment processes fail, which ultimately has a profound
effect on the banking system. The harmful consequences are
evidenced by *a widespread repayment of loans* by many demoralized businessmen assessing their losses and liquidating
unsound investment projects (thus provoking deflation and
the tightening of credit); they are also demonstrated by an
alarming and atypical rise in payment arrears on loans

(adversely affecting the banks' solvency). Just as the money supply was expanded according to the bank multiplier, artificial economic expansion fostered by the *ex nihilo* creation of loans eventually triggers an endogenous recession, which in the form of a widespread repayment of loans and an increase in arrears, reduces the money supply substantially. Therefore *the fractional-reserve banking system generates an extremely elastic money supply, which "stretches" with ease but then must contract just as effortlessly, producing the corresponding effects on economic activity, which is repeatedly buffeted by successive stages of boom and recession.* "Manic-depressive" economic activity, with all of its heavy, painful social costs, is undoubtedly the most severe, damaging effect the current banking system (based on a fractional reserve, in violation of universal legal principles) has on society.

In short, bank customers' economic difficulties, one of the inevitable consequences of all credit expansion, render many loans irrecoverable, accelerating even more the credit tightening process (the inverse of the expansion process). In fact, as in our accounting example, the bank may completely fail as a result, in which case the bills and deposits issued by it (which we know are economically equivalent) *will lose all value*, further aggravating the monetary squeeze (instead of the 9,000,000 m.u. decrease in the money supply caused by the return of a loan, here the money supply would drop by 10,000,000 m.u.; that is, including the 1,000,000 m.u. in primary deposits held by the bank). Furthermore, one bank's solvency problems are enough to sow panic among the customers of all other banks, leading them to suspend payments one by one, with tragic economic and financial consequences.

Moreover we must point out that, even if the public continues to trust banks (despite their insolvency), and even if a central bank created *ad hoc* for such situations provides all the liquidity necessary to assure depositors their deposits are fully protected, the inability to recover loans initiates a process of credit tightening that is spontaneously set off when loans are repaid and cannot be replaced by new ones at the same rate. This phenomenon is typical of periods of recession. When customers default on their loans, banks become more cautious about granting more. Hence the natural reluctance of the demoralized public to request loans is reinforced by banks' greater prudence and rigor when it comes to giving them. In addition, as bankers see their profitability fall along with the value of their assets as a result of irrecoverable loans, they will attempt to be more careful, and other things being equal, to increase their cash on hand by raising their reserve ratio, which will have an even greater tightening effect. Finally business failures and frustration arising from the inability to honor commitments to banks will contribute even more to the *demoralization* of economic agents and to their determination to avoid new investment projects financed with bank loans. In fact many businessmen eventually realize they allowed themselves to be carried away by unjustified optimism in the phases of expansion, *largely due to the excessively generous credit terms bankers initially offered*, and the businessmen correctly attribute their errors in judgment to these easy terms.[43] As a result they resolve not to commit the same errors again. (Whether or not their attempt at rectification is successful and in the future the businessmen remember their unpleasant experiences during the stage of recession is a different issue we will confront later.)

In conclusion, we have seen that the fractional-reserve banking system can contract and drastically reduce the money supply just as easily as it expands credit and increases the money supply. In other words, the system generates an elastic and extremely fragile stock of money which is subject to great

---

[43]See also chapter 5, sec. 4. The serious harm bankers do those customers they urge to "enjoy" new loans and get involved in business deals requiring bank financing should theoretically be admitted in legal cases in which banks would be sued for damages with respect to the injury they inflict upon borrowers in this way. If until now such suits have not been brought before the court, it is because economic theory had not been advanced enough to clearly identify the cause and nature of the injury. However nowadays theoretical developments make it possible to apply theory in court. A very similar, parallel case would be the use of breakthroughs in biology to facilitate judicial declarations of paternity which were impossible a few years ago.

convulsions that are very difficult, if not impossible, to mitigate or stop. This monetary and banking system contrasts with inelastic systems (for example, the one that combines the classic gold standard with a 100-percent reserve requirement), which do not permit disproportionate expansion of the money supply (the worldwide production of gold has been growing in recent centuries at the rate of 1 to 2 percent per year). Moreover they offer the following advantage: due to the fact that these systems are inelastic (gold is indestructible and throughout history the world has accumulated a very inflexible stock of it), they do not permit any abrupt decline, nor (logically) any credit or monetary squeezes which exert debilitating effects on the economy, as opposed to the current situation for which the existing banking system is responsible.[44]

---

[44]In the last chapter we will examine the comparative advantages of the classic gold standard based on a free banking system subject to legal principles; that is, with a 100-percent reserve requirement.

5

BANK CREDIT EXPANSION AND ITS EFFECTS ON THE ECONOMIC SYSTEM

I n the previous chapter we explained how the monetary bank-deposit contract with a fractional reserve leads to the creation of new money (deposits) and its infusion into the economic system in the form of new loans unbacked by a natural increase in voluntary saving (credit expansion). In this chapter we will focus on the effects of credit expansion on the economic system. We will analyze the distortions the expansion process causes: investment errors, credit squeezes, bank crises and eventually, unemployment and economic recessions. First, however, we must examine in detail both the theory of capital and the productive structure of a real economy, since a clear grasp of both is essential to understanding the processes triggered in the market by banks' concession of loans not derived from a previous increase in voluntary saving. Our analysis will reveal that the legal concept which concerns us (the monetary bank-deposit contract with a fractional reserve) does great harm to many economic agents (and to society in general) inasmuch as it is the principal root of recurring economic recessions. Moreover we will show that because credit expansion precipitates economic and bank crises, it renders the "law of large numbers" inapplicable in banking and therefore makes it technically impossible to ensure the completion of banks' fractional-reserve operations. This fact acquires great significance in light of the inevitable emergence of the central bank as a lender of last resort, which we will explore in depth in a later chapter. We will begin by explaining

the processes spontaneously set in motion in an economic system
when new loans originate from a voluntary increase in society's
real saving; then in contrast and by comparison it will be easier
to understand what happens when banks create loans *ex nihilo*
through a process of credit expansion.

1

THE FOUNDATIONS OF CAPITAL THEORY

In this section we will examine the basic tenets of capital
theory which are essential to understanding the effects credit
expansion exerts on the economic system.[1] We will begin by
considering the subjectivist conception of human action as a
series of productive stages intended to achieve an end.

HUMAN ACTION AS A SERIES OF SUBJECTIVE STAGES

We may begin by defining *human action* as any deliberate
behavior or conduct.[2] A person acts to attain certain *goals*
he/she feels are important. *Value* refers to the degree of subjective appreciation the actor assigns his goal, and the *means* is
anything the actor subjectively considers adequate to accomplish it. *Utility* represents the subjective *appraisal* the actor
makes of the means, in terms of the value of the goal he

---

[1]The capital theory we will expound is the key to understanding how
bank credit expansion distorts the economy's real productive structure.
In fact the usual error of the critics of the Austrian theory of the business
cycle (also called the circulation credit theory), which we present here,
is that they fail to take capital theory into account. This is the case, for
example, with Hans-Michael Trautwein and his two papers: "Money,
Equilibrium, and the Business Cycle: Hayek's Wicksellian Dichotomy,"
History of Political Economy 28, no. 1 (Spring, 1996): 27–55, and "Hayek's
Double Failure in Business Cycle Theory: A Note," chapter 4 of *Money
and Business Cycles: The Economics of F.A. Hayek*, M. Colonna and H.
Hagemann, eds. (Aldershot, U.K.: Edward Elgar, 1994), vol. 1, pp. 74–81.

[2]On the concepts of human action, plans of action, the subjective conception of time, and action understood as a set of successive stages, see
Huerta de Soto, *Socialismo, cálculo económico y función empresarial*, pp.
43 ff.

believes it will help him to achieve. Means must be *scarce* by definition: if the actor did not regard them as such in light of his objectives, he would not even take them into account before acting. Ends and means are not "given" (i.e., *data*) but instead result from the fundamental entrepreneurial activity of human beings, an activity which consists of creating, discovering or simply realizing which ends and means are relevant for the actor in each set of specific circumstances of time and place he encounters. Once the actor believes he has discovered which ends are worth accomplishing, he forms an idea of the means available to assist him. He then incorporates them, almost always tacitly, into a *plan* of action which he embarks upon through an *act of will*.

Consequently the *plan* is a mental picture, conjured up by the actor, of the different future *stages*, elements and circumstances his action may involve. The *plan* is the actor's personal evaluation of the practical information he possesses and gradually discovers within the context of each action. Moreover each action implies a continuous process of *individual* or *personal* planning through which the actor continually conceives, revises and modifies his plans, as he discovers and creates new subjective information on the goals he sets himself and the means he believes are available to assist him in reaching these goals.[3]

---

[3]The development of economics as a science which is always based on human beings, the creative actors and protagonists in all social processes and events (the subjectivist conception), is undoubtedly the most significant and characteristic contribution made by the Austrian School of economics, founded by Carl Menger. In fact Menger felt it vital to abandon the sterile objectivism of the classical (Anglo-Saxon) school whose members were obsessed with the supposed existence of external objective entities (social classes, aggregates, material factors of production, etc.). Menger held that economists should instead always adopt the subjectivist view of human beings who act, and that this perspective should invariably exert a decisive influence on the way all economic theories are formulated, in terms of their scientific content and their practical conclusions and results. On this topic see Huerta de Soto, "Génesis, esencia y evolución de la Escuela Austriaca de Economía," in *Estudios de economía política*, chap. 1, pp. 17–55.

All human action is directed toward the attainment of an *end*, or consumer good, which can be defined as a good that directly and subjectively satisfies the needs of the human actor. The term *first-order economic goods* has traditionally referred to those consumer goods which, in the specific, subjective context of each action, constitute the goal pursued by the actor in performing the action.[4] The achievement of these goals, consumer goods, or first-order economic goods, is necessarily preceded by a series of *intermediate stages* represented by "higher-order economic goods" (second, third, fourth, etc.). The higher the order of each stage, the further the good is from the final consumer good.

Furthermore all human action takes place in *time*, and we are not referring here to the deterministic or Newtonian sense of the word (i.e., merely physical or analogical), but to the subjective sense; that is, the actor's subjective perception of time within the context of his action. According to this subjectivist conception, the actor experiences the passage of time as he acts; in other words, as he realizes new ends and means, designs plans of action and completes the different stages which compose each action.

When human beings act, they inevitably synthesize memories of the past into new expectations and mental images for the future, regarding the different stages in the action process they will follow. This future is never predetermined, but instead the actor imagines, creates and *builds* it step by step. Therefore the future is always uncertain, since it has yet to be built, and the only part of it the actor possesses consists of specific ideas, mental images or expectations he hopes to realize through the completion of the stages he imagines will make

---

[4]This classification and terminology were conceived by Carl Menger, whose theory on economic goods of different order is one of the most important logical consequences of his subjectivist conception of economics. Carl Menger, *Grundsätze der Volkswirthschaftslehre* (Vienna: Wilhelm Braumüller, 1871). Menger uses the expression "Güter der ersten Ordnung" (p. 8) to refer to consumer goods or first-order goods. English translation by J. Dingwall and B. Hoselitz, *Principles of Economics* (New York: New York University Press, 1981).

up his personal action process. Furthermore the future is *open* to man's every creative possibility, and at any point the actor may modify his objectives or vary, rearrange and revise the stages of the action processes in which he is involved.

Hence in economics time is inseparable from human action. It is impossible to conceive of an action which does not take place in time, one that does not take time. Moreover the actor perceives the passage of time as he acts and goes through the different stages in his action process. Human action, which is always directed toward the attainment of a goal or the alleviation of a discomfort, invariably takes time, in the sense that it requires the realization and completion of a series of successive stages. Therefore what separates the actor from the achievement of his goal is the period of time required by the series of successive stages that compose his action process.[5]

The following tendency always exists with respect to the actor's subjective view of the future: as the time period required by an action increases (i.e., as the number and complexity of the successive stages which constitute the action increase), the result or aim of the action becomes more valuable. An action can acquire a greater subjective value—in terms of the number, duration, and complexity of stages involved—in two ways: by enabling the actor to achieve results he subjectively values more and could not achieve via shorter human actions; or by facilitating the attainment of more results than would be possible through shorter action processes.[6] It is easy to understand the economic principle

---

[5]On the subjective, experimental and dynamic conception of time as the only conception applicable to human action in economics, see chapter 4 of the book by Gerald P. O'Driscoll and Mario J. Rizzo, *The Economics of Time and Ignorance* (Oxford: Basil Blackwell, 1985), pp. 52–70.

[6]As Ludwig M. Lachmann has correctly stated, economic development entails not only an increase in the number of productive stages, but also an increase in their complexity, and therefore a change in their composition. Ludwig M. Lachmann, *Capital and its Structure* (Kansas City: Sheed Andrews and McMeel, 1978), p. 83. See also Peter Lewin, "Capital in Disequilibrium: A Reexamination of the Capital Theory of Ludwig M.

that human action processes tend to achieve aims of greater value the longer the processes last. Indeed if this were not the case, i.e., if the actor did not attach greater value to the results of longer actions, he would never undertake them and would opt for shorter actions instead. In other words, an actor is separated from his goal precisely by a certain length of time (i.e., by the time necessary to complete the set of stages in his action process). Thus, other things being equal, it is evident that human beings will always try to accomplish their goals as soon as possible, and they will only be willing to postpone the attainment of their ends when they subjectively believe that by doing so they will achieve more valuable objectives.[7]

We are now ready to discuss the logical notion of *time preference*, which establishes that, other things being equal, the actor prefers to satisfy his needs or reach his objectives as soon as possible. In other words, when the actor is faced with two goals of equal subjective value to him, he will always prefer the one he can attain in less time. Or to put it even more briefly, other things being equal, "present goods" are always preferable to "future goods." The law of time preference is just another way of expressing the following essential principle: any actor, in the course of his action, tries to achieve the results of the action as soon as possible, and he is separated from his ends by a series of intermediate stages involving a certain time period. Hence time preference is not a psychological

---

Lachmann," *History of Political Economy* 29, no. 3 (Fall, 1997): 523–48; and Roger W. Garrison, *Time and Money: The Macroeconomics of Capital Structure* (London and New York: Routledge, 2001), pp. 25–26.

[7]José Castañeda eloquently states:

> As more auxiliary means are introduced into the production process, the process becomes more lengthy, and in general, more productive. Of course more indirect processes may exist; that is, ones that are longer or more drawn-out, yet no more productive. Nevertheless these are not taken into account since they are not applied, and a longer process is only introduced when it improves productivity.

José Castañeda Chornet, *Lecciones de teoría económica* (Madrid: Editorial Aguilar, 1972), p. 385.

or physiological concept, but necessarily follows from the logical structure of action present in the mind of all human beings. In short, human action is directed toward certain ends and the actor chooses the means to accomplish them. The goal is the actor's purpose in performing any action, and in any action, time is what separates the actor from the goal. Therefore the closer the actor is in time to his goal, the closer he is to achieving the objectives he values. The tendency described above and the time preference we have just explained are simply two different ways of expressing the same reality. According to the former, actors undertake time-consuming actions because they expect to thus achieve more valuable ends; according to the latter, other things being equal, actors always prefer the goods closer to them in time.[8]

Hence it is impossible to imagine a human action to which the principle of time preference does not apply. A world without time preference is inconceivable and would be absurd: it would mean people always preferred the future to the present, and objectives would be postponed, one after the other,

---

[8]The law of time preference may even date back to Saint Thomas Aquinas, and it was expressly stated in 1285 by one of his most brilliant disciples, Giles Lessines, who maintained that

> res futurae per tempora non sunt tantae existimationis, sicut eadem collectae in instanti nec tantam utilitatem inferunt possidentibus, propter quod oportet quod sint minoris existimationis secundum iustitiam.

In other words,

> future goods are not valued as highly as goods available immediately, nor are they as useful to their owners, and therefore justice dictates they should be considered less valuable.

Aegidius Lessines, *De usuris in communi et de usurarum contractibus*, opuscule 66, 1285, p. 426; quoted by Dempsey, *Interest and Usury*, note 31 on p. 214. This idea was later presented by Saint Bernardine of Siena, Conrad Summenhart, and Martín Azpilcueta in 1431, 1499, and 1556 respectively (see Rothbard, *Economic Thought Before Adam Smith*, pp. 85, 92, 106–07 and 399–400). The implications this concept has for economic theory were later worked out by Turgot, Rae, Böhm-Bawerk, Jevons, Wicksell, Fisher, and especially Frank Albert Fetter and Ludwig von Mises.

just before they were reached, and therefore no end would ever be achieved and human action would be senseless.[9]

CAPITAL AND CAPITAL GOODS

We may use the term *capital goods* to designate the intermediate stages of each action process, subjectively regarded as such by the actor. Or to put it another way, each of the intermediate stages in an actor's production process is a capital good. Hence this definition of capital goods fits in perfectly with the subjectivist conception of economics presented above. The economic nature of a capital good does not depend on its physical properties, but on the opinion of an actor, who believes the good will enable him to reach or complete a stage in his action process. Therefore capital goods, as we have defined them, are simply the intermediate stages the actor believes he needs to go through before achieving the purpose of his action. Capital goods should always be placed in a *teleological* context, in which the essential defining elements are the aim pursued and the actor's subjective view on the stages necessary to fulfill it.[10]

---

[9]In a world without time preference people would consume nothing and save everything, and eventually humans would die of starvation and civilization would disappear. "Exceptions" to the law of time preference are merely apparent and invariably result from a disregard for the *ceteris paribus* condition inherent in the law. Thus a careful examination of any supposed "counter-example" suffices to reveal that refutations of time preference do not involve identical circumstances. This is the case with goods that cannot be simultaneously enjoyed, or those which, although they appear physically equivalent, are not identical from the actor's subjective viewpoint (for instance, ice cream, which we prefer in summer, even when winter is closer). On the theory of time preference, see Mises, *Human Action*, pp. 483–90 (pp. 480–87 of the Scholar's Edition).

[10]   The principal point to be emphasized is that capital goods, thus defined, are distinguished in that they fall neatly into place in a *teleological* framework. They are the interim goals aimed at in earlier plans; they are the means toward the attainment of still further ends envisaged by the earlier plans. It is here maintained that the perception of this aspect of tangible things now available provides the key to the unravelling

Hence capital goods are "higher-order economic goods," or factors of production which subjectively materialize at each intermediate stage in a particular action process. Moreover capital goods arise from the union of three essential elements: natural resources, labor and time, all of which are combined in entrepreneurial action conceived and processed by human beings.[11]

The *sine qua non* for producing capital goods is *saving*, or the relinquishment or postponement of immediate consumption. Indeed in an action process the actor will only be able to

---

of the problems generally attempted to be elucidated by capital theory.

Israel M. Kirzner, *An Essay on Capital* (New York: Augustus M. Kelley, 1966), p. 38; reproduced in Israel M. Kirzner's book, *Essays on Capital and Interest: An Austrian Perspective* (Aldershot, U.K.: Edward Elgar, 1996), pp. 13–122.

[11]This explains the traditional notion of three factors of production: land or natural resources, labor, and capital goods or higher-order economic goods. In each process of action or production, the actor, using his entrepreneurial sense, generates and combines these factors or resources. The processes culminate in the market in four different types of income: pure entrepreneurial profit, stemming from the actor's alertness and creativity; rent from land or natural resources, in terms of their productive capacity; labor income or wages; and rent derived from the use of capital goods. Even though all capital goods ultimately consist of combinations of natural resources and labor, they also incorporate (apart from the entrepreneurial alertness and creativity necessary to conceive and generate them), the time required to produce them. Furthermore from an economic standpoint capital goods cannot be differentiated from natural resources solely in terms of their distinct physical form. Only purely economic criteria, such as the unaltered permanence of a good with respect to the achievement of goals and the fact that no further action is required of the actor, enable us from an economic standpoint to clearly distinguish between land (or a natural resource), which is always permanent, and capital goods, which strictly speaking, are not permanent and are spent or "consumed" during the production process, making it necessary to take their depreciation into account. This is why Hayek has affirmed that, despite appearances, "Permanent improvements in land is land." F.A. Hayek, *The Pure Theory of Capital* (London: Routledge and Kegan Paul, [1941] 1976), p. 57; reedited by Lawrence H. White, as vol. XII of *The Collected Works of F.A. Hayek* (Chicago: University of Chicago Press, 2007). See also p. 298 and footnote 31.

reach successive and increasingly time-consuming intermediate stages if he has first sacrificed the chance to undertake actions which would produce a more immediate result. In other words, he must give up the achievement of immediate ends which would satisfy current human needs (consumption). To illustrate this important concept, we will use the example given by Böhm-Bawerk to explain the process of saving and investment in capital goods carried out by an individual actor in an isolated situation, such as Robinson Crusoe on his island.[12]

Let us suppose that Robinson Crusoe has just arrived on his island and spends his time picking berries by hand, his only means of subsistence. Each day he devotes all of his efforts to gathering berries, and he picks enough to survive and can even eat a few extra daily. After several weeks on this diet, Robinson Crusoe makes the entrepreneurial discovery that with a wooden stick several meters long, he could reach higher and further, strike the bushes with force and gather the necessary berries much quicker. The only problem is that he estimates it could take him five whole days to find a suitable tree from which to take the stick and then to prepare it by pulling off its branches, leaves, and imperfections. During this time he will be compelled to interrupt his berry picking. If he wants to produce the stick, he will have to reduce his consumption of berries for a time and store the remainder in a basket until he has enough to survive for five days, the predicted duration of the production process of the wooden stick. After planning his action, Robinson Crusoe decides to undertake it, and therefore he must first *save* a portion of the berries he picks by hand each day, reducing his consumption by that amount. This clearly means he must make an inevitable *sacrifice*, which he nevertheless deems well worth

---

[12]This is the classic example given by Eugen von Böhm-Bawerk, *Kapital und Kapitalzins: Positive Theorie des Kapitales* (Innsbruck: Verlag der Wagner'schen Universitäts-Buchhandlung, 1889), pp. 107–35. This work has been translated into English by Hans F. Sennholz, *Capital and Interest*, vol. 2: *Positive Theory of Capital* (South Holland, Ill.: Libertarian Press, 1959), pp. 102–18.

his effort in relation to the goal he longs to achieve. So he decides to reduce his consumption (in other words, to save) for several weeks while storing his leftover berries in a basket until he has accumulated an amount he believes will be sufficient to sustain him while he produces the stick.

This example shows that each process of investment in capital goods requires prior saving; that is, a decrease in consumption, which must fall below its potential level.[13] Once Robinson Crusoe has saved enough berries, he spends five days searching for a branch from which to make his wooden stick, separating it from the tree and perfecting it. What does he eat during the five days it takes him to prepare the stick, a production process which forces him to interrupt his daily harvest of berries? He simply consumes the berries he accumulated in the basket over the preceding several-week period during which he saved the necessary portion from his hand-picked berries and experienced some hunger. In this way, if Robinson Crusoe's calculations were correct, at the end of five days he will have the stick (a capital good), which represents an intermediate stage removed in time (by five days of saving) from the immediate processes of the berry production (by hand) which up to that point had occupied him. With the finished stick Robinson Crusoe can reach places inaccessible to him by hand and strike the bushes with force, multiplying his production of berries by ten. As a result, from that point on his stick enables him to gather in one-tenth of a day the berries he

---

[13]Saving always results in capital goods, even when initially these merely consist of the consumer goods (in our example the "berries") which remain unsold (or are not consumed). Then gradually some capital goods (the berries) are replaced by others (the wooden stick), as the workers (Robinson Crusoe) combine their labor with natural resources through a process which takes time and which humans are able to go through due to their reliance on the unsold consumer goods (the saved berries). Hence saving produces capital goods first (the unsold consumer goods that remain in stock) which are gradually used up and replaced by another capital good (the wooden stick). On this important point, see Richard von Strigl, *Capital and Production*, edited with an introduction by Jörg Guido Hülsmann (Auburn, Ala.: Mises Institute, 2000), pp. 27 and 62.

needs to survive, and he can spend the rest of his time resting or pursuing subsequent goals that are much more important to him (like building a hut or hunting animals to vary his diet and make clothes).

Robinson Crusoe's production process, like any other, clearly arises from an act of entrepreneurial creativity, the actor's realization that he stands to benefit, i.e., he can accomplish ends more valuable to him, by employing action processes which require a longer period of time (because they include more stages). Thus action or production processes yield capital goods, which are simply intermediate economic goods in an action process whose aim has not yet been reached. The actor is only willing to sacrifice his immediate consumption (i.e., to save) if he thinks that by doing so he will achieve goals he values more (in this case, the production of ten times more berries than he could gather by hand). Furthermore *Robinson Crusoe must attempt to coordinate as well as possible his present behavior with his foreseeable future behavior.* More specifically, he must avoid initiating action processes that are excessively long in relation to his savings: it would be tragic for him to run out of berries (that is, to consume all he has saved) halfway through the process of producing a capital good and without reaching his goal. He must also refrain from saving too much with respect to his future investment needs, since by doing so he would only unnecessarily sacrifice his immediate consumption. Robinson Crusoe's subjective assessment of his time preference is precisely what enables him to adequately coordinate or adjust his present behavior in relation to his future needs and behavior. On the one hand, the fact that his time preference is not absolute makes it possible for him to forfeit some of his present consumption over a period of several weeks with the hope of thus being able to produce the stick. On the other hand, the fact that he does have a time preference explains why he only devotes his efforts to creating a capital good he can produce in a limited period of time and which requires sacrificing and saving for a *limited* number of days. If Robinson Crusoe had no time preference, nothing would stop him from dedicating all of his efforts to building a hut right away (which, for example, might take him a month minimum), a plan he would not be able to carry out without first having saved a large quantity of berries. Therefore he would either starve to death or the project, out of all proportion to his potential saving, would soon be interrupted and abandoned. At any rate, it is important to understand that the real saved resources (the berries in the basket) are precisely the ones which enable Robinson Crusoe to survive during the time period he spends producing the capital good and during which he ceases to gather berries directly. Even though Robinson Crusoe is undoubtedly much more productive harvesting berries with his wooden stick than he is with his bare hands, there is also no doubt that the process of berry production using the stick is a more lengthy one in terms of time (it includes more stages) than the production process of berry picking by hand. Production processes tend to increase in length and duration (i.e., to become more complex and include more stages) as a result of the saving and entrepreneurial activity of humans; and the longer and more time-consuming these processes become, the more productive they tend to be.

In a modern economy, in which many economic agents simultaneously perform different functions, we will use the term *capitalist* to denote that economic agent whose function is precisely to save; in other words, to consume less than he creates or produces and to make available to workers the resources they need to live for the duration of the production process in which they participate. (Robinson Crusoe also behaved like a capitalist when he saved berries that later enabled him to survive *while* he produced his wooden stick.) Thus when the capitalist saves, he frees up resources (consumer goods) which can be used to sustain workers who direct their energies to productive stages further removed from final consumption, i.e., the production of capital goods.

Unlike in the example of Robinson Crusoe, production processes in a modern economy are extremely complex, and in terms of time, very lengthy. They incorporate a multitude of stages, all of which are interrelated and divide into numerous secondary processes that humans employ in the innumerable action projects they constantly launch.

For instance the process of producing a car consists of hundreds or even thousands of productive stages requiring a very prolonged period of time (even several years) from the moment the car company begins to design the vehicle (the stage furthest from final consumption), orders the corresponding materials from its suppliers, runs these materials through the different assembly lines, orders the different parts for the motor and all accessories, etc., until it arrives at the stages closest to consumption, such as transport and distribution to dealers, the development of advertising campaigns and the presentation and sale of the car to the public. So although when we visit the factory we see a finished vehicle emerge every minute, we must not deceive ourselves by thinking the production process of each car lasts one minute. Instead we should be aware that each car calls for a process of production lasting several years, a process comprised of numerous stages, beginning when the model is conceived and designed and ending when the car is presented to its proud owner as a consumer good. In addition, in modern societies humans have a tendency to specialize in different stages of the production process. An increasing division of labor (or to be more precise, of knowledge), both horizontal and vertical, causes the stages in the production process to be continuously broken down into other stages as the division of knowledge spreads and deepens. Specific companies and economic agents tend to specialize in each one of these stages. Apart from a stage-by-stage analysis, we can also examine the process by considering the many phases which occur at once. At all times each of the stages coexists with the others and therefore some people spend their time designing vehicles (the cars which will be available to the public in ten years), while others simultaneously order materials from suppliers, others work on assembly lines, and others devote their efforts to the commercial field (very close to final consumption), promoting the sale of vehicles that have already been produced.[14]

---

[14]Mark Skousen, in his book *The Structure of Production* (London and New York: New York University Press, 1990), reproduces a simplified outline of the stages in the production process used in the textile and oil industries in the United States (pp. 168–69). He illustrates in detail the

Therefore it is clear that, just as the difference between the "rich" Robinson Crusoe with the stick and the "poor" Robinson Crusoe without it lay in the capital good the former had obtained through prior saving, the essential difference between rich societies and poor societies does not stem from any greater effort the former devote to work, nor even from any greater technological knowledge the former hold. Instead it arises mainly from the fact that *rich nations possess a more extensive network of capital goods wisely invested from an entrepreneurial standpoint. These goods consist of machines, tools, computers, buildings, semi-manufactured goods, software, etc., and they exist due to prior savings of the nation's citizens.* In other words, comparatively rich societies possess more wealth because they have more *time accumulated* in the form of capital goods, which places them closer in time to the achievement of much more valuable goals. There is no doubt that an American worker earns a much higher wage than an Indian worker, but this is chiefly because the former has at his disposal and uses many more capital goods (tractors, computers, machines, etc.) than the Indian worker, and the goods he uses are of much higher quality. To put it another way, the longer the production process, the more productive it tends to be, as we have seen. The modern tractor plows the earth much more productively than the Roman plow. Nevertheless the tractor is a capital good whose production requires a set of stages much more numerous, complex and lengthy than those necessary to produce a Roman plow.

Capital goods in the extremely complex network which composes the real productive structure of a modern economy *are not perpetual*, but are always temporary in the sense that they are physically used up or consumed during the production process, or they become obsolete. In other words, wear on

---

complexity of both processes as well as the significant number of stages they comprise and the very prolonged time period they require. This type of flow chart can be used to provide a simplified description of the activity in any other sector or industry. Skousen takes the diagrams of the above-mentioned industries from the book by E.B. Alderfer and H.E. Michel, *Economics of American Industry*, 3rd ed. (New York: McGraw-Hill, 1957).

capital equipment is not only physical, but technological and economic as well (obsolescence). Hence capital goods must be preserved and maintained (in Robinson Crusoe's case, he must take care of his stick and protect it from wear). This means entrepreneurs must repair existing capital goods; and, even more importantly, they must constantly produce new capital goods to replace the old ones they are in the process of consuming. *Depreciation* refers to the wear capital goods undergo during the production process. A certain minimum level of saving is essential in order to compensate for depreciation by producing the capital goods necessary to replace ones that have worn out or depreciated. This is the only way for the actor to maintain his productive capacity intact. Moreover if he wishes to further increase the number of stages, lengthen the processes and make them more productive, he will have to accumulate *even more than the minimum savings required to counteract the strict amortization rate*, the accounting term for the depreciation of capital goods. To save, the actor must reduce consumption in relation to production. If his output is constant, he must curtail his actual consumption; however if his output is growing, he will be able to save (to accumulate capital goods) by keeping his volume of consumption relatively constant. Nevertheless even in this last case saving requires the sacrifice (as always) of the increasing volumes of potential consumption which a growing output would permit.

In every production process (i.e., series of successive stages or capital goods) it is possible to distinguish the stages which are relatively closer in time to the final consumer good from those which are relatively further from it. As a general rule capital goods are difficult to convert, and the closer they are to the final stage of consumption, the more difficult is their convertibility. Nonetheless the fact that capital goods are difficult to adapt does not mean the actor, in his action process, is not often forced to modify the objectives of his action, and consequently, to review and convert the stages he has already completed (i.e., to convert his capital goods as far as is practicable). In any case, when circumstances change or the actor changes his mind and modifies the aim of his action, the capital goods he has produced up to that point may become utterly useless or they may be useful only after a costly conversion. The actor could also find a way to use the goods, yet still feel that had he known in advance they would eventually be needed in a different production process, he would have made them in quite a different way. Finally, it is very rare for a capital good to be so removed from consumption, or for the circumstances to be such, that the good is perfectly useful in any alternative project.

Thus we see the influence of the past on actions carried out today. Action, as we have defined it, is always prospective, never retrospective; and an actor considers a good a capital good based on a planned future action, not on the good's material properties nor on former action projects.[15] Nevertheless the past undoubtedly *influences* future action, to the extent that it determines the current starting point. Humans commit countless entrepreneurial errors when conceiving, undertaking, and completing their actions; and consequently, they embark on subsequent actions from a present position they would have attempted to make different had they known about it in advance. However once events have unfolded in a certain way, humans always strive to make the best of their present circumstances with a view to accomplishing their goals for the future. While capital goods are difficult to convert,

---

[15]For this reason Hayek is especially critical of the traditional definition of a capital good as an intermediate good produced by humans, a definition he considers

> a remnant of the cost of production theories of value, of the old views which sought the explanation of the economic attributes of a thing in the forces embodied in it. . . . Bygones are bygones in the theory of capital no less than elsewhere in economics. And the use of concepts which see the significance of a good in past expenditure on it can only be misleading.

Hayek, *The Pure Theory of Capital,* p. 89. Hayek concludes that

> For the problems connected with the demand for capital, the possibility of producing new equipment is fundamental. And all the time concepts used in the theory of capital, particularly those of the various investment periods, refer to prospective periods, and are always "forward-looking" and never "backward-looking." (Ibid., p. 90)

investors manage to provide them with considerable "mobility" through the juridical institutions of property and contract law, which regulate the different forms of transferring such goods. Thus the (extremely complex and prolonged) productive structure permits the constant mobility of investors, through the exchange and sale of capital goods in the market.[16]

We are now ready to consider the concept of *capital*, which from an economic viewpoint differs from the concept of "capital goods." In fact we will define "capital" *as the market value of capital goods*, a value estimated by the individual actors who buy and sell capital goods in a free market.[17] Thus we see that capital is simply an abstract concept or instrument of economic calculation; in other words, a subjective valuation of or judgment on the market value entrepreneurs attribute to capital goods and on the basis of which they continually buy and sell them, attempting to make a pure entrepreneurial profit with each transaction. Therefore in a socialist economy in which neither free markets nor market prices exist, it is perhaps feasible to speak of capital goods, but not of capital: the latter always requires a market and prices which are freely determined by the economic agents who participate in it. If it were not for market prices and the subjective estimation of the capital value of goods that compose the intermediate stages in production processes, in a modern society it would be impossible to estimate or calculate whether or not the final value of the goods to be produced using capital goods offsets

---

[16]A demoralized entrepreneur who wishes to abandon his business and settle elsewhere can find sure, constant mobility in the market: legal contracts permit him to put his business up for sale, liquidate it and use his new liquidity to acquire another company. In this way he achieves real, effective mobility that is much greater than the mere physical or technical mobility of the capital good (which, as we have seen, is usually rather limited).

[17]Nonetheless on various occasions we will be forced to use the term capital less strictly, to refer to the set of capital goods which make up the productive structure. This loose sense of "capital" is the one intended by, among others, Hayek in *The Pure Theory of Capital*, p. 54; it is also the meaning intended by Lachmann in *Capital and its Structure*, where on page 11 "capital" is defined as "the heterogeneous stock of material resources."

the cost involved in the production processes, neither would it be possible to direct in a coordinated way the efforts of people who contribute to the different action processes.[18]

We have attempted elsewhere to demonstrate that all systematic coercion which impedes the free exercise of entrepreneurship prevents humans from discovering the information they need to carry out their actions.[19] It also keeps them from spontaneously transmitting this information and coordinating their behavior with respect to the needs of others. This means that the coercive intervention which is characteristic of socialism, of state interventionism in the economy, and of the granting of privileges to certain groups against traditional legal principles, prevents to a greater or lesser extent the exercise of entrepreneurship, and hence the coordinated action of human beings; it also tends to generate systematic maladjustments in the framework of society. Systematic discoordination can be intratemporal; or, as in the case of human actions related to different stages of production processes or capital goods, *intertemporal*, such that *human beings who cannot act freely tend to adjust their present behavior poorly to their future behavior and needs.*

As we saw from Robinson Crusoe's isolated production process, intertemporal coordination is fundamental to all human action which takes time and especially to those actions related to capital goods; thus the great importance of permitting the free exercise of entrepreneurship in this area. In this way entrepreneurs constantly discover profit opportunities in the market, believing they see new possible combinations of capital goods, and considering these combinations to be undervalued with respect to the market price they estimate they will be able to obtain in the future for the consumer goods they produce. In short we are referring to a process of continual buying and selling, "recombination" and production of new kinds of capital goods, a process which generates

---

[18]This is precisely the fundamental argument Mises raises concerning the impossibility of economic calculation in a socialist economy. See Huerta de Soto, *Socialismo, cálculo económico y función empresarial*, chaps. 3–7.

[19]Ibid., chaps. 2 and 3, pp. 41–155.

a dynamic and very complex productive structure which always tends to expand horizontally and vertically.[20] Without free entrepreneurship, nor free markets for capital goods and money, it is impossible to make the necessary economic calculation regarding the horizontal and vertical extension of the different stages in the production process, resulting in widespread discoordinated behavior that throws society off balance and prevents its harmonious development. In entrepreneurial processes of intertemporal coordination, a leading role is played by an important market price: the price of present goods in relation to future goods, more commonly known as the interest rate, which regulates the relationship between consumption, saving and investment in modern societies, and which we will study in detail in the next section.

THE INTEREST RATE

As we have seen, other things being equal, humans always place present goods higher than future goods on their scale of value. However the relative *intensity* of this difference in subjective valuation varies substantially from one person to another; and it can even vary greatly throughout the life of one person based on changes in his circumstances. Some people have a high time preference and value the present greatly in relation to the future; thus they are only willing to sacrifice the immediate achievement of their ends if they expect or believe they will accomplish in the future goals they subjectively value very highly. Other people have a more limited time preference, and although they also value present goods more than future goods, they are more predisposed to relinquish the immediate achievement of their aims in exchange for objectives which they value only a little more and which will be reached tomorrow. This difference in the *psychic intensity* of the subjective valuation of present goods in relation to future goods, a difference reflected on each human actor's

---

[20]This is the terminology used, for example, by Knut Wicksell in *Lectures on Political Economy* (London: Routledge and Kegan Paul, 1951), vol. 1, p. 164, where Wicksell expressly mentions a "horizontal-dimension" and a "vertical-dimension" to the structure of capital goods.

scale of value, means that in a market comprising many economic agents, each of which has his own distinct and variable time preference, multiple opportunities arise for mutually beneficial exchanges.

Hence people with a low time preference will be willing to give up present goods in exchange for future goods valued only a bit higher, and they will perform exchanges in which they will hand over their present goods to people with a higher time preference, i.e., people who value the present more intensely than they do. The creativity and alertness inherent in entrepreneurship give rise to a market process that tends to establish a *market price* for present goods with respect to future goods. *We will use the term "interest rate" to denote the market price of present goods in relation to future goods.* Given that in the market many actions are carried out using money as a generally-accepted medium of exchange, the interest rate is the price one must pay to obtain a certain number of m.u. immediately; this price reflects the number of units one must return in exchange at the end of the set term or time period. Generally, for reasons of custom, the price is expressed as a certain yearly percentage. For instance, an interest rate of 9 percent indicates that market transactions are conducted in such a way that it is possible to obtain 100 m.u. immediately (present good) in exchange for a promise to turn over 109 m.u. at the end of one year (future good).[21]

Therefore the interest rate is the price established in a market in which the suppliers or sellers of present goods are

---

[21]The interest rate can actually be interpreted in two different ways. It can be seen as a ratio of today's prices (of which one corresponds to the good available today and the other corresponds to the same good available tomorrow); or it can be considered the price of present goods in terms of future goods. Both ideas yield the same result. The former is the one advocated by Ludwig von Mises, for whom the interest rate "is a ratio of commodity prices, not a price in itself" (*Human Action*, p. 526). We prefer to favor the latter here, following Murray N. Rothbard. A detailed analysis of how the interest rate is determined as the market price of present goods in terms of future goods, along with other studies, can be found in Murray N. Rothbard's book, *Man, Economy, and*

precisely the savers; that is, all those relatively more willing to relinquish immediate consumption in exchange for goods of greater value in the future. The buyers of present goods are all those who consume immediate goods and services (be they workers, owners of natural resources or capital goods, or any combination of these). Indeed the market of present and future goods, in which the interest rate is determined, *consists of society's entire structure of productive stages,* in which savers or capitalists give up immediate consumption and offer present goods to owners of the primary or original factors of production (workers and owners of natural resources) and to owners of capital goods, in exchange for the full ownership of consumer (and capital) goods of a supposedly higher value once the production of these goods has been completed in the future. If we eliminate the positive (or negative) effect of pure entrepreneurial profits (or losses), this difference in value tends to coincide with the interest rate.

State: A Treatise on Economic Principles, 3rd ed. (Auburn, Ala.: Ludwig von Mises Institute, 1993), chaps. 5–6, pp. 273–387. In any case the interest rate is determined in the same way as any other market price. The only difference lies in the fact that, rather than reflect an established price for each good or service in terms of m.u., the interest rate is based on the sale of present goods in exchange for future goods, each in the form of m.u. Although we defend the idea that the interest rate is determined exclusively by time preference (i.e., by the subjective valuations of utility which time preference entails), the acceptance of another theory (for example, that to a greater or lesser degree the interest rate is set by the marginal productivity of capital) does not affect this book's essential argument concerning the disruptive effects which banks' expansive creation of loans has on the productive structure. In this regard, Charles E. Wainhouse states:

> Hayek establishes that his monetary theory of economic fluctuations is consistent with any of the "modern interest theories" and need not be based on any particular one. The key is the monetary causes of deviations of the current from the equilibrium rate of interest.

"Empirical Evidence for Hayek's Theory of Economic Fluctuations," chapter 2 in *Money in Crisis: The Federal Reserve, the Economy and Monetary Reform,* Barry N. Siegel, ed. (San Francisco: Pacific Institute for Public Policy Research, 1984), p. 40.

From a legal standpoint, exchanges of present goods for future goods can take many forms. For instance, in a cooperative the workers themselves simultaneously act as capitalists, waiting until the end of the entire production process to acquire the ownership of the final good and its full value. Nevertheless in most cases workers are not willing to wait until the production process ends nor to take on the risks and uncertainties it entails. Thus instead of forming cooperatives, they prefer to sell the services of their productive effort in exchange for immediate present goods. They agree on a labor contract (an employment contract for another's account) according to which the person who advances them the present goods (the capitalist, saver or supplier of present goods) receives the full ownership of the final good once it has been produced. Combinations of these two different types of contract are also possible. This is not the proper place to analyze the different legal forms which the exchange of present goods for future goods takes in a modern society. Furthermore these forms do not affect the fundamental argument we advance in this book, though they are undoubtedly of great interest from a theoretical and practical standpoint.

It is worth noting that the "loan market," in which one may obtain a loan by agreeing to pay the corresponding interest rate, constitutes a relatively small part of the general market, in which present goods are exchanged for future goods and which encompasses the entire productive structure of society. Here owners of the original means of production (labor and natural resources) and capital goods act as demanders of present goods, and savers act as suppliers of them. Therefore the short-, medium-, and long-term loan market is simply a subset of that much broader market in which present goods are exchanged for future goods and with respect to which it plays a mere secondary and dependent role, despite the fact that the loan market is the most visible and obvious to the general public.[22] In fact it is entirely possible to conceive

---

[22]What we colloquially refer to as the "money market" is actually just a short-term loan market. The true money market encompasses the entire

of a society in which no loan market exists, and all economic
agents invest their savings in production *directly* (via internal
financing and retained earnings through partnerships, corporations, and cooperatives). Although in this case no interest
rate would be established in a (nonexistent) loan market, an
interest rate would still be determined by the ratio at which
present goods are exchanged for future goods in the different
intermediate stages in production processes. Under these circumstances the interest rate would be determined by the *"rate
of profit"* which would tend to equal the net income at each
stage in the production process, per unit of value and time
period. Although this interest rate is not directly observable in
the market, and even though in each company and in each specific production process it incorporates important external factors (such as the components of pure entrepreneurial profits or
losses, and the risk premium), the profit generated in each
stage of the entire economic system would tend to correspond
to the interest rate, due to the typical entrepreneurial process of
equalizing accounting profits over the different stages of the
productive structure, assuming no further changes occur and
all creative possibilities and opportunities for entrepreneurial
profit have already been discovered and exploited.[23]

---

market in which goods and services are exchanged for m.u. and in
which the price or purchasing power of money, and the monetary price
of each good and service are simultaneously determined. This is why
the following affirmation, made by Marshall, is wholly misleading:
"The 'money market' is the market for command over money: 'the value
of money' in it at any time is the rate of discount, or of interest for short
period loans charged in it." Alfred Marshall, *Money Credit and Commerce*
(London: Macmillan, 1924), p. 14. Mises, in *Human Action*, p. 403, completely clears up Marshall's confusion of terms.

[23]However, strictly speaking, the concept of a "rate of profit" makes no
sense in real life, and we have only introduced it by way of illustration
and to aid the reader in understanding the theory of the cycle. As Mises
states:

> [I]t becomes evident that it is absurd to speak of a "rate of
> profit" or a "normal rate of profit" or an "average rate of
> profit." . . . There is nothing "normal" in profits and there can
> never be an "equilibrium" with regard to them. (Mises,
> *Human Action*, p. 297)

In the outside world, the only directly-observable figures are what we could call the *gross interest rate* or *market rate of interest* (which coincides with the interest rate in the credit market) and the *gross accounting profits* generated by each production activity (i.e., net income). The first consists of the interest rate as we have defined it (also sometimes called the *originary* or *natural rate of interest*), plus the *risk premium* corresponding to the operation in question, plus or minus a *premium for expected inflation or deflation*; that is, for the expected decrease or increase in the purchasing power of the monetary unit used in exchanges of present goods for future goods and in calculations regarding such transactions.

The second figure, which is also directly observable in the market, represents *gross accounting profits* (i.e., net income) derived from the specific productive activity carried out at each stage of the production process. These profits tend to match the gross interest rate (or market rate of interest) as we have defined it in the preceding paragraph, plus or minus pure entrepreneurial profits or losses.[24] As in all markets entrepreneurial profits and losses tend to disappear as a result of competition between entrepreneurs, the accounting profits of each productive activity by time period tend to match the gross market interest rate. Indeed the accounting profits reported by each company for a financial year could be considered to include an implicit interest-rate component, with respect to the resources saved and invested by the capitalists

---

[24]In fact the interest rate at which loans are negotiated in the credit market also includes an entrepreneurial component we have not mentioned in the text. This arises from the inescapable uncertainty (not "risk") regarding, for instance, the possibility that systematic changes could occur in society's rate of time preference or other disturbances impossible to insure against:

> The granting of credit is necessarily always an entrepreneurial speculation which can possibly result in failure and the loss of a part of the total amount lent. Every interest stipulated and paid in loans includes not only originary interest but also entrepreneurial profit. (Mises, *Human Action*, p. 536)

who own the company. This implicit component, together with the risk factor and entrepreneurial profits or losses which result from the purely entrepreneurial activity of the business, give rise to accounting profits. From this perspective it is possible for a company to report accounting profits (i.e., net income) when it has actually suffered entrepreneurial losses, if accounting profits fail to reach the amount necessary to exceed the implicit gross-market-interest-rate component that applies to resources capitalists invest in their businesses throughout the financial year.

In any case, regardless of the external form interest takes, the key is to remember that as a market price or social rate of time preference, interest plays a vital role in the coordination of the behavior of consumers, savers, investors, and producers in a modern society. Just as it was crucial for Robinson Crusoe to coordinate his actions and refrain from dedicating to future goals an effort disproportionate to his stock of saved present goods, the same issue, *intertemporal coordination*, arises constantly in society.

In a modern economy, present and future behaviors are reconciled through entrepreneurial activity in the market where present goods are exchanged for future goods and the interest rate, the market price of one type of goods in terms of the other, is established. Thus the more plentiful the savings, i.e., the greater the quantity of present goods sold or offered for sale, other things being equal, the lower their price in terms of future goods; and consequently, the lower the market rate of interest. This indicates to entrepreneurs that more present goods are available, which enables them to increase the length and complexity of the stages in their production processes, making these stages more productive. In contrast, the fewer the savings, i.e., other things being equal, the less economic agents are willing to give up immediate consumption of present goods, the higher the market rate of interest. Thus a high market rate of interest shows that savings are relatively scarce, an unmistakable sign entrepreneurs should heed to avoid unduly lengthening the different stages in the production process and generating as a result discoordination or maladjustments which pose a great danger to the sustained, healthy and harmonious development of society.[25] In short the interest rate conveys to entrepreneurs which new productive stages or investment projects they can and should embark on and which they should not, in order to keep coordinated, as much as humanly possible, the behavior of savers, consumers, and investors, and to prevent the different productive stages from remaining unnecessarily short or becoming too long.

Finally we must point out that the market rate of interest tends to be the same throughout the entire time market or productive structure in society, not only *intratemporally*, i.e., in different areas of the market, but also *intertemporally*, i.e., in some productive stages relatively close to consumption as in other productive stages further from it. Indeed if the interest rate one can obtain by advancing present goods in some stages (for example, those closest to consumption) is higher than that one can obtain in other stages (for example, those furthest from consumption), then the entrepreneurial force itself, driven by a desire for profit, will lead people to *disinvest* in stages in which the interest rate or "rate of profit" is lower, relatively speaking, and to invest in stages in which the expected interest rate or "rate of profit" is higher.

THE STRUCTURE OF PRODUCTION

Although it is nearly impossible to illustrate with charts the extremely complex structure of productive stages that make up a modern economy, Chart V-1 represents a simplified version of this structure, and we include it with the purpose of clarifying the theoretical arguments we will later develop.

---

[25]This same idea is focal in Roger Garrison's latest book, which we read after the first edition of our book had been published in Spanish. Garrison states:

> [T]he intertemporal allocation may be internally consistent and hence sustainable, or it may involve some systematic internal inconsistency, in which case its sustainability is threatened. The distinction between sustainable and unsustainable patterns of resource allocation is, or should be, a major focus of macroeconomic theorizing. (Garrison, *Time and Money*, pp. 33–34)

Moreover although this chart is not strictly necessary for explaining the essential theoretical arguments, and in fact, authors of the stature of Ludwig von Mises never used it in their presentation of the theory of capital and of business cycles,[26] traditionally many theorists have considered it helpful to use simplified charts of the stages in real production processes (like Chart V-1) in order to clarify their arguments.[27]

---

[26]Mises, *The Theory of Money and Credit* and also *Human Action*.

[27]The first theorist to propose an illustration basically identical to that of Chart V-1 was William Stanley Jevons in his book *The Theory of Political Economy*, the 1st edition of which was published in 1871. We have used a reprint of the 5th edition (Kelley and Millman, eds.), published in 1957 in New York; page 230 includes a diagram where, according to Jevons, "line ox indicates the duration of investment and the height attained at any point, i, is the amount of capital invested." Later, in 1889, Eugen von Böhm-Bawerk gave more in-depth consideration to the theoretical issue of the structure of successive stages of capital goods and to using charts to illustrate this structure. He proposed to represent it by successive annual concentric circles (the expression Böhm-Bawerk uses is *konzentrische Jahresringe*), each of which depicts a productive stage; the circles overlap other larger ones. This type of chart appears, along with Böhm-Bawerk's explanation of it, on pp. 114–15 of his book, *Kapital und Kapitalzins*, vol. 2: *Positive Theorie des Kapitales*; the corresponding pages of the English edition, *Capital and Interest*, are pp. 106–07, vol. 2. The chief problem with Böhm-Bawerk's chart is that it depicts the passage of time in a very clumsy way and therefore reveals the need for a second dimension (vertical). Böhm-Bawerk could easily have gotten around this difficulty by replacing his "concentric rings" with a number of cylinders placed one on top of the other, so that each cylinder has a base smaller than the one below it (like a circular wedding cake whose layers are smaller in diameter the higher their position). Hayek later overcame this difficulty, in 1931, in the first edition of his now classic book, *Prices and Production*, foreword by Lionel Robbins (London: Routledge, 1931; 2nd rev. ed., in 1935); p. 36 of the first edition and p. 39 of the second. From this point on, unless we indicate otherwise, all quotations taken from this book will come from the 2nd edition. The book contains a chart very similar to Chart V-1. Hayek used this type of illustration again in 1941 (but this time in continuous terms) in his book, *The Pure Theory of Capital* (see, for example, p. 109). Moreover in 1941 Hayek also developed a prospective three-dimensional chart of the different stages in the production process. What this chart gains in accuracy, precision, and elegance, it loses in comprehensibility (p. 117 of the 1941 English edition).

The stages of the productive structure reflected in Chart V-1 do not represent the production of capital goods and consumer goods in physical terms, but rather their value in monetary units (m.u.). To the left of the chart we assume that the productive structure is composed of five stages whose "order

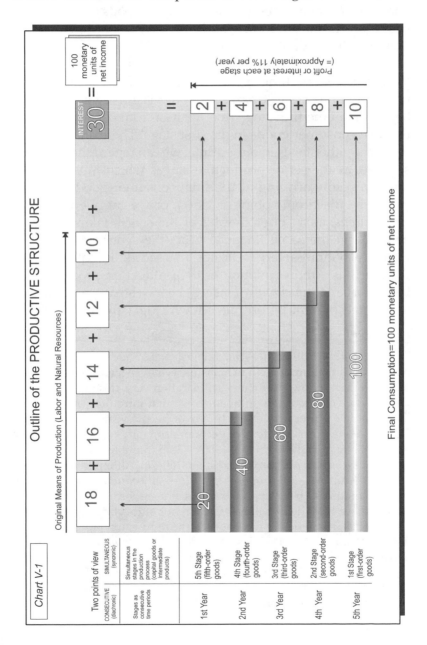

Chart V-1

Outline of the PRODUCTIVE STRUCTURE

number," in keeping with Menger's classic contribution, increases with the distance from the final stage of consumption. Thus the *first stage* comprises "first-order economic goods" or consumer goods which, in our chart, are exchanged for the value of one hundred m.u. The *second stage* is composed of "second-order economic goods," or the capital goods closest to consumption. The third, fourth, and fifth stages continue this pattern, and the fifth stage is the furthest from consumption. In order to simplify the explanation, we have supposed that each stage requires the time period of one year, and therefore the production process in Chart V-1 would last five years from its beginning in the fifth stage (the furthest from consumption) to the final consumer goods in the first stage. There are two ways to consider the stages in our outline: we can regard them as consecutive, as the set of productive stages which must be gone through before arriving at the final consumer good after five years (the diachronic point of view); or we can view them as *simultaneous*, as a "photograph" of the stages taking place at one time in the same financial year (the synchronic point of view). As Böhm-Bawerk indicates, this second interpretation of the chart (as a representation of the production process in the form of a set of *synchronized* stages) bears a strong resemblance to the age pyramids formulated with data from the census.

In 1962 Murray Rothbard (*Man, Economy, and State*, chaps. 6–7) proposed a depiction similar and in many aspects even superior to Hayek's. Mark Skousen follows Rothbard's illustration very closely in his book, *The Structure of Production*. In Spanish we first introduced the chart of the stages in the productive structure over twenty years ago in the article, "La teoría austriaca del ciclo económico," originally published in *Moneda y crédito*, no. 152 (March 1980): 37–55 (republished in our book, *Estudios de economía política*, chap. 13, pp. 160–76). Although the triangular charts Knut Wicksell proposes in *Lectures on Political Economy* (vol. 1, p. 159) could also be interpreted as an illustration of the productive structure, we have deliberately left them out of this brief outline of the history of charts depicting the stages in the production process. See also Alonso Neira, M.A., "Hayek's Triangle," *An Eponymeus Dictionary of Economics: A Guide to Laws and Theorems Named after Economists*, Julio Segura and Carlos Rodriquez Braun, eds. (Cheltenham, U.K.: Edward Elgar, 2004). Finally a critical analysis of Hayekian triangles from the Austrian point of view can be seen in Walter Block and William Barnett, "Hayekian Triangles," *Procesos de Mercado* 3, no. 2 (2006).

These pyramids represent cross-sections of the real population, which is classified by ages. In them we can also see the change in the number of people of each age who remain alive (mortality table); this second interpretation means viewing the stages as consecutive.[28]

The arrows in our diagram represent the *flows* of monetary income which at each stage in the production process reach the owners of the original means of production (labor and natural resources) in the form of wages and rents, and the owners of capital goods (capitalists or savers) in the form of interest (or accounting profit). Indeed if we begin at the first stage in our example, consumers spend 100 m.u. on consumer goods, and this money becomes the property of the capitalists who own the consumer goods industries. One year earlier, these capitalists had advanced from their savings 80 m.u. corresponding to the services of fixed capital goods and to circulating capital goods produced by other capitalists in the second stage of the production process. The first capitalists also pay 10 m.u. to the owners of the original means of production (labor and natural resources) which they hire directly in the last stage, corresponding to the production of consumer goods (this payment to the owners of the original means of production is represented on our chart by the *vertical* arrow that begins to the right of the last step [100 m.u.] and extends to the upper right-hand box containing 10 m.u.). Since the capitalists of the consumer goods stage advanced eighty m.u. to the owners of the capital goods of the second stage, and ten m.u. to workers and owners of natural resources (a total of 90 m.u.), at the end of one year when these capitalists sell the

---

28 The inventory of capital constitutes, so to speak, a cross section of the many processes of production which are of varying length and which began at different times. It therefore cuts across them at very widely differing stages of development. We might compare it to the census which is a cross section through the paths of human life and which encounters and which arrests the individual members of society at widely varying ages and stages. (Böhm-Bawerk, *Capital and Interest*, vol. 2: *Positive Theory of Capital*, p. 106)

In the original edition, this quotation appears on p. 115.

consumer goods for 100 units, they obtain an accounting profit or interest derived from having advanced 90 m.u. from savings a year earlier. This difference between the total amount they advanced, 90 m.u. (which they could have consumed, yet they saved and invested it), and the amount they receive at the end of a year, 100 m.u., is equal to an interest rate of approximately 11 percent per year (10:90 = 0.11). From an accounting standpoint, this sum appears as profit on the income statement drawn up to reflect the entrepreneurial activity of capitalists of the consumer goods stage (represented by the box at the lower right-hand corner of Chart V-1).

We can follow the same reasoning with respect to the rest of the stages. Hence for example, the capitalists who own the intermediate goods of the third stage advanced at the beginning of the period 40 m.u. in payment for capital goods produced in the fourth stage, as well as 14 m.u. to owners of the original means of production (labor and natural resources). In exchange for the 54 m.u. they have advanced, the capitalists become owners of the product which, once it is finished, they sell to capitalists of the second stage for 60 m.u., earning a differential of six m.u., which is their accounting profit or interest; it is also close to 11 percent. This pattern repeats itself in each stage.

The upper portion of the chart shows the amounts which the capitalists advance at each stage to the original means of production (workers and owners of natural resources) and which add up to a total of 70 m.u. (18+16+14+12+10=70 m.u.). In a column on the right-hand side, we indicate the monetary sums obtained as accounting profits at each stage. These profits reflect the accounting difference between the m.u. advanced by the capitalists of each stage and those they receive for the sale of their product in the following stage. As we know, this accounting profit tends to coincide with the interest derived from the amount the capitalists of each stage save and advance to capitalists of earlier stages and to the owners of the original means of production. The total of the accounting differences between income and expenses at each stage adds up to 30 m.u., which when added to the 70 m.u. received by the original means of production, equals 100 m.u.

of net income, which coincides exactly with the amount spent on final consumer goods during the period.

Some Additional Considerations

We must now discuss some important additional considerations regarding our outline of the stages in the production process:

1. *The arbitrary selection of the time period of each stage.*

First we must state that the decision to make each stage last one year was purely arbitrary, and any other time period could have been chosen. We decided on one year because that is the business and accounting period most commonly used, and therefore it makes the proposed illustrative outline of productive stages easier to understand.

2. *The avoidance of the erroneous concept of "average period of production."*

Second, we should indicate that the five-year duration of the production process in our example is also purely arbitrary. Modern production processes are highly complex, as we know, and they vary greatly from one sector or business to another, with respect to the number and duration of stages. At any rate, it is unnecessary and pointless to refer to an "average period of production," since *a priori* estimates of the length of any particular production process depend on the specific process itself. We know that capital goods are actually the intermediate stages in a production process initiated by an entrepreneur. From a subjective point of view, a production process always has a *beginning*, the specific moment at which the actor first perceives that a particular goal is worthwhile to him, and a certain set of intermediate stages which he conceives in advance and later attempts to carry out as he acts. Hence our analysis is not based on the idea of an "average period of production" and is therefore immune to criticism of that concept.[29] In fact all production periods have a specific

---

[29]John B. Clark, "The Genesis of Capital," *Yale Review* 2 (November 1893): 302–15; and "Concerning the Nature of Capital: A Reply," *Quarterly*

origin and cannot be traced back indefinitely in time; instead
each stops at the very moment a certain entrepreneur took up
the pursuit of an aim which constituted the imagined final
stage in his process.[30] Thus the first stage of production begins
precisely at the moment the entrepreneur conceives of the
final stage in the process (a consumer good or a capital good).
In identifying the beginning of the first stage, it is totally irrelevant whether or not the production process in question
involves the use of capital goods or factors of production completed in advance, yet which no one had ever imagined would
eventually be used in such a process. Moreover it is unnecessary to trace back indefinitely in time the conception of a set
of stages in a production process because any capital good
produced in advance which nevertheless remains unused for
a specific purpose for any length of time, ultimately becomes
another "original" resource, so to speak, similar in this respect
to all other natural resources that generate income, yet are
viewed by the actor as just another initial factor in his course
of action.[31] In short all production processes are invariably
prospective, they have an identifiable beginning and a foreseeable end, and their duration varies according to the process
in question yet is never infinite nor undetermined. Therefore
the retrospective calculation of supposed, phantasmagoric
average periods of production is meaningless.

Journal of Economics (May 1907). Frank H. Knight, "Capitalist Production, Time and the Rate of Return," in *Economic Essays in Honour of Gustav Cassel* (London: George Allen and Unwin, 1933).

[30]Ludwig von Mises very clearly states that

> The length of time expended in the past for the production of
> capital goods available today does not count at all. These cap-
> ital goods are valued only with regard to their usefulness for
> future satisfaction. The "average period of production" is an
> empty concept. (Mises, *Human Action*, p. 489)

Rothbard expresses a similar opinion in his book, *Man, Economy, and
State*, pp. 412–13.

[31]Furthermore Rothbard points out that

3. *Fixed and circulating capital goods.*

A third pertinent observation about our portrayal of productive stages is that it includes not only fixed capital goods, but also circulating capital goods and durable consumer goods. From a human actor's prospective point of view, the distinction between fixed and circulating capital goods is irrelevant, since it is largely based on the *physical* characteristics of the goods in question and depends especially upon whether or not these goods are considered to have been "completed." Indeed when fixed capital goods are incorporated into a production process, they are considered "completed," while circulating capital goods are thought to be semi-manufactured or in an "intermediate" process of production. However according to the subjectivist view on production processes aimed at consumption, *both fixed and circulating capital goods constitute intermediate stages in an action process which only concludes when the final consumer good satisfies the desires of consumers*; therefore, economically speaking, it is senseless to distinguish between the two.

The same can be said for "inventories" or stocks of intermediate goods held on hand at each of the productive stages. These stocks, which are considered a part of circulating capital, constitute one of the most significant components of the value of each stage in a process of production. Furthermore it has been demonstrated that as the economy evolves and prospers, these stocks become more important because they enable different businesses to minimize the ever-latent risk of unexpected shortages or "bottlenecks" which prolong delivery

---

[l]and that has been irrigated by canals or altered through the chopping down of forests has become a present, permanent *given*. Because it is a present given, not worn out in the process of production, and not needing to be replaced, it becomes a *land* factor under our definition. (Italics in original)

Rothbard concludes that once

the permanent are separated from the nonpermanent alterations, we see that *the structure of production no longer stretches back infinitely in time, but comes to a close within a relatively brief span of time.* (*Man, Economy and State*, p. 414; italics added)

periods. In this way, inventories make it possible for clients at all levels (not only at the level of consumption, but also at the level of intermediate goods) to have at their disposal a growing variety of products to choose from and acquire immediately. Hence one manifestation of the lengthening of production processes is precisely a continual increase in inventories or stocks of intermediate goods.

4. *The role of durable consumer goods.*

Fourth, durable consumer goods satisfy human needs over a very prolonged period of time. Therefore they simultaneously form a part of several stages at once: the final stage of consumption and various preceding stages, according to their duration. In any case, for our purposes it is irrelevant whether the consumer himself must wait a certain number of years or stages before taking advantage of the latest *services* his durable consumer good can perform. Only when these services are directly received do we reach the last stage of Chart V-1, the stage of consumption. The years the owner spends caring for and maintaining his durable consumer good so that it will continue to perform consumer services for him in the future correspond to the stages which appear above and are increasingly distant from consumption: stage two, three, four, etc.[32] Thus one of the manifestations of the lengthening of production

---

[32]As F.A. Hayek has explained,

> The different installments of future services which such goods are expected to render will in that case have to be imagined to belong to different "stages" of production corresponding to the time interval which will elapse before these services mature.

Prices and Production, p. 40; footnote on p. 2. In this respect the equivalence between durable consumer goods and capital goods had already been revealed by Eugen von Böhm-Bawerk, according to whom, "The value of the remoter installments of the renditions of service is subject to the same fate as is the value of future goods." *Capital and Interest*, vol. 2: *Positive Theory of Capital*, pp. 325–37, esp. p. 337. In the German edition see the chapter dedicated to "Der Zins aus ausdauernden Gütern," on pp. 361–82 of the 1889 edition already cited. Böhm-Bawerk expresses this principle in German in the following way: "In Folge davon verfällt der Werth der entlegeneren Nutzleistungsraten demselben Schicksale,

processes and of the increase in their number of stages consists precisely of the production of a larger number of durable consumer goods of increasing quality and durability.[33]

5. *The trend toward the equalization of the rate of accounting profit or interest at each stage.*

The fifth fundamental point we must emphasize is the following: In the market there exists a trend (driven by the force of entrepreneurship) toward the equalization of the "rate of profit" in all economic activities. This occurs not only *horizontally*, within each production stage, but also *vertically*, between stages. Indeed when there are disparities in profits, businessmen will devote their effort, creative capacity and investment to those activities which generate relatively higher profits, and they will stop devoting these things to activities which yield lower profits. Significantly, in the example from Chart V-1, the rate of accounting profit, or relative difference between income and expenses, is the same at each stage, i.e., approximately 11 percent per year. If the situation

---

wie der Werth künftiger Güter." See *Kapital und Kapitalzins*, vol. 2: *Positive Theorie des Kapitales*, p. 365. In Spain José Castañeda Chornet reveals that perhaps he has been the one who has best understood this essential idea when he affirms that

> Durable consumer goods, which generate a flow of consumer services over time, may be included in an economy's fixed capital. In a strict sense they constitute fixed consumer capital, not productive capital. So capital, in a broad sense, comprises productive or true capital as well as consumer capital, or capital for use. (Castañeda, *Lecciones de teoría económica*, p. 686)

[33]Roger W. Garrison has put forward the additional argument that all consumer goods for which a secondhand market exists should be classified, from an economic standpoint, as investment goods. In fact consumer goods classified as "durable" simultaneously form a part of consecutive stages in the production process, although they legally belong to "consumers," since consumers take care of, protect and maintain them in their productive capacity so they will render direct consumer services over a period of many years. Roger Garrison, "The Austrian-Neoclassical Relation: A Study in Monetary Dynamics," doctoral thesis presented at the University of Virginia, 1981, p. 45. On the possibility and convenience of representing consumer durables in our chart, see Garrison, *Time and Money*, pp. 47–48.

were otherwise; that is, if in one of the stages the rate of accounting profit or interest were higher, then disinvestment would take place, and productive resources would be withdrawn from the stages with a lower rate of profit and directed to those with a higher rate of accounting profit. This redirection of resources takes place until the greater demand for capital goods and original means of production in the receiving stage results in an increase in spending on these components in that stage; and the greater influx of its final goods tends to reduce their prices, until the differential between income and expenses decreases, giving rise to a rate of profit equal to that of other productive stages. *This microeconomic reasoning is key to understanding modifications made to the number and length of productive stages; we will later examine these changes.*

6. *Gross and net investment and saving.*

Sixth, although in the example from Chart V-1 the total *net income* received by owners of the original means of production and by capitalists in the form of profit or interest (100 m.u.) coincides exactly with the sum spent over the period in consumer goods (and thus *net saving* is equal to zero), there is a significant volume of gross saving and investment. In fact gross saving and investment are reflected in Table V-1, which indicates for each stage, at the left-hand side of the table, the supply of present goods offered by savers in exchange for future goods. At the right-hand side, we find the corresponding demand for present goods experienced by the providers of future goods, mainly owners of the original means of production (labor and natural resources) and the capitalists of earlier stages. We can observe from the table that gross saving, or the total supply of present goods, equals 270 m.u.: overall gross saving which takes place in the economic system and is 2.7 times greater than the amount spent during the year on final consumer goods. This *gross saving* is identical to the *gross investment* of the financial year in the form of spending by the capitalists on natural resources, labor, and capital goods from prior stages in the production process.[34]

---

[34]Tables such as Table V-1 have been constructed for the same purpose by Böhm-Bawerk (*Capital and Interest*, vol. 2, pp. 108–09, where in 1889

TABLE V-1
THE SUPPLY OF AND DEMAND FOR PRESENT GOODS

Suppliers of Present Goods
(Savers, or demanders of future goods)

Capitalists 1st stage   = 80+10 = 90 →
Capitalists 2nd stage   = 60+12 = 72 →
Capitalists 3rd stage   = 40+14 = 54 →
Capitalists 4th stage   = 20+16 = 36 →
Capitalists 5th stage   =   0+18 = 18 →

Demanders of Present Goods
(Suppliers of future goods)

80 to Capitalists 2nd stage + 10 to original means
60 to Capitalists 3rd stage + 12 to original means
40 to Capitalists 4th stage + 14 to original means
20 to Capitalists 5th stage + 16 to original means
                                18 to original means

200 Total demand from the owners of capital goods

70 Total demand from the owners of original means (land and labor)

Total supply of present goods = 270 m.u. = SAVING AND INVESTMENT = 270 m.u.   Total demand for present goods
(GROSS)

7. Gross and net income for the year.

Seventh, we could view Chart V-1, our outline of the different stages in the production process, as an illustration of the flow of both capital goods and money. Indeed capital goods "flow downward," i.e., from the stages furthest from consumption to the stages closest to it, and money "flows" in the opposite direction. In other words, m.u. are first used to pay for final consumer goods, and from that point they gradually move up the scale of productive stages until they reach those stages furthest from consumption. Therefore to obtain the gross monetary income for the period, we total, from bottom to top, all of the transactions (in terms of m.u.) conducted during the period. Details appear in Table V-2.

We see from this table that the *gross income* for the period is equal to 370 m.u. Of this amount, 100 m.u. correspond to *net income*, which is spent entirely on final consumer goods; and 270 m.u. correspond to the total supply of present goods or gross saving, which coincides with the total gross demand for present goods during the period. The following relationship exists between gross income and net income for the period, according to the calculation made in Table V-2: gross income is equal to 3.7 times the net income for the period. That is, a relationship exists between the number of m.u. spent on consumer goods and the much larger number spent on capital goods. This proportion is represented in Chart V-1 by the

---

he first recorded for each stage of production the value in "years of labor" of the products of the corresponding stage). Later, in 1929, F.A. Hayek performed the same task with greater precision in his article "Gibt es einen 'Widersinn des Sparens'?" (*Zeitschrift Für Nationalökonomie*, Bd. 1, Heft 3, 1929), which was translated with the title "The 'Paradox' of Saving" and published in English in *Economica* (May 1931) and later included as an appendix to the book, *Profits, Interest and Investment and Other Essays on the Theory of Industrial Fluctuations*, 1st ed. (London: George Routledge and Sons, 1939 and Clifton, N.J.: Augustus M. Kelley, Clifton 1975), pp. 199–263, esp. pp. 229–31. As Hayek himself admits, it was precisely the desire to simplify the awkward presentation of these tables that led him to introduce the chart of production stages we have displayed in Chart V-1 (see *Prices and Production*, p. 38, note 1).

unshaded area corresponding to the final stage, that of consumer goods, versus the shaded areas pertaining to the other stages (including the net monetary income of the factors of production, shown at the top). Hence it is an unquestionable fact that *the amount of money spent on intermediate goods during any time period is much larger by far than the amount spent during the same period on consumer goods and services.* It is interesting to note that even minds as brilliant as Adam Smith committed unfortunate errors when it came to recognizing this fundamental economic fact. Indeed, according to Adam Smith,

> the value of the goods circulated between the different dealers, never can exceed the value of those circulated between the dealers and the consumers; whatever is bought by the dealers, being ultimately destined to be sold to the consumers.[35]

CRITICISM OF THE MEASURES USED IN NATIONAL INCOME ACCOUNTING

The sum of gross income, as we have defined and calculated it, along with its distribution over the different stages in the production process, is crucial for a correct understanding of the economic process which takes place in society. In fact the structure of the stages of capital goods and their value in m.u. are not measures which, once obtained, can be automatically and indefinitely maintained regardless of human decisions made by entrepreneurs who must deliberately and continually choose whether to increase, hold steady or reduce the productive stages undertaken in the past. In other words, whether a

---

[35]Adam Smith, *The Wealth of Nations,* book 2, chap. 2, p. 390 of vol. 1 of the original 1776 edition cited earlier, p. 306 of the E. Cannan edition (New York: Modern Library, 1937 and 1965); and p. 322 of vol. 1 of the Glasgow edition, (Oxford: Oxford University Press, 1976). As Hayek points out (*Prices and Production,* p. 47), it is important to note that Adam Smith's authority on this subject has misled many authors. For example, Thomas Tooke, in his book, *An Inquiry into the Currency Principle* (London 1844, p. 71), and others have used Smith's argument to justify the erroneous doctrines of the Banking School.

TABLE V-2
GROSS OUTPUT AND NET INCOME FOR THE YEAR

Gross Output for the Year
100 m.u. of final consumption +270 m.u. of total
supply of present goods
(Gross Saving and Investment as shown
in detail in Table V-1)

Total Gross Output: 370 m.u.

Net Income for the Year

a) Net Income Received by Capitalists (the accounting profit or interest at each stage)	Capitalists 1st stage: 100-90:	= 10
	Capitalists 2nd stage: 80-72:	= 8
	Capitalists 3rd stage: 60-54:	= 6
	Capitalists 4th stage: 40-36:	= 4
	Capitalists 5th stage: 20-18:	= 2
	Total accounting profits (interest), or net income received by capitalists at all stages:	____ 30 m.u.
b) Net income Received by Owners of the Original Means of Production	From stage 1:	10
	From stage 2:	12
	From stage 3:	14
	From stage 4:	16
	From stage 5:	18
	Total net income received by owners of the original means of production:	____ 70 m.u.
	Total Net Income = Total Consumption	____ 100 m.u.

CONCLUSION: The Gross Output for the Year is equal to 3.7 times
the Net Income.

certain structure of productive stages remains the same or changes, becoming narrower or broader, depends solely upon whether the entrepreneurs of each stage subjectively decide it is worthwhile to reinvest the same percentage of the monetary income they have received, or instead, they believe it is more beneficial to them to modify this proportion by increasing or decreasing it. In the words of Hayek:

> The money stream which the entrepreneur representing any stage of production receives at any given moment is always composed of net income which he may use for consumption without disturbing the existing method of production, and of parts which he must continuously re-invest. But it depends entirely upon him whether he re-distributes his total money receipts in the same proportions as before. And the main factor influencing his decisions will be the magnitude of the profits he hopes to derive from the production of his particular intermediate product.[36]

Therefore no natural law forces entrepreneurs to reinvest their income in the same proportion in which they have invested in capital goods in the past. Instead, this proportion depends on the specific circumstances present at each moment, and in particular on the entrepreneurs' expectations regarding the profit they hope to obtain at each stage of the production process. This means that, from an analytical standpoint, it is very important to focus on the evolution of the amounts of gross income as reflected in our diagram, and to avoid concentrating exclusively on net values, as is the custom. So we see that even when net saving equals zero, a productive structure is maintained by considerable gross saving and investment, the sum of which is several times larger than

---

[36]Hayek, *Prices and Production*, p. 49. This is precisely why the conception of capital as a homogeneous fund that reproduces by itself is meaningless. This view of capital is defended by J.B. Clark and F.H. Knight and is the theoretical basis (along with the concept of general equilibrium) for the extremely stale model of the "circular flow of income" that appears in almost all economics textbooks, despite the fact that it is misleading, as it does not reflect the temporal structure by stages in the production process, as in Chart V-1 (see also footnote 39).

even the amount spent on consumer goods and services during each productive period. Therefore the key is to study gross saving and investment, i.e., the aggregated value, in monetary terms, spent in the stages of intermediate goods prior to final consumption, an amount which remains hidden if we focus exclusively on the evolution of accounting figures in net terms.

This is precisely why we should be especially critical of traditional national income accounting measures. For example, the traditional definition of "gross national product" (GNP) contains the word "gross," yet in no way reflects the true gross income spent during the year on the entire productive structure. On the one hand, GNP figures hide the existence of different stages in the production process. On the other hand, what is even more serious and consequential is that the gross national product, despite the "gross" in its name, *does not reflect the total gross monetary spending which takes place in all productive stages and sectors of the economy.* This is because it is based solely on the production of goods and services delivered to *final* users. In fact it rests on a narrow accounting criterion of added value which is foreign to the fundamental truths of the economy; it only adds the value of consumer goods and services and of the *final* capital goods completed during the year. *It does not incorporate the other intermediate products which make up the stages in the production process and which pass from one stage to another during the financial year.*[37] Hence gross national product figures only include a small percentage of the total

---

[37]For instance as Ramón Tamames indicates, the gross national product at market prices

> can be defined as the sum of the value of all the final goods and services produced in a nation in one year. I speak of final goods and services because intermediate ones are excluded to avoid the double computation of any value.

Fundamentos de estructura económica, 10th revised ed. (Madrid: Alianza Universidad, 1992), p. 304. Also see the book by Enrique Viaña Remis, *Lecciones de contabilidad nacional* (Madrid: Editorial Cívitas, 1993), in which he states that

> the distinction between intermediate inputs and depreciation has given rise to the convention of excluding the former and including the latter in the value added. Therefore we distinguish between gross value added, which includes depreciation,

production of capital goods. Indeed GNP incorporates the value of the sales of fixed or durable capital goods, such as real estate, industrial vehicles, machinery, tools, computers, etc., which are finished and sold to their final users during the year, and thus are considered *final* goods. However it in no way includes the value of circulating capital goods, intermediate non-durable products, nor of capital goods which are not yet finished or if so, pass from one stage to another during the process of production. These intermediate goods are obviously different from the similar ones included in final goods (for instance, the carburator produced as an intermediate product *is not the same* carburator included in the car sold as a final product.) In contrast, our *gross output* figure from Table V-2 incorporates the gross production of *all* capital goods, whether completed or not, fixed, durable or circulating, as well as all consumer goods and services produced during the financial year.

> and net value added, which excludes it. Consequently both product and income can be gross or net, depending upon whether they include or exclude depreciation. (p. 39)

As we see, the label "gross" is used to describe a figure that continues to be net, given that it excludes the entire value of intermediate inputs. National income accounting textbooks have not always ignored the fundamental importance of intermediate products. The classic work, *The Social Framework of the American Economy: An Introduction to Economics,* by J.R. Hicks and Albert G. Hart (New York: Oxford University Press, 1945), includes an explicit reference to the great importance of the time span in any process of production of consumer goods (the concrete example used is that of the production of a loaf of bread). The authors give a detailed explanation of the different stages of intermediate products necessary to arrive at the final consumer good. Hicks and Hart conclude (pp. 33–34):

> The products which result from these early stages are useful products, but not products which are directly useful for satisfying the wants of consumers. Their use is to be found in their employment in the further stages, at the end of which a product which is directly wanted by consumers will emerge. . . . A producers' good may be technically finished, in the sense that the particular operation needed to produce it is completed. . . . Or it may not be technically finished, but still in process, even so far as its own stage is concerned. In either case it is a producers' good, because further stages are needed before the result of the whole process can pass into the consumers' hands. *The consumers' good is the end of the whole process; producers' goods are stages on the road toward it.* (Italics added)

In short the Gross National Product is an aggregate figure representing added values, and it excludes intermediate goods. The only reason national accounting theorists offer for using this figure is that with this criterion they avoid the problem of "double counting." Yet from the standpoint of macroeconomic theory, this argument rests on a narrow accounting concept applicable to individual companies and is very dangerous, as it excludes from the computation the enormous volume of entrepreneurial effort which each year is dedicated to the production of intermediate capital goods, the bulk of economic activity but not at all worth evaluating, according to GNP figures. To get an idea of the amounts involved, it suffices to consider that the gross output (calculated according to our criterion) of an advanced country like the United States is equal to more than twice the country's official GNP.[38]

Therefore traditional national income accounting figures tend to eliminate at a stroke the central role intermediate stages play in the process of production; specifically, these measures ignore the undeniable fact that the continuance of intermediate

---

[38]Skousen, in his book, *The Structure of Production*, pp. 191–92, proposes the introduction of "gross national output," a new measure in national income accounting. With respect to the possible gross national output of the United States, Skousen concludes the following:

> First, Gross National Output (GNO) was nearly double [Gross National Product] (GNP), thus indicating the degree to which GNP underestimates total spending in the economy. Second, consumption represents only 34 percent of total national output, far less than what GNP figures suggest (66 percent). Third, business outlays, including intermediate inputs and gross private investment, is the largest sector of the economy, 56 percent larger than the consumer-goods industry. GNP figures suggest that the capital-goods industry represents a minuscule 14 percent of the economy.

All of these figures refer to 1982 national income accounting data for the United States. As we will later see when we focus on business cycles, traditional gross national product figures have the glaring theoretical defect of hiding the important oscillations which take place in the intermediate stages of the production process throughout the cycle. Gross national output, however, would reflect all of these fluctuations. See also the data for 1986, found at the end of footnote 20, chapter 6.

stages is not guaranteed, but results from a constant, uncertain series of concrete entrepreneurial decisions which depend on expected accounting profits and on the social rate of time preference or interest rate. The use of GNP in national income accounting almost inevitably implies that production is instantaneous and requires no time, i.e., that there are no intermediate stages in the production process and that time preference is irrelevant with respect to determining the interest rate. In short the standard measures of national income completely do away with the largest, most significant part of the production process, and moreover they do so in a disguised manner, since, paradoxically and despite the label "gross," they cause non-experts (and even most experts) in the field to overlook the most significant part of each country's productive structure.[39]

If national income accounting measures were modified and made truly "gross," they would include all intermediate

---

[39]As Murray Rothbard indicates, the net quality of GNP invariably leads one to identify capital with a perpetual fund that reproduces by itself without the need for any particular decision-making on the part of entrepreneurs. This is the "mythological" doctrine defended by J.B. Clark and Frank H. Knight, and it constitutes the conceptual basis for the current national income accounting system. Thus this system is simply the statistical, accounting manifestation of the mistaken understanding of capital theory promoted by these two authors. Rothbard concludes: "To maintain this doctrine it is necessary to deny the stage analysis of production and, indeed, to deny the very influence of *time* in production" (Rothbard, *Man, Economy, and State*, p. 343). Furthermore the current method of calculating GNP also strongly reflects Keynes's influence, enormously exaggerating the importance of consumption in the economy and conveying the false impression that the most significant portion of the national product exists in the form of consumer goods and services, instead of investment goods. In addition this explains why most agents involved (economists, businessmen, investors, politicians, journalists, and civil servants) have a distorted idea of the way the economy functions. Since they believe the sector of final consumption to be the largest in the economy, they very easily conclude that the best way to foster the economic development of a country is to stimulate consumption and not investment. On this point see Hayek, *Prices and Production*, pp. 47–49, esp. note 2 on p. 48, Skousen, *The Structure of Production*, p. 190, and also George Reisman, "The Value of 'Final Products' Counts Only Itself," *American Journal of Economics and Sociology* 63, no. 3 (July 2004): 609– 25, and *Capitalism* (Ottawa, Ill.: Jameson Book, 1996), pp. 674ff. See also next footnote 55.

products, and it would be possible to follow the proportion of the amount spent each year on consumer goods and services to the amount spent at all intermediate stages. This ratio is ultimately determined by the social rate of time preference, which establishes the proportion of gross saving and investment to consumption. Clearly the weaker the time preference, and therefore the more savings generated in society, the larger the proportion of gross saving and investment to final consumption. At the same time, a strong time preference means interest rates will be high, and the ratio of gross saving and investment to consumption will decrease. Adequate intertemporal coordination of the decisions of economic agents in a modern society requires that the productive structure adapt to different social rates of time preference quickly and efficiently, something the entrepreneurial spirit itself, driven by the search for profit, tends to guarantee, as entrepreneurs try to equalize profit over all stages. If we wish to find a statistical measure which, instead of concealing, sheds as much light as possible on this important intertemporal coordination process, we must replace the current gross national product estimate with another such as gross national output, as defined here.[40]

---

[40]Input-output tables partially escape the inadequacies of traditional national income accounting by permitting the calculation of the amount corresponding to all intermediate products. However even though input-output analysis is a step in the right direction, it also has very serious limitations. In particular, it reflects only two dimensions: it relates the different industrial sectors with the factors of production used directly in them, but not with the factors of production which are used but correspond to more distant stages. In other words, input-output analysis does not reflect the set of consecutive intermediate stages leading up to any intermediate stage or capital good or to the final consumer good. Instead it only relates each sector with its direct provider. Furthermore due to the great cost and complexity of input-output tables, they are only compiled every certain number of years (in the United States, every five years), and therefore the statistics they contain are of very slight value with respect to calculating the gross national output for each year. See Skousen, *The Structure of Production*, pp. 4–5.

2

THE EFFECT ON THE PRODUCTIVE STRUCTURE
OF AN INCREASE IN CREDIT FINANCED UNDER
A PRIOR INCREASE IN VOLUNTARY SAVING

THE THREE DIFFERENT MANIFESTATIONS OF THE
PROCESS OF VOLUNTARY SAVING

In this section we will examine what happens within the structure of production when, for whatever reason, economic agents reduce their rate of time preference; that is, when they decide to increase their saving or supply of present goods to others. This can take place in any of the following ways:

First, capitalists of the different stages in the productive structure may decide, beginning at a certain point, to modify the proportion in which they had been *reinvesting* the gross income derived from their productive activity. In other words, nothing guarantees the continuity, from one period to the next, of the ratio in which the capitalists of one productive stage spend the income they receive from that stage on the purchase of capital goods from earlier stages and on labor and natural resources. Capitalists may very possibly decide to increase their supply of present goods to others. That is, they may decide to reinvest a greater percentage of the income they receive per period, acquiring capital goods and services as well as original means of production (labor and natural resources). In that case, in the short run, their accounting profit margin will decrease, which is equivalent to a downward trend in the market interest rate. The profit margin falls as a result of an increase in monetary costs in relation to income. The capitalists are willing to *temporarily* accept this drop in accounting profits, since they expect to generate in this way, in a more or less distant future, total profits larger than those they would have earned had they not modified their behavior.[41] Given that the market in which present goods

---

[41]The expected increase in profit is considered in absolute, not relative, terms. Indeed profits representing, for example, 10 percent of 100 m.u.

are exchanged for future goods encompasses society's entire structure of productive stages, such increases in saving and their manifestation in new investments are often the most important in society.

Second, owners of the original means of production (workers and owners of natural resources) may decide not to consume, as in the past, the entire sum of their social net income (which in Chart V-1 was 70 m.u.). They may instead decide to reduce their consumption beginning at a certain point and to invest the m.u. they no longer spend on final consumer goods and services, in the productive stages they decide to launch *directly* as capitalists (a category which includes members of cooperatives). Though this procedure takes place in the market, the resulting savings are not normally very substantial in real life.

Third, it could occur that both the owners of the original means of production (workers and the owners of natural resources) as well as capitalists (to the extent they receive net income in the form of accounting profits or market interest) decide beginning at a certain point not to consume their entire net income, but to *loan* a portion of it to capitalists of the different stages in the production process, enabling them to broaden their activities by purchasing more capital goods from prior stages and more natural resources, and by hiring more labor. This third procedure is carried out through the *credit market*, which, despite being the most visible and conspicuous in real economic life, is of *secondary* importance and plays a *subsidiary* role in relation to the more general market in

---

(10 m.u.) are smaller than profits representing 8 percent of 150 m.u. (12 m.u.). Even though the interest rate or rate of accounting profit decreases as the result of the weaker time preference which causes an increase in saving and investment, in absolute terms the accounting profits rise by 20 percent, i.e., from 10 to 12 m.u. This is what generally occurs in the stages furthest from consumption during the process we are considering. Regarding the stages closest to consumption, it is important to remember that, as we will indicate in the main text, the comparison is not drawn with past profits, but with an estimate of those which would have been produced had the entrepreneurial investment strategy not been modified.

which present goods are exchanged for future goods through self-financing or capitalists' direct reinvestment of present goods in their productive stages (the first and second procedures of saving-investment mentioned above). Though this system of saving is important, it is usually secondary to the first two procedures for increasing saving we described above. Nevertheless a very strong connection exists between the flows of saving and investment of both procedures, and in fact both sectors of the "time market"—the general sector of the productive structure and the particular sector of the credit market—behave as if they were communicating vessels.

ACCOUNT RECORDS OF SAVINGS CHANNELLED INTO LOANS

From an economic standpoint, all three of these procedures for increasing saving invariably entail the following: an increase in the supply of present goods by savers, who transfer these present goods to the owners of original resources and material means of production (capital goods) from previous productive stages. For instance, if we follow the accounting example from chapter 4, which involves the third procedure described above, the following journal entries result:

The saver who loans his resources in the form of present goods records this entry in his journal:

(72)	Debit		Credit	
1,000,000	Loan granted	Cash		1,000,000

This entry is clearly the accounting record of the fact that the saver offers 1,000,000 m.u. of present goods, which he relinquishes. In doing so he loses the complete availability of the goods and transfers it to a third person; for instance, the entrepreneur of a certain productive stage. The entrepreneur receives the m.u. as a loan, which he records in his journal via the following entry:

(73)	Debit	Credit	
1,000,000	Cash	Loan received	1,000,000

The entrepreneur who receives these present goods uses them to acquire: (1) capital goods from prior productive stages; (2) labor services; (3) natural resources. Through this third procedure, savers who do not wish to involve themselves directly in the activity of any of the productive stages can save and invest through the credit market by entering into a loan contract. Although this method is indirect, it ultimately produces a result identical to that of the first two procedures for voluntarily increasing saving.

THE ISSUE OF CONSUMER LOANS

It could be argued that sometimes loans are not granted to entrepreneurs of productive stages, to enable them to lengthen their production processes through investment, but are instead granted to *consumers who purchase final goods.* First, we must note that the very nature of the initial two saving procedures described above precludes the use of the saved resources for consumption. It is only possible to conceive of a consumer loan in the credit market, which as we know plays a subsidiary role and is secondary to the total market where present goods are offered and purchased in exchange for future goods. Second, in most cases consumer loans are granted to finance the purchase of *durable consumer goods,* which as we saw in previous sections,[42] *are ultimately comparable to capital goods maintained over a number of consecutive stages of production, while the durable consumer good's capacity to provide services to its owner lasts.* Under these circumstances, by far the most common, the economic effects of consumer loans, with respect to encouraging investment and lengthening productive stages, are *identical to and indistinguishable from* the effects of any increase in savings directly invested in the capital

---

[42]See pages 300–01 and footnotes 32 and 33.

goods of any stage in the productive structure. Therefore only a hypothetical consumer loan allocated for financing a household's *current expenditure* on non-durable consumer goods would have the effect of immediately and directly increasing final current consumption. Nonetheless despite the fact that relatively little credit is allotted to final current consumption, the existence of such consumer loans in the market indicates a certain latent consumer demand for them. Given the connection between all sectors of the market of present and future goods, once this residual demand for loans for *current* consumption is satisfied, most real resources saved are freed to be invested in the productive stages furthest from consumption.

THE EFFECTS OF VOLUNTARY SAVING ON THE PRODUCTIVE STRUCTURE

We will now explain how the price system and the coordinating role of entrepreneurs in a free market spontaneously channel decreases in the social rate of time preference and the resulting increases in saving into modifications of society's structure of productive stages, making this structure more complex and lasting, and in the long run, appreciably more productive. In short we will explain one of the most significant coordinating processes which exist in all economies. Unfortunately, as a result of monetarist and Keynesian economic theories (which we will examine critically in chapter 7), for at least two generations of economists the majority of economics textbooks and study programs have almost completely ignored this process. Consequently most of today's economists are unfamiliar with the functioning of one of the most important processes of coordination present in all market economies.[43]

---

[43]While studying economics in the late seventies, we noticed that in no Economic Theory course did the instructor explain how an increase in saving affects the productive structure; professors described only the Keynesian model of the "paradox of thrift," which as is widely known, outright condemns increases in social saving, because they reduce effective demand. Although Keynes did not expressly refer to the "paradox

For analytical purposes we will begin by considering an extreme situation which nevertheless will be of great assistance in graphically illustrating and better understanding the processes involved. We will suppose that economic agents *suddenly* decide to save 25 percent of their net income. Our starting point will be the clear, numerical example of the last section, in which we assumed net income was equal to 100 m.u., which corresponded to the original means of production and the interest capitalists received, and which was spent entirely on consumer goods. We will now suppose that, as a result of a fall in time preference, economic agents decide to *relinquish* 25 percent (i.e., one-fourth) of their consumption and to save the corresponding resources, offering this excess of present goods to potential demanders of them. Three effects simultaneously follow from this increase in voluntary saving. Given their great importance, we will now consider them separately.[44]

---

of thrift," this concept follows when Keynes's economic principles are carried to their "logical" conclusion:

> If governments should increase their spending during recessions, why should not households? If there were no principles of "sound finance" for public finance, from where would such principles come for family finance? Eat, drink and be merry, for in the long-run all are dead. (Clifford F. Thies, "The Paradox of Thrift: RIP," *Cato Journal* 16, no. 1 [Spring–Summer, 1996]: 125)

See also our comments in footnote 58 on the treatment this subject receives in different editions of Samuelson's textbook.

[44]Following Turgot, Eugen von Böhm-Bawerk was the first to confront and resolve this issue. His analysis was rudimentary, yet contained all the essential elements of a definitive explanation. It is found in volume 2 of his *magnum opus, Capital and Interest*, published in 1889 (*Kapital und Kapitalzins: Positive Theorie des Kapitales*, pp. 124–25). Due to its significance, we include here the passage from *Capital and Interest* in which Böhm-Bawerk poses the question of growth in voluntary saving in a market economy and the forces involved which lead to a lengthening of the productive structure: let us suppose, says Böhm-Bawerk, that

> each individual consumes, on the average, only three-quarters of his income and saves the other quarter, then obviously there will be a falling off in the desire to buy consumption goods and in the demand for them. Only three-quarters as

First: The Effect Produced by the New Disparity in Profits Between the Different Productive Stages

If there is an increase in social saving of one-fourth of net income, clearly the total monetary demand for consumer goods will decrease by the same proportion. Chart V-2 illustrates the effect this has on the final stage, that of consumption, and on the accounting profits of companies devoted to that stage.

---

great a quantity of consumption goods as in the preceding case will become the subject of demand and of sale. If the entrepreneurs were nevertheless to continue for a time to follow the previous disposition of production and go on bringing consumption goods to the market at a rate of a full 10 million labor-years annually, the oversupply would soon depress the prices of those goods, render them unprofitable and hence induce the entrepreneurs to adjust their production to the changed demand. They will see to it that in one year only the product of 7.5 million labor-years is converted into consumption goods, be it through maturation of the first annual ring or be it through additional present production. The remaining 2.5 million labor-years left over from the current annual allotment can be used for increasing capital. *And it will be so used.* . . . In this way it is added to the nation's productive credit, increases the producer's purchasing power for productive purposes, and so becomes the cause of an increase in the demand for production goods, which is to say intermediate products. And that demand is, in the last analysis, what induces the managers of business enterprises to invest available productive forces in desired intermediate product. . . . [I]f individuals do save, then the change in demand, once more through the agency of price, forces the entrepreneurs into a changed disposition of productive forces. In that case fewer productive powers are enlisted during the course of the year for the service of the present as consumption goods, *and there is a correspondingly greater quantity of productive forces tied up in the transitional stage of intermediate products.* In other words, there is an increase in capital, which redounds to the benefit of an enhanced enjoyment of consumption goods in the future. (Böhm-Bawerk, *Capital and Interest*, vol. 2: *Positive Theory of Capital*, pp. 112–13; italics added)

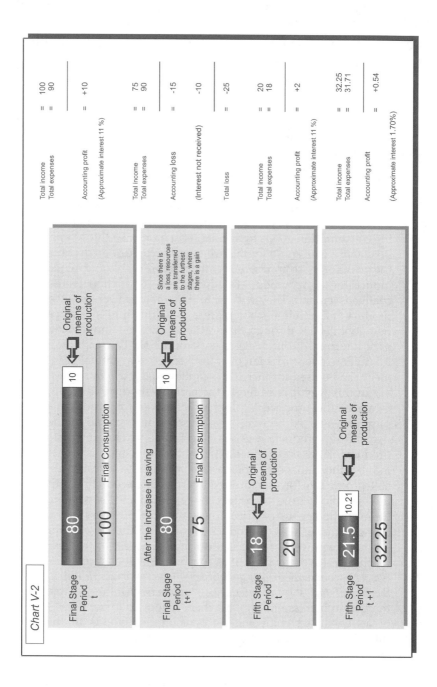

Chart V-2

Final Stage
Period
t

80

100   Final Consumption

→ 10   Original means of production

Total income   = 100
Total expenses   = 90
                              ─────
Accounting profit   = +10

(Approximate interest 11 %)

After the increase in saving

Final Stage
Period
t+1

80

75   Final Consumption

→ 10   Original means of production

Total income   = 75
Total expenses   = 90
                              ─────
Accounting loss   = -15

(Interest not received)   = -10
                              ─────
Total loss   = -25

Since there is a loss, resources are transferred to the furthest stages, where there is a gain

Fifth Stage
Period
t

18

20

→   Original means of production

Total income   = 20
Total expenses   = 18
                              ─────
Accounting profit   = +2

(Approximate interest 11 %)

Fifth Stage
Period
t+1

21.5   10.21

32.25

→   Original means of production

Total income   = 32.25
Total expenses   = 31.71
                              ──────
Accounting profit   = +0.54

(Approximate interest 1.70%)

Chart V-2 shows that before the increase in saving, 100 m.u. of net income were spent on final consumer goods produced by companies which first incurred expenses totaling 90 m.u. Of this amount, 80 m.u. corresponded to the purchase of capital goods from the stage immediately preceding, and 10 m.u. were paid for original means of production hired or purchased in the last stage (labor and natural resources). This determined an accounting profit of 10 m.u., roughly equal to an interest rate of 11 percent, which as we saw in the last section, was the *market rate of interest which accounting profits of all productive stages, both those closest to and those furthest from final consumption, tended to match.*

If we suppose there is an increase in saving equal to 25 percent of net income, the situation in the final stage (consumption) is reflected in Chart V-2 at period of time t+1. Immediately following the rise in saving, we see that the monetary demand for final consumer goods decreases from 100 to 75 m.u. in each time period. Nevertheless a reduction in expenditures does not immediately accompany this fall in cash income which businesses devoted to the final stage of production experience. On the contrary, in their account books these companies record *unchanged* expenditures of 90 m.u. Just as in the previous case, 80 m.u. of this amount is spent on capital goods from the preceding stage (machinery, suppliers, intermediate products, etc.) and 10 m.u. are paid to the owners of the original means of production (workers and the owners of natural resources). As a result of this increase in saving, companies devoted to the final stage (consumption) suffer an accounting loss of 15 m.u. This sum becomes 25 m.u. when we consider the *opportunity cost* derived from the fact that the entrepreneurs not only experience the above accounting loss, but also *fail to earn* the 10 m.u. which capital invested in other productive stages generates as interest. Therefore we could conclude that all *increases in saving cause considerable relative losses to or decreases in the accounting profits of the companies which operate closest to final consumption.*

However let us now remember that the sector of consumption constitutes only a relatively small part of society's total productive structure and that the sum of the m.u. spent on final consumption makes up only a fraction of the value of the gross national output, which encompasses all stages of the production process. Therefore the fact that accounting losses occur in the final stage does not immediately affect the stages prior to consumption, in which a positive difference continues to exist between income and expenditures, a difference similar to the one which preceded the increase in saving. Only after a prolonged period of time will the depressive effect which the rise in saving exerts upon the final stage (that of consumer goods) begin to be felt in the stages closest to it, and this negative influence will increasingly weaken as we "climb" to productive stages relatively more distant from final consumption. At any rate the accounting profits of the stages furthest from consumption will tend to remain constant, as shown in Chart V-2, stage five, period of time t. Here we observe that activity in this stage continues to yield an accounting profit of 11 percent, the result of a total income of 20 m.u. and total expenses of 18 m.u. Hence the increase in saving clearly gives rise to a great disparity between the accounting profits received by companies devoted to the first stage, that of consumer goods, and those earned by companies operating in the stages furthest from final consumption (in our example, the fifth stage in the productive structure). In the consumer goods sector an accounting loss follows from the upsurge in saving, while the industries of the fifth stage, which are further from consumption (now are helping to produce consumer goods that only will be available five years from now), continue to enjoy profits roughly equal to 11 percent of the capital invested (the current decrease in consumption does not affect consumption five years from now).

   This disparity in profits acts as a warning sign and an incentive for entrepreneurs to restrict their investments in the stages close to consumption and to channel these resources into other stages which still offer relatively higher profits and which are, given the circumstances, the stages furthest from final consumption. Therefore entrepreneurs will tend to transfer a portion of their demand for productive resources, in the form of capital goods and primary factors of production, from the final stage (consumption) and those closest to it, to the stages furthest from consumption, where they discover they can still obtain comparatively much higher profits. The increased investment or demand for more productive resources in the stages furthest from consumption produces the effect shown in Chart V-2 for stage five, period of time t+1. Indeed entrepreneurs from the fifth stage increase their investment in original factors and productive resources from 18 m.u. to 31.71 m.u., a figure nearly double their initial outlay. (Of this amount 21.5 m.u. are spent on the productive services of capital goods and 10.21 m.u. are spent on labor services and natural resources).[45] This leads to a rise in the production of goods in the fifth stage, which in monetary terms, increases from 20 m.u. to 32.35 m.u., resulting in an accounting profit of 0.54 m.u. Although in terms of percentage this amount is lower than former profits (1.70 percent as opposed to the 11 percent earned previously), it is comparatively a much higher profit than that which the industries producing final consumer goods obtain (industries which, as we saw, are sustaining absolute losses of 15 m.u.).

Consequently growth in saving gives rise to a disparity between the rates of profit in the different stages of the productive structure. This leads entrepreneurs to reduce immediate production of consumer goods and to increase production in the stages furthest from consumption. A *temporary lengthening* of production processes tends to ensue, lasting until the new social rate of time preference or interest rate, in the form of differentials between accounting income and expenditures in each stage, now appreciably lower as a result of the substantial increase in saving, spreads uniformly, throughout the entire productive structure.

The entrepreneurs of the fifth stage have been able to increase their supply of present goods to others from 18 m.u. during period t to 31.71 m.u. in period t+1. This has been possible due to greater social saving, or a greater supply of present goods in society. The entrepreneurs finance this larger investment in part through the increase in their own saving, i.e., by investing a portion of the money which in the past they earned as interest and spent on consumption, and in part through new saving they receive from the credit market in the form of loans *fully backed by a prior rise in voluntary saving*. In other words, the increase in investment in the fifth stage materializes by any of the three procedures described in the last section.

---

[45]These amounts correspond to the numerical example in Chart V–3.

Moreover the increase one might expect to observe in the prices of the factors of production (capital goods, labor and natural resources) as a result of the greater demand for them in the fifth stage does not necessarily occur (with the possible exception of very specific means of production). In fact each increase in the demand for productive resources in the stages furthest from consumption is mostly or even completely neutralized or offset by a parallel increase in the supply of these inputs which takes place as they are gradually freed from the stages closest to consumption, where entrepreneurs are incurring considerable accounting losses and are consequently obliged to restrict their investment expenditure on these factors. Thus for entrepreneurial coordination to exist between the stages in the productive structure of a society which is immersed in a process of increased saving and economic growth, it is particularly important that the corresponding factor markets, especially the markets for original means of production (labor and natural resources), be very flexible and permit at a minimum economic and social cost the gradual transfer of these factors from certain stages of production to others.

Finally the drop in investment in the consumer goods sector, which tends to stem from accounting losses generated by the increase in voluntary saving, normally accounts for a certain *slowdown* in the arrival of new consumer goods to the market (regardless of the increase in the stock of them). This slowdown lasts until the rise in the complexity and number of stages in the production process unquestionably improves productivity, which in turn brings a significantly larger quantity of consumer goods to the market. One might expect the *temporary* reduction in the supply of consumer goods to push up their price, other things being equal. However this rise in prices does not materialize, precisely because from the outset the decrease in supply is more than compensated for by the parallel fall in the demand for consumer goods, a result of the prior increase in voluntary saving.

To sum up, the increase in voluntary saving is invested in the productive structure, either through direct investments or through loans granted to the entrepreneurs of the productive stages relatively distant from consumption. These loans are backed by real voluntary saving and lead to an increase in the monetary demand for original means of production and capital goods used in such stages. As we saw at the beginning of this chapter, production processes tend to be more productive the more stages distant from consumption they contain, and the more complex these stages are. Therefore this more capital-intensive structure will eventually bring about a considerable increase in the final production of consumer goods, once the newly-initiated processes come to an end. Hence growth in saving and the free exercise of entrepreneurship are the necessary conditions for and the motor which drives all processes of economic growth and development.

SECOND: THE EFFECT OF THE DECREASE IN THE
INTEREST RATE ON THE MARKET PRICE OF CAPITAL GOODS

The increase in voluntary saving, i.e., in the supply of present goods, gives rise, other things being equal, to a decrease in the market rate of interest. As we know, this interest rate tends to manifest itself as the accounting difference between income and expenses in the different productive stages and is also visible in the interest rate at which loans are granted in the credit market. It is important to note that the fall in the interest rate caused by all rises in voluntary saving greatly affects the value of capital goods, especially all of those used in the stages furthest from final consumption, goods which, relatively speaking, have a long life and make a large contribution to the production process.

Let us consider a capital good with a long life, such as a building owned by a company, an industrial plant, a ship or airplane used for transport, a blast furnace, a computer or high-tech communications device, etc., which has been produced and performs its services in different stages of the productive structure, all of which are relatively distant from consumption. The *market value* of this capital good tends to equal the value of its expected future flow of rents, discounted by the interest rate. An inverse relationship exists between the present (discounted) value and the interest rate. By way of illustration, a decrease in the interest rate from 11 to 5 percent, brought about by an increase in saving, causes the present value of a capital good with a very long life to more than double (the present value of a perpetual unitary rent at 11 percent interest is equal to $1/0.11 = 9.09$; and the present value of a perpetual rent at 5 percent interest is equal to $1/0.05 = 20$). If the capital good lasts, for example, twenty years, a drop in the interest rate from 11 to 5 percent produces an increase of 56 percent in the market or capitalized value of the good.[46]

Therefore if people begin to value present goods less in relative terms, then the market price of capital goods and durable consumer goods will tend to increase. Moreover it will tend to increase in proportion to the duration of a good; i.e., to the number of productive stages in which it is used and to the distance of these stages from consumption. Capital goods already in use will undergo a significant rise in price as a result of the drop in the interest rate and will be produced in greater quantities, bringing about a horizontal *widening* of the capital goods structure (that is, an increase in the production of *pre-existing* capital goods). At the same time, the fall in the interest rate will reveal that many production processes or capital goods which until then were not considered profitable begin to be so, and consequently entrepreneurs will start to introduce them. In fact in the past entrepreneurs refrained from adopting many technological innovations and new projects because they expected the cost involved to be higher than the resulting market value (which tends to equal the value of the estimated future rent of each capital good, discounted by the interest rate). However when the interest rate falls, the

---

[46]The formula is $a_n = \dfrac{1 - (1 + i)^{-n}}{i} = \dfrac{(1 + i)^n - 1}{i(1 + i)^n},$

which in terms of compound capitalization at interest i, corresponds to the present value of a temporary annuity, payable in arrears, of n periods, where the capitalization period coincides with the rent period. It is clear that as period n becomes longer and approaches infinity, the value of the rent will approach $1/i$, which as a mnemonic rule, is applicable in practice to all capital goods with a very long life (and to land, due to its permanence). See Lorenzo Gil Peláez, *Tablas financieras, estadísticas y actuariales*, 6th revised updated ed. (Madrid: Editorial Dossat, 1977), pp. 205–37.

market value of projects for lengthening the productive structure through new, more modern stages further from consumption begins to rise and may even come to exceed the cost of production, rendering these projects worthwhile. Hence the second effect of a decrease in the interest rate caused by an increase in voluntary saving is the deepening of the investment goods structure, in the form of a vertical lengthening involving *new* stages of capital goods increasingly distant from consumption.[47]

Both the widening and deepening of the capital goods structure follow from the role of entrepreneurs and their collective capacity for creativity and coordination. They are able to recognize an opportunity and a potential profit margin when a difference arises between the market price of capital goods (determined by the present value of their expected future rent, which increases appreciably when the interest rate falls) and the cost necessary to produce them (a cost which remains constant or may even decrease, given the greater market supply of original means of production coming from the stage of final consumption, which initially shrank when saving increased).

Thus this *second effect* also entails a lengthening of the capital goods structure, just as we saw with the first effect.

Fluctuations in the value of capital goods, which arise from variations in saving and the interest rate, also tend to spread to the *securities* which represent these goods, and thus to the stock markets where they are traded. Hence an increase in voluntary saving, which leads to a drop in the interest rate, will further boost the price of stocks of companies which operate in the capital goods stages furthest from consumption, and in general, the price of all securities representing capital

---

[47]It should be noted that technological innovations which boost productivity (in the form of a greater quantity and/or quality of goods and services) by reducing the length of production processes will be introduced in any case, whether or not society's net saving increases. However such an increase makes possible the application of new technologies which, due to a marginal lack of resources, cannot be adopted prior to the rise in saving.

goods. Only securities which represent the property of the companies closest to consumption will undergo a temporary, relative decline in price, as a result of the immediate, negative impact of the decrease in the demand for consumer goods that is generated by the upsurge in saving. Therefore it is clear that, contrary to popular opinion, and in the absence of other monetary distortions we have not yet touched on, the stock market does not necessarily reflect mainly companies' profits. In fact, in relative terms with the capital invested, the accounting profits earned by the companies of the different stages tend to match the interest rate. Thus an environment of high saving and low relative profits (i.e., with a low interest rate) constitutes the setting for the greatest growth in the market value of securities representing capital goods. Moreover the further the capital goods are from final consumption, the higher the market price of the corresponding securities.[48] In contrast, growth in relative accounting profits throughout the productive structure, and thus in the market rate of interest, other things being equal, will manifest itself in a drop in the value of securities and a consequent fall in their market value. This theoretical explanation sheds light on many general stock-market reactions which ordinary people and many "experts" in finance and economics fail to understand, since they simply apply the naive theory that the stock market must merely reflect, automatically and faithfully, the level of accounting profits earned by all companies participating in the production process, without considering the stages in which the profits are earned nor the evolution of the social time preference (interest rates).

---

[48]The ceiling price will be reached when the effect of the reduction in the interest rate subsides and is counteracted by the larger number and volume of securities issued in the primary stock and bond market, which will tend to cause the market price *per security* to stabilize at a lower level. In the next chapter we will see that all prolonged market buoyancy and in general, all sustained, constant rises in stock-market indexes, far from indicating a very healthy underlying economic situation, stem from an inflationary process of credit expansion which sooner or later will provoke a stock-market crisis and an economic recession.

Third: The Ricardo Effect

All increases in voluntary saving exert a particularly important, immediate effect on the level of *real* wages. Chart V-2 shows how the monetary demand for consumer goods falls by one-fourth (from 100 m.u. to 75 m.u.), due to the rise in saving. Hence it is easy to understand why increases in saving are generally followed by decreases in the prices of final consumer goods.[49] If, as generally occurs, the wages or rents of the original factor labor are initially held constant in nominal terms, a decline in the prices of final consumer goods will be followed by a rise in the *real* wages of workers employed in all stages of the productive structure. With the same money income in nominal terms, workers will be able to acquire a greater quantity and quality of final consumer goods and services at consumer goods' new, more reduced prices.

This increase in real wages, which arises from the growth in voluntary saving, means that, relatively speaking, it is in the interest of entrepreneurs of all stages in the production process to replace labor with capital goods. To put it another way, via an increase in real wages, the rise in voluntary saving sets a trend throughout the economic system toward longer and more capital-intensive productive stages. In other words, entrepreneurs now find it more attractive to use, relatively speaking, more capital goods than labor. This constitutes a third powerful, additional effect tending toward the lengthening of the stages in the productive structure. It adds to and overlaps the other two effects mentioned previously.

---

[49]As Hayek indicates, these reductions in prices may take some time, depending upon the rigidity of each market, and at any rate, they will be less than proportional to the fall in demand that accompanies saving. If this were not the case, saving would not entail any actual sacrifice and the stock of consumer goods necessary to sustain economic agents while more capital-intensive processes are completed would not be left unsold. See F.A. Hayek, "Reflections on the Pure Theory of Money of Mr. J.M. Keynes (continued)," *Economica* 12, no. 35 (February 1932): 22–44, republished in *The Collected Works of F.A. Hayek*, vol. 9: *Contra Keynes and Cambridge: Essays, Correspondence*, Bruce Caldwell, ed. (London: Routledge, 1995), pp. 179–80.

The first to explicitly refer to this third effect was David Ricardo. He did so in his book, *On the Principles of Political Economy and Taxation*, the first edition of which was published in 1817. Here Ricardo concludes that

> [e]very rise of wages, therefore, or, which is the same thing, every fall of profits, would lower the relative value of those commodities which were produced with a capital of a durable nature, and would proportionally elevate those which were produced with capital more perishable. A fall of wages would have precisely the contrary effect.[50]

In the well-known appendix "On Machinery," which was added in the third edition, published in 1821, Ricardo concludes that "[m]achinery and labour are in constant competition, and the former can frequently not be employed until labour rises."[51]

The same idea was later recovered by F.A. Hayek, who, beginning in 1939, applied it extensively in his writings on business cycles. Here we will for the first time use it, integrated with the prior two effects, to explain the consequences an upsurge in voluntary saving has on the productive structure and to detract from theories on the so-called "paradox of thrift" and the supposedly negative influence of saving on effective demand. Hayek offers a very concise explanation of the "Ricardo Effect" when he states that

> [w]ith high real wages and a low rate of profit investment will take highly capitalistic forms: entrepreneurs will try to meet the high costs of labour by introducing very labour-saving machinery—the kind of machinery which it will be profitable to use only at a very low rate of profit and interest.[52]

---

[50]See David Ricardo, *The Works and Correspondence of David Ricardo*, vol. 1: *On the Principles of Political Economy and Taxation*, Piero Sraffa and M.H. Dobb, eds. (Cambridge: Cambridge University Press, 1982), pp. 39–40.

[51]Ibid., p. 395.

[52]See Hayek, *"Profits, Interest and Investment" and Other Essays on the Theory of Industrial Fluctuations*, p. 39. Shortly afterward, in 1941, F.A. Hayek briefly touched on this effect in relation to the impact an increase

Hence the "Ricardo Effect" is a third microeconomic explanation for the behavior of entrepreneurs, who react to an upsurge in voluntary saving by boosting their demand for

---

in voluntary saving exerts on the productive structure, though he did not expressly quote Ricardo. This is the only instance we know of in which the "Ricardo Effect" is directly applied to an analysis of the consequences of a rise in voluntary saving, and not to the role the effect plays in the different phases of the business cycle, theorists' predominant concern up until now. The excerpt in question is found on p. 293 of *The Pure Theory of Capital* (London: Macmillan, 1941), and successively reprinted thereafter (we quote from the 1976 Routledge reprint). It reads as follows: "The fall in the rate of interest may . . . drive up the price of labour to such an extent as to enforce an extensive substitution of machinery for labour." Hayek later returned to the topic in his article, "The Ricardo Effect," published in *Economica* 34, no. 9 (May 1942): 127–52, and republished as chapter 11 of *Individualism and Economic Order* (Chicago: University of Chicago Press, 1948), pp. 220–54. Thirty years later he dealt with it again in his article, "Three Elucidations of the Ricardo Effect," published in the *Journal of Political Economy* 77, no. 2 (1979), and reprinted as chapter 11 of the book *New Studies in Philosophy, Politics, Economics and the History of Ideas* (London: Routledge and Kegan Paul, 1978), pp. 165–78. Mark Blaug recently admitted that his criticism of the "Ricardo Effect" in his book, *Economic Theory in Retrospect* (Cambridge: Cambridge University Press, 1978), pp. 571–77, was based on an error in interpretation regarding the supposedly static nature of Hayek's analysis. See Mark Blaug's article entitled "Hayek Revisited," published in *Critical Review* 7, no. 1 (Winter, 1993): 51–60, and esp. note 5 on pp. 59–60. Blaug acknowledges that he discovered his error thanks to an article by Laurence S. Moss and Karen I. Vaughn, "Hayek's Ricardo Effect: A Second Look," *History of Political Economy* 18, no. 4 (Winter, 1986): 545–65. For his part, Mises (*Human Action*, pp. 773–77) has criticized the emphasis placed on the Ricardo Effect in order to justify a forced increase in wages through union or government channels with the purpose of raising investment in capital goods. He concludes that such a policy only gives rise to unemployment and a poor allocation of resources in the productive structure, since the policy does not stem from an increase in society's voluntary saving, but rather from the simple coercive imposition of artificially high wages. Rothbard expresses a similar view in *Man, Economy, and State* (pp. 631–32). Hayek does so as well in *The Pure Theory of Capital* (p. 347), where he concludes that dictatorially-imposed growth in wages produces not only a rise in unemployment and a fall in saving, but also generalized consumption of capital combined with an artificial lengthening and narrowing of the stages in the productive structure.

capital goods and by investing in new stages further from final consumption.

It is important to remember that all increases in voluntary saving and investment initially bring about a decline in the production of new consumer goods and services *with respect to the short-term maximum which could be achieved* if inputs were not diverted from the stages closest to final consumption. This decline performs the function of freeing productive factors necessary to lengthen the stages of capital goods furthest from consumption.[53] Furthermore the consumer goods and services left unsold as a result of the rise in voluntary saving play a role remarkably similar to that of the accumulated berries in our Robinson Crusoe example. The berries permitted Crusoe to sustain himself for the number of days required to produce his capital equipment (the wooden stick); during this time period he was not able to devote himself to picking berries "by hand." In a modern economy, consumer goods and services which remain unsold when saving increases fulfill the important function of making it possible for the different economic agents (workers, owners of natural resources and capitalists) to sustain themselves during the time periods that follow. During these periods the recently-initiated lengthening of the productive structure causes an inevitable slowdown in the arrival of new consumer goods and services to the market. This "slowdown" lasts until the completion of all of the new, more capital-intensive processes that have been started. If it were not for the consumer goods and services that remain unsold due to saving, the temporary drop in the supply of new consumer goods would trigger a substantial rise in the relative price of these goods and considerable difficulties in the provision of them.[54]

---

[53]See Hayek, *The Pure Theory of Capital*, p. 256.

[54]In the words of Hayek himself:

> All that happens is that at the earlier date the savers consume less than they obtain from current production, and at the later date (when current production of consumers' goods has decreased and additional capital goods are turned out . . .) they are able to consume more consumers' goods than they

CONCLUSION: THE EMERGENCE OF A NEW, MORE
CAPITAL-INTENSIVE PRODUCTIVE STRUCTURE

The three effects we have just examined are provoked by
the entrepreneurial process of seeking profit, and the combination of the three tends to result in a new, narrower and more
elongated structure of capital goods stages. Moreover the differential between income and costs at each stage, i.e., the
accounting profit or interest rate, tends to even out *at a lower
level* over all stages of the new productive structure (as naturally corresponds to a larger volume of saving and a lower
social rate of time preference). Therefore the shape of the productive structure comes to closely resemble that reflected in
Chart V-3.

Chart V-3 reveals that final consumption has fallen to 75
m.u. This reduction has also affected the value of the product
of the second stage (the previous stage closest to consumption), which has dropped from 80 m.u. in Chart V-1 to 64.25
m.u. in Chart V-3. A similar decrease occurs in the third stage
(from 60 m.u. to 53.5 m.u.), though this time the reduction is
proportionally smaller. However beginning in the fourth stage
(and upward, each stage further from consumption than the
one before it), the demand in monetary terms grows. The
increase is gradual at first. In the fourth stage, the figures rise
from 40 m.u. to 42.75 m.u. It then becomes proportionally
much more substantial in the fifth stage, where the value of
the product grows from 20 m.u. to 32.25 m.u., as we saw in
Chart V-2. Furthermore two *new stages*, stages six and seven,
appear in the area furthest from consumption. These stages
did not exist before.

After all necessary adjustments have been made, the rate
of profit for the different stages tends to even out at a significantly lower level than that reflected in Chart V-1. This phenomenon derives from the fact that the upsurge in voluntary
saving generates a much lower market rate of interest, and the
rate of accounting profit for each stage (in our example,

---

get from current production. (Hayek, *The Pure Theory of Capital*, p. 275. See also footnote 13 above)

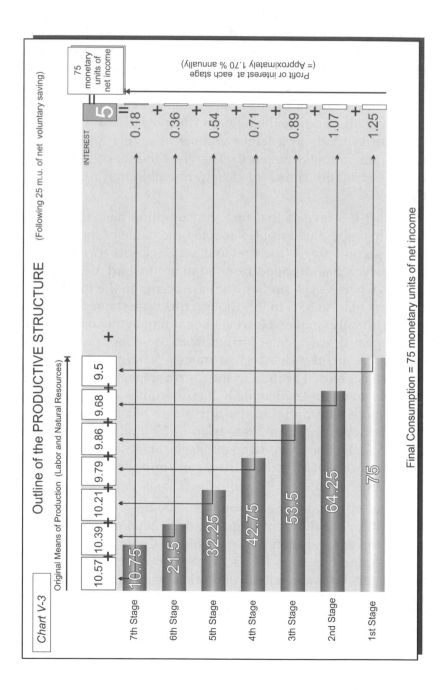

Chart V-3

Outline of the PRODUCTIVE STRUCTURE (Following 25 m.u. of net voluntary saving)

approximately 1.70 percent annually) approaches this figure. The *net income* received by the owners of the original means of production (workers and owners of natural resources) and by the capitalists of each stage, according to the net interest rate or differential, amounts to 75 m.u., which coincides with the monetary income spent on consumer goods and services. It is important to point out that even if only 75 m.u. are spent on consumer goods and services, i.e., 25 units less than in Chart V-1, once all new production processes are completed, the production of new final consumer goods and services will increase substantially in real terms. This is because production processes tend to become more productive as they become more roundabout and capital-intensive. Moreover a larger quantity, in real terms, of produced consumer goods and services can only be sold for a lower total number of m.u. (in our example, 75). Therefore there is a dramatic decline in the unit price of new consumer goods and services reaching the market, and correspondingly the income received by owners of the original means of production (specifically, workers' wages and hence, their living standard) undergoes a sharp increase in real terms.

Tables V-3 and V-4 reflect both the supply of and the demand for present goods, as well as the composition of the gross national output for the year, after all adjustments provoked by the increase in voluntary saving. We see that the supply of and demand for present goods rests at 295 m.u., i.e., 25 m.u. more than in Table V-1. This is because gross saving and investment have grown by precisely the 25 m.u. of additional net saving voluntarily carried out. However as Table V-4 shows, the gross national output for the year remains unaltered at 370 m.u., of which 75 m.u. correspond to the demand for final consumer goods, and 295 m.u. to the total supply of present goods. In other words, even though the gross national output is identical in monetary terms to its value in the last example, *it is now distributed in a radically different manner:* over a narrower and more elongated productive structure (that is, a more capital-intensive one with more stages).

The distinct distribution of the same gross national output (in monetary terms) in each of the two productive structures is more apparent in Chart V-4.

Chart V-4 is simply the result of superimposing Chart V-1 (line) on Chart V-3 (bar), and it shows the impact on the productive structure of the 25 m.u. growth in voluntary net saving. Hence we see that the voluntary increase in saving provokes the following effects:

- *First*: a *deepening* of the capital goods structure. This outcome manifests itself as a *vertical* "lengthening" of the productive structure via the addition of new stages (in our example, stages six and seven, which did not exist before).

- *Second*: a *widening* of the capital goods structure, embodied in a broadening of the existing stages (as in stages four and five).

- *Third*: a *relative narrowing* of the capital goods stages closest to consumption.

- *Fourth*: In the final stage, the stage of consumer goods and services, the jump in voluntary saving invariably generates an initial drop in consumption (in monetary terms). However the lengthening of the productive structure is followed by a substantial real increase (in terms of quantity and quality) in the production of consumer goods and services. Given that the monetary demand for these goods is invariably reduced, and given that these two effects (the drop in consumption and the upsurge in the production of consumer goods) exert similar influences, the increase in production gives rise to a *sharp drop in the market prices of consumer goods*. Ultimately this drop in prices makes it possible for a significant real rise in wages to occur, along with a general increase in all real income received by owners of the original means of production.[55]

---

[55]The above considerations reveal once again the extent to which traditional national income statistics and the measures of growth in national income are theoretically inadequate. We have already pointed out that the indicators of national income do not measure the gross national output and tend to exaggerate the importance of consumption, while overlooking the intermediate stages in the production process. It is also true that the statistical measures of economic growth and of the evolution of

TABLE V-3

THE SUPPLY OF AND DEMAND FOR PRESENT GOODS

(FOLLOWING 25 M.U. OF VOLUNTARY NET SAVING)

Suppliers of Present Goods
(Savers or demanders of future goods)

Capitalists 1st stage = 64.25 + 9.50 = 73.75 ↑
Capitalists 2nd stage = 53.50 + 9.68 = 63.18 ↑
Capitalists 3rd stage = 42.75 + 9.86 = 52.61 ↑
Capitalists 4th stage = 32.25 + 9.79 = 42.04 ↑
Capitalists 5th stage = 21.50 + 10.21 = 31.71 ↑
Capitalists 6th stage = 10.75 + 10.39 = 21.14 ↑
Capitalists 7th stage = 0 + 10.57 = 10.57 ↑

Total Supply   295.00 m.u. =
of Present Goods

Demanders of Present Goods
(Suppliers of future goods)

64.25 to Capitalists 2nd stage + 9.50 to original means
53.50 to Capitalists 3rd stage + 9.68 to original means
42.75 to Capitalists 4th stage + 9.86 to original means
32.25 to Capitalists 5th stage + 9.79 to original means
21.50 to Capitalists 6th stage + 10.21 to original means
10.75 to Capitalists 7th stage + 10.39 to original means
                                     10.57 to original means

225.00 Total demand   70.00 Total demand
        from the owners of   from the owners
        capital goods   of o.m. (land
                                        and labor)

SAVING AND   295.00 m.u. Demand
INVESTMENT (GROSS)   for present goods
Total

TABLE V-4
GROSS INCOME AND NET INCOME FOR THE YEAR
(following 25 m.u. of voluntary net saving)

Gross Income for the Year

75 m.u. of final consumption + 295 m.u.
of total supply of present goods
(Gross Saving and Investment as shown in detail in Table V-3)

(Note: Gross saving and investment grow by 25 m.u., from 270 to
295; and consumption shrinks by 25 m.u., from 100 to 75)

Total Gross Income: 370 m.u.

Net Income for the Year

a) Net Income	Capitalists 1st stage:	75.00	− 73.75	= 1.25
Received by	Capitalists 2nd stage:	64.25	− 63.18	= 1.07
Capitalists	Capitalists 3rd stage:	53.50	− 52.61	= 0.89
(Profit or interest	Capitalists 4th stage:	42.75	− 42.04	= 0.71
at each stage)	Capitalists 5th stage:	32.25	− 31.71	= 0.54
	Capitalists 6th stage:	21.50	− 21.14	= 0.36
	Capitalists 7th stage:	10.75	− 10.57	= 0.18

Total profits, interest or   _____
net income received by
capitalists at all stages: =   5.00 m.u.

b) Net Income	From stage 1:	9.50
Received by	From stage 2:	9.68
Owners of the	From stage 3:	9.86
Original Means	From stage 4:	9.79
of Production	From stage 5:	10.21
(labor and	From stage 6:	10.39
natural resources)	From stage 7:	10.59

Total net income received   _____
by owners of the original
means of production: 70.00 m.u.

                                                      ═════
Total Net Income = Total Consumption   75.00 m.u.

CONCLUSION: The Gross Income for the Year is equal to 4.9 times
               the Net Income

In short, in our example there has been no drop in the money supply (and therefore no external deflation, strictly-speaking), nor has the demand for money risen. So if we assume both of these factors remain constant, then the general fall in the price of consumer goods and services arises exclusively from the upsurge in saving and the increase in productivity, itself a consequence of the more capital-intensive productive structure. Moreover this brings about marked growth in wages (in real terms), which, though their nominal value

---

the price index are both distorted because they focus mainly on the final stage, consumption. Therefore it is easy to see how, in the initial phases of the process triggered when voluntary saving rises, a statistical decrease in economic growth is registered. In fact there is often an initial decline in final consumer and investment goods, while national accounting statistics fail to reflect the parallel increase in investment in the stages furthest from consumption, the creation of new stages, not to mention the growth in investment in non-final intermediate products, stocks and inventories of circulating capital. Moreover the consumer price index falls, since it merely reflects the effect the reduced monetary demand has on consumer goods stages, yet no index adequately records the growth in prices in the stages furthest from consumption. Consequently different agents (politicians, journalists, union leaders, and employers' representatives) often make an erroneous popular interpretation of these economic events, based on these statistical national accounting measures. Hayek, toward the end of his article on "The Ricardo Effect" (*Individualism and Economic Order*, pp. 251–54), offers a detailed description of the great statistical difficulties which exist with respect to using national accounting methods to record the effects on the productive structure of an increase in voluntary saving; or in this case, the influence of the "Ricardo Effect." More recently, in his Nobel Prize acceptance speech, F.A. Hayek warned against the particularly widespread custom of regarding unsound theories as valid simply because there appears to be empirical support for them. Hayek cautioned against rejecting or even ignoring true theoretical explanations merely because it is quite difficult, from a technical standpoint, to collect the statistical information necessary to confirm them. These are precisely the errors committed in the application of national income accounting to the process by which the productive stages furthest from consumption grow wider and deeper, a process always due to a rise in voluntary saving. See "The Pretence of Knowledge," Nobel Memorial Lecture, delivered December 11, 1974 and reprinted in *The American Economic Review* (December 1989): 3–7.

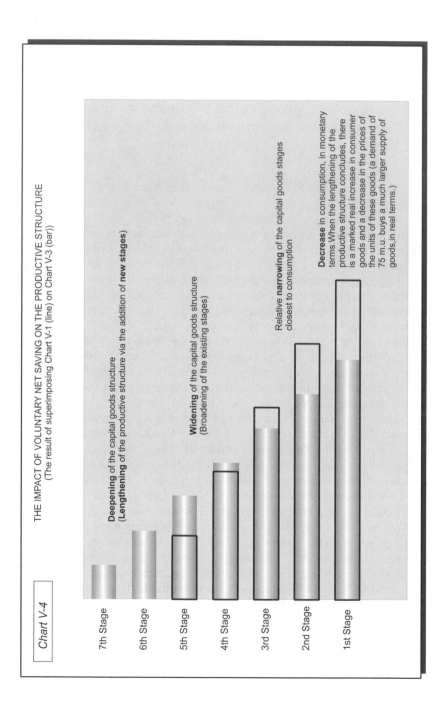

Chart V-4

THE IMPACT OF VOLUNTARY NET SAVING ON THE PRODUCTIVE STRUCTURE
(The result of superimposing Chart V-1 (line) on Chart V-3 (bar))

Deepening of the capital goods structure
(**Lengthening** of the productive structure via the addition of **new stages**)

Widening of the capital goods structure
(Broadening of the existing stages)

Relative **narrowing** of the capital goods stages
closest to consumption

Decrease in consumption, in monetary terms. When the lengthening of the productive structure concludes, there is a marked real increase in consumer goods and a decrease in the prices of the units of these goods (a demand of 75 m.u. buys a much larger supply of goods, in real terms.)

7th Stage

6th Stage

5th Stage

4th Stage

3rd Stage

2nd Stage

1st Stage

remains the same or even diminishes somewhat, permit the earner to acquire an increasing quantity of consumer goods and services of higher and higher quality: the decline in the price of these goods is proportionally much sharper than the possible decline in wages. In brief this is the healthiest, most sustained process of economic growth and development imaginable. In other words, it involves the fewest economic and social maladjustments, tensions, and conflicts and historically has taken place on various occasions, as the most reliable studies have shown.[56]

---

[56]Milton Friedman and Anna J. Schwartz, in reference to the period from 1865 to 1879 in the United States, during which practically no increase in the money supply occurred, conclude that,

> [T]he price level fell to half its initial level in the course of less than fifteen years and, at the same time, economic growth proceeded at a rapid rate. . . . [T]heir coincidence casts serious doubts on the validity of the now widely held view that secular price deflation and rapid economic growth are incompatible. (Milton Friedman and Anna J. Schwartz, *A Monetary History of the United States 1867–1960* [Princeton, N.J.: Princeton University Press, 1971], p. 15, and also the important statistical table on p. 30)

In addition Alfred Marshall, in reference to the period 1875–1885 in England, stated that

> It is doubtful whether the last ten years, which are regarded as years of depression, but in which there have been few violent movements of prices, have not, on the whole, *conduced more to solid progress and true happiness* than the alternations of feverish activity and painful retrogression which have characterised every preceding decade of this century. In fact, *I regard violent fluctuations of prices as a much greater evil than a gradual fall of prices.* (Alfred Marshall, *Official Papers*, p. 9; italics added)

Finally, see also George A. Selgin, *Less Than Zero: The Case for a Falling Price Level in a Growing Economy*, Hobart Paper 132 (London: Institute of Economic Affairs, 1997).

THE THEORETICAL SOLUTION TO THE "PARADOX OF THRIFT"[57]

Our analysis also allows us to solve the problems posed by the supposed dilemma of the paradox of thrift or saving. This "paradox" rests on the concept that, though saving by

---

[57]The essential argument against the thesis that saving adversely affects economic development and that it is necessary to stimulate consumption to foster growth was very brilliantly and concisely expressed by Hayek in 1932 when he demonstrated that *it is a logical contradiction to believe that an increase in consumption manifests itself as an increase in investment, since investment can only rise due to a rise in saving, which must always go against consumption.* In his own words:

> Money spent today on consumption goods does not immediately increase the purchasing power of those who produce for the future; in fact, it actually competes with their demand and their purchasing power is determined not by current but by past prices of consumer goods. This is so because the alternative always exists of investing the available productive resources for a longer or a shorter period of time. *All those who tacitly assume that the demand for capital goods changes in proportion to the demand for consumer goods ignore the fact that it is impossible to consume more and yet simultaneously to defer consumption with the aim of increasing the stock of intermediate products.* (F.A. Hayek, "Capital Consumption," an English translation of the article previously published under the German title "Kapitalaufzehrung," in *Weltwirtschaftliches Archiv* 36, no. 2 (1932): 86–108; italics added)

The English edition appears as chapter 6 of *Money, Capital and Fluctuations: Early Essays* (Chicago: University of Chicago Press, 1984), pp. 141–42. Hayek himself reminds us that this fundamental principle was put forward by John Stuart Mill, who in his fourth proposition on capital established that: "demand for commodities is not demand for labour." Nevertheless Hayek indicates that John Stuart Mill failed to adequately justify this principle, which only became fully accepted by theorists upon the development of the theory of capital by Böhm-Bawerk and the theory of the cycle by Mises and Hayek himself (see John Stuart Mill, *Principles of Political Economy* (Fairfield, N.J.: Augustus M. Kelley, 1976), book 1, chap. 5, no. 9, pp. 79–88). According to Hayek, the understanding of this basic idea is the true test of any economist: "More than ever it seems to me to be true that the complete apprehension of the doctrine that 'demand for commodities is not demand for labor' . . . is 'the best test of an economist.'" Hayek, *The Pure Theory of*

individuals is positive in the sense that it allows them to augment their income, socially speaking, when the aggregate demand for consumer goods diminishes, the decrease eventually exerts a negative effect on investment and production.[58] In contrast we have presented the theoretical arguments

---

Capital (1976 ed.), p. 439. In short it means understanding that it is perfectly feasible for an entrepreneur of consumer goods to earn money even when his sales do not increase and even decrease, if the entrepreneur reduces his costs by substituting capital equipment for labor. (The increased investment in capital equipment creates jobs in other stages and makes society's productive structure more capital-intensive.) See also J. Huerta de Soto, "Hayek's Best Test of a Good Economist," *Procesos de Mercado* 5, no. 2 (Autumn 2004): 121–24.

[58]To F.A. Hayek goes the credit for being the first to have theoretically demolished the supposed "paradox of thrift" in 1929, in his article, "Gibt es einen 'Widersinn des Sparens'?" ("The 'Paradox' of Saving," *Economica* 2, no. 2 [May 1931], and reprinted in *Profits, Interest and Investment*, pp. 199–263). In Italy Augusto Graziani defended a position very similar to Hayek's in his article, "Sofismi sul risparmio," originally published in *Rivista Bancaria* (December 1932), and later reprinted in his book, *Studi di Critica Economica* (Milan: Società Anonima Editrice Dante Alighieri, 1935), pp. 253–63. It is interesting to note that an author as distinguished as Samuelson has continued to defend the old myths of the theory of underconsumption which constitute the basis for the paradox of thrift. He does so in various editions of his popular textbook, and as one might expect, relies on the fallacies of Keynesian theory, which we will comment on in chapter 7. It is not until the thirteenth edition that the doctrine of the "paradox of thrift" becomes optional material and the corresponding diagram justifying it disappears (Paul A. Samuelson and William N. Nordhaus, *Economics*, 13th ed. [New York: McGraw-Hill, 1989], pp. 183–85). Later, in the 14th edition (New York: McGraw-Hill, 1992), all references to the topic are silently and prudently eliminated. Unfortunately, however, they reappear in the 15th edition (New York: McGraw-Hill, 1995, pp. 455–57). See also Mark Skousen "The Perseverance of Paul Samuelson's *Economics*," *Journal of Economic Perspectives* 2, no. 2 (Spring, 1997): 137–52. The main error in the theory of the paradox of thrift consists of the fact that it ignores the basic principles of capital theory and does not treat the productive structure as a series of consecutive stages. Instead it contains the implicit assumption that only two stages exist, one of final aggregate consumer demand and another made up of a single set of intermediate investment stages. Thus in the simplified model of the "circular flow of income," it is assumed that the negative effect on consumption of an upsurge in saving immediately and automatically spreads to all investment. On this topic see Skousen, *The Structure of Production*, pp. 244–59.

which demonstrate that this interpretation, based on the old myth of underconsumption, is faulty. Indeed, even assuming that gross national output in monetary terms remains constant, we have shown how society grows and develops through an increase in real wages, even when the monetary demand for consumer goods declines. We have also demonstrated how, in the absence of state intervention and increases in the money supply, an immensely powerful market force, driven by entrepreneurs' search for profit, leads to the lengthening of and growing complexity in the productive structure. In short, despite the *initial* relative decrease in the demand for consumer goods which stems from growth in saving, the productivity of the economic system is boosted, as is the final production of consumer goods and services, and real wages.[59]

THE CASE OF AN ECONOMY IN REGRESSION

Our reasoning up to this point can be reversed, with appropriate changes, to explain the effects of a hypothetical

---

[59]Rothbard (*Man, Economy, and State*, pp. 467–79) has revealed that, as a result of the lengthening of the productive structure (a phenomenon we have examined and one which follows from an increase in voluntary saving), it is impossible to determine in advance whether or not the income capitalists receive in the form of interest will rise. In our detailed example this does not occur in monetary terms and perhaps not in real terms either. This is due to the fact that, even when saving and gross investment grow, we cannot establish, simply on the basis of economic theory, whether or not the value of income derived from interest will fall, rise or remain constant, since each of these alternatives is feasible. It is also impossible to ascertain what will happen to the monetary income received by owners of the original means of production. In our example it stays the same, which results in a dramatic increase in the owners' real income once the prices of consumer goods decline. Nonetheless a drop in the income (in monetary terms) received by the owners of the original means of production is possible, although such a drop will always be less marked than the reduction in the prices of consumer goods and services. Nowadays it is clearly a challenge for us to conceive of an economy in rapid development, yet where the monetary income received by owners of the factors of production (especially labor) diminishes, however this scenario is perfectly feasible if the prices of final consumer goods and services fall even faster.

decrease in society's voluntary saving. Let us begin by supposing that the productive structure closely resembles that reflected in Chart V-3. If society as a whole decides to save less, the result will be an increase, of for instance 25 m.u., in the monetary demand for consumer goods and services. Therefore the monetary demand will rise from 75 m.u. to 100 m.u., and the industries and companies of the stages closest to consumption will tend to grow dramatically, which will drive up their accounting profits. Though these events may appear to provoke the effects of a consumer boom, in the long run they will lead to a "flattening" of the productive structure, since productive resources will be withdrawn from the stages furthest from consumption and transferred to those closest to it. In fact the increased accounting profits of the stages close to final consumption will, relatively speaking, discourage production in the most distant stages, which will tend to bring about a reduction in investment in these stages. Moreover the drop in saving will push up the market rate of interest and diminish the corresponding present value of durable capital goods, deterring investment in them. Finally a reverse "Ricardo Effect" will exert its influence: growth in the prices of consumer goods and services will be accompanied by an immediate decline in real wages and in the rents of the other original factors, which will encourage capitalists to replace capital equipment with labor, now relatively cheaper.

The combined result of all these influences is a flattening of the productive structure, which comes to resemble that described in Chart V-1, which, although it reflects a greater demand for consumer goods and services in monetary terms, shows *there has been a generalized impoverishment of society in real terms*. In fact the less capital-intensive productive structure will result in the arrival of fewer consumer goods and services to the final stage, which nevertheless undergoes a considerable rise in monetary demand. Hence there is a decrease in the production of consumer goods and services, along with a substantial increase in their price, a consequence of the two previous effects combined. The result is the generalized impoverishment of society, especially of workers, whose wages shrink in real terms, since, while in monetary terms they may remain constant or even increase, such a rise never reaches the level of growth undergone by monetary prices of consumer goods and services.

According to John Hicks, Giovanni Boccaccio, in an interesting passage in the Introduction to *Decameron*, written around the year 1360, was the first to describe, in rather precise terms, a process very similar to the one we have just analyzed when he related the impact the Great Plague of the fourteenth century had on the people of Florence. In fact the epidemic caused people to anticipate a drastic reduction in life expectancy, and thus entrepreneurs and workers, instead of saving and "lengthening" the stages in their production process by working their lands and tending their livestock, devoted themselves to increasing their present consumption.[60] After Boccaccio, the first economist to seriously consider the effects of a decline in saving and the resulting economic setback was Böhm-Bawerk in his book, *Capital and Interest*,[61] where he explains in detail that a general decision by individuals to consume more and save less triggers a phenomenon of capital consumption, which ultimately lowers productive capacity and the production of consumer goods and services, giving rise to the generalized impoverishment of society.[62]

---

[60]In the words of John Hicks himself:

> Boccaccio is describing the impact on people's minds of the Great Plague at Florence, the expectation that they had not long to live. "Instead of furthering the future products of their cattle and their land and their own past labour, they devoted all their attention to the consumption of present goods." [John Hicks asks:] "Why does Boccaccio write like Böhm-Bawerk? The reason is surely that he was trained as a merchant."
> (Hicks, *Capital and Time: A Neo-Austrian Theory*, pp. 12–13)

[61]Böhm-Bawerk, *Capital and Interest*, vol. 2: *The Positive Theory of Capital*, pp. 113–14. At the end of this analysis, Böhm-Bawerk concludes that saving is the necessary prior condition for the formation of capital. In the words of Böhm-Bawerk himself: "Ersparung [ist] eine unentbehrliche Bedingung der Kapitalbildung" (Böhm-Bawerk, German edition, p. 134).

[62]Fritz Machlup clearly exposed the error committed by the theorists of the paradox of thrift when he made reference to the concrete historical case of the Austrian economy after World War I. At that time everything

3

THE EFFECTS OF BANK CREDIT EXPANSION UNBACKED BY AN INCREASE IN SAVING: THE AUSTRIAN THEORY OR CIRCULATION CREDIT THEORY OF THE BUSINESS CYCLE

In this section we will examine the effects banks exert on the productive structure when they create loans unbacked by a prior increase in voluntary saving. These circumstances differ radically from those we studied in the last section, where loans were fully backed by a corresponding rise in voluntary saving. In accordance with the credit expansion process triggered by fractional-reserve banking (a process we examined in detail in chapter 4), a bank's creation of credit would result in an accounting entry which, in its simplest form, would resemble this one:

(73)	Debit	Credit	
1,000,000	Cash	Demand deposits	1,000,000

(74)			
900,000	Loans granted	Demand deposits	900,000

These book entries, which are identical to numbers (17) and (18) in chapter 4, record in a simplified and concise fashion the unquestionable fact that the bank is able to generate

---

possible was done to foster consumption, however the country became extremely impoverished. Machlup ironically states:

> Austria had most impressive records in five lines: she increased public expenditures, she increased wages, she increased social benefits, she increased bank credits, she increased consumption. After all these achievements she was on the verge of ruin. (Fritz Machlup, "The Consumption of Capital in Austria," *Review of Economic Statistics* 17, no. 1 [1935]: 13–19)

Other examples of this kind of generalized impoverishments were the Argentina of General Perón and Portugal after the 1973 Revolution.

from nothing new m.u. in the form of deposits or fiduciary media which are granted to the public as loans or credit even when the public has not first decided to increase saving.[63] We will now consider the effects this important event has on social processes of coordination and economic interaction.

THE EFFECTS OF CREDIT EXPANSION ON THE PRODUCTIVE STRUCTURE

The creation of money by the banking system in the form of loans has some real effects on the economy's productive structure, and it is necessary to clearly distinguish between these effects and those we studied in the last section with respect to loans backed by saving. More specifically, the generation of loans *ex nihilo* (i.e., in the absence of an increase in saving) raises the supply of credit to the economy, especially to the different capital goods stages in the productive structure. From this standpoint, the increased supply of loans which results from bank credit expansion will initially exert an effect very similar to that produced by the flow of new loans from saving which we analyzed in detail in the last section: it will tend to cause a widening and lengthening of the stages in the productive structure.

The "widening" of the different stages is easy to understand, since basically the loans are granted for the production processes which constitute each of the stages. Credit extended to finance durable consumer goods also leads to a widening and lengthening of the productive structure, because (as we have seen) durable consumer goods are economically comparable to capital goods throughout the period during which they are fit to render their services. Therefore even in the case of consumer loans (to finance durable consumer goods), the greater influx of loans will tend to increase both the quantity and quality of such goods.

------

[63]"So far as deposits are created by the banks, money means are created, and the command of capital is supplied, without cost or sacrifice on the part of the saver." F.W. Taussig, *Principles of Economics*, 3rd ed. (New York: Macmillan, 1939), vol. 1, p. 357.

The "lengthening" of the productive structure derives from the fact that the only way banks can introduce into the economy the new money they create from nothing and grant as loans is by temporarily and artificially reducing the interest rate in the credit market and by easing the rest of the economic and contractual conditions they insist on when granting loans to their customers. This lowering of the interest rate in the credit market does not necessarily manifest itself as a decrease in absolute terms. Instead a decrease in relative terms, i.e., in relation to the interest rate which would have predominated in the market *in the absence of credit expansion*, is sufficient.[64] Hence the reduction is even compatible with an increase in the interest rate in nominal terms, if the rate climbs less than it would have in an environment without credit expansion (for instance, if credit expansion coincides with a generalized drop in the purchasing power of money). Likewise such a reduction is compatible with a decline in the interest rate, if the rate falls even more than it would have had there been no credit expansion (for example, in a process in which, in contrast, the purchasing power of money is growing). Therefore this lowering of the interest rate is a fact accounted for by theory, and one it will be necessary to interpret historically while considering the circumstances particular to each case.

The relative reduction credit expansion causes in the interest rate boosts the present value of capital goods, since the flow of rents they are expected to produce increases in value when discounted using a lower market rate of interest. In addition, the lowering of the interest rate gives the appearance

---

64　It does not matter whether this drop in the gross market rate expresses itself in an arithmetical drop in the percentage stipulated in the loan contracts. It could happen that the nominal interest rates remain unchanged and that the expansion manifests itself in the fact that at these rates loans are negotiated which would not have been made before on account of the height of the entrepreneurial component to be included. Such an outcome too amounts to a drop in gross market rates and brings about the same consequences. (Mises, *Human Action*, p. 552)

of profitability to investment projects which until that point were not profitable, giving rise to new stages further from consumption. The process through which these stages come into existence closely resembles the one involved when society's voluntary saving actually increases. Nevertheless we must emphasize that although the *initial* effects may be very similar to those which, as we saw, follow an upsurge in voluntary saving, *in this case the productive stages are lengthened and widened*[65] *only as a consequence of the easier credit terms banks offer at relatively lower interest rates yet without any previous growth in voluntary saving.* As we know, a sustainable lengthening of the productive structure is only possible if the necessary prior saving has taken place in the form of a drop in the final demand for consumer goods. This drop permits the different productive agents to sustain themselves using the unsold consumer goods and services while the new processes introduced reach completion and their more productive result begins to reach the market in the form of consumer goods.[66]

In short, entrepreneurs decide to launch new investment projects, widening and lengthening the capital goods stages in

---

[65]   When under the conditions of credit expansion the whole amount of the additional money substitutes is lent to business, production is expanded. The entrepreneurs embark either upon lateral expansion of production (viz., the expansion of production without lengthening the period of production in the individual industry) or upon longitudinal expansion (viz., the lengthening of the period of production). In either case, the additional plants require the investment of additional factors of production. But the amount of capital goods available for investment has not increased. Neither does credit expansion bring about a tendency toward a restriction of consumption. (Ibid., p. 556)

[66]   A lengthening of the period of production is only practicable, however, either when the means of subsistence have increased sufficiently to support the laborers and entrepreneurs during the longer period or when the wants of producers have decreased sufficiently to enable them to make the same means of subsistence do for the longer period. (Mises, *The Theory of Money and Credit*, p. 400)

the productive structure; that is, they act *as if* society's saving had increased, when in fact such an event has not occurred. In the case of an upsurge in voluntary saving, which we examined in the last section, the individual behavior of the different economic agents tended to become compatible, and thus the real resources that were saved and not consumed made the preservation and lengthening of the productive structure possible. Now the fact that entrepreneurs respond to credit expansion by behaving as if saving had increased *triggers a process of maladjustment or discoordination in the behavior of the different economic agents.* Indeed entrepreneurs rush to invest and to widen and lengthen the real productive structure even though economic agents have not decided to augment their saving by the volume necessary to finance the new investments. In a nutshell, this is a typical example of an inducement to mass entrepreneurial error in economic calculation or estimation regarding the outcome of the different courses of action entrepreneurs adopt. This error in economic calculation stems from the fact that one of the basic indicators entrepreneurs refer to before acting, the interest rate (along with the attractiveness of terms offered in the credit market), is temporarily manipulated and artificially lowered by banks through a process of credit expansion.[67] In the words of Ludwig von Mises,

> But now the drop in interest falsifies the businessman's calculation. Although the amount of capital goods available did not increase, the calculation employs figures which would be utilizable only if such an increase had taken place. The result of such calculations is therefore misleading. They make some projects appear profitable and realizable which a correct calculation, based on an interest rate not manipulated by credit expansion, would have shown as

---

[67]Elsewhere we have explained why systematic coercion and manipulation of market indicators, the result of government intervention or the granting of privileges by the government to pressure groups (unions, banks, etc.), prevent people from producing and discovering the information necessary to coordinate society, and serious maladjustments and social discoordination systematically follow. See Huerta de Soto, *Socialismo, cálculo económico y función empresarial*, chaps. 2 and 3.

unrealizable. Entrepreneurs embark upon the execution of such projects. Business activities are stimulated. A boom begins.[68]

At first the discoordination expresses itself in the emergence of a period of exaggerated and disproportionate optimism, which stems from the fact that economic agents feel able to expand the productive structure without at the same time having to make the sacrifice of reducing their consumption to generate savings. In the last section the lengthening of the productive structure was shown to be made possible precisely by the prior sacrifice required by all increases in saving. Now we see that entrepreneurs hasten to widen and lengthen the stages in production processes when no such prior saving has taken place. The discoordination could not be more obvious nor the initial excess of optimism more justified, since it seems possible to introduce longer production processes without any sacrifice or previous accumulation of capital. In short a mass error is committed by entrepreneurs, who adopt production processes they consider profitable, but which are not. This error feeds a generalized optimism founded on the belief that it is possible to widen and lengthen the stages in production processes without anyone's having to save. *Intertemporal discoordination* increasingly mounts: entrepreneurs invest *as if* social saving were constantly growing;

---

[68]Mises, *Human Action*, p. 553 (p. 550 of the Scholar's Edition). As all saving takes the form of capital goods, even when initially these goods are merely the consumer goods which remain unsold when saving rises, Mises's explanation is completely valid. See footnotes 13 and 54. Lionel Robbins, in his book, *The Great Depression* (New York: Macmillan, 1934), lists the following ten characteristics typical of any boom: *first*, the interest rate falls in relative terms; *second*, short-term interest rates begin to decline; *third*, long-term interest rates also drop; *fourth*, the current market value of bonds rises; *fifth*, the velocity of the circulation of money increases; *sixth*, stock prices climb; *seventh*, real estate prices begin to soar; *eighth*, an industrial boom takes place and a large number of securities are issued in the primary market; *ninth*, the price of natural resources and intermediate goods rises; and last, *tenth*, the stock exchange undergoes explosive growth based on the expectation of an *uninterrupted* increase in entrepreneurial profits (pp. 39–42).

consumers continue to consume at a steady (or even increased) pace and do not worry about stepping up their saving.[69]

To illustrate the initial effect credit expansion exerts on the real productive structure, we will follow the system used in the last section to present several graphs and tables which reflect the impact of credit expansion on the productive structure. A word of caution is necessary, however: it is practically impossible to represent in this way the complex effects produced in the market when credit expansion triggers the generalized process of discoordination we are describing. Therefore it is important to exercise great care in interpreting the following tables and charts, which should only be valued insofar as they illustrate and facilitate understanding of the fundamental economic argument. It is nearly impossible to reflect with charts anything other than strictly static situations, since charts invariably conceal the dynamic processes which take place between situations. Nonetheless the tables and graphs we propose to represent the stages in the productive structure may well help illustrate the essential theoretical argument and greatly facilitate an understanding of it.[70]

---

[69]Roger Garrison interprets this phenomenon as an unsustainable departure from the production possibilities frontier (PPF). See his book, *Time and Money*, pp. 67–76.

[70]Our intention is to warn readers of the error which threatens anyone who might attempt to make a strictly theoretical interpretation of the charts we present. Nicholas Kaldor committed such an error in his critical analysis of Hayek's theory, as was recently revealed by Laurence S. Moss and Karen I. Vaughn, for whom

> the problem is not to learn about adjustments by comparing states of equilibrium but rather to ask if the conditions remaining at T_1 make the transition to T_2 at all possible. Kaldor's approach indeed assumed away the very problem that Hayek's theory was designed to analyze, the problem of the transition an economy undergoes in moving from one coordinated capital structure to another.

See their article, "Hayek's Ricardo Effect: A Second Look," p. 564. The articles in which Kaldor criticizes Hayek are "Capital Intensity and the Trade Cycle," *Economica* (February 1939): 40–66; and "Professor Hayek

Chart V-5 provides a simplified illustration of the effect exerted on the structure of productive stages by credit expansion brought about by the banking system without the necessary increase in social saving. When we compare it with Chart V-1 of this chapter, we see that final consumption remains unchanged at 100 m.u., in keeping with our supposition that no growth in net saving has taken place. However new money is created (deposits or fiduciary media) and enters the system through credit expansion and the relative reduction in the interest rate (along with the typical easing of the contractual conditions and the requirements for obtaining a loan) necessary to persuade economic agents to take out the newly-created loans. Therefore the rate of profit in the different productive stages, which as we know tends to coincide with the interest rate obtained at each stage by advancing present goods in exchange for future goods, now drops from the 11 percent shown in Chart V-1 to slightly over 4 percent yearly. Moreover the new loans allow the entrepreneurs of each productive stage to pay more for the corresponding original means of production, as well as for the capital goods from earlier stages which they obtain for their own productive processes.

Table V-5 reflects the supply of and demand for present goods following bank credit expansion unbacked by saving. We see that the supply of present goods increases from the 270 m.u. shown in Table V-1 to slightly over 380 m.u., which are in turn composed of the 270 m.u. from the example in the last section (m.u. originating from real saved resources) *plus slightly over 113 m.u. which banks have created through credit*

---

and the Concertina Effect," *Economica* (November 1942): 359–82. Curiously, Kaldor had translated from German to English Hayek's book, *Monetary Theory and the Trade Cycle*, first published in 1933 (London: Routledge). Rudy van Zijp recently pointed out that the criticism Kaldor and others have leveled against Hayek's "Ricardo Effect" has derived from the assumption of a hypothetical state of general equilibrium which does not permit a dynamic analysis of the intertemporal discoordination credit expansion inevitably provokes in the market. See Rudy van Zijp, *Austrian and New Classical Business Cycle Theory* (Aldershot, U.K.: Edward Elgar, 1994), pp. 51–53.

expansion without the backing of any saving. Thus credit expansion has the effect of artificially raising the supply of present goods, which are demanded at lower interest rates by owners of the original means of production and by capitalists of the earlier stages further from consumption. Furthermore Table V-5 reveals that the gross income for the year is over 483 m.u., 113 units more than the gross income for the year prior to credit expansion. (See Table V-2.)

Chart V-6 offers a simplified representation of the effect of credit expansion (i.e., unbacked by a *prior* rise in voluntary saving) on the productive structure. In our example, this effect expresses itself in the lengthening of the productive structure via the appearance of two new stages, six and seven. Prior to the expansion of credit these stages did not exist, and they are the furthest from final consumption. In addition the preexisting productive stages (two through five) are widened. The sum of the m.u. which represent the monetary demand embodied in each new widening or lengthening of productive stages, and which on the chart is reflected by the shaded areas, amounts to 113.75 m.u., the exact rise in gross monetary income for the year, an increase which stems exclusively from the creation of new money through credit expansion brought about by banks.

Let us not be deceived by Chart V-5: the new structure of productive stages it illustrates rests on generalized intertemporal discoordination, in turn the result of the mass entrepreneurial error provoked by the introduction of a large volume of new loans which are granted at artificially reduced interest rates, without the backing of real prior saving. This anomalous state of discoordination cannot be maintained, and the next section will include a detailed explanation of the reaction credit expansion inevitably sets off in the market. *In other words, from the standpoint of pure microeconomic theory, we will examine the factors that will cause the reversal of the "macroeconomic" discoordination we have revealed.*

Hence we will study the reasons the intertemporal discoordination process, initially set in motion by credit expansion, will completely reverse. Any attack on the social process, be it intervention, systematic coercion, manipulation of essential

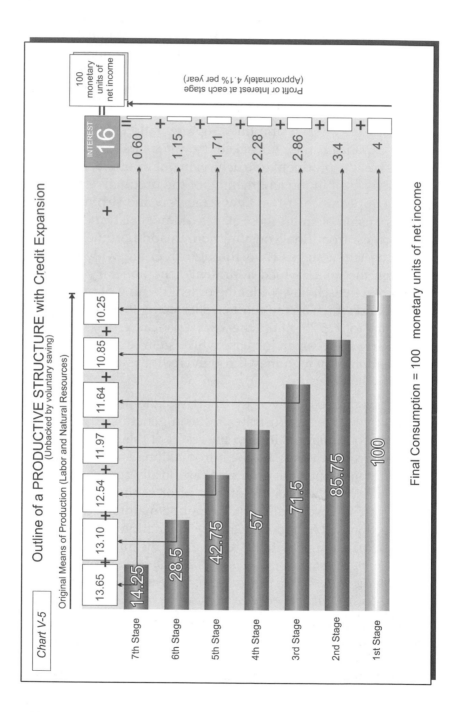

Chart V-5

Outline of a PRODUCTIVE STRUCTURE with Credit Expansion
(Unbacked by voluntary saving)

Original Means of Production (Labor and Natural Resources)

Profit or Interest at each stage
(Approximately 4.1% per year)

100 monetary units of net income

INTEREST 16

Final Consumption = 100   monetary units of net income

indicators (such as the price of present goods in terms of future goods, or the market rate of interest), or the granting of privileges against traditional legal principles, spontaneously triggers certain processes of social interaction which, as they are driven precisely by entrepreneurship and its capacity to coordinate, tend to halt and rectify errors and discoordination. Great credit goes to Ludwig von Mises for being the first to reveal, in 1912, that credit expansion gives rise to booms and optimism which sooner or later invariably subside. In his own words:

> The increased productive activity that sets in when the banks start the policy of granting loans at less than the natural rate of interest at first causes the prices of production goods to rise while the prices of consumption goods, although they rise also, do so only in a moderate degree, namely, only insofar as they are raised by the rise in wages. Thus the tendency toward a fall in the rate of interest on loans that originates in the policy of the banks is at first strengthened. *But soon a countermovement sets in: the prices of consumption goods rise, those of production goods fall. That is, the rate of interest on loans rises again, it again approaches the natural rate.*[71]

---

[71]Mises, *The Theory of Money and Credit*, p. 401; italics added. The last two sentences are so important that it is worthwhile to consider Ludwig von Mises's expression of the essential idea in his original German edition:

> Aber bald setzt eine rückläufige Bewegung ein: Die Preise der Konsumgüter steigen, die der Produktivgüter sinken, das heißt der Darlehenszinsfuß steigt wieder, er nähert sich wieder dem Satze des natürlichen Kapitalzinses. (Ludwig von Mises, *Theorie des Geldes und der Umlaufsmittel*, 2nd German ed. [Munich and Leipzig: Duncker and Humblot, 1924], p. 372)

Mises, who was strongly influenced by Wicksell's doctrine of "natural interest," bases his theory on the disparities which emerge throughout the cycle between "natural interest" and "gross interest in the credit (or 'monetary') market." Banks temporarily reduce the latter in their process of credit expansion. Though we view Mises's analysis as impeccable, we prefer to base our presentation of the theory of the cycle

TABLE V-5

THE SUPPLY OF AND DEMAND FOR PRESENT GOODS (WITH CREDIT EXPANSION)

Suppliers of Present Goods
(270 m.u. come from savers and 113.75 m.u.
have been created ex nihilo via bank credit)

Demanders of Present Goods
(Suppliers of future goods)

Capitalists 1st stage	=	85.75	+	10.25	= 96.00 ↑	85.75 to Capitalists 2nd stage	+ 10.25 to original means
Capitalists 2nd stage	=	71.50	+	10.85	= 82.35 ↑	71.50 to Capitalists 3rd stage	+ 10.85 to original means
Capitalists 3rd stage	=	57.00	+	11.64	= 68.64 ↑	57.00 to Capitalists 4th stage	+ 11.64 to original means
Capitalists 4th stage	=	42.75	+	11.97	= 54.72 ↑	42.75 to Capitalists 5th stage	+ 11.97 to original means
Capitalists 5th stage	=	28.50	+	12.54	= 41.04 ↑	28.50 to Capitalists 6th stage	+ 12.54 to original means
Capitalists 6th stage	=	14.25	+	13.10	= 27.35 ↑	14.25 to Capitalists 7th stage	+ 13.10 to original means
Capitalists 7th stage	=	0	+	13.65	= 13.65 ↑		13.65 to original means

299.75 Total demand from the
owners of capital goods

84.00 Total demand from
the owners of o.m.
(land and labor)

Total Supply of Present Goods   383.75 m.u.   383.75 m.u. Total Demand
Of which: for Present Goods

1) 270.00 m.u. derive from real saved resources (real gross saving as shown in Table V-1)

2) 113.75 m.u. derive from credit expansion (unbacked by saving)   383.75 m.u. TOTAL

*Gross Income for the Year (including 100 m.u. of net income):   483.75

*Gross Income for the Year, prior to Credit Expansion (See Table V-2):   370.00

Nominal Increase in Gross Income caused by Credit Expansion (unbacked by saving):   113.75

As we will have the opportunity to study later, prior to Mises various scholars of the School of Salamanca (Saravia de la Calle for instance) and others of the nineteenth century, mainly intellectuals of the Currency School (Henry Thornton, Condy Raguet, Geyer, etc.), sensed that booms provoked by credit expansion ultimately and spontaneously reversed, causing economic crises. Nonetheless Mises was the first to correctly formulate and explain, from the standpoint of economic theory, the reasons this is necessarily so. Despite Mises's momentous initial contribution, a completely formulated analysis of the different economic effects which comprise the market's reaction to credit expansion first became available with the writings of Mises's most brilliant student, F.A. Hayek.[72] In the next section we will examine these effects in detail.[73]

---

directly on the effects credit expansion exerts on the productive structure, and to somewhat minimize the importance of Mises's analysis of the disparities between "natural interest" and "monetary interest." Knut Wicksell's main work in this area is *Geldzins und Güterpreise: Eine Studie über die den Tauschwert des Geldes bestimmenden Ursachen* (Jena: Verlag von Gustav Fischer, 1898), translated into English by R.F. Kahn with the title *Interest and Prices: A Study of the Causes Regulating the Value of Money* (London: Macmillan, 1936 and New York: Augustus M. Kelley, 1965). Nevertheless Wicksell's analysis is much inferior to Mises's, particularly because it rests almost exclusively on changes in the general price level, rather than on variations in relative prices in the capital goods structure, which is the essence of our theory. Mises summarized and completed the exposition of his own theory in *Geldwertstabilisierung und Konjunkturpolitik* (Jena: Gustav Fischer, 1928); English translation by Bettina Bien Greaves, "Monetary Stabilization and Cyclical Policy," included in *On the Manipulation of Money and Credit* (New York: Free Market Books, 1978).

[72]Hayek's most important works are: *Geldtheorie und Konjunkturtheorie*, (Beitrage zur Konjunkturforschung, herausgegeben vom Österreichisches Institut für Konjunkturforschung, no. 1 [Vienna 1929]), translated into English by Nicolas Kaldor and published as *Monetary Theory and the Trade Cycle* (London: Routledge, 1933, and New Jersey: Augustus M. Kelley, 1975); *Prices and Production*, the first edition of which appeared in 1931 and the second, revised, updated edition of which appeared in 1935 and was later reprinted more than ten times in England and the United States; *Profits, Interest, and Investment* (1939, 1969, 1975); the series of essays published in *Money, Capital and Fluctuations: Early Essays,*

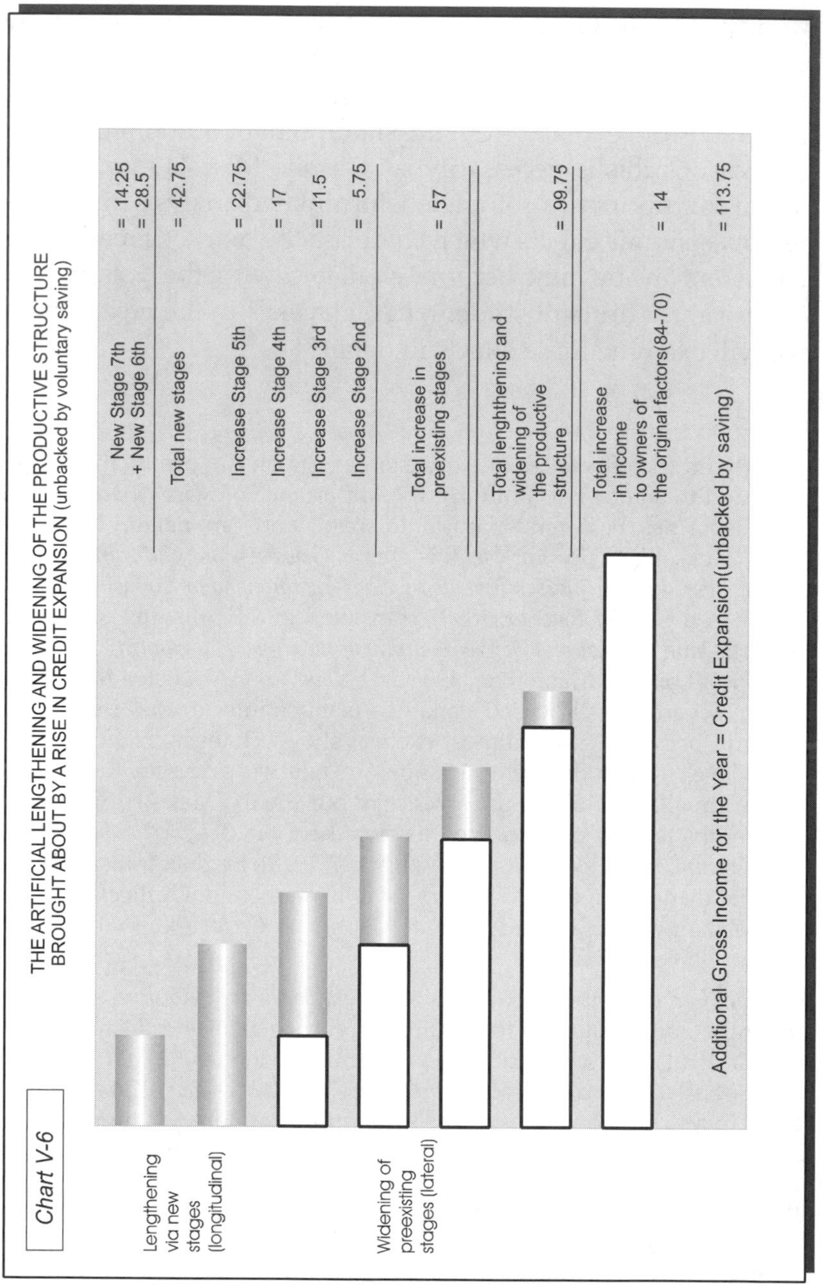

Chart V-6

THE ARTIFICIAL LENGTHENING AND WIDENING OF THE PRODUCTIVE STRUCTURE
BROUGHT ABOUT BY A RISE IN CREDIT EXPANSION (unbacked by voluntary saving)

Lengthening
via new
stages
(longitudinal)

New Stage 7th = 14.25
+ New Stage 6th = 28.5

Total new stages = 42.75

Increase Stage 5th = 22.75

Increase Stage 4th = 17

Increase Stage 3rd = 11.5

Increase Stage 2nd = 5.75

Widening of
preexisting
stages (lateral)

Total increase in
preexisting stages = 57

Total lenghthening and
widening of
the productive
structure = 99.75

Total increase
in income
to owners of
the original factors(84-70) = 14

Additional Gross Income for the Year = Credit Expansion(unbacked by saving) = 113.75

THE MARKET'S SPONTANEOUS REACTION TO CREDIT EXPANSION

We will now consider the *microeconomic* factors which will halt the process of exaggerated optimism and unsustainable

Roy McCloughry, ed. (Chicago: University of Chicago Press, 1984); and last, *The Pure Theory of Capital* (1941; four later editions, and vol. XII of Hayek's *Collected Works).* Hayek himself, in an "Appendix" to *Prices and Production* (pp. 101–04), lists the main forerunners of the Austrian theory or circulation credit theory of the business cycle, which can be traced back to Ricardo himself (the first to describe the effect Hayek christened the "Ricardo Effect"), Condy Raguet, James Wilson, and Bonamy Price in England and the United States; J.G. Courcelle-Seneuil, V. Bonnet, and Yves Guyot in France; and curiously, in German, ideas very similar to those of the theorists of the Austrian School can be found in the writings of Karl Marx and especially in those of Mijail Tugan-Baranovsky (see his work, *Industrial Crises in England*, St. Petersburg, 1894), and of course in those of Böhm-Bawerk *(Capital and Interest,* vol. 2: *Positive Theory of Capital*, pp. 316ff.). Later these contemporaries of Hayek worked along the same lines: Richard von Strigl, in *Kapital und Produktion* (Munich and Vienna: Philosophia Verlag, 1934, 1982; English translation, Auburn, Ala.: Ludwig von Mises Institute, 2000); Bresciani-Turroni in Italy, *The Economics of Inflation: A Study of Currency Depreciation of Post-War Germany* (1931, 1937; London and New York: Augustus M. Kelley 1968); Gottfried Haberler, "Money and the Business Cycle," published in 1932 and reprinted in *The Austrian Theory of the Trade Cycle and Other Essays* (Washington, D.C: Ludwig von Mises Institute, 1978), pp. 7–20; Fritz Machlup, *The Stock Market, Credit and Capital Formation*, originally published in German in 1931 and reprinted in English (London: William Hodge, 1940). Notable writings in the English-speaking world include: Davenport, *The Economics of Enterprise* (New York: Augustus M. Kelley, [1913] 1978), chap. 13; Frederick Benham, *British Monetary Policy* (London: P.S. King and Shaw, 1932); H.F. Fraser, *Great Britain and the Gold Standard* (London: Macmillan, 1933); Theodore E. Gregory, *Gold, Unemployment and Capitalism* (London: P.S. King and Shaw, 1933); E.F.M. Durbin, *Purchasing Power and Trade Depression: A Critique of Under-Consumption Theories* (London and Toronto: Johnathan Cape, 1933), and *The Problem of Credit Policy* (London: Chapman and Hall, 1935); M.A. Abrams, *Money in a Changing Civilisation* (London: John Lain, 1934); and C.A. Phillips, T.F. McManus and R.W. Nelson, *Banking and the Business Cycle,* (New York: Arno Press, 1937). And also in the United States, the work of Frank Albert Fetter, esp. his article, "Interest Theory and Price Movements," *American Economic Review* 17, no. 1 (1926): 72ff. (included in F.A. Fetter, *Capital, Interest, and Rent*, Murray N. Rothbard, ed. [Kansas City: Sheed Andrews and McMeel, 1977]).

[73]It is important to remember that in 1974 the Swedish Academy awarded F.A. Hayek the Nobel Prize in Economics precisely for his

economic expansion that follows the granting of bank loans unbacked by a previous increase in voluntary saving. In this way we will be fully able to take typically macroeconomic

---

"pioneering work in the theory of money and economic fluctuations." See William J. Zahka, *The Nobel Prize Economics Lectures* (Aldershot, U.K.: Avebury, 1992), pp. 19 and 25–28. Writings in Spanish on the Austrian theory of the business cycle are few but can be traced back to the article by Mises published in the *Revista de Occidente* in 1932 ("La causa de las crisis económicas," *Revista de Occidente*, February 1932) and to Luis Olariaga's translation of *Monetary Theory and the Trade Cycle*, by F.A. Hayek *(La teoría monetaria y el ciclo económico* [Espasa-Calpe, 1936]). Olariaga's edition of this book of Hayek's contains, as an appendix, a translation into Spanish (entitled "Previsiones de Precios, Perturbaciones Monetarias e Inversiones Fracasadas") of "Price Expectations, Monetary Disturbances and Malinvestments" from the original English version. This article appears as chapter 4 of *Profits, Interest and Investment* and undoubtedly holds one of Hayek's clearest presentations of his theory of the business cycle (fortunately it is included in the Spanish translation of *Prices and Production* published in 1996 [*Precios y producción*], Unión Editorial, Madrid). The fateful first year of the Spanish Civil War also coincided with the publication of the first Spanish translation (by Antonio Riaño) of *The Theory of Money and Credit*, by Ludwig von Mises *(Teoría del dinero y del crédito* (Madrid: Editorial Aguilar, 1936). It is not surprising that the war reduced the impact of these writings in Spain to a minimum. A notable achievement from the period following the civil war is Richard von Strigl's outline of the Austrian theory of the cycle in his book, *Curso medio de economía*, M. Sánchez Sarto, Spanish trans. (Mexico: Fondo de Cultura Económica, 1941). The year 1947 saw the publication of *Teoría de los ciclos económicos* (Madrid: CSIC, 1947), by Emilio de Figueroa. In volume 2 of this work Figueroa compares Hayek's and Keynes's theories of the cycle (pp. 44–63). The Fondo de Cultura Económica also published the translation of J.A. Estey's book, *Business Cycles* (*Tratado sobre los ciclos económicos* [Mexico: Fondo de Cultura Económica, 1948]), chapter 13 of which contains a detailed explanation of the Austrian theory. The only other works on this subject to be translated into Spanish are Gottfried Haberler's book, *Prosperity and Depression* (*Prosperidad y depresión: análisis teórico de los movimientos cíclicos*, translated by Gabriel Franco and Javier Márquez and published by the Fondo de Cultura Económica in 1942; chapter 3 of this book is devoted to the Austrian School's theory of circulation credit); F.A. Hayek's book, *The Pure Theory of Capital* (*La teoría pura del capital*, published by Aguilar in 1946); and Ludwig von Mises's work, *Human Action* (*La acción humana: tratado de economía*, the first edition of which was published in 1960 by the Fundación Ignacio Villalonga). Apart from these

phenomena (economic crises, depression, and unemployment) back to their fundamental microeconomic roots. We will now study, one by one, the six microeconomic causes of the reversal of the boom that credit expansion invariably triggers:

1. *The rise in the price of the original means of production.*

The first temporary effect of credit expansion is an increase in the relative price of the original means of production (labor and natural resources). This rise in price stems from two separate causes which reinforce each other. On the one hand, capitalists from the different stages in the production process show a greater monetary demand for original resources, and this growth in demand is made possible by the new loans the banking system grants. On the other hand, with respect to supply, we must keep in mind that when credit expansion takes place without the backing of a prior increase in saving, no original means of production are freed from the stages closest to consumption, as occurred in the process we studied earlier, which was initiated by a real upsurge in voluntary saving. Therefore the rise in the demand for original means of production in the stages furthest from consumption and the absence of an accompanying boost in supply inevitably result in a gradual increase in the market price of the factors of production. Ultimately this increase tends to accelerate due to competition among the entrepreneurs of the different stages in the production process. The desire of these entrepreneurs to attract original resources to their projects makes them willing to pay higher and higher prices for these resources, prices they are able to offer because they have just received new liquidity from the banks in the form of loans the banks have created from nothing. This rise in the relative price of the original factors of production begins to push the cost of the newly

books, the only other work in Spanish on the topic is our article, "La teoría austriaca del ciclo económico," which was published over twenty years ago in *Moneda y Crédito* 152 (March 1980), and which includes a comprehensive bibliography on the subject; and the series of essays by F.A. Hayek published as *¿Inflación o Pleno Empleo?* (Madrid: Unión Editorial, 1976). Last, in 1996 Carlos Rodríguez Braun's translation of Hayek's *Prices and Production* (*Precios y producción*) appeared, published by Ediciones Aosta and Unión Editorial in Madrid.

launched investment projects above the amount originally budgeted. Nevertheless this effect alone is still not sufficient to end the wave of optimism, and entrepreneurs, who continue to feel safe and supported by the banks, usually go ahead with their investment projects without a second thought.[74]

2. *The subsequent rise in the price of consumer goods.*

Sooner or later the price of consumer goods begins to gradually climb, while the price of services offered by the original factors of production starts to mount at a slower pace (in other words, it begins to fall in relative terms). The combination of the following three factors accounts for this phenomenon:

(a) First, *growth in the monetary income of the owners of the original factors of production.* Indeed if, as we are supposing, economic agents' rate of time preference remains stable, and therefore they continue to save the same proportion of their income, the monetary demand for consumer goods increases as a result of the increase in monetary income received by the owners of the original factors of production. Nonetheless this effect would only explain a similar rise in the price of consumer goods if it were not for the fact that it combines with effects (b) and (c).

(b) Second, a *slowdown* in the production of new consumer goods and services in the short- and medium-term, a consequence of the lengthening of production processes and the greater demand for original means of production in the stages furthest from final consumption. This decline in the speed at which new consumer goods arrive at the final stage in the production process derives from the fact that original factors of production are withdrawn from the stages closest to consumption, causing a relative shortage of these factors in those stages. This shortage affects the *immediate* production and delivery of final consumer

---

[74]In section 11 of chapter 6 (p. 440) we will see that our analysis does not change substantially even when a large volume of unused factors of production exists prior to credit expansion.

goods and services. Furthermore as the capital theory outlined at the beginning of the chapter explains, the generalized lengthening of production processes and the incorporation into them of a greater number of stages further from consumption invariably leads to a short-term decrease in the rate at which new consumer goods are produced. This slowdown lasts the length of time necessary for newly initiated investment processes *to reach completion*. It is clear that the longer production processes are, i.e., the more stages they contain, the more productive they tend to be. However it is also clear that until new investment processes conclude, they will not allow a larger quantity of consumer goods to reach the final stage. Hence the growth in income experienced by the owners of the original factors of production, and thus the increase in monetary demand for consumer goods, combined with the short-term slowdown in the arrival of new consumer goods to the market, accounts for the fact that the price of consumer goods and services eventually climbs more than proportionally; that is, faster than the increase in monetary income experienced by the owners of the original means of production.

(c) Third, the rise in monetary demand for consumer goods which is triggered by *artificial* entrepreneurial profits that result from the credit expansion process. Banks' creation of loans ultimately entails an increase in the money supply and a rise in the price of the factors of production and of consumer goods. These increases eventually distort entrepreneurs' estimates of their profits and losses. In fact entrepreneurs tend to calculate their costs in terms of the historical cost and purchasing power of m.u. prior to the inflationary process. However they compute their earnings based on income comprised of m.u. with less purchasing power. All of this leads to considerable and purely fictitious profits, the appearance of which creates an *illusion of entrepreneurial prosperity* and explains why businessmen begin to spend profits that have not actually

been produced, which further increases the pressure
of the monetary demand for final consumer goods.[75]

It is important to underline the effect of the more-than-
proportional rise in the price of consumer goods with respect
to the rise in the price of original factors of production. Theoretically this is the phenomenon which has most escaped the
notice of many scholars. As they have not fully comprehended
capital theory, the analyses of these theorists have not
accounted for the fact that when more productive resources
are devoted to processes further from consumption, processes
which begin to yield results only after a prolonged period of
time, there is a reduction in the speed at which new consumer
goods arrive at the last stage in the production process. Moreover this is one of the most significant distinguishing features
of the case we are now considering (in which the lengthening
of production processes is financed with loans the banks create *ex nihilo*) with respect to the process initiated by an
upsurge in voluntary saving (which by definition produced
an increase in the stock of consumer goods that remained

---

[75]   The additional demand on the part of the expanding entre-
    preneurs tends to raise the prices of producers' goods and
    wage rates. With the rise in wage rates, the prices of con-
    sumers' goods rise too. Besides, the entrepreneurs are con-
    tributing a share to the rise in the prices of consumers' goods
    as they too, deluded by the illusory gains which their busi-
    ness accounts show, are ready to consume more. The general
    upswing in prices spreads optimism. If only the prices of pro-
    ducers' goods had risen and those of consumers' goods had
    not been affected, the entrepreneurs would have become
    embarrassed. They would have had doubts concerning the
    soundness of their plans, as the rise in costs of production
    would have upset their calculations. But they are reassured
    by the fact that the demand for consumers' goods is intensi-
    fied and makes it possible to expand sales in spite of rising
    prices. Thus they are confident that production will pay,
    notwithstanding the higher costs it involves. They are
    resolved to go on. (Mises, *Human Action*, p. 553)

Furthermore, assuming the existence of a (constant) supply curve of
savings, the decrease in interest rates will reduce savings and increase
consumption. See Garrison, *Time and Money*, p. 70.

unsold and which sustained the owners of the original factors of production while new processes of production could be completed). When there is no prior growth in saving, and therefore consumer goods and services are not freed to support society during the lengthening of the productive stages and the transfer of original factors from the stages closest to consumption to those furthest from it, the relative price of consumer goods inevitably tends to rise.[76]

3. *The substantial relative increase in the accounting profits of the companies from the stages closest to final consumption.*

The price of consumer goods escalates faster than the price of original factors of production, and this results in relative growth in the accounting profits of the companies from the stages closest to consumption with respect to the accounting profits of companies who operate in the stages furthest from consumption. Indeed the relative price of the goods and services sold in the stages closest to consumption increases very rapidly, while costs, though they also rise, do not rise as fast. Consequently accounting profits, or the differential between income and costs, mount in the final stages. In contrast, in the stages furthest from consumption the price of the intermediate goods produced at each stage does not show a major change, while the cost of the original factors of production employed at each stage climbs continuously, due to the greater monetary demand for these factors, which in turn originates directly from credit expansion. Hence companies operating in the stages furthest from consumption tend to

---

[76]Hayek expresses the concept in this concise manner:

> [F]or a time, consumption may even go on at an unchanged rate after the more roundabout processes have actually started, because the goods which have already advanced to the lower stages of production, being of a highly specific character, will continue to come forward for some little time. But this cannot go on. When the reduced output from the stages of production, from which producers' goods have been withdrawn for use in higher stages, has matured into consumers' goods, a scarcity of consumers' goods will make itself felt, and the prices of those goods will rise. (Hayek, *Prices and Production*, p. 88)

bring in less profit, an accounting result of a rise in costs more
rapid than the corresponding increase in income. These two
factors produce the following combined effect: it gradually
becomes evident throughout the productive structure that *the
accounting profits generated in the stages closest to consumption are
higher in relative terms than the accounting profits earned in the
stages furthest from it.* This prompts entrepreneurs to rethink
their investments and even to doubt their soundness. It com-
pels them to again consider the need to reverse their initial
investment of resources by withdrawing them from more capital-intensive projects which have barely gotten off the ground
and returning them to the stages closest to consumption.[77]

4. The *"Ricardo Effect."*

In addition, the more-than-proportional rise in the price of
consumer goods with respect to the increase in original-factor
income begins to drive down (in relative terms) the real
income of these factors, particularly wages. This real reduction

---

[77]   Sooner or later, then, the increase in the demand for con-
       sumers' goods will lead to an increase of their prices and of
       the profits made on the production of consumers' goods. But
       once prices begin to rise, the additional demand for funds
       will no longer be confined to the purposes of new additional
       investment intended to satisfy the new demand. At first—and
       this is a point of importance which is often overlooked—only
       the prices of consumers' goods, and of such other goods as
       can rapidly be turned into consumers' goods, will rise, and
       consequently profits also will increase only in the late stages
       of production. . . . [T]he prices of consumers' goods would
       always keep a step ahead of the prices of factors. *That is, so
       long as any part of the additional income thus created is spent on
       consumers' goods (i.e., unless all of it is saved), the prices of con-
       sumers' goods must rise permanently in relation to those of the var-
       ious kinds of input.* And this, as will by now be evident, cannot
       be lastingly without effect on the relative prices of the various
       kinds of input and on the methods of production that will
       appear profitable. (Hayek, *The Pure Theory of Capital,* pp.
       377–78; italics added)

In an environment of increasing productivity (such as the one experienced during the period from 1995 to 2000), the (unit) prices of consumer goods will not rise significantly, yet the (monetary) amount companies closest to consumption bring in in sales and total profits will soar.

in wages provokes the "Ricardo Effect," which we have covered in detail, but which now exerts an impact contrary to the one it exerted in our last example, where real growth took place in voluntary saving. In the case of voluntary saving, the temporary decrease in the demand for consumer goods brought about a real increase in wages, which tended to give rise to the substitution of machines for labor and therefore to lengthen the productive stages, distancing them from consumption and making them more capital-intensive. However *now the effect is just the opposite*: the more-than-proportional growth in the price of consumer goods with respect to the rise in factor income drives this income, particularly wages, down in real terms, providing entrepreneurs with a powerful financial incentive to substitute labor for machinery or capital equipment, in keeping with the "Ricardo Effect." This results in a relative drop in the demand for the capital goods and intermediate products of the stages furthest from consumption, which in turn further aggravates the underlying problem of the fall in accounting profits (even losses) which begins to be perceived in the stages furthest from consumption.[78]

In short, here the "Ricardo Effect" exerts an impact contrary to the one it exerted when there was an upsurge in voluntary saving.[79] Then we saw that an increase in saving brought about

---

[78]As is logical, the fact that, due to coercion and union action, wages may rise at a rate similar to that of the increase in the price of consumer goods, in no way detracts from our argument, since the other five factors we have mentioned in the text will continue to exert their influence. The "Ricardo Effect" may do so as well, given that, at least in relative terms, the price of the factors of production employed in the stages closest to consumption will always be lower than that of the resources used in the stages furthest from it, and therefore the "Ricardo Effect," which is based on a comparison of relative costs, will continue to operate (entrepreneurs of the stages closest to consumption will begin to use, in *relative terms*, more labor than capital equipment). When coercion is used to improve the income of owners of the original factors, ultimately the only possible outcome is an important rise in involuntary unemployment among members of this group. This effect is especially acute in the stages furthest from consumption.

[79]The first time Hayek expressly mentioned the "Ricardo Effect" to explain the process by which the initial effects of credit expansion

a short-term decrease in the demand for consumer goods and
in their price, and thus a boost in real wages which encouraged
the substitution of machinery for workers, growth in the
demand for capital goods and a lengthening of productive
stages. Now we see that the relative rise in the price of consumer goods causes a drop in real wages, motivating entrepreneurs to substitute labor for machinery, which lessens the
demand for capital goods and further reduces the profits of
companies operating in the stages furthest from consumption.[80]

---

reverse was in his essay, "Profits, Interest and Investment," included in
pp. 3–71 of the book of the same title. Hayek offers a very concise description of the "Ricardo Effect" on pp. 13–14 of this essay, where he states:

> It is here that the "Ricardo Effect" comes into action and
> becomes of decisive importance. The rise in the prices of con-
> sumers' goods and the consequent fall in real wages means a
> rise in the rate of profit in the consumers' goods industries,
> but, as we have seen, a very different rise in the time rates of
> profit that can now be earned on more direct labour and on the
> investment of additional capital in machinery. A much higher
> rate of profit will now be obtainable on money spent on labour
> than on money invested in machinery. The effect of this rise in
> the rate of profit in the consumers' goods industries will be
> twofold. On the one hand it will cause a tendency to use more
> labour with the existing machinery, by working over-time and
> double shifts, by using outworn and obsolete machinery, etc.,
> etc. On the other hand, in so far as new machinery is being
> installed, either by way of replacement or in order to increase
> capacity, this, so long as real wages remain low compared with
> the marginal productivity of labour, will be of a less expensive,
> less labour-saving or less durable type.

Hayek also deals with the action of the "Ricardo Effect" in the most expansive phases of the boom in the following papers: "The Ricardo Effect"
(1942, pp. 127–52), and the previously-cited "Three Elucidations of the
Ricardo Effect" (1969). Other interesting writings on this topic include the
article by Laurence S. Moss and Karen I. Vaughn, "Hayek's Ricardo Effect:
A Second Look" (1986, pp. 545–65) and the one by G.P. O'Driscoll, "The
Specialization Gap and the Ricardo Effect: Comment on Ferguson," published in *History of Political Economy* 7 (Summer, 1975): 261–69. See also
Jesús Huerta de Soto, "Ricardo Effect," *Eponymous Dictionary of Economics:
A Guide to Laws and Theorems Named after Economists,* Julio Segura and Car-
los Rodriquez Braun, eds. (Cheltenham, U.K.: Edward Elgar, 2004).

[80]Or as Mises explains:

5. *The increase in the loan rate of interest. Rates even exceed pre-credit-expansion levels.*

The last temporary effect consists of an escalation in interest rates in the credit market. This rise occurs sooner or later, when the pace of credit expansion unbacked by real saving stops accelerating. When this happens the interest rate will tend to return to the relatively higher levels which prevailed prior to the beginning of credit expansion. In fact if, for instance, the interest rate is around 10 percent before credit expansion begins and the new loans the banking system creates *ex nihilo* are placed in the productive sectors via a reduction in the interest rate (for example, to 4 percent) and an easing of the rest of the "peripheral" requirements for the granting of loans (contractual guarantees, etc.), it is clear that when credit expansion comes to a halt, if, as we are supposing, no increase in voluntary saving takes place, *interest rates will climb to their previous level* (in our example, they will rise from 4 to 10 percent). They will even exceed their pre-credit-expansion level (i.e., they will rise above the originary rate of 10 percent) as a result of the combined effect of the following two phenomena:

(a) Other things being equal, credit expansion and the increase in the money supply which it involves will tend to drive up the price of consumer goods, i.e., to reduce the purchasing power of the monetary unit. Consequently if lenders wish to charge the same

---

[W]ith further progress of the expansionist movement the rise in the prices of consumers' goods will outstrip the rise in the prices of producers' goods. The rise in wages and salaries and the additional gains of the capitalists, entrepreneurs, and farmers, although a great part of them is merely apparent, intensify the demand for consumers' goods. . . . At any rate, it is certain that the intensified demand for consumers' goods affects the market at a time when the additional investments are not yet in a position to turn out their products. The gulf between the prices of present goods and those of future goods widens again. A tendency toward a rise in the rate of originary interest is substituted for the tendency toward the opposite which may have come into operation at the earlier stages of the expansion. (Mises, *Human Action*, p. 558)

interest rates in real terms, they will have to add (to
the interest rate which prevails prior to the beginning
of the credit expansion process) a component for
"inflation," or in other words, for the expected drop in
the purchasing power of the monetary unit.[81]

(b) There is another powerful reason interest rates climb
to and even exceed their prior level: entrepreneurs
who have embarked upon the lengthening of production processes despite the rise in interest rates will, to
the extent that they have already committed substantial resources to new investment projects, *be willing to
pay very high interest rates, provided they are supplied
with the funds necessary to complete the projects they have
mistakenly launched.* This is an important aspect which
went completely unnoticed until Hayek studied it in

---

[81]As Ludwig von Mises wrote in 1928:

> The banks can no longer make additional loans at the same
> interest rates. As a result, they must raise the loan rate once
> more for two reasons. In the first place, the appearance of the
> positive price premium forces them to pay higher interest for
> outside funds which they borrow. Then also they must dis-
> criminate among the many applicants for credit. Not all enter-
> prises can afford this increased interest rate. Those which can-
> not run into difficulties. (See *On the Manipulation of Money and
> Credit*, p. 127)

This is Bettina Bien Greaves's translation into English of the book published in 1928 by Ludwig von Mises with the title, *Geldwertstabilisierung
und Konjunkturpolitik.* The above passage is found on pp. 51–52 of this
German edition, which contains a detailed explanation of all of Mises's
theory on business cycles. It was published before *Prices and Production*
and the German edition of *Monetary Theory and the Trade Cycle* by Hayek
(1929). It is odd that Hayek almost never cites this important work, in
which Mises formulates and develops the theory of the cycle, which he
only had the opportunity to outline in his book, *The Theory of Money and
Credit*, published sixteen years earlier. Perhaps this oversight was deliberate and arose from a desire to convey to the scientific community the
impression that the first attempt to develop Mises's theory was made by
Hayek in his writings on *Monetary Theory and the Trade Cycle* and *Prices
and Production*, when Mises had already covered the topic very thoroughly in 1928.

detail in 1937.[82] Hayek demonstrated that the process of investment in capital goods generates an autonomous demand for subsequent capital goods, precisely ones which are *complementary* to those already produced. Furthermore this phenomenon will last as long as the belief that the production processes can be completed. Thus entrepreneurs will rush to demand new loans regardless of their cost, before being forced to admit their failure and altogether abandon investment projects in which they have allocated very important resources and with respect to which they have jeopardized their prestige. As a result, the growth in the interest rate which takes place in the credit market at the end of the boom is not only due to monetary phenomena, as Hayek had previously thought, but also to *real factors* that affect the demand for new loans.[83] In short, entrepreneurs, determined to complete the new capital goods stages they have

---

[82]See F.A. Hayek, "Investment that Raises the Demand for Capital," published in *Review of Economics and Statistics* 19, no. 4 (November 1937) and reprinted in *Profits, Interest and Investment*, pp. 73–82.

[83]Hayek himself, in reference to the rise in interest rates in the final stage of the boom, indicates that:

> [T]he most important cause practically of such false expectations probably is a temporary increase in the supply of such funds through credit expansion at a rate which cannot be maintained. In this case, the increased quantity of current investment will induce people to expect investment to continue at a similar rate for some time, and in consequence to invest now in a form which requires for its successful completion further investment at a similar rate. . . . And the greater the amount of investment which has already been made compared with that which is still required to utilise the equipment already in existence, the greater will be the rate of interest which can advantageously be borne in raising capital for these investments completing the chain. (Hayek, "Investment that Raises the Demand for Capital," pp. 76 and 80)

Mises points out the boom ends precisely when the entrepreneurs begin to experience difficulties in obtaining the increasing amount of financing they need for their investment projects:

begun and which they begin to see threatened, turn to banks and demand additional loans, offering a higher and higher interest rate for them. Thus they start a "fight to the death" to obtain additional financing.[84]

> The entrepreneurs cannot procure the funds they need for the further conduct of their ventures. The gross market rate of interest rises because the increased demand for loans is not counterpoised by a corresponding increase in the quantity of money available for lending. (Mises, *Human Action*, p. 554)

[84]   Entrepreneurs determined to complete their endangered long-term capital projects turn to the banks for more bank credit, and a tug-of-war begins. Producers seek new bank loans, the banking system accommodates the new loan demand by creating new money, product prices rise ahead of wage costs. In each market period the process repeats itself, with product prices always rising ahead of wages. (Moss and Vaughn, "Hayek's Ricardo Effect: A Second Look," p. 554)

In *Human Action* Mises explains the process in this way:

> This tendency toward a rise in the rate of originary interest and the emergence of a positive price premium explain some characteristics of the boom. The banks are faced with an increased demand for loans and advances on the part of business. The entrepreneurs are prepared to borrow money at higher gross rates of interest. They go on borrowing in spite of the fact that banks charge more interest. Arithmetically, the gross rates of interest are rising above their height on the eve of the expansion. Nonetheless, they lag catalactically behind the height at which they would cover originary interest plus entrepreneurial component and price premium. The banks believe that they have done all that is needed to stop "unsound" speculation when they lend on more onerous terms. They think that those critics who blame them for fanning the flames of the boom-frenzy of the market are wrong. They fail to see that in injecting more and more fiduciary media into the market they are in fact kindling the boom. It is the continuous increase in the supply of the fiduciary media that produces, feeds, and accelerates the boom. The state of the gross market rates of interest is only an outgrowth of this increase. If one wants to know whether or not there is credit expansion, one must look at the state of the supply of fiduciary media, not at the arithmetical state of the interest rates. (Mises, *Human Action*, pp. 558–59)

6. *The appearance of accounting losses in companies operating in the stages relatively more distant from consumption: the inevitable advent of the crisis.*

The above five factors provoke the following combined effect: sooner or later companies which operate in the stages relatively more distant from consumption begin to incur heavy accounting losses. These accounting losses, when compared with the relative profits generated in the stages closest to consumption, finally reveal beyond all doubt the serious entrepreneurial errors committed and the urgent need to correct them by paralyzing and then liquidating the investment projects mistakenly launched, withdrawing productive resources from the stages furthest from consumption and transferring them back to those closest to it.

In a nutshell, entrepreneurs begin to realize a massive readjustment in the productive structure is necessary. Through this "restructuring" in which they withdraw from the projects they began in the stages of capital goods industries and which they were unable to successfully complete, they transfer what is left of their resources to the industries closest to consumption. It has now become obvious that certain investment projects are unprofitable, and entrepreneurs must liquidate these and make a massive transfer of the corresponding productive resources, particularly labor, to the stages closest to consumption. *Crisis and economic recession have hit, essentially due to a lack of real saved resources with which to complete investment projects which, as has become apparent, were too ambitious.* The crisis is brought to a head by *excessive investment* ("overinvestment") in the stages furthest from consumption, i.e., in capital goods industries (computer software and hardware, high-tech communications devices, blast furnaces, shipyards, construction, etc.), and in all other stages with a widened capital goods structure. It also erupts due to a parallel *relative shortage in investment* in the industries closest to consumption. The combined effect of the two errors is generalized *malinvestment* of productive resources; that is, investment of a style, quality, quantity, and geographic and entrepreneurial distribution typical of a situation in which much more voluntary saving has taken place. In short, entrepreneurs have invested an inappropriate amount in an inadequate manner in the wrong places in the productive structure because they were under the impression, *deceived as they were by bank credit expansion*, that social saving would be much greater. Economic agents have devoted themselves to lengthening the most capital-intensive stages in the hope that once the new investment processes have, with time, reached completion, the final flow of consumer goods and services will increase significantly. However the process by which the productive structure is lengthened requires a very prolonged period of time. Until this time has passed, society cannot profit from the corresponding rise in the production of consumer goods and services. Yet economic agents are not willing to wait until the end of that more prolonged period of time. Instead they express their preferences through their actions and demand the consumer goods and services *now*, i.e., much sooner than would be possible were the lengthening of the productive structure to be completed.[85]

Society's savings can be either wisely or foolishly invested. Credit expansion brought about by the banking system *ex nihilo* encourages entrepreneurs to act *as if* social saving had increased substantially, precisely by the amount the bank has created in the form of new loans or fiduciary media. The

---

[85]In the words of F.A. Hayek:

> The crux of the whole capital problem is that while it is almost always possible to postpone the use of things now ready or almost ready for consumption, it is in many cases impossible to anticipate returns which were intended to become available at a later date. The consequence is that, while a relative deficiency in the demand for consumers' goods compared with supply will cause only comparatively minor losses, a relative excess of this demand is apt to have much more serious effects. It will make it altogether impossible to use some resources which are destined to give a consumable return only in the more distant future but will do so only in collaboration with other resources which are now more profitably used to provide consumables for the more immediate future. (Hayek, *The Pure Theory of Capital*, pp. 345–46)

microeconomic processes examined above invariably and spontaneously bring to light the error committed. This error derives from the fact that for a prolonged period of time economic agents believed available savings to be much more considerable than they actually were. This situation is very similar to the one in which our Robinson Crusoe from section 1 would find himself if, having saved a basket of berries large enough to permit him to spend a maximum of five days producing a capital good without having to devote himself to the collection of more berries, *through an error in calculation*[86] he were to believe that this amount of savings would allow him to undertake the construction of his cabin. After five days spent just digging the foundations and gathering materials, he would have consumed all of his berries and would therefore be unable to complete his illusory investment project. Mises likens the general error committed to the one a builder would make if he were to misjudge the amount of materials available to him and use them all up laying the foundations of a building, which he would then be forced to leave unfinished.[87] As Hayek puts it, we are thus dealing with a crisis of *overconsumption*, or in other words, *insufficient saving*. It has become

---

[86]Precisely for this reason we have argued elsewhere that business cycles are a practical example of the errors in economic calculation which result from state interventionism in the economy (in this case in the monetary and credit field). See Huerta de Soto, *Socialismo, cálculo económico y función empresarial*, pp. 111ff. In other words, we could consider the entire content of this book as simply the application of the theorem of the impossibility of socialist economic calculation to the particular case of the credit and financial sector.

[87]   The whole entrepreneurial class is, as it were, in the position of a master-builder whose task it is to erect a building out of a limited supply of building materials. If this man overestimates the quantity of the available supply, he drafts a plan for the execution of which the means at his disposal are not sufficient. He oversizes the groundwork and the foundations and only discovers later in the progress of the construction that he lacks the material needed for the completion of the structure. It is obvious that our master-builder's fault was not overinvestment, but an inappropriate employment of the means at his disposal. (Mises, *Human Action*, p. 560)

See also the curious Biblical reference in Luke 14, 28–30.

obvious that saving is inadequate to permit the completion of the more capital-intensive investments made by mistake. The situation would resemble that of the imaginary inhabitants of an island who, having undertaken the construction of an enormous machine capable of completely satisfying their needs, had exhausted all of their savings and capital before finishing it and had been left with no other choice but to temporarily abandon the project and return all of their energy to the daily search for food at a mere subsistence level, i.e., without the assistance of any capital equipment.[88] In our society such a shortage of savings leads to the following: many factories are closed, particularly in the stages furthest from consumption, numerous investment projects launched in error are paralyzed, and many workers are laid off. Furthermore pessimism spreads throughout society, and the notion that an *inexplicable* economic crisis has erupted, shortly after people had begun to believe that the boom and optimism, far from reaching their peak, would last indefinitely, demoralizes even the most persistently high-spirited.[89]

---

[88]See Huerta de Soto, "La teoría austriaca del ciclo económico," in *Estudios de Economía Política*, chap. 13, p. 175. In Hayek's own words:

> The situation would be similar to that of a people of an isolated island, if, after having partially constructed an enormous machine which was to provide them with all necessities, they found out that they had exhausted all their savings and available free capital before the new machine could turn out its product. They would then have no choice but to abandon temporarily the work on the new process and to devote all their labour to producing their daily food without any capital. (Hayek, *Prices and Production*, p. 94)

[89] The entrepreneurs must restrict their activities because they lack the funds for their continuation on the exaggerated scale. Prices drop suddenly because these distressed firms try to obtain cash by throwing inventories on the market dirt cheap. Factories are closed, the continuation of construction projects in progress is halted, workers are discharged. As on the one hand many firms badly need money in order to avoid bankruptcy, and on the other hand no firm any longer enjoys confidence, the entrepreneurial component in the gross market rate of interest jumps to an excessive height. (Mises, *Human Action*, p. 562)

Chart V-7 reflects the state of the productive structure once the crisis and economic recession provoked by credit expansion (i.e., unbacked by a prior increase in voluntary saving) have become evident and the necessary readjustments have been made. As the chart makes clear, the new productive structure is *flatter* and contains only five stages, since the two stages furthest from consumption have disappeared. As Charts V-5 and V-6 show, initially credit expansion, in error, permitted entrepreneurs to embark on these stages. Furthermore Table V-6 demonstrates that although the gross income for the year is identical to that reflected in Table V-5 (483.7 m.u.), the distribution of the portion allocated to the direct demand for final consumer goods and services and to the demand for intermediate goods has varied in favor of the former. In fact now there are 132 m.u. of monetary demand for consumer goods, an amount one-third larger than the 100 units of monetary demand which appeared in the example shown in Chart V-5 and Table V-5. Meanwhile the overall monetary demand for intermediate goods has diminished from 383 to 351 units. In short there is a "flatter" structure which is less capital-intensive and therefore leads to the production of fewer consumer goods and services, yet these goods and services are the object of greater monetary demand, all of which gives rise to a strong jump in the price of consumer goods and services and the generalized impoverishment of society. This is revealed in the fall, *in real terms*, in the price of the different original factors of production. Though the nominal value of the monetary income received by their owners has mounted substantially, the even more rapid

---

Mark Skousen indicates that in the recession phase the price of goods from the different stages undergoes the following changes: *first*, the most serious decreases in price and employment normally affect the companies operating furthest from consumption; *second*, the prices of products from the intermediate stages fall as well, though not as dramatically; *third*, wholesale prices drop, yet less sharply in comparison; and *fourth and last*, the prices of consumer goods also tend to decline, though much less noticeably than the rest of the above goods. Moreover if stagflation occurs the price of consumer goods may even rise instead of declining. See Skousen, *The Structure of Production*, p. 304.

increase in the price of consumer goods places the owners of these factors at a considerable disadvantage in real terms. Moreover the interest rate, or rate of accounting profit approached at each stage, has risen above 13.5 percent, i.e., to a level which even exceeds that of the interest in the credit market *prior to* credit expansion (11 percent per year). This higher rate reflects a premium to compensate for the drop in the purchasing power of money; the keener competition among the different entrepreneurs, who desperately wish to obtain new loans; and the increase in the components of risk and entrepreneurial uncertainty which influences the interest rate whenever pessimism and economic distrust are rampant.

We must emphasize that the productive structure which remains following the necessary readjustment, and which Chart V-7 illustrates, cannot continue to match the structure that existed *prior to* credit expansion. This is due to the fact that *circumstances have changed significantly*. Heavy inevitable losses of specific capital goods have been incurred to the extent that society's scarce resources have been channeled into investments that cannot be restructured and therefore are devoid of economic value. This gives rise to general impoverishment of society, a state which manifests itself as a decline in capital equipment per capita, resulting in a decrease in the productivity of labor, and consequently, a further reduction in real wages. Furthermore there has been a shift in the distribution of income among the different factors of production, as well as a realignment of all the investment processes which, though initiated in error, are still of some use and economic value. All of these new circumstances make the productive structure qualitatively very different from and quantitatively much flatter and poorer than the one that existed before banks brought about credit expansion.[90]

---

[90]Fritz Machlup has closely studied the factors which provoke the flattening of the productive structure and has examined the reasons it is different and poorer after the readjustment than before credit expansion:

> (1) Many capital goods are specific, i.e., not capable of being used for other purposes than those they were originally planned for; major losses follow then from the change in

In summary, we have described the microeconomic basis for the spontaneous market reaction which consistently tends to follow credit expansion. This reaction gives rise to the consecutive cycles of boom and recession which have regularly affected western economies for nearly two centuries (and even much longer, as we saw in chapter 2). We have also demonstrated that *there is no theoretical possibility that banks'*

---

production structure. (2) Capital values in general—i.e., anticipated values of the future income—are reduced by higher rates of capitalization; the owners of capital goods and property rights experience, therefore, serious losses. (3) The specific capital goods serviceable as "complementary" equipment for those lines of production which would correspond to the consumers' demand are probably not ready; employment in these lines is, therefore, smaller than it could be otherwise. (4) Marginal-value productivity of labour in shortened investment periods is lower, wage rates are, therefore, depressed. (5) Under inflexible wage rates unemployment ensues from the decreased demand prices for labour. (See Fritz Machlup, "Professor Knight and the 'Period of Production,'" *Journal of Political Economy* 43, no. 5 [October 1935]: 623)

The comments of Ludwig von Mises regarding the possibility that the new productive structure will resemble the one which existed prior to credit expansion are perhaps even more specific:

These data, however, are no longer identical with those that prevailed on the eve of the expansionist process. A good many things have changed. Forced saving and, to an even greater extent, regular voluntary saving may have provided new capital goods which were not totally squandered through malinvestment and overconsumption as induced by the boom. Changes in the wealth and income of various individuals and groups of individuals have been brought about by the unevenness inherent in every inflationary movement. Apart from any causal relation to the credit expansion, population may have changed with regard to figures and the characteristics of the individuals comprising them; technological knowledge may have advanced, demand for certain goods may have been altered. The final state to the establishment of which the market tends is no longer the same toward which it tended before the disturbances created by the credit expansion. (Mises, *Human Action*, p. 563)

increase in loans, if not backed by a corresponding prior rise in voluntary saving, will permit society to reduce the necessary sacrifices all processes of economic growth require, and foster and accelerate sustainable growth in the absence of a voluntary decision made by citizens to sacrifice and save.[91] Given that these are highly significant conclusions, in the next section we will analyze their implications for the banking sector, particularly, the manner in which they explain that this sector cannot operate independently (i.e., without a central bank) while maintaining a fractional reserve. Thus we will conclude the theoretical analysis we set out to produce in chapter 3: to demonstrate on the basis of economic theory that it is impossible for the banking system to insure itself against suspensions of payments and bankruptcy via a fractional-reserve requirement, since the supposed insurance (the fractional-reserve requirement) is precisely what triggers a process of credit expansion, boom, crisis and economic recession which invariably has a detrimental effect on banks' solvency and ability to pay.

---

[91]In the eloquent words of Moss and Vaughn:

> Any real growth in the capital stock takes time and requires voluntary net savings. *There is no way for an expansion of the money supply in the form of bank credit to short-circuit the process of economic growth.* ("Hayek's Ricardo Effect: A Second Look," p. 555; italics added)

Perhaps the article in which Hayek most concisely and clearly explains this entire process is "Price Expectations, Monetary Disturbances and Malinvestment," published in 1933 and included in his book, *Profits, Interest and Investment*, pp. 135–56. Along these lines we should also mention the work of Roger W. Garrison, who vividly illustrated the Austrian theory of capital and of the cycle and compared it with the most common diagrams used in macroeconomics textbooks to present the classical and Keynesian models, especially, "Austrian Macroeconomics: A Diagrammatical Exposition," originally published on pp. 167–201 of the book, *New Directions in Austrian Economics*, Louis M. Spadaro, ed. (Kansas City: Sheed Andrews and McMeel, 1978; The Institute for Humane Studies, 1978, as an independent monograph), and the article by Ludwig M. Lachmann, "A Reconsideration of the Austrian Theory of Industrial Fluctuations," originally published in *Economica* 7 (May 1940), and included on pp. 267–84 of Lachmann's book, *Capital, Expectations and the Market Process: Essays on the Theory of the Market Economy* (Kansas City: Sheed Andrews and McMeel, 1977). Finally, see Garrison's book, *Time and Money*.

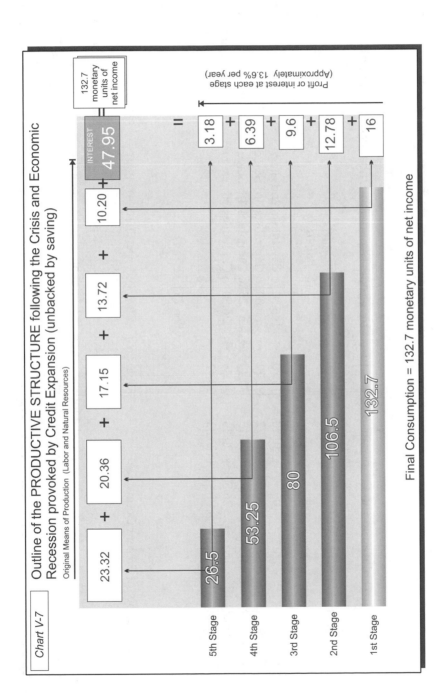

Chart V-7   Outline of the PRODUCTIVE STRUCTURE following the Crisis and Economic Recession provoked by Credit Expansion (unbacked by saving)

Original Means of Production (Labor and Natural Resources)

132.7 monetary units of net income

INTEREST **47.95**

Profit or interest at each stage (Approximately 13.6% per year)

$23.32 + 20.36 + 17.15 + 13.72 + 10.20 + 47.95 =$

$3.18 + 6.39 + 9.6 + 12.78 + 16$

5th Stage — 26.5
4th Stage — 53.25
3rd Stage — 80
2nd Stage — 106.5
1st Stage — 132.7

Final Consumption = 132.7 monetary units of net income

TABLE V-6

THE SUPPLY OF AND DEMAND FOR PRESENT GOODS

(Following the Economic Crisis Caused by Credit Expansion Unbacked by Saving)

Suppliers of Present Goods
(Savers)

Demanders of Present Goods
(Suppliers of Future Goods)

Capitalists 1st Stage	=	106.50	+ 10.20 = 116.70	→	106.50 to Capitalists 2nd Stage	+ 10.20 to original means
Capitalists 2nd Stage	=	80.00	+ 13.72 = 93.72	→	80.00 to Capitalists 3rd Stage	+ 13.72 to original means
Capitalists 3rd Stage	=	53.25	+ 17.15 = 70.40	→	53.25 to Capitalists 4th Stage	+ 17.15 to original means
Capitalists 4th Stage	=	26.50	+ 20.36 = 46.86	→	26.50 to Capitalists 5th Stage	+ 20.36 to original means
Capitalists 5th Stage	=	0	+ 23.32 = 23.32	→		23.32 to original means

266.25   84.75

Total Supply of Present Goods   =   351.00 m.u. = SAVING AND INVESTMENT = 351.00 m.u.
                                                         (GROSS)   Total Demand
                                                                            For Present Goods

Gross Income for the Year = 483.7 (identical to that of Table V-5)

132.7 m.u. of final consumption + 351 m.u. of supply of and demand for present goods
(gross saving and investment = 483.7 m.u.)

4

BANKING, FRACTIONAL-RESERVE RATIOS,
AND THE LAW OF LARGE NUMBERS

Our analysis up to this point permits us to comment on whether it is possible, as certain scholars maintain, to *insure* through the application of the law of large numbers the practice of fractional-reserve banking. Essentially we will respond to the argument that banks, in order to fulfill their customers' normal requests for liquidity, and in accordance with the law of large numbers, only need to keep on hand, in the form of a cash reserve, a fraction of the money deposited with them in cash. This argument lies at the heart of legal doctrines aimed at justifying the monetary irregular bank-deposit contract with a fractional reserve. We critically examined this contract in chapter 3.

The reference in this area to the law of large numbers is equivalent to an attempt to apply the principles of insurance techniques to guard against the risk of deposit withdrawals, a risk assumed in advance to be quantifiable and thus technically insurable. However, this belief is mistaken, and as we will see, it is based on a misconceived idea of the nature of the phenomena before us. Indeed, far from the type of events which correspond to the natural world and represent an insurable risk, banking related phenomena fall within the realm of human action and are therefore immersed in *uncertainty* (not risk), which by its very nature is not technically insurable.

For in the field of human action the future is always *uncertain*, in the sense that it has yet to be built and the only part of it possessed by the actors which will be its protagonists are certain ideas, mental images, and expectations they hope to realize through their personal action and interaction with other actors. Moreover the future is open to man's every creative possibility; hence each actor faces it with a *permanent uncertainty* which can be reduced through the patterned behaviors of the actor and others (institutions) and the alert exercise of entrepreneurship. Nevertheless the actor will not be able to totally eliminate this uncertainty.[92] The open, permanent nature of the uncertainty we are referring to makes both traditional notions of objective and subjective probability, and the Bayesian conception of the latter inapplicable to the field of human interaction. In fact Bayes's theorem requires a stable, underlying stochastic structure incompatible with the human capacity for entrepreneurial creativity.[93] This is so for two reasons: first, it is not even possible to know all of the potential alternatives or cases; and second, the actor only possesses certain subjective beliefs or convictions—termed by Mises *case probabilities* (of unique events)[94]—which as they are modified or broadened tend to change by surprise, i.e., in a radical, divergent manner, the actor's entire map of beliefs and knowledge. Thus the actor continually discovers completely new situations of which previously he had not even been able to conceive.

This concept of uncertainty, which corresponds to single events in the field of human action and hence of economics, differs radically from the notion of *risk* applicable within the sphere of physics and natural science. Table V-7 provides a summary.

Clearly the events related to customers' more or less massive and unexpected withdrawal of deposits from a bank correspond to the sphere of human action and are immersed in uncertainty, which by its very nature is not technically

---

[92]On this topic see Huerta de Soto, *Socialismo, cálculo económico y función empresarial*, pp. 46–47.

[93]"The Bayesian approach rules out the possibility of surprise." J.D. Hey, *Economics in Disequilibrium* (New York: New York University Press, 1981), p. 99. Along the same lines, Emiel F.M Wubben, in his article, "Austrian Economics and Uncertainty," a manuscript presented at the First European Conference on Austrian Economics (Maastricht, April 1992, p. 13), states:

> the conclusion to be drawn is the impossibility of talking about subjective probabilities that tend to objective probabilities. The dimensions are not on the same footing but cover different levels of knowledge.

[94]Mises, *Human Action*, pp. 110–18.

insurable. The technical-economic reason it is impossible to insure uncertainty stems basically from the fact that *human action itself brings about or creates the events which an attempt is made to insure*. In other words, withdrawals of deposits are invariably influenced by the very existence of the insurance, and therefore the necessary stochastic independence between the existence of the "insurance" (a fractional-reserve requirement supposedly established according to the law of large numbers and bankers' experience) and the occurrence of the phenomenon (bank crises and runs which provoke the massive withdrawal of deposits), precisely what is meant to be insured against, does not exist.[95] A detailed demonstration of the close connection between the attempt to apply the law of large numbers in the form of a fractional-reserve requirement and the fact that this "insurance" inevitably triggers massive withdrawals of deposits is simple. The development of the Austrian theory, or circulation credit theory of the business cycle (covered in this chapter), makes it possible. Indeed fractional-reserve banking permits the large-scale granting of loans

---

[95]In short we are referring to the phenomenon of *moral hazard*, which M.V. Pauly has already theoretically analyzed. According to Pauly, the optimality of complete insurance is no longer valid when the method of insurance influences the demand for the services provided by the insurance policy ("The Economics of Moral Hazard," *American Economic Review* 58 (1968): 531–37). Another relevant article is Kenneth J. Arrow's "The Economics of Moral Hazard: Further Comments," originally published in *American Economic Review* 58 (1968): 537–53. Here Arrow continues the research he started on this phenomenon in his 1963 article, "Uncertainty in the Welfare Economics of Medical Care," *American Economic Review* 53 (1963): 941–73. Arrow holds the view that moral hazard is involved whenever "the insurance policy might itself change incentives and therefore the probabilities upon which the insurance company has relied." These two articles by Arrow appear in his book, *Essays in the Theory of Risk-Bearing* (Amsterdam, London and New York: North Holland Publishing Company, 1974), pp. 177–222; see esp. pp. 202–04. Finally two further sources which warrant consideration are: chapter 7 (devoted to uninsurable risks) of Karl H. Borch's important book, *Economics of Insurance* (Amsterdam and New York: North Holland, 1990), esp. pp. 317 and 325–30; as well as Joseph E. Stiglitz's article, "Risk, Incentives and Insurance: The Pure Theory of Moral Hazard," published in *The Geneva Papers on Risk and Insurance* 26 (1983): 4–33.

TABLE V-7

The Field of Natural Science	*The Field of Human Action*
1. *Class probability*: The behavior of the class is known or knowable, while the behavior of its individual elements are not.	1. *"Probability" of a unique case or event*: class does not exist, and while some of the factors which affect the unique event are known, others are not. Action itself may bring about or create the event.
2. A situation of *insurable risk* exists for the whole class.	2. Permanent *uncertainty* exists, given the creative nature of human action. Thus uncertainty is not insurable.
3. Probability can be expressed in *mathematical terms*.	3. Probability cannot be expressed in *mathematical terms*.
4. Probability is gauged through logic and *empirical research*. Bayes's theorem makes it possible to estimate the probability of class as new information appears.	4. It is discovered through insight, understanding, and *entrepreneurial estimation*. Each new bit of information modifies *ex novo* the entire map of beliefs and expectations (concept of *surprise*).
5. It is an object of research to the natural *scientist*.	5. A concept typically used by the *actor-entrepreneur* and by the historian.

unbacked by a prior increase in saving (credit expansion) and initially provokes artificial widening and lengthening of the productive structure (illustrated by the shaded areas in Chart V-6). Nevertheless sooner or later the microeconomic factors explained in detail in the previous section set in motion social processes which tend to reverse the entrepreneurial errors committed, and consequently the productive structure comes to resemble that illustrated in Chart V-7. There we see that the new stages by which an attempt was made to lengthen the productive structure (stages six and seven of Chart V-6) disappear altogether. Furthermore the "widenings" of stages two through five are liquidated, bringing about the general impoverishment of society, a result of the unwise investment of its scarce real saved resources. Accordingly a highly significant number of the recipients of loans derived from credit expansion are ultimately unable to repay them and become defaulters, initiating a process in which both suspensions of payments and bankruptcies multiply. Hence default comes to affect a very large percentage of bank loans. In fact once the crisis hits and it becomes evident that the investment projects launched in error should not have been undertaken, the market value of these projects is reduced to a fraction of their initial value, when it does not disappear completely.

The extent to which this generalized decrease in the value of many capital goods is carried over to banks' assets is graphically illustrated precisely by the loan amounts which correspond to the shaded areas in Chart V-6. This chart reflects, in monetary terms, the erroneous lengthening and widening of the productive structure: changes attempted in the expansive phases of the economic cycle, due to the cheap, easy financing of bank loans (unbacked by a prior increase in voluntary real saving). *Inasmuch as the errors committed are revealed and the "lengthenings" and "widenings" of the productive structure are abandoned, liquidated, or realigned, the value of the assets of the entire banking system diminishes dramatically.* Moreover this decline in value is gradually accompanied by the credit tightening process we analyzed in accounting terms at the end of chapter 4 and which tends to aggravate even further the negative effects the recession exerts on the assets of the banking system. In fact those entrepreneurs who fortunately manage to save their companies from a suspension of payments and bankruptcy restructure the investment processes they initiated. They paralyze them, liquidate them and accumulate the liquidity necessary to return the loans they obtained from the bank. Furthermore the pessimism and demoralization of economic agents[96] means that new loan requests and their approval cannot compensate for the speed at which loans are repaid. A serious credit squeeze results.

Therefore one must draw the conclusion that the economic recession caused by credit expansion results in a generalized decline in the value of the accounting assets of the banking system, just when depositors' optimism and confidence are lowest. In other words, recession and default drive down the value of banks' loans and other assets, while banks' corresponding liabilities, the deposits now in the hands of third parties, remain unchanged. With respect to accounting, the financial situation of many banks becomes particularly problematic and difficult, and they begin to announce suspensions of payments and failures. As is logical, from a theoretical standpoint it is impossible to determine in advance which specific banks will be relatively more affected. However we can safely predict that those banks which are marginally less solvent will face a serious liquidity squeeze, a suspension of payments and even bankruptcy. Such a situation can very easily precipitate a generalized crisis of confidence in the entire banking system, prompting individuals to withdraw their deposits en masse, not only from the banks which, relatively speaking, experience the greatest difficulties, but by contagion, from all the rest as well. Indeed all banks which operate with a fractional reserve are inherently *insolvent*, and their differences are relatively

---

[96]   The boom produces impoverishment. But still more disastrous are its moral ravages. It makes people despondent and dispirited. The more optimistic they were under the illusory prosperity of the boom, the greater is their despair and their feeling of frustration. (Mises, *Human Action*, p. 576)

Remember also what we said in chapter 4, sec. 8, pp. 254–63.

minor and merely a matter of degree, making a significant financial and credit squeeze inevitable. Events of this sort (such as the economic crisis Florentine banks provoked in the four-teenth century) have repeatedly occurred since the dawn of fractional-reserve banking. At any rate it has been demon-strated that the fractional-reserve system *endogenously* triggers processes which make it impossible to insure banking via the application of the law of large numbers. These processes cause systematic crises in the banking system, which sooner or later plague it with insuperable difficulties. This invalidates one of the stalest arguments to technically justify the existence of a contract which, like that of the monetary bank deposit with a fractional reserve, is of an inadmissible legal nature (as we saw in chapter 3), given that it originates solely from a *privilege* granted by public authorities to private banks.

One might mistakenly believe that the high incidence of default and the generalized loss of value on the asset side of bank balance sheets, both products of the economic crisis, could from an accounting standpoint be offset with no prob-lem by eliminating the corresponding deposits which balance these loans on the liability side. Not in vain did chapter 4 show that the credit expansion process entails banks' creation of such deposits. Nonetheless economically speaking this argument is invalid. While banks' creation of money in the form of deposits initially coincides with their creation of loans, and both are granted to the same actors, loan recipients imme-diately part with the m.u. received as deposits, using them to pay their suppliers and owners of the original means of pro-duction. Hence the direct recipients continue to owe the loan amounts to the bank, yet the deposits change hands at once. This precisely is the root of banks' *inherent insolvency* which endangers their survival in the stages of severe economic recession. In fact the businessmen who receive loans commit en masse entrepreneurial errors which the crisis reveals. They mistakenly instigate processes of investment in capital goods, in which the loans materialize, loans whose value falls dra-matically or is completely lost. Substantial default results, and the value of a large portion of banks' assets plummets. How-ever at the same time, the deposit holders, now third parties, maintain their claims intact against the banks that brought about credit expansion, and therefore banks are unable to eliminate their liabilities at the same rate the value of their assets drops. An accounting maladjustment ensues, leading to suspensions of payments and to the bankruptcy of marginally less solvent banks. If pessimism and the lack of confidence spread, all banks may become insolvent, ending in the disastrous failure of the banking system and of the monetary system based on fractional-reserve banking. This instability intrinsic to the fractional-reserve banking system is what makes the existence of a central bank as lender of last resort inevitable, just as the correct functioning of a system of complete banking freedom requires a return to traditional legal principles and thus a 100-percent reserve requirement.

If a monetary bank-deposit contract which allows bankers to neglect their obligation to maintain a 100-percent reserve ratio may eventually even lead to the downfall of the banking system (and of many of its customers), how is it possible that historically bankers have insisted upon acting in this manner? In the first three chapters we studied the historical factors and circumstances which gave rise to the bank-deposit contract with a fractional reserve. There we saw that this contract originated from a privilege governments granted bankers, allowing them to use in their own interest the money of their depositors, most often in the form of loans given to the very granter of the privilege, i.e., the government or state, continually overwhelmed by financial pressures. If governments had fulfilled their essential purpose and had adequately defined and defended the property rights of depositors, such an anomalous institution would never have emerged.

Let us now ponder some additional considerations with respect to the emergence of the monetary bank-deposit contract with a fractional reserve. One relevant issue is the great theoretical difficulty which, given the complex, abstract nature of social processes related to credit and money, renders a great many people, even those most involved in these processes, unable to analyze and comprehend the effects which credit expansion ultimately provokes. In fact throughout history most people have generally considered the effects of credit expansion on the economy positive and have merely focused on its most visible, short-term results (waves of optimism, economic booms). However what can be said of the bankers themselves, who throughout history have experienced numerous bank runs and crises that have repetitively and seriously endangered their business or even ended it? Given that bankers have suffered first-hand the consequences of operating with a fractional-reserve ratio, one might think it is *in their own best interest* to modify their practices and adapt them to traditional legal principles (that is, a 100-percent cash reserve). Even Ludwig von Mises held this idea at first,[97] yet historical experience, which shows that again and again banks have relapsed into holding a fractional reserve (in spite of the huge risks it entails), does not justify it, nor does the theoretical analysis. Indeed even when bankers are aware that fractional-reserve banking is condemned to failure in the long run,

---

[97]In 1928 Ludwig von Mises admitted:

> I could not understand why the banks didn't learn from experience. I thought they would certainly persist in a policy of caution and restraint, if they were not led by outside circumstances to abandon it. Only later did I become convinced that it was useless to look to an outside stimulus for the change in the conduct of the banks. Only later did I also become convinced that fluctuations in general business conditions were completely dependent on the relationship of the quantity of fiduciary media in circulation to demand. . . . We can readily understand that the banks issuing fiduciary media, in order to improve their chances for profit, may be ready to expand the volume of credit granted and the number of notes issued. What calls for a special explanation is why attempts are made again and again to improve general economic conditions by the expansion of circulation credit in spite of the spectacular failure of such efforts in the past. The answer must run as follows: According to the prevailing ideology of businessman and economist-politician, the reduction of the interest rate is considered an essential goal of economic policy. Moreover, the expansion of circulation credit is assumed to be the appropriate means to achieve this goal. ("Monetary Stabilization and Cyclical Policy," included in the book, *On the Manipulation of Money and Credit*, pp. 135–36)

This work is the English translation of the important book Mises published in 1928 with the title, *Geldwertstabilisierung und Konjunkturpolitik*.

the *ex nihilo* creation of money, an ability all credit expansion involves, generates such large profits that bankers eventually succumb to the temptation to revert to a fractional reserve. In addition *no particular banker* can be absolutely certain his bank will be one of those that eventually suspend payments or fail, since he can always hope to be able to withdraw from the process before the crisis hits, demand the repayment of loans, and avoid defaulters. Thus a typical *tragedy of the commons*, a process known to be triggered whenever the property rights of third parties are inadequately defined or defended (as in the case which concerns us), is set in motion. We will study the process in greater depth in chapter 8. In light of the above it is unsurprising banks face an irresistible temptation to expand their credit before other banks and hence to take full advantage of the profits of the expansion while leaving the rest of the banks, and the entire economic system in general, to jointly bear the extremely harmful consequences which ultimately follow.[98]

To conclude, the technical impossibility of insuring against the risk of deposit withdrawal via a fractional-reserve ratio also explains, as we will see in chapter 8, that bankers themselves have been the chief defenders of the existence of *a central bank* which, as lender of last resort, could guarantee their

---

[98]We first had the opportunity to defend the thesis that the theory of the "tragedy of the commons" should be applied to fractional-reserve banking at the Regional Meeting of the Mont-Pèlerin Society which took place in Rio de Janeiro, September 5–8, 1993. There we pointed out that the typical "tragedy of the commons" clearly applies to banking, given that the entire expansive process derives from a privilege against property rights, since each bank entirely internalizes the benefits of expanding its credit while letting the other banks and the whole economic system share the corresponding costs. Moreover as we will see in chapter 8, an interbank clearing mechanism within a free banking system may thwart individual, isolated attempts at expansion, but it is useless if all banks, moved by the desire for profit in a typical "tragedy of the commons" process, are more or less carried away by "optimism" in the granting of loans. On this topic see our "Introducción Crítica a la Edición Española" to Vera C. Smith's book, *Fundamentos de la banca central y de la libertad bancaria* [*The Rationale of Central Banking and the Free Banking Alternative*] (Madrid: Unión Editorial/Ediciones Aosta, 1993), footnote 16 on p. 38.

survival during panic stages.[99] From this point of view, the historical emergence of the central bank as an institution was an inevitable result of the very privilege which allows banks to loan most of the money they receive on deposit, through the maintenance of a fractional-reserve ratio. Furthermore it is evident that until traditional legal principles, and thus a 100-percent reserve requirement, are reestablished, it will be impossible to manage without the central bank and to introduce a true free-banking system which is subject to the law and does not adversely affect the course of the economy by regularly provoking destabilizing phases of artificial expansion and economic recession.[100]

---

[99]The standard analysis of the "public-choice school" could also be mentioned here to explain how banks, as a powerful pressure group, have mobilized to protect their privilege, establish a legal foundation for it and obtain government support whenever necessary. Thus it is not surprising authors such as Rothbard conclude that "bankers are inherently inclined toward statism." Murray N. Rothbard, *Wall Street, Banks, and American Foreign Policy* (Burlingame, Calif.: Center for Libertarian Studies, 1995), p. 1. See also the literature on the economic effects of demand deposits in current monetary systems based on central banks (among others Douglas W. Diamond and Phillip H. Dybvig, "Bank Runs, Deposit Insurance, and Liquidity," *Journal of Political Economy* 91 [1983]: 401–19; and Itay Goldstein and Ady Pauzner, "Demand-Deposit Contracts and the Probability of Bank Runs," *Journal of Finance* 60, no. 3 [June 2005]: 1293–1327).

[100]Therefore the central bank constitutes the most concrete historical proof of the practical and theoretical failure of the attempt to insure against deposit withdrawal via a fractional reserve. The fact that a lender of last resort, to create and provide the liquidity required in times of panic, is considered necessary shows that such insurance is impossible and that the only way to avoid the inevitable, damaging consequences that the institution of fractional-reserve banking produces for banks is by creating and preserving an institution with absolute control over the monetary system and the ability to create the necessary liquidity at any time. In other words, the fractional-reserve privilege is also ultimately responsible for the central bank's strong, frequent intervention in the financial system, which is thus excluded from the processes of the free market subject to traditional legal principles. This book began with the assertion that the main practical and theoretical challenge facing the economy at the start of this new century is precisely to put an end to the intervention and systematic coercion of the state and to privileges within the financial system, by subjecting it to the same traditional legal principles which are invariably demanded of all other economic agents operating in a free market. This assertion is now perfectly understandable.

6

ADDITIONAL CONSIDERATIONS ON THE THEORY OF THE BUSINESS CYCLE

his chapter presents some additional considerations to clarify various aspects of the circulation credit theory of the business cycle. These reflections are intended to further our analysis as much as possible and to shed light on different peripheral matters of great theoretical and practical interest. The final part of the chapter is devoted to a review of the empirical evidence which illustrates and supports the theory put forward in the previous chapters.

1

WHY NO CRISIS ERUPTS WHEN NEW INVESTMENT IS FINANCED BY REAL SAVING (AND NOT BY CREDIT EXPANSION)

No economic crisis and consequent recession hit when the lengthening of the stages in the productive structure, a process we studied in the last chapter, results from a prior increase in voluntary saving, rather than from credit expansion banks bring about without the backing of any growth in real saving. Indeed if a sustained rise in voluntary saving triggers the process, this saving prevents all of the six microeconomic phenomena which spontaneously arise in reaction to credit expansion and which reverse the artificial boom that credit expansion initially creates. In fact in such a case there is no increase in the price of the original means of production. On the contrary, if the loans originate from an upsurge in real saving, the relative decrease in immediate consumption which this saving invariably entails frees a large volume of productive resources in the market of original means of production. These resources become available for use in the stages furthest from consumption and *there is no need to pay higher prices for them*. In the case of credit expansion we saw that prices rose precisely because such expansion did not arise from a prior increase in saving, and therefore original productive resources were not freed in the stages close to consumption, and the only way entrepreneurs from the stages furthest from consumption could obtain such resources was by offering relatively higher prices for them.

In addition if the lengthening of the productive structure derives from growth in voluntary saving, there is no increase in the price of consumer goods which is more than proportional to a corresponding increase in the price of the factors of production. Quite the opposite is true; at first there tends to be a sustained drop in the price of these goods. Indeed a rise in saving always involves a certain short-term drop in consumption. Hence there will be no relative increase in the accounting profits of the industries closest to consumption, nor a decrease in the profits, or even an accounting loss, in the stages furthest from consumption. Therefore the process will not reverse and there will be nothing to provoke a crisis. Moreover as we saw in chapter 5, the "Ricardo Effect" plays a role, as it becomes advantageous for entrepreneurs to substitute capital equipment for labor, due to the growth in real wages following the relative decrease in the price of consumer goods, which in turn tends to arise from an upsurge in saving. Market rates of interest do not mount; on the contrary, they tend to decline *permanently*, reflecting society's new rate of time preference, now even lower, given the increased desire to save. Furthermore if a component is to be included in the market interest rate to compensate for a change in the purchasing power of money, when voluntary saving climbs, the component will be *negative*. This is because, as we have seen, the tendency is toward a fall in the price of consumer goods (in the short- and long-term), which tends to drive up the purchasing power of money, an event which will exert even further downward pressure on nominal interest rates. In addition economic growth based on voluntary saving is healthy and sustained, and therefore entrepreneurial and risk components implicit in the interest rate will also tend to drop.

The above considerations confirm that the recession always originates from an absence of the voluntary saving necessary to sustain a productive structure which thus proves too capital-intensive. The recession is caused by the credit expansion the banking system undertakes without the corresponding support of economic agents, who in general do not wish to augment their voluntary saving. Perhaps Moss and Vaughn have most concisely expressed the conclusion of the entire theoretical analysis of this process:

> Any real growth in the capital stock takes time and requires voluntary net savings. There is no way for the expansion of the money supply in the form of bank credit to short-circuit the process of economic growth.[1]

2

THE POSSIBILITY OF POSTPONING THE ERUPTION OF THE CRISIS: THE THEORETICAL EXPLANATION OF THE PROCESS OF STAGFLATION

The arrival of the economic recession can be *postponed* if additional loans unbacked by real saving are granted at an ever-increasing rate, i.e., if credit expansion reaches a speed at which economic agents cannot completely anticipate it. The procedure consists of administering additional doses of bank credit to the companies which have launched new investment projects and have widened and lengthened the stages in the production process. This new credit may defer

---

[1]Moss and Vaughn, "Hayek's Ricardo Effect: A Second Look," p. 555. See also footnote 91 on p. 382.

the six phenomena we explained in chapter 5, which always tend to spontaneously reverse the initial consequences of all credit expansion in the market. However, while this procedure may postpone the depression, and may even do so for relatively long periods of time,[2] this strategy is condemned to inevitable failure and involves a huge additional cost: once the recession hits, it will be much deeper and much more painful and prolonged.[3]

---

[2]Hayek himself, while commenting on the eruption of the economic crisis at the end of the 1970s, admitted:

> [m]y expectation was that the inflationary boom would last five or six years, as the historical ones had done, forgetting that then their termination was due to the gold standard. If you had no gold standard—if you could continue inflating for much longer—it was very difficult to predict how long it would last. Of course, it has lasted very much longer than I expected. The end result was the same.

Hayek is referring to the inflationary process which in the 1960s and 1970s spread throughout the world and was encouraged by historical circumstances which, like the Vietnam War and other events, fostered almost unlimited credit expansion worldwide, thus triggering a process that would later give rise to the severe stagflation and high unemployment of the late 1970s and early 1980s. See *Hayek on Hayek: An Autobiographical Dialogue*, Stephen Kresge and Leif Wenar, eds. (London: Routledge, 1994), p. 145.

[3]Murray Rothbard assesses the possibility of deferring the arrival of the depression in the following terms:

> Why do booms, historically, continue for several years? What delays the reversion process? The answer is that as the boom begins to peter out from an injection of credit expansion, the banks inject a further dose. In short, the only way to *avert* the onset of the depression-adjustment process is to continue inflating money and credit. For only continual doses of new money on the credit market will keep the boom going and the new stages profitable. Furthermore, only *ever increasing* doses can step up the boom, can lower interest rates further, and expand the production structure, for as the prices rise, more and more money will be needed to perform the same amount of work. . . . But it is clear that prolonging the boom by ever larger doses of credit expansion will have only one result: to make the inevitably ensuing depression longer and more grueling. (Rothbard, *Man, Economy, and State*, pp. 861–62)

The success of this strategy of postponing the crisis through additional loans hinges on a continuously-growing rate of credit expansion. Hayek already revealed this principle in 1934 when he stated: "[I]n order to bring about constant additions to capital, [credit] would have to . . . increase *at a constantly increasing rate*."[4] The need for this ever-escalating increase in the rate of credit expansion rests on the fact that in each time period the rate must *exceed* the rise in the price of consumer goods, a rise which results from the greater monetary demand for these goods following the jump in the nominal income of the original factors of production. Therefore given that a large portion of the new income received by owners of the original means of production originates directly from credit expansion, this expansion must progressively intensify so that *the price of the factors of production is always ahead of the price of consumer goods*. The moment this ceases to be true, the six microeconomic processes which reverse the changes made to the productive structure, shortening and flattening it, are spontaneously set in motion and the crisis and economic recession irrevocably hit.

In any case credit expansion must accelerate at a rate which does not permit economic agents to adequately predict it, since if these agents begin to correctly anticipate rate increases, the six phenomena we are familiar with will be triggered. Indeed if expectations of inflation spread, the prices of consumer goods will soon begin to rise even faster than the prices of the factors of production. Moreover market interest rates will soar, even while credit expansion continues to intensify (given that the expectations of inflation and of growth in the interest rate will immediately be reflected in its market value).

Hence the strategy of increasing credit expansion in order to postpone the crisis cannot be indefinitely pursued, and sooner or later the crisis will be provoked by any of the following three factors, which will also give rise to the recession:

---

[4]Hayek, *Prices and Production*, p. 150.

(a) The rate at which credit expansion accelerates either slows down or *stops*, due to the fear, experienced by bankers and economic authorities, that a crisis will erupt and that the subsequent depression may be even more acute if inflation continues to mount. The moment credit expansion ceases to increase at a growing rate, begins to increase at a steady rate, or is completely halted, the six microeconomic processes which lead to the crisis and the readjustment of the productive structure are set in motion.

(b) Credit expansion is *maintained* at a rate of growth which, nevertheless, does not accelerate fast enough to prevent the effects of reversion in each time period. In this case, despite continual increases in the money supply in the shape of loans, the six effects described will inevitably develop. Thus the crisis and economic recession will hit. There will be a sharp rise in the prices of consumer goods; simultaneous inflation and crisis; depression; and hence, high rates of unemployment. To the great surprise of Keynesian theorists, the western world has already experienced such circumstances and did so both in the inflationary depression of the late 1970s and, to a lesser extent, in the economic recession of the early 1990s. The descriptive term used to refer to them is *stagflation*.[5]

---

[5]Mark Skousen correctly indicates that, in relative terms, *stagflation* is a *universal phenomenon*, considering that in all recessions the price of consumer goods climbs more (or falls less) *in relative terms* than the price of the factors of production. Widespread growth in the nominal prices of consumer goods during a *phase of recession* first took place in the depression of the 1970s, and later in the recession of the 1990s. It sprang from the fact that the credit expansion which fed both processes was great enough in the different stages of the cycle to create and maintain expectations of inflation in the market of consumer goods and services even during the deepest stages of the depression (apart from the typical recent phenomena of relentless growth in public spending and in the deficit, and of massive social transfer payments which foster direct growth in the demand for, and therefore, in the prices of consumer goods and services). See Skousen, *The Structure of Production*, pp. 313–15.

Hayek revealed that the increasing speed at which the rise in the monetary income of the factors of production pushes up the demand for consumer goods and services ultimately limits the chances that the inevitable eruption of the crisis can be deferred via the subsequent acceleration of credit expansion. Indeed sooner or later a point will be reached at which growth in the prices of consumer goods will actually start to outstrip the increase in the monetary income of the original factors, even though this may only be due to the emergence of a slowdown in the arrival of consumer goods and services to the market, as a result of the "bottlenecks" caused by the attempt to make society's productive structure more capital-intensive. Beginning at that point, the income generated by the factors of production, specifically wages, will begin to decline in relative terms, and therefore entrepreneurs will find it advantageous to substitute labor (now relatively cheaper) for machinery, and the "Ricardo Effect" will enter into action, hindering the projects of investment in capital-intensive goods, and thus ensuring the outbreak of the recession.[6]

---

[6]Hayek draws the following analogy to explain this phenomenon:

The question is rather similar to that whether, by pouring a liquid fast enough into one side of a vessel, we can raise the level at that side above that of the rest to any extent we desire. How far we shall be able to raise the level of one part above that of the rest will clearly depend on how fluid or viscid the liquid is; we shall be able to raise it more if the liquid is syrup or glue than if it is water. But in no case shall we be at liberty to raise the surface in one part of the vessel above the rest to any extent we like. Just as the viscosity of the liquid determines the extent to which any part of its surface can be raised above the rest, so the speed at which an increase of incomes leads to an increase in the demand for consumers' goods limits the extent to which, by spending more money on the factors of production, we can raise their prices relative to those of the products. (Hayek, "The Ricardo Effect," pp. 127–52; *Individualism and Economic Order*, p. 241)

(c) Finally let us suppose that the banking system at no
    time reduces the rate at which it accelerates credit
    expansion, and instead does just the opposite: it con-
    stantly and progressively intensifies it, with the pur-
    pose of quashing any symptom of an emerging
    depression. In this case, the moment economic agents
    begin to realize that the rate of inflation is certain to
    continue growing, a widespread flight toward real
    values will commence, along with an astronomical
    jump in the prices of goods and services, and finally,
    the collapse of the monetary system, an event which

In 1969 Hayek again used this analogy in his article, "Three Elucidations of the Ricardo Effect," in which he reiterates that the distorting
effect of credit expansion on the productive structure must continue as
long as banks create new money and this money enters the economic
system at certain points at a progressively increasing rate. Hayek criticizes Hicks for assuming the inflationary shock will "uniformly" affect
the entire productive structure, and he demonstrates that if credit
expansion escalates at a rate exceeding the rise in prices, this process
"can evidently go on indefinitely, at least as long as we neglect changes
in the manner in which expectations concerning future prices are
formed." He concludes:

> I find it useful to illustrate the general relationship by an anal-
> ogy which seems worth stating here, though Sir John [Hicks]
> (in correspondence) did not find it helpful. The effect we are
> discussing is rather similar to that which appears when we
> pour a viscous liquid, such as honey, into a vessel. There will,
> of course, be a tendency for it to spread to an even surface. But
> if the stream hits the surface at one point, a little mound will
> form there from which the additional matter will slowly spread
> outward. Even after we have stopped pouring in more, it will
> take some time until the even surface will be fully restored. It
> will, of course, not reach the height which the top of the mound
> had reached when the inflow stopped. But as long as we pour
> at a constant rate, the mound will preserve its height relative to
> the surrounding pool—providing a very literal illustration of
> what I called before a fluid equilibrium. (Hayek, *New Studies in
> Philosophy, Politics, Economics and the History of Ideas*, pp.
> 171–73)

On the important role of expectations in this entire process, see especially Garrison, *Time and Money*, chaps. 1–4.

will ensue when the hyperinflation process destroys the purchasing power of the monetary unit and economic agents spontaneously start to use another type of money. At that point the six microeconomic reversion effects we are familiar with will appear in all of their intensity, as will an acute economic depression, which to the painful readjustment of a totally distorted productive system will add the tremendous cost and social harm involved in any general failure of the monetary system.[7]

---

[7]Ludwig von Mises examines this process in his analysis of the hyperinflation which assailed Germany from 1920 to 1923. Mises concludes:

> Suppose the banks still did not want to give up the race? Suppose, in order to depress the loan rate, they wanted to satisfy the continuously expanding desire for credit by issuing still more circulation credit? Then they would only hasten the end, the collapse of the entire system of fiduciary media. The inflation can continue only so long as the conviction persists that it will one day cease. Once people are persuaded that the inflation will *not* stop, they turn from the use of this money. They flee then to "real values," foreign money, the precious metals, and barter. (Mises, "Monetary Stabilization and Cyclical Policy," p. 129)

Later, in *Human Action*, Mises states:

> The boom can last only as long as the credit expansion progresses at an ever-accelerated pace. The boom comes to an end as soon as additional quantities of fiduciary media are no longer thrown upon the loan market. But it could not last forever even if inflation and credit expansion were to go on endlessly. It would then encounter the barriers which prevent the boundless expansion of circulation credit. It would lead to the crack-up boom and breakdown of the whole monetary system. (p. 555)

The classical treatment of Germany's hyperinflation process is the one Bresciani-Turroni gives in *The Economics of Inflation: A Study of Currency Depreciation in Post-War Germany*. See also Richard M. Ebeling, "The Great Austrian Inflation," *The Freeman* (April 2006): 2–3.

3
Consumer Credit and the Theory of the Cycle

We are now able to identify the modifications, if any, to be made to our analysis when, as in modern economies, a significant portion of the credit expansion banks bring about without the support of voluntary saving takes the form of consumer credit. This analysis is of great theoretical and practical importance, since it has at times been argued that, to the extent credit expansion initially falls on consumption and not on investment, the economic effects which trigger a recession would not necessarily appear. Nevertheless this opinion is erroneous for reasons this section will explain.

It is first necessary to point out that most consumer credit is extended by banks to households for the purchase of *durable* consumer goods. We have already established that durable consumer goods are actually true capital goods which permit the rendering of direct consumer services over a very prolonged period of time. Therefore *from an economic standpoint, the granting of loans to finance durable consumer goods is indistinguishable from the direct granting of loans to the capital-intensive stages furthest from consumption*. In fact an easing of credit terms and a decline in interest rates will provoke, among other effects, an increase in the quantity, quality and duration of so-called "durable consumer goods," which will simultaneously require a widening and lengthening of the productive stages involved, especially those furthest from consumption.

Hence we have only to consider how to revise our theory of the business cycle if a significant portion of credit expansion is devoted (contrary to the usual practice) to financing not durable consumer goods, but the *current consumption* of each financial year (in the form of goods and services which directly satisfy human needs and are exhausted in the course of the period in question). Substantial modifications to our analysis are unnecessary in this case as well, since one of the following is true: either credit expansion satisfies a more or less constant demand for credit to finance existing direct consumption in the economic system, and given that credit markets are like "communicating vessels," such expansion frees the capacity to grant loans in favor of the stages furthest from consumption, thus instigating the typical processes of expansion and recession we are familiar with; or the loans exert their impact on current consumption while no additional capacity is freed for granting loans to industries from the stages furthest from consumption.

Only in this second case, insignificant in practice, is there a direct effect on the monetary demand for consumer goods and services. Indeed the new money immediately pushes up the prices of consumer goods and diminishes, in relative terms, the prices of the factors of production. The "Ricardo Effect" is set in motion, and entrepreneurs begin to hire more workers, in relative terms, and substitute them for machinery. Thus *a trend toward the flattening of the productive structure is established without a prior expansionary boom in the stages furthest from consumption*. Therefore the only modification to be made to our analysis is the following: if consumption is directly encouraged through credit expansion, the existing productive structure furthest from consumption clearly ceases to be profitable in relative terms, creating a trend toward the liquidation of these stages and the general flattening of the productive structure. This constitutes an economic process of impoverishment which initially manifests itself in a bubble, not only due to the increased consumer demand, but also because many entrepreneurs try to complete the investment projects they have already committed to. This process is just the opposite of the one we examined at the beginning of chapter 5, where we studied the beneficial effects an increase in voluntary saving (or a decrease in the immediate consumption of goods and services) exerts on economic development.[8]

---

[8]Perhaps Fritz Machlup has most clearly and concisely explained this phenomenon. He states:

> The view that the expansion of credit for financing the production of consumers' goods will not lead to disproportionalities of the kind associated with inflation can be disproved by the following argument. *Either* the consumers' goods industries would have borrowed on the money market, or the capital market, in the absence of any expansion of bank credit, in which case the satisfaction of their demand for funds by

At any rate credit expansion always gives rise to the same widespread malinvestment in the productive structure, whether by artificially lengthening the existing structure (when expansion directly affects the capital goods stages, financing durable consumer goods) or shortening it (when credit expansion directly finances non-durable consumer goods).[9]

> means of the credit expansion obviously implies that there is so much less pressure on the credit market, and that some producers' goods industry, which would not otherwise have obtained credit to finance an expansion, will be enabled to do so by this means. . . . *Or* the consumers' goods industries would not have had any incentive to extend production in the absence of the credit expansion; in this case the fact that they now enter the market for producers' goods with relatively increased buying power as against all other industries . . . may lead to a change in the distribution of productive factors involving a shift from the stages far from consumption to the stages near to consumption. (Machlup, *The Stock Market, Credit and Capital Formation*, pp. 192–93)

In *Prices and Production* (pp. 60–62 of the 1935 edition) Hayek uses his triangular diagrams to explain how the productive structure will inevitably become flatter and less capital-intensive, and therefore, less productive and poorer, if consumption is directly promoted through the granting of loans to finance non-durable consumer goods and services.

[9]In the 1970s this phenomenon, along with the need to provide a simplified explanation of the process of malinvestment without relying on the complicated reasoning inherent in capital theory, led F.A. Hayek to slightly modify the popular presentation of his theory of the cycle. In his article, "Inflation, the Misdirection of Labor, and Unemployment," written in 1975 (and included in the book, *New Studies in Philosophy, Politics, Economics and the History of Ideas*, pp. 197–209), he states:

> [T]he explanation of extensive unemployment ascribes it to a discrepancy between the distribution of labour (and the other factors of production) between the different industries (and localities) and the distribution of demand among their products. This discrepancy is caused by a distortion of the system of relative prices and wages. (p. 200)

In the recent "biography" of Hayek, we see that in the last years of his life he believed modern cycles to be characterized by the very distinct forms of malinvestment involved, not only credit expansion in the stages furthest from consumption, but also artificial stimulation of consumption and, in

4

THE SELF-DESTRUCTIVE NATURE OF THE ARTIFICIAL
BOOMS CAUSED BY CREDIT EXPANSION:
THE THEORY OF "FORCED SAVING"

In the *broad sense* of the term, "forced saving" arises whenever there is an increase in the quantity of money in circulation or an expansion of bank credit (unbacked by voluntary
saving) which is injected into the economic system at a specific point. If the money or credit were evenly distributed
among all economic agents, no "expansionary" effect would
appear, except the decrease in the purchasing power of the
monetary unit in proportion to the rise in the quantity of
money. However if the new money enters the market at certain specific points, as always occurs, then in reality a relatively small number of economic agents initially receive the
new loans. Thus these economic agents temporarily enjoy
greater purchasing power, given that they possess a larger
number of monetary units with which to buy goods and services at market prices that still have not felt the full impact of
the inflation and therefore have not yet risen. Hence the
process gives rise to a *redistribution of income* in favor of those
who first receive the new injections or doses of monetary
units, *to the detriment of the rest of society*, who find that with the
same monetary income, the prices of goods and services begin
to go up. "Forced saving" affects this second group of economic agents (the majority), since their monetary income
grows at a slower rate than prices, and they are therefore

---

general, all public spending which generates in the productive structure a
change that cannot ultimately become permanent because the behavior of
consumers does not support it. Hayek concludes:

> [S]o much of the credit expansion has gone to where govern-
> ment directed it that the misdirection may no longer be of an
> overinvestment in industrial capital but may take any number of
> forms. You must really study it separately for each particular
> phase and situation. . . . But you get very similar phenomena
> with all kinds of modifications. (Hayek, *Hayek on Hayek: An
> Autobiographical Dialogue*, p. 146)

obliged to reduce their consumption, other things being equal.[10]

Whether this phenomenon of forced saving, which is provoked by an injection of new money at certain points in the market, leads to a net increase or decrease in society's overall, voluntary saving will depend on the circumstances specific to

---

[10]Consequently in its broadest sense, "forced saving" refers to the forced expropriation to which banks and monetary authorities subject most of society, producing a diffuse effect, when they decide to expand credit and money, diminishing the purchasing power of the monetary units individuals possess, in relation to the value these units would have in the absence of such credit and monetary expansion. The funds derived from this social plunder can either be completely squandered (if their recipients spend them on consumer goods and services or sink them into utterly mistaken investments), or they can become business or other assets, which either directly or indirectly come, *de facto*, under the control of banks or the state. The first Spaniard to correctly analyze this inflationary process of expropriation was the scholastic Father Juan de Mariana, in his work, *De monetae mutatione*, published in 1609. In it he writes:

> If the prince is not a lord, but an administrator of the goods of individuals, neither in that capacity nor in any other will he be able to seize a part of their property, *as occurs each time the currency is devalued*, since they are given less in place of what is worth more; and if the prince cannot impose taxes against the will of his vassals nor create monopolies, he will not be able to do so in this capacity either, because it is all the same, and it is all depriving the people of their goods, no matter how well disguised by giving the coins a legal value greater than their actual worth, which are all deceptive, dazzling fabrications, and all lead to the same outcome. (Juan de Mariana, *Tratado y discurso sobre la moneda de vellón que al presente se labra en Castilla y de algunos desórdenes y abusos* [*Treatise and Discourse on the Copper Currency which is now Minted in Castile and on Several Excesses and Abuses*], with a preliminary study by Lucas Beltrán [Madrid: Instituto de Estudios Fiscales, Ministerio de Economía y Hacienda, 1987], p. 40; italics added)

A somewhat different translation from the original text in Latin has been more recently published in English. Juan de Mariana, S.J., *A Treatise on the Alteration of Money*, translation by Patrick T. Brannan, S.J. Introduction by Alejandro A. Chafuen, *Journal of Markets and Morality* 5, no. 2 (Fall, 2002): 523–93. The quotation is on page 544 (12 of the translation).

each historical case. In fact if those whose income rises (those who first receive the new money created) consume a proportion of it greater than that previously consumed by those whose real income falls, then overall saving will drop. It is also conceivable that those who benefit may have a strong inclination to save, in which case the final amount of saving might be positive. At any rate the inflationary process unleashes other forces which impede saving: inflation falsifies economic calculation by generating fictitious accounting profits which, to a greater or lesser extent, will be consumed. Therefore it is impossible to theoretically establish in advance whether the injection of new money into circulation at specific points in the economic system will result in a rise or a decline in society's overall saving.[11]

In a *strict sense*, "forced saving" denotes the lengthening (longitudinal) and widening (lateral) of the capital goods

---

[11]Joseph A. Schumpeter attributes the appropriate expression "forced saving" (in German, *Erzwungenes Sparen* or *Zwangssparen*) to Ludwig von Mises in his book, *The Theory of Economic Development*, first published in German in 1911 (*The Theory of Economic Development* [Cambridge, Mass.: Harvard University Press, 1968], p. 109). Mises acknowledges having described the phenomenon in 1912 in the first German edition of his book, *The Theory of Money and Credit*, though he indicates he does not believe he used the particular expression Schumpeter attributes to him. In any case Mises carefully analyzed the phenomenon of forced saving and theoretically demonstrated that it is impossible to predetermine whether or not net growth in voluntary saving will follow from an increase in the amount of money in circulation. On this topic see *On the Manipulation of Money and Credit*, pp. 120, 122 and 126–27. Also *Human Action*, pp. 148–50. Mises first dealt with the subject in *The Theory of Money and Credit*, p. 386. Though we will continue to attribute the term "forced saving" to Mises, a very similar expression, "forced frugality," was used by Jeremy Bentham in 1804 (see Hayek's article, "A Note on the Development of the Doctrine of 'Forced Saving,'" published as chapter 7 of *Profits, Interest and Investment*, pp. 183–97). As Roger Garrison has aptly revealed, a certain disparity exists between Mises's concept of forced saving (what we refer to as "the broad sense" of the term) and Hayek's concept of it (which we will call "the strict sense"), and thus "what Mises termed malinvestment is what Hayek called forced savings." See Garrison, "Austrian Microeconomics: A Diagrammatical Exposition," p. 196.

stages in the productive structure, changes which stem from credit expansion the banking system launches without the support of voluntary saving. As we know, this process initially generates an increase in the monetary income of the original means of production, and later, a more-than-proportional rise in the price of consumer goods (or in the gross income of consumer goods industries, if productivity increases). In fact, the circulation credit theory of the business cycle explains the theoretical microeconomic factors which determine that the attempt to force a more capital-intensive productive structure, without the corresponding backing of voluntary saving, is condemned to failure and will invariably reverse, provoking economic crises and recessions. This process is almost certain to entail an eventual redistribution of resources which in some way modifies the overall voluntary saving ratio that existed prior to the beginning of credit expansion. *However unless the entire process is accompanied by a simultaneous, independent, and spontaneous increase in voluntary saving of an amount at least equal to the newly-created credit banks extend* ex nihilo, *it will be impossible to sustain and complete the new, more capital-intensive stages undertaken, and the typical reversion effects we have examined in detail will appear, along with a crisis and economic recession.* Moreover the process involves the squandering of numerous capital goods and society's scarce resources, making society poorer. As a result, by and large, society's *voluntary* saving ultimately tends to shrink rather than grow. At any rate, barring dramatic, spontaneous, unforeseen increases in voluntary saving, which for argument's sake we exclude at this point from the theoretical analysis (which furthermore always involves the assumption that other things remain equal), credit expansion will provoke a self-destructive boom, which sooner or later will revert in the form of an economic crisis and recession. This demonstrates the impossibility of *forcing* the economic development of society by artificially encouraging investment and initially financing it with credit expansion, if economic agents are unwilling to voluntarily back such a policy by saving more. Therefore society's investment cannot possibly exceed its voluntary saving for long periods (this would constitute an alternative definition of "forced saving," one more in line with the Keynesian analysis, as F.A. Hayek correctly indicates).[12] Instead, regardless of the final amount of saving and investment in society (*always* identical *ex post*), all that is achieved by an attempt to *force* a level of investment which exceeds that of saving is the general malinvestment of the country's saved resources and an economic crisis always destined to make it poorer.[13]

5

THE SQUANDERING OF CAPITAL, IDLE CAPACITY, AND MALINVESTMENT OF PRODUCTIVE RESOURCES

The chief effect credit expansion exerts on the productive structure is ultimately that it *discoordinates* the behavior of the different economic agents. Indeed entrepreneurs rush to lengthen and widen the productive stages and make them more capital-intensive, while the remaining economic agents *are unwilling to cooperate* by sacrificing their consumption and raising their overall voluntary saving. This maladjustment or discoordination, which stems from a systematic attack on the process of social interaction (the privilege governments grant banks, allowing them to use a fractional reserve on demand deposits), invariably triggers a crisis process that eventually corrects the entrepreneurial mistakes committed. Nevertheless the process takes time, and inevitably, by its end, serious errors will have been made that will have become *irreversible*.

The errors consist of launching and attempting to complete a series of investment projects which entail a lengthening and widening of the capital goods structure, projects which nonetheless cannot come to fruition, due to a lack of real saved resources. Moreover once resources and original

---

[12]See Hayek, "A Note on the Development of the Doctrine of 'Forced Saving,'" p. 197. See also the comments on Cantillon and Hume's contributions in chapter 8, pp. 615–20.

[13]Fritz Machlup has compiled up to 34 different concepts of "forced saving" in his article, "Forced or Induced Saving: An Exploration into its Synonyms and Homonyms," *The Review of Economics and Statistics* 25, no. 1 (February 1943); reprinted in Fritz Machlup, *Economic Semantics* (London: Transaction Publishers, 1991), pp. 213–40.

factors of production have been transformed into capital goods, these goods become *non-convertible* to a certain extent. In other words, many capital goods will lose all of their value once it becomes clear there is no demand for them, they were manufactured in error and they should never have been produced. It will be possible to continue using others, but only after spending a large amount of money redesigning them. The production of yet others may reach completion, but given that the capital goods structure requires that the goods be *complementary*, they may never be operated if the necessary complementary resources are not produced. Finally, it is conceivable that certain capital goods may be remodeled at a relatively low cost, though such goods are undoubtedly in the minority.[14] Hence a widespread malinvestment of society's scarce productive resources takes place, and a loss of many of its scarce capital goods follows. This loss derives from the *distorted information* which, during a certain period of time, entrepreneurs received in the form of easier credit terms and relatively lower interest rates.[15] Many investment processes

---

[14]As a general rule, the closer a capital good is to the final consumer good, the more difficult it will be to convert. In fact all human actions are more irreversible the closer they are to their final objective: a house built in error is an almost irreversible loss, while it is somewhat easier to modify the use of the bricks if it becomes obvious during the course of the construction that using them to build a specific house is a mistake (see comments on pp. 280–82 previously).

[15]Thus the theory of the cycle is simply the application, to the specific case of credit expansion's impact on the productive structure, of the theory on the discoordinating effects of institutional coercion, a theory we present in *Socialismo, cálculo económico y función empresarial* (esp. pp. 111–18). Lachmann arrives at the same conclusion when he states that malinvestment is "the waste of capital resources in plans prompted by misleading information," adding that, though many capital goods reach completion, they

> will lack complementary factors in the rest of the economy. Such lack of complementary factors may well express itself in lack of demand for its services, for instance where these factors would occupy "the later stages of production." To the untrained observer it is therefore often indistinguishable from "lack of effective demand." (Lachmann, *Capital and its Structure*, pp. 66 and 117–18)

may also be left half-completed, as their promoters abandon them upon realizing they cannot continue to obtain the new financial resources necessary to complete them, or though they may be able to continue to secure loans, they recognize that the investment processes lack economic viability. In short the widespread malinvestment expresses itself in the following ways: many capital goods remain unused, many investment processes cannot be completed, and capital goods produced are used in a manner not originally foreseen. A large portion of society's scarce resources has been squandered, and as a result, society becomes poorer in general and the standard of living drops, in relative terms.

Many economists have misunderstood the fact that a significant number of the errors committed manifest themselves as completed capital goods which, nonetheless, cannot be used, due to the absence of the complementary capital goods or working capital necessary. Indeed many see this phenomenon of "idle capacity" as clear proof of a necessity to boost overall consumption with the purpose of putting into operation an *idle capacity* which has been developed but is not yet used. They do not realize that, as Hayek indicates,[16] the

---

[16]In the words of F.A. Hayek himself:

> The impression that the already existing capital structure would enable us to increase production almost indefinitely is a deception. Whatever engineers may tell us about the supposed immense unused capacity of the existing productive machinery, there is in fact no possibility of increasing production to such an extent. These engineers and also those economists who believe that we have more capital than we need, are deceived by the fact that many of the existing plant and machinery are adapted to a much greater output than is actually produced. What they overlook is that durable means of production do not represent all the capital that is needed for an increase of output and that in order that the existing durable plants could be used to their full capacity it would be necessary to invest a great amount of other means of production in lengthy processes which would bear fruit only in a comparatively distant future. The existence of unused capacity is, therefore, by no means a proof that there exists an

existence of "idle capacity" in many production processes (but especially in those furthest from consumption, such as high technology, construction, and capital goods industries in general) in no way constitutes proof of oversaving and insufficient consumption. Quite the opposite is true: it is a *symptom* of the fact that we cannot completely use fixed capital produced in error, because the immediate demand for consumer goods and services is so urgent that we cannot allow ourselves the luxury of producing the complementary capital goods nor the working capital necessary to take advantage of such idle capacity. In short the crisis is provoked by a relative excess of consumption, i.e., a relative shortage of saving, which does not permit the completion of the processes initiated, nor the production of the complementary capital goods or working capital necessary to maintain the ongoing investment processes and to employ the capital goods which, for whatever reason, entrepreneurs were able to finish during the expansion process.[17]

---

excess of capital and that consumption is insufficient: on the contrary, it is a symptom that we are unable to use the fixed plant to the full extent because the current demand for consumers' goods is too urgent to permit us to invest current productive services in the long processes for which (in consequence of "misdirections of capital") the necessary durable equipment is available. (Hayek, *Prices and Production*, pp. 95–96)

[17] After the boom period is over, what is to be done with the malinvestments? The answer depends on their profitability for further use, i.e., on the degree of error that was committed. Some malinvestments will have to be abandoned, since their earnings from consumer demand will not even cover the current costs of their operation. Others, though monuments of failure, will be able to yield a profit over current costs, although it will not pay to replace them as they wear out. Temporarily working them fulfills the economic principle of always making the best of even a bad bargain. Because of the malinvestments, however, the boom always leads to general *impoverishment*, i.e., reduces the standard of living below what it would have been in the absence of the boom. For the credit expansion has caused the squandering of scarce

6

CREDIT EXPANSION AS THE CAUSE
OF MASSIVE UNEMPLOYMENT

The *direct* cause of massive unemployment is labor market inflexibility. In fact state intervention in the labor market and union coercion, made possible by the privileges the legal system confers on unions, result in a series of regulations (minimum wages, entry barriers to maintain wages artificially high, very strict, interventionist rules on hiring and dismissal, etc.) which make the labor market one of the most rigid. Furthermore due to the artificial costs labor legislation generates, the discounted value of a worker's real marginal productivity tends to fall short of the total labor costs the entrepreneur incurs (in the form of monetary costs, such as wages, and other costs, such as subjective inconveniences) in hiring the worker. This leads to markedly high unemployment, which will affect all workers whose expected marginal productivity yields a discounted value lower than the cost involved in employing them. Therefore they will either be dismissed or not hired at all.

Whereas the direct cause of unemployment is clearly that indicated above, the indirect cause is still inflation; more specifically, credit expansion initiated by the banking system without the backing of real saving. Credit expansion is ultimately what gives rise to massive unemployment, since it instigates the entire process of widespread discoordination and malinvestment described. It does so by extensively allocating original means of production to parts of the productive structure where they do not belong, considering that entrepreneurs attract them to lengthen and widen the capital goods structure, without realizing that in doing so they commit a

---

resources and scarce capital. Some resources have been completely wasted, and even those malinvestments that continue in use will satisfy consumers less than would have been the case without the credit expansion. (Rothbard, *Man, Economy, and State*, p. 863)

serious, large-scale entrepreneurial error. When the crisis hits
and the errors come to light, new massive transfers of original
factors of production and labor from the stages furthest from
consumption to those closest to it will be necessary and will
require an especially flexible labor market, one free of any
institutional or union restrictions or coercion. Therefore those
societies with a more rigid labor market will experience
higher and more sustained unemployment upon the
inevitable exposure of the entrepreneurial errors provoked in
the productive structure by credit expansion.[18]

Thus the only way to fight unemployment is, in the short
term, to make the labor market more flexible in every sense,
and in the medium and long term, to prevent the initiation of
any process of artificial expansion which arises from the banking system's granting of loans in the absence of a prior
increase in voluntary saving.

7

NATIONAL INCOME ACCOUNTING IS INADEQUATE TO REFLECT THE DIFFERENT STAGES IN THE BUSINESS CYCLE

The statistics of gross national product (GNP), and in general, the definitions and methodology of national income
accounting do not provide a reliable indication of economic
fluctuations. Indeed gross national product figures systematically conceal both the artificial expansionary effects of banks'
creation of loans and the tightening effects the crisis exerts on
the stages furthest from consumption.[19] This phenomenon can

---

[18]We are referring to involuntary (or institutional) unemployment, not
to the so-called "natural rate of unemployment" (or voluntary and
"catallactic" unemployment) which has grown so spectacularly in modern times as a result of generous unemployment compensation and
other measures which act as a strong disincentive to the desire of workers to return to work.

[19]See pp. 305–12 and 336 note 55. As Mark Skousen has pointed out:

   Gross Domestic Product systematically underestimates the
   expansionary phase as well as the contraction phase of the

be explained in the following manner: contrary to the very implications of the term gross, which is added to the expression "National Product," GNP is actually a *net* figure that excludes the value of all *intermediate* capital goods which at the end of the measurement period become available as inputs for the next financial year. Hence gross national product figures exaggerate the importance of consumption[20] over national

---

business cycle. For example, in the most recent recession, real GDP declined 1–2 percent in the United States, even though the recession was quite severe according to other measures (earnings, industrial production, employment). . . . A better indicator of total economic activity is Gross Domestic Output (GDO), a statistic I have developed to measure spending in all stages of production, including intermediate stages. According to my estimates, GDO declined at least 10–15 percent during most of the 1990–92 recession. (See "I Like Hayek: How I Use His Model as a Forecasting Tool," presented at The Mont Pèlerin Society General Meeting, which took place in Cannes, France, September 25–30, 1994, manuscript awaiting publication, p. 12.)

[20]Most conventional economists, along with political authorities and commentators on economic issues, tend to magnify the importance of the sector of consumer goods and services. This is primarily due to the fact that national income accounting measures tend to exaggerate the importance of consumption over total income, since they exclude most products manufactured in the intermediate stages of the production process, thus representing consumption as the most important sector of the economy. In modern economies this sector usually accounts for 60 to 70 percent of the entire national income, while it does not normally reach a third of the gross domestic output, if calculated in relation to the total spent in all stages of the productive structure. Moreover it is evident that Keynesian doctrines continue to strongly influence the methodology of the national income accounts as well as the statistical procedures used to collect the information necessary to prepare them. From a Keynesian standpoint, it is advantageous to magnify the role of consumption as an integral part of aggregate demand, thus centering national income accounting on this phenomenon, excluding from its calculations the portion of the gross domestic output which fails to fit well into Keynesian models and making no attempt to reflect the development of the different stages devoted to the production of intermediate capital goods, which is much more volatile and difficult to predict than consumption. On these interesting topics see Skousen, *The Structure of*

income, relegate to third place, after government expenditure, the production of *final* capital goods completed throughout the period (the only capital goods reflected in the GNP by definition) and absurdly exclude approximately half of all of society's entrepreneurial, labor and productive effort, that devoted to the manufacture of intermediate products.

The gross domestic output (GDO) of a financial year would be a much more precise indicator of the influence business cycles exert on the market and society. This measure would be calculated as described in tables from chapter 5, i.e., in *truly gross* terms, including *all* monetary spending, not merely that related to final goods and services, but all inter-mediate products manufactured in all stages in the production process. A measure of this sort would reveal the true effects exerted on the productive structure by credit expansion and by the economic recession it inevitably causes.[21]

Production, p. 306. According to a study carried out by the U.S. Depart-ment of Commerce, entitled, "The Interindustry Structure of the United States," and published in 1986, 43.8 percent of the American gross domestic output (3,297,977 million dollars) comprised intermediate products which were not reflected by GDP figures (merely equal to 56.2 percent of the gross domestic output, i.e., 4,235,116 million dollars). See Arthur Middleton Hughes, "The Recession of 1990: An Austrian Expla-nation," *Review of Austrian Economics* 10, no. 1 (1997): 108, note 4. Com-pare this data with that provided for 1982 in footnote 38 of chapter 5.

[21]Hayek, on the last pages of his 1942 article on the Ricardo Effect ("The Ricardo Effect," pp. 251–54), examines the ways in which traditional consumer price index statistics tend to obscure or prevent the empirical description of the evolution of the cycle, in general, and of the operation of the Ricardo Effect during the cycle, in particular. In fact the statistics in use do not reflect price changes in the products manufactured in the different stages of the production process, nor the relationship which exists in each stage between the price paid for the original factors of pro-duction involved and the price of the products made. Fortunately recent statistical studies have in all cases confirmed the Austrian analysis, revealing how the price of goods from the stages furthest from con-sumption is much more volatile than the price of consumer goods. Mark Skousen, in his (already cited) article presented before the general meet-ing of the Mont Pèlerin Society of September 25–30, 1994 in Cannes, showed that in the United States over the preceding fifteen years the

8
ENTREPRENEURSHIP AND THE THEORY OF THE CYCLE

The conception of entrepreneurship developed by Ludwig von Mises, Friedrich A. Hayek, and Israel M. Kirzner lies at the very root of a theory of entrepreneurship which we have presented elsewhere.[22] An entrepreneur is any human actor who performs each of his actions with shrewdness, remains alert to the opportunities for subjective profit which arise in his environment and tries to act so as to take advantage of them. Human beings' innate entrepreneurial capacity not only leads them to constantly *create* new information concerning their ends and means, but also spontaneously triggers a process by which this information tends to *spread* throughout society, accompanied by the spontaneous *coordination* of disparate human behaviors. The coordinating capacity of entrepreneurship sparks the emergence, evolution and coordinated development of human society and civilization, as long as entrepreneurial action is not systematically coerced (interventionism and socialism) nor are entrepreneurs obliged to act in an environment in which traditional legal norms are not respected because the government has granted privileges to certain social groups. When entrepreneurship cannot be incorporated into a framework of general legal principles or is systematically coerced, not only does it cease to create and transmit a large volume of social information, but it also generates corrupt and distorted information and provokes discoordinated

---

price of the goods *furthest* from consumption had oscillated between a +30 percent increase and a –10 percent decrease, depending on the year and the stage of the cycle; while the price of products from the intermediate stages had fluctuated between +14 percent and –1 percent, depending on the particular stage in the cycle, and the price of consumer goods vacillated between +10 percent and –2 percent, depending on the particular stage. These results are also confirmed by V.A. Ramey's important article, "Inventories as Factors of Production and Economic Fluctuations," *American Economic Review* (June 1989): 338–54.

[22]See Huerta de Soto, *Socialismo, cálculo económico y función empresarial*, chaps. 2 and 3.

and irresponsible behaviors. From this point of view our theory of the cycle could be considered *an application of the more general theory of entrepreneurship to the specific case of the intertemporal discoordination (i.e., between different time periods) which follows from banking activity not subject to general legal principles* and therefore based on the privilege of granting loans unbacked by a prior rise in voluntary saving (the monetary bank-deposit contract with a fractional reserve). Hence our theory explains how the violation of legal principles, which invariably causes serious social discoordination, exerts the same effect in a field as complex and abstract as that of money and bank credit. Thus economic theory has made it possible to connect legal and economic phenomena (the granting of privileges in violation of legal principles; and crises and recessions) which until now were thought to be completely unrelated.

One might wonder how entrepreneurs can possibly fail to recognize that the theory of the cycle developed by economists and presented here pertains to them, and to modify their behavior by ceasing to accept the loans they receive from the banking sector and avoiding investment projects which, in many cases, will bankrupt them. However, entrepreneurs cannot refrain from participating in the widespread process of discoordination bank credit expansion sets in motion, even if they have a perfect theoretical understanding of how the cycle will develop. This is due to the fact that individual entrepreneurs do not know whether or not a loan offered them originates from growth in society's voluntary saving. In addition though hypothetically they might suspect the loan to be created *ex nihilo* by the bank, they have no reason to refrain from requesting the loan and using it to expand their investment projects, *if they believe they will be able to withdraw from them before the onset of the inevitable crisis.* In other words the possibility of earning considerable entrepreneurial profit exists for those entrepreneurs who, though aware the entire process is based on an artificial boom, are shrewd enough to withdraw from it in time and to liquidate their projects and companies before the crisis hits. (This is, for instance, what Richard Cantillon did, as we saw in chapter 2.) Therefore the entrepreneurial spirit itself, and the profit motive on which it rests, destines entrepreneurs to participate in the cycle even when they are aware of the theory concerning it. Logically no one can predict precisely when and where the crisis will erupt, and a large number of entrepreneurs will undoubtedly be "surprised" by the event and will encounter serious difficulties. Nonetheless, in advance, from a theoretical standpoint, we can never describe as "irrational" those entrepreneurs who, though familiar with the theory of the cycle, get carried away by the new money they receive, funds which the banking system has created from nothing, and which from the start provide the entrepreneurs with a great additional ability to pay and the chance to make handsome profits.[23]

Another connection links the theory of entrepreneurship to the theory of the business cycle, and it involves the stage of recession and readjustment in which the grave errors committed in earlier phases of the cycle are exposed. Indeed economic recessions are the periods in which historically the seeds of the greatest entrepreneurial fortunes have been sown. This phenomenon is due to the fact that the deepest stages of the recession are accompanied by an abundance of capital goods produced in error, goods with a market price reduced to a fraction of its original amount. Therefore the opportunity to make a large entrepreneurial profit presents

---

[23]However Mises makes the following astute observation:

> it may be that businessmen will in the future react to credit expansion in a manner other than they have in the past. It may be that they will avoid using for an expansion of their operations the easy money available because they will keep in mind the inevitable end of the boom. Some signs forebode such a change. But it is too early to make a definite statement. (Mises, *Human Action*, p. 797)

Nevertheless, for reasons supplied in the main text, this augural presentation Mises made in 1949 of the hypothesis of *rational expectations* is not entirely justified, considering that even when entrepreneurs have a perfect understanding of the theory of the cycle and wish to avoid being trapped by it, they will always continue to be tempted to participate in it by the excellent profits they can bring in if they are perceptive enough to withdraw in time from the corresponding investment projects. On this topic, see also the section entitled, "A Brief Note on the Theory of Rational Expectations" from chapter 7 in this volume, pp. 535–42.

itself to those entrepreneurs shrewd enough to arrive at this recession stage in the cycle with liquidity and to very selectively acquire those capital goods which have lost nearly all of their commercial value but which will again be considered very valuable once the economy recovers. Hence entrepreneurship is essential to salvaging whatever can be saved and to getting the best possible use, depending upon the circumstances, from those capital goods produced in error, by selecting and keeping them for the more or less distant future in which the economy will have recovered and they can again be useful to society.

9

THE POLICY OF GENERAL-PRICE-LEVEL STABILIZATION AND ITS DESTABILIZING EFFECTS ON THE ECONOMY

Theorists are particularly interested in the following question, which has carried practical significance in the past and appears to be acquiring it again: If the banking system brings about credit expansion unbacked by real saving, and as a result the money supply increases, but just enough to maintain the purchasing power of money (or the "general price level"), then does the recession we are analyzing in this chapter follow? This question applies to those economic periods in which productivity jumps due to the introduction of new technologies and entrepreneurial innovations, and to the accumulation of capital wisely invested by diligent, insightful entrepreneurs.[24] As we have seen, when bank credit is not

---

[24]This appears to be the case of the American economic boom of the late 1990s, when to a large extent the upsurge in productivity hid the negative, distorting effects of great monetary, credit and stock market expansion. The parallel with the development of economic events in the 1920s is striking, and quite possibly, the process will again be interrupted by a recession, which will again surprise all who merely concentrate their analysis on the evolution of the "general price level" and other macroeconomic measures that conceal the underlying microeconomic situation (disproportion in the real productive structure of the economy). At the time of this writing (the end of 1997), the first symptoms of a new recession have already manifested themselves, at least

artificially expanded and the quantity of money in circulation remains more or less constant, growth in voluntary saving gives rise to a widening (lateral) and lengthening (longitudinal) of the capital goods stages in the productive structure. These stages can be completed with no problem, and once concluded, they yield a new rise in the quantity and quality of final consumer goods and services. This increased production of consumer goods and services must be sold to a decreased monetary demand (which has fallen by precisely the amount saving has risen), and consequently the unit prices of consumer goods and services tend to decline. This reduction is always more rapid than the possible drop in the nominal income of the owners of the original means of production, whose income therefore increases very significantly in real terms.

The issue we now raise is whether or not a policy aimed at increasing the money supply by credit expansion or another procedure, and *at maintaining the price level of consumer goods and services constant*, triggers the processes which lead to intertemporal discoordination among the different economic agents, and ultimately, to economic crisis and recession. The American economy faced such a situation throughout the 1920s, when dramatic growth in productivity was nevertheless not accompanied by the natural decline in the prices of consumer goods and services. These prices did not fall, due to the expansionary policy of the American banking system, a policy orchestrated by the Federal Reserve to stabilize the purchasing power of money (i.e., to prevent it from rising).[25]

---

through the serious banking, stock market, and financial crises which have erupted in Asian markets. [The evolution of the world economy since 1998 has confirmed entirely the analysis of this book as already mentioned in its Preface to the 2nd English edition.]

[25]See, for example, Murray N. Rothbard's detailed analysis of this historical period in his notable book, *America's Great Depression*, 5th ed. (Auburn, Ala.: Ludwig von Mises Institute, 2000). Mises (*Human Action*, p. 561) indicates that in the past, economic crises have generally hit during periods of continual improvement in productivity, due to the fact that

At this point it should be evident that a policy of credit expansion unbacked by real saving must inevitably set in motion all of the processes leading to the eruption of the economic crisis and recession, even when expansion coincides with an increase in the system's productivity and nominal prices of consumer goods and services do not rise. Indeed the issue is not the *absolute* changes in the general price level of consumer goods, but how these changes evolve *in relative terms* with respect to the prices of the intermediate products from the stages furthest from consumption and of the original means of production. In fact in the 1929 crisis, the relative prices of consumer goods (which in nominal terms did not rise and even fell slightly) escalated in comparison with the prices of capital goods (which plummeted in nominal terms). In addition the overall income (and hence, profits) of the companies close to

---

[t]he steady advance in the accumulation of new capital made technological improvement possible. Output per unit of input was increased and business filled the markets with increasing quantities of cheap goods.

Mises explains that this phenomenon tends to partially counteract the rise in prices which follows from an increase in credit expansion, and that in certain situations the price of consumer goods may even fall instead of rise. He concludes:

As a rule the resultant of the clash of opposite forces was a preponderance of those producing the rise in prices. But there were some exceptional instances too in which the upward movement of prices was only slight. The most remarkable example was provided by the American boom of 1926–29.

In any case Mises warns against policies of general price level stabilization, not only because they mask credit expansion during periods of increasing productivity, but also due to the theoretical error they contain:

It is a popular fallacy to believe that perfect money should be neutral and endowed with unchanging purchasing power, and that the goal of monetary policy should be to realize this perfect money. It is easy to understand this idea . . . against the still more popular postulates of the inflationists. But it is an excessive reaction, it is in itself confused and contradictory, and it has worked havoc because it was strengthened by an inveterate error inherent in the thought of many philosophers and economists. (*Human Action*, p. 418)

consumption soared throughout the final years of the expansion, as a result of the substantial increase in their productivity. Their goods were sold at constant nominal prices in an environment of great inflationary expansion. Therefore the factors which typically trigger the recession (relative growth in profits in consumption and a mounting interest rate), including the "Ricardo Effect," are equally present in an environment of rising productivity, insofar as increased profits and sales in the consumer sector (more than the jump in nominal prices, which at that point did not take place) reveal the decline in the relative cost of labor in that sector.

The theoretical articles Hayek wrote on the occasion of his first scholarly trip to the United States in the 1920s were aimed at analyzing the effects of the policy of stabilizing the monetary unit. Fisher and other monetarists sponsored the policy, and at that time its effects were considered harmless and very beneficial to the economic system. Upon analyzing the situation in the United States, Hayek arrives at the opposite conclusion and presents it in his well-known article, "Intertemporal Price Equilibrium and Movements in the Value of Money," published in 1928.[26] There Hayek demonstrates that a policy

---

[26]The article was first printed in German with the title, "Das intertemporale Gleichgewichtssystem der Preise und die Bewegungen des 'Geldwertes,'" and published in *Weltwirtschaftliches Archiv* 2 (1928): 36–76. It was not translated nor published in English until 1984, when it was included in the book, *Money, Capital and Fluctuations: Early Essays*, pp. 71–118. A second English translation, by William Kirby, appeared in 1994. It is superior to the first and is entitled, "The System of Intertemporal Price Equilibrium and Movements in the 'Value of Money,'" chapter 27 of *Classics in Austrian Economics: A Sampling in the History of a Tradition*, Israel M. Kirzner, ed., vol. 3: *The Age of Mises and Hayek* (London: William Pickering, 1994), pp. 161–98. Prior to this article, Hayek dealt with the same topic in "Die Währungspolitik der Vereinigten Staaten seit der Überwindung der Krise von 1920," *Zeitschrift für Volkswirtschaft und Sozialpolitik* 5 (1925): vols. 1–3, pp. 25–63 and vols. 4–6, pp. 254–317. The theoretical portion of this article has appeared in English with the title, "The Monetary Policy of the United States after the Recovery from the 1920 Crisis," in *Money, Capital and Fluctuations: Early Essays*, pp. 5–32. Here Hayek first criticizes the stabilization policies adopted in the United States.

of stabilizing the purchasing power of the monetary unit is incompatible with the necessary function of money with respect to coordinating the decisions and behaviors of economic agents at different points in time. Hayek explains that if the quantity of money in circulation remains constant, then in order to maintain intertemporal equilibrium among the actions of the different economic agents, widespread growth in the productivity of the economic system must give rise to a drop in the price of consumer goods and services, i.e., in the general price level. Thus a policy which prevents an upsurge in productivity from reducing the price of consumer goods and services inevitably generates expectations on the maintenance of the price level in the future. These expectations invariably lead to an artificial lengthening of the productive structure, a modification bound to reverse in the form of a recession. Although in 1928 Hayek had yet to make his polished contributions of the 1930s, writings which we have used in our analysis and which make this phenomenon much easier to understand, it is especially commendable that at that point he arrived at the following conclusion (in his own words):

> [I]t must be assumed, in sharpest contradiction to the prevailing view, that it is not a deficiency in the stability of the purchasing power of money that constitutes one of the most important sources of disturbances of the economy from the side of money. On the contrary, it is the tendency peculiar to all commodity currencies to stabilize the purchasing power of money even when the general state of supply is changing, a tendency alien to all the fundamental determinants of economic activity.[27]

---

[27]F.A. Hayek, "Intertemporal Price Equilibrium and Movements in the Value of Money," p. 97; italics removed. Even more specifically, Hayek concludes that

> [t]here is no basis in economic theory for the view that the quantity of money must be adjusted to changes in the economy if economic equilibrium is to be maintained or—what signifies the same—if monetary disturbances to the economy are to be prevented. (p. 106)

Hence it is not surprising that F.A. Hayek and the other theorists of his school during the latter half of the 1920s, upon examining the expansionary monetary policy of the United States (which, nonetheless, given the increase in productivity, did not manifest itself as a rise in prices), were the only ones capable not only of correctly interpreting the largely artificial nature of the expansionary American boom and its accompanying impact in the form of what appeared to be unlimited growth in the New York stock market indexes, but also of predicting, against the tide and to the surprise of all, the arrival of the Great Depression of 1929.[28] Therefore we can conclude with Fritz Machlup that

---

[28]See Mark Skousen, "Who Predicted the 1929 Crash?" included in *The Meaning of Ludwig von Mises*, Jeffrey M. Herbener, ed. (Amsterdam: Kluwer Academic Publishers, 1993), pp. 247–84. Lionel Robbins, in his "Foreword" to the first edition of *Prices and Production* (p. xii), also expressly refers to the prediction of Mises and Hayek of the arrival of the Great Depression. This prediction appeared in writing in an article by Hayek published in 1929 in *Monatsberichte des Österreichischen Instituts für Konjunkturforschung*. More recently, in 1975, Hayek was questioned on this subject and answered the following (*Gold & Silver Newsletter* [Newport Beach, Calif.: Monex International, June 1975]):

I was one of the only ones to predict what was going to happen. In early 1929, when I made this forecast, I was living in Europe which was then going through a period of depression. I said that there [would be] no hope of a recovery in Europe until interest rates fell, and interest rates would not fall until the American boom collapses, which I said was likely to happen within the next few months. What made me expect this, of course, is one of my main theoretical beliefs, that you cannot indefinitely maintain an inflationary boom. Such a boom creates all kinds of artificial jobs that might keep going for a fairly long time but sooner or later must collapse. Also, I was convinced after 1927, when the Federal Reserve made an attempt to stave off a collapse by credit expansion, the boom had become a typically inflationary one. So in early 1929 there was every sign that the boom was going to break down. I knew by then that the Americans could not prolong this sort of expansion indefinitely, and as soon as the Federal Reserve was no longer to feed it by more inflation, the thing would collapse. In addition, you must remember that at the time the Federal Reserve was not only unwilling but was unable to

[t]he creation of new circulating media so as to keep constant a price level which would otherwise have fallen in
response to technical progress, may have the same unstabi-
lizing effect on the supply of money capital that has been
described before, and thus be liable to lead to a crisis. In
spite of their stabilizing effect on the price level, the emergence of the new circulating media in the form of money
capital may cause roundabout processes of production to be
undertaken which cannot in the long run be maintained.[29]

Though in the past these considerations could be thought
of little practical importance, given the chronic increase in the
general price level in western economies, today they are again
significant and demonstrate that even with a policy of monetary "stability" guaranteed by central banks, in an environment of soaring productivity economic crises will inevitably

---

> continue the expansion because the gold standard set a limit
> to the possible expansion. Under the gold standard, therefore,
> an inflationary boom could not last very long.

This entire process, which Austrian economists found so easy to understand and predict because they already had the necessary analytical
tools, took place in an environment in which the general price level of
consumer goods not only did not rise, but tended to fall slightly. In fact
in the 1920s the general price level in the United States was very stable:
the index went from 93.4 (100 in the base year, 1926) in June 1921, to 104.5
in November 1925, and fell again to 95.2 in June 1929. However during
this seven-year period, the money supply grew from 45.3 to 73.2 trillion
dollars, i.e., more than 61 percent. See Rothbard, *America's Great Depression*, pp. 88 and 154. Rothbard, with his natural insight, concludes:

> The ideal of a stable price level is relatively innocuous during
> a price rise when it can aid sound money advocates in trying
> to check the boom; but it is highly mischievous when prices
> are tending to sag, and the stabilizationists call for inflation.
> And yet, stabilization is always a more popular rallying cry
> when prices are falling. (p. 158)

Incidentally a great parallel exists between the situation Hayek
described and that which is developing seventy years later, at the time
of this writing (1997). Thus the American economic and stock-market
boom may soon very possibly reverse in the form of a worldwide recession (which has already begun to manifest itself in Asian markets).

[29]Machlup, *The Stock Market, Credit and Capital Formation*, p. 177.

hit if all credit expansion is not prevented. Thus in the near future these considerations may very well regain their very important practical significance. At any rate, they are of great use in understanding many economic cycles of the past (the most consequential of which was the Great Depression of 1929), and as an application of the theoretical conclusions of our analysis.[30]

---

[30]Gottfried Haberler demonstrated that a fall in the general price level caused by improvements in all lines of production does not lead to the same adverse consequences as monetary deflation. See his monograph, *Der Sinn der Indexzahlen: Eine Untersuchung über den Begriff des Preisniveaus und die Methoden seiner Messung* (Tübingen: Verlag von J.C.B. Mohr [Paul Siebeck], 1927), pp. 112ff. See also his article, "Monetary Equilibrium and the Price Level in a Progressive Economy," published in *Economica* (February 1935): 75–81 (this article has been reprinted in Gottfried Haberler, *The Liberal Economic Order*, vol. 2: *Money and Cycles and Related Things*, Anthony Y.C. Koo, ed. [Aldershot: Edward Elgar, 1993], pp. 118–25). Gottfried Haberler later qualified his position on the Austrian theory of the business cycle. This led some to believe, in our opinion unjustifiably, that Haberler had recanted his position entirely. The most substantial concession he made consisted of the statement that the theorists of the Austrian School had not *rigorously* shown that the stabilization of prices in an improving economy would necessarily *always* lead to an economic crisis (see Haberler, *Prosperity and Depression*, pp. 56–57). Furthermore Haberler did not base his change of opinion on any theoretical consideration, but merely on the possibility that during the evolution of the cycle, additional, unforeseen phenomena might occur (such as an increase in voluntary saving, etc.), which would tend to neutralize to an extent the forces indicated by the economic analysis. Therefore it is the responsibility of Haberler and his supporters to explain, in reference to each specific cycle, what particular circumstances may have neutralized the typical effects of credit expansion, effects, on the whole, predicted by the Austrians, whose formal theory Haberler and his followers have not been able to discredit at all (see also our comments on the similar thesis of D. Laidler, in chapter 7, pp. 528–30). Another author of relevant work is L. Albert Hahn, who, in his book, *Common Sense Economics* (New York: Abelard-Schumann, 1956, p. 128), asks whether or not a rise in productivity justifies a policy of inflationary credit expansion. He arrives at the conclusion that such a policy, which generates *inflation without inflation* and is generally considered totally harmless, can have very disturbing effects and cause a deep economic crisis. According to Hahn, theorists who consider such a policy innocuous err because they "overlook the fact that productivity

10
HOW TO AVOID BUSINESS CYCLES: PREVENTION OF
AND RECOVERY FROM THE ECONOMIC CRISIS

At this point we can easily deduce that once banks have initiated a policy of credit expansion, or the money supply has increased in the form of new loans granted without the support of new voluntary saving, processes which eventually provoke a crisis and recession are spontaneously triggered. Thus economic crises and depressions *cannot be avoided* when credit expansion has taken place. The only possible measure is to *prevent* the process from beginning, by precluding the adoption of policies of credit expansion or of growth in the money supply in the shape of new bank loans. The final chapter of this book contains an explanation of the institutional modifications necessary to immunize modern economies against the successive stages of boom and recession they regularly undergo. These institutional reforms essentially involve restoring banking to the traditional legal principles which regulate the contract of irregular deposit of fungible goods and which require the continuous maintenance of the *tantundem*; in other words, a 100-percent reserve requirement. This is the only way to guarantee that the system will not independently initiate any credit expansion unbacked by real saving, and that the loans granted will always originate from a prior increase in society's voluntary saving. Thus entrepreneurs will only undertake the lengthening of the productive structure when, barring unusual circumstances, they are able to complete and maintain it in the absence of systematic discoordination between the entrepreneurial decisions of investors and those of the other economic agents with respect to the amount and proportion of their income they wish to consume and save.

---

increases mean profit increases for the entrepreneurs as long as costs— for labor as well as for capital—are not fully raised accordingly." Hence Murray Rothbard concludes that the important factor is not so much the evolution of the general price level, but whether via a policy of credit expansion the interest rate is reduced to a level lower than the one which would prevail in a free market in the absence of such a policy (*Man, Economy, and State*, pp. 862–63).

Assuming credit expansion has taken place in the past, we know the economic crisis will inevitably hit, regardless of any attempts to postpone its arrival through the injection of new doses of credit expansion at a progressively increasing rate. In any case the eruption of the crisis and recession ultimately constitutes the beginning of the *recovery*. In other words the economic recession is the start of the *recovery* stage, since it is the phase in which the errors committed are revealed, the investment projects launched in error are liquidated, and labor and the rest of the productive resources begin to be transferred toward those sectors and stages where consumers value them most. Just as a hangover is a sign of the body's healthy reaction to the assault of alcohol, an economic recession marks the beginning of the recovery period, which is as healthy and necessary as it is painful. This period results in a productive structure more in tune with the true wishes of consumers.[31]

The recession hits when credit expansion slows or stops and as a result, the investment projects launched in error are liquidated, the productive structure narrows and its number of stages declines, and workers and other original means of production employed in the stages furthest from consumption, where they are no longer profitable, are laid off or no longer demanded. Recovery is consolidated when economic agents, in general, and consumers, in particular, decide to reduce their consumption in relative terms and to increase their saving in order to repay their loans and face the new stage of economic uncertainty and recession. The boom and

---

[31] One point should be stressed: the *depression* phase is actually the *recovery* phase; . . . it is the time when bad investments are liquidated and mistaken entrepreneurs leave the market—the time when "consumer sovereignty" and the free market reassert themselves and establish once again an economy that benefits every participant to the maximum degree. The depression period ends when the free-market equilibrium has been restored and expansionary distortion eliminated. (Rothbard, *Man, Economy, and State*, p. 860)

Therefore even though upcoming Table VI-1 (pp. 506–07) distinguishes between the phases of "depression" and "recovery" as in the text, strictly speaking, the stage of depression marks the beginning of the true recovery.

the beginning of the readjustment are naturally followed by a drop in the interest rate. This drop arises from the reduction and even the disappearance of the premium based on the expectation of a decrease in the purchasing power of money, and also from the increased relative saving the recession provokes. The slowing of the frantic pace at which goods and services from the final stage are consumed, together with the rise in saving and the reorganization of the productive structure at all levels, furthers the recovery. Its effects initially appear in stock markets, which are generally the first to undergo a certain improvement. Moreover the real growth in wages which takes place during the stage of recovery sets the "Ricardo Effect" in motion, thus reviving investment in the stages furthest from consumption, where labor and productive resources are again employed. In this spontaneous manner the recovery concludes. It can be strengthened and maintained indefinitely in the absence of a new stage of credit expansion unbacked by real saving, an event which is usually repeated, giving rise to new recurring crises.[32]

Nevertheless now that we have established that economic crises cannot be avoided once the seeds of them are sown, and that the only alternative is to prevent them, what would be the most appropriate policy to apply once an inevitable crisis and recession have hit? The answer is simple if we remember the origin of the crisis and what the crisis implies: the need to readjust the productive structure and adapt it to consumers'

---

[32]A detailed study of recovery and its different phases can be found on pp. 38–82 of Hayek's book, *Profits, Interest and Investment*. See also pp. 315–17 of Skousen's book, *The Structure of Production*, where Skousen refers to a statement of Hayek's, according to which:

> It is a well-known fact that in a slump the revival of final demand is generally an effect rather than a cause of the revival in the upper reaches of the stream of production— activities generated by savings seeking investment and by the necessity of making up for postponed renewals and replacements. (Skousen, *The Structure of Production*, p. 315)

Hayek made this astute observation in the journal, *The Economist*, in an article printed June 11, 1983 and entitled "The Keynes Centenary: The Austrian Critic," no. 7293, p. 46.

true desire with regard to saving, to liquidate the investment projects undertaken in error and to massively transfer factors of production toward the stages and companies closest to consumption, where consumers demand they be employed. Therefore the only possible and advisable policy in the case of a crisis consists of *making the economy as flexible as possible*, particularly the different factor markets, and especially the labor market, so the adjustment can take place as quickly and with as little pain as possible. Hence the more rigid and controlled an economy is, the more prolonged and socially painful its readjustment will be. The errors and recession could even persist indefinitely, if it is institutionally impossible for economic agents to liquidate their projects and regroup their capital goods and factors of production more advantageously. Thus *rigidity is the chief enemy of recovery and any policy aimed at mitigating the crisis and initiating and consolidating recovery as soon as possible must center on the microeconomic goal of deregulating all factor markets, particularly the labor market, as much as possible, and on making them as flexible as possible.*[33]

This is the only measure advisable during the stage of economic crisis and recession, and it is particularly important to avoid any policies which, to a greater or lesser extent, actively hinder or prevent the necessary spontaneous process of readjustment.[34] Also to be especially avoided are certain measures

---

[33]As Ludwig M. Lachmann indicates,

> [w]hat is needed is a policy which promotes the necessary readjustments. . . . Capital regrouping is thus the necessary corrective for the maladjustment engendered by a strong boom. (*Capital and its Structure*, pp. 123 and 125)

[34]We agree with Murray N. Rothbard when he recommends that once the crisis erupts, the economy should be made as flexible as possible and the scope and influence of the state with respect to the economic system be reduced at all levels. In this way not only is entrepreneurship fostered in the sense that businessmen are encouraged to liquidate erroneous projects and appropriately redesign them, but a higher rate of social saving and investment is also promoted. According to Rothbard,

> Reducing taxes that bear most heavily on savings and investment will further lower social time preferences. Furthermore,

which always acquire great popularity and political support
during crises, in view of the socially painful nature of such
phenomena. The following are among the main steps which
are normally proposed and should be averted:

(a) The granting of new loans to companies from the
    capital goods stages to keep them from going
    through a crisis, suspending payments and having to

> depression is a time of economic strain. Any reduction of
> taxes, or of any regulations interfering with the free-market,
> will stimulate healthy economic activity.

He concludes,

> There is one thing the government can do positively, how-
> ever: it can drastically *lower* its relative role in the economy,
> slashing its own expenditures and taxes, particularly taxes
> that interfere with saving and investment. Reducing its tax-
> pending level will automatically shift the societal saving-
> investment-consumption ratio in favor of saving and invest-
> ment, thus greatly lowering the time required for returning to
> a prosperous economy. (*America's Great Depression*, p. 22)

Rothbard also provides us with a list of typical government measures
which are highly counterproductive and which, in any case, tend to prolong the depression and make it more painful. The list is as follows:

> (1) *Prevent or delay liquidation.* Lend money to shaky busi-
> nesses, call on banks to lend further, etc. (2) *Inflate further.* Fur-
> ther inflation blocks the necessary fall in prices, thus delaying
> adjustment and prolonging depression. Further credit expan-
> sion creates more malinvestments, which, in their turn, will
> have to be liquidated in some later depression. A government
> "easy-money" policy prevents the market's return to the nec-
> essary higher interest rates. (3) *Keep wage rates up.* Artificial
> maintenance of wage rates in a depression insures permanent
> mass unemployment. . . . (4) *Keep prices up.* Keeping prices
> above the free-market levels will create unsalable surpluses,
> and prevent a return to prosperity. (5) *Stimulate consumption
> and discourage saving.* . . . [M]ore saving and less consumption
> would speed recovery; more consumption and less saving
> aggravate the shortage of saved capital even further. . . . (6)
> *Subsidize unemployment.* Any subsidization of unemployment
> . . . will prolong unemployment indefinitely, and delay the
> shift of workers to the fields where jobs are available. (*Amer-
> ica's Great Depression*, p. 19)

reorganize. The granting of new loans simply post-pones the eruption of the crisis, while making the nec-essary subsequent readjustment much more severe and difficult. Furthermore, the systematic concession of new loans to repay the old ones delays the painful investment liquidations, postponing, even indefi-nitely, the arrival of the recovery. Therefore any policy of further credit expansion should be avoided.

(b) Also very harmful are the inappropriately-named policies of "full employment," which are intended to guarantee jobs to all workers. As Hayek very clearly states,

> [A]ll attempts to create full employment with the existing distribution of labour between industries will come up against the difficulty that with full employment people will want a larger share of the total output in the form of consumers' goods than is being produced in that form.[35]

Thus it is impossible for a government policy of spending and credit expansion to successfully protect all *current* jobs if workers spend their income, origi-nating from credit expansion and artificial demand from the public sector, in a way that requires a different productive structure, i.e., one incapable of keeping them in their current jobs. Any policy of artificially preserving jobs which is financed with inflation or credit expansion is *self-destructive*, insofar as con-sumers spend the new money created, once it reaches

---

[35]Hayek, *Profits, Interest and Investment*, p. 60. Hayek also mentions that the rate of unemployment fails to reflect differences between the various stages in production processes. He points out that normally, in the deep-est stage of the crisis, up to 25 or 30 percent of workers who dedicate their efforts to the stages furthest from consumption may be unem-ployed, while unemployment among workers from the stages closest to consumption is noticeably reduced, and may reach 5 or 10 percent. See also footnote 2 on pp. 59–60 of Hayek's book.

their pockets, in a way that makes it impossible for those very jobs to be profitable. Hence the only labor policy possible is to facilitate the dismissal and rehiring of workers by making labor markets highly flexible.

(c) Likewise, any policy aimed at restoring the status quo with respect to macroeconomic aggregates should also be avoided. Crises and recessions are by nature microeconomic, not macroeconomic, and thus such a policy is condemned to failure, to the extent it makes it difficult or impossible for entrepreneurs to review their plans, regroup their capital goods, liquidate their investment projects and rehabilitate their companies. As Ludwig M. Lachmann articulately puts it,

> [A]ny policy designed merely to restore the *status quo* in terms of "macro-economic" aggregate magnitudes, such as incomes and employment, is bound to fail. The state prior to the downturn was based on plans which have failed; hence a policy calculated to discourage entrepreneurs from revising their plans, but to make them "go ahead" with the same capital combinations as before, cannot succeed. Even if business men listen to such counsel they would simply repeat their former experience. What is needed is a policy which promotes the necessary readjustments.[36]

Therefore monetary policies intended to maintain at all costs the economic boom in the face of the early symptoms of an impending crisis (generally, a downturn in the stock market and real estate market), will not prevent the recession, even when they are sufficient to postpone its arrival.

(d) In addition the price of present goods in terms of future goods, which is reflected by the social rate of time preference, or the interest rate, should not be

---

[36]Lachmann, *Capital and its Structure*, p. 123.

manipulated. Indeed in the recovery phase the interest rate in the credit market will spontaneously tend to decline, given the drop in the price of consumer goods and the increase in saving brought about by the reorganization the recession entails. Nevertheless any manipulation of the market rate of interest is counterproductive and exerts a negative effect on the liquidation process or generates new entrepreneurial errors. In fact we can conclude with Hayek that any policy which tends to maintain interest rates at a fixed level will be highly detrimental to the stability of the economy, since interest rates must evolve spontaneously according to the real preferences of economic agents with respect to saving and consumption:

> [T]he tendency to keep the rates of interest stable, and especially to keep them low as long as possible, must appear as the arch-enemy of stability, causing in the end much greater fluctuations, probably even of the rate of interest, than are really necessary. Perhaps it should be repeated that this applies especially to the doctrine, now so widely accepted, that interest rates should be kept low till "full employment" in general is reached.[37]

(e) Finally any policy involving the creation of artificial jobs through public works or other investment projects financed by the government should be avoided. It is evident that if such projects are financed by taxes or via the issuance of public debt, they will simply draw resources away from those areas of the economy where consumers desire them and toward the public works financed by the government, thus creating a new layer of widespread malinvestment. Moreover if these works or "investments" are financed through the mere creation of new money, generalized malinvestment also takes place, in the sense that, if workers

---

[37]Hayek, *Profits, Interest and Investment*, p. 70.

employed through this procedure dedicate most of their income to consumption, the price of consumer goods tends to rise in relative terms, causing the delicate situation of companies from the stages furthest from consumption to deteriorate even further. In any case, in their contracyclical policies of public spending, it is nearly impossible for governments to resist the influence of all kinds of political pressures which tend to render these policies even more inefficient and harmful, as indicated by the conclusions of public-choice theory. Furthermore there is no guarantee that by the time governments diagnose the situation and decide to take the supposedly remedial measures, they will not err with respect to the timing or sequence of the different phenomena and tend with their measures to worsen rather than solve the maladjustments.[38]

11

THE THEORY OF THE CYCLE AND IDLE RESOURCES: THEIR ROLE IN THE INITIAL STAGES OF THE BOOM

Critics of the Austrian theory of the business cycle often argue that the theory is based on the assumption of the *full employment* of resources, and that therefore the existence of *idle resources* means credit expansion would not necessarily give rise to their widespread malinvestment. However this criticism is completely unfounded. As Ludwig M. Lachmann has insightfully revealed, the Austrian theory of the business cycle does not start from the assumption of full employment. On the contrary, almost from the time Mises began formulating the theory of the cycle, in 1928, he started from the premise that at any time a very significant volume of resources could

---

[38]On this topic see Ludwig von Mises, "The Chimera of Contracyclical Policies," pp. 798–800 of *Human Action*. See also the pertinent observations of Mark Skousen on "The Hidden Drawbacks of Public Works Projects," pp. 337–39 of his book, *The Structure of Production*.

be idle.[39] In fact Mises demonstrated from the beginning that the unemployment of resources was not only compatible with the theory he had developed, but was actually one of its essential elements. In market processes in which entrepreneurs undertake plans that involve the production of heterogeneous and complementary capital goods, errors are continually committed and due to "bottlenecks," not all productive factors and resources are fully employed. Thus the necessity of a flexible market conducive to the exercise of entrepreneurship, which tends to reveal existing maladjustments and restore coordination in a never-ending process. Indeed the theory explains how bank credit expansion interrupts and complicates the coordinating process by which existing maladjustments are remedied.[40]

---

[39]   [T]he Austrian theory does not, as is often suggested, assume "Full Employment." It assumes that in general, at any moment, some factors are scarce, some abundant. It also assumes that, for certain reasons connected with the production and planned use of capital goods, some of these scarcities become more pronounced during the upswing. Those who criticize the theory on the ground mentioned merely display their inability to grasp the significance of a fundamental fact in the world in which we are living: the heterogeneity of all resources. Unemployment of some factors is not merely compatible with Austrian theory; unemployment of those factors whose complements cannot come forward in the conditions planned is an essential feature of it. (Lachmann, *Capital and its Structure*, pp. 113–14)

[40]In 1928 Mises stated:

At times, even on the unhampered market, there are some unemployed workers, unsold consumers' goods and quantities of unused factors of production, which would not exist under "static equilibrium." With the revival of business and productive activity, these reserves are in demand right away. However, once they are gone, the increase of the supply of fiduciary media necessarily leads to disturbances of a special kind. (Mises, *On the Manipulation of Money and Credit*, p. 125)

This is the English translation of a passage found on p. 49 of the book Mises originally published in Jena in 1928. It is entitled, *Geldwertstabilisierung und Konjunkturpolitik*. Hayek, in his book, *Profits, Interest and Investment*, pp. 3–73, presents his theory of the business cycle, starting

The theory of the business cycle teaches precisely that credit expansion unbacked by an increase in real saving will encourage the malinvestment of productive resources *even when there is a significant volume of idle resources, specifically, unemployed labor.* In other words, contrary to opinions expressed by many critics of the theory, full employment is not a prerequisite of the microeconomic distortions of credit expansion. When credit expansion takes place, economic projects which are not actually profitable appear so, regardless of whether they are carried out with resources that were unemployed prior to their commencement. The only effect is that the nominal price of the original means of production may not rise as much as it would if full employment existed beforehand. Nevertheless the other factors which give rise to malinvestment and a spontaneous reversal, in the form of a crisis and recession, of the errors committed eventually appear, regardless of whether the errors have been committed with originally-unemployed resources.

An artificial boom based on bank credit expansion which reallocates previously-unemployed original means of production merely interrupts the process of readjustment of those factors, a process not yet complete. Consequently a new layer of widespread malinvestment of resources overlaps a previous layer which has yet to be completely liquidated and reabsorbed by the market.

Another possible effect of the use of previously-idle resources is the following: apart from the fact that their price does not increase as rapidly in absolute terms, they may make a short-term slowdown in the production of consumer goods and services unnecessary. Nonetheless a poor allocation of resources still takes place, since resources are invested in unprofitable projects, and the effects of the cycle eventually appear when the monetary income of the previously-unemployed original means of production begins to be spent on

---

from the existence of idle resources. There he expressly reminds us that from the time Mises began developing the theory of the cycle in 1928, he assumed some labor and other resources would be unemployed (see also the footnote 1 on p. 42).

consumer goods and services. The relative prices of these goods and services rise more rapidly than the prices of products from the stages furthest from consumption, thus diminishing real relative wages and setting off the "Ricardo Effect" and the other effects which lead to crisis and recession. In any case credit expansion will always, from the outset, cause a more-than-proportional increase in the relative price of products from the stages furthest from consumption. This rise stems from the new monetary demand credit generates for these goods and from the artificial reduction in the interest rate, which makes such projects more attractive. This results in a lengthening of the productive structure, a change which cannot be maintained in the long run and which is completely independent of whether previously-idle resources have been used in some of such projects.

Therefore the common argument that the theory developed by Mises, Hayek, and the Austrian School rests on the existence of a full employment of resources is fallacious. Even if we suppose high unemployment exists, the credit expansion process invariably leads to a recession.[41]

---

41   Thus it becomes obvious how vain it is to justify a new credit expansion by referring to unused capacity, unsold—or, as people say incorrectly, "unsalable"—stocks, and unemployed workers. The beginning of a new credit expansion runs across remainders of preceding malinvestment and malemployment, not yet obliterated in the course of the readjustment process, and seemingly remedies the faults involved. In fact, however, this is merely an interruption of the process of readjustment and of the return to sound conditions. The existence of unused capacity and unemployment is not a valid argument against the correctness of the circulation credit theory. (Mises, *Human Action*, p. 580)

Hayek arrives at a similar conclusion, though his reasoning differs slightly:

If the proportion as determined by the voluntary decisions of individuals is distorted by the creation of artificial demand, it must mean that part of the available resources is again led into a wrong direction and a definite and lasting adjustment is again postponed. And, even if the absorption of the unemployed resources were to be quickened in this way, it would

12

THE NECESSARY TIGHTENING OF CREDIT IN THE RECESSION STAGE: CRITICISM OF THE THEORY OF "SECONDARY DEPRESSION"

We will now consider three different types of *deflation*, defined as any decrease in the quantity of money "in circulation."[42] Deflation consists of a drop in the money supply or a rise in the demand for money, and other things being equal, it tends to cause an increase in the purchasing power of the monetary unit (i.e., a decline in the "general price level"). Nevertheless it is important to avoid confusing deflation with its most typical, pronounced effect (the fall in the general price level), given that in certain cases the prices of goods and services decrease in the absence of deflation. As we have seen, this is part of the healthy growth process of an economy whose productivity is improving due to the incorporation of new technologies and to capital accumulation which arises from the entrepreneurial spirit and from the natural increase in the voluntary saving of its agents. We studied this process in previous sections, and without any decrease in the quantity of money in circulation, it gives rise to a widespread increase in the production of consumer goods and services, which can only be sold at lower prices. Thus the process results in a real rise in wages and in the income of the other original means of

---

only mean that the seed would already be sown for new disturbances and new crises. The only way permanently to "mobilise" all available resources is, therefore, not to use artificial stimulants—whether during the crisis or thereafter—but to leave it to time to effect a permanent cure by the slow process of adapting the structure of production to the means available for capital purposes. (Hayek, *Prices and Production*, pp. 98–99)

Mark Skousen also makes some very shrewd observations on this subject in his book, *The Structure of Production*, pp. 289–90.

[42]This expression, though quite vivid, is not theoretically rigorous, since money is never "in circulation," but always forms part of the cash balances of someone.

production, because although the income of workers and of the other owners of original factors may remain fairly constant in nominal terms, the prices of the consumer goods and services workers acquire drop considerably. In this case the decline in the general price level is not monetary in origin, but real,[43] and it derives from the generalized increase in the productivity of the economy. Hence this phenomenon is completely unrelated to deflation as we have defined it, and is simply a sign of the healthiest and most natural process of economic development.

Nonetheless we will now examine *three distinct types of deflation* (strictly defined as any decline in the supply of or increase in the demand for money) which have radically different causes and consequences. Let us analyze these types of deflation in detail:[44]

---

[43]See the section entitled, "Cash-Induced and Goods-Induced Changes in Purchasing Power," from chapter 17 of Mises, *Human Action*, 3rd ed., pp. 419ff.

[44]In short we attempt to fill an important theoretical gap in the economic theory of deflation. In 1933 Ludwig von Mises revealed this gap when he stated,

> Unfortunately, economic theory is weakest precisely where help is most needed—in analyzing the effects of declining prices. . . . Yet today, even more than ever before, the rigidity of wage rates and the costs of many other factors of production hamper an unbiased consideration of the problem. Therefore, it would certainly be timely now to investigate thoroughly the effects of declining money prices and to analyze the widely held idea that declining prices are incompatible with the increased production of goods and services and an improvement in general welfare. The investigation should include a discussion of whether it is true that only inflationistic steps permit the progressive accumulation of capital and productive facilities. So long as this naive inflationist theory of development is firmly held, proposals for using credit expansion to produce a boom will continue to be successful.

Ludwig von Mises, "Die Stellung und der nächste Zukunft der Konjunkturforschung," published in *Festschrift in honor of Arthur Spiethoff* (Munich: Duncker and Humblot, 1933), pp. 175–80, and translated into English as "The Current Status of Business Cycle Research and its Prospects for the Immediate Future," published in *On the Manipulation of Money and Credit*, pp. 207–13 (the excerpt is taken from pp. 212–13).

(a) The first type consists of policies adopted by public authorities to deliberately reduce the quantity of money in circulation. Such policies have been implemented on various historical occasions[45] and trigger a process by which the purchasing power of the monetary unit tends to increase. Moreover this forced decrease in the quantity of money in circulation distorts the structure of society's productive stages. Indeed the reduction in the quantity of money initially brings about a decline in loan concession and an artificial increase in the market interest rate, which in turn leads to a flattening of the productive structure, a modification forced by strictly monetary factors (and not by the true desires of consumers). Consequently many profitable capital goods stages in the productive structure erroneously appear unprofitable (especially those furthest from consumption and most capital-intensive). As a result the most specialized companies in capital-intensive sectors sustain widespread accounting losses. Furthermore in all sectors the reduced monetary demand is unaccompanied by a parallel, equally-rapid decline in costs, and thus accounting losses arise and pessimism becomes generalized. In addition the increase in the purchasing power of the monetary unit and the decrease in the products' selling price cause a substantial rise in the real income of the owners of the original means of production, who, to the extent their prices are rigid and do not fall at the same rate as those of consumer goods, will tend to become unemployed. Therefore a prolonged, painful adjustment period begins and lasts until the entire productive structure and all original factors have adjusted to the new monetary conditions.

---

[45]For example on May 13, 1925, Winston Churchill, at that time Chancellor of the Exchequer of the United Kingdom, decided to restore the pre-World War I gold parity of the pound sterling. In other words, the parity which had existed since 1717, when Sir Isaac Newton fixed it at 1 pound per 4.86 dollars of gold.

This whole process of *deliberate deflation* contributes nothing and merely subjects the economic system to unnecessary pressure. Regrettably, politicians' lack of theoretical knowledge has led them on various historical occasions to deliberately initiate such a process.[46]

---

[46]The most typical examples of deflation deliberately initiated by governments are found in the United Kingdom: first, following the Napoleonic wars, and then, as mentioned above, under the auspices of Winston Churchill in 1925 when, despite the tremendous inflation which affected pound sterling notes in World War I, he decided to restore the currency's prewar parity with gold. In short Churchill blatantly disregarded the advice Ricardo had given 100 years earlier in a very similar situation, following the Napoleonic wars: "I should never advise a government to restore a currency which had been depreciated 30 per cent to par." Letter from David Ricardo to John Wheatley, dated September 18, 1821, *The Works of David Ricardo*, Piero Sraffa, ed. (Cambridge: Cambridge University Press, 1952), vol. 9, p. 73. Ludwig von Mises, in reference to these two historical cases, states:

> The outstanding examples were provided by Great Britain's return, both after the wartime inflation of the Napoleonic wars and after that of the first World War, to the prewar gold parity of the sterling. In each case Parliament and Cabinet adopted the deflationist policy without having weighed the pros and cons of the two methods open for a return to the gold standard. In the second decade of the nineteenth century they could be exonerated, as at that time monetary theory had not yet clarified the problems involved. More than a hundred years later it was simply a display of inexcusable ignorance of economics as well as of monetary history. (Mises, *Human Action*, pp. 567–68 and also p. 784)

F.A. Hayek points out the grave error of returning to the pre-World War I parity between gold and the pound and also mentions that this policy was implemented slowly and gradually, instead of in the form of a rapid shock, as took place in the United States between 1920 and 1921. Hayek concludes:

> Though the clear determination of the government to restore the gold standard made it possible to do so as early as 1925, internal prices and wages were then still far from being adapted to the international level. To maintain this parity, a slow and highly painful process of deflation was initiated, bringing lasting and extensive unemployment, to be abandoned only when it became intolerable when intensified by

(b) The second type of deflation, which should be clearly distinguished from the first, occurs when economic agents decide to save; that is, to refrain from consuming a significant portion of their income and to devote all or part of the monetary total saved to increasing their cash balances (i.e., to *hoarding*).[47] In this case, the rise in the demand for money tends to push up the purchasing power of the monetary unit (in other words, it tends to push down the "general price level"). However this type of deflation differs radically from the former in the sense that it does make a contribution, since it originates from an increase in the saving of economic agents, who thus free resources in the form of unsold consumer goods and services. This provokes the effects we studied in chapter 5, where we considered a rise in voluntary saving. More specifically the "Ricardo Effect" appears, due to the drop in the relative prices of consumer goods, which in turn leads to an increase, other things being equal, in the real wages of workers and in the income of the other original means of production. Hence the processes which trigger a lengthening of the productive structure are set in motion. The productive structure becomes more capital-intensive, due to the new investment projects undertaken, projects entrepreneurs will be able to complete because productive

---

the world crisis of 1931—but, I am still inclined to believe, just at the time when the aim of that painful struggle had been nearly achieved. (F.A. Hayek, *1980s Unemployment and the Unions: The Distortion of Relative Prices by Monopoly in the Labour Markets*, 2nd ed. [London: Institute of Economic Affairs, 1984], p. 15. See also footnote 43 in chapter 8)

[47]It is also possible, in theory and in practice, for economic agents to raise their cash balances (demand for money) without at all modifying their volume of monetary consumption. They can do this by disinvesting in productive resources and selling capital goods. This leads to a flattening of the productive structure and brings about the widespread impoverishment of society through a process which is the exact opposite of the one we analyzed in chapter 5 with respect to a lengthening (financed by growth in voluntary saving) of the productive structure.

resources have been freed in the stages closest to consumption. The only difference between this situation and that of an increase in voluntary saving which is immediately and directly invested in the productive structure or capital markets is as follows: when saving manifests itself as a rise in cash balances, there is a necessary decline in the price of consumer goods and services and in the price of products from the intermediate stages, as well as an inevitable reduction in the nominal income of the original means of production and in wages, all of which adapt to the increased purchasing power of the monetary unit. Nevertheless unlike the first type of deflation mentioned, this type does not entail a painful process which contributes nothing. Instead here it is based on effective saving which causes a rise in society's productivity. The lengthening of the productive structure and the reallocation of the factors of production occur to the extent there is a change, as explained in chapter 5, in the relative prices of the products from the intermediate stages and from the final stage, consumption. Such a change is independent of whether, in *absolute, nominal terms*, all prices must drop (to a varying extent) as a consequence of the increased purchasing power of the monetary unit.[48]

---

[48]   Whenever an individual devotes a sum of money to saving instead of spending it for consumption, the process of saving agrees perfectly with the process of capital accumulation and investment. It does not matter whether the individual saver does or does not increase his cash holding. The act of saving always has its counterpart in a supply of goods produced and not consumed, of goods available for further production activities. A man's savings are always embodied in concrete capital goods. . . . The effect of our saver's saving, i.e., the surplus of goods produced over goods consumed, does not disappear on account of his hoarding. The prices of capital goods do not rise to the height they would have attained in the absence of such hoarding. But the fact that more capital goods are available is not affected by the striving of a number of people to increase their cash holdings. . . . The two

(c) The third type of deflation we will consider results
from the *tightening of credit* which normally occurs in
the crisis and recession stage that follows all credit
expansion. This process was mentioned in chapters 4
and 5, where we analyzed the following: just as credit
expansion increases the quantity of money in circulation, the massive repayment of loans and the loss of
value on the assets side of banks' balance sheets, both
caused by the crisis, trigger an inevitable, cumulative
process of credit tightening which reduces the quantity of money in circulation and thus generates deflation. This third type of deflation arises when, as the
crisis is emerging, not only does credit expansion stop
increasing, but there is actually a credit squeeze and
thus, deflation, or a drop in the money supply, or
quantity of money in circulation. Nevertheless this
sort of deflation differs from that analyzed in (a)
above and produces various *positive effects* which
merit our attention. First, deflation caused by the
tightening of credit does not give rise to the unnecessary maladjustments referred to in section (a); instead
it facilitates and accelerates the liquidation of the
investment projects launched in error during the
expansionary phase. Therefore it is the natural market
reaction necessary for a rapid liquidation of the
investment projects undertaken in error during the
expansionary stage. A second positive effect of credit
deflation is that it in a sense reverses the redistribution of income which took place in the expansionary
stage of the inflationary boom. In fact inflationary
expansion tended to bring about a decrease in the
purchasing power of money, which in turn reduced
the real income of everyone on a fixed income (savers,
widows, orphans, pensioners) in favor of those who
first received the loans of the banking system and first

---

processes—increased cash holding of some people and
increased capital accumulation—take place side by side.
(Mises, *Human Action*, pp. 521–22)

experienced an increase in monetary income. Now, in the stage of credit tightening, this forced redistribution of income reverses in favor of those who in the expansionary stage were the first harmed, and thus people on a fixed income (widows, orphans, and pensioners) will gain an advantage over those who most exploited the situation in the earlier stage. Third, credit deflation generally makes business ventures appear less profitable, since historical costs are recorded in monetary units with less purchasing power, and later, accounting income is recorded in monetary units with more purchasing power. As a result entrepreneurial profits are artificially diminished in account books, prompting entrepreneurs to save more and distribute less in the form of dividends (exactly the opposite of what they did in the expansionary phase). This tendency to save is highly favorable to the commencement of economic recovery.[49] The decline, provoked by the tightening of credit, in the quantity of money in circulation undoubtedly tends to drive up the purchasing power of the monetary unit. An inevitable drop in the wages and income of the original means of production follows, though at first this decrease will be more rapid

---

[49]An analysis of the positive effects of this third type of deflation (caused by the tightening of credit in the recession stage of the cycle) can be found in Rothbard, *Man, Economy, and State*, pp. 863–71. See also Mises, *Human Action*, pp. 566–70. Furthermore Mises indicates that despite its negative effects, the deflationary squeeze is never as damaging as credit expansion, because

> contraction produces neither malinvestment nor overconsumption. The temporary restriction in business activities that it engenders may by and large be offset by the drop in consumption on the part of the discharged wage earners and the owners of the material factors of production the sales of which drop. No protracted scars are left. When the contraction comes to an end, the process of readjustment does not need to make good for losses caused by capital consumption. (Mises, *Human Action*, p. 567)

than the reduction in the price of consumer goods and services, if such a reduction takes place. Consequently, in relative terms, the wages and income of the original means of production will decline, leading to an increased hiring of workers over machines and a massive transfer of workers toward the stages closest to consumption. In other words the credit squeeze reinforces and accelerates the necessary "flattening" of the productive structure, a process which accompanies the recession. It is essential that labor markets be flexible in every aspect, in order to facilitate the massive transfers of productive resources and labor. The sooner the readjustment is completed and the effect of loans granted for erroneous investment projects is eliminated, the sooner the foundations of the subsequent recovery will be laid. The recovery will be characterized by a restoration of the relative price of the original means of production, i.e., by a decrease in the price of consumer goods and services. This reduction in the price of consumer goods and services will be greater, in relative terms, than the drop in wages, due to an increase in society's general saving, which will again stimulate growth in the capital goods stages. This growth will be achievable, given that it will originate from a rise in voluntary saving. As Wilhelm Röpke reasonably concludes, this third type of deflation (the result of the credit squeeze that follows the crisis)

> is the unavoidable reaction to the inflation of the boom and must not be counteracted, otherwise a prolongation and aggravation of the crisis will ensue, as the experiences in the United States in 1930 have shown.[50]

Under certain conditions, government and union intervention, along with the institutional rigidity of the markets, may prevent the necessary readjustments which precede any

---

[50]Wilhelm Röpke, *Crises and Cycles* (London: William Hodge, 1936), p. 120.

recovery of economic activity. If wages are inflexible, hiring conditions very rigid, union power great and governments succumb to the temptation of protectionism, then extremely high unemployment can actually be maintained indefinitely, without any adjustment to new economic conditions on the part of the original means of production. Under these circumstances a cumulative process of contraction may also be triggered. By such a process the massive growth of unemployment would give rise to a widespread decrease in demand, which in turn would provoke new doses of unemployment, etc. Some theorists have used the term *secondary depression* to refer to this process, which does not arise from spontaneous market forces, but from coercive government intervention in labor markets, products, and international trade. In some instances, "secondary depression" theorists have considered the mere possibility of such a situation a *prima facie* argument to justify government intervention, encouraging new credit expansion and public spending. However the only effective policy for avoiding a "secondary depression," or for preventing the severity of one, is to broadly liberalize markets and resist the temptation of credit expansion policies. Any policy which tends to keep wages high and make markets rigid should be abandoned. These policies would only make the readjustment process longer and more painful, even to the point of making it politically unbearable.[51]

What should be done if, under certain circumstances, it appears politically "impossible" to take the measures necessary to make labor markets flexible, abandon protectionism and promote the readjustment which is the prerequisite of any recovery? This is an extremely intriguing question of

---

[51]Wilhelm Röpke, the chief "secondary depression" theorist, in his hesitant and at times contradictory treatment of the topic, acknowledges that in any case, in the absence of outside intervention or rigidity, spontaneous market forces prevent a "secondary depression" from hitting and developing. Even when the rigidity of labor markets and the implementation of protectionist policies causes such a depression and it develops, the market ultimately, invariably and spontaneously establishes a "floor" to the cumulative process of depression. See Röpke, *Crises and Cycles*, pp. 128–29.

economic policy, and its answer must depend on a correct evaluation of the severity of each particular set of circumstances. Although theory suggests that any policy which consists of an artificial increase in consumption, in public spending and in credit expansion is counterproductive, no one denies that, in the short run, it is possible to absorb any volume of unemployment by simply raising public spending or credit expansion, albeit at the cost of interrupting the readjustment process and aggravating the eventual recession. Nonetheless Hayek himself admitted that, under certain circumstances, a situation might become so desperate that politically the only remaining option would be to intervene again, which is like giving a drink to a man with a hangover. In 1939 Hayek made the following related comments:

> it has, of course, never been denied that employment can be rapidly increased, and a position of "full employment" achieved in the shortest possible time by means of monetary expansion. . . . All that has been contended is that the kind of full employment which can be created in this way is inherently unstable, and that to create employment by these means is to perpetuate fluctuations. There may be desperate situations in which it may indeed be necessary to increase employment at all costs, even if it be only for a short period—perhaps the situation in which Dr. Brüning found himself in Germany in 1932 was such a situation in which desperate means would have been justified. But the economist should not conceal the fact that to aim at the maximum of employment which can be achieved in the short run by means of monetary policy is essentially the policy of the desperado who has nothing to lose and everything to gain from a short breathing space.[52]

---

[52]Hayek, *Profits, Interest and Investment*, footnote 1 on pp. 63–64. Hayek later amplified his ideas on the subject, indicating that in the thirties he was opposed to Germany's expansionary policy and even wrote an article that he never actually published. He sent the article to Professor Röpke with a personal note in which he stated the following:

> Apart from political considerations I feel you ought not—not yet at least—to start expanding credit. But if the political situation is so serious that continuing unemployment would

Now let us suppose politicians ignore the economist's recommendations and circumstances do not permit the liberalization of the economy, and therefore unemployment becomes widespread, the readjustment is never completed and the economy enters a phase of cumulative contraction. Furthermore let us suppose it is politically impossible to take any appropriate measure and the situation even threatens to end in a revolution. What type of monetary expansion would be the least disturbing from an economic standpoint? In this case the policy with the least damaging effects, though it would still exert some very harmful ones on the economic system, would be the adoption of a program of public works which would give work to the unemployed at relatively reduced wages, so workers could later move on quickly to other more profitable and comfortable activities once circumstances improved. At any rate it would be important to refrain from the direct granting of loans to companies from the productive stages furthest from consumption. Thus a policy of government aid to the unemployed, in exchange for the actual completion of works of social value at low pay (in order to avoid providing an incentive for workers to remain chronically

---

> lead to a political revolution, please do not publish my article. That is a political consideration, however, the merits of which I cannot judge from outside Germany but which you will be able to judge.

Hayek concludes:

> Röpke's reaction was not to publish the article, because he was convinced that at that time the political danger of increasing unemployment was so great that he would risk the danger of causing further misdirections by more inflation in the hope of postponing the crisis; at that particular moment, this seemed to him politically necessary and I consequently withdrew my article. (F.A. Hayek, "The Campaign Against Keynesian Inflation," chapter 13 of *New Studies in Philosophy, Politics, Economics and the History of Ideas*, p. 211)

At any rate desperate measures such as this can only procure a brief respite, while postponing the resolution of problems, which become much more serious over time. Indeed despite Röpke's consequentialist decision, the situation in Germany continued to deteriorate and it was impossible to prevent Hitler's accession to power in 1933.

unemployed) would be the least debilitating under the extreme conditions described above.[53]

13

THE "MANIC-DEPRESSIVE" ECONOMY:
THE DAMPENING OF THE ENTREPRENEURIAL SPIRIT
AND OTHER NEGATIVE EFFECTS RECURRING BUSINESS
CYCLES EXERT ON THE MARKET ECONOMY

The economic crises credit expansion repeatedly provokes lead to other consequences which are more subtle, yet no less damaging to the harmonious cooperation among people and to their economic and social development.[54] Specifically it is

---

[53]F.A. Hayek himself mentions that, under such circumstances, the least damaging policy would consist of offering

> employment through public works at relatively low wages so that workers will wish to move as soon as they can to other and better paid occupations, and not by directly stimulating particular kinds of investment or similar kinds of public expenditure which will draw labour into jobs they will expect to be permanent but which must cease as the source of the expenditure dries up. (Hayek, "The Campaign against Keynesian Inflation," p. 212)

However the risk of this type of concession is that, in current democratic systems, it is almost certain to be used by politicians in a less than rigorous manner to justify their measures of intervention in any economic recession. A possible solution might be to include as an article in the constitution the principle, supported by classical experts of public finance, of a balanced budget. As the agreement of all political forces would be required in order to modify the article, and this would only occur in the case of a unanimous belief in the "critical" nature of the situation, the risk of the unjustified implementation of artificial expansionary measures in times of crisis could be reduced.

[54]The fact that new crises erupt every few years shows that they originate from the credit expansion process, which necessarily sets off the spontaneous readjustments we have studied. In the absence of credit expansion, economic crises would be specific, isolated events which would result only from unusual phenomena of a physical sort (poor crops, earthquakes, etc.) or of a social sort (wars, revolutions, etc.). They

necessary to highlight the way in which the current monetary system, based on credit expansion, has made it customary for booms and crises to disturb economic development. In other words, it appears as if "manic-depressive" behavior were required of a market economy.

Indeed businessmen, journalists, politicians, union members, and economic agents in general have come to consider the artificial expansionary phase characteristic of a boom to be the normal stage of prosperity, which should be sought and maintained in any way possible. By the same token, expansion's inevitable consequences, i.e., crisis and recession, are considered a very negative stage which should be avoided at all costs.[55] Economic agents do not recognize the recession as the inevitable result of artificial expansion, and they fail to realize it has the virtue of revealing the errors committed and facilitating the recovery and readjustment of the productive structure.

Furthermore credit expansion excessively and unjustifiably forces economic agents' reflexes and the pace at which they work. While the expansion lasts, people's capacity for work is pushed to the limit and their entrepreneurial spirit becomes corrupted. Psychological stress and wear follow and are of high human and personal cost. Moreover the new money created via the expansionary granting of loans is used

---

would not arise regularly, nor would they be as geographically widespread as they normally are.

[55]   The boom is called good business, prosperity, and upswing. Its unavoidable aftermath, the readjustment of conditions to the real data of the market, is called crisis, slump, bad business, depression. People rebel against the insight that the disturbing element is to be seen in the malinvestment and the overconsumption of the boom period and that such an artificially induced boom is doomed. (Mises, *Human Action*, p. 575)

Thus it is a grave error to believe real wealth is destroyed by the stock market crash which announces the crisis. On the contrary, the economic destruction takes place much earlier, in the form of generalized malinvestment during the previous stage, the credit boom. The fall in the stock market merely indicates economic agents have finally taken notice of this phenomenon. See also section 14.

to finance all sorts of speculative operations, takeover bids and financial and trade wars in which the culture of short-sighted speculation prevails. In other words the misconceived idea that it is possible and desirable to accumulate astronomical profits with astonishing ease and swiftness spreads. This discourages the traditional entrepreneurial spirit and a job well done, both of which are based on prudent business management with an attitude of constancy and commitment to the achievement of long-term goals. This is what we have in mind when we refer to the widespread demoralization caused by artificial credit expansion. This discouragement is especially devastating to society's youngest, most dynamic generations.[56]

The problem is made worse if, as theorists who have analyzed the cycle from a political standpoint have shown,[57] politicians make their decisions entirely on a short-term basis and with the aim of attaining immediate support to guarantee them victory in the next election, and therefore they never hesitate to advocate and initiate those policies of monetary expansion which will most help them achieve electoral success in the short run. Furthermore as any deviation from artificial expansion and the excessive optimism it produces is viewed unfavorably, immediately attacked by the media and used as a political weapon to be hurled by the opposition, unions and business organizations, no one dares to condemn the

---

[56]The effect of credit expansion is more harmful the more accustomed economic agents are to an austere economy, the sustained growth of which depends solely on voluntary saving. It is under these circumstances that credit expansion is most damaging. Nevertheless under current conditions, in which artificial booms alternate with recessions, economic agents begin to learn from experience and the expansionary effects of the granting of loans are increasingly reduced or are achieved solely at the cost of injecting mounting volumes of credit at an escalating rate.

[57]William D. Nordhaus, "The Political Business Cycle," *Review of Economic Studies* 42, no. 130 (April 1975): 169–90. See also Edward R. Tufte, *Political Control of the Economy* (Princeton, N.J.: Princeton University Press, 1978); and C. Duncan MacRae, "A Political Model of the Business Cycle," published in *Journal of Political Economy* 85 (1977): 239–63. See also footnote 56 of chapter 9.

evils of the credit policy. This creates an environment of monetary irresponsibility which tends to aggravate problems and makes it highly unlikely they will be resolved through a sensible readjustment and liquidation which lay the foundations for a sustained recovery that does not depend on credit expansion.

The recurrent economic crises credit expansion provokes exert another very destructive effect on market economies and the principles of freedom of enterprise. Indeed each expansion process is invariably followed by a painful stage of readjustment, which is the ideal breeding ground for justifications of subsequent state intervention in the economy and for popular arguments that it is precisely the economic recession which reveals the inadequacies of a market economy and "proves" the necessity for the state to intervene more in the economy at all levels to mitigate the consequences of the recession and prevent further crises. Thus the recession provides a favorable environment for the resurgence of proposals of trade protectionism, market intervention, increases in the government budget deficit, and regulation of the economy. As we know, these interventionist policies only serve to prolong and aggravate the recession, and to hamper the necessary recovery. Sadly, the timid beginnings of the recovery are accompanied by such public pressure in favor of new credit expansion that expansion begins again and the entire process is repeated. As Mises eloquently concludes: "But the worst is that people are incorrigible. After a few years they embark anew upon credit expansion, and the old story repeats itself."[58]

14

THE INFLUENCE EXERTED ON THE STOCK MARKET BY ECONOMIC FLUCTUATIONS

The stock market is an important part of the marketplace in which securities representing loans to companies are traded (also called the "capital market"). Securities are the legal

---

[58]Mises, *Human Action*, p. 578.

embodiment of investments which savers, or capitalists, make in the following type of transaction: Capitalists concede present goods to demanders of present goods, who are willing to hand over a larger quantity of future goods to savers, or lenders, in the future in exchange for the ability to use the present goods in production processes. These securities may take on a wide variety of legal forms; they may be stocks, bonds, etc. In any case the stock market has the great virtue of facilitating the exchange of ownership of such securities, and hence of the corresponding capital goods of which the securities represent a share. Another main advantage of the stock market is that it allows the holders of securities to obtain rapid liquidity should they wish to part with them.[59] In addition it permits economic agents to temporarily invest their excess cash on hand, which they can use to purchase securities, and though these securities may represent long-term investments, they can be held for shorter periods and sold at any time.[60]

---

[59]Another essential function of the stock market and the options and futures market has been revealed, in accordance with the most hallowed tradition of the Austrian School, by Ludwig M. Lachmann, who states:

> [T]he Stock Exchange by facilitating the exchange of knowledge tends to make the expectations of large numbers of people consistent with each other, at least more consistent than they would have been otherwise; and that through the continual revaluation of yield streams it promotes *consistent capital change* and therefore economic progress. (Lachmann, *Capital and its Structure*, p. 71; italics added)

[60]It is important to point out that the banking sector has largely usurped this important role of the stock market. Since the banking sector can expand credit, generate deposits and pay them out, it has become a popular tool for investing a temporary excess of cash. This is very harmful, as it permits an even greater increase in credit expansion, along with the negative effects we are familiar with. However if excess cash were placed in the stock market, it would lead to an effective rise in voluntary saving, which would permit the lengthening of investment processes, and no inevitable subsequent crisis would force entrepreneurs to suspend these processes (yet savers would never have the guarantee of receiving the same monetary sum for their securities, should they sell them, as they pay when they buy them). A common criticism against the stock market is that its small size and limited development make the

In an economy which shows healthy, sustained growth, voluntary savings flow into the productive structure by two routes: either through the self-financing of companies, or through the stock market. Nevertheless the arrival of savings via the stock market is slow and gradual and does not involve stock market booms or euphoria.[61]

Only when the banking sector initiates a policy of credit expansion unbacked by a prior increase in voluntary saving do stock market indexes show dramatic and sustained overall growth. In fact newly-created money in the form of bank loans reaches the stock market at once, starting a purely speculative upward trend in market prices which generally affects most securities to some extent. Prices may continue to mount as long as credit expansion is maintained at an accelerated rate. Credit expansion not only causes a sharp, artificial relative drop in interest rates, along with the upward movement in market prices which inevitably follows. It also allows securities with continuously rising prices to be used as collateral for new loan requests in a *vicious circle* which feeds on continual, speculative stock market booms, and which does not come to

---

issuance of bank deposits necessary for the financing of production projects. We are now in a position to grasp why this criticism is unjustified. The reality is actually quite the opposite: banks' ability to finance investment projects via credit expansion unbacked by real saving is precisely what places banks in a position of prominence in many investment projects, to the detriment of the stock market, which loses importance in the process of investment and in many instances becomes a secondary market which, throughout the cycle, follows the guidelines set by the banking sector.

[61]Only a sudden, improbable drop in society's rate of time preference would allow stock-market indexes, in the absence of credit expansion, to jump to a new, consolidated level, from which point, at most, slow, gradual stock-market growth could take place. Thus continuously-prolonged stock-market booms and euphoria are invariably artificial and fed by credit expansion. Moreover such episodes of euphoria encourage the public to postpone consumption for the short term and invest cash balances in the stock market. Therefore while expectations of stock-market booms fed by credit expansion last, the crisis and recession can be temporarily postponed. This is what happened at the end of the 1990s, before the severe stock-market adjustment of 2000–2001.

an end as long as credit expansion lasts. As Fritz Machlup
explains:

> If it were not for the elasticity of bank credit, which has often
> been regarded as such a good thing, the boom in security
> values could not last for any length of time. In the absence
> of inflationary credit the funds available for lending to the
> public for security purchases would soon be exhausted.[62]

Therefore (and this is perhaps one of the most important
conclusions we can reach at this point) uninterrupted stock
market growth never indicates favorable economic conditions. Quite the contrary: all such growth provides the most
unmistakable sign of credit expansion unbacked by real savings, expansion which feeds an artificial boom that will invariably culminate in a severe stock market crisis.

By the same token, as Hayek has shown, the significant
capital gains acquired on the stock market during the expansion stage, to the extent economic agents consider them an
addition to their wealth and spend them on the purchase of
consumer goods and services, imply substantial consumption
of capital, an event which will ultimately make society
poorer.[63]

Even when, analytically speaking, it is perfectly easy to
identify the processes which tend to reverse the investment
projects undertaken in error as a result of credit expansion, it
is impossible to determine in advance exactly when and under

---

[62]Machlup, *The Stock Market, Credit and Capital Formation,* p. 92. This
book by Machlup is essential to understanding the cycle's influence on
the stock market.

[63]   Stock Exchange profits made during such periods of capital
       appreciation in terms of money, which do not correspond to
       any proportional increase of capital beyond the amount
       which is required to reproduce the equivalent of current
       income, are not income, and their use for consumption pur-
       poses must lead to a destruction of capital. (F.A. Hayek, "The
       Maintenance of Capital," *Economica* 2 [August 1934])

This article appears as chapter 3 of *Profits, Interest and Investment,* pp.
83–134. The above excerpt is found on p. 133.

what specific circumstances the artificial nature of the expansion will become evident in the stock market, ultimately setting off a crisis. However the stock market will definitely offer the first sign that the expansion is artificial and has "feet of clay," and then quite possibly, the slightest trigger will set off a stock market crash.[64] The crash will take place as soon as economic agents begin to doubt the continuance of the expansionary process, observe a slowdown or halt in credit expansion and in short, become convinced that a crisis and recession will appear in the near future. At that point the fate of the stock market is sealed.

The first symptoms of a stock market crisis seriously frighten politicians, economic authorities and the public in general, and a widespread clamor in favor of enough further credit expansion to consolidate and maintain the high stock market indexes is usually heard. High security prices are mistakenly viewed as a sign of good economic "health," and therefore it is wrongly believed that all possible measures should be taken to prevent the stock market from collapsing.[65]

---

[64]Regardless of its specific historical trigger, the stock market crisis will erupt after credit expansion decreases, since, as Fritz Machlup states,

> The most probable result in this case is a quick recession of security prices. For higher stock prices will invite a new supply of securities, and the corporations, which want to take advantage of the higher prices in order to draw funds from the stock exchange and use them for real investment, will find that there are no additional funds to be had. (Machlup, *The Stock Market, Credit and Capital Formation*, p. 90)

[65]We make no mention of the unquestionable fact that the interests of many speculative security holders are behind a large part of the "public clamor" in favor of institutional support of the stock market. Likewise it is highly significant that when a stock market crisis erupts, the media almost unanimously convey "reassuring" messages which insist the phenomenon is transient and "unjustified" and advise the public not only to refrain from getting rid of their stocks, but also to take advantage of the situation to acquire more securities at a good price. The discordant voices of those who view the situation differently and believe it is wisest to sell (voices which, in crisis situations, represent precisely the majority of those who go to the market) are always discreetly and conveniently silenced.

Indeed neither the public nor the majority of specialists wish to accept that the stock market decline is the initial warning of the inevitable recession and that stock market indexes cannot remain unchanged in the absence of new doses of credit.[66] Such credit would only postpone the crisis and make the eventual recession much more severe.

When the crisis erupts, the stock market also acts as an indicator of its development. Other things being equal, indexes corresponding to the securities of companies that operate in the stages furthest from consumption reflect a more dramatic fall in market prices than those which represent companies that produce consumer goods and services. This is the stock market's confirmation of the fact that the greatest entrepreneurial errors have been committed in the capital goods stages and of the necessity to liquidate these errors, save what can be saved and transfer the corresponding resources and original means of production toward other companies closer to consumption.

Once the recession period has begun, market sluggishness will continue for the duration of the readjustment process, indicating not only that this process is still painfully in motion, but also that market interest rates have risen to their pre-credit-expansion level (or even to a higher level, if, as usually occurs, they incorporate an additional premium for risk and inflation).[67] In any case, market sluggishness will last as

---

[66]Hence, for example, just prior to the stock market crash of October 24, 1929, Irving Fisher himself confidently stated, on October 17, 1929, "We are in a 'higher plateau' of stock exchange prices," that a fully consolidated level had been reached and would never necessarily drop. See the remarks he made to the *Commercial & Financial Chronicle*, remarks which appeared on October 26, 1929, pp. 2618–19. Cited by Benjamin M. Anderson, *Economics and the Public Welfare: A Financial and Economic History of the United States, 1914–1946* (Indianapolis, Ind.: Liberty Press, 1979), p. 210. Wesley C. Mitchell, R.G. Hawtrey and even John Maynard Keynes committed the same error as Fisher. See Skousen, "Who Predicted the 1929 Crash?" pp. 254–57 (see also footnote 100 below).

[67] This is clearly seen on the Stock Exchange which discounts future yield streams on the basis of the present rate of interest. A sensitive and well-informed market witnessing the

long as the readjustment, and could last indefinitely if the readjustment never concludes because new loans prolong malinvestment, and labor and all other markets are highly controlled and rigid.[68]

When the readjustment has ended the recovery can begin, assuming economic agents regain confidence and again increase their rate of voluntary saving. In this case the price of consumer goods and services will tend to decline, in relative terms, with respect to the wages and income of the original means of production. This will set off the "Ricardo Effect," and entrepreneurs will again become interested in launching new investment projects to lengthen and widen the capital goods stages in the productive structure. This rise in saving will stimulate growth in the price of securities, which will indicate the recovery has begun and entrepreneurs are again embarking on new processes of investment in capital goods. Nonetheless the upturn in stock market indexes will not be spectacular as long as new credit expansion is not initiated.[69]

> spectacle of a strong boom will of course in any case sooner or later have its misgivings about future yields and the cost of present projects. But we need not doubt that where this is not so, a rising rate of interest would strongly reinforce the discounting factor and thus damp excessive optimism. (Lachmann, *Capital and Its Structure*, pp. 124–25)

Lachmann explains the great importance of the stock market and futures market in spreading the dispersed knowledge and information of the different economic agents, thus enhancing the inter- and intratemporal coordination among them. Hence both the stock market and the futures market facilitate economic coordination and stability, *as long as they are not distorted by the inflationary impact of credit expansion.* At any rate futures markets will be the first to predict the successive phases of the business cycle. Even if this should not be the case, the events themselves (an increase in interest rates, accounting losses in capital-goods industries, etc.) will eventually put an end to the stock market boom and precipitate the economic crisis.

[68]This is true of the current (2001) Japanese recession.

[69]Therefore it should not surprise us that the recovery stage combines a relative drop in the price of consumer goods and services, and hence, in

Although many additional considerations regarding the evolution of the stock market during the business cycle could be presented, the most important idea is this: in general, no significant, continuous rise in the price of securities can be accounted for by an improvement in production conditions nor by an increase in voluntary saving; such a rise can only be indefinitely maintained as a result of inflationary growth in credit expansion. A sustained improvement in the economy and an increase in voluntary saving generate a greater monetary influx into the stock market, but this inflow is slower and more gradual and is rapidly absorbed by the new securities issued by companies with an aim to finance their new investment projects. Only continuous, disproportionate growth in the money supply in the form of credit expansion can feed the speculative mania (or "irrational exuberance") which characterizes all stock market booms.[70]

-----

the price of the listed securities which correspond to the companies closest to the last stage in the productive structure, with an increase in the price of the securities which correspond to the companies which operate furthest from consumption. As Fritz Machlup indicates,

> A shift of demand from consumers' goods to securities is "saving." It is usually assumed that a significant price shift takes place not only between consumers' goods and securities but also between consumers' goods and producers' goods. It may seem strange that the price fall in consumers' goods should correspond on the other side to price rises in *two* categories of things at the same time. But there is nothing complicated about this, for the rise in price of *titles* to capital goods may actually involve the rise in prices of the *capital goods* themselves. (Machlup, *The Stock Market, Credit and Capital Formation*, pp. 70–71)

[70]   A continual rise of stock prices cannot be explained by improved conditions of production or by increased voluntary savings, but only by an inflationary credit supply. A lasting boom can result only from inflationary credit supply. (Ibid., pp. 99 and 290)

15

Effects the Business Cycle Exerts
on the Banking Sector

At this point in our analysis it should be easy to identify the effects and relationships which link the business cycle and the banking sector. To begin with, we must recognize that the business cycle stems from credit expansion the banking sector brings about as a result of its legal privilege of implementing monetary demand-deposit contracts with a fractional reserve ratio. Moreover in chapter 4 we saw that this privilege explains the trend toward mergers in the banking industry, since the larger a bank's relative size is in the market, the greater are its possibilities for credit expansion unlimited by the corresponding bank clearing house. Furthermore bank consolidation makes it possible to better "manage" fractional cash reserves, allowing banks to satisfy normal withdrawals with lower central cash balances.

Nevertheless in chapter 5 we saw how the credit expansion process inevitably provokes a crisis and readjustment period, during which much of the book value of banks' assets evaporates, and in addition a widespread increase occurs in the demand for money and in the withdrawal of deposits (at least in the marginally less solvent banks). Therefore this accounts for the fact that bankers have forced the creation of a public institution, called the "central bank," designed to act basically as lender of last resort in the stages of economic recession which are so dangerous for banks. Also the difficulties and overwhelming worries which beset bankers as a consequence of default and the withdrawal of deposits during the stage of readjustment and economic recession reinforce even further the trend toward bank mergers. In fact in this way banks are able to treat defaulters more uniformly, achieve significant economies of scale in the management of payment arrears and avoid the marginally more insolvent situation in which they would find themselves if a higher percentage of their loans were non-performing or if the public had less confidence in them.

Hence we can conclude that an inherent trend in the *privileged* exercise of fractional-reserve banking leads to bank *consolidation* and encourages bankers to develop and maintain close relations with the central bank as the only institution capable of guaranteeing banks' survival in moments of crisis, situations banks themselves create regularly. Furthermore the central bank directs, orchestrates, and organizes credit expansion, making sure that banks expand more or less in unison and that none stray far from the established pace.

16

MARX, HAYEK, AND THE VIEW THAT ECONOMIC CRISES ARE INTRINSIC TO MARKET ECONOMIES

It is interesting to note that Marx, in his analysis of the capitalist economic system, basically concentrates on the study of the imbalances and maladjustments which occur in the market. This accounts for the fact that Marxist theory is primarily a theory of market disequilibrium and that occasionally it even coincides remarkably with the dynamic analysis of market processes which was developed by economists of the Austrian School, and particularly by Mises and Hayek themselves. One of the more curious points on which a certain agreement exists relates precisely to the theory of the crises and recessions which systematically ravage the capitalist system. Thus it is interesting to observe that certain authors of the Marxist tradition, such as the Ukrainian Mikhail Ivanovich Tugan-Baranovsky (1865–1919), reached the conclusion that economic crises originate from a tendency toward a *lack of proportion* among the different branches of production, a lack Tugan-Baranovsky believed inherent in the capitalist system.[71] According to Baranovsky, crises occur because

> the distribution of production ceases to be proportional: the machines, tools, tiles and wood used in construction are

---

[71]Tugan-Baranovsky, *Industrial Crises in Contemporary Britain*. Spanish translation included in *Lecturas de economía política*, Francisco Cabrillo, ed. (Madrid: Minerva Ediciones, 1991), pp. 190–210. See also chapter 7, footnote 87.

requested less than before, given that new companies are less numerous. However the producers of the means of production cannot withdraw their capital from their companies, and in addition, the importance of the capital involved in the form of buildings, machines, etc., obliges producers to continue producing (if not, the idle capital would not bear interest). *Thus there is excessive production of the means of production.*[72]

Clearly part of the underlying economic reasoning behind this analysis bears a strong resemblance to that behind the Austrian theory of the business cycle. In fact Hayek himself mentions Tugan-Baranovsky as one of the forerunners of the theory of the cycle he presents in *Prices and Production*.[73]

Furthermore it is interesting to note that Hayek himself, for a time, came to believe, like Marx, *that economic crises were inherent in the capitalist economic system*, although Hayek considered them the necessary cost of maintaining an elastic

---

[72]Excerpt translated from Spanish edition. Ibid., p. 205; italics added.

[73]   In the German literature similar ideas were introduced mainly by the writings of Karl Marx. It is on Marx that M.v. Tougan-Baranovsky's work is based which in turn provided the starting point for the later work of Professor Spiethoff and Professor Cassel. The extent to which the theory developed in these lectures corresponds with that of the two last-named authors, particularly with that of Professor Spiethoff, need hardly be emphasised. (Hayek, *Prices and Production*, p. 103)

See also Hayek, *The Pure Theory of Capital*, p. 426. On Tugan-Baranovsky and the content of his doctoral thesis, *The Industrial Crises in England*, see the biographical article on this author by Alec Nove, published in *The New Palgrave: A Dictionary of Economics*, John Eatwell, Murray Milgate, and Peter Newman, eds. (London: Macmillan, 1987), vol. 4, pp. 705–06. The error in all of these doctrines of a "lack of proportion" lies in the fact that they disregard the monetary and interventionist origin (in the form of the privileged operation of the banking system) of such a lack, they fail to recognize the entrepreneurial tendency to detect and correct maladjustments (in the absence of state intervention) and they naively assume that government economic authorities possess a deeper knowledge of these effects than the network of entrepreneurs which act freely in the market. See Mises, *Human Action*, pp. 582–83.

monetary and credit system, the expansion of which, at all times, would "guarantee" economic development. Specifically, Hayek asserted that economic crises arose

> from the very nature of the modern organization of credit. So long as we make use of bank credit as a means of furthering economic development we shall have to put up with the resulting trade cycles. They are, in a sense, the price we pay for a speed of development exceeding that which people would voluntarily make possible through their savings, and which therefore has to be extorted from them. And even if it is a mistake—as the recurrence of crises would demonstrate—to suppose that we can, in this way, overcome all obstacles standing in the way of progress, it is at least conceivable that the non-economic factors of progress, such as technical and commercial knowledge, are thereby benefited in a way which we should be reluctant to forgo.[74]

---

[74]Hayek, *Monetary Theory and the Trade Cycle*, pp. 189–90. In 1929 the young Hayek added that, in his opinion, a rigid banking system would prevent crises, but "the stability of the economic system would be obtained at the price of curbing economic progress." He concluded,

> It is no exaggeration to say that not only would it be impossible to put such a scheme into practice in the present state of economic enlightenment of the public, but even its theoretical justification would be doubtful. (Ibid., p. 191)

Hayek himself recognized that his conclusion rested more on intuition and non-economic factors than on a rigorous theoretical analysis, and therefore it is not surprising that only a few years later, in *Prices and Production* and in *Monetary Nationalism and International Stability*, he changed his mind, proposed a constant money supply and advocated the demand for a 100-percent reserve requirement in banking. In "Hayek, Business Cycles and Fractional Reserve Banking: Continuing the De-Homogenization Process," *The Review of Austrian Economics* 9, no. 1 (1996): 77–94, Walter Block and Kenneth M. Garschina level penetrating criticism against these statements the young Hayek made in 1929. However, on reflection, perhaps Hayek's comments should be understood in a different light. As early as 1925 he proposed, as a radical solution to economic cycles, a return to the prescriptions of the Bank Charter Act of 1844 and the establishment of a 100-percent reserve requirement for demand deposits held by banks. Thus maybe it would be wiser to interpret the assertions Hayek made in 1929 (in *Monetary Theory and the Trade Cycle*) in the context of the lecture given before the

This early thesis of Hayek's, which partially coincides with that of Marx, would only be valid if the very Austrian theory of business cycles had not revealed that economic crises cause great damage to the productive structure and widespread consumption of accumulated capital. These effects seriously hinder the harmonious economic development of any society. Moreover (and this is even more important) the theoretical, legal, and economic analysis carried out here is aimed at demonstrating that economic crises are not an inevitable by-product of market economies, but on the contrary, result from a *privilege* governments have granted banks, allowing them, with respect to monetary demand deposits, to act outside the traditional legal principles of private property, principles vital to market economies. Thus credit expansion and economic cycles arise from an institutionally-forced violation of the property rights involved in the monetary bank-deposit contract. Therefore *crises are in no way inherent in the capitalist system, nor do they inevitably emerge in a market economy subject to the general legal principles that constitute its essential legal framework, an economy in which no privileges are conferred.*

A second link connects Marxism and the Austrian theory of business cycles. Indeed if any ideology has justified and fed the class struggle, strengthening the popular belief that it is

---

Verein für Sozialpolitik which took place in Zurich in September 1928, instead of in the context of his other research studies. (This lecture formed the basis of his 1929 book.) Hayek's speech was subject to a rigorous examination by professors who were little inclined to accept conclusions they viewed as too original or revolutionary. Hayek's first endorsement of a 100-percent reserve requirement is found in note 12 of his article, "The Monetary Policy of the United States after the Recovery from the 1920 Crisis," p. 29 (see also upcoming footnote 94). Hayek's erroneous and short-lived concession regarding the supposedly beneficial effect of credit expansion on technological innovation echoes the naive inflationism implicit in Joseph Schumpeter's book, *Theory of Economic Development*. A brilliant critical evaluation of Schumpeter's unorthodox nature as viewed from the perspective of the Austrian theory of capital and business cycles is presented by José Antonio Aguirre in his "Introducción" to the Spanish edition of Böhm-Bawerk's book, *Capital and Interest*, vol. 2: *Positive Theory of Capital* (*Teoría positiva del capital*) (Madrid: Ediciones Aosta/Unión Editorial, 1998), pp. 19–22.

necessary to strictly regulate and control labor markets to "protect" workers from entrepreneurs and their capacity for exploitation, it has precisely been Marxist ideology. Hence Marxism has played a key and perhaps unintentional[75] role in justifying and fostering the rigidity of labor markets, and therefore in making the readjustment processes which inevitably follow any stage of bank credit expansion much more prolonged and painful. If labor markets were much more flexible (a situation which will only be politically possible once the general public realizes how damaging labor regulation is), the necessary readjustment processes which follow credit expansion would be much less lasting and painful.

There is a third possible connection between the Austrian theory of economic cycles and Marxism: the absence of economic crises in systems of "real socialism," an absence many authors have highly praised in the past. Nevertheless there is no point in arguing that economic crises do not arise in systems in which the means of production are never privately owned and all economic processes are "coordinated" from above through a coercive plan which public authorities deliberately impose. We must remember that depression appears in a market economy precisely because credit expansion distorts the productive structure, so that it no longer matches the one consumers would voluntarily maintain. Thus wherever consumers lack the freedom to choose and the productive structure is imposed on them from above, it is not that successive stages of boom and recession cannot occur, but rather, with all theoretical justification *we may consider that such economies are continually and permanently in a situation of crisis and recession.* This is due to the fact that the productive structure is imposed

---

[75]In fact Marx himself considered the interventionist and syndicalist versions of socialism "utopian" and even stated that welfare and labor legislation aimed at benefiting workers would invariably be ineffective. In this sense he fully accepted the classical school's arguments against state regulation of the market economy. Marx's position on this issue in no way lessens the fact that Marxism, quite unintentionally, was the main ideological force behind the "reformist" movements that justified intervention in the labor market.

from above and does not coincide with the desires of citizens and it is theoretically impossible for the system to correct its maladjustments and discoordination.[76] Therefore to contend that an economy of real socialism offers the advantage of eliminating economic crises is tantamount to affirming that the advantage of being dead is immunity to disease.[77] Indeed after the fall of the socialist regimes of Eastern Europe, when consumers were again given the opportunity to freely establish the productive structure most in line with their desires, it immediately became clear that the scale and magnitude of past investment errors would make the readjustment process much deeper and much more prolonged and painful than is common in the stages of recession which affect market economies. It has become evident that most of the capital goods structure which existed in socialist economies was completely useless with respect to the needs and objectives characteristic of a modern economy. In short socialism provokes a widespread, intense, and chronic malinvestment of society's factors of production and capital goods, a malinvestment much more severe than that caused by credit expansion. Hence we may conclude that "real socialism" is immersed in a deep "chronic depression," i.e., in a situation of constant

---

[76]We have completely devoted the book, *Socialismo, cálculo económico y función empresarial*, to demonstrating why it is impossible for a system of real socialism to exert a coordinating effect through its policies even under the most favorable conditions.

[77]   A dictator does not bother about whether or not the masses approve of his decision concerning how much to devote for current consumption and how much for additional investment. If the dictator invests more and thus curtails the means available for current consumption, the people must eat less and hold their tongues. No crisis emerges because the subjects have no opportunity to utter their dissatisfaction. Where there is no business at all, business can be neither good nor bad. There may be starvation or famine, but no depression in the sense in which this term is used in dealing with the problems of a market economy. Where the individuals are not free to choose, they cannot protest against the methods applied by those directing the course of production. (Mises, *Human Action*, pp. 565–66)

malinvestment of productive resources, a phenomenon which has even been accompanied by cyclical adverse changes and which has been studied in certain detail by various theorists from the former Eastern economies.[78]

The appalling economic difficulties presently confronting the economies of the former Eastern bloc stem from many decades of systematic economic errors. These errors have been much more serious (and have been committed at a much more rapid pace) than those which have regularly appeared in the West due to credit expansion by the banking system and to the monetary policy of public authorities.

17

TWO ADDITIONAL CONSIDERATIONS

On various historical occasions credit expansion has been used as an instrument to help finance the national budget deficit. This can occur in two ways: either banks may be instructed to acquire treasury bonds with part of their credit expansion, or the government may borrow money directly from banks. Though technically these are examples of credit expansion, here it does not directly influence the loan market, but rather acts as a perfect substitute for the creation of money. In fact in this case, credit expansion amounts to the simple creation of money to finance the public deficit and leads to the traditional effects of any inflationary process: an initial redistribution of income similar to that which follows any inflationary process; and a distortion of the productive structure, to the extent the government finances expenditures and public works which temporarily modify the productive structure and later cannot be permanently maintained via economic agents' current spending on consumer goods and services. At any rate it is necessary to distinguish true credit expansion,

---

[78]Among others, Tomask Stankiewicz in his article, "Investment under Socialism," *Communist Economies* 1, no. 2 (1989): 123–30. See also Jan Winiecki's book, *The Distorted World of Soviet-Type Economies* (London: Routledge, 1988 and 1991).

which gives rise to an artificial boom and to the business cycle, from the mere creation of new money and the placing of it in the hands of the state, a procedure which exerts the effects typical of an inflationary tax.[79]

Another final consideration relates to the *international nature* of business cycles. Economies as internationally integrated as modern ones usually are initiate credit expansion processes simultaneously, and the effects spread rapidly to all the world's markets. While the gold standard prevailed, each country's capacity for domestic credit expansion was automatically limited, and this limit was determined by the invariable outflow of gold from the relatively more inflationary economies. With the abandonment of the gold standard, the arrival of flexible exchange rates and the triumph of monetary nationalism, each country became able to freely adopt credit expansion policies, triggering an *inflationary contest* which pitted all countries against all others. Only a very large and integrated economic area comprising various nations which have renounced credit expansion and maintain among themselves fixed exchange rates will be able to free itself, relatively speaking (not completely), from the damaging effects of a general expansion of credit initiated outside its borders. Nevertheless the effects of inflation may be felt even inside this area if a flexible exchange rate is not established between it and the countries outside of it which suffer a process of monetary expansion. It is true that fixed exchange rates act as an (imperfect) substitute for the limits the gold standard set on each country's ability to independently expand its money supply in the form of loans. However this is consistent with the fact that the negative effect external expansion has on nations with more prudent monetary policies can only be lessened by the establishment of flexible exchange rates.

---

[79]The massive increase in budget deficits was a common characteristic of the 1980s (especially in Spain), and it served to prolong expansionary periods and to postpone and aggravate subsequent recessions. The negative effects of these indirectly-monetized deficits have combined with the harmful effects of credit expansion, and the result has been even greater maladjustments in the allocation of resources and a delay in the beginning of the necessary readjustment.

In any case the definitive elimination of economic crises will require a *worldwide* reform of the monetary system. Such a reform is outlined in the ninth and final chapter of this book.

18
EMPIRICAL EVIDENCE FOR THE THEORY OF THE CYCLE

In this section we will study how the theory of the business cycle presented in former sections fits in with the history of economic events. In other words we will consider whether or not our theoretical analysis provides an outline suitable for use in interpreting the phenomena of boom and recession which have occurred in history and still continue to occur. Thus we will contemplate how historical events, both those in the distant past and those more recent, illustrate or fit in with the theory we have developed.

Nonetheless it is necessary to begin with a word of caution regarding the historical interpretation of business cycles. Contrary to the assumptions of the "positivist" school, we do not consider empirical evidence alone sufficient to confirm or refute a scientific theory in the field of economics. We deliberately stated that we aim to study how historical events "illustrate" or "fit in with" the theoretical conclusions reached in our analysis, not to carry out an empirical test allowing us to falsify, confirm or demonstrate the validity of our analysis. Indeed though this may not be an appropriate place to reproduce the entire critical analysis of the logical inadequacies of "positivist methodology,"[80] it is clear that experience in the

---

[80]A summary of the critical analysis of positivist methodology, along with a brief bibliography of the most important writings on the topic, appears in our article, "Método y crisis en la ciencia económica," *Hacienda pública española* 74 (1982): 33–48, reprinted in Jesús Huerta de Soto, *Estudios de economía política* (Madrid: Unión Editorial, 1994), chap. 3, pp. 59–82. See also our article, "The Ongoing Methodenstreit of the Austrian School," pp. 75–113. The methodological ideas of the Austrian School evolved in parallel with the debate on socialist economic calculation, and criticism of positivist methodology is one of the

social realm is always "historical," i.e., it consists of extremely complex events in which innumerable "variables" are involved. It is not possible to observe these variables directly; we can only interpret them in light of a prior theory. Furthermore both events (with their infinite complexity) and their specific structure vary from one situation to another, and hence, though the typical, underlying forces of greatest significance may be considered the same, their *specific historical nature* varies substantially from one particular case to another.

Each theory of the cycle will determine a different selection and interpretation of historical events, and this fact gives great significance to the prior establishment, by methodological procedures other than positivist ones, of

---

most interesting byproducts of this debate. The very factors which make socialism an intellectual error (the impossibility of obtaining the necessary practical information in a centralized way, for example) actually explain why it is not possible in economics to directly observe empirical events, nor to empirically test any theory, nor in short, to make specific predictions with respect to the time and place of future events. This is because the object of research in economics consists of the ideas and knowledge which human beings possess and create in connection with their actions, and this information changes constantly, is highly complex and cannot be measured, observed nor grasped by a scientist (nor by a central planning agency). If it were possible to measure social events and empirically test economic theories, socialism would be possible. The very factors which make socialism impossible demonstrate that positivist methodology is inapplicable. Thus "events" in the social realm, given their "spiritual" nature, can only be interpreted from a historical perspective, and this always requires a prior theory. For more on these controversial and thought-provoking issues, see the 33 bibliographical sources mentioned in our article, "Método y crisis en la ciencia económica," and especially Mises's book, *Theory and History* (New Haven, Conn.: Yale University Press, 1957), Hayek's article, "The Facts of the Social Sciences," in *Individualism and Economic Order*, pp. 57–76, and *The Counter-Revolution of Science* (Glencoe, Ill.: Free Press, 1952; Indianapolis, Ind.: Liberty Press, 1979). A favorable and unbiased explanation of the Austrian methodological paradigm appears in Bruce Caldwell, *Beyond Positivism: Economic Methodology in the Twentieth Century* (London: George Allen and Unwin, 1982; 2nd ed., London: Routledge, 1994), esp. pp. 117–38.

valid theories which permit the adequate interpretation of reality. Hence no irrefutable historical evidence exists, much less evidence capable of confirming that a theory is valid or invalid. Therefore we should be very cautious and humble in our hopes of empirically corroborating a theory. At most we must be satisfied with developing a logically-coherent theory which is as free as possible of logical defects in its corresponding chain of analytical arguments and is based on the essential principles of human action ("subjectivism"). With this theory at our disposal, the next step is to check how well it fits in with historical events and allows us to interpret actual occurrences in a manner more general, balanced and suitable than other, alternative theories.

These considerations are particularly relevant to the theory of the business cycle. As F.A. Hayek has indicated, the "scientistic" attitude which has so far dominated economics has determined that only economic theories formulated in empirical terms and applicable to measurable magnitudes are heeded. In Hayek's words:

> It can hardly be denied that such a demand quite arbitrarily limits the facts which are to be admitted as possible causes of the events which occur in the real world. This view, which is often quite naively accepted as required by scientific procedure, has some rather paradoxical consequences. We know, of course, with regard to the market and similar social structures, a great many facts which we cannot measure and on which indeed we have only some very imprecise and general information. And because the effects of these facts in any particular instance cannot be confirmed by quantitative evidence, they are simply disregarded by those sworn to admit only what they regard as scientific evidence: they thereupon happily proceed on the fiction that the factors which they can measure are the only ones that are relevant. The correlation between aggregate demand and total employment, for instance, may only be approximate, but as it is the *only* one on which we have quantitative data, it is accepted as the only causal connection that counts. On this standard there may thus well exist better "scientific" evidence for a false theory, which will be accepted because it is more "scientific," than for a valid

explanation, which is rejected because there is no sufficient quantitative evidence for it.[81]

While taking the above warnings and considerations into account, in this section we will see that the available historical data concerning past cycles of boom and recession fits in excellently with our theory of the cycle. In addition at the end of this section we will review the studies conducted to empirically test the Austrian theory of the business cycle.

BUSINESS CYCLES PRIOR TO THE INDUSTRIAL REVOLUTION

(a) It would be impossible to cover here (even in condensed form) all cycles of boom and recession which affected the world's economies prior to the Industrial Revolution. Nevertheless we are fortunate enough to have available to us a growing number of works on economic history which greatly facilitate the application of the theory of the business cycle to specific economic events from the past. We could begin by mentioning Carlo M. Cipolla's works on the crises which gripped the Florentine economy in the mid-fourteenth century and in the sixteenth century, crises we covered in chapter 2.[82] Indeed we saw that Cipolla,

---

[81]Hayek made these important observations regarding the difficulty of empirically testing economic theories, particularly the theory of the cycle, in the acceptance speech he made on receiving the Nobel Prize December 11, 1974. See his article, "The Pretence of Knowledge," *The American Economic Review* (December 1989): 3. Hayek concludes in the same place:

> [W]hat is probably the true cause of extensive unemployment has been disregarded by the scientistically minded majority of economists, because its operation could not be confirmed by directly observable relations between measurable magnitudes, and that an almost exclusive concentration on quantitatively measurable surface phenomena has produced a policy which has made matters worse. (p. 5)

[82]Carlo M. Cipolla, *The Monetary Policy of Fourteenth-Century Florence* (Berkeley: University of California Press, 1982); and *Money in Sixteenth-Century Florence* (Berkeley: University of California Press, 1989).

following R.C. Mueller's studies,[83] documented the substantial credit expansion Florentine banks brought about starting at the beginning of the fourteenth century.[84] The result was a significant economic boom that made Florence the center of financial and trade activity in the Mediterranean. Nonetheless a series of events, such as the bankruptcy in England, the withdrawal of funds in Naples, and the crash of Florentine treasury bills triggered the beginning of the inevitable crisis, which manifested itself in widespread bank failure and a strong tightening of credit in the market (or as it was then known, *mancamento della credenza*). Cipolla points out that the crisis resulted in the destruction of a great stock of wealth, and real estate prices, which had skyrocketed, plummeted to half their former value, and even such a reduction in price was insufficient to attract enough buyers. According to Cipolla, it took thirty years (from 1349 to 1379) for a recovery to begin. In his opinion a major role in the recovery was played by the disastrous plague, which

> broke the vicious spiral of deflation. Since the number of capita was suddenly and dramatically reduced, the average per capita amount of currency available rose. In addition, during the three years that followed the plague, the output of the mint remained high. Consequently, cash balances were unusually large, and they were not hoarded: the prevailing mood among the survivors was that of spending. Thus prices and wages increased.[85]

---

[83]R.C. Mueller, "The Role of Bank Money in Venice: 1300–1500," pp. 47–96. And more recently, *The Venetian Money Market: Bank, Panics, and the Public Debt, 1200–1500*.

[84]As Carlo Cipolla literally states: "The banks of that time had already developed to the point of creating money besides increasing its velocity of circulation." Cipolla, *The Monetary Policy of Fourteenth-Century Florence*, p. 13.

[85]Ibid., p. 48.

In chapter 2 we critically analyzed Cipolla's use of the monetarist theory which underlies his interpretation of Florentine monetary processes.

(b) The second economic crisis Cipolla has studied in depth can also be fully accounted for in terms of the Austrian theory of the business cycle. It involves credit expansion which took place during the second half of the sixteenth century in Florence. Specifically, Cipolla explains,

> the managers of the Ricci bank used the public funds as a monetary base for a policy of credit expansion. The preeminence of the Ricci bank in the Florentine market must have lured the other banks into emulating its policy of credit expansion.[86]

According to Cipolla, during the 1560s the Florentine economy was quite active and was boosted by credit euphoria. However at the beginning of the 1570s the situation culminated in a severe liquidity squeeze which affected the entire banking system. Bankers, as the chroniclers colorfully put it, "only paid in ink." The crisis gradually grew worse and then violently exploded in the mid-1570s, when a "great shortage of money" (deflation) and a tightening of credit were felt in the city. Cipolla states,

> The credit multiplier suddenly worked perversely, and the Florentine market was throttled by a liquidity crisis, induced by the credit squeeze, that was exceptionally serious both in intensity and length. In the chronicler's pages, in the merchants' letters, and in the contemporary bans we find continual, concerned references to the monetary and credit "stringency," to the banks that did not "count" (that is, did not pay

---

[86]Cipolla, *Money in Sixteenth-Century Florence*, p. 106.

out cash), and to the lack of cash to pay workers on Saturdays.[87]

Therefore credit expansion and the boom were followed by a depression, due to which trade shrank rapidly and bankruptcies were frequent. At that point the Florentine economy fell into a long process of decline.

(c)   In chapter 2 we also mentioned other credit expansion processes which inevitably gave rise to subsequent economic crises. For example we covered the case of the Venetian Medici Bank, which expanded credit and eventually failed in 1492. In addition we studied, following Ramón Carande, the processes of expansion and bank failure which affected all of Charles V's bankers in the Seville square. Likewise we reflected on the major depression which stemmed from John Law's speculative and financial expansion in France at the beginning of the eighteenth century, expansion which several authors, including Hayek himself, have analyzed in detail.[88]

BUSINESS CYCLES FROM THE INDUSTRIAL REVOLUTION ONWARD

With the Napoleonic Wars, the start of the Industrial Revolution and the spread of the fractional-reserve banking system, business cycles began to reappear with great regularity and acquired the most significant typical features identified by the theory we have presented in this book. We will now briefly touch on the dates and features of the most substantial cycles since the beginning of the nineteenth century.

1. *The Panic of 1819.* This particularly affected the United States and has been studied chiefly by Murray N. Rothbard in

---

[87]Ibid., p. 111.

[88]See Hayek's article, "First Paper Money in Eighteenth Century France," printed as chapter 10 of the book, *The Collected Works of F.A. Hayek*, vol. 3: *The Trend of Economic Thinking*, pp. 155–76. See also Kindleberger, *A Financial History of Western Europe*, pp. 98ff.

a now classic book on the subject. The panic was preceded by an expansion of credit and of the money supply, both in the form of bank bills and of loans, neither of which were backed by real saving. The newly-created Bank of the United States played a leading role in this process. This produced great artificial economic expansion which was sharply inter-rupted in 1819, when the bank ceased to expand credit and demanded the payment of other banks' bills it possessed. The typical tightening of credit followed, along with a deep, widespread economic depression which halted the investment projects initiated during the boom and pushed up unemploy-ment.[89]

2. *The Crisis of 1825.* This was essentially an English crisis. It was characterized by marked credit expansion, which was used to finance a lengthening of the productive structure, i.e., an addition to the stages furthest from consumption. Such financing consisted basically of investments in the first rail-road lines and in the development of the textile industry. In 1825 the crisis erupted, triggering a depression which lasted until 1832.

3. *The Crisis of 1836.* Banks began again to expand credit, and this led to a boom in which banking companies and cor-porations multiplied. New loans financed railroads, the iron and steel industry and coal, and the steam engine was devel-oped as a new source of power. At the beginning of 1836 prices

---

[89]See Rothbard, *The Panic of 1819: Reactions and Policies*. Rothbard made another important contribution with this book: in it he revealed that the crisis aroused a highly intellectual controversy regarding bank paper. Rothbard highlights the emergence of a large group of politicians, jour-nalists and economists who were able to correctly diagnose the origins of the crisis and to propose appropriate measures to prevent it from recurring in the future. All of this occurred years before Torrens and oth-ers in England defined the essential principles of the Currency School. The following are among the most important figures who identified credit expansion as the origin of economic evils: Thomas Jefferson, Thomas Randolph, Daniel Raymond, Senator Condy Raguet, John Adams, and Peter Paul de Grand, who even defended the call for banks to follow the model of the Bank of Amsterdam and to constantly main-tain a 100-percent reserve ratio (p. 151).

began to shoot up. The crisis came to a halt when banks decided
to stop increasing their loans in light of the fact that they were
losing more and more gold reserves, which were leaving the
country, headed mainly for the United States. Starting in 1836
prices plunged and banks failed or suspended payments. The
result was a deep depression which lasted until 1840.

4. *The Crisis of 1847.* As of 1840 credit expansion resumed
in the United Kingdom and spread throughout France and the
United States. Thousands of miles of railroad track were built
and the stock market entered upon a period of relentless
growth which mostly favored railroad stock. Thus began a
speculative movement which lasted until 1846, when economic crisis hit in Great Britain.

It is interesting to note that on July 19, 1844, under the auspices of Peel, England had adopted the Bank Charter Act, which
represented the triumph of Ricardo's Currency School and prohibited the issuance of bills not backed 100 percent by gold. Nevertheless this provision was not established in relation to deposits
and loans, the volume of which increased five-fold in only two
years, which explains the spread of speculation and the severity
of the crisis which erupted in 1846. The depression spread to
France and the price of railroad stock plummeted in the different
stock exchanges. In general profits decreased, particularly in the
capital goods industries. Unemployment grew, especially in the
sector of railroad construction. It is in this historical context that
we should view the (clearly working-class and socialist) revolution which broke out in France in 1848.

5. *The Panic of 1857.* Its structure resembled that of previous
crises. The panic originated in a prior boom which lasted five
years, from 1852 to 1857, and which rested on widespread
credit expansion of worldwide consequences. Prices, profits
and nominal wages rose, and a stock market boom took place.
The boom especially favored mining companies and railroad
construction companies (the most important capital goods
industries of the period). Moreover speculation became generalized. The first signs of the end of the boom appeared with the
start of the decline in mining and railroad profits (the stages
furthest from consumption); and the increase in production
costs weakened profits further. Subsequently the slowdown

impacted the iron, steel and coal industries and the crisis hit. It spread quickly, triggering a worldwide depression. August 22, 1857 was a day of true panic in New York and many banks suspended their operations.

6. *The Crisis of 1866.* The expansionary stage began in 1861. The evolution of banking in England, and credit expansion initiated by the Credit Foncier in France played a key role. Expansion drove up the price of intermediate goods, construction and cotton-related industries and persisted at a rapid pace until panic broke out in 1866, due to a series of spectacular failures, the most famous of which was that of Overend Gurney in London. At this time, as occurred in 1847 and 1857, Peel's Bank Charter Act was temporarily suspended with the purpose of injecting liquidity into the economy and defending the Bank of England's gold reserves. France's first investment bank, the Crédit Mobiliaire, failed. The above gave rise to a depression which, as always, affected principally the sector of railroad construction, and unemployment spread mostly to capital-goods industries. Between 1859 and 1864, Spain engaged in substantial credit expansion which fostered widespread malinvestment, particularly in railroads. Beginning in 1864 it suffered a recession which reached its peak in 1866. Gabriel Tortella Casares has analyzed this entire process, and although in light of our theory some of his interpretative conclusions should be modified, the events he presents in his writings fit in perfectly with it.[90]

7. *The Crisis of 1873.* The pattern of this crisis also closely resembled that of prior crises. Expansion was initiated in the United States due to the high costs involved in the Civil War. The railroad network was dramatically enlarged and the iron

---

[90]Tortella points out, quoting Vicens, that the Spanish crisis of 1866 "was at the origin of the Catalonian businessmen's proverbial mistrust towards banks and large corporations." See Gabriel Tortella-Casares, *Banking, Railroads, and Industry in Spain 1829–1874* (New York: Arno Press, 1977), p. 585. For more information on the Spanish economy during this period, see Juan Sardá, *La política monetaria y las fluctuaciones de la economía española en el siglo XIX* (Barcelona: Ariel, 1970; first ed., Madrid: C.S.I.C., 1948), esp. pp. 131–51.

and steel industries underwent intensive development. Expansion spread to the rest of the world and in Europe there was tremendous stock market speculation in which industrial sector securities soared. Crisis hit first on the Continent in May of 1873 and following the summer in the United States, when recession had become obvious and one of the great American banks, Jay Cook & Co., failed. Notably, France, having abstained from the prior credit expansion, escaped this panic and the serious depression which followed.

8. *The Crisis of 1882.* Credit expansion resumed in 1878 in the United States and France. In the latter the issuance of industrial shares soared and an ambitious public works program was introduced. Banks played a very active role in attracting family savings and in the massive granting of loans to industry. The crisis erupted in 1882 with the failure of the Union Générale. Also on the verge of failure, the Crédit Lyonnais faced a massive withdrawal of deposits (around half). In the United States over 400 banks (from a total of 3,271) failed, and unemployment and crisis spread mostly to the industries furthest from consumption.

9. *The Crisis of 1890–1892.* Credit expansion spread throughout the world in the form of loans directed mainly to South America. Shipbuilding and heavy industry developed rapidly. The crisis arose in 1890, and the depression lasted until 1896. The usual bankruptcies of railroad companies, collapse of the stock market, crisis in the iron and steel industries, and unemployment made a violent appearance, as is typical in all depression years following a crisis.

10. *The Crisis of 1907.* In 1896 credit expansion was again initiated and lasted until 1907. In this case the new loan funds (created *ex nihilo*) were invested in electric power, telephone, subways, and shipbuilding. Electricity took on the leading role previously played by the railroads. Moreover for the first time the chemical industry took advantage of bank loans and the first automobiles appeared. In 1907 the crisis hit. It was particularly severe in the United States and many banks failed.

Following the crisis of 1907 a new boom began, and in 1913 it culminated in a new crisis similar to previous ones. This new crisis was interrupted by the outbreak of World War I, which altered the productive structure of nearly all countries in the world.[91]

THE ROARING TWENTIES AND THE GREAT DEPRESSION OF 1929

The years following the First World War were characterized by the great credit expansion initiated in the United States. The newly-established Federal Reserve (founded in 1913) orchestrated this bout of credit expansion, which revolved around programs to stabilize the value of the monetary unit. Theorists such as Irving Fisher and other monetarists supported these programs, which acquired great, enduring popularity at this point. Given that the decade of the 1920s saw a considerable increase in productivity, in which many new technologies were employed and a large quantity of capital was accumulated, in the absence of such an expansion of the money supply in the form of loans, there would have been a significant decrease in the price of consumer goods and services, and thus a substantial rise in real wages. However credit expansion kept the prices of consumer goods practically constant throughout the entire period.

Benjamin M. Anderson, in his notable financial and economic history of this period in the United States, gives a detailed account of the volume of credit expansion brought about by the American banking system. In little over five years, the amount of the loans created *ex nihilo* by the banking system grew from $33 billion to over $47 billion. Anderson expressly states that

> Between the middle of 1922 and April 1928, without need, without justification, lightheartedly, irresponsibly, we

---

[91]For a more detailed historical outline of the crises and economic cycles from the dawn of the Industrial Revolution until World War I, see, for example, Maurice Niveau, *Historia de los hechos económicos contemporáneos*, Spanish trans. Antonio Bosch Doménech (Barcelona: Editorial Ariel, 1971), pp. 143–60.

expanded bank credit by more than twice as much, and in
the years which followed we paid a terrible price for this.[92]

Murray N. Rothbard calculates that the money supply in
the United States grew from $37 billion in 1921 to over $55 billion in January 1929.[93] These figures closely approximate the
estimates of Milton Friedman and Anna J. Schwartz, according to whom the money supply increased from over $39 bil-
lion in January 1921 to $57 billion in October 1929.[94]

---

[92]Anderson, *Economics and the Public Welfare*, pp. 145–57. The above
excerpt appears on p. 146.

[93]Rothbard, *America's Great Depression*, p. 88, column 4. Rothbard examines all peculiarities of the inflationary process, specifically their correspondence with a deliberate policy of the Federal Reserve, a policy
endorsed by, among others, the Secretary of the Treasury, William G.
McAdoo, according to whom,

> The primary purpose of the Federal Reserve Act was to alter
> and strengthen our banking system that the enlarged credit
> resources demanded by the needs of business and agricul-
> tural enterprises will come almost automatically into exis-
> tence and at rates of interest low enough to stimulate, protect
> and prosper all kinds of legitimate business. (p. 113)

Also see George A. Selgin, "The 'Relative' Inflation of the 1920's," in *Less
Than Zero*, pp. 55–59.

[94]Milton Friedman and Anna J. Schwartz, *A Monetary History of the
United States, 1867–1960* (Princeton, N.J.: Princeton University Press,
1963), pp. 710–12 (Table A-1, column 8). In the chapter they devote to the
1920s, Friedman and Schwartz indicate that one of the principal changes
of the period was the decision, for the first time in history, to use

> central-bank powers to promote internal economic stability as
> well as to preserve balance in international payments and to
> prevent and moderate strictly financial crises. In retrospect,
> we can see that this was a major step toward the assumption
> by government of explicit continuous responsibility for eco-
> nomic stability. (p. 240)

Although Friedman and Schwartz put their finger on the issue with this
observation, the inadequacy of the monetary analysis with which they
interpret their data leads them to consider the cause of the Great
Depression of 1929 to be monetary policy errors committed by the Federal Reserve as of that date and not, as the theory of the Austrian School
reveals, the credit expansion of the 1920s. Friedman and Schwartz

F.A. Hayek himself was a qualified first-hand witness of the expansionary credit policy the Federal Reserve followed in the 1920s. Indeed between 1923 and 1924 he spent fifteen months studying *in situ* the monetary policy of the U.S. Federal Reserve. One outcome of that stay was his article on American monetary policy following the crisis of 1920.[95] In this article Hayek critically analyzes the Federal Reserve's objective, according to which

> Any rise in the index by a definite percentage is immediately to be met with a rise in the discount rate or other restrictions on credit, and every fall in the general price level by a reduction of the discount rate.[96]

Hayek indicates that the proposal to stabilize the general price level originated with Irving Fisher in the United States and J.M. Keynes and Ralph Hawtrey in England, and that various economists, headed by Benjamin M. Anderson, fiercely criticized it. Hayek's essential theoretical objection to the stabilization project is that, when the general price level is declining, attempts at stabilization invariably take the form of credit expansion, which inevitably provokes a boom,

---

completely overlook and fail to grasp the influence such expansion exerts on the productive structure.

[95]F.A. Hayek, "The Monetary Policy of the United States after the Recovery from the 1920 Crisis," chapter 1 of *Money, Capital and Fluctuations*, pp. 5–32. This article is an extract from a much more extensive German version which appeared in 1925 in *Zeitschrift für Volkswirtschaft und Sozialpolitik* (no. 5, 1925, vols. 1–3, pp. 25–63, and vols. 4–6, pp. 254–317). It is important to point out that it is in note 4 of this article (pp. 27–28) that Hayek first presents the fundamental argument which he later develops in detail in *Prices and Production* and which he bases on the work of Mises. Moreover note 12 of this article contains Hayek's first explicit statement in favor of reestablishing a 100-percent reserve requirement for banking. Hayek concludes:

> The problem of the prevention of crises would have received a radical solution if the basic concept of Peel's Act had been consistently developed into the prescription of 100-percent gold cover for bank deposits as well as notes. (p. 29)

[96]Hayek, *Money, Capital and Fluctuations*, p. 17.

a poor allocation of resources in the productive structure and subsequently, a deep depression. This is what actually happened.

Indeed the goal of stability in the general price level of consumer goods was very nearly achieved throughout the 1920s, at the cost of great credit expansion. This generated a boom which, in keeping with our theoretical predictions, affected mainly capital goods industries. Thus the price of securities increased four-fold in the stock market, and while the production of goods for current consumption grew by 60 percent throughout the period, the production of durable consumer goods, iron, steel, and other fixed capital goods increased by 160 percent.[97]

Another fact which illustrates the Austrian theory of the cycle is the following: during the 1920s wages rose mainly in the capital goods industries. Over an eight-year period they increased in this sector by around 12 percent, in real terms, while they showed an average of 5 percent real growth in the consumer goods industries. In certain capital goods industries wages rose even more. For instance, they increased by 22 percent in the chemical industry and by 25 percent in the iron and steel industry.

Apart from John Maynard Keynes and Irving Fisher, Ralph Hawtrey, the British Treasury's Director of Financial Studies, was another particularly influential economist in

---

[97]In other words high "inflation" was definitely a factor during this period, but it manifested itself in the sector of financial assets and capital goods, not in the consumer goods sector (Rothbard, *America's Great Depression*, p. 154). In his article, "The Federal Reserve as a Cartelization Device: The Early Years: 1913–1930," chapter 4 in *Money in Crisis*, Barry N. Siegel, ed., pp. 89–136, Murray Rothbard offers us a fascinating account of the development of the Federal Reserve's policy from 1913 to 1930, together with an analysis of the close, expansion-related cooperation between Strong, governor of the Federal Reserve, and Montagu Norman, governor of the Bank of England. The large-scale open market operations of the 1920s followed. Their purpose was to inflate the American money supply in order to help the United Kingdom resolve its self-inflicted deflation problem.

terms of justifying credit expansion with the supposedly beneficial goal of keeping the general price level constant. According to Hawtrey,

> The American experiment in stabilization from 1922 to 1928 showed that early treatment could shake a tendency either to inflation or to depression in a few months, before any serious damage had been done. The American experiment was a great advance upon the practice of the 19th century.[98]

The policy of credit expansion which was deliberately adopted to keep the general price level stable initially provoked a boom. This boom, along with a lack of the analytical tools necessary to comprehend that the plan would actually cause a deep depression, led authorities to go ahead with the policy, which as we know, was doomed to fail.[99]

The eruption of the crisis surprised monetarists (Fisher, Hawtrey, etc.), who, imbued with a mechanistic concept of the quantity theory of money, believed that once the money supply had been increased, its impact on prices would become stable and irreversible. These theorists did not realize that the

---

[98]Ralph G. Hawtrey, *The Art of Central Banking* (London: Longman, 1932), p. 300. Rothbard describes Hawtrey as "one of the evil geniuses of the 1920s." Rothbard, *America's Great Depression*, p. 159. The most serious error committed by Fisher, Hawtrey, and the rest of the "stabilizing" theorists is their failure to understand that the principal function of money is to serve as a vehicle for the creative exercise of entrepreneurship by leaving all creative possibilities for human action open with respect to the future. Therefore the demand for money and the purchasing power of money must never cease to vary. As Mises states,

> With the real universe of action and unceasing change, with the economic system which cannot be rigid, neither neutrality of money nor stability of its purchasing power are compatible. A world of the kind which the necessary requirements of neutral and stable money presuppose would be a world without action. (Mises, *Human Action*, p. 419)

[99]According to Phillips, McManus, and Nelson, "The end result of what was probably the greatest price-level stabilization experiment in history proved to be, simply, the greatest depression." Phillips, McManus, and Nelson, *Banking and the Business Cycle*, p. 176.

expansionary growth in loans exerted a highly unequal effect on the productive structure and relative prices. Professor Irving Fisher was perhaps the most famous American economist at the time, and his comments were among those which most stood out. Fisher obstinately defended the theory that the stock market had reached a level (a high plateau) below which it would never again fall. The 1929 crisis took him by surprise and nearly ruined him.[100]

The New York Stock Exchange disaster occurred in stages. Between 1926 and 1929 the share index more than doubled, increasing from 100 to 216. The first warning appeared on Thursday, October 24, 1929, when a supply of thirteen million shares was met with an almost nonexistent demand, and prices collapsed. Banks intervened and were able to momentarily suspend the fall, and prices dropped between twelve and twenty-five points. Though the panic was expected to cease over the weekend, the morning of Monday, October 28 brought a new, unstoppable disaster. Over nine million shares were offered for sale, and the market plunged by forty-nine points. The most devastating day was Tuesday, October 29, when thirty-three million shares were offered and the market plummeted by another forty-nine points.

At that point the depression hit and had the typical characteristics. More than 5,000 banks (out of a total of 24,000) failed or suspended payments between 1929 and 1932.[101]

---

[100]On October 17, 1929, Fisher asserted: "Stocks have reached what looks like a permanently high plateau." Anderson, *Economics and the Public Welfare*, p. 210. On the fortune Fisher made developing a calculator, and his inability to theoretically explain events he experienced and to predict the stock market crash in which he lost practically everything, see Robert Loring Allen's enthralling biography, *Irving Fisher: A Biography* (Oxford: Blackwell, 1993). Fisher's major forecasting errors account for the damage to his academic and popular reputation and for the fact that his subsequent theory on the causes of the Great Depression was not taken very seriously. See Robert W. Dimand, "Irving Fisher and Modern Macroeconomics," *American Economic Review* 87, no. 2 (May 1997): 444.

[101]Elmus Wicker, *The Banking Panics of the Great Depression* (Cambridge: Cambridge University Press, [1996] 2000).

Furthermore a drastic credit squeeze took place, and gross private investment shrank from over $15 billion in 1929 to barely $1 billion in 1932. In addition unemployment reached its peak in 1933 at around 27 percent of the active population.

The duration and particular severity of the Great Depression, which lasted an entire decade, can only be understood in terms of the economic and monetary policy errors committed principally by the Hoover administration (President Hoover was reelected in 1928), but also by Roosevelt, an interventionist democrat. Virtually all of the most counterproductive measures possible were taken to exacerbate the problems and hinder the arrival of recovery. Specifically a forced and artificial wage support policy drove up unemployment and prevented the transfer of productive resources and labor from one industry to another. Moreover a colossal increase in public spending in 1931 constituted another grave error in economic policy. That year public spending rose from 16.4 percent of the gross domestic product to 21.5 percent, and a deficit of over $2 billion ensued. Authorities mistakenly decided to balance the budget by raising taxes (instead of reducing expenses): income taxes increased from 1.5 percent–5 percent to 4 percent–8 percent, many deductions were eliminated and marginal tax rates for the highest income levels jumped. Likewise corporate taxes climbed from 12 to nearly 14 percent, and estate and gift taxes doubled, reaching a maximum rate of 33.3 percent.

Furthermore the public works considered necessary to mitigate the problems of unemployment were financed by the large-scale issuance of government securities, which ultimately absorbed the scarce supply of available capital, crippling the private sector.

Franklin D. Roosevelt, who succeeded Hoover in the 1932 election, continued these harmful policies and carried their disastrous results a step further.[102]

---

[102]Murray N. Rothbard concludes his analysis of the Great Depression in this way:

> Economic theory demonstrates that only governmental inflation can generate a boom-and-bust cycle, and that the depression will be prolonged and aggravated by inflationist and

THE ECONOMIC RECESSIONS OF THE LATE 1970s AND EARLY 1990s

The most characteristic feature of the business cycles which have followed World War II is that they have originated in deliberately inflationary policies directed and coordinated by central banks. During the post-war decades and well into the late sixties Keynesian theory led to the belief that an "expansive" fiscal and monetary policy could avert any crisis. Grim reality sank in with the arrival of severe recession in the 1970s, when stagflation undermined and discredited Keynesian assumptions. Moreover the 1970s and the emergence of stagflation actually marked the rebirth of interest in Austrian economics, and Hayek received the 1974 Nobel Prize in Economics precisely for his studies on the theory of the business cycle. As a matter of fact, the crisis and stagflation of the seventies were a "trial by fire" which Keynesians did not survive, and which earned great recognition for Austrian School theorists, who had been predicting it for some time. Their only error, as Hayek admits, lay in their initial misjudgment of the duration of the inflationary process, which, unrestricted by old gold-standard requirements, was prolonged by additional doses of credit expansion and spanned two decades. The result

---

other interventionary measures. In contrast to the myth of *laissez-faire*, we have shown how government intervention generated the unsound boom of the 1920's, and how Hoover's new departure aggravated the Great Depression by massive measures of interference. The guilt for the Great Depression must, at long last, be lifted from the shoulders of the free market economy, and placed where it properly belongs: at the doors of politicians, bureaucrats, and the mass of "enlightened" economists. And in any other depression, past or future, the story will be the same. (Rothbard, *America's Great Depression*, p. 295)

We have not yet mentioned the European side of the Great Depression, an analysis of which appears in Lionel Robbins's book, *The Great Depression* (1934). In a recent work, *The Credit-Anstalt Crisis of 1931* (Cambridge: Cambridge University Press, 1991), Aurel Schubert provides a clear account of the crisis of the Austrian banking system (though the underlying theory at times leaves much to be desired).

was an unprecedented phenomenon: an acute depression accompanied by high rates of inflation and unemployment.[103]

The crisis of the late seventies belongs to recent economic history and we will not discuss it at length. Suffice it to say that the necessary worldwide adjustment was quite costly. Perhaps after this bitter experience, with the recovery underway, western financial and economic authorities could have been required to take the precautionary measures necessary to avoid a future widespread expansion of credit and thus, a future recession. Unfortunately this was not the case, and despite all of the effort and costs involved in the realignment of western economies following the crisis of the late seventies, the second half of the eighties saw the beginnings of another significant credit expansion which started in the United States

---

[103]In an article in which he examines data from the crises between 1961 and 1987, Milton Friedman states that he sees no correlation between the amount of expansion and the subsequent contraction and concludes that these results "would cast grave doubt on those theories that see as the source of a deep depression the excesses of the prior expansion (the Mises cycle theory is a clear example)." See Milton Friedman, "The 'Plucking Model' of Business Fluctuations Revisited," *Economic Inquiry* 31 (April 1993): 171–77 (the above excerpt appears on p. 172). Nevertheless Friedman's interpretation of the facts and their relationship to the Austrian theory is incorrect for the following reasons: (a) As an indicator of the cycle's evolution, Friedman uses GDP magnitudes, which as we know conceal nearly half of the total gross national output, which includes the value of intermediate products and is the measure which most varies throughout the cycle; (b) The Austrian theory of the cycle establishes a correlation between credit expansion, microeconomic malinvestment and recession, *not* between economic expansion and recession, both of which are measured by an aggregate (GDP) that conceals what is really happening; (c) Friedman considers a very brief time period (1961–1987), during which any sign of recession was met with energetic expansionary policies which made subsequent recessions short, except in the two cases mentioned in the text (the crisis of the late seventies and early nineties), in which the economy entered the trap of stagflation. Thanks to Mark Skousen for supplying his interesting private correspondence with Milton Friedman on this topic. See also the demonstration of the perfect compatibility between Friedman's aggregate data and the Austrian theory of business cycles, in Garrison, *Time and Money*, pp. 222–35.

and spread throughout Japan, England, and the rest of the world. Despite the stock market's "warnings," particularly the collapse of the New York Stock Exchange on October 19, 1987, "Black Monday," (when the New York Stock Exchange Index tumbled 22.6 percent), monetary authorities reacted by nervously injecting massive new doses of credit into the economy to bolster stock market indexes.

In an empirical study on the recession of the early nineties,[104] W.N. Butos reveals that between 1983 and 1987 the average rate of annual growth in the reserves provided by the Federal Reserve to the American banking system increased by 14.5 percent per year (i.e., from $25 billion in 1985 to over $40 billion three years later). This led to great credit and monetary expansion, which in turn fed a considerable stock market boom and all sorts of speculative financial operations. Moreover the economy entered a phase of marked expansion which entailed a substantial lengthening of the capital goods stages and a spectacular increase in the production of durable consumer goods. This stage has come to be called the "Golden Age" of the Reagan-Thatcher years, and it rested mainly on the shaky foundation of credit expansion.[105] An empirical study by Arthur Middleton Hughes also confirms

---

[104]William N. Butos, "The Recession and Austrian Business Cycle Theory: An Empirical Perspective," in *Critical Review* 7, nos. 2–3 (Spring and Summer, 1993). Butos concludes that the Austrian theory of the business cycle provides a valid analytical explanation for the expansion of the eighties and the subsequent crisis of the early nineties. Another interesting article which applies the Austrian theory to the most recent economic cycle is Roger W. Garrison's "The Roaring Twenties and the Bullish Eighties: The Role of Government in Boom and Bust," *Critical Review* 7, nos. 2–3 (Spring and Summer, 1993): 259–76. The money supply grew dramatically during the second half of the 1980s in Spain as well, where it increased from thirty trillion pesetas to nearly sixty trillion between 1986 and 1992, when a violent crisis erupted in Spain ("Banco de España," *Boletín estadístico* [August 1994]: 17).

[105]Margaret Thatcher herself eventually admitted, in her autobiography, that all of the economic problems of her administration emerged when money and credit were expanded too quickly and the prices of consumer goods rocketed. Thatcher, *The Downing Street Years*.

these facts. Furthermore Hughes examines the impact of credit expansion and recession on different sectors belonging to various stages of the productive structure (some closer to and some further from consumption). His empirical time-series study confirms the most important conclusions of our theory of the cycle.[106] Moreover this recession was accompanied by a severe bank crisis which in the United States became apparent due to the collapse of several important banks and especially to the failure of the savings and loan sector, the analysis of which has appeared in many publications.[107]

This last recession has again surprised monetarists, who cannot understand how such a thing happened.[108] However the expansion's typical characteristics, the arrival of the crisis and the ensuing recession all correspond to the predictions of the Austrian theory of the cycle.

Perhaps one of the most interesting, distinguishing characteristics of the last cycle has been the key role the Japanese

---

[106]Hughes, "The Recession of 1990: An Austrian Explanation," pp. 107–23.

[107]For example, Lawrence H. White, "What has been Breaking U.S. Banks?" pp. 321–34, and Catherine England, "The Savings and Loan Debacle," in *Critical Review* 7, nos. 2–3 (Spring and Summer, 1993): 307–20. In Spain, the following work of Antonio Torrero Mañas stands out: *La crisis del sistema bancario: lecciones de la experiencia de Estados Unidos* (Madrid: Editorial Cívitas, 1993).

[108]On this topic Robert E. Hall arrives at a most illustrative conclusion:

> Established models are unhelpful in understanding this recession, and probably most of its predecessors. There was no outside force that concentrated its effects over the few months in the late summer and fall of 1990, nor was there a coincidence of forces concentrated during that period. Rather, there seems to have been a cascading of negative responses during that time, perhaps set off by Iraq's invasion of Kuwait and the resulting oil-price spike in August 1990. (Hall, "Macrotheory and the Recession of 1990–1991," *American Economic Review* (May 1993): 275–79; above excerpt appears on pp. 278–79)

It is discouraging to see such a prestigious author so confused about the emergence and evolution of the 1990s crisis. This situation says a lot about the pitiful current state of macroeconomic theory.

economy has played in it. Particularly in the four-year period between 1987 and 1991, the Japanese economy underwent enormous monetary and credit expansion which, as theory suggests, affected mainly the industries furthest from consumption. In fact although the prices of consumer goods rose only by around 0 to 3 percent each year during this period, the price of fixed assets, especially land, real estate, stocks, works of art and jewelry, escalated dramatically. Their value increased to many times its original amount and the respective markets entered a speculative boom. The crisis hit during the second quarter of 1991, and the subsequent recession has lasted more than ten years. A widespread malinvestment of productive resources has become evident, a problem unknown in Japan in the past, and has made it necessary for the Japanese economy to initiate a painful, comprehensive realignment process in which it continues to be involved at the time of this writing (2001).[109]

Regarding the effect this worldwide economic crisis has exerted in Spain, it is necessary to note that it violently gripped the country in 1992 and the recession lasted almost five years. All of the typical characteristics of expansion, crisis and recession have again been present in Spain's immediate economic environment, with the possible exception that the artificial expansion was even more exaggerated as a

---

[109]The Nikkei 225 index of the Tokyo Stock Exchange dropped from over 30,000 yen at the beginning of 1990 to less than 12,000 yen in 2001, following the failure of a number of banks and stock market firms (such as Hokkaido Takushoku, Sanyo and Yamaichi Securities and others). These bankruptcies have seriously harmed the credibility of the country's financial system, which will take a long time to recover. Furthermore the Japanese bank and stock market crises have fully spread to the rest of the Asian markets (the failure of the Peregrine Bank of Hong Kong, of the Bangkok Bank of Commerce, and of the Bank Korea First come to mind, among others), and in 1997 they even threatened to spread to the rest of the world. On the application of the Austrian theory to the Japanese recession see the interesting article Yoshio Suzuki presented at the regional meeting of the Mont Pèlerin Society, September 25–30, 1994 in Cannes, France. See also the pertinent comments of Hiroyuki Okon in *Austrian Economics Newsletter* (Winter, 1997): 6–7.

consequence of Spain's entrance into the European Economic Community. Moreover the recession hit within a context of an overvalued peseta, which had to be devalued on three consecutive occasions over a period of twelve months. The stock market was seriously affected, and well-known financial and bank crises arose in an environment of speculation and get-rich-quick schemes. It has taken several years for Spain to recover entirely from these events. Even today, Spanish authorities have yet to adopt all necessary measures to increase the flexibility of the economy, specifically the labor market. Together with a prudent monetary policy and a decrease in public spending and the government deficit, such measures are essential to the speedy consolidation of a stable, sustained recovery process in Spain.[110] Finally, following the great Asian economic crisis of 1997, the Federal Reserve orchestrated an expansion of credit in the United States (and throughout the world) which gave rise to an intense boom and stock-market bubble. At this time (late 2001), it appears this situation will very probably end in a stock-market crash (already evident for stocks in the so-called "New Economy" of electronic commerce, new technologies and communications) and a new, deep, worldwide economic recession.[111]

---

[110]We will not also go into the devastating effect of the economic and bank crisis in developing countries (for example, Venezuela), and on the economies of the former Eastern bloc (Russia, Albania, Latvia, Lithuania, the Czech Republic, Romania, etc.), which with great naivete and enthusiasm have raced down the path of unchecked credit expansion. As an example, in Lithuania at the end of 1995, following a period of euphoria, a bank crisis erupted and led to the closure of sixteen of the twenty-eight existing banks, the sudden tightening of credit, a drop in investment, and unemployment and popular malaise. The same can be said for the rest of the cases mentioned (in many of them the crisis has even been more severe).

[111]As explained in the Preface, when the English edition of this book was prepared (2002–2003), a worldwide economic recession was simultaneously affecting Japan, Germany, and (very probably) the United States.

SOME EMPIRICAL TESTING OF THE AUSTRIAN THEORY
OF THE BUSINESS CYCLE

Several fascinating studies have lent strong empirical support to the Austrian theory of the business cycle. This has
occurred despite the difficulties in testing a theory based on
the impact of credit expansion on the productive structure and
the irregular manner in which such expansion affects the relative prices of products of the different production stages. It is
difficult to empirically test these economic processes, especially
while an attempt is made to continue using national accounting statistics, which, as we know, exclude most of the gross
value produced in the intermediate stages of the production
process. Charles E. Wainhouse has carried out one of these
outstanding empirical studies.[112] Wainhouse lists nine propositions which he deduces from the Austrian theory of the cycle
and empirically tests them one by one.[113] These tests yield several main conclusions. Wainhouse *first* empirically tests the
proposition that changes in the supply of voluntary savings
are independent of changes in bank credit. He uses statistical
series which date from January 1959 to June 1981 and finds
that in all cases but one the empirical evidence confirms this

---

[112]Wainhouse, "Empirical Evidence for Hayek's Theory of Economic
Fluctuations," pp. 37–71. See also his article, "Hayek's Theory of the
Trade Cycle: The Evidence from the Time Series" (Ph.D. dissertation,
New York University, 1982).

[113]Wainhouse states:

> Within the constellation of available tests of causality,
> Granger's notion of causality—to the extent that it requires
> neither the "true" model nor controllability—seems to offer
> the best prospects for practical implementation. (Wainhouse,
> "Empirical Evidence for Hayek's Theory of Economic Fluctu-
> ations," p. 55)

Wainhouse mentions the following articles of Granger's and bases his
empirical testing of the Austrian theory on them: Clive W.J. Granger,
"Investigating Causal Relations by Econometric Models and Cross-
Spectral Methods," *Econometrica* 37, no. 3 (1969): 428 ff.; and "Testing for
Causality: A Personal Viewpoint," *Journal of Economic Dynamics and Con-
trol* 2, no. 4 (November 1980): 330 ff.

first proposition. Wainhouse's *second* proposition is that modifications in the supply of credit give rise to changes in the interest rate, and that the two are inversely related. Abundant empirical evidence also exists to support this second proposition. Wainhouse's *third* proposition states that changes in the rate at which loans are granted cause an increase in the output of intermediate goods, an idea he believes is also corroborated by the evidence he analyzes. The last three propositions Wainhouse empirically tests are these: that the ratio of the price of intermediate goods to the price of consumer goods rises following the beginning of credit expansion; that in the expansion process the price of the goods closest to final consumption tends to decrease in relation to the price of intermediate goods; and lastly, that in the final stage of expansion the price of consumer goods increases more rapidly than that of intermediate goods, thus reversing the initial trend. Wainhouse also believes that in general these last three propositions agree with the empirical data, and he therefore concludes that the data supports the theoretical propositions of the Austrian School of economics. Wainhouse leaves three propositions untested, thus leaving open an important field of possible future study for econometricians.[114]

---

[114]In his book, *Prices in Recession and Recovery* (New York: National Bureau of Economic Research, 1936), Frederick C. Mills presents another relevant empirical study which centers on the years of the Great Depression of 1929. Here Mills empirically confirms that the evolution of relative prices during the period of crisis, recession, and recovery which followed the crash of 1929 closely resembled that outlined by the Austrian theory of the business cycle. Specifically, Mills concludes that during the depression "Raw materials dropped precipitously; manufactured goods, customarily sluggish in their response to a downward pressure of values, lagged behind." With respect to consumer goods, Mills states that they "fell less than did the average of all commodity prices." Regarding the recovery of 1934–1936, Mills indicates that "the prices of industrial raw materials, together with relatively high prices of finished goods, put manufacturers in an advantageous position on the operating side" (pp. 25–26, see also pp. 96–97, 151, 157–58 and 222).

A helpful evaluation of Mills's writings appears in Skousen's book, *The Structure of Production*, pp. 58–60.

Another empirical study pertinent to the Austrian theory of the cycle is one conducted by Valerie Ramey, of the University of California at San Diego.[115] Ramey has developed an intertemporal model which breaks down into different stages the inventories which correspond to: consumer goods, wholesale goods, manufactured equipment goods, and intermediate manufactured products. Ramey draws the conclusion that the price of inventories oscillates more the further they are from the final stage of consumption. The inventories closest to consumption are the most stable and vary the least throughout the cycle.

Mark Skousen arrives at a similar conclusion in his analysis of trends in the prices of products from three different production stages: that of finished consumer goods, that of intermediate products, and that of material factors of production. Skousen indicates, as stated in footnote 21, that during the period from 1976 to 1992, the prices of products from the stages furthest from consumption varied from +30 percent to –10 percent, the prices of intermediate goods only oscillated between +14 percent and –1 percent, and the prices of final consumer goods varied from +10 to –2 percent.[116] Moreover Mark Skousen himself estimates that in the crisis of the early nineties, the gross national output of the United States, a measure which includes all goods from intermediate stages, fell by between 10 and 15 percent, and not by the significantly lower percentage (between 1 and 2 percent) reflected by traditional national accounting figures, like gross national product, which exclude all intermediate products, and therefore enormously exaggerate the relative importance of final consumption with respect to the total national productive effort.[117]

---

[115]Valerie A. Ramey, "Inventories as Factors of Production and Economic Fluctuations," *American Economic Review* (July 1989): 338–54.

[116]Mark Skousen, "I Like Hayek: How I Use His Model as a Forecasting Tool," presented at the general meeting of the Mont Pèlerin Society which took place September 25–30, 1994 in Cannes, France, pp. 10–11.

[117]Other empirical studies have also revealed the non-neutral nature of monetary growth and the fact that it exerts a relatively greater impact on the industries in which the most durable goods are produced. See,

Hopefully the future will bring more frequent and abundant historical-empirical research on the Austrian theory of the business cycle. With luck this research will rest on data from input-output tables and permit the use of the Austrian theory to reform the methodology of the national accounts, thus permitting the gathering of statistical data on variations in relative prices, variations which constitute the microeconomic essence of the business cycle. Table VI-1 is designed to simplify and facilitate this type of empirical research in the future. It summarizes and compares the different phases in the market processes triggered by an increase in society's voluntary saving and those triggered by an expansion of bank credit unbacked by a prior rise in voluntary saving.

CONCLUSION

In light of the theoretical analysis carried out and the historical experience accumulated, it is surprising that at the dawn of the twenty-first century doubts still exist with respect to the recessive nature of credit expansion. We have seen that stages of boom, crisis, and recession recur with great regularity, and we have examined the key role bank credit expansion plays in these stages. Despite these truths, a large number of theorists persist in denying that economic crises stem from an underlying theoretical cause. These theorists fail to realize that

---

for example, Peter E. Kretzmer, "The Cross-Industry Effects of Unanticipated Money in an Equilibrium Business Cycle Model," *Journal of Monetary Economics* 23, no. 2 (March 1989): 275–396; and Willem Thorbecke, "The Distributional Effects of Disinflationary Monetary Policy," Jerome Levy Economics Institute Working Paper No. 144 (Fairfax, Va.: George Mason University, 1995). Tyler Cowen, commenting on these and other studies, concludes:

> [T]he literature on sectoral shifts presents some of the most promising evidence in favor of Austrian approaches to business cycles. The empirical case for monetary non-neutrality across sectors is relatively strong, and we even see evidence that monetary shocks have greater real effects on industries that produce highly durable goods. (Tyler Cowen, *Risk and Business Cycles: New and Old Austrian Perspectives* [London: Routledge, 1997], chap. 5, p. 134)

their own analysis (be it Keynesian, monetarist, or of any other tendency) relies on the implicit assumption that the monetary factors related to credit play a leading role. These factors are fundamental to understanding the expansion and initial boom, that excessive, continuous increase which invariably takes place in the stock market, and, with the arrival of the crisis, the inevitable credit squeeze and recession, which particularly affects capital-goods industries.

Furthermore it should be obvious that such cycles perpetually recur due to an institutional cause, one capable of accounting for this inherent behavior of (controlled) market economies. As we have been arguing from the beginning of chapter 1, the cause lies in the privilege granted to bankers, allowing them, in violation of traditional legal principles, to loan out the money placed with them on demand deposit, thus operating with a fractional reserve. Governments have also taken advantage of this privilege in order to obtain easy financing in moments of difficulty, and later, via central banks, to guarantee easy credit terms and inflationary liquidity, which until now have been considered necessary and favorable as a stimulus of economic development.

The "gag rule" which has generally been imposed on the Austrian theory of the business cycle is highly significant, as is the widespread public ignorance of the functioning of the financial system. It is as if the two corresponded to an unspoken strategy to avoid change, a strategy which may originate from the desire of many theorists to maintain a justification for government intervention in financial and banking markets, together with the fear and awe most people feel at the idea of confronting banks. Thus we conclude with Mises:

> For the nonmonetary explanations of the trade cycle the experience that there are recurrent depressions is the primary thing. Their champions first do not see in their scheme of the sequence of economic events any clue which could suggest a satisfactory interpretation of these enigmatic disorders. They desperately search for a makeshift [explanation] in order to patch it onto their teachings as an alleged cycle theory. The case is different with the monetary or circulating credit theory. Modern monetary theory has finally

cleared away all notions of an alleged neutrality of money. It has proved irrefutably that there are in the market economy factors operating about which a doctrine ignorant of the driving force of money has nothing to say. . . . It has been mentioned already that every nonmonetary explanation of the cycle is bound to admit that an increase in the quantity of money or fiduciary media is an indispensable condition of the emergence of a boom. . . . The fanaticism with which the supporters of all these nonmonetary doctrines refuse to acknowledge their errors is, of course, a display of political bias. . . . [T]he interventionists are . . . anxious to demonstrate that the market economy cannot avoid the return of depressions. They are the more eager to assail the monetary theory as currency and credit manipulation is today the main instrument by means of which the anticapitalist governments are intent upon establishing government omnipotence.[118]

---

[118]Mises, "Fallacies of the Nonmonetary Explanations of the Trade Cycle," in *Human Action*, pp. 580–82.

TABLE VI-1
A SUMMARY OF STAGES

(1) An Increase in Voluntary Saving	(2) Credit Expansion (No increase in saving)

S1	The rate of consumption slows. Consumer goods drop in price.	S1	Consumption does not decline.
		S1	Banks grant new loans on a massive scale and the interest rate drops.
S2	Accounting profits decline in the consumer sector.		
		S2	Capital goods rise in price.
S2	Real wages tend to climb (unchanged nominal amount; lower-priced consumer goods).	S2	Prices climb on the stock market.
		S2	The productive structure is artificially lengthened.
S2	The Ricardo Effect: workers are replaced by capital equipment.	S2	Large accounting profits appear in the capital-goods sector.
S2	The interest rate decreases (due to the rise in saving). The stock market shows moderate growth.	S3	The capital-goods sector demands more workers.
		S3	Wages rise.
S2	Capital goods rise in price (due to the increase in the demand for them, the Ricardo Effect, and the reduction in the interest rate).	S3	The expansionary and stock market boom becomes widespread. Rampant speculation.
S3	The production of capital goods mounts.	S4	Monetary demand for consumer goods begins to grow (increased earned and entrepreneurial income is devoted to consumption).
S3	Workers are laid off in the consumer sector and hired in capital-goods industries.		
S4	The productive structure is permanently lengthened.	S4	At some point the rate of growth in credit expansion ceases to mount: the interest rate climbs. The stock market crashes.
S5	The production of consumer goods and services soars, while their price falls (increased supply and decreased monetary demand). Wages and national income rise permanently in real terms.	S4	Accounting profits appear in the consumer sector (demand increases).
		S4	The prices of consumer goods begin to grow faster than wages, in relative terms.

Expansion — *Boom* — *Crisis*

(Continued on the next page)

(Continued from previous page)

S4 Real wages fall. The Ricardo Effect: capital equipment is replaced by workers.

Depression

S5 The capital-goods sector sustains heavy accounting losses. (Demand decreases, the Ricardo Effect, and costs rise. The interest rate and the prices of commodities increase.)

S5 Workers are laid off in capital-goods industries.

S5 Entrepreneurs liquidate erroneous investment projects: bankruptcies and suspensions of payments. Widespread pessimism.

S5 Bank default mounts: Marginally less solvent banks face serious difficulties. Credit squeeze.

S5 Workers are again employed in stages close to consumption.

S5 Capital is consumed, and the productive structure becomes shorter.

S5 The production of consumer goods and services slows.

S5 The relative prices of consumer goods rise even further (decreased supply and increased monetary demand).

S5 National income and wages drop in real terms.

Recovery

S6 Once the readjustment has occurred, an increase in voluntary saving may bring recovery. See column (1). Or credit expansion may begin again. See column (2).

Notes on Table VI-1

1. All references to "increases" and "decreases" in prices refer to relative prices, not nominal prices or absolute magnitudes. Thus, for example, an "increase in the prices" of consumer goods indicates that such prices rise, in relative terms, with respect to those of intermediate goods.

2. It is simple to introduce the necessary modifications in the stages of the theoretical processes summarized in the table to include the historical peculiarities of each cycle. Hence if a rise in voluntary saving is accompanied by an increase in hoarding or the demand for money, the phases will remain the same, yet there will be a greater nominal decrease in the price of consumer goods, and a lesser increase in the nominal price of the factors of production. Nonetheless all relationships among relative prices remain just as depicted in the table. In the case of credit expansion, if "idle capacity" exists at its initiation, the nominal price of the factors of production and capital goods will not rise as significantly in the beginning, though the rest of the stages will follow as described, and foolish investments will also pile up.

3. Though the number which follows the letter "S" denotes the order of the stages, in certain cases this numbering is relatively arbitrary, depending upon each particular historical situation and whether or not the stages take place more or less simultaneously.

4. In real life the process could come to an indefinite halt during any of the phases, if government intervention makes markets highly rigid, and specifically if the prices of intermediate goods, wages or labor legislation are successfully manipulated. Furthermore a progressive increase in credit expansion may postpone the eruption of the crisis (and/or the liquidation of the malinvestments), but it will make it deeper and more painful when it inevitably hits.

7

A CRITIQUE OF MONETARIST AND KEYNESIAN THEORIES

I n this chapter we will criticize alternative theoretical developments aimed at explaining economic cycles. More specifically, we will consider the theories of the two most deeply-rooted schools of macroeconomics: the Monetarist School and the Keynesian School. According to the general view, these two approaches offer alternative, competing explanations of economic phenomena. However from the standpoint of the analysis presented here, they suffer from very similar defects and can thus be criticized using the same arguments. Following an introduction in which we identify what we believe to be the unifying element of the macroeconomic approaches, we will study the monetarist position (including some references to new classical economics and the school of rational expectations) and then the Keynesian and neo-Ricardian stances. With this chapter we wrap up the most important analytical portion of the book. At the end, as an appendix, we include a theoretical study of several peripheral financial institutions unrelated to banking. We are now fully prepared to grasp the different effects they exert on the economic system.

1
INTRODUCTION

Though most textbooks on economics and the history of economic thought contain the assertion that the subjectivist

revolution Carl Menger started in 1871 has been fully
absorbed by modern economic theory, to a large extent this
claim is mere rhetoric. The old "objectivism" of the Classical
School which dominated economics until the eruption of the
marginalist revolution continues to wield a powerful influence. Moreover various important fields within economic theory have until now remained largely unproductive due to the
imperfect reception and assimilation of the "subjectivist
view."[1]

Perhaps money and "macroeconomics" (a term of varying
accuracy) constitute one of the most significant areas of economics in which the influence of the marginalist revolution
and subjectivism has not yet been noticeable. In fact with the
exception of Austrian School theorists, in the past macroeconomic scholars have not generally been able to trace their theories and arguments back to their true origin: the action of
human individuals. More specifically, they have not incorporated the following essential idea of Menger's into their models:
every action involves a series of consecutive stages which the
actor must complete (and which take time) before he reaches
his goal in the future. Menger's most important conceptual

---

[1]For example, when Oskar Lange and other theorists developed the
neoclassical theory of socialism, they intended it to apply Walras's
model of general equilibrium to solve the problem of socialist economic
calculation. The majority of economists believed for many years that
this issue had been successfully resolved, but recently it became clear
their belief was unjustified. This error would have been obvious had
most economists understood from the beginning the true meaning and
scope of the subjectivist revolution and had they completely imbued
themselves with it. Indeed if all volition, information, and knowledge is
created by and arises from human beings in the course of their free interaction with other actors in the market, it should be evident that, to the
extent economic agents' ability to act freely is systematically limited (the
essence of the socialist system is embodied in such institutional coercion), their capacity to create, to discover new information and to coordinate society diminishes, making it impossible for actors to discover the
practical information necessary to coordinate society and make economic calculations. On this topic see Huerta de Soto, *Socialismo, cálculo
económico y función empresarial*, chaps. 4–7, pp. 157–411.

contribution to economics was his theory of economic goods of different order (consumer goods, or "first-order" economic goods, and "higher-order" economic goods). According to this theory, higher-order economic goods are embodied in a number of successive stages, each of which is further from final consumption than the last, ending in the initial stage in which the actor plans his whole action process. The entire theory of capital and cycles we have presented here rests on this concept of Menger's. It is a basic idea which is easy to understand, given that all people, simply by virtue of being human, recognize this concept of human action as the one they put into practice daily in all contexts in which they act. In short Austrian School theorists have developed the whole theory of capital, money and cycles which is implicit in the subjectivism that revolutionized economics in 1871.

Nevertheless in economics antiquated patterns of thinking have been at the root of a very powerful backlash against subjectivism, and this reaction is still noticeable today. Thus it is not surprising that Frank H. Knight, one of the most important authors of one of the two "objectivist" schools we will critically examine in this chapter, has stated:

> Perhaps the most serious defect in Menger's economic system . . . is his view of production as a process of converting goods of higher order to goods of lower order.[2]

We will now consider the ways in which the ideas of the Classical School have continued to predominate in the Monetarist and Keynesian Schools, the developers of which have thus far disregarded the subjectivist revolution started in 1871. Our analysis will begin with an explanation of the errors in the concept of capital proposed by J.B. Clark and F.H. Knight. Then we will critically examine the mechanistic version of the quantity theory of money supported by monetarists. Following a brief digression into the school of rational expectations, we will study the ways in which Keynesian economics, today

---

[2]Frank H. Knight, in his introduction to the first English edition of Carl Menger's book, *Principles of Economics*, p. 25.

in the grip of a crisis, shares many of the theoretical errors of monetarist macroeconomics.[3]

2
A CRITIQUE OF MONETARISM

THE MYTHICAL CONCEPT OF CAPITAL

In general the Neoclassical School has followed a tradition which predated the subjectivist revolution and which deals with a productive system in which the different factors

---

[3]The following words of John Hicks offer compelling evidence that the subjectivist revolution sparked off by the Austrian School lay at the core of economic development until the eruption of the neoclassical-Keynesian "counterrevolution":

> I have proclaimed the "Austrian" affiliation of my ideas; the tribute to Böhm-Bawerk, and to his followers, is a tribute that I am proud to make. I am writing in their tradition; yet I have realized, as my work has continued, that it is a wider and bigger tradition than at first appeared. The "Austrians" were not a peculiar sect, out of the main stream; they were in the main stream; it was the others who were out of it. (Hicks, *Capital and Time*, p. 12)

It is interesting to observe the personal scientific development of Sir John Hicks. The first edition of his book, *The Theory of Wages* (London: Macmillan, 1932), reflects a strong Austrian influence on his early work. Chapters 9 to 11 were largely inspired by Hayek, Böhm-Bawerk, Robbins, and other Austrians, whom he often quotes (see, for example, the quotations on pp. 190, 201, 215, 217 and 231). Hicks later became one of the main architects of the doctrinal synthesis of the neoclassical-Walrasian School and the Keynesian School. In the final stage of his career as an economist, he returned with a certain sense of remorse to his subjectivist origins, which were deeply rooted in the Austrian School. The result was his last work on capital theory, from which the excerpt at the beginning of this note is taken. The following statement John Hicks made in 1978 is even clearer, if such a thing is possible: "I now rate Walras and Pareto, who were my first loves, so much below Menger." John Hicks, "Is Interest the Price of a Factor of Production?" included in *Time, Uncertainty, and Disequilibrium: Exploration of Austrian Themes*, Mario J. Rizzo, ed. (Lexington, Mass.: Lexington Books, 1979), p. 63.

of production give rise, in a homogenous and horizontal manner, to consumer goods and services, without at all allowing for the immersion of these factors in time and space throughout a temporal structure of productive stages. This was more or less the basic framework for the research of classical economists from Adam Smith, Ricardo, Malthus, and John Stuart Mill to Marshall.[4] It also ultimately provided the structure for

---

[4]Alfred Marshall is undoubtedly the person most responsible for the failure of both monetarist and Keynesian School theorists, his intellectual heirs, to understand the processes by which credit and monetary expansion affect the productive structure. Indeed Marshall was unable to incorporate the subjectivist revolution (started by Carl Menger in 1871) into Anglo Saxon economics and to carry it to its logical conclusion. On the contrary, he insisted on constructing a "decaffeinated" *synthesis* of new marginalist contributions and Anglo-Saxon Classical School theories which has plagued neoclassical economics up to the present. Thus it is interesting to note that for Marshall, as for Knight, the key subjectivist distinction between first-order economic goods, or consumer goods, and higher-order economic goods "is vague and perhaps not of much practical use" (Alfred Marshall, *Principles of Economics*, 8th ed. [London: Macmillan, 1920], p. 54). Moreover Marshall was unable to do away with the old, pre-subjectivist ways of thinking, according to which costs determine prices, not vice versa. In fact Marshall believed that while marginal utility determined the demand for goods, supply ultimately depended on "real" factors. He neglected to take into account that costs are simply the actor's subjective valuation of the goals he relinquishes upon acting, and hence both blades of Marshall's famous "pair of scissors" have the same subjectivist essence based on utility (Rothbard, *Man, Economy, and State*, pp. 301–08). Language problems (the works of Austrian theorists were belatedly translated into English, and then only partially) and the clear intellectual chauvinism of many British economists have also helped significantly to uphold Marshall's doctrines. This explains the fact that most economists in the Anglo-Saxon tradition are not only very distrustful of the Austrians, but they have also insisted on keeping the ideas of Marshall, and therefore those of Ricardo and the rest of the classical economists as part of their models (see, for example, H.O. Meredith's letter to John Maynard Keynes, dated December 8, 1931 and published on pp. 267–68 of volume 13 of *The Collected Writings of John Maynard Keynes: The General Theory and After*, Part I, *Preparation*, Donald Moggridge, ed. [London: Macmillan, 1973]. See also the criticism Schumpeter levels against Marshall in Joseph A. Schumpeter, *History of Economic Analysis* [Oxford and New York: Oxford University Press, 1954], pp. 920–24).

the work of John Bates Clark (1847–1938). Clark was Professor of Economics at Columbia University in New York, and his strong anti-subjectivist reaction in the area of capital and interest theory continues even today to serve as the foundation for the entire neoclassical-monetarist edifice.[5] Indeed Clark considers production and consumption to be *simultaneous*. In his view production processes are not comprised of stages, nor is there a need to wait any length of time before obtaining the results of production processes. Clark regards capital as a *permanent fund* which "automatically" generates a productivity in the form of interest. According to Clark, the larger this social fund of capital, the lower the interest. The phenomenon of time preference in no way influences interest in his model.

It is evident that Clark's concept of the production process consists merely of a transposition of Walras's notion of general equilibrium to the field of capital theory. Walras developed an economic model of general equilibrium which he expressed in terms of a system of *simultaneous* equations intended to explain how the market prices of different goods and services are determined. The main flaw in Walras's model is that it involves the interaction, within a system of simultaneous equations, of magnitudes (variables and parameters) which are not simultaneous, but which occur *sequentially* in time as the actions of the agents participating in the economic system drive the production process. In short, Walras's model of general equilibrium is a strictly static model which fails to account for the passage of time and which describes the interaction of supposedly concurrent variables and parameters which never arise simultaneously in real life.

Logically, it is impossible to explain real economic processes using an economic model which ignores the issue of time and in which the study of the sequential generation of

---

5The following are J.B. Clark's most important writings: "The Genesis of Capital," pp. 302–15; "The Origin of Interest," *Quarterly Journal of Economics* 9 (April 1895): 257–78; *The Distribution of Wealth* (New York: Macmillan, 1899, reprinted by Augustus M. Kelley, New York 1965); and "Concerning the Nature of Capital: A Reply."

processes is painfully absent.[6] It is surprising that a theory such as the one Clark defends has nevertheless become the most widely accepted in economics up to the present day and appears in most introductory textbooks. Indeed nearly all of these books begin with an explanation of the "circular flow of income,"[7] which describes the interdependence of production, consumption and exchanges between the different economic agents (households, firms, etc.). Such explanations completely overlook the role of time in the development of economic events. In other words, this model relies on the

---

[6]Perhaps the theorist who has most brilliantly criticized the different attempts at offering a functional explanation of price theory through static models of equilibrium (general or partial) has been Hans Mayer in his article, "Der Erkenntniswert der funktionellen Preistheorien," published in *Die Wirtschaftstheorie der Gegenwart* (Vienna: Verlag von Julius Springer, 1932), vol. 2, pp. 147–239b. This article was translated into English at the request of Israel M. Kirzner and published with the title, "The Cognitive Value of Functional Theories of Price: Critical and Positive Investigations Concerning the Price Problem," chapter 16 of *Classics in Austrian Economics: A Sampling in the History of a Tradition*, vol. 2: *The InterWar Period* (London: William Pickering, 1994), pp. 55–168. Hans Mayer concludes:

> In essence, there is an immanent, more or less disguised, fiction at the heart of mathematical equilibrium theories: that is, *they bind together, in simultaneous equations, non-simultaneous magnitudes operative in genetic-causal sequence as if these existed together at the same time.* A state of affairs is *synchronized* in the "static" approach, whereas in reality we are dealing with a *process*. But one simply cannot consider a *generative process* "statically" as a *state of rest*, without eliminating precisely that which makes it what it is. (Mayer, p. 92 in the English edition; italics in original)

Mayer later revised and expanded his paper substantially at the request of Gustavo del Vecchio: Hans Mayer, "Il concetto di equilibrio nella teoria economica," in *Economía Pura*, Gustavo del Vecchio, ed., *Nuova Collana di Economisti Stranieri e Italiani* (Turin: Unione Tipografico-Editrice Torinese, 1937), pp. 645–799.

[7]A standard presentation of the "circular flow of income" model and its traditional flow chart appears, for example, in Paul A. Samuelson and William D. Nordhaus, *Economics*. According to Mark Skousen the inventor of the circular-flow diagram (under the name of "wheel of wealth") was precisely Frank H. Knight. See Skousen, *Vienna and Chicago: Friends or Foes* (Washington, D.C.: Capital Press, 2005), p. 65.

assumption that all actions occur *at once*, a false and totally groundless supposition which not only avoids solving important, real economic issues, but also constitutes an almost insurmountable obstacle to the discovery and analysis of them by economics scholars. This idea has also led Clark and his followers to believe interest is determined by the "marginal productivity" of that mysterious, homogenous fund they consider capital to be, which explains their conclusion that as this fund of capital increases, the interest rate will tend to fall.[8]

---

[8]For our purposes, i.e., the analysis of the effects credit expansion exerts on the productive structure, it is not necessary to take a stand here on which theory of interest is the most valid, however it is worth noting that Böhm-Bawerk refuted the theories which base interest on the productivity of capital. In fact according to Böhm-Bawerk the theorists who claim interest is determined by the marginal productivity of capital are unable to explain, among other points, why competition among the different entrepreneurs does not tend to cause the value of capital goods to be identical to that of their corresponding output, thus eliminating any value differential between costs and output throughout the production period. As Böhm-Bawerk indicates, the theories based on productivity are merely a remnant of the objectivist concept of value, according to which value is determined by the historical cost incurred in the production process of the different goods and services. However prices determine costs, not vice versa. In other words, economic agents incur costs because they believe the value they will be able to obtain from the consumer goods they produce will exceed these costs. The same principle applies to each capital good's marginal productivity, which is ultimately determined by the *future* value of the consumer goods and services which it helps to produce and which, by a discount process, yields the *present* market value of the capital good in question. Thus the origin and existence of interest must be independent of capital goods, and must rest on human beings' subjective time preference. It is easy to comprehend why theorists of the Clark-Knight School have fallen into the trap of considering the interest rate to be determined by the marginal productivity of capital. We need only observe that interest and the marginal productivity of capital become equal in the presence of the following: (1) an environment of perfect equilibrium in which no changes occur; (2) a concept of capital as a mythical fund which replicates itself and involves no need for specific decision-making with respect to its depreciation; and (3) a notion of production as an "instantaneous" process which takes no time. In the presence of these three conditions, which are as absurd as they are removed from reality, the rent of a capital good is always equal to the interest rate. In light of this fact it is perfectly understandable that

After John Bates Clark, another American economist, Irving Fisher, the most visible exponent of the mechanistic version of the quantity theory of money, also defended the thesis that capital is a "fund," in the same way income is a "flow." He did so in his book, *The Nature of Capital and Income*, and his defense of this thesis lent support to Clark's markedly "macroeconomic" view involving general equilibrium.[9]

In addition Clark's objectivist, static concept of capital was also advocated by Frank H. Knight (1885–1962), the founder of the present-day Chicago School. In fact Knight, following in Clark's footsteps, viewed capital as a permanent fund which automatically and synchronously produces income, and he considered the production "process" to be instantaneous and not comprised of different temporal stages.[10]

---

theorists, imbued with a synchronous, instantaneous conception of capital, have been deceived by the mathematical equality of income and interest in a hypothetical situation such as this, and that from there they have jumped to the theoretically unjustifiable conclusion that productivity determines the interest rate (and not vice versa, as the Austrians assert). On this subject see: Eugen von Böhm-Bawerk, *Capital and Interest*, vol. 1, pp. 73–122. See also Israel M. Kirzner's article, "The Pure Time-Preference Theory of Interest: An Attempt at Clarification," printed as chapter 4 of the book, *The Meaning of Ludwig von Mises: Contributions in Economics, Sociology, Epistemology, and Political Philosophy*, Jeffrey M. Herbener, ed. (Dordrecht, Holland: Kluwer Academic Publishers, 1993), pp. 166–92; republished as essay 4 in Israel M. Kirzner's book, *Essays on Capital and Interest*, pp. 134–53. Also see Fetter's book, *Capital, Interest and Rent*, pp. 172–316.

[9]Irving Fisher, *The Nature of Capital and Income* (New York: Macmillan, 1906); see also his article, "What Is Capital?" published in the *Economic Journal* (December 1896): 509–34.

[10]George J. Stigler is another author of the Chicago School who has gone to great lengths to support Clark and Knight's mythical conception of capital. In fact Stigler, in his doctoral thesis (written, interestingly enough, under the direction of Frank H. Knight in 1938), vigorously attacks the subjectivist concept of capital developed by Menger, Jevons, and Böhm-Bawerk. In reference to Menger's groundbreaking contribution with respect to goods of different order, Stigler believes "the classification of goods into ranks was in itself, however, of dubious value."

AUSTRIAN CRITICISM OF CLARK AND KNIGHT

Austrian economists reacted energetically to Clark and Knight's erroneous, objectivist conception of the production process. Böhm-Bawerk, for instance, describes Clark's concept of capital as *mystical* and *mythological*, pointing out that production processes never depend upon a mysterious, homogeneous fund, but instead invariably rely on the joint operation of specific capital goods which entrepreneurs must always first conceive, produce, select, and combine within the economic process. According to Böhm-Bawerk, Clark views capital as a sort of "value jelly," or fictitious notion. With remarkable foresight, Böhm-Bawerk warned that acceptance of such an idea was bound to lead to grave errors in the future development of economic theory.[11]

He thus criticizes Menger for not formulating a concept of the production "process" as one in which capital goods yield "a perpetual stream of services (income)." George J. Stigler, *Production and Distribution Theories* (London: Transaction Publishers, 1994), pp. 138 and 157. As is logical, Stigler concludes that "Clark's theory of capital is fundamentally sound, in the writer's opinion" (p. 314). Stigler fails to realize that a mythical, abstract fund which replicates itself leaves no room for entrepreneurs, since all economic events recur again and again without change. However in real life capital only retains its productive capacity through concrete human actions regarding all aspects of investing, depreciating and consuming specific capital goods. Such entrepreneurial actions may be successful, but they are also subject to error.

[11]Eugen von Böhm-Bawerk, "Professor Clark's Views on the Genesis of Capital," *Quarterly Journal of Economics* IX (1895): 113–31, reprinted on pp. 131–43 of *Classics in Austrian Economics*, Kirzner, ed., vol. 1. Böhm-Bawerk, in particular, predicted with great foresight that if Clark's static model were to prevail, the long-discredited doctrines of underconsumption would revive. Keynesianism, which in a sense stemmed from Marshall's neoclassical theories, is a good example:

> When one goes with Professor Clark into such an account of the matter, the assertion that capital is not consumed is seen to be another inexact, shining figure of speech, which must not be taken at all literally. Any one taking it literally falls into a total error, into which, for sooth, science has already fallen once. I refer to the familiar and at one time widely disseminated doctrine that saving is a social evil and the class of

Years after Böhm-Bawerk, fellow Austrian Fritz Machlup voiced his strong criticism of the Clark-Knight theory of capital, concluding that

> [t]here was and is always the choice between maintaining, increasing, or consuming capital. And past and "present" experience tells us that the decision in favour of consumption

---

> spendthrifts a useful factor in social economy, because what is saved is not spent and so producers cannot find a market. (Böhm-Bawerk quoted in *Classics in Austrian Economics*, Kirzner, ed., vol. 1, p. 137)

Mises reaches the same conclusion when he censures Knight for his

> chimerical notions such as "the self-perpetuating character" of useful things. In any event their teachings are designed to provide a justification for the doctrine which blames oversaving and underconsumption for all that is unsatisfactory and recommends spending as a panacea. (*Human Action*, p. 848)

Further Böhm-Bawerk criticism of Clark appears mainly in his essays, "Capital and Interest Once More," printed in *Quarterly Journal of Economics* (November 1906 and February 1907): esp. pp. 269, 277 and 280–82; "The Nature of Capital: A Rejoinder," *Quarterly Journal of Economics* (November 1907); and in the above-cited *Capital and Interest*. Moreover the fact that Böhm-Bawerk's "average production period" idea was misconceived, a fact recognized by Menger, Mises, Hayek, and others, in no way justifies the mythical concept of capital Clark and Knight propose. The members of the Austrian School have unanimously acknowledged that Böhm-Bawerk made a "slip" when he introduced the (non-existent) "average production period" in his analysis, since the entire theory of capital may be easily constructed from a prospective viewpoint; that is, in light of actors' subjective estimates regarding the time periods their future actions will take. In fact Hayek states,

> Professor Knight seems to hold that to expose the ambiguities and inconsistencies involved in the notion of an average investment period serves to expel the idea of time from capital theory altogether. But it is not so. In general it is sufficient to say that the investment period of some factors has been lengthened, while those of all others have remained unchanged. (F.A. Hayek, "The Mythology of Capital," *Quarterly Journal of Economics* [February 1936]: 206)

of capital is far from being impossible or improbable. Capital is not necessarily perpetual.[12]

Realizing the debate between the two sides is not pointless, as it involves the clash of two radically incompatible conceptions of economics (namely subjectivism versus objectivism based on general equilibrium), Hayek also attacked Clark and Knight's position, which he felt rested on the following essential error:

> This basic mistake—if the substitution of a meaningless statement for the solution of a problem can be called a mistake—is the idea of capital as a fund which maintains itself automatically, and that, in consequence, once an amount of capital has been brought into existence the necessity of reproducing it presents no economic problem.[13]

Hayek insists that the debate on the nature of capital is not merely terminological. On the contrary, he emphasizes that the mythical conception of capital as a self-sustaining fund in a production "process" which involves no time prevents its own proponents from identifying, on the whole, the important economic issues in real life. In particular it blinds them to variations in the productive structure which result from changes in the level of voluntary saving, and to the ways credit expansion affects the structure of production. In other words the mythical concept of capital keeps its supporters from understanding the close relationship between the *micro* and *macro* aspects of economics, since the connection between

---

[12]Fritz Machlup, "Professor Knight and the 'Period of Production,'" p. 580, reprinted in Israel M. Kirzner, ed., *Classics in Austrian Economics*, vol. 2, chap. 20, pp. 275–315.

[13]F.A. Hayek, "The Mythology of Capital," *Quarterly Journal of Economics* (February 1936): 203. Several years later, Hayek added:

> I am afraid, with all due respect to Professor Knight, I cannot take this view seriously because I cannot attach any meaning to this mystical "fund" and I shall not treat this view as a serious rival of the one here adopted. (Hayek, *The Pure Theory of Capital*, p. 94)

the two is composed precisely of the temporal plans of creative entrepreneurs who, by definition, are excluded from the Walrasian model of the economic system, the model Clark and Knight incorporate into their theory of capital.[14]

Ludwig von Mises later joined the debate, showing his disapproval of the "new chimerical notions such as the 'self-perpetuating character' of useful things."[15] Mises echoes Böhm-Bawerk's[16] views when he points out that such notions are eventually put forward to justify doctrines based on the myth of "underconsumption" and on the supposed "paradox of thrift," and to thus provide a theoretical basis for economic policies which foster increased consumption to the detriment of saving. Mises explains that the entire current structure of capital goods is the result of concrete entrepreneurial decisions made in the past by real people who on specific occasions opted to invest in certain capital goods, and on others, to replace them or group them differently, and on yet others to even relinquish or consume capital goods already produced. Hence "we are better off than earlier generations because we are equipped with the capital goods they have accumulated for us."[17] Incredibly, it appears this theoretical principle and others equally obvious have yet to sink in.

In his more recent book, *An Essay on Capital*, Israel M. Kirzner emphasizes that Clark and Knight's concept of capital rules out human, entrepreneurial decision-making in the

---

[14]The negative consequences of disregarding the time factor and the stages involved in any action process were stressed by Hayek as early as 1928, when he pointed out that,

> [I]t becomes evident that the customary abstraction from time does a degree of violence to the actual state of affairs which casts serious doubt on the utility of the results thereby achieved. (F.A. Hayek, "Intertemporal Price Equilibrium and Movements in the Value of Money," originally published in German in 1928, chapter 4 of *Money, Capital and Fluctuations*, p. 72)

[15]Mises, *Human Action*, p. 848.

[16]See footnote 11 above.

[17]Mises, *Human Action*, p. 492.

production process. Individuals' different *plans* regarding the specific capital goods they may decide to create and employ in their production processes are not even considered. In short Clark and Knight assume that the course of events flows "by itself" and that the future is an objective given which follows a set pattern and is not influenced by individual agents' microeconomic actions and decisions, which they deem fully predetermined. Kirzner concludes that the view of Clark and Knight ignores "the planned character of capital goods maintenance," adding that their model requires acceptance of the notion that

> the future will take care of itself so long as the present "sources" of future output flows are appropriately maintained. . . . The Knightian approach reflects perfectly the way in which this misleading and unhelpful notion of "automaticity" has been developed into a fully articulated and self-contained theory of capital.[18]

A CRITIQUE OF THE MECHANISTIC MONETARIST VERSION OF THE QUANTITY THEORY OF MONEY

Monetarists not only overlook the role time and stages play in the economy's productive structure. They also accept a *mechanistic* version of the quantity theory of money, a version they base on an equation which supposedly demonstrates the existence of a *direct* causal link between the total quantity of money in circulation, the "general level" of prices and total production. The equation is as follows:

$$MV = PT$$

where M is the stock of money, V the "velocity of circulation" (the number of times the monetary unit changes hands on average in a certain time period), P the general price level, and T the "aggregate" of all quantities of goods and services exchanged in a year.[19]

---

[18]Kirzner, *An Essay on Capital*, p. 63; italics deleted.

[19]This is the transaction version of the equation of exchange. According to Irving Fisher (*The Purchasing Power of Money: Its Determination and*

Supposing the "velocity of circulation" of money remains relatively constant over time, and the gross national product approximates that of "full employment," monetarists believe money is *neutral* in the long run, and that therefore an expansion of the money supply (*M*) tends to *proportionally* raise the corresponding general price level. In other words, though in nominal terms the different factor incomes and production and consumption prices may increase by the same percentage as the money supply, in real terms they remain the same over time. Hence monetarists believe inflation is a monetary phenomenon that affects all economic sectors *uniformly and proportionally*, and that therefore it does not disrupt or discoordinate the structure of productive stages. It is clear that the monetarist viewpoint is purely "macroeconomic" and ignores the microeconomic effects of monetary growth on the productive structure. As we saw in the last section, this approach stems from the lack of a capital theory which takes the time factor into account.

Relation to Credit Interest and Crises [New York: Macmillan, 1911 and 1925], p. 48 in the 1925 edition), the left side of the equation can also be separated out into two parts, *MV* and *M'V'*, where *M'* and *V'* denote respectively the supply and velocity of money with respect to bank deposits:

$$MV + M'V' = PT$$

A national income version of the equation of exchange has also been proposed. In this case *T* represents a "real" national income measure (for example, the "real" gross national product), which, as we know, only includes consumer goods and services and *final* capital goods (see, for instance, Samuelson and Nordhaus, *Economics*). This version is particularly faulty, since it excludes all products of intermediate stages in the productive structure, products *which are also exchanged in units of the money stock, M*. Thus the equation more than halves the true, real value of *T* which *MV* supposedly influences. Finally, the Cambridge cash balance version is as follows:

$$M = kPT$$

where *M* is the stock of money (though it can also be interpreted as the *desired* cash balance) and *PT* is a measure of national income. See Milton Friedman, "Quantity Theory of Money," in *The New Palgrave: A Dictionary of Economics*, vol. 4, esp. pp. 4–7.

The English economist R.G. Hawtrey, a main exponent of the Monetarist School in the early twentieth century, is one whose position illustrates the theoretical difficulties of monetarism. In his review of Hayek's book, *Prices and Production,* which appeared in 1931, Hawtrey expressed his inability to understand the book. To comprehend this assertion, one must take into account that Hayek's approach presupposes a capital theory; but monetarists lack such a theory and therefore fail to grasp how credit expansion affects the productive structure.[20] Furthermore against all empirical evidence, Hawtrey declares that the first symptom of all depressions is a decline in sales in the sector of final consumer goods, thus overlooking the fact that a much sharper drop in the price of capital goods always comes first. Thus the prices of consumer goods fluctuate relatively little throughout the cycle when compared to those of capital goods produced in the stages furthest from consumption. Moreover, in keeping with his monetarist position, Hawtrey believes credit expansion gives rise to excess monetary demand which is *uniformly* distributed among all goods and services in society.[21]

---

[20]To be precise, Hawtrey stated that Hayek's book was "so difficult and obscure that it is impossible to understand." See R.G. Hawtrey, "Review of Hayek's *Prices and Production,*" *Economica* 12 (1932): 119–25. Hawtrey was an officer of the British Treasury and a monetarist who competed with Keynes in the 1930s for prominence and influence on government economic policy. Even today the Austrian theory of the cycle continues to baffle monetarists. Modern monetarists keep repeating Hawtrey's *boutade*: for instance, Allan Meltzer, in reference to Hayek's *Prices and Production*, has stated:

> The book is obscure and incomprehensible. Fortunately for all of us, and for political economy and social science, Hayek did not spend his life trying to explain what *Prices and Production* tried to do. (Allan Meltzer, "Comments on Centi and O'Driscoll," manuscript presented at the General Meeting of the Mont Pèlerin Society, Cannes, France, September 25–30, 1994, p. 1)

[21]R.G. Hawtrey, *Capital and Employment* (London: Longmans Green, 1937), p. 250. Hayek levels penetrating criticism against Hawtrey in his review of Hawtrey's book, *Great Depression and the Way Out*, in *Economica* 12 (1932): 126–27. That same year Hayek wrote an article ("Das

More recently other monetarists have also revealed their lack of an adequate capital theory and have thus expressed the same bewilderment as Hawtrey with respect to studies on the effects of monetary expansion on the productive structure. Milton Friedman and Anna J. Schwartz, in reference to the possible effects of money on the productive structure, state:

> We have little confidence in our knowledge of the transmission mechanism, except in such broad and vague terms as to constitute little more than an impressionistic representation rather than an engineering blueprint.[22]

Furthermore, surprisingly, these authors maintain that no empirical evidence exists to support the thesis that credit expansion exerts an irregular effect on the productive structure. Therefore they disregard not only the theoretical analysis presented in detail here, but also the different empirical studies reviewed in the last chapter. Such studies identify *typical*,

---

Schicksal der Goldwährung," printed in the *Deutsche Volkswirt* 20 (February 1932): 642–45, and no. 21, pp. 677–81; English translation entitled "The Fate of the Gold Standard," chapter 5 of *Money, Capital and Fluctuations*, pp. 118–35) in which he strongly criticizes Hawtrey for being, along with Keynes, one of the key architects and defenders of the program to stabilize the monetary unit. According to Hayek, such a program, based on credit expansion and implemented in an environment of rising productivity, will inevitably cause profound discoordination in the productive structure and a serious recession. Hayek concludes that

> Mr. Hawtrey seems to be one of the stabilization theorists referred to above, to whose influence the willingness of the managements of the central banks to depart more than ever before from the policy rules traditionally followed by such banks can be attributed. (Hayek, *Money, Capital and Fluctuations*, p. 120)

[22]See Milton Friedman, *The Optimum Quantity of Money and Other Essays* (Chicago: Aldine, 1979), p. 222, and the book by Milton Friedman and Anna J. Schwartz, *Monetary Trends in the United States and United Kingdom: Their Relation to Income, Prices and Interest Rates, 1867–1975* (Chicago: University of Chicago Press, 1982), esp. pp. 26–27 and 30–31. The mention of "engineering" and the "transmission mechanism" betrays the strong scientific leaning of these two authors.

empirical features which largely coincide with those observed in all cycles from the time they began.

Friedrich A. Hayek stated that his

> chief objection against [monetarist] theory is that, as what is called a "macrotheory," it pays attention only to the effects of changes in the quantity of money on the general price level and not to the effects on the structure of relative prices. In consequence, it tends to disregard what seems to me the most harmful effects of inflation: the misdirection of resources it causes and the unemployment which ultimately results from it.[23]

It is easy to understand why a theory such as the one monetarists hold, which is constructed in strictly macroeconomic terms with no analysis of underlying microeconomic factors, must ignore not only the effects of credit expansion on the productive structure, but also, in general, the ways in which "general price level" fluctuations influence the structure of *relative* prices.[24] Rather than simply raise or lower the general

---

[23]Hayek, *New Studies in Philosophy, Politics, Economics and the History of Ideas*, p. 215. Near the end of his life, Fritz Machlup commented on the same topic:

> I don't know why a man as intelligent as Milton Friedman doesn't give more emphasis to relative prices, relative costs, even in an inflationary period. (Joseph T. Salerno and Richard M. Ebeling, "An Interview with Professor Fritz Machlup," *Austrian Economics Newsletter* 3, no. 1 [Summer, 1980]: 12)

[24] The main fault of the old quantity theory as well as the math-ematical economists' equation of exchange is that they have ignored this fundamental issue. Changes in the supply of money must bring about changes in other data too. The mar-ket system before and after the inflow or outflow of a quan-tity of money is not merely changed in that the cash holdings of the individuals and prices have increased or decreased. There have been effected also changes in the reciprocal exchange ratios between the various commodities and serv-ices which, if one wants to resort to metaphors, are more ade-quately described by the image of price revolution than by the misleading figure of an elevation or sinking of the "price level." (Mises, *Human Action*, p. 413)

price level, fluctuations in credit constitute a "revolution" which affects all relative prices and eventually provokes a crisis of malinvestment and an economic recession. The inability to perceive this fact led the American economist Benjamin M. Anderson to assert that the fundamental flaw in the quantity theory of money is merely that it conceals from the researcher the underlying microeconomic phenomena influenced by variations in the general price level. Indeed monetarists content themselves with the quantity theory's equation of exchange, deeming all important issues to be adequately addressed by it and subsequent microeconomic analyses to be unnecessary.[25]

The above sheds light on monetarists' lack of a satisfactory theory of economic cycles and on their belief that crises and depressions are caused merely by a "monetary contraction." This is a naive and superficial diagnosis which confuses the cause with the effect. As we know, economic crises arise because credit expansion and inflation first distort the productive structure through a complex process which *later* manifests itself in a crisis, monetary squeeze, and recession. Attributing crises to a monetary contraction is like attributing measles to the fever and rash which accompany it. This explanation of cycles can only be upheld by the scientistic, ultra-empirical methodology of monetarist macroeconomics, an approach which lacks a temporal theory of capital.[26]

---

[25]   The formula of the quantity theorists is a monotonous "tit-tat-toe"—money, credit, and prices. With this explanation the problem was solved and further research and further investigation were unnecessary, and consequently stopped—for those who believed in this theory. It is one of the great vices of the quantity theory of money that it tends to check investigation for underlying factors in a business situation.

Anderson concludes:

The quantity theory of money is invalid. . . . We cannot accept a predominantly monetary general theory either for the level of commodity prices or for the movements of the business cycle. (Anderson, *Economics and the Public Welfare*, pp. 70–71)

[26]The Spanish monetarist Pedro Schwartz once stated:

Furthermore not only are monetarists incapable of explaining economic recessions except by resorting to the effects of the monetary contraction;[27] they have also been unable to present any valid theoretical argument against the Austrian theory of economic cycles: they have simply ignored it or, as Friedman has done, have only mentioned it in passing, falsely indicating that it lacks an "empirical" basis. Thus David Laidler, in a recent critique of the Austrian theory of the cycle, had no choice but to turn to the old, worn-out Keynesian arguments which center on the supposedly healthy influence of effective demand on real income. The basic idea is this: that an increase in effective demand could ultimately give rise to an increase in income, and hence, supposedly, in savings, and that therefore the artificial lengthening based on credit expansion could be maintained indefinitely, and the process of poor allocation of resources would not necessarily reverse in the form of a recession.[28] The essential error

---

> There is no proven theory of cycles: it is a phenomenon we simply do not understand. However with money becoming elastic and expansions and recessions leaving us speechless, it is easy to see how we macroeconomists became unpopular. (Pedro Schwartz, "Macro y Micro," *Cinco Días* [April 12, 1993], p. 3)

It is regrettable that the effects of credit "elasticity" on the real economy continue to befuddle monetarists, and that they still insist on disregarding the Austrian theory of economic cycles, which not only fully *integrates* the "micro" and "macro" aspects of economics, but also explains how credit expansion, a product of fractional-reserve banking, invariably provokes a widespread poor allocation of resources in microeconomic terms, a situation which inevitably leads to a macroeconomic recession.

[27]See, for instance, Leland Yeager, *The Fluttering Veil: Essays on Monetary Disequilibrium*, George Selgin, ed. (Indianapolis, Ind.: Liberty Fund, 1997).

[28]   It is now a commonplace that, if saving depends upon real income, and if the latter is free to vary, then variations in the rate of investment induced by credit creation, among other factors, will bring about changes in the level of real income and therefore the rate of voluntary saving as an integral part of the mechanisms that re-equilibrate intertemporal choices.

in Laidler's argument was clearly exposed by Hayek already in 1941, when he explained that the *only* possible way for production processes financed by credit expansion to be maintained without a recession would be for economic agents to voluntarily save *all* new monetary income created by banks and used to finance such processes. The Austrian theory of the cycle suggests that cycles occur when *any portion* of the new monetary income (which banks create in the form of loans and which reaches the productive structure) is spent on consumer goods and services by the owners of capital goods and the original means of production. Thus the spending of a share on consumption, which is surely always the case, is sufficient to trigger the familiar microeconomic processes which irrevocably lead to a crisis and recession. In the words of Hayek himself:

> All that is required to make our analysis applicable is that, when incomes are increased by investment, the share of the additional income spent on consumers' goods during any period of time should be larger than the proportion by which the new investment adds to the output of consumers' goods during the same period of time. And there is of course no reason to expect that more than a fraction of the new income, and certainly not as much as has been newly invested, will be saved, because this would mean that practically all the income earned from the new investment would have to be saved.[29]

(See David Laidler, "Hayek on Neutral Money and the Cycle," printed in *Money and Business Cycles: The Economics of F.A. Hayek*, M. Colonna and H. Hagemann, eds., vol. 1, p. 19.)

[29]In other words, it would be necessary for economic agents to save *all* monetary income corresponding to the shaded area in Chart V-6, which reflects the portion of the productive structure lengthened and widened as a result of credit expansion. Understandably it is nearly impossible for such an event to occur in real life. The above excerpt appears on p. 394 of *The Pure Theory of Capital*. In short, credit expansion provokes a *maladjustment* in the behavior of the different productive agents, and the only remedy is an increase in voluntary saving and a decrease in artificially-lengthened investments, until the two can again become coordinated. As Lachmann eloquently puts it:

It is interesting to note that one of today's most prominent monetarists, David Laidler, is forced to resort to Keynesian arguments in a fruitless attempt to criticize the Austrian theory of economic cycles. Nevertheless the author himself correctly recognizes that from the standpoint of the Austrian theory, the differences between monetarists and Keynesians are merely trivial and mostly apparent, since both groups apply very similar "macroeconomic" methodologies in their analyses.[30]

The above reflections on monetarism (its lack of a capital theory and the adoption of a macroeconomic outlook which masks the issues of true importance) would not be complete without a criticism of the equation of exchange, $MV=PT$, on which monetarists have relied since Irving Fisher proposed it in his book, *The Purchasing Power of Money*.[31] Clearly this

---

> What the Austrian remedy—increasing voluntary savings— amounts to is nothing but *a change of data* which will turn data which originally were purely imaginary—entrepreneurs' profit expectations induced by the low rate of interest—into real data. (Lachmann, "On Crisis and Adjustment," *Review of Economics and Statistics* [May 1939]: 67)

[30]David Laidler, *The Golden Age of the Quantity Theory* (New York: Philip Allan, 1991). Laidler specifically concludes:

> I am suggesting, more generally, that there is far less difference between neoclassical and Keynesian attitudes to policy intervention, particularly in the monetary area, than is commonly believed. The economists whose contributions I have analyzed did not regard any particular set of monetary arrangements as sacrosanct. For most of them, the acid test of any system was its capacity to deliver price level stability and hence, they believed, output and employment stability too.

Laidler adds:

> The consequent adoption of Keynesian policy doctrines, too, was the natural product of treating the choice of economic institutions as a political one, to be made on pragmatic grounds. (p. 198)

Laidler's book is essential for understanding current monetarist doctrines and their evolution.

[31]Irving Fisher, *The Purchasing Power of Money*, esp. pp. 25ff. in the 1925 edition. Mises, with his customary insight, points out that defenders of the quantity theory of money have done it more damage than their

"equation of exchange" is simply an *ideogram* which rather awkwardly represents the relationship between growth in the money supply and a decline in the purchasing power of money. The origin of this "formula" is a simple *tautology* which expresses that the total amount of money *spent* on transactions conducted in the economic system during a certain time period must be identical to the quantity of money *received* on the same transactions during the same period ($MV=\Sigma pt$). However monetarists then take a leap in the dark when they assume the other side of the equation can be represented as PT, where T is an absurd "aggregate" which calls for adding up *heterogeneous*

---

opponents. This is due to the fact that the great majority of the theory's defenders have accepted the mechanistic equation of exchange which, at best, merely represents a tautology: that the income and expenditure involved in all transactions must be equal. Furthermore they attempt to supply a comprehensive explanation of economic phenomena by adding up the prices of goods and services exchanged in different time periods and assuming the value of the monetary unit is determined by, among other factors, the "velocity" of circulation of money. They fail to realize that the value of money originates with humans' subjective desire to maintain certain cash balances, and to focus exclusively on aggregate concepts and averages like the velocity of money conveys the impression that money only fulfils its function when transactions are carried out, and not when it remains "idle" in the form of cash balances held by economic agents. Nonetheless economic agents' demand for money comprises both the cash balances they retain at all times, as well as the additional amounts they demand when they make a transaction. Thus money performs its function in both cases and always has an owner; in other words, it is included in the cash balance of an economic agent, regardless of whether the agent *plans* to increase or decrease the balance at any point in the future. According to Mises, another crucial defect of the equation of exchange is that it conceals the effects variations in the quantity of money have on relative prices and the fact that new money reaches the economic system at very specific points, distorting the productive structure and favoring certain economic agents, to the detriment of the rest. Ludwig von Mises, "The Position of Money Among Economic Goods," first printed in *Die Wirtschaftstheorie der Gegenwart*, Hans Mayer, ed. (Vienna: Julius Springer, 1932), vol. 2. This article has been translated into English by Albert H. Zlabinger and published in the book, *Money, Method, and the Market Process: Essays by Ludwig von Mises*, Richard M. Ebeling, ed. (Dordrecht, Holland: Kluwer Academic Publishers, 1990), pp. 55ff.

quantities of goods and services exchanged over a period of time. The lack of homogeneity makes this an impossible sum.[32] Mises also points out the absurdity of the concept of "velocity of money," which is defined simply as the variable which, dependent on the others, is necessary to maintain the balance of the equation of exchange. The concept makes no economic sense because individual economic agents cannot possibly act as the formula indicates.[33]

Therefore the fact that monetarists' equation of exchange makes no mathematical or economic sense reduces it to a mere ideogram at most, or, as the *Shorter Oxford English Dictionary* puts it, "a character or figure symbolizing the idea of a thing without expressing the name of it, as the Chinese characters, etc."[34] This ideogram contains an undeniable element of truth inasmuch as it reflects the notion that variations in the money supply eventually influence the purchasing power of money (i.e., the price of the monetary unit in terms of every good and

---

[32]Murray N. Rothbard argues that the "general price level," P, is a weighted average of prices of goods which vary in quantity and quality in time and space, and the denominator is intended to reflect the sum of *heterogeneous* amounts expressed in different units (the year's total production in real terms). Rothbard's brilliant, perceptive critical treatment of monetarists' equation of exchange appears in his book, *Man, Economy, and State*, pp. 727–37.

[33]"For individual economic agents, it is impossible to make use of the formula: total volume of transactions divided by velocity of circulation." Mises, *The Theory of Money and Credit*, p. 154. The concept of velocity of money only makes sense if we intend to measure the general price level over a certain time period, which is patently absurd. It is pointless to consider the prices of goods and services over a period of time, e.g., a year, during which the quantity and quality of goods and services produced vary, as does the purchasing power of the monetary unit. It so happens that from an individual's point of view prices are determined in each transaction, each time a certain amount of money changes hands, so an "average velocity of circulation" is inconceivable. Moreover from a "social" standpoint, at most we might consider a "general price level" with respect to a *certain point in time* (not a period), and thus the "velocity of circulation of money" concept is totally meaningless in this case as well.

[34]*The Shorter Oxford English Dictionary*, 3rd ed. (Oxford: Oxford University Press, 1973), vol. 1, p. 1016.

service). Nevertheless its use as a supposed aid to explaining economic processes has proven highly detrimental to the progress of economic thought, since it prevents analysis of underlying microeconomic factors, forces a mechanistic interpretation of the relationship between the money supply and the general price level, and in short, masks the true microeconomic effects monetary variations exert on the real productive structure. The harmful, false notion that money is neutral results. However, as early as 1912, Ludwig von Mises demonstrated that all increases in the money supply invariably modify the structure of relative prices of goods and services. Aside from the purely imaginary case in which the new money is evenly distributed among all economic agents, it is always injected into the economy in a sequential manner and at various specific points (via public expenditure, credit expansion, or the discovery of new gold reserves in particular places). To the extent this occurs, only certain people will be the first to receive the new monetary units and have the chance to purchase new goods and services at prices not yet affected by monetary growth. Thus begins a process of *income redistribution* in which the first to receive the monetary units benefit from the situation at the expense of all other economic agents, who find themselves purchasing goods and services at rising prices before any of the newly-created monetary units reach their pockets. This process of income redistribution not only inevitably alters the "structure" of economic agents' value scales but also their weights in the market, which can only lead to changes in society's entire structure of relative prices. The specific characteristics of these changes in cases where monetary growth derives from credit expansion have been covered in detail in previous chapters.[35]

---

[35]Mises, *The Theory of Money and Credit*, p. 162 ff. Mises concludes:

> The prices of commodities after the rise of prices will not bear the same relation to each other as before its commencement; the decrease in the purchasing power of money will not be uniform with regard to different economic goods. (p. 163)

Before Mises, the same idea was also expressed by Cantillon, Hume, and Thornton, among others. For instance, see "Of Money," one of Hume's essays contained in *Essays*, pp. 286ff. Hume takes the idea from Cantillon who was the first one to express it in his *Essai sur la nature du commerce en général*, chap. VII, part II, pp. 232–39.

What policy do monetarists advocate to prevent and counter crises and economic recessions? They generally confine themselves to recommending policies that merely treat the symptoms, not the ultimate causes, of crises. In other words they suggest increasing the quantity of money in circulation, and thus reinflating the economy to fight the monetary contraction which, to a greater or lesser degree, always takes place following the crisis. They fail to realize that this macroeconomic policy hinders the liquidation of projects launched in error, prolongs the recession and may eventually lead to stagflation, a phase we have already analyzed.[36] In the long run, as we know, the expansion of new loans during a crisis can, at most, only postpone the inevitable arrival of the recession, making the subsequent readjustment even more severe. As Hayek quite clearly states:

> Any attempt to combat the crisis by credit expansion will, therefore, not only be merely the treatment of symptoms as causes, but may also prolong the depression by delaying the inevitable real adjustments.[37]

Finally, some monetarists propose the establishment of a constitutional rule which would predetermine the growth of the money supply and "guarantee" monetary stability and economic growth. However this plan would also be ineffective in averting economic crises if new doses of money continued, to any degree, to be injected into the system through credit expansion. In addition whenever a rise in general productivity "required" increased credit expansion to stabilize

---

[36]Hans F. Sennholz, *Money and Freedom* (Spring Mills, Penn.: Libertarian Press, 1985), pp. 38–39. Sennholz explains Friedman's lack of a true theory of the cycle and his attempt to disguise this gap by designing a policy aimed simply at breaking out of a recession by monetary means, without accounting for its causes.

[37]F.A. Hayek, "A Rejoinder to Mr. Keynes," *Economica* 11, no. 34 (November 1931): 398–404. Reprinted as chapter 5 of *Friedrich A. Hayek: Critical Assessments*, John Cunningham Wood and Ronald N. Woods, eds. (London and New York: Routledge, 1991), vol. 1, pp. 82–83; see also *Contra Keynes and Cambridge*, pp. 159–64.

the purchasing power of money, this action would trigger and intensify all of the processes which inexorably lead to investment errors and crisis, and which monetarists are incapable of understanding, due to the obvious deficiencies in the macroeconomic analytical tools they use.[38]

A Brief Note on the Theory of Rational Expectations

The analysis carried out here can also be applied to make some comments on both the hypothesis of rational expectations and other contributions of new classical economics. According to the hypothesis of rational expectations, economic agents tend to make correct predictions based on an appropriate use of all relevant information and on scientific knowledge made available by economic theory. Those who accept this hypothesis argue that government attempts to influence production and employment through monetary and fiscal policy are fruitless. Supporters therefore hold that, to the extent that economic agents foresee the consequences of traditional policies, these policies are ineffective in influencing real production or employment.[39]

Nevertheless there are serious flaws in the economic logic of these analytical developments in new classical economics. On the one hand, we must take into account that economic agents cannot possibly obtain all of the relevant information, both with respect to the particular circumstances of the current cycle (practical knowledge), and with respect to which economic theory best explains the course of events (scientific knowledge). This is due, among other factors, to a lack of unanimity as to which theory of cycles is the most valid: though the arguments presented here indicate that the correct explanation is the one provided by the Austrian theory of the business cycle, as long as the scientific community as a whole fails to accept it, we cannot expect all other economic agents

---

[38]See section 9 of chapter 6 (pp. 424–31), which covered the harmful effects of policies to stabilize the purchasing power of money.

[39]See the explanation on the evolution of the school of rational expectations in Garrison, *Time and Money*, chap. 2, pp. 15–30.

to recognize it as an acceptable explanation.[40] Furthermore for exactly the same reasons the economic theory of socialism has proven it is impossible for a hypothetical benevolent dictator-scientist to obtain all *practical* information concerning his subjects, it is equally impossible for each economic agent to obtain all practical information concerning his fellow citizens, and all *scientific* knowledge available at any one time.[41]

On the other hand, even if, for the sake of argument, we allow that economic agents can obtain the relevant information and hit the mark with respect to the theoretical explanation of the cycle (unanimously understanding the essential elements of our circulation credit theory), "rational expectations" theorists are still incorrect when they conclude that government fiscal and monetary policies can produce no real consequences. This is the strongest argument against the theory of rational expectations. Even if entrepreneurs have "perfect" knowledge of events to come, they cannot shy away from the effects of an expansion of credit, since their very

---

[40]As Leijonhufvud eloquently states:

> When theorists are not sure they understand, or cannot agree, it is doubtful that they are entitled to the assumption that private sector agents understand and agree. (Axel Leijonhufvud, "What Would Keynes Have Thought of Rational Expectations?" UCLA Department of Economics Discussion Paper No. 299 [Los Angeles: University of California, Los Angeles, 1983], p. 5)

[41]This argument parallels the one we employ in *Socialismo, cálculo económico y función empresarial*, to explain the theoretical impracticability of socialism. This reasoning is based on the radical difference between practical (subjective) information or knowledge and scientific (objective) information or knowledge. Therefore rational expectations theorists commit the same type of error as the neoclassical theorists who sought to prove socialism was possible. There is only one difference: instead of assuming a scientist or dictator can obtain all practical information concerning his subjects, new classical economists start from the premise that the subjects themselves are capable of obtaining all relevant information, both *practical* (concerning the rest of the economic agents), and *scientific* (concerning the valid theories on the evolution of the cycle). See Huerta de Soto, *Socialismo, cálculo económico y función empresarial*, pp. 52–54 and 87–110.

profit motive will inevitably lead them to take advantage of the newly-created money. In fact even if they understand the dangers of lengthening the productive structure without the backing of real savings, they can easily derive large profits by accepting the newly-created loans and investing the funds in new projects, *provided they are capable of withdrawing from the process in time and of selling the new capital goods at high prices before their market value drops, an event which heralds the arrival of the crisis.*[42] Indeed entrepreneurial profits arise

---

[42]In light of the above considerations, the following remark Ludwig von Mises makes seems a bit exaggerated (see his article, "Elastic Expectations in the Austrian Theory of the Trade Cycle," published in *Economica* [August 1943]: 251–52):

> The teachings of the monetary theory of the trade cycle are today so well known even outside of the circle of economists, that the naive optimism which inspired the entrepreneurs in the boom periods has given way to a greater skepticism. It may be that businessmen will in the future react to credit expansion in another manner than they did in the past. It may be that they will avoid using for an expansion of their operations the easy money available, because they will keep in mind the inevitable end of the boom. Some signs forebode such a change. But it is too early to make a positive statement.

Although it is obvious that "correct" expectations of the course events will take will hasten their arrival and make credit expansion less "effective" than it would be under other circumstances, even if entrepreneurs have "perfect" knowledge of the typical characteristics of the cycle, they cannot forgo the profits which, in the short run, credit expansion gives them, especially if they believe they are capable of predicting the appropriate time to sell their capital goods and avoid the corresponding losses. Mises himself, in *Human Action* (p. 871), makes the following clarification:

> What the individual businessman needs in order to avoid losses is knowledge about the date of the turning point at a time when other businessmen still believe that the crash is farther away than is really the case. Then his superior knowledge will give him the opportunity to arrange his own operations in such a way as to come out unharmed. But if the end of the boom could be calculated according to a formula, all businessmen would learn the date at the same time. Their endeavors to adjust their conduct of affairs to this information would immediately result in the appearance of all the

from knowledge of *specific* conditions with respect to time and
place, and entrepreneurs may well discover significant opportunities for profit in each historical process of credit expansion, despite their theoretical knowledge of the processes
which inexorably lead to a depression, a stage they may quite
legitimately expect to escape from, due to their superior
knowledge as to when the first symptoms of the recession will
appear. Gerald P. O'Driscoll and Mario J. Rizzo make a similar
observation:

> Though entrepreneurs understand this [theory] at an
> abstract (or macro-) level, they cannot predict the exact fea-
> tures of the next cyclical expansion and contraction. That is,
> they do not know how the unique aspects of one cyclical
> episode will differ from the last such episode or from the
> "average" cycle. They lack the ability to make micro-predic-
> tions, . . . even though they can predict the general sequence
> of events that will occur. These entrepreneurs have no rea-
> son to foreswear the temporary profits to be garnered in an
> inflationary episode. In the end, of course, all profits are
> purely temporary. And each individual investment oppor-
> tunity carries with it a risk. For one thing, other entrepre-
> neurs may be quicker. Or so many may have perceived an
> opportunity that there is a temporary excess supply at some
> point in the future.[43]

> phenomena of the depression. It would be too late for any of
> them to avoid being victimized. *If it were possible to calculate
> the future state of the market, the future would not be uncertain.
> There would be neither entrepreneurial loss nor profit.* What peo-
> ple expect from the economists is beyond the power of any
> mortal man. (Italics added)

[43]Gerald P. O'Driscoll and Mario J. Rizzo, *The Economics of Time and Ignorance*, p. 222. Further criticism of the theory of rational expectations
appears in Gerald P. O'Driscoll's article, "Rational Expectations, Politics
and Stagflation," chapter 7 of the book, *Time, Uncertainty and Disequilibrium: Exploration of Austrian Themes*, Mario J. Rizzo, ed. (Lexigton, Mass.:
Lexington Books, 1979), pp. 153–76. Along the same lines, Roger Garrison has remarked:

> Feedback loops, multiple alternatives for inputs, and multiple
> uses of outputs . . . are complexities [that] preclude the hedg-
> ing against crisis and downturn on a sufficiently widespread

In addition rational expectations theorists still do not comprehend the Austrian theory of the cycle, and, like monetarists, they lack an adequate capital theory. In particular they fail to see how credit expansion affects the productive structure and why a recession inevitably results, even when expectations regarding the *general* course of events are flawless. After all, if entrepreneurs think they possess more (subjective) information than all other economic agents and believe themselves capable of withdrawing from an expansionary process before they sustain any losses, it would go against the grain for them to dismiss the possibility of making short-term gains in a market where such a process had been initiated. In other words, no one is going to turn his nose up at created money just because it will ultimately usher in a recession. One does not look a gift horse in the mouth, especially if one plans to get rid of the horse before the catastrophe hits.

The role of expectations in the cycle is much more subtle than new classical economists assert, as Mises and Hayek reveal in their treatment of the Austrian theory of the cycle, covered in chapter 6. Indeed Mises explains that there is often a certain time lag between the beginning of credit expansion

---

basis as to actually nullify the process that would have led to the crisis. The idea that entrepreneurs know enough about their respective positions to hedge against the central bank is simply not plausible. It all but denies the existence of an economic problem that requires for its solution a market process. (Roger W. Garrison, "What About Expectations?: A Challenge to Austrian Theory," an article presented at the 2nd Austrian Scholars Conference [Mises Institute, Auburn, Alabama, April 4–5, 1997, manuscript pending publication], p. 21; see also *Time and Money*, pp. 15–30)

Our stance on the theory of rational expectations is, however, even more radical than that of O'Driscoll and Rizzo. As we have already stated, even if economic agents know not only the typical shape of the cycle, but also the specific moments and values at which the most important changes are to come about, they will still be inclined to accept the newly-created money to cash in on the myriad of opportunities for profit which crop up throughout the capital goods structure as the market process advances through the different stages in the cycle. See an illustration of this strategy in Peter Temin and Hans-Joachim Voth, "Riding the South Sea Bubble," *American Economic Review* 94, no. 5 (December 2004): 1654–68, esp. p. 1666.

and the appearance of expectations regarding its consequences. In any case the formation of realistic expectations
merely speeds up the processes that trigger the crisis and
makes it necessary for new loans to be granted at a progressively increasing speed, if the policy of loan creation is to continue producing its expansionary effect. Therefore, other
things being equal, the more accustomed economic agents
become to a stable institutional environment, the more damaging credit expansion will be, and the more maladjustments
it will cause in the stages of the production process. (This particularly applies to the expansion of the 1920s, which led to the
Great Depression). Moreover, *ceteris paribus*, as economic
agents become more and more accustomed to credit expansion, larger and larger doses of it will have to be injected into
the economic system to induce a boom and avoid the reversion effects we are familiar with. This constitutes the only element of truth in the hypothesis of rational expectations. (In the
well-chosen words of Roger W. Garrison, it is "the kernel of
truth in the rational expectations hypothesis."[44]) Nevertheless
the assumptions on which the theory rests are far from being
proven right, and entrepreneurs will never be able to completely refrain from taking advantage of the immediate profit
opportunities which arise from the newly-created money they
receive. Thus even with "perfect" expectations, credit expansion will always distort the productive structure.[45]

In short the underlying thesis behind the theory of rational
expectations is that money is *neutral*, given that agents tend to

---

[44]Garrison, "What About Expectations?, p. 1.

[45]   The crucial question devolves around the source of errors in
       cyclical episodes. In Hayek's analysis, misallocations and
       errors occur as economic actors respond to genuine price sig-
       nals. . . . Entrepreneurs are being offered a larger command
       over the real resources in society; the concomitant changes in
       relative prices make investing in these real resources gen-
       uinely profitable. There is surely nothing "irrational" in entre-
       preneurs grasping real profit opportunities. (O'Driscoll,
       "Rational Expectations, Politics and Stagflation," in *Time,
       Uncertainty and Disequilibrium*, p. 166)

precisely predict the course of events.[46] Defenders of this hypothesis fail to realize that, as Mises correctly explained, the concept of neutral money is a contradiction in terms:

> The notion of a neutral money is no less contradictory than that of a money of a stable purchasing power. Money without a driving force of its own would not, as people assume, be a perfect money; it would not be money at all.[47]

Under these circumstances it is not surprising that new classical economists lack a satisfactory theory of the cycle, as did their monetarist predecessors, that their only explanation for the cycle is based on mysterious, unpredictable, real shocks,[48] and that they are ultimately incapable of explaining

---

[46]See Robert E. Lucas's, refined and concise exposition in his "Nobel Lecture: Monetary Neutrality," *Journal of Political Economy* 104, no. 4 (August 1996): 661–82. Lucas has described cycles as the real results of monetary shocks unanticipated by economic agents. Consequently various authors have pointed out supposed similarities between the theorists of the Austrian School and those of new classical economics. In view of the fact that new classical economists lack a capital and malinvestment theory, and that Austrians consider the equilibrium model, maximizing representative agent and aggregates their new classical economist colleagues use unrealistic and/or meaningless, we may reasonably conclude that the "similarities" are more apparent than real. See Richard Arena, "Hayek and Modern Business Cycle Theory," in *Money and Business Cycles: The Economics of F.A. Hayek*, M. Colonna and H. Hagemann, eds., vol. 1, chap. 10, pp. 203–17; see also Carlos Usabiaga Ibáñez and José María O'Kean Alonso, *La nueva macroeconomía clásica* (Madrid: Ediciones Pirámide, 1994), pp. 140–44. A detailed analysis of the profound differences between the Austrian approach and the neoclassical perspective, which constitutes the microeconomic basis for Lucas's views, appears in Huerta de Soto, "The Ongoing Methodenstreit of the Austrian School"; see also Garrison, *Time and Money*, esp. chaps. 10–12.

[47]Mises, *Human Action*, p. 418. We must emphasize that Austrians do not consider money neutral even in the long term, since the productive structure which remains following all of the readjustments credit expansion provokes bears no resemblance to the one which would have formed in the absence of inflation.

[48]See Finn E. Kydland and Edward C. Prescott, "Time to Build and Aggregate Fluctuations," *Econometrica* 50 (November 1982): 1345–70;

why such shocks recur regularly and consistently exhibit the same typical features.[49]

3

CRITICISM OF KEYNESIAN ECONOMICS

After our examination of monetarism, it seems appropriate to embark on a critical analysis of Keynesian theory. We have chosen this approach for two reasons. First, the "Keynesian revolution" erupted *after* old neoclassical monetarism (a mechanistic conception of the quantity theory of money, the lack of a capital theory, etc.) had gained a firm foothold. Second, nowadays Keynesian economics has undoubtedly been pushed into the background with respect to the Monetarist School. Despite these facts, we must emphasize that from the analytical viewpoint we adopt in this book, i.e., that of the Austrian School, monetarists and Keynesians use very similar approaches and methodologies. Like monetarists, Keynes held no capital theory to enable him to understand the division of economic processes into productive stages and the role time plays in such processes. Furthermore his macroeconomic theory of prices rests on such concepts as the general price level, the overall quantity of money, and even the velocity of circulation of money.[50] Nevertheless

---

and also "Business Cycles: Real Facts and Monetary Myth," *Federal Reserve Bank of Minneapolis Quarterly Review* 14 (1990): 3–18. Authors of these and the other explanations for the economic cycle which are not based on the effects of credit expansion are obliged to acknowledge, at least implicitly, that credit expansion is always a factor and is a necessary element in any explanation for the sustained growth of an expansionary boom. See Mises, "The Fallacies of the Nonmonetary Explanations of the Trade Cycle," in *Human Action*.

[49]Furthermore if rational expectations theorists are right and any government economic measure is "useless," what sense is there in adopting expansionary policies again and again? The answer lies in the (seemingly beneficial) short-term effects, which always reverse, sabotaging the economy in the medium and long term.

[50]John Maynard Keynes, *The General Theory of Employment, Interest and Money* (London: Macmillan, 1936 and 1970), chap. 21, pp. 292–309. It is

certain significant peculiarities of Keynesian thought warrant discussion.

Before we begin, however, let us remember that Keynes possessed only a very limited knowledge of economics in general, and of the market processes of entrepreneurial coordination in particular. According to F.A. Hayek, Keynes's theoretical background was limited almost exclusively to the work of Alfred Marshall, and he was unable to understand economics books written in foreign languages (with the possible exception of those in French). Hayek wrote:

---

obvious in Keynes's book, *The General Theory*, that his macroeconomic theory of prices is simply a variant of the monetarist conception. In his book Keynes makes the following explicit assertion:

> The Theory of Prices, that is to say, *the analysis of the relation between changes in the quantity of money and changes in the price-level* with a view to determining the elasticity of prices in response to changes in the quantity of money, must, therefore, direct itself to the five complicating factors set forth above. (Keynes, *The General Theory*, pp. 296–97; italics are added)

The best modern exposition of Keynes's theoretical framework is that of Roger Garrison (*Time and Money*, chaps. 7–9), who shows that Keynes was ultimately a socialist who did not believe in free markets for investment. Keynes himself acknowledged this fact when he wrote that his theories were "more easily adapted to the conditions of a totalitarian state" (*Collected Writings* [London: Macmillan, 1973], vol. 7, p. xxvi). This statement appears in the prologue (which Keynes wrote on September 7, 1936) to the German edition of *The General Theory*. The exact words follow:

> Trotzdem kann die Theorie der Produktion als Ganzes, die den Zweck des folgenden Buches bildet, viel leichter den Verhältnissen eines totalen Staates angepasst werden als die Theorie der Erzeugung und Verteilung einer gegebenen, unter Bedingungen des freien Wettbewerbes und eines grossen Masses von *Laissez-faire* erstellten Produktion. (See John Maynard Keynes, *Allgemeine Theorie der Beschäftigung, des Zinses und des Geldes* [Berlin: Dunker and Humblot, 1936 and 1994], p. ix)

Footnote 76 of this chapter contains Keynes's explicit acknowledgement of his lack of an adequate theory of capital.

Keynes was not a highly trained or a very sophisticated economic theorist. He started from a rather elementary Marshallian economics and what had been achieved by Walras and Pareto, the Austrians and the Swedes was very much a closed book to him. I have reason to doubt whether he ever fully mastered the theory of international trade; I don't think he had ever thought systematically on the theory of capital, and even in the theory of the value of money his starting point—and later the object of his criticism— appears to have been a very simple, equation-of-exchange-type of the quantity theory rather than the much more sophisticated cash-balances approach of Alfred Marshall.[51]

Keynes himself admitted there were gaps in his training, especially with respect to his inferior ability to read German. When referring to Mises's works in his book, *A Treatise on Money*, Keynes had no choice but to confess that his poor knowledge of German had prevented him from grasping their content as fully as he would have liked. He went on to say:

> In German I can only clearly understand what I know already!—so that *new* ideas are apt to be veiled from me by the difficulties of language.[52]

SAY'S LAW OF MARKETS

John Maynard Keynes begins his book, *The General Theory*, by condemning Say's law as one of the fundamental principles

---

[51]F.A. Hayek, *A Tiger by the Tail: A 40-Years' Running Commentary on Keynesianism by Hayek*, compiled and edited by Sudha R. Shenoy (London: Institute of Economic Affairs, 1972), p. 101.

[52]John Maynard Keynes, *A Treatise on Money*, vol. 1: *The Pure Theory of Money*, in *The Collected Writings of John Maynard Keynes* (London: Macmillan, 1971), vol. 5, p. 178, footnote 2. In the last piece of writing he published before his death, Haberler commented ironically on the weakness of the critical remarks Keynes directs at Mises in his review of the book, *Theorie des Geldes und der Umlaufsmittel*, printed in *The Economic Journal* (September 1914) and republished on pp. 400–03 of volume 11 of *The Collected Writings*. See Gottfried Haberler, "Reviewing a Book Without Reading It," *Austrian Economics Newsletter* 8 (Winter, 1995); also *Journal of Economic Perspectives* 10, no. 3 (Summer, 1996): 188.

upon which the classical analysis rests. Nonetheless Keynes overlooked the fact that the analysis carried out by Austrian School theorists (Mises and Hayek) had already revealed that processes of credit and monetary expansion ultimately distort the productive structure and create a situation in which the supply of capital goods and consumer goods and services no longer corresponds with economic agents' demand for them. In other words a *temporal* maladjustment in the economic system results.[53] In fact the entire Austrian theory of the economic cycle merely explains why, under certain circumstances, and as a consequence of credit expansion, Say's law repeatedly fails to hold true. The theory also accounts for the spontaneous reversion effects which, in the form of a crisis and the necessary recession or readjustment of the productive system, tend to cause the system to again become coordinated. Thus upon receiving from Keynes a copy of *The General Theory*, Hayek responded that although

> I fully agree about the importance of the problem which you outline at the beginning, I cannot agree that it has always been as completely neglected as you suggest.[54]

When members of the Austrian School developed the theory of capital, they shed light for the first time on the maladjustment process the productive structure often goes through. Hence the Austrians were the first to identify the microeconomic processes by which an increase in saving manifests itself in a lengthening and widening of the productive structure of

---

[53]   Say's law is violated in the short run by a fiat credit inflation. Of course, the short run may take some time to work itself out! True, the larger supply created by the fiat money also creates its own excessive demand, but it is the *wrong* kind of demand in the case of a business credit expansion, an ephemeral demand which cannot last. (Skousen, *The Structure of Production*, p. 325)

[54]Letter from F.A. Hayek to John Maynard Keynes, dated February 2, 1936 and printed on p. 207 of vol. 29 of *The Collected Writings of John Maynard Keynes: The General Theory and After: A Supplement* (London: Macmillan, 1979), p. 207.

capital goods. Therefore it is not surprising that the absence of an elaborate capital theory in Marshallian economics and Keynes's ignorance of Austrian contributions led Keynes to criticize all classical economists for assuming that "supply must always *automatically* create its own demand." Indeed, according to Keynes, classical economists

> are fallaciously supposing that there is a nexus which unites decisions to abstain from present consumption with decisions to provide for future consumption; . . . whereas the motives which determine the latter are not linked in any simple way with the motives which determine the former.[55]

Although this assertion may be justified with respect to the neoclassical economics of Keynes's time, it in no way applies to Austrian economics, if we consider the level of development Austrians had already reached with their theory of capital and cycles when *The General Theory* was published. Thus Keynes was mistaken when he called Hayek a neoclassical author.[56] Hayek came from a subjectivist tradition which differed sharply from Marshall's neoclassical background. Furthermore, aided by Mises's subjective theory of money, capital and cycles (a theory typically Austrian), he had already closely analyzed the extent to which Say's law is temporally unsound and had studied the disruptive effect on the economic system of regular, credit-related shocks.

KEYNES'S THREE ARGUMENTS ON CREDIT EXPANSION

Keynes conspicuously attempted to deny bank credit plays any role in disrupting the relationship between saving

---

[55]Keynes, *The General Theory*, p. 21.

[56]John Maynard Keynes, *The General Theory and After*, part 2: *Defence and Development*, in *The Collected Writings of John Maynard Keynes*, vol. 14 (London: Macmillan, 1973), pp. 24 and 486. Here Keynes refers to "recent figures like Hayek, whom I should call 'neoclassicals'" (p. 24) and to "the neo-classical school of Professor Hayek and his followers" (p. 486).

and investment. Indeed by the time Keynes published *The General Theory*, he had already debated enough with Hayek to identify Hayek's main argument: that credit expansion gives rise to a temporal, *unsustainable* separation between entrepreneurial investment and society's real, voluntary saving. If Hayek's thesis is correct, it deals a fatal blow to Keynes's theory. Thus it was crucial for Keynes to invalidate Hayek's argument. Nevertheless Keynes's reasoning on the issue of bank credit was too confused and faulty to refute Hayek's theory. Let us review his arguments one by one.

First, Keynes claims bank credit has no expansionary effect whatsoever on aggregate investment. He bases this assertion on the absurd accounting argument that the corresponding creditor and debtor positions cancel each other out:

> We have, indeed, to adjust for the creation and discharge of debts (including *changes in the quantity of credit or money*); but since for the community as a whole the increase or decrease of the aggregate creditor position is always exactly equal to the increase or decrease of the aggregate debtor position, this complication also cancels out when we are dealing with aggregate investment.[57]

Nonetheless a statement like this one cannot obscure the strong distorting influence credit expansion exerts on investment. It is indeed true that a person receiving a loan from a bank is the bank's debtor for the amount of the loan, and creditor for the amount of the deposit. However, as B.M. Anderson points out, the borrower's debt with the bank is not money, whereas his credit is a demand deposit account which *clearly is money* (or to be more precise, a perfect money substitute, as Mises maintains). Once the borrower decides to invest the loan funds in capital goods and in services offered by the factors of production, he uses the money (created *ex nihilo* by the bank) to increase investment, while no corresponding increase in voluntary saving takes place. He does so without altering the stability of his debt with the bank.[58]

---

[57]Keynes, *The General Theory*, p. 75; italics added.

[58]Anderson, *Economics and the Public Welfare*, p. 391.

Second, Keynes, realizing the great weakness of his "accounting argument," puts forward an even more preposterous one. He maintains that new loan funds the bank creates and grants its customers are not used to finance new investment above the level of voluntary saving, since the newly-created money borrowers receive could be used to purchase consumer goods instead. To the extent the new money is not used to purchase consumer goods and services, Keynes reasons, it is implicitly "saved" and thus when invested, its amount corresponds exactly to that of "genuine, prior" savings. This is how Keynes himself expresses this argument:

> [T]he savings which result from this decision are just as genuine as any other savings. No one can be compelled to own the additional money corresponding to the new bank-credit, unless he deliberately prefers to hold more money rather than some other form of wealth.[59]

Keynes clearly relies on the *ex post facto* equivalence between saving and investment to ward off the harmful effects credit expansion exerts on investment and the productive structure.[60] Nevertheless all saving requires discipline and the sacrifice of the *prior* consumption of goods and services, not merely the renunciation of the potential consumption afforded by new monetary units created *ex nihilo*. Otherwise

---

[59]Keynes, *The General Theory*, p. 83.

[60]Benjamin Anderson, in reference to Keynes's theory that credit expansion does not lead to a disproportion between investment and voluntary savings, since new money invested could be spent on consumer goods and services instead and therefore must first be "saved," concludes:

> One must here protest against the dangerous identification of bank expansion with savings, which is part of the Keynesian doctrine. . . . This doctrine is particularly dangerous today, when we find our vast increase in money and bank deposits growing out of war finance described as "savings," just because somebody happens to hold them at a given moment of time. On this doctrine, the greater the inflation, the greater the savings! (Anderson, *Economics and the Public Welfare*, pp. 391–92)

any increase in the money supply via credit expansion would be tantamount to an "increase in saving," which is sheer nonsense.[61] Even if we concede for the sake of argument that all investment financed by new credit has been immediately and simultaneously "saved," a problem still faces us. Once the new money reaches its final holders (workers and owners of capital goods and original means of production), if these people decide to spend all or part of it on consumer goods and services, the productive structure will be revealed as too capital-intensive and recession will hit. For all his sophistry, Keynes cannot deny the obvious fact that artificial credit expansion does not guarantee economic agents will be compelled to save and invest more than they normally would.[62] Furthermore it is paradoxical that Keynes should insist that voluntary saving does not guarantee more investment, while at the same time claiming all investment implies prior saving. If we admit that the agents who save and those who invest are different, and that a lack of coordination in their decisions may prevent equilibrium, then we must admit that such discoordination may exist not only on the side of

---

[61]George Selgin essentially bases his doctrine of monetary equilibrium on this second argument of Keynes's (without specifically citing it). We will critically examine Selgin's doctrine in the next chapter. It is paradoxical that Selgin, an economist from an Austrian background, should fall into the Keynesian trap in an attempt to prove that credit expansion in the context of a free-banking system would be harmless for the economic system. Perhaps this fact provides the clearest evidence that the Old Banking School has been reincarnated today in the figures of theorists like Selgin, defenders of fractional-reserve free banking. See George A. Selgin, *The Theory of Free Banking: Money Supply under Competitive Note Issue* (Totowa, N.J.: Rowman and Littlefield, 1988), esp. pp. 54–55.

[62]In other words, although *ex post facto* all invested resources have been saved (I=S), Keynes overlooks the fact that, microeconomically speaking, saved resources can be invested either wisely or foolishly. In fact credit expansion misleads entrepreneurs with respect to the true rate of voluntary saving. Thus society's meager savings are unwisely invested in processes which are excessively capital-intensive and cannot be completed or sustained, and society grows poorer as a result (see pp. 375–84 of chapter 5).

voluntary saving (more voluntary saving without investment), but also on that of investment (more investment without prior saving). In the first case there is an increase in the
demand for money. As we saw in the last chapter, such an
increase provokes several overlapping effects: both those
characteristic of all voluntary saving (changes in the relative-
price structure which lead to a lengthening of investment
processes) and those due to a rise in the purchasing power of
money.[63] In the second case (more investment without prior
saving) an artificially long structure of production is created.
It is one which cannot be maintained indefinitely, since economic agents are not willing to save enough. It also accounts
for the onset of crises and recessions following periods of
credit expansion.

In his attempt to counteract the Austrian hypothesis on the
harmful effects of credit expansion, Keynes puts forward a
third and final argument. He alleges that credit expansion may
ultimately be used to finance an increase in investment

---

[63]Jacques Rueff has pointed out that in an economy on a pure gold standard, an increase in the demand for money (or "hoarding") does not
push up unemployment at all. In fact, in accordance with the price system, it channels a greater proportion of society's productive resources
(labor, capital equipment, and original means of production) into the
mining, production, and distribution of more monetary units (gold).
This is the market's natural, spontaneous reaction to economic agents'
new desire for higher cash balances. Therefore it is not necessary to initiate a program of public works (even if, as Keynes ironically remarked,
it consisted merely of digging ditches and then filling them in again),
since society will spontaneously use its productive resources to dig
deeper mines and extract gold, thus more effectively satisfying the
desires of consumers and economic agents for higher cash balances.
Hence an increased "liquidity preference" cannot possibly produce a
situation of permanent, combined equilibrium and unemployment. A
combination of equilibrium and unemployment can only stem from a
rigid labor market in which the coercive power of the state, the unions
or both, prevents flexibility in wages and other employment contract
and labor market conditions. See Jacques Rueff's article, "The Fallacies
of Lord Keynes' General Theory," printed in *The Critics of Keynesian Economics*, Henry Hazlitt, ed. (New York: Arlington House, 1977), pp.
239–63, esp. p. 244.

which would lead to a rise in income and therefore eventually also boost saving. Thus Keynes believes entrepreneurs *cannot possibly* invest loaned funds at a rate faster than that at which the public decides to increase savings. In Keynes's own words:

> The notion that the creation of credit by the banking system allows investment to take place to which "no genuine saving" corresponds can only be the result of isolating one of the consequences of the increased bank-credit to the exclusion of the others. If the grant of a bank credit to an entrepreneur additional to the credits already existing allows him to make an addition to current investment which would not have occurred otherwise, incomes will necessarily be increased and at a rate which will normally *exceed* the rate of increased investment. Moreover, except in conditions of full employment, there will be an increase of real income as well as of money-income. The public will exercise a "free choice" as to the proportion in which they divide their increase of income between saving and spending; *and it is impossible that the intention of the entrepreneur who has borrowed in order to increase investment can become effective . . . at a faster rate than the public decide to increase their savings.*[64]

Keynes clearly states that it is impossible for the rate of investment to exceed the rate of saving. His claim is conditioned by his tautological belief that investment and saving are always equal, a concept which keeps him from appreciating the disruptive effect investment financed by newly-created loans exerts on the productive structure. Nonetheless if a rise in investment leads hypothetically to an increase in real income, we may still wonder whether or not such an increase in income could stimulate enough growth in saving to permanently sustain new investments initially financed by credit expansion.

We must remember that Hayek showed it to be practically impossible for the income growth which arises from investment financed by new credit expansion to provoke enough voluntary saving to sustain initial investment. Indeed if such

---

[64]Keynes, *The General Theory*, pp. 82–83; italics added.

investment is to be upheld by a subsequent rise in voluntary saving, *economic agents will ultimately have to save absolutely all monetary income derived from the new investment.* In other words when the portion of gross income shaded in Chart V-6 reaches the pockets of consumers, they will have to save all of it. (The shaded portion reflects the artificial lengthening and widening of the productive structure, modifications made possible by new loans the bank creates from nothing.) Obviously consumers will almost never save all such income, since they will spend at least part (and usually the largest part) of the new monetary income created by banks on consumer goods and services. In accordance with the theory presented in detail in the last two chapters, such spending will necessarily reverse the new investment processes of monetary origin, and the crisis and recession will hit. In Hayek's own words:

> [S]o long as any part of the additional income thus created is spent on consumers' goods (*i.e.* unless all of it is saved), the prices of consumers' goods must rise permanently in relation to those of various kinds of input. And this, as will by now be evident, cannot be lastingly without effect on the relative prices of the various kinds of input and on the methods of production that will appear profitable.

Elsewhere in the same work Hayek concludes:

> All that is required to make our analysis applicable is that, when incomes are increased by investment, the share of the additional income spent on consumers' goods during any period of time should be larger than the proportion by which the new investment adds to the output of consumers' goods during the same period of time. And there is of course no reason to expect that more than a fraction of the new income [created by credit expansion], and certainly not as much as has been newly invested, will be saved, because this would mean that practically all the income earned from the new investment would have to be saved.[65]

---

[65]Hayek, *The Pure Theory of Capital*, pp. 378 and 394. In the footnote on page 395 of the original English edition of *The Pure Theory of Capital*, Hayek emphasizes his thesis even more when he states:

KEYNESIAN ANALYSIS AS A PARTICULAR THEORY

As Austrian economists in general and Mises in particular demonstrated as early as 1928, in the specific event that idle resources and unemployment are widespread, entrepreneurs, relying on new loans, may continue to lengthen the productive structure without provoking the familiar reversion effects, until the moment one of the complementary factors in the production process becomes scarce.[66] At the very least, this fact shows Keynes's so-called *general* theory to be, in the best case, a *particular* theory, applicable only when the economy is in the deepest stages of a depression with generalized idle capacity in *all* sectors.[67] However, as we saw in the last chapter, even under these conditions credit expansion will stimulate a widespread malinvestment of resources. This malinvestment will add to previous errors not yet liquidated owing to the institutional rigidity of the labor market and of the other productive resources. If holders of the new jobs created in these stages of acute depression begin to spend their earnings on consumer goods and services at a pace more rapid than that at which final consumer goods are arriving on the market (due to a relative shortage of some factor or to bottlenecks related to any of the complementary factors or resources of production), the familiar microeconomic processes which tend to reverse the initial expansionary effects of new bank-credit will be triggered. Under such conditions, it will be possible to create new jobs only if real wages fall, a phenomenon we observe when

---

> [T]he essential thing . . . is that we must always compare the result of investment embodied in concrete goods with the money expenditure on these goods. It is never the investment which is going on at the same time as the saving, but the result of *past* investment, that determines the supply of capital goods to which the monetary demand may or may not correspond.

[66]Mises, *On the Manipulation of Money and Credit*, p. 125 (p. 49 of *Geldwertstabilisierung und Konjunkturpolitik*, the German edition).

[67]For Roger Garrison, the true general theory is that of the Austrians and "Keynesian theory [we would also say monetarist theory] becomes a special case of Austrian theory." See Garrison, *Time and Money*, p. 250.

the price of consumer goods and services begins to rise faster
than wages.[68]

---

[68]It is interesting to remember how Keynes defines "involuntary"
unemployment:

> Men are involuntarily unemployed if, in the event of a small
> rise in the price of wage-goods relative to the money-wage,
> both the aggregate supply of labour willing to work for the
> current money-wage and the aggregate demand for it at that
> wage would be greater than the existing volume of employ-
> ment. (Keynes, *The General Theory*, p. 15; italics deleted)

By this convoluted definition, Keynes simply means that "involuntary"
unemployment exists whenever a drop in relative wages would give
rise to an increase in employment. However there are two possible
routes to a relative reduction in wages: either a worker may accept
lower nominal wages, or he may agree to work in an environment
where nominal wages remain unchanged, but the prices of consumer
goods rise. The latter is the more indirect route. In neither case is unemployment involuntary: it is purely voluntary in both. In the first, a
worker remains unemployed because he voluntarily chooses not to
work for a lower nominal wage. In the second, he only agrees to work
if he has deceived himself, since his real wages fall even though his
nominal wages remain the same. (In other words, in the second case he
agrees to work in an environment in which the prices of consumer
goods and services increase faster than wages). In fact most of Keynes's
policy prescriptions amount to an attempt to reduce unemployment by
lowering real wages via the indirect route of increasing inflation, and
thus the prices of consumer goods, while maintaining nominal wages
constant. This remedy has failed, not only because workers are no
longer fooled by the money illusion and demand nominal wage
increases which at least compensate for decreases in the purchasing
power of money, but also because the proposed "medicine," apart from
being ineffective, entails the enormous social cost of the economic crises
and recessions credit expansion provokes. Furthermore we must realize
that to a great extent, Keynes's own prescriptions, which consist of
boosting effective demand through fiscal and monetary measures, are
the main culprits in keeping labor markets rigid and even in making
them gradually more so, since economic agents, specifically workers
and unions, have come to believe that adjustments in real wages must
always take the form of increases in the general price level. Hence Keynesian doctrine, rather than a "remedy" for the disease, has become an
aggravating factor which worsens it. It will take much time and effort
for economic agents to again become accustomed to living in a stable
environment where the price system can again operate without the

THE SO-CALLED MARGINAL EFFICIENCY OF CAPITAL

We find another indication that Keynes's is a specific theory, rather than a general one, in his definition of the "marginal efficiency of capital," which he expresses as

> that rate of discount which would make the present value of the series of annuities given by the returns expected from the capital-asset during its life just equal to its supply price.[69]

The most important error Keynes commits is to consider investment determined by the "marginal efficiency of capital" as defined above, *viewing the supply price of the capital good as a given, an unchanging, constant amount*, even when entrepreneurs' profit outlook varies. Indeed Keynes, succumbing to the classical "objectivist" tradition passed down by Marshall, believes the supply price of capital goods does not fluctuate when entrepreneurs' profit outlook improves or worsens. This belief is based on the implicit notion that such prices are ultimately determined by the historical cost of producing the capital good. Thus Keynes clings to a remnant of the old objective theory of value, according to which value is determined by cost. This doctrine, clearly on the decline in relation to the Austrian subjectivist conception, was partially revived by

---

inflexibility that hinders it today. On this topic see Hans-Hermann Hoppe's article, "Theory of Employment, Money, Interest and the Capitalist Process: The Misesian Case Against Keynes," chapter 5 in *The Economics of Ethics and Private Property* (London: Kluwer Academic Publishers, 1993), pp. 111–38, esp. pp. 124–26.

Similarly, in the banking sector, as Jörg Guido Hülsmann has written,

> [t]he public no longer perceives business cycles and breakdown of the entire banking system as upshots of the fractional-reserve principle run amok under the protection of the law, but as a "macroeconomic" problem requiring action by the central-bank managers.

See his article, "Has Fractional-Reserve Banking Really Passed the Market Test?" p. 416.

[69]Keynes, *The General Theory*, p. 135.

Marshall, at least regarding the supply side of price determination.[70]

Hayek has conclusively demonstrated that the entire Keynesian doctrine of the "marginal efficiency of capital" as the determining factor in investment is acceptable only if we assume that there is absolutely no shortage of capital goods, and hence that any quantity can be acquired at a constant, set price. However, this would only be conceivable in a mythical economy in which no shortage ever occurs, or in a hypothetical economy in the deepest stages of an extraordinarily severe depression, and thus where an immense degree of excess capacity exists. In real life at least some of the complementary goods necessary to produce a capital good will always become relatively scarce at some point, and entrepreneurs, in keeping with their profit expectations, will increase the amount they are willing to pay for the good in question until the marginal efficiency or productivity of capital becomes equal to the interest rate. In other words, as Hayek indicates, competition among entrepreneurs will ultimately lead them to push up the cost or offering price of capital goods to the exact point where it coincides with the present value (the value discounted by the interest rate) of the marginal productivity of the equipment in question. Hence the "marginal efficiency of capital" will always tend to coincide with the interest rate.[71] This is precisely the essence of the Austrian theory on the influence of the interest rate on the

---

[70]   Mr. Keynes . . . is presumably . . . under the influence of the "real cost" doctrine which to the present day plays such a large rôle in the Cambridge tradition, he assumes that the prices of all goods except the more durable ones are even in the short run determined by costs. (Hayek, *The Pure Theory of Capital*, p. 375, footnote 3)

[71]   Entrepreneurs will still tend to bid up the prices of the various kinds of input to the discounted value of their respective marginal products, and, if the rate at which they can borrow money remains unchanged, the only way in which this equality between the price of the input and the discounted value of its marginal product can be restored, is evidently by reducing that marginal product. (Hayek, *The Pure Theory of Capital*, p. 383)

productive structure, a theory we covered in chapter 5. In fact we know that the interest rate is the price of present goods in terms of future goods, and that it tends to manifest itself throughout the productive structure in the accounting profit differential which arises between the different stages in the production process. To put it another way, the interest rate expresses itself in the difference between income and costs at each stage, and there is always an inexorable tendency for the profits at each stage to match the interest rate (that is, for the cost of production at each stage to equal the present value of the stage's marginal productivity).

KEYNES'S CRITICISM OF MISES AND HAYEK

In light of the above, the explicit criticism Keynes levels against Mises and Hayek on pages 192 and 193 of *The General Theory* is absurd. Keynes accuses Mises and Hayek of confusing the interest rate with the marginal efficiency of capital. As we know, the Austrians believe that the interest rate is determined independently by the value scales of time preference (the supply and demand of present goods in exchange for future goods), and that the marginal productivity or efficiency of capital merely affects the present value of capital goods. In the market, the price (cost) of a capital good *tends* to equal the value (discounted by the interest rate) of its future flow of rents, or the series of values corresponding to the marginal productivity of the capital equipment. The Austrians therefore consider that the marginal productivity of capital tends to follow the interest rate and not vice versa, and that only in equilibrium (which is never reached in real life) do the two become equal. Keynes's fundamental error lies in his failure to realize that the purchase price of capital goods will vary when expectations of the profit or productivity associated with them improve. This is how events unfold in real life, and Austrian economists have always taken this fact into account in their analysis. Hence when Keynes boldly claims Austrian economists "confuse" the interest rate with the marginal productivity of capital, he scandalously twists the facts.[72]

---

[72]Denis H. Robertson, among others, agrees. When critically analyzing *The General Theory*, Robertson wrote the following directly to Keynes:

CRITICISM OF THE KEYNESIAN MULTIPLIER

Keynes commits such errors because he lacks a capital theory to help him grasp how saving converts into investment through a series of microeconomic processes he overlooks entirely. Therefore it is not surprising that Keynes is simply incapable of understanding the Hayekian argument, and that, when referring to the schools of economic thought which, like the Austrian School, analyze the effects credit expansion exerts on the productive structure, he concludes: "I can make

----

> I don't think these pages (192–93) are at all a fair account of Hayek's own exposition. In his own queer language he is saying that the fall in the rate of interest will so much increase the demand price for machines (in spite of the fall in the price of their products) as to make it profitable to produce more machines. (See the letter from Denis H. Robertson to John Maynard Keynes dated February 3, 1935 and reprinted on pp. 496ff. of volume 13 of *The Collected Writings of John Maynard Keynes*. The above excerpt appears on page 504)

In his correspondence with Robertson (February 20, 1935), Keynes actually admitted that in the above-mentioned paragraphs of *The General Theory* he misinterpreted Hayek's words:

> Thanks for the reference to Hayek which I will study. I do not doubt that Hayek says somewhere the opposite to what I am here attributing to him. (Ibid., p. 519)

Nonetheless Keynes lacked sufficient intellectual honesty to correct the manuscript prior to its definitive publication in 1936. Ludwig M. Lachmann also comments on the criticism Keynes directs at Mises and Hayek on pages 192 and 193 of *The General Theory*, where Keynes concludes that "Professor von Mises and his disciples have got their conclusions exactly the wrong way round." Lachmann responds:

> In reality, however, the Austrians were merely following Wicksell in drawing a distinction between the "natural rate of interest" and the money rate, and Keynes' own distinction between marginal efficiency of capital and the latter is exactly parallel to it. The charge of simple confusion of terms is groundless. (Ludwig M. Lachmann, "John Maynard Keynes: A View from an Austrian Window," *South African Journal of Economics* 51, no. 3 (1983): 368–79, esp. pp. 370–71)

no sense at all of these schools of thought."[73] Keynes's lack of an adequate theory of capital also explains his development of a mechanistic conception of the investment multiplier, which he defines as the reciprocal of one minus the marginal propensity to consume. Thus according to Keynes, the greater the marginal propensity to consume, the more an increase in investment will boost the national income. However the investment multiplier hinges on a purely mathematical argument which contradicts the most basic economic logic of capital theory. Indeed the multiplier indicates that any increase in credit expansion will cause a rise in real national income equal to the reciprocal of the marginal propensity to save (one minus the marginal propensity to consume). Hence according to Keynesian logic, the less people save, the more real income will grow. Nevertheless we know that the mathematical automatism which lies at the root of the multiplier concept bears no relation to the real processes at work in the productive structure. Credit expansion will stimulate investment that will drive up the price of the factors of production and bring about a subsequent, more-than-proportional increase in the price of consumer goods and services. Even if gross income in money terms rises as a result of the injection of new money created by the banking system, the multiplier, owing to its mechanical and macroeconomic nature, *is inadequate to depict the disruptive microeconomic effects credit expansion always exerts on the productive structure.* Consequently the multiplier masks the widespread malinvestment of resources which in the long run impoverishes society as a whole (rather than enriching it, as Keynes alleges). We agree with Gottfried Haberler when he concludes that the multiplier

> turns out to be not an empirical statement which tells us something about the real world, but a purely analytical statement about the consistent use of an arbitrarily chosen terminology—a statement which does not explain anything about reality. . . . Mr. Keynes' central theoretical idea about

---

[73]Keynes, *The General Theory*, p. 329. Monetarist writers such as Hawtrey, Friedman, and Meltzer have made the same explicit acknowledgement.

the relationships between the propensity to consume and the multiplier, which is destined to give shape and strength to those observations, turns out to be not an empirical statement which tells us something interesting about the real world, but a barren algebraic relation which no appeal to facts can either confirm or disprove.[74]

Hayek, in his detailed critique of both volumes of Keynes's *A Treatise on Money* (1930), accuses Keynes of entirely ignoring the theory of capital and interest, particularly the work of Böhm-Bawerk and the other theorists of the Austrian School in this regard.[75] According to Hayek, Keynes's lack of knowledge in this area accounts for the fact that he overlooks the existence of different stages in the productive structure (as Clark had done and Knight later would) and that he ultimately fails to realize that the essential decision facing entrepreneurs is not whether to invest in consumer

---

[74]Gottfried Haberler, "Mr. Keynes' Theory of the 'Multiplier': A Methodological Criticism," originally published in the *Zeitschrift für Nationalökonomie* 7 (1936): 299–305, and reprinted in English as chapter 23 of the book *Selected Essays of Gottfried Haberler*, Anthony Y. Koo, ed. (Cambridge, Mass.: The MIT Press, 1985), pp. 553–60, and esp. pp. 558–59. It is interesting to note that Hawtrey, a monetarist, was a forerunner of Keynes in the development of the multiplier theory. See Robert B. Dimand's account in "Hawtrey and the Multiplier," *History of Political Economy* 29, no. 3 (Autumn, 1997): 549–56.

[75]Hayek wrote three articles in which he criticizes the monetary theories Keynes includes in his book, *A Treatise on Money*. The articles are: "Reflections on The Pure Theory of Money of Mr. J.M. Keynes (1)," published in *Economica* 11, no. 33 (August 1931): 270–95; "A Rejoinder to Mr. Keynes," pp. 398–403; and finally, "Reflections on The Pure Theory of Money of Mr. J.M. Keynes (continued) (2)," also published in *Economica* 12, no. 35 (February 1932): 22–44. These articles and Keynes's responses to them appear in *Friedrich A. Hayek: Critical Assessments*, John Cunningham Wood and Ronald N. Woods, eds. (London: Routledge, 1991), pp. 1–86 and also in *The Collected Works of F.A. Hayek*, vol. 9: *Contra Keynes and Cambridge: Essays, Correspondence* (London: Routledge, 1995). In the first of these articles (Wood and Woods, eds., p. 7), Hayek concludes that Keynes's main problem is methodological and stems from the fact that the macroeconomic aggregates which form the basis of his analysis conceal from him the microeconomic processes essential to understanding changes in the productive structure.

goods or in capital goods, but *whether to invest in production processes which will yield consumer goods in the near future or in those which will yield them in a more distant future.* Thus Keynes's notion of a productive structure comprised of only two stages (one of consumer goods and another of capital goods) and his failure to allow for the temporal aspect of the latter, nor for the consecutive stages which compose it, lead him into the trap of the "paradox of thrift," the fallacious theoretical rationale which we explained in chapter 5.[76]

Hence Keynesians hold no theory to explain why crises recur in a hampered market economy that suffers credit expansion (that is, one in which traditional legal principles are violated). Keynesians simply attribute crises to sudden halts in investment demand, interruptions caused by irrational behavior on the part of entrepreneurs or by an unexpected loss of confidence and optimism on the part of economic agents. Moreover Keynesians neglect to recognize in their analyses that crises are an *endogenous* consequence of the very credit expansion process which first feeds the boom. Unlike their fellow macroeconomists, the monetarists, Keynesians believe the results of monetary expansion policies to be relatively less effective and important than those of fiscal policy, and they advocate public spending as the means to directly increase effective demand. They fail to comprehend that such a policy

---

[76]It is important to remember that John Maynard Keynes himself explicitly and publicly admitted to Hayek that he lacked an adequate theory of capital. In Keynes's own words:

> Dr. Hayek complains that I do not myself propound any satisfactory theory of capital and interest and that I do not build on any existing theory. He means by this, I take it, the theory of capital accumulation relatively to the rate of consumption and the factors which determine the natural rate of interest. This is quite true; and I agree with Dr. Hayek that a development of this theory would be highly relevant to my treatment of monetary matters and likely to throw light into dark corners. (John Maynard Keynes, "The Pure Theory of Money: A Reply to Dr. Hayek," *Economica* 11, no. 34 [November 1931]: 394; p. 56 in the Wood and Woods edition)

further complicates the process by which the productive structure readjusts, and it worsens the outlook for the stages furthest from consumption. As a result of Keynesian "remedies," entrepreneurs will surely encounter even greater difficulty in consistently financing these stages using voluntary savings. As to the likelihood that Keynesian policies could cure "secular" unemployment through the complete socialization of investment, the Austrian theorem on the impossibility of economic calculation under socialism is entirely applicable, as illustrated by the massive industrial malinvestment accumulated during the decades of government-directed investments in the former socialist economies of Eastern Europe.

Short-term unemployment can only be eliminated through "active" policies if workers and unions let themselves be deceived by the money illusion, and thus maintain nominal salaries constant in an inflationary atmosphere of soaring consumer prices. Experience has shown that the Keynesian remedy for unemployment (the reduction of real wages through increases in the general price level) has failed: workers have learned to demand raises which at least compensate them for decreases in the purchasing power of their money. Therefore the expansion of credit and effective demand, an action Keynesians supported, has gradually ceased to be a useful tool for generating employment. It has also entailed a cost: *increasingly grave distortions of the productive structure.* In fact a stage of deep depression combined with high inflation (stagflation) followed the crisis of the late seventies and was the empirical episode which most contributed to the invalidation of all Keynesian theory.[77]

---

[77]This is not the appropriate place to carry out an exhaustive analysis of the rest of the Keynesian theoretical framework, for instance his conception of the interest rate as a strictly monetary phenomenon determined by the money supply and "liquidity preference." Nonetheless we know that the supply of and demand for money determine its price or purchasing power, not the interest rate, as Keynes maintains, concentrating merely on the effects credit expansion exerts on the credit market in the immediate short term. (Besides, with his liquidity preference theory, Keynes resorts to the circular reasoning characteristic of the functional analysis of mathematician-economists. Indeed first he asserts

Hence we must concur with Hayek's statement that the doctrines of John Maynard Keynes take us

> back to the pre-scientific stage of economics, when the whole working of the price mechanism was not yet understood, and only the problems of the impact of a varying money stream on a supply of goods and services with given prices aroused interest.[78]

---

that the interest rate is determined by the demand for money or liquidity preference, and then he states that the latter in turn depends on the former.) Another considerable shortcoming of Keynesian doctrine is the assumption that economic agents first decide how much to consume and then, from the amount they have decided to save, they determine what portion they will use to increase their cash balances and then what portion they will invest. Nevertheless economic agents *simultaneously* decide how much they will allot to all three possibilities: consumption, investment and the increase of cash balances. Hence if there is a rise in the amount of money each economic agent hoards, the additional amount could come from any of the following: (a) funds previously allocated for consumption; (b) funds previously allocated for investment; or (c) any combination of the above. It is obvious that in case (a) the interest rate will fall; in case (b) it will rise; and in case (c) it may remain constant. Therefore no direct relationship exists between liquidity preference or demand for money and the interest rate. An increase in the demand for money may not affect the interest rate, if the relationship between the value allotted for present goods and that allotted for future goods (time preference) does not vary. See Rothbard, *Man, Economy, and State*, p. 690. A list of all relevant critical references on Keynesian theory, including various articles on its different aspects, appears in *Dissent on Keynes: A Critical Appraisal of Keynesian Economics*, Mark Skousen, ed. (New York and London: Praeger, 1992). See also the previously cited chapters 7–9 of Garrison's *Time and Money*.

[78]Hayek, *The Pure Theory of Capital*, pp. 409–10. Hayek concludes:

> It is not surprising that Mr. Keynes finds his views anticipated by the mercantilist writers and gifted amateurs: concern with the surface phenomena has always marked the first stage of the scientific approach to our subject. But it is alarming to see that after we have once gone through the process of developing a systematic account of those forces which in the long run determine prices and production, we are now called upon to scrap it, in order to replace it by the short-sighted philosophy of the business man raised to the dignity of a science. Are we not even

In fact Keynesian remedies which consist of increasing effective demand and credit expansion do not begin to relieve unemployment. Instead they inevitably worsen it, as they result in a poor allocation of jobs and factors of production throughout a series of productive stages which consumers do not wish to maintain in the long run.[79]

> told that, "since in the long run we are all dead," policy should be guided entirely by short-run considerations? I fear that these believers in the principle of *après nous le déluge* may get what they have bargained for sooner than they wish. (p. 410)

[79]Hayek's main objection to macroeconomics (both Keynesian and monetarist versions) is that macroeconomists work with macroaggregates and thus do not take into account the harmful microeconomic effects of credit expansion, which as we have seen, leads to the malinvestment of resources and ultimately, to crisis and unemployment. Moreover, as Keynesians assume excess availability of all factors exists (due to idle capacity and unemployment of resources), *they tend to ignore the price system, the functioning of which they consider unnecessary. The price system is therefore rendered a vague, incomprehensible redundancy.* To the extent that all is determined by macroaggregate functions, the traditional microeconomic theory of relative-price determination and the theory of capital, interest and distribution, which are the backbone of economic theory, become unintelligible. Unfortunately, as Hayek points out, an entire generation of economists have learned nothing other than Keynesian [and monetarist] macroeconomics ("I fear the theory will still give us a lot of trouble: it has left us with a lost generation of economists who have learnt nothing else," F.A. Hayek, "The Campaign against Keynesian Inflation," in *New Studies*, p. 221). Hayek believes Keynes was aware he had developed a weak theoretical framework. Hayek indicates that the last time he saw Keynes prior to his death, he asked him if he was becoming alarmed at the poor use most of his disciples were making of his theories:

> His reply was that these theories had been greatly needed in the 1930s; but if these theories should ever become harmful, I could be assured that he would quickly bring about a change in public opinion. (Hayek, "Personal Recollections of Keynes and the Keynesian Revolution," p. 287)

Hayek states that Keynes died two weeks later without ever having the chance to alter the course of events. Hayek criticizes him for giving the name *"general* theory" to an erroneous conceptual framework which, as its own author eventually recognized, had been conceived *ad hoc* based

CRITICISM OF THE "ACCELERATOR" PRINCIPLE

Our theory on the impact of credit expansion on the structure of production rests on a capital theory we examined in detail in chapter 5. According to this theory, a healthy, permanent "lengthening" of the productive structure is contingent on a prior increase in saving. Therefore we must criticize the so-called "accelerator principle," developed by the Keynesian School. Those who accept this principle assert that any increase in consumption leads to a *more-than-proportional* increase in investment, which is contrary to what our theory suggests.

In fact, according to the accelerator principle, a rise in the demand for consumer goods and services provokes an exaggerated upsurge in the demand for capital goods. The argument centers around the notion that a fixed relationship exists between the output of consumer goods and the number of machines necessary to produce them. Thus any rise in the demand for consumer goods and services causes a proportional increase in the number of machines necessary to produce them. When we compare this new number with that normally demanded to compensate for the customary depreciation of the machines, we see an upturn in the demand for capital goods which is far more than proportional to the rise in the demand for consumer goods and services.[80]

---

on the specific circumstances of the 1930s. Today so-called "new Keynesian macroeconomists" (Stiglitz, Shapiro, Summers, Romer, etc.) focus on the analysis of the real and monetary rigidities they observe in the market. However they still do not understand that such rigidities and their chief effects appear and worsen precisely as a result of credit expansion and government intervention, nor do they recognize that certain spontaneous, microeconomic forces exist in the market which, in the absence of government intervention, tend to reverse, coordinate, and resolve maladjustments by a process of crisis, recession, and recovery. On the new Keynesians, see also upcoming footnote 94.

[80]Samuelson provides the following example to illustrate the accelerator principle:

> Imagine a typical textile firm whose stock of capital equipment is always kept equal to about 2 times the value of its

We know that according to the accelerator principle, an increase in the demand for consumer goods and services brings about tremendously magnified growth in the demand for capital goods. However the principle also implies that if the demand for capital goods is to remain constant, the demand for consumer goods and services will have to continue to rise at a progressively increasing rate. This is due to the fact that a steady demand for consumer goods and services, i.e., a demand which does not increase, will provoke a marked contraction in the demand for equipment goods. The demand for these goods will return to the level necessary for replacements only. The accelerator principle clearly and perfectly fits the Keynesian prescriptions of an unlimited expansion of consumption and aggregate demand: indeed, the accelerator doctrine indicates that any rise in consumption causes a huge upsurge in investment, and that saving is of no importance! Thus the accelerator principle acts as a false substitute for the capital theory the Keynesian model lacks; it eases the theoretical conscience of Keynesians, and it reinforces their belief that voluntary saving is counterproductive and unnecessary for economic development (the "paradox of

---

yearly sales of cloth. Thus, when its sales have remained at $30 million per year for some time, its balance sheet will show $60 million of capital equipment, consisting of perhaps 20 machines of different ages, with 1 wearing out each year and being replaced. Because replacement just balances depreciation, there is no *net* investment or saving being done by the corporation. *Gross* investment takes place at the rate of $3 million per year, representing the yearly replacement of 1 machine. . . . Now let us suppose that, in the fourth year, sales rise 50 per cent—from $30 to $45 million. Then the number of machines must also rise 50 per cent, or from 20 to 30 machines. In that fourth year, instead of 1 machine, 11 machines must be bought—10 new ones in addition to the replacement of the worn-out one. Sales rose 50 per cent. How much has machine production gone up? From 1 machine to 11; or by 1,000 percent! (Samuelson, *Economics*, 11th ed. [New York: McGraw-Hill, 1980], pp. 246–47)

Interestingly, the analysis of the accelerator principle was eliminated from the 15th edition of the book, published in 1992.

thrift"). Therefore it is particularly important that we thoroughly expose the errors and fallacies which form the basis of the principle.[81]

The theory based on the accelerator not only omits the most elementary principles of capital theory; it was also developed based on a *mechanistic*, automatic and fallacious conception of economics. Let us analyze each of the reasons behind this assertion.

First, the accelerator theory excludes the real functioning of the entrepreneurial market process and suggests that entrepreneurial activities are nothing more than a blind, automatic response to momentary impulses in the demand for consumer goods and services. However entrepreneurs are not robots, and their actions are not mechanical. On the contrary, entrepreneurs predict the course of events, and with the purpose of obtaining a profit, they act in light of what they believe may happen. *Hence no transmitter mechanism automatically and instantaneously determines that growth in the demand for consumer goods and services will trigger an immediate, proportional increase in the demand for capital goods.* Quite the opposite is true. In view of potential variations in the demand for consumer goods and services, entrepreneurs usually maintain a certain amount of idle capacity in the form of capital equipment. This idle capacity allows them to satisfy sudden increases in demand when they occur. The accelerator principle proves to be much less sound when, as in real life, companies keep some capital goods in reserve.

Therefore it is obvious that the accelerator principle would only be sound if capital goods were in full use, such that it would be impossible to raise the output of consumer goods at all without increasing the number of machines. Nevertheless, and *second*, the great fallacy of the accelerator principle is that it depends on the existence of fixed, unchanging proportions between capital goods, labor and the output of consumer

---

[81]Antecedents of the "accelerator principle" appear in the works of Karl Marx, Albert Aftalion, J.M. Clark, A.C. Pigou, and Roy F. Harrod. See P.N. Junankar, "Acceleration Principle," in *The New Palgrave: A Dictionary of Economics*, Eatwell, Milgate and Newman, eds., vol. 1, pp. 10–11.

goods and services. The accelerator principle *fails to take into account that the same result in terms of consumer goods and services can be achieved using many different combinations of fixed capital, variable capital and especially, labor.* The specific combination an entrepreneur may choose in any given case depends on the structure of relative prices. Hence, to assume fixed proportions exist between the output of consumer goods and services and the quantity of capital goods necessary to produce them is an error, and it contradicts the basic principles of the theory of prices in the factor market. Indeed, as we saw when we analyzed the "Ricardo Effect," a drop in the relative price of labor will lead companies to produce consumer goods and services in a more labor-intensive manner, i.e., using fewer capital goods in relative terms. The reverse is also true: a rise in the relative cost of labor will trigger a relative increase in the use of capital goods. Because the accelerator principle rests on the assumption that fixed proportions exist between the factors of production, it totally excludes the role entrepreneurship, the price system and technological change play in market processes.

Furthermore, and *third*, even if, for the sake of argument, we suppose fixed ratios exist between consumption and capital equipment used, and we even assume there to be no idle capacity with respect to capital goods, we must ask ourselves the following question: *How can the output of capital goods possibly rise in the absence of the saving necessary to finance such an investment?* It is an insoluble logical contradiction to consider that an increase in the demand for consumer goods and services will automatically and instantaneously provoke a much-more-than-proportional rise in the output of capital goods, given that in the absence of excess capacity the production of these goods is contingent on growth in voluntary saving. Moreover such growth inevitably entails a momentary drop in the demand for consumer goods (which clearly contradicts the premise on which the accelerator theory is based). Therefore the accelerator theory contradicts the most fundamental principles of capital theory.

Fourth, it is important to realize that an investment in capital goods which is far more than proportional to the increase in the demand for consumer goods can only be financed if substantial credit expansion is initiated and sustained. In other words, the accelerator principle ultimately presupposes that the increase in credit expansion necessary to stimulate an enormously exaggerated investment in capital goods takes place. We are already familiar with the effects such credit expansion exerts on the productive structure and with the way in which the relative-price system invariably limits the expansion and forces a reversal that manifests itself in a crisis and recession.[82]

Fifth, it is absurd to expect a rise in the demand for consumer goods and services to cause an instantaneous upsurge in the output of capital goods. We know that during the boom, which is financed by credit expansion, companies and industrial sectors devoted to the production of equipment and capital goods *operate at maximum capacity*. Orders pile up and companies are unable to satisfy the increased demand, except with very lengthy time lags and dramatic increases in the price of equipment goods. Therefore it is impossible to imagine that a rise in the output of capital goods could take place as soon as the accelerator principle presupposes.

Sixth, the accelerator theory rests on peculiar mechanistic reasoning by which an attempt is made to relate growth in the demand for consumer goods and services, measured in *monetary terms*, with a rise, in *physical terms*, in the demand for equipment and capital goods. Entrepreneurs never base their decisions on a comparison between monetary and physical magnitudes; instead they always compare estimated income and costs, measured strictly in monetary terms. To compare

---

[82]   [I]f, for the sake of argument, we were ready to admit that capitalists and entrepreneurs behave in the way that the disproportionality doctrines describe, it remains inexplicable how they could go on in the absence of credit expansion. The striving after such additional investments raises the prices of the complementary factors of production and the rate of interest on the loan market. These effects would curb the expansionist tendencies very soon if there were no credit expansion. (Mises, *Human Action*, p. 586)

heterogeneous magnitudes is absurd and makes entrepreneurial economic calculation utterly impossible. Obviously, if the price of capital goods begins to increase, entrepreneurial decisions will not mechanically manifest themselves in "fixed proportions" of inputs. Instead entrepreneurs will carefully monitor the evolution of costs to determine the extent to which production will continue at the old proportions, or they will start using a higher proportion of alternative factors, specifically labor.[83]

Seventh, William Hutt has shown that the entire accelerator theory rests on the choice of a purely arbitrary time period of analysis.[84] Indeed, why calculate the supposed relative increase in the demand for capital goods based on a one-year period? The shorter the time period chosen, the more "amplified" the supposed automatic rise in the demand for machines, an upsurge which results from any fixed ratio between the output of consumer goods and services and capital goods. However if we consider a longer time period, such as the estimated life of the machine, the marked oscillations which appear to arise from the accelerator principle disappear altogether. In addition, this long-term perspective is always the one considered by entrepreneurs. In order to be able to momentarily raise output if necessary in the future, they usually increase their demand for capital goods more than would be strictly necessary to produce a certain volume of consumer goods. Thus when we take into account society as a whole and entrepreneurial expectations, increases in the demand for equipment and machines in the stages closest to consumption are much more modest than the doctrine of the accelerator principle indicates.

In short the accelerator principle rests on fallacious, mechanistic reasoning which excludes the most elementary principles of the market process, specifically the nature of entrepreneurship. The doctrine ignores the functioning and

---

[83]See, for instance, Jeffrey M. Herbener's interesting article, "The Myths of the Multiplier and the Accelerator," chapter 4 of *Dissent on Keynes*, pp. 63–88, esp. pp. 84–85.

[84]William H. Hutt, *The Keynesian Episode: A Reassessment* (Indianapolis, Ind.: Liberty Press, 1979), pp. 404–08.

effects of the price system, the possibility of substituting certain inputs for others, the most essential aspects of capital theory and of the analysis of the productive structure, and finally, the microeconomic principles which govern the relationship between saving and the lengthening of the productive structure.[85]

4

THE MARXIST TRADITION AND THE AUSTRIAN THEORY OF ECONOMIC CYCLES. THE NEO-RICARDIAN REVOLUTION AND THE RESWITCHING CONTROVERSY

In his critical analysis of capitalism, Karl Marx accepts the Classical School's objectivist conception of two essential factors of production (capital and labor) and a production process comprised of only two stages (consumption and production). Nevertheless in Friedrich Engels's preface to the third volume of Karl Marx's *Capital*, Engels makes explicit reference to the different stages in the production process. He portrays them in a manner similar to that of the Austrian School, though he uses the argument with the purpose of better illustrating the supposed injustice of the capitalist economic system. Engels states:

> The capitalist sellers, such as the producer of raw materials, the manufacturer, the wholesale dealer, the retail dealer, all make a profit on their transactions, each selling his product at a higher price than the purchase price, each adding a certain percentage to the price paid by him. The laborer alone is unable to raise the price of his commodity, he is compelled, by his oppressed condition, to sell his labor to the capitalist at a price corresponding to its cost of production, that is to say, for the means of his subsistence.[86]

---

[85]Rothbard, *Man, Economy, and State*, pp. 759–64.

[86]Friedrich Engels, Preface to the English edition of Karl Marx's *Capital: A Critique of Political Economy*, vol. 3: *The Process of Capitalist Production as a Whole*, Frederick Engels, ed., Ernest Untermann, trans. (Chicago: Charles H. Kerr and Company, 1909), pp. 19–20.

The Marxist theorist Mijail Ivanovich Tugan-Baranovsky later expanded on and reworked Engels's comments with the aim of developing a theory of economic cycles based on the phenomenon of "overproduction" in the stages of investment. As we have already indicated, this theory is very closely related to the Austrian theory of economic cycles presented here. Indeed though Tugan-Baranovsky is unable to identify the monetary origin (credit expansion) of overinvestment and disequilibrium between the different stages in the production process, his interpretation is basically correct with respect to capital theory, and Hayek himself has recognized it as an antecedent to the Austrian theory of economic cycles.[87]

Therefore it is not surprising that an author such as Howard J. Sherman, of clear Marxist leanings, has maintained that Hayek's theory on the different stages in the production process fits in perfectly with the Marxist theoretical framework. This framework has traditionally highlighted a tendency toward a significant disproportion between the different industrial stages in the capitalist system. As one might expect, the purpose has not been to demonstrate the harmful effects credit expansion and government and central banks' monetary policy exert on the productive structure, but merely to illustrate the supposed inherent instability in the capitalist system.[88] According to the Austrian School, Marxists' error lies not in their diagnosis of the symptoms of the disease (basically accurate), but in their analysis of its causes, which Austrians see in the credit expansion which derives from the violation of legal principles in the monetary bank-deposit contract (fractional-reserve cash ratio).

In addition, the neo-Ricardian and neoclassical controversy regarding the possibility of technique reswitching also has favorable implications for the Austrian theory of economic cycles. Indeed the reswitching debate has emphasized

---

[87]Hayek's explicit reference to Tugan-Baranovsky appears in *Prices and Production*, p. 103, and also in *The Pure Theory of Capital*, p. 426. See also chapter 6, footnote 71.

[88]See Howard J. Sherman's book, *Introduction to the Economics of Growth, Unemployment and Inflation* (New York: Appleton, 1964), esp. p. 95.

the heterogeneous, complementary nature of different capital goods (in the purest Austrian tradition), versus the neoclassical conception of capital as a homogeneous fund. Furthermore Austrians, and Hayek in particular, showed from the beginning that the lengthening of the productive structure could often provoke seemingly paradoxical instances of reswitching which nevertheless, when interpreted prospectively, are simply another manifestation of the normal lengthening process.[89]

The jump between two alternate production techniques, an occurrence which may accompany continuous variations in the interest rate, and which has quite dismayed neoclassical theorists, presents no difficulties whatsoever for the Austrian theory of capital. In fact an increase in saving, and thus a decrease in the interest rate, always manifests itself in a change in the temporal perspective of consumers, who begin to view their actions in terms of a more distant future. Hence the productive structure is lengthened *regardless* of whether changes or even reswitching occur with respect to the different specific production techniques. In other words, within the Austrian School model, if, at a drop in the interest rate, a former technique is revived in connection with a new investment

---

[89] It is evident and has usually been taken for granted that methods of production which were made profitable by a fall of the rate of interest from 7 to 5 per cent may be made unprofitable by a further fall from 5 per cent to 3 per cent, because the former method will no longer be able to compete with what has now become the cheaper method. . . . It is only via price changes that we can explain why a method of production which was profitable when the rate of interest was 5 per cent should become unprofitable when it falls to 3 per cent. Similarly, it is only in terms of price changes that we can adequately explain why a change in the rate of interest will make methods of production profitable which were previously unprofitable. (Hayek, *The Pure Theory of Capital*, pp. 388–89 [also pp. 76–77, 140ff., 191ff., and 200])

Augusto Graziani, for his part, asserts that Hayek "had shown the possibility of reswitching." See Graziani's book review of *"Hayek on Hayek: An Autobiographical Dialogue,"* in *The European Journal of the History of Economic Thought* 2, no. 1 (Spring, 1995): 232.

project, this occurrence is merely a concrete sign, in the context of a particular production process, that this process has become longer as a result of the rise in saving and the fall in the interest rate.[90]

Therefore we must not be deceived by the "comparative static equilibrium analysis" carried out by neoclassical theorists who, like Mark Blaug, consider that the reswitching controversy somehow refutes the Austrian theory of capital.[91] On the contrary, we know that the real world Austrian theorists study is one of continual change and that growth in voluntary saving always causes, in prospective terms, a "lengthening" of the productive structure, irrespective of whether techniques which were only profitable at higher interest rates are readopted in certain new investment processes.[92] From the point of view of an individual actor or entrepreneur, once the prospective decision has been made to lengthen production

---

[90]O'Driscoll and Rizzo, *The Economics of Time and Ignorance*, p. 183.

[91]Mark Blaug mistakenly calls the reswitching theorem "the final nail in the coffin of the Austrian theory of capital." Blaug, *Economic Theory in Retrospect*, p. 552. Blaug fails to comprehend that once the objectivist remains Böhm-Bawerk brought to the Austrian theory of capital (the concept of a measurable average production period) are eliminated and the production process is viewed in strictly prospective terms, the Austrian theory of capital becomes immune to the attack of the reswitching theorists and is even strengthened by it. On this topic see Ludwig M. Lachmann, "On Austrian Capital Theory," published in *The Foundations of Modern Austrian Economics*, Edwin E. Dolan, ed. (Kansas City: Sheed and Ward, 1976), p. 150; see also Israel M. Kirzner, "Subjectivism, Reswitching Paradoxes and All That," in *Essays on Capital and Interest*, pp. 7–10. Kirzner concludes that

> we should understand that comparing the complex, multidimensional waiting requirements for different techniques *simply does not permit us to pronounce* that one technique involves unambiguously less waiting than a second technique. (p. 10)

[92]The chief inadequacy of the neo-Ricardian theory of reswitching is not only that it rests on a comparative static equilibrium analysis which does not entail a prospective approach to dynamic market processes, but also that it fails to identify the ultimate causes of the interest-rate variations which provoke the supposed reswitching in the most profitable techniques. An increase in saving (and thus a decrease in the interest rate, other things being equal) may result in the replacement of

plans (due to a rise in saving), all initial factors (land, labor, and *existing capital goods*) are subjectively deemed to be "original means of production" which merely determine the starting point of the production process. *It is therefore irrelevant whether or not the new investment process incorporates techniques which, considered individually, may have been profitable at higher rates of interest.*[93]

---

a certain technique (the Roman plow, for instance) by a more capital-intensive one (the tractor). Even so, a subsequent drop in the interest rate may permit the reintroduction of the Roman plow in *new* production processes formerly prevented by a lack of saving (in other words, the established processes are not affected and still involve the use of tractors). Indeed a new lengthening of production processes may give rise to *new* stages in agriculture or gardening that incorporate techniques which, even assuming that production processes are effectively lengthened, may appear less capital-intensive when considered separately in a comparative static equilibrium analysis.

[93]We must not forget that although neo-Ricardians may have been circumstantial allies to the Austrians in their criticism of the neoclassical trend, the neo-Ricardians' stated objective is precisely to neutralize the influence (which is not yet strong enough, in our opinion) exerted on economics since 1871 by the subjectivist revolution Menger started. The Ricardian counterrevolution erupted with Piero Sraffa's review of Hayek's book, *Prices and Production* (see "Doctor Hayek on Money and Capital," *Economic Journal* 42 [1932]: 42–53), as Ludwig M. Lachmann points out in his article, "Austrian Economics under Fire: The Hayek-Sraffa Duel in Retrospect," printed in *Austrian Economics: History and Philosophical Background*, Wolfgang Grassl and B. Smith, eds. (London and Sydney: Croom Helm, 1986), pp. 225–42. We should also mention Joan Robinson's work published in 1953 and devoted to criticizing the neoclassical production function (see Joan Robinson, *Collected Economic Papers* [London: Blackwell, 1960], vol. 2, pp. 114–31). Of particular relevance is chapter 12 of Piero Sraffa's book, *Production of Commodities by Means of Commodities: Prelude to a Critique of Economic Theory* (Cambridge: Cambridge University Press, 1960). The entire chapter deals with the "switch in methods of production." On the neoclassical side, see the famous article by Paul A. Samuelson, who declared his unconditional surrender to the Cambridge Switching Theorem. The article appeared in *Quarterly Journal of Economics* 80 (1966): 568–83, and was entitled "Paradoxes in Capital Theory: A Summing Up." On this point another interesting resource is Geoffrey C. Harcourt's book, *Some Cambridge Controversies in the Theory of Capital* (Cambridge: Cambridge University Press, 1972). Finally see also Ludwig Lachmann, *Macroeconomic Thinking and the Market Economy* (London: Institute of Economic Affairs, 1973).

5

CONCLUSION

From the standpoint of our analysis, it is clear that there
are far greater similarities than possible differences between
monetarists and Keynesians. Indeed Milton Friedman himself
has acknowledged: "We all use the Keynesian language and
apparatus. None of us any longer accept the initial Keynesian
conclusions."[94] Peter F. Drucker, for his part, indicates that
Milton Friedman is essentially and epistemologically a Keynesian:

---

[94]Milton Friedman, *Dollars and Deficits* (Englewood Cliffs, N.J.: Prentice
Hall, 1968), p. 15. The new Keynesians have in turn built on the foundations of neoclassical microeconomics to justify the existence of wage
rigidities in the market. Specifically they have formulated the efficiency-
wage hypothesis, according to which wages tend to determine a
worker's productivity and not vice versa. See, for example, Robert Gordon, "What is New-Keynesian Economics?" *Journal of Economic Literature* 28 (September 1990); and Lawrence Summers, *Understanding
Unemployment* (Cambridge, Mass.: The MIT Press, 1990). Our criticism
of the new Keynesians (for whom a more fitting name would be the
"new monetarists," according to Garrison in *Time and Money*, p. 232)
centers on the fact that their models, like those of monetarists, are
largely based on the concepts of equilibrium and maximization, and
their hypotheses are almost as unreal (experience teaches us that very
often, if not always, the wages of those talents in greatest demand are
the ones which tend to rise) as those of the new classical economists
who hold the theory of rational expectations. Peter Boettke, in reference
to both schools, concludes:

> Like rational-expectations theorists who developed elaborate
> "proofs" of how the (Neo-) Keynesian picture *could not* be
> true, the New Keynesians start with the assumption that it
> must be true, and then try to explain how this "reality" might
> have come to be. In the end, then, the New Keynesians are as
> ideological as the Chicago School. In the hands of both, eco-
> nomics is reduced to a game in which preconceived notions
> about the goodness or badness of markets are decked out in
> spectacular theory. (See Peter Boettke, "Where Did Economics
> Go Wrong? Modern Economics as a Flight From Reality,"
> *Critical Review* 1 [Winter, 1997]: 42–43)

His economics is pure macroeconomics, with the national government as the one unit, the one dynamic force, controlling the economy through the money supply. Friedman's economics are completely demand-focused. Money and credit are the pervasive, and indeed the only, economic reality. That Friedman sees money supply as original and interest rates as derivative, is not much more than minor gloss on the Keynesian scriptures.[95]

Furthermore even before the appearance of Keynes's *The General Theory*, the principal monetarist theorists of the

---

A good overview of the trends in diffuse modern macroeconomics appears in Olivier J. Blanchard and Stanley Fischer, *Lectures on Macroeconomics* (Cambridge, Mass.: The MIT Press, 1990); see also David Romer, *Advanced Macroeconomics* (New York: McGraw-Hill, 1996).

[95]Peter F. Drucker, "Toward the Next Economics," published in *The Crisis in Economic Theory*, Daniel Bell and Irving Kristol, eds. (New York: Basic Books, 1981), p. 9. Therefore, as Mark Skousen points out, it is not surprising that one of the most prominent monetarists of the 1930s, Ralph G. Hawtrey, allied himself with Keynes against Hayek, defending an anti-saving position and adopting viewpoints very similar to those of Keynesians with respect to capital theory and macroeconomics (see, among other sources, Hawtrey's *Capital and Employment*, pp. 270–86, and Skousen's *Capital and its Structure*, p. 263). The entire "consumption function" debate again reveals the obvious Keynesian and macroeconomic influence on monetarists. In fact Milton Friedman, while preserving all of the Keynesian analytical and theoretical tools, attempted with his "permanent-income hypothesis" to introduce an empirical variant which would make it possible to modify the conclusions reached through macroeconomic analysis. Indeed if economic agents plan their consumption in view of long-term permanent income, then according to Keynesian logic, more-than-proportional increases in saving will not accompany rises in income, and therefore the underconsumption issues Keynes analyzed will disappear. Nonetheless the use of this type of "empirical argument" suggests implicit acknowledgement of the validity of Keynesian hypotheses regarding the harmful effects of saving and the capitalist tendency toward underconsumption. Nevertheless we have already exposed the analytical errors of such a viewpoint, and we have based our reasoning on the microeconomic arguments which explain that certain market forces lead to the investment of saved amounts, regardless of the apparent historical form of the supposed consumption function. See Milton Friedman, *A Theory of the Consumption Function* (Princeton, N.J.: Princeton University Press, 1957).

Chicago School were already prescribing the typical Keynesian remedies for depression and fighting for large budget deficits.[96]

Table VII-1 recapitulates the differences between the Austrian perspective and the major macroeconomic schools. The table contains twelve comparisons that reveal the radical differences between the two approaches.[97]

---

[96]   Frank H. Knight, Henry Simons, Jacob Viner and their Chicago colleagues argued throughout the early 1930's for the use of large and continuous deficit budgets to combat the mass unemployment and deflation of the times. (J. Ronnie Davies, "Chicago Economists, Deficit Budgets and the Early 1930's," *American Economic Review* 58 [June 1968]: 476)

Even Milton Friedman confesses:

> So far as policy was concerned, Keynes had nothing to offer those of us that had sat at the feet of Simons, Mints, Knight and Viner. (Milton Friedman, "Comment on the Critics," included in Robert J. Gordon, ed., *Milton Friedman's Monetary Framework* [Chicago: Chicago University Press, 1974], p. 163)

Skousen, commenting on both perspectives, states:

> No doubt one of the reasons why the Chicago school gained greater acceptance was that there were some things they had in common with the Keynesians: they both used aggregate concepts; they both relied on empirical studies to support their models; and they both favoured some form of government involvement in the macroeconomic sphere. Granted, the Chicagoites favored monetary policy, while the Keynesians emphasized fiscal policy, *but both involved forms of state interventionism.* (Mark Skousen, "The Free Market Response to Keynesian Economics," included in *Dissent on Keynes*, p. 26; italics added)

On this topic see also Roger W. Garrison's article, "Is Milton Friedman a Keynesian?" published as chapter 8 of *Dissent on Keynes*, pp. 131–47. Also, Robert Skidelsky confirmed that the Keynesian "remedies" for recession were nothing new to the theorists of the Chicago School in the 1930s. See Robert Skidelsky, *John Maynard Keynes: The Economist as Saviour, 1920–1937* (London: Macmillan, 1992), p. 579. Finally, see the more recent, well-documented article by George S. Tavlas, "Chicago, Harvard and the Doctrinal Foundations of Monetary Economics," *Journal of Political Economy* 105, no. 1 (February 1997): 153–77.

[97] This table appeared in our preface to the Spanish edition of F.A. Hayek's *Contra Keynes and Cambridge* [*Contra Keynes y Cambridge*, p. xii].

Table VII-1 groups monetarists and Keynesians together because their similarities far outweigh their differences. Nevertheless we must acknowledge that certain important differences do separate these schools. Indeed, though both lack a capital theory[98] and apply the same "macro" methodology to the economy,[99] monetarists concentrate on the long term and

---

It is a personal adaptation of the tables included in Hayek's *The Pure Theory of Capital*, pp. 47–49, and Skousen's *The Structure of Production*, p. 370. Huerta de Soto, "The Ongoing Methodenstreit of the Austrian School," p. 96, also includes a table which contrasts the Austrian and neoclassical viewpoints, and the information contained there is essentially reproduced here as well.

[98] Except for the Austrian school and some sectors of the Swedish and early neoclassical school, the contending macro-economic theories are united by a common omission. They neglect to deal with capital or, more pointedly, the economy's intertemporal capital structure in any straightforward and satisfactory way. Yet capital theory offers the richest and most promising forum for the treatment of the critical time element in macroeconomics. (Roger W. Garrison, "The Limits of Macroeconomics," in *The Cato Journal: An Interdisciplinary Journal of Public Policy Analysis* 12, no. 1 [1993]: 166)

[99]Luis Ángel Rojo states:

On the whole, the current macroeconomic outlook is characterized by a high degree of confusion. Keynesian economics is in the grip of a deep crisis, as it has failed to adequately explain, much less control, the course of events. At the same time, new ideas have not yet taken root and are still an easy target in light of the empirical evidence.

Though we believe Rojo's diagnosis is correct, and he refers to the theoretical failings of both Keynesians and monetarists, it is unfortunate that he neglects to mention the need to base macroeconomics on an adequate capital theory which permits the correct integration of the "micro" and "macro" aspects of economics. See Luis Ángel Rojo, *Keynes: su tiempo y el nuestro* (Madrid: Alianza Editorial, 1984), pp. 365ff. In the same book Rojo makes a brief and largely insufficient reference to the Austrian theory of the economic cycle (see pp. 324–25). Ramón Febrero provides a useful summary of the current state of macroeconomics and attempts to bring some order to its chaotic and diffuse condition in his article, "El mundo de la macroeconomía: perspectiva general y concepciones originarias," in *Qué es la economía*, Ramón Febrero, ed. (Madrid: Ediciones Pirámide, 1997), chap. 13, pp. 383–424. Unfortunately Febrero does not

see a direct, immediate and effective connection between money and real events. In contrast Keynesians base their analysis on the short term and are very skeptical about a possible connection between money and real events, a link capable of somehow guaranteeing equilibrium will be reached and sustained. In comparison, the Austrian analysis presented here and the elaborate capital theory on which it rests suggest a healthy *middle ground* between monetarist and Keynesian extremes. In fact for Austrians, monetary assaults (credit expansion) account for the system's endogenous tendency to move away from "equilibrium" toward an unsustainable path. In other words they explain why the capital supply structure tends to be incompatible with economic agents' demand for consumer goods and services (and thus Say's law temporarily fails to hold true). Nonetheless certain inexorable, microeconomic forces, driven by entrepreneurship, the desire for profit, and variations in relative prices, tend to reverse the unbalancing effects of expansionary processes and return coordination to the economy. Therefore Austrians see a certain connection—a *loose joint*, to use Hayek's terminology[100]—between monetary phenomena and real phenomena, a link which is neither absolute, as monetarists claim, nor totally non-existent, as Keynesians assert.[101]

---

do justice to the alternative Austrian approach, which he hardly mentions at all.

[100]Hayek, *The Pure Theory of Capital*, p. 408.

[101] The conception of money as a loose joint suggests that there are two extreme theoretical constructs to be avoided. To introduce money as a "tight joint" would be to deny the special problem of intertemporal coordination. . . . At the other extreme, to introduce money as a "broken joint" would be to deny even the possibility of a market solution to the problem of intertemporal coordination. . . . Monetarism and Keynesianism, have tended to adopt one of the two polar positions with the result that, as a first approximation, macroeconomic problems are seen to be either trivial or insoluble. Between these extreme conceptions is Hayek's notion of loose-jointed money, which serves to recognize the problem while leaving the possibility of a market solution to it an open question.

In short, Austrians believe money is never neutral (not in the short, medium, nor long run), and institutions that deal with it (banks in particular) must be founded on universal legal principles which prevent a "falsification" of relative prices due to strictly monetary factors. Such falsifications lead to the widespread malinvestment of resources, and inevitably, to crisis and recession. Thus Austrian theorists consider the following to be the three essential principles of macroeconomic policy, in order of importance:

1. The quantity of money must remain as constant as possible (i.e., as in a pure gold standard), and credit expansion must be particularly avoided. These objectives require a return to the traditional legal principles which govern the monetary bank-deposit contract and the establishment of a 100-percent reserve requirement in banking.

2. Every attempt should be made to insure that the relative prices of different goods, services, resources, and factors of production remain flexible. In general the greater the credit and monetary expansion, the more rigid relative prices will tend to be, the more people will fail to recognize the true cost of a lack of flexibility, and the more corrupt the habits of economic agents will become. Agents will eventually come to accept the misconceived idea that the vital adjustments can and should always take the form of an increase in the quantity of money in circulation. In

---

(Roger W. Garrison, "Time and Money: The Universals of Macroeconomic Theorizing," *Journal of Macroeconomics* 6, no. 2 [Spring, 1984]: 203)

According to Garrison, the Austrians adopt a healthy middle ground in the area of expectations as well:

Assuming either superrational expectations or subrational expectations detract from the equally crucial role played by the market process itself, which alone can continuously inform expectations, and subtracts from the plausibility of the theory in which these unlikely expectational schemes are employed. (Garrison, "What About Expectations?, p. 22.)

TABLE VII-1
Two Contrasting Approaches to Economics

The Austrian School	Macroeconomists *(Monetarists and Keynesians)*
1. *Time* plays an essential role	1. The influence of time is ignored
2. "Capital" is viewed as a *heterogeneous* set of capital goods which receive constant wear and must be *replaced*	2. Capital is viewed as a *homogeneous* fund which *reproduces* on its own
3. The production process is *dynamic* and *is divided into multiple, vertical* stages	3. There is a notion of a *one-dimensional, horizontal* productive structure in *equilibrium* (circular flow of income)
4. Money affects the process by modifying the structure of *relative* prices	4. Money affects the *general* level of prices. Changes in relative prices are not considered
5. Macroeconomic phenomena are explained in *microeconomic* terms (variations in relative prices)	5. *Macroeconomic aggregates* prevent the analysis of underlying microeconomic factors (malinvestment)
6. Austrians hold a theory on the *endogenous* causes of economic crises which explains their *recurrent* nature (corrupt institutions: fractional-reserve banking and artificial credit expansion)	6. An endogenous theory of cycles is lacking. Crises have *exogenous* causes (psychological, technological and/or errors in monetary policy)
7. Austrians hold an elaborate *capital theory* (structure of production)	7. A theory of capital is lacking
8. *Saving* plays a decisive role. It causes a *longitudinal* change in the productive structure and determines the sort of technology to be used	8. Saving is *not* important. Capital reproduces *laterally* (more of the same), and the *production function* is fixed and is determined by the state of technology
9. There is an *inverse* relationship between the demand for capital goods and the demand for consumer goods. All investment requires saving and thus a temporary relative drop in consumption	9. The demand for capital goods is *directly* related to the demand for consumer goods
10. It is assumed that production costs are *subjective* and not predetermined	10. Production costs are *objective*, real and predetermined
11. Market prices tend to determine production costs, not vice versa	11. Historical costs of production tend to determine market prices
12. The interest rate is a market price determined by subjective valuations of time preference. The interest rate is used to arrive at the present value (toward which the market price of each capital good tends) by discounting its expected future flow of returns	12. The interest rate tends to be determined by the marginal productivity or efficiency of capital, understood as the internal rate of discount at which the expected flow of returns is equal to the historical cost of producing each capital good (which is considered invariable and predetermined). The short-term interest rate is believed to have a predominantly monetary origin

any case, as we have already argued, the indirect, underlying cause of economic maladjustments lies in credit expansion, which provokes a generalized malinvestment of resources, which in turn creates unemployment. The more rigid the markets, the higher the unemployment.

3. When economic agents enter into long-term contracts negotiated in monetary units, they must be able to adequately predict changes in the purchasing power of money. This last requirement appears the easiest to satisfy, both when the purchasing power of the monetary unit declines continuously, as has occurred since World War II, and when it gradually and predictably rises, as would occur following the adoption of a policy to maintain the quantity of money in circulation constant. In fact the condition is even more likely to be met in the second case.[102]

---

[102]See Hayek's article, "On Neutral Money," published as chapter 7 of *Money, Capital and Fluctuations*, pp. 159–62, esp. p. 161. This is the English translation of the original German article, "Über 'Neutrales Geld'" in *Zeitschrift für Nationalökonomie* 4 (1933): 659–61. Donald C. Lavoie has revealed that at any rate, the disruptive effects a simple variation in the general price level may provoke are less damaging and much easier to predict than those exerted on the productive structure by the type of monetary injection bank credit expansion entails:

> My own judgment would be that the price-level effects are less damaging and easier to adjust to than the injection effects; thus the optimal policy for monetary stability would be as close to zero money growth as can be practically attained. In my view the gradual deflation that this policy would permit would be preferable to the relative price distortion which would be caused by attempting to inject enough money into the economy to keep the price level constant.

He adds:

> Even gold money would undergo gradual increases in its supply over time. Some have estimated that about a two percent increase per year would be likely. To me this appears to be the best we can do. (Don C. Lavoie, "Economic Calculation

6

Appendix on Life Insurance Companies and Other Non-Bank Financial Intermediaries

The analysis of the last four chapters has put us in a position to understand the important role true financial intermediaries play in the economy. Logically, we use the term *true* to describe those non-bank financial intermediaries which create *ex nihilo* neither loans nor the corresponding deposits, and which merely act as middlemen in the market in which present goods are exchanged for future goods. In other words, financial intermediaries simply take money from lenders offering present goods and hand it over to borrowers. In return for their service as mere intermediaries they receive a profit, which is generally small. This slender profit margin contrasts with the disproportionate gains the aggregate of banks accumulate when they create money *ex nihilo* in the form of deposits, an activity they pursue thanks to the legal privilege which permits them to make self-interested use of most of the money deposited with them on demand.

Although with tiresome insistence banks are claimed to be the most important financial "intermediaries" in the economy, this is a baseless, unrealistic notion. Banks are essentially not financial intermediaries. Their main activity consists of creating loans and deposits from nothing (and is apart from their function as *true* financial intermediaries, a role of secondary importance, both quantitatively and qualitatively speaking).[103] In fact banks and the banking system have not taken

_____

and Monetary Stability," printed in *Cato Journal* 3, no. 1 [Spring, 1983]: 163–70, esp. p. 169)

In chapter 9 we suggest a process for reforming the monetary and banking system. Upon its culmination, this process would obviate the need to design and implement any more "macroeconomic policies."

[103]Luis Ángel Rojo has correctly pointed out that banks' central activity does not involve their function as financial intermediaries, but their ability to create loans and deposits from nothing. However he still refers to banks as financial "intermediaries" and overlooks the prominent role true financial intermediaries (which he describes as "non-bank") would

on a major role in modern economies because they act as financial intermediaries, but because they typically create loans, and thus deposits, *ex nihilo*, thereby increasing the money supply. Hence it is not surprising that banks are capable of distorting the productive structure and the behavior of economic agents, who find the great relative ease of acquiring present goods from a bank enormously tempting. In comparison, it is more difficult to obtain resources drawn from real voluntary savings. Saving always involves greater initial sacrifice and discipline on the part of third-party savers, and it is comparatively much harder to accomplish.

Therefore it is absurd to maintain, as is sometimes heard, that owing to the insufficient development of the capital market and of non-bank financial intermediaries, banks "have had no choice" but to take on a prominent role in the financing of production processes. Indeed the exact opposite is true. Banks' expansionary capacity to grant loans from nothing inevitably robs the capital market and non-bank financial intermediaries of a significant part of their economic prominence, since the banking system, which can expand loans without anyone's having to first sacrifice immediate consumption by voluntarily saving, is always much more likely to grant a loan.

Once the general public begins to correctly identify the evils of bank credit expansion, to understand that the expansion process depends on a legal privilege no other economic agent enjoys, and to see that the process inevitably provokes consecutive cycles of boom and depression, the public will be able to instigate a reform of the banking system. Such a reform will be founded on the reestablishment of a 100-percent reserve requirement for demand deposits, i.e., on the application of traditional legal principles to banking operations. Once this reform has been introduced, the proper status will be restored to the capital market and to true financial intermediaries, i.e., non-bank intermediaries, who by their very nature,

---

play in an economy free of special privileges for banks. See Luis Ángel Rojo, *Teoría económica III*, Class Notes and Syllabus, year 1970–1971 (Madrid, 1970), pp. 13ff., and 90–96.

are those entrepreneurs who specialize in convincing economic agents of the importance and necessity of short-,
medium- and long-term saving, as well as in efficiently con-
necting lenders and borrowers, spreading risk and taking
advantage of the corresponding economies of scale.

LIFE INSURANCE COMPANIES
AS TRUE FINANCIAL INTERMEDIARIES

The social significance of life insurance companies sets
them apart from other true financial intermediaries. In fact the
contracts offered by these institutions make it possible for
broad layers of society to undertake a genuine, disciplined
effort to save for the long term. Indeed life insurance provides
the perfect way to save, since it is the only method which
guarantees, precisely at those moments when households
experience the greatest need (in other words, in the case of
death, disability, or retirement), the immediate availability of
a large sum of money which, by other saving methods, could
only be accumulated following a very prolonged period of
time. With the payment of the first premium, the policyholder's beneficiaries acquire the right to receive, in the event
of this person's death, for instance, a substantial amount of
money which would have taken the policyholder many years
to save via other methods.

Moreover life insurers develop and operate large commercial networks which specialize in emphasizing to families the
fundamental importance of committing to long-term, disciplined saving, not only to prepare for the possible misfortunes
associated with death, disability, or illness, but also to guarantee a decent income in case of survival beyond a certain age.
Thus we could conclude that life insurance companies are the
quintessential "true financial intermediaries," because their
activity consists precisely of encouraging long-term saving in
families and channeling saved funds into very secure long-
term investments (mainly blue-chip bonds and real estate).[104]

---

[104]Austrian economists have always recognized the major role life
insurance plays in facilitating voluntary saving among broad sections of

The fact that life insurance companies do not expand credit nor create money is obvious, especially if one compares the contracts they market with banks' demand deposit operations. The accounting entries typical of a life insurance company are as follows:

Once the company has convinced its customers of the importance of initiating a long-term plan of disciplined saving, the customers pay a premium to the company each year for the duration of the life insurance contract. The premiums are considered part of the insurance company's income, as shown below:

(76) Debit	Credit
Cash	Life insurance premiums (On the revenues side of the income statement)

Life insurance companies use the premiums they receive to meet a series of operational costs, primarily claims costs, marketing and administrative expenses, and other expenses involved in the technical coverage of the risk of death, disability and survival. The entry which follows the payment of these technical costs appears below:

---

society. Thus Richard von Strigl makes explicit reference to the "life insurance business, which is of such extraordinary importance in capital formation." Strigl indicates that, in order for voluntary saving in general and life insurance in particular to prosper, it must be clear that the purchasing power of the monetary unit will at least remain constant. See Richard von Strigl, *Curso medio de economía*, pp. 201–02. In addition, in his classic article on saving, F.A. Hayek refers to life insurance and the purchase of a home as two of the most important sources of voluntary saving (see F.A. Hayek, "Saving," originally published for the 1933 edition of the *Encyclopedia of the Social Sciences*, and reprinted as chapter 5 of *Profits, Interest and Investment*, esp. pp. 169–70).

(77) Debit	Credit
Operational costs (Claims, administrative expenses, etc.)	Cash

We should point out that operational costs absorb only a portion of the total amount paid in premiums to life insurance companies, which must reserve a significant part of their premium income to cover not only future risks (since companies charge constant annual premiums for the coverage of risks which increase in probability as policyholders grow older), but also the important saving component usually incorporated in the most popular types of life insurance. This second share of the premium total generates *reserves* in the form of long-term investments recorded as the insurer's assets and counterbalanced on the liability side by a *mathematical reserve* account, which shows the present actuarial value of the future commitments the insurance company makes to its policyholders. The corresponding entries are as follows:

(78) Debit	Credit
Long-term investments	Cash
(79) Portion of premium income which is invested (expenses)	Mathematical reserves (future commitments to policyholders)

The life insurance company's balance sheet would look like this:

(80)   Life Insurance Company E
Balance Sheet
(End of the year)

Assets	Liabilities
Long-term investments	Mathematical reserves

    Obviously no money is created, and mathematical reserves, which represent the book value of future obligations to policyholders, correspond to the fact that the insured have handed over a certain quantity of present goods in exchange for a larger quantity of goods at an undetermined point in the future (when the contingency insured against—death, disability, or survival—takes place). Until the anticipated event occurs, policyholders lose the availability of their money, which becomes available to borrowers who receive it from the insurance companies. These borrowers are the issuers of the corresponding bonds and fixed-income securities the life insurance companies acquire. When life insurance companies invest in real estate, they do so directly, thus taking on the role of important real estate owners devoted to renting their properties to the public.

    The income statement of the life insurance company appears as follows:

(81)   Life Insurance Company E
Income Statement for the year

Expenses	Revenues
Operational costs	Premiums
Mathematical reserves (allowance)	Financial income
Profit	

It is clear that insurers' accounting profit arises from the difference between revenues (premiums and financial income) and expenses (operational costs and those resulting from increases in mathematical reserves). Insurance companies usually make a very modest profit which has three possible sources: claim profit (i.e., the company may overestimate the number of claims in its calculation of premiums), profit derived from operational, administrative costs (administrative expenses included in the calculation of premiums may be greater than the company's real costs), and finally, financial, profit (financial revenues may exceed the "technical interest rate" used in the calculation of premiums). Furthermore competition in the market has led life insurance companies to pass on a large part of their yearly profits to their policyholders, since life insurance contracts now commonly include profit-sharing clauses, which increase customers' insured capital annually without increasing premiums. Thus from an economic standpoint, regardless of its legal status (whether a corporation or a mutual company), a life insurance company becomes, at least partially, a sort of "mutual company" in which the policyholders themselves share in the company's profits.

The institution of life insurance has gradually and spontaneously taken shape in the market over the last two hundred years. It is based on a series of technical, actuarial, financial and juridical principles of business behavior which have enabled it to perform its mission perfectly and survive economic crises and recessions which other institutions, especially banking, have been unable to overcome. Therefore the high "financial death rate" of banks, which systematically suspend payments and fail without the support of the central bank, has historically contrasted with the health and technical solvency of life insurance companies. (In the last two hundred years, a negligible number of life insurance companies have disappeared due to financial difficulties.)

The following technical principles are traditional in the life insurance sector: assets are valued at historical cost, and premiums are calculated based on very prudent technical interest rates, which never include a component for inflation expectations. Thus life insurance companies tend to underestimate their assets, overestimate their liabilities, and reach a high level of static and dynamic solvency which makes them immune to the deepest stages of the recessions that recur with economic cycles. In fact when the value of financial assets and capital goods plunges in the most serious stages of recession in every cycle, life insurance companies are not usually affected, given the reduced book value they record for their investments. With respect to the amount of their liabilities, insurers calculate their mathematical reserves at interest rates much lower than those actually charged in the market. Hence they tend to overestimate the present value of their commitments on the liabilities side. Moreover policyholders take advantage of the profits insurance companies bring in, as long as the profits are distributed *a posteriori*, in accordance with the above-mentioned profit-sharing clauses. Logically the amounts of such profits cannot be guaranteed *a priori* in the corresponding contracts.[105]

SURRENDER VALUES AND THE MONEY SUPPLY

Life insurance contracts commonly offer an option by which the company, at the request of the policyholder, *redeems* the policy via the payment of a certain sum in cash. This

---

[105]We have attempted elsewhere to integrate the Austrian theory of economic cycles with an explanation of insurance techniques and have explained how insurance methods have spontaneously evolved to counter the harmful effects of recessions. At the same time, insurance companies have striven to constantly guarantee the fulfillment of their commitments to their customers (widows, orphans, and retired people). We conclude that this approach, which has been consistently successful, should be adopted with respect to uninsured "pension funds" as well, if we expect them to accomplish their purpose and be as immune as possible to the damaging consequences of the cycle. See our article, "Interés, ciclos económicos y planes de pensiones," published in the *Anales del Congreso Internacional de Fondos de Pensiones,* which took place in Madrid in April 1984, pp. 458–68. Jesús Huerta Peña has studied the essential principles behind the financial stability of life insurance companies in his book, *La estabilidad financiera de las empresas de seguros* (Madrid, 1954).

option, which is generally included in all types of life insurance, with the exception of those which cover solely the risk of death or survival, can be exercised whenever the policyholder desires, following the initial period stipulated in the policy (normally two or three years). This contractual clause could give the impression that a life insurance policy could also serve as a tool for legally implementing a monetary demand-deposit contract. Nevertheless we know that demand-deposit contracts are characterized by their essential cause, which lies in the safekeeping obligation and in the depositor's ability to withdraw the money deposited at any time. Therefore life insurance differs fundamentally from demand deposits. The following factors prevent any confusion between the two:[106]

First, life insurers have traditionally sold their products as long-term saving tools. Hence when customers buy life insurance they are undoubtedly motivated by a desire to begin setting aside and saving a portion of their income for the long term, in order to build up capital for use when their families need it most. From the standpoint of the contract's cause, as well as the policyholder's *subjective* ends, present goods are

---

[106] [T]he cash surrender values of life insurance policies are not funds that depositors and policy holders can obtain and spend without reducing the cash of others. These funds are in large part invested and thus not held in a monetary form. That part which is in banks or in cash is, of course, included in the quantity of money which is either in or out of banks and should not be counted a second time. Under present laws, such institutions cannot extend credit beyond sums received. If they need to raise more cash than they have on hand to meet customer withdrawals, they must sell some of their investments and reduce the bank accounts or cash holdings of those who buy them. Accordingly, *they are in no position to expand credit or increase the nation's quantity of money as can commercial and central banks, all of which operate on a fractional reserve basis and can lend more money than is entrusted to them.* (Percy L. Greaves, in his Introduction to Mises's book, *On the Manipulation of Money and Credit,* pp. xlvi–xlvii; italics added)

clearly handed over and the full availability of them lost, in exchange for the guarantee of a substantial income or capital under certain future circumstances (those in which a family's need may be greatest, such as the death of a provider or survival beyond a certain age).

Second, most life insurance operations do not permit the possibility of obtaining the surrender value immediately, i.e., from the moment the contract is signed and the money is paid. Instead there is generally a waiting period, which, depending upon the market and legislation, varies in length from two to three years. Only after this initial period does the customer acquire the right to a surrender value.

Third, surrender values do not approximate the total amount paid to the insurance company in premiums, since they are reduced by the initial costs of the policy, which are amortized over the entire duration of the policy and which, for technical and business reasons, tend to be rather high and are paid when the policy is purchased. Moreover the surrender value normally includes a penalty fee in favor of the insurer to further encourage customers to carry their policies to maturity. Thus it is obvious that life insurance operations have been designed to discourage the surrender option as much as possible, so that policyholders are only willing to exercise it in situations of urgent family need or when they wish to change insurance companies. Therefore subjectively speaking, we must conclude that for most customers traditional life-insurance operations do not mask deposit contracts.[107]

---

[107]Although the arguments expressed in the text are more than sufficient to show that traditional life insurance is not a mask for demand deposits, from a legal and economic standpoint we cannot be absolutely certain unless insurers cease to guarantee a *predetermined* surrender value and limit this amount to the market value acquired at any specific point by the investments corresponding to the mathematical reserves of any particular policy. In this case no one would be able to claim a right to a predetermined surrender value; a customer would only be entitled to the liquidation value of his policy at secondary market prices. Nevertheless the difficulties insurers encounter in assigning specific investments to each policy, difficulties which stem from the long-term nature

THE CORRUPTION OF TRADITIONAL LIFE-INSURANCE PRINCIPLES

Despite the above considerations, we must acknowledge that in recent times, under the pretext of a supposedly beneficial "deregulation of financial markets," the distinct boundaries between the institution of life insurance and the banking sector have often been blurred in many western countries. This blurring of boundaries has permitted the emergence of various supposed "life insurance" operations which, instead of following the traditional principles of the sector, have been designed to mask true demand-deposit contracts which involve an attempt to guarantee the immediate, complete availability to the policyholder of the money deposited as "premiums" and of the corresponding interest.[108] This corruption,

---

of life insurance contracts, have led companies to develop, from a legal and actuarial point of view, a series of contractual clauses (waiting periods, penalty fees in the event of surrender, etc.) which, *de facto*, have the same deterrent effect as the receipt of a reduced value at secondary market prices should the customer terminate the policy during an economic recession. A summary of the most typical surrender clauses appears in Jesús Huerta Ballester, *A Brief Comparison Between the Ordinary Life Contracts of Ten Insurance Companies* (Madrid, 1954).

[108]Thus traditional life insurance can also be corrupted, especially when its basic principles are to different degrees abandoned under the pretext of "financial deregulation" or when an attempt is made to combine the institution with a sector as foreign to life insurance as banking. John Maynard Keynes provided a historical example of this corruption of life insurance during the years he was chairman of the National Mutual Life Assurance Society of London. See related comments in chapter 3, footnote 47. While chairman, Keynes embraced an *ad hoc* investment policy centered on variable-yield securities, as opposed to the traditional policy of investing in fixed-yield securities. Furthermore he favored the use of unorthodox accounting principles, e.g., he valued assets at market prices, not at their historical cost, and he even authorized the distribution of profits to policyholders against unrealized gains. All of these typically Keynesian assaults on traditional insurance principles nearly cost him the solvency of his company with the arrival of the Great Depression. The negative influence Keynes exerted on the British life insurance industry can still be felt today, and to a certain extent, it has spread to the American insurance market as well. Those within the sector are now attempting to free themselves from such unhealthy influences and

which we touched on in chapter 3, has exerted a very negative influence on the insurance sector as a whole and has made it possible for some life insurance companies to market deposits in violation of traditional legal principles and thus to act, in different degrees, as banks, i.e., to loan money actually placed with them on demand deposit. Hence various life insurance companies have begun to take part in the banking process of credit expansion, which damages the productive structure

---

return to the traditional principles which from the beginning have guaranteed the smooth operation and solvency of the industry. On these issues, see the following references: Nicholas Davenport, "Keynes in the City," published in *Essays on John Maynard Keynes*, Milo Keynes, ed. (Cambridge: Cambridge University Press, 1975), pp. 224–25; Skidelsky, *John Maynard Keynes: The Economist as Saviour, 1920–1937*, esp. pp. 25–26 and 524; and D.E. Moggridge, *Maynard Keynes: An Economist's Biography* (London: Routledge, 1992), esp. pp. 410 and 411. Keynes had a *direct* corrupting effect as a highly influential leader in the British insurance industry of his time. However he also had a much more damaging *indirect* effect on the insurance sector in general in the sense that his economic theory helped to push up inflation and to discredit and destroy the saving habits of ordinary people, in keeping with his "euthanasia of the rentier" philosophy, which exerted a very harmful influence on the development of the life insurance and pension market worldwide. In this respect, the fact that Keynes was chairman of a life insurance company for many years constitutes one of the most remarkable ironies in the history of life insurance. See Ludwig von Mises, "Pensions, the Purchasing Power of the Dollar and the New Economics," included in *Planning for Freedom and Twelve Other Addresses* (South Holland, Ill.: Libertarian Press, 1974), pp. 86–93. See also the speeches Keynes delivered at the seventeen general meetings (1922–1938) while chairman of the National Mutual Life Assurance Society. The speeches make fascinating reading and superbly illustrate the highly disruptive effects which, by the irony of fate, followed from giving a speculative "wolf" and enemy of saving, like Keynes, power over some peaceful "sheep" (his life insurance company). See volume 12 of *The Collected Writings of John Maynard Keynes* (London: Macmillan, 1983), pp. 114–254. Hermann Heinrich Gossen was another famous economist involved in the insurance sector. Apart from his role as advisor in a financially-doomed crop-and-livestock insurance company, Gossen designed a blueprint for a German savings bank devoted to the life insurance business. The project never came to fruition, however. See the article F.A. Hayek wrote on Gossen and which appears in Hayek's *The Trend of Economic Thinking*, vol. 3, p. 356.

and causes economic cycles and recessions. Furthermore these companies have done serious harm to the insurance industry itself, which has been the object of increasing state and central-bank intervention and has lost many of the fiscal advantages it had always enjoyed in the past, advantages justified in light of the considerable benefit the institution produces in fostering long-term saving among broad sectors of society.[109] At any rate we intend the theoretical analysis performed in this book to give life insurers back their self-confidence and their trust in the positive nature of the traditional institution of which they form a part and to encourage a clear separation between life insurance and the banking "business," which is foreign to it. As we know, this "business" not only lacks the necessary juridical foundation, but also provokes economic effects highly detrimental to society. In contrast the institution of life insurance rests on an extraordinarily solid legal, technical-actuarial, and financial foundation. When life insurance companies are faithful to the traditional principles of the sector, not only do they not hamper peaceful economic growth; they are actually essential and extremely beneficial in terms of

---

[109]To the extent economic agents begin to subjectively view the surrender value of their policies as money available to them at all times, the recent "confusion" between the insurance and banking sectors warrants considering surrender values (which are generally lower than insurers' mathematical reserves) as part of the money supply. This is the thesis Murray N. Rothbard presents in his article, "Austrian Definitions of the Supply of Money," in *New Directions in Austrian Economics*, pp. 143–56, esp. pp. 151–52. Nevertheless we disagree with Rothbard's opinion that surrender values should automatically be included in the money supply, since this ultimately depends on whether actors in general subjectively regard the surrender value of their policies as part of their immediately-available cash balances, something which does not yet occur in most markets. Moreover we should note that confusion between the institutions of insurance and banking has not been complete, and even in those markets in which it was greatest, companies appear to be returning to traditional insurance principles, in particular the radical separation between insurance and banking. Regarding new life insurance operations and their similarities with bank deposits, see the book by Thierry Delvaux and Martin E. Magnee, *Les nouveaux produits d'assurance-vie* (Brussels: Editions de L'Université de Bruxelles, 1991).

fostering long-term saving and investment and hence, the sustainable economic development of society.

OTHER TRUE FINANCIAL INTERMEDIARIES: MUTUAL FUNDS AND HOLDING AND INVESTMENT COMPANIES

Other true financial intermediaries which would become even more developed if the privileges currently enjoyed by banks were eliminated are mutual funds, holding and investment companies, leasing and finance corporations, etc. All of these institutions receive present goods from savers and, in their capacity as intermediaries, transfer these goods to final borrowers. Though none of these institutions has the ability of life insurance to guarantee a substantial income from the first moment should a fortuitous event occur (death, disability, survival), it is obvious that they would all become more prominent, even more than they are now, if banks were obligated to maintain a 100-percent reserve ratio, and thus were to lose their power to create deposits and grant loans from nothing. In particular, mutual funds would take on a very important role, in the sense that economic agents would invest their excess cash balances through them and would be able to obtain immediate liquidity by selling their shares, though at secondary-market prices, never at their nominal value. The same applies to holding companies and other financial and investment institutions, which have on many occasions gone through a process of corruption and assault very similar to that of life insurance, a process of "innovation" consisting of the design of different formulas for "guaranteeing" the corresponding "investors" the immediate availability of their money, i.e., the possibility of retrieving their "savings" at the nominal value at any time. For instance, as we saw in chapter 3 in connection with different types of financial operations, clauses containing agreements of repurchase at a predetermined price are among the abusive legal devices generally used to mask true "demand deposit" contracts in other institutions completely unrelated to banking.[110] From an economic standpoint, as such procedures

---

[110]Economically speaking, it is easy to show that a financial operation which involves an agreement of guaranteed repurchase at any time at

have spread, the contracts and institutions in question have begun to produce the same harmful effects as fractional-reserve banking. Therefore as we will see in the following chapters, any proposal to reform the banking system must include a plan to quickly identify different abusive legal procedures which could be conceived to mask true fractional-reserve, demand-deposit contracts. Such procedures must be curtailed, as they go against general legal principles and seriously disrupt the harmonious process of economic coordination.

SPECIFIC COMMENTS ON CREDIT INSURANCE

Finally we should briefly mention credit insurance operations, which have spontaneously emerged in developed economies. In exchange for a premium, these policies guarantee that in the event that the customers of insured business and industrial enterprises cannot pay their debts, which are usually paid within a certain period (thirty, sixty, ninety days, etc.) using a given financial instrument (for example, a bill of exchange), the insurance company will pay a percentage of the total corresponding debt (between 75 and 95 percent), thus taking it over and later collecting the amount from the delinquent customer. Therefore credit insurance addresses a real need which arises in markets. It responds to a set of circumstances which derives from the credit that different industrial and business enterprises habitually extend to their customers. Such credit corresponds, economically speaking, to a traditional operation in which savers, generally capitalists who own a business, advance financial resources for a time to

---

its nominal value (not at the unpredictable, oscillating price of the secondary market) constitutes a demand deposit which requires a 100-percent reserve ratio. Indeed the only way for a company to guarantee at all times its ability to honor all its repurchase agreements is to keep available a monetary reserve equal in value to the total that would have to be paid if all agreements were exercised at once (100-percent reserve ratio). As long as companies fail to maintain such a reserve, they will always run the risk of being unable to immediately comply with the exercise of the repurchase option, a possibility which, during stages of recession in the economic cycle, will almost become a certainty without the unconditional support of a central bank to act as lender of last resort.

workers and owners of the original means of production, as well as to their customers, whom they grant a period of several days or months to pay their debts. Logically, this credit customers receive always requires a prior sacrifice on the part of certain economic agents, who must reduce their consumption and save the corresponding resources to make these easy payment terms possible. Hence customer credit cannot be generated from nothing, but always obliges someone (the owners of the company offering the credit) to save first. In the absence of distortions caused by bank credit expansion, credit insurance fulfills a particularly important economic function. The large databases of credit insurance companies enable them to classify customers according to their default risk. These credit insurance companies also provide legal collection services, taking advantage of significant economies of scale beyond the scope of their individual clients.

The problem emerges when bank credit expansion distorts all credit markets and provokes recurrent cycles of boom and recession. In fact in the boom stage fed by credit expansion, multiple unrealistic investment projects are artificially launched, and many market operations are financed in installments and covered by credit insurance. As a result, companies specializing in credit insurance take on *systematic* risks which, by their very nature, are not technically insurable. Indeed the process of expansion must reverse sooner or later, and widespread bankruptcies, suspensions of payments, and liquidations of unsuccessful investment projects will reveal the errors committed. Consequently, in modern economies subject to the distorting effects of credit expansion, credit insurance is of a cyclical nature, which prevents it from surviving recession stages in the absence of a series of safeguard clauses to protect it from the same fate suffered on a large scale by overoptimistic entrepreneurs who unduly lengthen their investment projects in the expansionary boom stage. Of these clauses the following stand out: those which establish deductibles and waiting periods on the payment of claims, depending upon the amount, and that which requires an adjudication of bankruptcy, which, due to the sheer length of bankruptcy proceedings, tends to involve a long delay, which allows the insurance company, meanwhile, to make the necessary collections and maintain the necessary financial stability.[111]

Successive cycles of boom and depression invariably pose a formidable challenge to credit insurance companies, which apart from their traditional services (collections, customer risk classification, etc.), perform an additional one: during economic booms they accumulate important financial reserves, which they later use in crises and recessions to systematically satisfy the much larger claims filed during these periods. In any case we must recognize that the legal precautionary measures adopted to this point have been insufficient to prevent the failure and liquidation of some of the most prominent credit insurers in the western world during each of the recent crises which have erupted in the West. We must also acknowledge that the institution of credit insurance will always be highly vulnerable to stages of recession, particularly while banks continue to operate with a fractional reserve.[112]

---

[111]Francisco Cabrillo, *Quiebra y liquidación de empresas* (Madrid: Unión Editorial, 1989).

[112]It is obviously impossible for credit insurance companies to technically insure loans the banking system itself grants during its expansionary phase, since, as we have already shown, the necessary independence between the existence of the insurance and the results of the hypothetically insured event is lacking. Indeed if bank loans were insured, there would be no limit to their expansion, and in the inevitable recession which credit expansion always causes, a systematic increase in the number of defaulters would render the policy technically unviable. Thus, for the same reasons the law of large numbers and a fractional-reserve ratio are inadequate to insure demand deposits, it is technically impossible to insure banks' credit operations through the credit insurance industry.

8

CENTRAL AND FREE BANKING THEORY

T
his chapter contains a theoretical analysis of the arguments raised for and against both central and free
banking throughout the history of economic thought.
To begin we will review the theoretical debate between those
in favor of a privileged banking system, i.e., one not subject to
traditional legal principles and therefore capable of expanding
credit (the Banking School), and those theorists who have
always contended that banks should follow universal rules
and principles (the Currency School).[1] The analysis and evaluation of the theoretical contributions of both schools will

---

[1]The definitions of "Banking School" and "Currency School" offered in
the text basically coincide with those Anna J. Schwartz proposes.
According to Schwartz, theorists of the Currency School believe monetary policy should be disciplined and subject to general legal rules and
principles, while members of the Banking School generally advocate
granting bankers (and eventually the central bank) complete discretionary freedom to act and even to disregard traditional legal principles.
In fact Anna J. Schwartz notes that the whole controversy centers on
whether

> policy should be governed by rules (espoused by adherents
> of the Currency School), or whether the authorities should
> allow discretion (espoused by adherents of the Banking
> School). (Anna J. Schwartz's article, "Banking School, Cur-
> rency School, Free Banking School," which appeared in vol-
> ume 1 of *The New Palgrave: Dictionary of Money and Finance*
> [London: Macmillan, 1992], pp. 148–51)

also provide us with a chance to study the controversy between supporters of the central bank and defenders of a free banking system. We will see that at first members of the Currency School by and large defended the central bank, and Banking School theorists favored a free banking system, yet in the end the inflationist doctrines of the Banking School prevailed, ironically under the auspices of the central bank. Indeed one of the most important conclusions of our analysis is that the central bank, far from being a result of the spontaneous process of social cooperation, emerged as the inevitable consequence of a fractional-reserve private banking system. In a fractional-reserve context it is private bankers themselves who eventually demand a lender of last resort to help them weather the cyclical economic crises and recessions such a system provokes. We will wrap up the chapter with a look at the theorem of the impossibility of socialist economic calculation. When applied to central bank operations, this theorem explains the problems of administrative banking laws as we know them. Finally we will argue that current free-banking advocates usually make the mistake of accepting and justifying fractional-reserve practices and fail to see that such a concession would not only inevitably lead to the resurgence of central banks, but would also trigger cyclical crises harmful to the economy and society.

1

A CRITICAL ANALYSIS OF THE BANKING SCHOOL

In this section we will examine the theoretical arguments advocates of fractional-reserve banking have constructed to justify such a system. Although these arguments have traditionally been considered a product of the Banking and Currency School controversy which arose in England during the first half of the nineteenth century, the earliest arguments on fractional-reserve banking and the two opposing sides (the banking view versus the currency view) can actually be traced back to contributions made by the theorists of the School of Salamanca in the sixteenth and seventeenth centuries.

The Banking and Currency Views and the
School of Salamanca

The theorists of the School of Salamanca made important contributions in the monetary field which have been studied in detail.[2]

The first Spanish scholastic to produce a treatise on money was Diego de Covarrubias y Leyva, who published *Veterum collatio numismatum* ("Compilation on old moneys") in 1550. In this work the famous Segovian bishop examines the history of the devaluation of the Castilian maravedi and compiles a large quantity of statistics on the evolution of prices. Although the essential elements of the quantity theory of money are already implicit in Covarrubias's treatise, he still lacks an explicit monetary theory.[3] It was not until 1556, several years later, that Martín de Azpilcueta unequivocally declared the increase in prices, or decrease in the purchasing power of money, to be the result of a rise in the money supply, an increase triggered in Castile by the massive influx of precious metals from America.

Indeed Martín de Azpilcueta's description of the relationship between the quantity of money and prices is faultless:

---

[2]See especially the research Marjorie Grice-Hutchinson published under the direction of F.A. Hayek, *The School of Salamanca: Readings in Spanish Monetary Theory, 1544–1605*; Rothbard, "New Light on the Prehistory of the Austrian School," pp. 52–74; Alejandro A. Chafuen, *Christians for Freedom: Late-Scholastic Economics* (San Francisco: Ignatius Press, 1986), pp. 74–86. On Marjorie Grice-Hutchinson see the laudatory comments Fabián Estapé makes in his introduction to the third Spanish edition of Schumpeter's book, *The History of Economic Analysis* (*Historia del análisis económico* [Barcelona: Editorial Ariel, 1994], pp. xvi–xvii).

[3]We have used the *Omnia opera* edition, published in Venice in 1604. Volume 1 includes Diego de Covarrubias's treatise on money under the complete title, *Veterum collatio numismatum, cum his, quae modo expenduntur, publica, et regia authoritate perpensa*, pp. 669–710. Davanzati often quotes this piece of writing, and Ferdinando Galiani does so at least once in chapter 2 of his famous work, *Della moneta*, p. 26. Carl Menger also refers to the treatise of Covarrubias in his book, *Principles of Economics* (New York and London: New York University Press, 1981), p. 317; p. 257 in the original version, *Grundsätze der Volkswirthschaftslehre*.

In the lands where there is a serious shortage of money, all other saleable items and even the labor of men are given for less money than where money is abundant; for example, experience shows that in France, where there is less money than in Spain, bread, wine, cloth and labor cost much less; and even when there was less money in Spain, saleable items and the labor of men were given for much less than after the Indies were discovered and covered Spain with gold and silver. *The reason is that money is worth more when and where it is scarce, than when and where it is abundant.*[4]

In comparison with the profound and detailed studies which have been conducted on the monetary theory of the School of Salamanca, up to this point very little effort has been made to analyze and evaluate the position of the scholastics on banking.[5] Nevertheless the theorists of the School of Salamanca carried out a penetrating analysis of banking practices, and by and large, they were forerunners of the different theoretical positions which more than two centuries later reappeared in the debate between members of the "Banking School" and those of the "Currency School."

As a matter of fact, in chapter 2 we mentioned the severe criticism of fractional-reserve banking voiced by Doctor Saravia de la Calle in the final chapters of his book, *Instrucción de mercaderes*. In a similar vein, though not as strongly critical as Saravia de la Calle, Martín de Azpilcueta and Tomás de Mercado undertake a rigorous analysis of banking which includes

---

[4]Azpilcueta, *Comentario resolutorio de cambios*, pp. 74–75; italics added. However Nicholas Copernicus preceded Martín de Azpilcueta by almost thirty years, since he formulated a (more embryonic) version of the quantity theory of money in his book, *De monetae cudendae ratio* (1526). See Rothbard, *Economic Thought Before Adam Smith*, p. 165.

[5]See, for instance, the comments Francisco Gómez Camacho makes in his introduction to Luis de Molina's work, *La teoría del justo precio* (Madrid: Editora Nacional, 1981), pp. 33–34; the remarks Sierra Bravo makes in *El pensamiento social y económico de la escolástica desde sus orígenes al comienzo del catolicismo social*, vol. 1, pp. 214–37; the article by Francisco Belda which we cover in detail on the following pages; and the more recent article by Huerta de Soto, "New Light on the Prehistory of the Theory of Banking and the School of Salamanca."

a catalog of the requirements for a fair and lawful monetary bank deposit. These early authors could be viewed as members of an incipient "Currency School," which had long been developing at the very heart of the School of Salamanca. These scholars typically adopt a consistent, firm stance on the legal requirements for bank-deposit contracts, as well as a generally critical, wary attitude toward banking.

A distinct second group of theorists is led by Luis de Molina and includes Juan de Lugo and Leonardo de Lesio and, to a lesser extent, Domingo de Soto. As stated in chapter 2, these authors follow Molina's example and, like him, they demand only a weak legal basis for the monetary bank-deposit contract and accept fractional-reserve practices, arguing that such a contract is more a "precarious" loan or mutuum than a deposit. We will not repeat here all arguments against Molina's position on the bank-deposit contract. Suffice it to say that underlying his position is a widespread misconception which dates back to the medieval glossators and their comments on the institution of the *depositum confessatum*. What concerns us now is the fact that this second group of scholastics was much more lenient in their criticism of bankers and went as far as to justify fractional-reserve banking. It is not, then, altogether far-fetched to consider this group an early "Banking School" within the School of Salamanca. As their English and Continental heirs would do several centuries later, members of this school of thought not only justified fractional-reserve banking, in clear violation of traditional legal principles, but also believed it exerted a highly beneficial effect on the economy.

Though Luis de Molina's arguments concerning the bank contract rest on a very shaky theoretical foundation and in a sense constitute a regression with respect to other attitudes held by members of the School of Salamanca, it should be noted that Molina was the first in the "Banking School" tradition to realize that checks and other documents which authorize the payment, on demand, of certain quantities against deposits fulfill exactly the same function as cash. Therefore it is not true, though it is widely believed, that the nineteenth-century theorists of the English Banking School were the first to discover that demand deposits in banks form part of the money supply in their entirety, and thus affect the economy in the same way as bank bills. Luis de Molina had already clearly illustrated this fact over two centuries earlier in Disputation 409 of his work, *Tratado sobre los cambios* ["Treatise on exchanges"]. In fact, Molina states:

> People pay bankers in two ways: both in cash, by giving them the coins; and with bills of exchange or any other type of draft, by virtue of which the one who must pay the draft becomes the bank's debtor for the amount which the draft indicates will be paid into the account of the person who deposits the draft in the bank.[6]

Specifically, Molina is referring to certain documents which he calls *chirographis pecuniarum* ("written money"), and which were used as payment in many market transactions. Thus:

> Though many transactions are conducted in cash, most are carried out using documents which attest either that the bank owes money to someone or that someone agrees to pay, and the money stays in the bank.

Moreover Molina indicates that these checks are considered "on demand": "The term 'demand' is generally used to describe these payments, because the money must be paid the moment the draft is presented and read."[7]

Most importantly, long before Thornton in 1797 and Pennington in 1826, Molina expressed the essential idea that the total volume of monetary transactions conducted at a market could not be carried out with the amount of cash which changes hands at the market, were it not for the money banks *create* with their deposit entries, and depositors' issuance of *checks* against these deposits. Hence banks' financial activities result in the *ex nihilo* creation of a new sum of money (in the form of deposits) which is used in transactions. Indeed Molina expressly tells us:

---

[6]Molina, *Tratado sobre los cambios*, p. 145.

[7]Ibid., p. 146.

Most of the transactions made in advance [are concluded] using signed documents, *since there is not enough money to permit the huge number of goods for sale at the market to be paid for in cash, if they must be paid for in cash, or to make so many business deals possible.*[8]

Finally, Molina distinguishes sharply between those operations which do involve the granting of a loan, since the payment of a debt is temporarily postponed, from those carried out *in cash* via check or bank deposit. He concludes:

We must warn that an item cannot be considered purchased on credit if the price is withdrawn from a bank account, even if an immediate cash payment is not made; for the banker will pay the amount owed in cash when the market is over, if not sooner.[9]

Juan de Lugo, for his part, strictly adheres to Molina's doctrine and views the monetary bank deposit as a "precarious" loan or mutuum which the banker may use in his private business dealings as long as the depositor does not claim it.[10]

Molina and Lugo are so confused as to the legal basis of the bank deposit contract that they actually claim it can have a distinct legal nature for each of the parties involved (i.e., that it can simultaneously be a deposit to the depositor and a loan to the banker). These two theorists apparently see no contradiction in this position, and with respect to bankers' activities, content themselves with cautioning bankers to act "prudently," so that, in keeping with the law of large numbers, their liquidity will always be sufficient to allow them to satisfy "customary" requests for deposit returns. They fail to realize

---

[8]Ibid., p. 147; italics added.

[9]Ibid., p. 149.

[10] Quare magis videntur pecuniam precario mutuo accipere, reddituri quotiscumque exigetur a deponente. Communiter tamen, pecunia illa interim negotiantur, et lucrantur, sine ad cambium dando, sine aliud negotiationis genus exercendo.

This is a direct quotation taken from p. 406, section 5, no. 60, "De Cambiis," by Lugo Hispalensis, *Disputationum de iustitia et iure*.

that their standard of *prudence* is not an objective criterion adequate to direct the actions of bankers. It certainly does not coincide with bankers' ability to return all deposits in their keeping at any time, and Molina and Lugo themselves are careful to point out that bankers commit "mortal sin" when they use their depositors' funds speculatively and imprudently, *even if such actions end well and they are able to return their depositors' money in time.*[11] Moreover the standard of prudence is not a sufficient condition: a banker may be very prudent yet not very perceptive, or he may even have bad luck in business, so that when the time comes to pay he lacks ample liquidity and cannot return deposits.[12] What, then, is an acceptable standard of prudence? This question clearly has no objective answer capable of serving as a guide in banking. Furthermore as we saw in earlier chapters, the law of large numbers is inapplicable to fractional-reserve banking, since the credit expansion involved in such banking practices leads to recurrent cycles of boom and recession which invariably cause difficulties for bankers. Indeed the banking business itself creates the liquidity crises and thus, the widespread insolvency of banks. At any rate, when the crisis hits it is highly likely that the bank will be unable to pay, i.e., that it will suspend payments, and even if in the end all its creditors are lucky enough to receive their money, in the best of circumstances this only happens after a long liquidation process in which the depositors' role is altered. They lose immediate availability of their money and become *forced lenders* with no choice but to postpone withdrawal of their deposits until the liquidation is over.

Tomás de Mercado was undoubtedly motivated by the above considerations when he emphasized that Molina and

---

[11]Perhaps it is Juan de Lugo who most clearly and concisely expresses this principle, as we saw in footnote 102 of chapter 2.

[12]In other words a banker may commit pure or genuine entrepreneurial errors (ones not insurable by the law of large numbers) which result in serious entrepreneurial losses, regardless of the degree of prudence he has shown. On the concept of "genuine error," see Israel Kirzner, "Economics and Error," in *Perception, Opportunity and Profit* (Chicago: University of Chicago Press, 1979), chap. 8, pp. 120–36.

Lugo's principles of prudence were an objective *no* bank fulfilled in practice. It seems as if Tomás de Mercado was aware that such principles do not constitute a practical guide to guaranteeing the solvency of banks. Moreover if these principles are ineffectual in consistently achieving the goal of solvency and liquidity, the fractional-reserve banking system will not be capable of honoring its commitments in all situations.

Two Jesuit economists recently examined the doctrine of the scholastics on banking; one did so from the perspective of the Banking School, and the other from that of the Currency School. The first is the Spanish Jesuit Francisco Belda, the author of an interesting paper entitled, "Ética de la creación de créditos según la doctrina de Molina, Lesio y Lugo" ["The ethics of the creation of loans, according to the doctrine of Molina, Lesio and Lugo"].[13] Indeed Father Belda considers it obvious that:

> It can be gathered from Molina's description that in the case of bankers there is a true creation of loans. The intervention of banks has lead to the creation of new purchasing power previously nonexistent. The same money is simultaneously used twice; the bank uses it in its business dealings, and the depositor uses it as well. The overall result is that the media of exchange in circulation are several times greater in quantity than the real amount of cash at their origin, and the bank benefits from all these operations.

Furthermore according to Belda, Molina believes

> banks can reasonably do business with the deposits of their clients, as long as they do so prudently and do not risk being unable to honor their own obligations on time.[14]

In addition, Belda states that Juan de Lugo offers

---

[13]Published in *Pensamiento*, a quarterly journal of philosophical research and information, published by the Facultades de Filosofía de la Compañía de Jesús en España 73, no. 19 (January–March 1963): 53–89.

[14]Belda, pp. 63 and 69.

a thorough description of the practices of money changers and bankers. Here we do find explicit approval of credit creation, though not with the formal appearance of *created* credit. Banks do business with the deposits of their clients, who at the same time do not give up the use of their own money. Banks expand the means of payment through loans, trade-bill discounting and other economic activities they carry out with the money of third parties. The final result is that the purchasing power in the market is pushed far beyond that represented by the cash deposits at its origin.[15]

Belda obviously concludes correctly that of all the scholastics' doctrines, those of Molina and Lugo are the most favorable to banking. Nevertheless we must criticize Father Belda for not explaining the positions of the other members of the School of Salamanca, for example Tomás de Mercado, and especially Martín de Azpilcueta and Saravia de la Calle, who as we know, are much harsher and more critical judges of the institution of banking. Furthermore Belda bases his analysis of the contributions of Molina and Lugo on a Keynesian view of economics, a perspective which not only ignores all the damaging effects credit expansion exerts on the productive structure, but also presents such practices as highly beneficial because they increase "effective demand" and national income. Therefore Belda adopts the Keynesian and Banking-School view and only analyzes the contributions of those members of the School of Salamanca who are the least strict concerning the legal justification for the monetary bank deposit and, thus, the most inclined to defend fractional-reserve banking.

Nonetheless another prominent Jesuit, Father Bernard W. Dempsey, is the author of an economic treatise, entitled *Interest and Usury*,[16] in which he also examines the position of the members of the School of Salamanca on the banking business.

---

[15]Ibid., p. 87. Belda refers to Juan de Lugo, *Disputationum de iustitia et iure*, vol. 2, provision 28, section 5, nos. 60–62.

[16]Dempsey, *Interest and Usury*. We must note that Father Belda actually intended his article to be a Keynesian criticism of the ideas Father Dempsey presents in this book. Our thanks to Professor James Sadowsky, of Fordham University, for supplying a copy of Dempsey's book, which we were unable to find in Spain.

Father Dempsey's theoretical knowledge of money, capital and cycles serves as the foundation of his study and represents a much sounder basis than the one Father Belda builds upon.[17]

Strangely, Dempsey does not develop his thesis with an analysis of the views of those members most against banking (Saravia de la Calle, Martín de Azpilcueta, and Tomás de Mercado), but instead focuses on the writings of those most favorable to the banking business (Luis de Molina, Juan de Lugo and Lesio). Dempsey carries out an exegesis on the works of these authors and concludes that *fractional-reserve banking would not be legitimate even from the standpoint of their own doctrines*. These Salamancan authors defend certain traditional principles concerning usury, and Dempsey supports his conclusion by applying such principles to banking and its economic consequences, which, though unknown in the age of these scholastics, had been revealed in the theories of Mises and Hayek before Dempsey produced his treatise. Indeed though we must acknowledge Molina and Lugo's more favorable treatment of banking, Dempsey expressly states that the loans banks generate *ex nihilo* in the course of their operation with a fractional-reserve entail the creation of buying power backed by no prior voluntary saving or sacrifice. As a result, considerable harm is done to a vast number of third parties, who see the purchasing power of their monetary units fall owing to the inflationary expansion of banks.[18] According to

---

[17]In his introduction to Father Dempsey's book, Schumpeter strongly emphasizes Dempsey's deep theoretical knowledge of and complete familiarity with the economic doctrines of Ludwig von Mises, Friedrich A. Hayek, Wicksell, Keynes and others. Moreover, in his monumental work, *The History of Economic Analysis*, Schumpeter makes laudatory mention of Dempsey.

[18]   The credit expansion results in the depreciation of whatever circulating medium the bank deals in. Prices rise; the asset appreciates. *The bank absolves its debt by paying out on the deposit a currency of lesser value.* . . . No single person would be convicted by a Scholastic author of the sin of usury. But the *process* has operated usuriously; again we meet systematic or

Dempsey, this *ex nihilo* generation of buying power, which implies no previous loss of purchasing power to other people, violates the essential legal principles Molina and Lugo themselves lay down and in this sense is reprehensible. Specifically, Dempsey asserts:

> We may conclude from this that a Scholastic of the seventeenth century viewing the modern monetary problems would readily favor a 100-percent reserve plan, or a time limit on the validity of money. A fixed money supply, or a supply altered only in accord with objective and calculated criteria, is a necessary condition to a meaningful just price of money.[19]

Dempsey insists that bank credit expansion drives down the purchasing power of money, and that therefore banks tend to return deposits in monetary units of increasingly reduced purchasing power. This leads him to conclude that if members of the School of Salamanca had possessed a detailed, theoretical understanding of the functioning and implications of the economic process which fractional-reserve banking triggers, then even Molina, Lesio, and Lugo would have condemned it as a vast, harmful, and illegitimate process of *institutional usury*.

Now that we have analyzed the main postures members of the School of Salamanca adopted on banking, we will see how their ideas were collected and developed in later centuries by both continental European and Anglo-Saxon thinkers.

> institutional usury. . . . The modern situation to which theorists have applied the concepts of diversion of natural and money interest, diversion of saving and investment, diversion of income disposition from tenable patterns by involuntary displacements, all these have a sufficient common ground with late medieval analysis to warrant the expression, "institutional usury," for the movements heretofore described in the above expressions. (Dempsey, *Interest and Usury*, pp. 225 and 227–28; italics added)

In short, Dempsey simply applies to banking the thesis Juan de Mariana presents in his work, *Tratado y discurso sobre la moneda de vellón*.

[19]Dempsey, *Interest and Usury*, p. 210.

THE RESPONSE OF THE ENGLISH-SPEAKING WORLD TO THESE IDEAS ON BANK MONEY

Although a comprehensive analysis of the evolution of monetary thought from the scholastics to the English Classical School would exceed the scope of this book,[20] it is fitting that we should comment briefly on the evolution of ideas concerning fractional-reserve banking up to the time the controversy between the Banking and Currency Schools officially arose, in nineteenth-century Britain.

The seminal monetary ideas conceived by members of the School of Salamanca later won the support of Italians Bernardo Davanzati[21] and Geminiano Montanari, whose book, *La moneta*, was published in 1683.[22] In their treatises these theorists take the contributions of the School of Salamanca as a starting point and go on to develop the quantity theory of money as presented by Azpilcueta and other scholastics. Although the influence of this intellectual monetary trend soon spread to England, basically through the works of Sir William Petty (1623–1687),[23] John Locke (1632–1704),[24] and

---

[20]A brilliant, concise summary of this monetary history appears with the title, "English Monetary Policy and the Bullion Debate," in chapters 9–14 (part 3) of volume 3 of F.A. Hayek's *The Collected Works*. See also D.P. O'Brien, *The Classical Economists* (Oxford: Oxford University Press, 1975), chap. 6; and Rothbard, *Classical Economics*, chaps. 5 and 6.

[21]An English translation of Davanzati's book, entitled *A Discourse upon Coins*, was published in 1696 (London: J. D. and J. Churchill, 1696).

[22]Montanari's book was originally entitled *La zecca in consulta di stato* and was reprinted as *La moneta* in *Scrittori classici italiani di economía política* (Milan: G. Destefanis, 1804), vol. 3.

[23]See Sir William Petty's *Quantulumcumque Concerning Money*, 1682, included in *The Economic Writings of Sir William Petty* (New York: Augustus M. Kelley, 1964), vol. 1, pp. 437–48.

[24]Locke's writings on monetary theory include "Some Considerations of the Consequences of the Lowering of Interest, and Raising the Value of Money" (London: Awnsham and John Churchill, 1692) and his "Further Considerations Concerning Raising the Value of Money" (London: Awnsham and John Churchill, 1695). Both of these pieces were reprinted in *The Works of John Locke*, 12th ed. (London: C. and J. Rivington, 1824),

others, it was not until John Law, Richard Cantillon, and David Hume had made their contributions that we find express reference to the problems posed by fractional-reserve banking with respect to both monetary issues and the real economic framework.

We have already referred to John Law (1671–1729) elsewhere in this book: in chapter 2 we pointed out his unusual personality, as well as his utopian, inflationist monetary proposals. Although he made some valuable original contributions, such as his opposition to Locke's nominalist, conventional theory on the origin of money,[25] John Law also made the first attempt to give a veneer of theoretical respectability to the fallacious and popular idea that growth in the quantity of money in circulation always stimulates economic activity. In fact, from the correct initial premise that money as a widely-accepted medium of exchange boosts commerce and encourages the division of labor, Law arrives at the erroneous conclusion that the greater the amount of money in circulation, the larger the number of transactions and the higher the level of economic activity. What follows would constitute another fatal error in his doctrine, namely the belief that the money supply must at all times match the "demand" for it, specifically the number of inhabitants and the level of economic activity. This implies that unless the amount of money in circulation keeps pace with economic activity, the latter will decline and unemployment will rise.[26] This theory of Law's,

---

vol. 4; and also in *Several Papers Relating to Money, Interest, and Trade, Etcetera* (New York: Augustus M. Kelley, 1968). Locke was the first in England to introduce the idea that the value of the monetary unit is ultimately determined by the amount of money in circulation.

[25]We must remember that, according to Carl Menger, Law was the first to correctly formulate the evolutionist theory on the origin of money.

[26]See John Law, *Money and Trade Considered: With a Proposal for Supplying the Nation with Money* (Edinburgh: A. Anderson, 1705; New York: Augustus M. Kelley, 1966). In Law's own words:

> The quantity of money in a state must be adjusted to the number of its inhabitants, . . . One million can create employment for only a limited number of persons . . . a larger amount of money can create employment for more people than a smaller

later discredited by Hume and Austrian School monetary theorists, has in one form or another survived up to the present, not only through the work of nineteenth-century Banking-School theorists, but also through many modern-day monetarists and Keynesians. In short, Law attributes Scotland's poor level of economic activity in his time to the "reduced" money supply and thus carries the ideas of the Mercantilist School to their logical conclusion. For this reason, Law claims the primary objective of any economic policy must be to increase the amount of money in circulation, an aim he attempted to accomplish in 1705 by introducing paper money backed by what then was the most important real asset: land.[27] Law later changed his mind and centered all his economic-policy efforts on the establishment of a fractional-reserve banking system which, through the issuance of paper money redeemable in specie, was expected to increase the money supply as needed in any given situation to sustain and foster economic activity. We will not dwell here on the details of the inflationary boom Law's proposals generated in eighteenth-century France, nor on the collapse of his entire system, which brought great social and economic harm to that nation.

A contemporary of John Law was fellow banker Richard Cantillon (*c.* 1680–1734), whose life and adventures we have already covered. Cantillon, also a speculator and banker, was endowed with great insight for theoretical analysis. He produced a highly significant study of the influence an increase in the quantity of money in circulation exerts on prices, an influence which first becomes evident in the prices of certain goods and services and gradually spreads throughout the entire economic system. Therefore Cantillon argued, as Hume later would, that variations in the quantity of money mainly affect the *relative price* structure, rather than the general price

---

amount, and each reduction in the money supply lowers the employment level to the same extent. (Quoted by Hayek in "First Paper Money in Eighteenth-century France," chapter 10 of *The Trend of Economic Thinking*, p. 158)

[27]See John Law's *Essay on a Land Bank*, Antoin E. Murphy, ed. (Dublin: Aeon Publishing, 1994).

level. Cantillon, a banker first and foremost, justified fractional-reserve banking and his self-interested use of any
money or securities his customers entrusted to him as an
irregular deposit of fungible goods indistinguishable from
one another. In fact chapter 6 ("Des Banques, et de leur
credit") of part 3 of his notable work, *Essai sur la nature du commerce en général,* contains the first theoretical analysis of fractional-reserve banking, in which Cantillon not only justifies
the institution but also draws the conclusion that banks, under
normal conditions, can smoothly conduct business with a 10-
percent cash reserve. Cantillon states:

> If an individual has to pay a thousand ounces to another, he
> will pay him with a banker's note for that sum. Possibly this
> other person will not claim the money from the banker, but
> will keep the note and, when the occasion requires it, hand
> it over to a third person as payment. Thus the note in ques-
> tion may be exchanged many times to make large payments,
> without anyone's thinking of demanding the money from
> the banker for a long time. There will hardly be anyone who,
> due to a lack of complete trust or to a need to make small
> payments, will demand the sum. *In this first case, a banker's
> cash does not represent as much as 10 percent of his business.*
> (Italics added)[28]

---

[28]   Si un particulier a mille onces à païer à un autre, il lui donnera
       en paiement le billet du Banquier pour cette somme: cet autre
       n'ira pas peut-être demander l'argent au Banquier; il gardera le
       billet et le donnera dans l'occasion à un troisième en paiement,
       et ce billet pourra passer dans plusieurs mains dans les gros
       paiements, sans qu'on en aille de long-temps demander l'argent
       au banquier: il n'y aura que quelqu'un qui n'y a pas une parfaite
       confiance, ou quelqu'un qui a plusieurs petites sommes à païer
       qui en demandera le montant. *Dans ce premier exemple la caisse
       d'un Banquier ne fait que la dixième partie de son commerce.* (Cantil-
       lon, *Essai sur la nature du commerce en général,* pp. 399–400)

Cantillon obviously makes the same observation the theorists of the
School of Salamanca had almost two centuries earlier with respect to
bankers in Seville and other cities. Because these bankers enjoyed the
public's trust, they could consistently conduct their business while
maintaining only a small fraction in cash to cover current payments.
And, most importantly, that loans extended against deposits increase
the money supply and create "disorders" (pp. 408–13).

After Cantillon, and aside from some interesting monetary analysis by Turgot, Montesquieu, and Galiani,[29] no important references to banking appear until Hume makes his essential contributions.

David Hume's (1711–1776) treatment of monetary matters is contained in three brief but comprehensive and illuminating essays entitled "Of Money," "Of Interest" and "Of the Balance of Trade."[30] Hume deserves special recognition for having successfully refuted John Law's mercantilist fallacies by proving that *the quantity of money in circulation is irrelevant to economic activity.* Indeed Hume argues that the volume of money in circulation is unimportant and ultimately influences only the trend in nominal prices, as stated by the quantity theory of money. To quote Hume: "The greater or less plenty of money is of no consequence; since the prices of commodities are always proportioned to the plenty of money."[31] Nevertheless Hume's

---

[29]Ferdinando Galiani follows in Davanzati and Montanari's footsteps, and his writings, included in *Della moneta*, rival even the works of Cantillon and Hume.

[30]These essays have been reprinted in splendid editions by Liberty Classics. See Hume, *Essays: Moral, Political and Literary*, pp. 281–327.

[31]See "Of Money," ibid., p. 281. Even today this essential observation of Hume's escapes some highly distinguished economists, as is clear from the following assertion Luis Ángel Rojo makes:

> From a social standpoint, the real money balances held by the public should be at a level where the social marginal productivity of the money is equal to the social marginal cost of producing it—a cost which is very low in a modern economy. From a private perspective, the overall possession of real money balances will reach a level where their private marginal productivity—which, for the sake of simplicity, we may assume to be equal to their social marginal productivity—is equal to the private opportunity cost of holding riches in money form. As the public will decide, based on personal standards, the volume of real money balances they wish to maintain, the amount actually held will tend to be lower than that which would be ideal from a social viewpoint. (Luis Ángel Rojo, *Renta, precios y balanza de pagos* [Madrid: Alianza Universidad, 1976], pp. 421–22)

unqualified acknowledgment that the volume of money is inconsequential does not prevent him from correctly recognizing that *rises* and *falls* in the amount of money in circulation do have a profound effect on real economic activity, since these changes always influence primarily the structure of *relative* prices, rather than the "general" price level. Indeed certain businessmen are always the first to receive the new money (or to experience a slump in their sales as a result of a decrease in the money supply), and thus begins an artificial process of boom (or recession) with far-reaching consequences for economic activity. Hume maintains:

> In my opinion, it is only in this interval or intermediate situation, between the acquisition of money and rise of prices, that the encreasing quantity of gold and silver is favourable to industry.[32]

Although Hume lacks a theory of capital to show him how artificial rises in the quantity of money damage the productive structure and trigger a recession, the inevitable reversal of the initial expansionary effects of such rises, he correctly intuits the process and doubts that increases in credit expansion and in the issuance of paper money offer any long-term economic advantage: "This has made me entertain a doubt concerning the benefit of *banks* and *paper-credit*, which are so generally esteemed advantageous to every nation."[33] For this reason Hume condemns credit expansion in general and fractional-reserve banking in particular and advocates a strict 100-percent reserve requirement in banking, as we saw in chapter 2. Hume concludes:

> [T]o endeavour artificially to encrease such a credit, can never be the interest of any trading nation; but must lay them

---

In this excerpt Luis Ángel Rojo not only views money as if it were a sort of factor of production, but he also fails to take into account that money fulfills both its individual and social functions perfectly, *regardless of its volume*. As Hume established, *any amount of money is optimal.*

[32]Hume, *Essays*, p. 286.

[33]Ibid., p. 284; italics added.

under disadvantages, by encreasing money beyond its natural proportion to labour and commodities, and thereby
heightening their price to the merchant and manufacturer.
And in this view, it must be allowed, that no bank could be
more advantageous, than such a one as locked up all the
money it received [this is the case with the Bank of AMS-
TERDAM], and never augmented the circulating coin, as is
usual, by returning part of its treasure into commerce.[34]

Equally valuable is Hume's essay, "Of Interest," devoted
entirely to criticizing the mercantilist (now Keynesian) notion
that a connection exists between the quantity of money and
the interest rate. Hume's reasoning follows:

For suppose, that, by miracle, every man in GREAT
BRITAIN should have five pounds slipt into his pocket in
one night; this would much more than double the whole
money that is at present in the kingdom; yet there would not
next day, nor for some time, be any more lenders, nor any
variation in the interest.[35]

According to Hume, the influence of money on the interest rate is only temporary (i.e., short-term) when money is
increased through credit expansion and a process is initiated
which, once completed, causes interest to revert to the previous rate:

The encrease of lenders above the borrowers sinks the
interest; and so much the faster, if those, who have
acquired those large sums, find no industry or commerce in
the state, and no method of employing their money but by
lending it at interest. *But after this new mass of gold and silver
has been digested, and has circulated through the whole state,
affairs will soon return to their former situation;* while the land-
lords and new money-holders, living idly, squander above
their income; and the former daily contract debt, and the
latter encroach on their stock till its final extinction. The
whole money may still be in the state, and make itself felt

---

[34]Ibid., pp. 284–85.

[35]Hume, "Of Interest," *Essays,* p. 299.

by the encrease of prices: But not being now collected into any large masses or stocks, the disproportion between the borrowers and lenders is the same as formerly, and consequently the high interest returns.[36]

Hume's two brief essays constitute as concise and correct an economic analysis as can be found. We may wonder how different economic theory and social reality would have been if Keynes and other such writers had read and understood from the start these important contributions of Hume's, and had thus become immune to the outdated mercantilist ideas which, time and again, reappear and gain new acceptance.[37]

Compared to Hume's, Adam Smith's contributions must largely be considered an obvious step backward. Not only does Smith express a much more positive opinion of paper money and bank credit, but he also openly supports fractional-reserve banking. In fact Smith claims:

> What a bank can with propriety advance to a merchant or undertaker of any kind, is not, *either the whole capital with which he trades, or even any considerable part of that capital; but that part of it only, which he would otherwise be obliged to keep by him unemployed, and in ready money for answering occasional demands.*[38]

The only restriction Smith places on the granting of loans against demand deposits is that banks must use

---

[36]Ibid., pp. 305–06; italics added.

[37]Hayek has pointed out the surprising gaps in Keynes's knowledge of the history of economic thought concerning monetary matters in eighteenth- and nineteenth-century England and has indicated that, had Keynes's knowledge been deeper, we would have been spared much of the clear regression Keynesian doctrines have represented. See F.A. Hayek, "The Campaign against Keynesian Inflation," in *New Studies in Philosophy, Politics, Economics and the History of Ideas*, p. 231.

[38]Adam Smith, *An Inquiry into the Nature and Causes of the Wealth of Nations*, vol. 1, p. 304; italics added. On the evolution of Adam Smith's ideas on banking, see James A. Gherity, "The Evolution of Adam Smith's Theory of Banking," *History of Political Economy* 26, no. 3 (Autumn, 1994): 423–41.

deposits "prudently," for if they abandon caution, they lose the confidence of their customers and fail. As was the case with those Salamancan scholastics (Molina and Lugo) whose views were closest to those of the Banking School, nowhere does Smith define his criterion of "prudence," nor does he ever comprehend the devastating effects temporary credit expansion (beyond the level of voluntary saving) exerts on the productive structure.[39]

After Adam Smith, the most important thinkers on banking activities are Henry Thornton and David Ricardo. In 1802 Thornton, a banker, published a noteworthy book on monetary theory entitled *An Inquiry into the Nature and Effects of the Paper Credit of Great Britain.*[40] Thornton produced a highly precise analysis of the effects credit expansion exerts on prices in the different stages of the productive structure. He even guesses that whenever banks' interest rate is lower than the "average rate" of profit companies derive, an undue increase in the issuance of bills results, triggering inflation and, in the long run, recession. Thornton's intuitions foreshadowed not

---

[39]Edwin G. West has noted that Perlman believes Smith was aware of the problems of expanding credit beyond voluntary saving, even though Smith was unable to resolve the contradiction between his favorable treatment of fractional-reserve banking and his sound thesis that only investment financed by voluntary saving is beneficial for the economy. See Edwin G. West, *Adam Smith and Modern Economics: From Market Behaviour to Public Choice* (Aldershot, U.K.: Edward Elgar, 1990), pp. 67–69. Pedro Schwartz mentions that "Adam Smith did not express his thoughts on credit and monetary matters as clearly as Hume did" and that, in fact, "he misled several of his followers . . . by not always identifying his institutional assumptions." Pedro Schwartz also indicates that Adam Smith knew much less about banking and paper money than James Steuart and even states: "Some of the criteria in Smith's presentation may have come from reading Steuart's book, *Political Economy.*" See the article by Pedro Schwartz, "El monopolio del banco central en la historia del pensamiento económico: un siglo de miopía en Inglaterra," printed in *Homenaje a Lucas Beltrán* (Madrid: Editorial Moneda y Crédito, 1982), p. 696.

[40]See F.A. Hayek's edition of this book and the introduction (New York: Augustus M. Kelley, 1978).

only Wicksell's theory on the natural rate of interest, but also much of the Austrian theory of the economic cycle.[41]

After Thornton's, the most notable work was produced by David Ricardo, whose distrust of banks parallels Hume's. Ricardo may be regarded as the official father of the English *Currency School*. In fact Ricardo strongly disapproved of the abuses committed by bankers in his day and particularly resented the harm done to the lower and middle classes when banks were unable to honor their commitments. He deemed such phenomena the result of banking offenses, and while he did not anticipate the precise development of the Austrian, or circulation credit theory of the business cycle, he at least understood that artificial processes of expansion and depression stem from certain banking practices, namely the unchecked issuance of paper money unbacked by cash and the injection of this money into the economy via credit expansion.[42] In the following section we will examine in detail the key principles of the Currency School, started by Ricardo, as well as the main postulates of the Banking School.[43]

THE CONTROVERSY BETWEEN THE CURRENCY SCHOOL AND THE BANKING SCHOOL

The popular arguments raised by defenders of fractional-reserve banking from the days of the School of Salamanca

---

[41]Hayek, *The Trend of Economic Thinking*, pp. 194–95.

[42]Schwartz, "El monopolio del banco central en la historia del pensamiento económico: un siglo de miopía en Inglaterra," p. 712.

[43]Ricardo's chief banking contributions appear in his well-known book, *Proposals for an Economical and Secure Currency* (1816), which has been reprinted in *The Works and Correspondence of David Ricardo*, Piero Sraffa, ed. (Cambridge: Cambridge University Press, 1951–1973), vol. 4, pp. 34–106. Ricardo's criticism of banks is present in, among other documents, a letter he wrote to Malthus on September 10, 1815. This letter is included in volume 4 of *The Works*, edited by Sraffa, p. 177. Again, we must remember that Ricardo would never have advised a government to restore the parity of its devalued currency to predepreciation levels, as he clearly implies in his letter to John Wheatley of September 18, 1821 (contained in volume 9 of *The Works*, pp. 71–74). Hayek himself wrote in 1975:

became more widespread and systematic in England during the first half of the nineteenth century, owing to the efforts of the so-called Banking School.[44] During that period a sizeable group of theorists (Parnell, Wilson, MacLeod, Tooke, Fullarton, etc.) formed, bringing together and systematizing the three main tenets of the Banking School, namely: (a) that fractional-reserve banking is juridically and doctrinally justified and highly beneficial to the economy; (b) that the ideal monetary system is one which permits the expansion of the money supply as required by the "needs of trade," and particularly to adjust to population and economic growth (this is the idea John Law initially developed); and (c) that the fractional-reserve banking system, through credit expansion and the

---

> I ask myself often how different the economic history of the world might have been if in the discussion of the years preceding 1925 one English economist had remembered and pointed out this long-before published passage in one of Ricardo's letters. (Hayek, *New Studies in Philosophy, Politics, Economics and the History of Ideas*, p. 199)

In fact the fatal mistake manifest in the British post-war attempt to return to the gold standard abandoned during the First World War and to restore the pound to its previous value, lowered by wartime inflation, had already been revealed in a remarkably similar situation (following the Napoleonic wars) by David Ricardo a hundred years earlier. Ricardo stated at that time that he

> never should advise a government to restore a currency which had been depreciated 30 percent to par; I should recommend, as you propose, but not in the same manner, that the currency should be fixed at the depreciated value by lowering the standard, and that no farther deviations should take place. (David Ricardo, in the above-mentioned letter to John Wheatley dated September 18, 1821, included in *The Works and Correspondence of David Ricardo*, Sraffa, ed., vol. 9, p. 73; see also chap. 6, footnote 46)

[44]Actually, the main doctrines of the Banking School had already been put forward, at least in embryonic form, by theorists of the Anti-Bullionist School in eighteenth-century England. See chapter 5 ("The Early Bullionist Controversy") from Rothbard's book, *Classical Economics* (Aldershot, U.K.: Edward Elgar 1995), pp. 159–274; and Hayek, *The Trend of Economic Thinking*, vol. 3, chaps. 9–14.

issuance of paper bills unbacked by commodity-money, permits increases in the money supply to meet the "needs of trade" without producing inflationary effects or distortions in the productive structure.

John Fullarton (*c.* 1780–1849) was undoubtedly the most prominent of Banking School representatives. He was among the school's most persuasive authors and in 1844 published a widely-read book entitled *On the Regulation of Currencies.*[45] Here Fullarton puts forward what would become a famous doctrine, Fullarton's law of reflux of banknotes and credit. According to Fullarton, credit expansion in the form of bills issued by a fractional-reserve banking system poses no danger of inflation because the bills banks issue are injected into the economic system as loans, rather than direct payment for goods and services. Thus, Fullarton reasons, when the economy "needs" more means of payment it demands more loans, and when it needs less, loans are repaid and flow back to banks, and therefore credit expansion has no negative effects whatsoever on the economy. This doctrine became quite popular, yet it was a clear step backward with respect to advances Hume and other authors had already made in monetary theory. Nevertheless it surprisingly gained the unexpected support of even John Stuart Mill, who eventually, by and large, endorsed Fullarton's theories on the issue.

We have already explained at length why the essential principles of the Banking School are fundamentally unsound. Only ignorance of the simplest basics of monetary and capital

---

[45]John Fullarton, *On the Regulation of Currencies, being an examination of the principles on which it is proposed to restrict, within certain fixed limits, the future issues on credit of the Bank of England and of the other banking establishments throughout the country* (London: John Murray, 1844; 2nd rev. ed., 1845). Fullarton's law of reflux appears on p. 64 of the book. In continental Europe, Adolph Wagner (1835–1917) popularized Fullarton's version of the Banking School inflationist creed. John Fullarton was a surgeon, publisher, tireless traveler, and also a banker. On the influence Fullarton exerted on such diverse authors as Marx, Keynes, and Rudolph Hilferding, see Roy Green's essay published in *The New Palgrave: A Dictionary of Economics*, vol. 2, pp. 433–34.

theory might make the inflationist fallacies of this school appear somewhat credible. The main error in Fullarton's law of reflux lies in its failure to account for the nature of fiduciary loans. We know that when a bank discounts a bill or grants a loan, it exchanges a present good for a future good. Since banks which expand loans create present goods *ex nihilo*, a natural limit to the volume of fiduciary media the banking system could create would only be conceivable under one condition: if the quantity of future goods offered in the market in exchange for bank loans were somehow limited. However, as Mises has eloquently pointed out, this is never the case.[46] In fact banks may expand credit *without limit* simply by reducing the interest rate they apply to the corresponding loans. Moreover, given that loan recipients pledge to return a greater amount of *monetary units* at the end of a certain time period, there is no limit to credit expansion. Indeed borrowers can repay their loans with new monetary units the banking system itself creates *ex nihilo* in the future. As Mises puts it, "Fullarton overlooks the possibility that the debtor may procure the necessary quantity of fiduciary media for the repayment by taking up a new loan."[47]

Although the monetary theories of the Banking School were invalid, in one particular respect they were accurate. Banking School theorists were the first to recover a monetary doctrine of the "banking" sector of the School of Salamanca, namely that bank deposit balances fulfil exactly the same economic function as banknotes. As we will later see, throughout the debate between the Banking and Currency Schools, in which the latter focused solely on the damaging effects of unbacked paper bills, Banking School defenders correctly argued that if the recommendations of the Currency School were sensible (and they were), they should also be applied to all bank deposits, since, as bank money, deposits play a role identical to that of unbacked banknotes. Even though this

---

[46]Mises, *The Theory of Money and Credit*, pp. 340–41.

[47]Ibid., p. 342. For more on Mises's criticism of the Banking School, see *On the Manipulation of Money and Credit*, pp. 118–19 and *Human Action*, pp. 429–40.

doctrine (i.e., that bank deposits are part of the monetary supply) had already been espoused by the Salamancan group
most favorable to banking (Luis de Molina, Juan de Lugo,
etc.), in nineteenth-century England it had been practically
forgotten when Banking School theorists rediscovered it. Perhaps the first to refer to this point was Henry Thornton himself, who, on November 17, 1797, before the *Committee on the
Restriction of Payments in Cash by the Bank*, testified: "The balances in the bank are to be considered in very much the same
light with the paper circulation."[48] Nonetheless, in 1826 James
Pennington made the clearest assertion on this matter:

> The book credits of a London banker, and the promissory
> notes of a country banker *are essentially the same thing, that
> they are different forms of the same kind of credit; and that they are
> employed to perform the same function* . . . both the one and the
> other are substitutes for a metallic currency and are suscep-
> tible of a considerable increase or diminution, without the
> corresponding enlargement or contraction of the basis on
> which they rest. (Italics added)[49]

In the United States, in 1831, Albert Gallatin revealed the
economic equivalence of bank bills and deposits and did so
more explicitly than even Condy Raguet. Specifically, Gallatin
wrote:

---

[48]Reprinted in the *Records from Committees of the House of Commons, Mis-
cellaneous Subjects, 1782, 1799, 1805*, pp. 119–31.

[49]James Pennington's contribution is dated February 13, 1826 and entitled "On Private Banking Establishments of the Metropolis." It appeared
as an appendix to Thomas Tooke's book, *A Letter to Lord Grenville; On the
Effects Ascribed to the Resumption of Cash Payments on the Value of the Currency* (London: John Murray, 1826); it was also included in Tooke's work,
History of Prices and of the State of the Circulation from 1793–1837, vol. 2, pp.
369 and 374. Murray N. Rothbard points out that before Pennington,
Pennsylvania Senator Condy Raguet, an American theorist of the Currency School and defender of a 100-percent reserve requirement, had
already shown (in 1820) that paper money is equivalent to deposits created by banks which operate with a fractional reserve. On this topic see
Rothbard, *The Panic of 1819*, p. 149 and footnote 52 on pp. 231–32, as well
as p. 3 of Rothbard's book, *The Mystery of Banking*.

> The credits in current accounts or deposits of our banks are also in their origin and effect perfectly assimilated to banknotes, and we cannot therefore but consider the aggregate amount of credits payable on demand standing on the books of the several banks as being part of the currency of the United States.[50]

Nevertheless despite this valuable contribution from the Banking School, i.e., the rediscovery that bank deposits and paper money perform exactly the same economic function as specie and cause the same problems, the rest of the Banking School doctrines were, as Mises asserted, seriously faulty. Banking School theorists were unable to coherently defend their contradictory ideas; they tried in vain to refute the quantity theory of money; and they failed in their attempt to develop an articulate interest rate theory.[51]

These Banking School doctrines met with fierce opposition from defenders of the Currency School, who carried on a time-honored tradition which dates back not only to the Salamancan scholastics who were most uncompromising in their views on banking (Saravia de la Calle, Martín Azpilcueta and, to a lesser extent, Tomás de Mercado), but also, as we have seen, to Hume and Ricardo. The leading theorists of the nineteenth-century Currency School were Robert Torrens, S.J. Lloyd (later Lord Overstone), J.R. McCulloch, and George W. Norman.[52]

---

[50] Albert Gallatin, *Considerations on the Currency and Banking System of the United States* (Philadelphia: Carey and Lea, 1831), p. 31.

[51] It was the only merit of the Banking School that it recognized that what is called deposit currency is a money-substitute no less than banknotes. But except for this point, all the doctrines of the Banking School were spurious. It was guided by contradictory ideas concerning money's neutrality; it tried to refute the quantity theory of money by referring to a *deus ex machina*, the much talked about hoards, and it misconstrued entirely the problems of the rate of interest. (Mises, *Human Action*, p. 440)

[52] The most valuable contributions from these authors are covered in Hayek's recently-published summary of the controversy between the Banking and Currency Schools. See chapter 12 of *The Trend of Economic*

Currency School theorists provided a valid explanation of the recurring phases of boom and recession which plagued the British economy in the 1830s and 1840s: the booms had their roots in credit expansion which the Bank of England initiated and the other British banks continued. Gold systematically flowed out of the United Kingdom whenever her trading partners either did not engage in credit expansion or did so at a slower pace than Britain, where the fractional-reserve banking system was comparatively more developed. Each of the arguments Banking School theorists devised in their attempt to refute the Currency School's central idea (i.e., that the outflow of gold and cash from Great Britain was the inevitable consequence of domestic credit expansion) failed miserably. However defenders of the Currency School position made three serious mistakes which in the long run proved fatal. *First*, they failed to realize that bank deposits play exactly the same role as banknotes unbacked by specie. *Second*, they were unable to combine their sound monetary theory with a complete explanation of the trade cycle. They merely scratched the surface of the problem, and, lacking an adequate theory of capital, were unable to perceive that bank credit expansion exerts a negative influence on the different capital-goods stages in a nation's productive structure. They did not analyze in detail the existing relationship between variations in the money supply and the market rate of interest, and thus they implicitly relied on the naive, mistaken assumption that money could be

---

Thinking. In particular we must cite the following: Samuel Jones Lloyd (Lord Overstone), *Reflections Suggested by a Perusal of Mr. J. Horseley Palmer's Pamphlet on the Causes and Consequences of the Pressure on the Money Market* (London: P. Richardson 1837); later reprinted by J.R. McCulloch in his *Tracts and Other Publications on Metallic and Paper Currency*, by the Right Hon. Lord Overstone (London: Harrison and Sons 1857). Also George Warde Norman, *Remarks upon some Prevalent Errors with respect to Currency and Banking, and Suggestions to the Legislature and the Public as to the Improvement in the Monetary System* (London: P. Richardson 1838); and especially Robert Torrens (perhaps the finest Currency School theorist), *A Letter to the Right Hon. Lord Viscount Melbourne, on the Causes of the Recent Derangement in the Money Market, and on Bank Reform* (London: Longman, Rees, Orme, Brown and Green, 1837).

neutral, an idea today's monetarists have supported. Therefore it was not until 1912, when Ludwig von Mises reformu-
lated Currency School teachings, that monetary theory was
finally fully integrated with capital theory, within a general
theory of the economic cycle. The *third* fatal error of the Currency School lay in the notion that, in keeping with Ricardo's
suggestions, the best way to curtail the Banking School's inflationary excesses was to grant an official central bank a monopoly on the issuance of banknotes.[53] Currency School theorists
failed to realize that in the long run such an institution was
bound to be used by Banking School members themselves to
speed up credit expansion in the form of banknotes and
deposits in circulation.

These three mistakes of the Currency School proved fatal:
they were the reason Sir Robert Peel's famous Bank Charter
Act (passed on July 19, 1844), despite the highly honorable
intentions of its drafters, failed to ban the creation of fiduciary
media (deposits unbacked by metallic money) though it did
ban the issuance of unbacked bills. As a result, even though
Peel's Act marked the beginning of a central bank monopoly
on the issuance of paper currency, and although the central
bank theoretically issued only banknotes fully backed by
specie (100 percent reserve), private banks were free to expand
money by granting new loans and creating the corresponding
deposits *ex nihilo*. Hence expansionary booms and the subsequent stages of crisis and depression continued, and during
these periods the Bank of England was obliged time and again
to suspend the provisions of the Peel Act and to issue the
paper currency necessary to satisfy private banks' demand for
liquidity, thus, when possible, saving them from bankruptcy.
Therefore it is ironic that the Currency School supported the
creation of a central bank which, gradually and due mainly to
political pressures and the negative influence of predominant
Banking School theorists, was eventually used to justify and

---

[53]Nevertheless Ricardo foresaw the importance of making the central
bank independent of the government. See José Antonio de Aguirre, *El
poder de emitir dinero: de J. Law a J.M. Keynes* (Madrid: Unión Editorial,
1985), pp. 52–62 and footnote 16.

encourage policies of monetary recklessness and financial excesses much worse than those it was originally designed to prevent.[54]

Consequently, *even though in terms of theory the Banking School was utterly defeated, in practice it ultimately triumphed.* Indeed Peel's Bank Charter Act failed because it did not prohibit the issuance of new loans and deposits in the absence of a 100 percent reserve. As a result, recurrent cycles of boom and recession continued, and the proposals and theories of the Currency School understandably lost a tremendous amount of prestige. Therefore popular demands for inflationary policies which facilitate credit expansion, demands backed by the ever handy mercantilist theories of the Banking School, found a breeding ground in the central-bank-based system, which ultimately became an essential instrument of an interventionist, planned credit and monetary policy invariably aimed at virtually unchecked monetary and credit expansion.

Only Modeste, Cernuschi, Hübner, and Michaelis, followed by Ludwig von Mises and his much more profound analysis, saw that the Currency School's recommendation of central banking was mistaken and that the best, indeed the only, way to uphold the school's principles of sound money was to adopt a free banking system subject to private law (i.e., to a 100-percent reserve requirement) and unbenefited by privileges. However we will study this point in greater detail in the next section, in which we will examine the debate between supporters of free banking and those of central banking.

---

[54]We agree entirely with Pedro Schwartz when he classifies Keynes (and to a lesser extent, Marshall) as "Banking School" theorists who nonetheless defended the central bank system (precisely to gain the maximum "flexibility" to expand the money supply). See Schwartz's article, "El monopolio del banco central en la historia del pensamiento económico: un siglo de miopía en Inglaterra," pp. 685–729, esp. p. 729.

2

THE DEBATE BETWEEN DEFENDERS OF THE
CENTRAL BANK AND ADVOCATES OF FREE BANKING

An analysis of the nineteenth-century debate between
defenders of the central bank and advocates of free banking
must begin with an acknowledgment of the indisputable,
close connection which initially existed between the Banking
School and the Free-Banking School, on the one hand, and
between the Currency School and the Central-Banking School,
on the other.[55] Indeed it is easy to understand why supporters
of fractional-reserve banking, on the whole, initially championed a banking system free from any kind of interference: they
wished to continue to do business based on a fractional reserve.
Likewise it was only natural for Currency School theorists,
ever distrustful of bankers, to naively embrace government

---

[55]See Vera C. Smith, *The Rationale of Central Banking and the Free Banking
Alternative*. Leland B. Yeager has written the preface to this magnificent
edition. This work is a doctoral thesis written by the future Vera Lutz
under the direction of F.A. Hayek. In fact Hayek had already devoted
some time to a projected book on money and banking when, following
his famous lecture series at the London School of Economics which
yielded his book *Prices and Production*, he was appointed Tooke Professor of Economic Science and Statistics at that prestigious institution and
was forced to interrupt his research. Hayek had completed four chapters: the history of monetary theory in England, money in eighteenth-
century France, the evolution of paper currency in England, and the
controversy between the Banking and Currency Schools. It was at this
point he decided to hand over the work he had completed thus far, as
well as the notes for a fifth and final chapter, to one of his most brilliant
students, Vera C. Smith (later Vera Lutz), who, as a doctoral thesis,
expanded on them and produced the above-mentioned book. Fortunately Hayek's original manuscript was recovered by Alfred Bosch and
Reinhold Weit, and an English translation by Grete Heinz has been published as chapters 9, 10, 11, and 12 of volume 3 of *The Collected Works of
F.A. Hayek*. See F.A. Hayek, *The Trend of Economic Thinking*. On pp. 112–13
(2nd English ed.) of her book, Vera C. Smith mentions the initial general
agreement between the Banking and Free-Banking Schools, and
between the Currency and Central-Banking Schools. On this matter see
also Rothbard, *Classical Economics*, vol. 2, chap 7.

regulation in the form of a central bank intended to avoid the abuses the Banking School attempted to justify.

PARNELL'S PRO-FREE-BANKING ARGUMENT AND THE
RESPONSES OF MCCULLOCH AND LONGFIELD

We will not embark here on a comprehensive account of the controversy between the Free-Banking and Central-Banking Schools: Vera C. Smith and others have already come up with excellent studies on this topic. Nonetheless a few additional points merit discussion. One thought we must keep in mind is that most advocates of free banking based their doctrine on the spurious, inflationist Banking School arguments covered in the last section. Therefore, regardless of the effects a free-banking system might actually exert on the economy, the theoretical foundation on which most free-banking advocates built their arguments was either entirely fallacious or, at best, highly questionable. Consequently, during this period the Free-Banking School made few contributions of any doctrinal value. One such contribution was the correct acknowledgment that, economically speaking, deposits and unbacked bills play the same role. Another, one of particular analytical interest, was made by Sir Henry Parnell as early as 1827. According to Parnell, a free-banking system would place natural limits on the issuance of banknotes, due to the influence of the corresponding interbank clearing house, which, on the model of the Scottish banking system, Parnell believed would develop wherever banks freely competed in the issuance of banknotes. Parnell argued that banks in a totally free banking system would be unable to endlessly expand their paper-money base without prompting their competitors to demand payment of the bills, in specie, through a clearing house. Thus banks, for fear of being unable to weather the corresponding outflow of gold, would, in their own interest, adopt strict limitations on the issuance of fiduciary media.[56] Parnell's

---

[56]Henry Parnell, *Observations on Paper Money, Banking and Other Trading, including those parts of the evidence taken before the Committee of the House of Commons which explained the Scotch system of banking* (London: James Ridgway, 1827), esp. pp. 86–88.

analysis has considerable merit and lies at the heart of the arguments invoked to date in favor of free banking. His analysis was used and developed even by certain authors of the Currency School (like Ludwig von Mises) who were nonetheless highly skeptical of the central-bank system.[57]

A FALSE START FOR THE CONTROVERSY BETWEEN CENTRAL BANKING AND FREE BANKING

Two distinguished theorists of the Currency School, J.R. McCulloch and S.M. Longfield, challenged Parnell's claim. McCulloch argued that the mechanism Parnell described would not curb inflation if all banks in a free-banking system should collectively yield to a wave of expansion in the issuance of banknotes.[58] Samuel Mountifort Longfield carried McCulloch's objection even further and contended that even if a single bank expanded its paper-money base, in a free-banking system the rest would inevitably be forced to follow suit lest their financial-market share or their profits drop.[59] Longfield's argument contains an important kernel of truth, since the liquidation of excess banknotes through a clearing house

---

[57]See, for example, Mises, "The Limitation of the Issuance of Fiduciary Media," section 12 of chapter 17 of *Human Action*, pp. 434–48; see esp. "Observations on the Discussions Concerning Free Banking," p. 444.

[58]J.R. McCulloch, *Historical Sketch of the Bank of England with an Examination of the Question as to the Prolongation of the Exclusive Privileges of that Establishment* (London: Longman, Rees, Orme, Brown and Green, 1831). See also his *A Treatise on Metallic and Paper Money and Banks* (Edinburgh: A. and C. Black, 1858).

[59]Longfield's contributions appeared in a series of four articles on "Banking and Currency" published by the *Dublin University Magazine* in 1840. Vera C. Smith concludes:

> The point raised by the Longfield argument is by far the most important controversial point in the theory of free banking. No attempt was made in subsequent literature to reply to it. (Smith, *The Rationale of Central Banking and the Free Banking Alternative*, p. 88)

See also our analysis supporting the initial Longfield insight on pp. 664–71.

takes time, and there is always a (perhaps irresistible) temptation to overissue on the assumption that all other banks will sooner or later do the same. In this way the first bank to launch an expansionary policy derives the most profit and eventually establishes a position of advantage over its competitors.

Regardless of the theoretical basis for the arguments of Parnell, or for those of McCulloch and Longfield, one thing seems certain: their debate sparked off a *false controversy* between central-bank and free-banking supporters. We use the term "false" because the theoretical discussion between these two sides misses the heart of the whole problem. Indeed Parnell is correct when he states that in a free-banking context, the clearinghouse system tends to act as a buffer against isolated cases of expansion in the issuance of banknotes. At the same time, McCulloch, and Longfield as well, are right in pointing out that Parnell's argument fails if all banks simultaneously embark on a policy of expansion. Nevertheless Currency School theorists felt their arguments against Parnell's views lent *prima facie* support to the establishment of a central bank, which they believed would offer the most effective protection against the abuses of fractional-reserve banking. Parnell, for his part, contented himself with defending free banking, though with the limits the interbank clearinghouse system would set as a safeguard against banks' reckless expansion of their paper-money base. Nonetheless he failed to realize that, regardless of the arguments of McCulloch and Longfield, a return to traditional legal principles and a 100-percent reserve requirement would be much simpler and more effective than any clearinghouse system. Having overlooked this option, at least with regard to bank deposits, is the most crucial error committed by McCulloch and Longfield's branch of the Currency School as well. By endorsing the creation of a central bank, this faction inadvertently paved the way for the future strengthening of the very inflationary policies its adversaries favored.[60]

---

[60]A debate parallel to this one took place in Belgium and France between proponents of Free-Banking and the Banking School (Courcelle-Seneuil,

THE CASE FOR A CENTRAL BANK

Thus began a prolonged controversy between free-banking champions and central-bank promoters. The latter offered the following arguments to support their case against the position of the Banking and Free-Banking School:

First, a free-banking system, by its very nature, even under optimal conditions, would be prone to occasional, isolated bank crises which would harm customers and holders of banknotes and deposits. Therefore, under such circumstances, there is a need for an official central bank with the power to step in to protect noteholders and depositors in the event of a crisis. This argument is clearly paternalistic and aimed at justifying the existence of a central bank. It ignores the fact that when support is provided to those hit by a crisis, in the long run such support merely tends to further hamper the smooth running of the banking system, which requires constant and active supervision and confidence on the part of the public. Supervision is relaxed and confidence bolstered when the general public takes for granted the intervention of the central bank to avoid any damage in the case of a bank failure. Moreover bankers actually tend to exercise less responsibility when they too are sure of the central bank's support should they need it. Hence it is quite credible that the existence of a central bank tends to aggravate bank crises, as has been revealed even recently in several cases. The "deposit insurance" system in many countries has played a major role in fostering perverse behavior among bankers and in facilitating and aggravating bank crises. Nevertheless, from a political standpoint the above paternalistic argument can become extremely influential, even nearly irresistible, in a democratic environment. At any rate, this first argument marks the beginning of the false

---

Coquelin, Chevalier, and others) and Currency School theorists in favor of a central bank (such as Lavergne, D'Eichtal, and Wolowsky). In Germany the quarreling factions were led by Adolph Wagner and Lasker, on the side of free banking, and Tellkampf, Geyer, Knies, and Neisser, on the side of the pro-central-bank Currency School. On this matter, see chapters 8 and 9 of Smith, *The Rationale of Central Banking*, pp. 92–132.

start in the free-banking/central-banking debate, in the sense that the argument would be meaningless if traditional legal principles were respected and a 100-percent reserve requirement were reestablished for banking. Under these conditions, no harm would be done to holders of banknotes and deposits, who would always be able to withdraw their money, regardless of the fate of their bank. Therefore the paternalistic argument that a central bank is necessary to protect the interests of injured parties makes no sense. If we follow the logic of a fractional-reserve banking system, this first argument in favor of a central bank is at least very doubtful, while in the context of a free-banking system based on traditional legal principles and a 100-percent reserve requirement, it is completely irrelevant.

The *second* argument expressed in favor of central banks rests on the notion that a banking system controlled by a central bank provokes fewer economic crises than a free-banking system. This argument, like the first one, represents an inappropriate approach to the debate. We already know that the fractional-reserve free-banking system may stimulate growth in the money supply in the form of loans, and that this growth invariably distorts the productive structure of capital goods and endogenously and repetitively triggers a reversion process that manifests itself as an economic recession that hits banks particularly hard. In fact it was the very desire to protect banks from the effects of the repetitive crises created by fractional-reserve banking which prompted *bankers themselves* to demand the establishment of a central bank to loan them money as a last resort. Experience has shown that far from defusing economic crises, the advent of the central bank has exacerbated them. In a fractional-reserve free-banking system (with no central bank), even though the expansionary processes which provoke crises cannot be avoided, the reversion mechanisms which lead to the necessary readjustment and correction of economic errors operate much sooner and more quickly than in the central-bank-based system. Indeed the loss of public confidence is not the only factor to endanger the most expansionist banks, the reserves of which rapidly diminish as the holders of their bills withdraw their countervalue in specie. Interbank clearing mechanisms related to deposits also jeopardize those banks which expand their credit base faster than the rest. Even if most banks expand their deposits and bills simultaneously, the spontaneous processes identified by the theory of economic cycles soon gather momentum and tend to reverse the initial expansionary effects and bankrupt marginally less solvent banks. In contrast, the existence of a central bank, a lender of last resort, may prolong the process of credit and monetary expansion much further in relation to the independent process which would be set in motion in a free-banking system. It is impossible to ignore the *contradiction inherent* in the institution of the central bank, which was theoretically created to curb monetary expansion, maintain economic stability and prevent crises, but which in practice is devoted to providing new liquidity on a massive scale when banks face crises and panics. If we also consider political influences and the inflationary desires of the public, we will understand why inflationary processes and their distortion of the productive structure have been aggravated and the historical result has been much more severe and profound economic crises and recessions than those which would have arisen in a free-banking system. Therefore we can conclude that this second argument in favor of the central bank is groundless, since the very existence of the central bank tends to exacerbate economic crises and recessions. Nevertheless we must also acknowledge that crises would erupt even in a fractional-reserve free-banking system, though they would not cause as many repercussions as in a monetary system directed by a central bank. We have made this point in previous chapters and will demonstrate it further on. In any case, we do not have to resign ourselves to living with recurrent economic crises and recessions, since the mere re-establishment of general legal principles (100-percent reserve requirement) would prevent a free-banking system from exerting any negative effects on economic processes, and in this way the most common pretext for creating a central bank would disappear.

The *third* argument in favor of a central bank is that in supplying the liquidity necessary, it provides the best way to deal with crises once they have hit. Again it is evident that the failure to clearly identify the essential root of the economic problems of banking leads theorists to err substantially in their approach to the debate between central-banking and free-banking supporters. Although interbank clearing mechanisms and continuous public supervision would tend to limit credit expansion in a fractional-reserve free-banking system, they would be unable to prevent it completely, and bank crises and economic recessions would inevitably arise. There is no doubt that crises and recessions provide politicians and technocrats with an ideal opportunity to orchestrate central-bank intervention. Therefore it is obvious that *the very existence of a fractional-reserve banking system invariably leads to the emergence of a central bank as a lender of last resort.* Until traditional legal principles are reestablished, along with a 100-percent reserve requirement in banking, it will be practically inconceivable for the central bank to disappear (in other words, it will inevitably arise and endure).

At the same time, the establishment of a central bank to meet crises tends to worsen economic recessions. The existence of a lender of last resort aggravates expansionary processes and makes them much more rapid and lengthy than they would be in a fractional-reserve free-banking system (i.e., with no central bank). Therefore it is paradoxical to claim that the correct treatment of economic and bank crises depends on the existence of a central bank, when the central bank is ultimately the main culprit in dragging out and exacerbating crises. Nevertheless let us remember that even if the introduction of a fractional-reserve free-banking system were to tame crises somewhat, it could not completely eliminate them, and the different economic agents involved (mainly the bankers and citizens potentially harmed in each crisis) would inevitably urge the establishment of a central bank. *The only way to end this vicious circle is to recognize that the origin of the entire problem lies in fractional-reserve banking.* In fact the reestablishment of a 100-percent reserve requirement would not only avoid bank crises and recurrent economic recessions, but it would also invalidate this third argument, one of the stalest invoked to justify the existence of the central bank.

Finally, two additional, subsidiary arguments in favor of the central bank have been expressed. The first refers to the supposed "need" for a "rational" monetary policy imposed from above through the central bank. The second argument is related to the first and centers around the need to establish an adequate policy of monetary cooperation among different countries. Supposedly this goal also requires the existence of different, coordinated central banks. We will examine the theoretical impossibility of implementing a monetary and banking policy in a centralized, coercive manner through a central bank in a forthcoming section, where we will apply the theory of the impossibility of socialism to the banking and financial sector. Therefore we will refrain from analyzing these last two arguments in depth here.

THE POSITION OF THE CURRENCY SCHOOL THEORISTS WHO DEFENDED A FREE-BANKING SYSTEM

Unfortunately, due to their inability to equate the economic effects of deposits with those of banknotes, and to their naiveté in proposing the creation of a central bank to check the abuses of fractional-reserve banking, Currency School theorists were unable to foresee that the remedy they prescribed would necessarily prove much worse than the sickness they had correctly diagnosed. Only a handful of Currency School theorists understood that their goals of monetary stability and solvency would be at much greater risk if a central bank were created, and as a lesser evil and in order to prevent abuses as far as possible, these theorists recommended the maintenance or establishment of a free-banking system with no central bank. Nonetheless most Currency School writers who defended free banking were not deceived as to the expansionary possibilities of such a system, and they always maintained that the *final* solution to the problems posed would only be achieved with the prohibition of the issuance of new fiduciary media (i.e., with the prohibition of credit expansion unbacked by an increase in real voluntary saving). In proposing a system in which banks could freely issue bills and deposits, they basically hoped that interbank clearing mechanisms, customer supervision and control through the market, and the immediate failure of banks which lost public confidence would serve to more effectively limit the issuance of unbacked banknotes and deposits.[61] By this indirect route, they planned an effective move toward the objective of a 100-percent reserve requirement (for both bills and deposits), an aim to be pursued by all legal means available in each historical context.

This idea was first defended in France by Victor Modeste.[62] With the same goal in mind, Henri Cernuschi, on October 24, 1865, before a commission appointed to investigate banking activities, stated:

> I believe that what is called freedom of banking would result in a total suppression of banknotes in France. I want to give everybody the right to issue banknotes so that nobody should take any banknotes any longer.[63]

---

[61]The future development of payment and clearing systems through the Internet and other forms of computer-based communications will make the "emptying" of those banks which operate with a fractional reserve almost immediate upon the emergence of the *slightest doubt* concerning their solvency. In this respect the technological revolution in the field of computer communications will tend to promote private banking with a reserve requirement close to 100 percent (assuming the current system were to be completely privatized and the central bank were to disappear). See the paper by our pupil, Jesper N. Katz, "An Austrian Perspective on the History and Future of Money and Banking," Erasmus Programme in Law and Economics, Summer 1997. See also *The Future of Money in the Information Age*, James A. Dorn, ed. (Washington, D.C.: Cato Institute, 1997). As for credit cards, or "plastic" or "electronic" money, as they are commonly known, we should note that *they are not money*, but mere instruments which, like paper checks, provide the ability to pay by charging to real money (or perfect money substitutes, such as bank deposits).

[62]Victor Modeste, "Le billet des banques d'émission et la fausse monnaie," *Le Journal des Économistes* n.s. 3 (August 15, 1866).

[63]   Je crois que ce qu'on appelle liberté bancaire aurait pour résultat la disparition complète des billets de banque en France. Je souhaite donner à tout le monde le droit d'émettre des billets, de sorte que plus personne désormais n'en accepterait. (Henri Cernuschi, *Contre le billet de banque* [Paris: Guillaumin, 1866], p. 55)

See also Cernuschi's interesting work, *Mécanique de l'échange* (Paris: A. Lacroix, 1865). Ludwig von Mises fully accepts Modeste's and Cernuschi's views as expressed above and includes the excerpt in *Human*

Cernuschi's doctrine had only two flaws: it referred merely to banknotes and ignored bank deposits. And furthermore, it was not so radical as Modeste's who considered fractional-reserve free banking a fraudulent business that should not be allowed at all.

While the French Currency School was establishing this position in favor of free banking and a 100-percent reserve ratio, a number of German economists, among them Hübner and Michaelis, were carrying out a more in-depth theoretical analysis which led to the same conclusions. In the United States, the panic of 1819 had sparked the formulation of a doctrine against both fractional-reserve banking and the establishment of a central bank, and this doctrine strongly influenced the above school of German-speakers. As we already know, in the U.S., Condy Raguet and others (William M. Gouge, John Taylor, John Randolph, Thomas Hart Benton, Martin Van Buren, etc.) developed a body of monetary doctrine highly critical of banking.[64] These men correctly identified fractional-reserve banking as the ultimate cause of crises and concluded that a return to a 100-percent reserve ratio was

---

Action, with the following comment: "[F]reedom in the issuance of banknotes would have narrowed down the use of banknotes considerably if it had not entirely suppressed it." Mises, *Human Action,* p. 446. Banking School theorists in favor of free banking opposed Cernuschi. In France this school was led by Jean-Gustav Courcelle-Seneuil. See especially his book, *La banque libre: exposé des fonctions du commerce de banque et de son application à l'agriculture suivi de divers écrits de controverse sur la liberté des banques* (Paris: Guillaumin, 1867). The best account of Modeste's and Cernuschi's doctrines (including an analysis of their differences) is that of Oskari Juurikkala's "The 1866 False Money Debate, in the *Journal des Économistes*: Déjà Vu for Austrians?" *Quarterly Journal of Austrian Economics* 5, no. 4 (Winter, 2002): 43–55.

[64]Another voice in support of a banking system subject to a 100-percent reserve requirement was that of the famous Davy Crockett, the frontier hero-turned-senator, for whom fractional-reserve banking systems were "species of swindling on a large scale" (Skousen, *The Economics of a Pure Gold Standard,* p. 32). Similar views were held by Andrew Jackson, the above-cited Martin Van Buren, Henry Harrison, and James K. Polk, all of whom would later become U.S. presidents.

the only way to eradicate them.[65] Tellkampf, who had visited the U.S. as a young man, witnessed the abuses and highly damaging effects of fractional-reserve banking there and was imbued with the rigorous monetary doctrine being developed in America at the time. When he returned to Germany and was appointed professor of economics at Breslau, he wrote several papers in which he called for a ban on banks' issuance of fiduciary media.[66] Otto Hübner also shared some of the

---

[65]An outline of the evolution of this school in the United States during the first half of the nineteenth century appears in James E. Philbin's article, "An Austrian Perspective on Some Leading Jacksonian Monetary Theorists," *The Journal of Libertarian Studies: An Interdisciplinary Review* 10, no. 1 (Autumn 1991): 83–95. Another book which covers the different Banking and Monetary Schools which emerged in the first half of the nineteenth century in the United States is Harry E. Miller's *Banking Theory in the United States Before 1860* (1927; New York: Augustus M. Kelley, 1972).

[66]Johann Ludwig Tellkampf, *Essays on Law Reform, Commercial Policies, Banks, Penitentiaries, etc., in Great Britain and the United States of America* (London: Williams and Norgate, 1859). See also his *Die Prinzipien des Geld- und Bankwesens* (Berlin: Puttkammer and Mühlbrecht, 1867). As early as 1912 Mises made reference to Tellkampf's (and Geyer's) proposals in the following rather puzzling passage:

> The issue of fiduciary media has made it possible to avoid the convulsions that would be involved in an increase in the objective exchange value of money, and reduced the cost of the monetary apparatus. (Mises, *The Theory of Money and Credit*, p. 359)

This does not seem to square with other comments made by Mises, who at the end of the book proposes a return to a 100-percent reserve ratio and a ban on the creation of new fiduciary media, just as Tellkampf and Geyer (among the defenders of a central bank), and Hübner and Michaelis (among the defenders of free banking) do. As we observed in chapter 7, a parallel contradiction exists between the Hayek of *Monetary Theory and The Trade Cycle* (1929) and that of *Prices and Production* (1931). The only explanation lies in the process of intellectual development followed by the two authors, who were at first reluctant to vigorously defend the implications of their own analysis. Moreover we must keep in mind that, as we will see in the next chapter, Mises defends the establishment of a 100-percent reserve requirement, but only on *newly-created* banknotes and deposits, in the same vein as Peel's Bank Charter Act. Therefore it is somewhat comprehensible that he should mention the "advantages" of the past issuance of fiduciary media, though it is surprising that he neglects to explain why the system he considers most suitable

views of Tellkampf and the American school. Hübner observed that the less regulated banks were, the less frequent their solvency problems tended to be. He felt the choice was between a system of privileged banks protected by a central bank and apt to encourage irresponsible practices, and a free-banking system with no central bank to confer any privileges or protection. In this second system, each bank would necessarily be responsible for its own policies, and consequently bankers would act in a more prudent way. According to Hübner, the final objective should be an end to the issuance of banknotes not backed 100 percent by specie. Nevertheless, in light of the current situation, he believed the fastest and most effective way to move toward the ideal system was through free banking, in which each bank would be required to fulfill its obligations entirely.[67]

As early as 1867, the notable theorist Philip Joseph Geyer formulated a theory to explain economic cycles (a precursor to the theory proposed in this book) which Mises and Hayek would later carry to its logical conclusion. In fact Geyer impeccably summarises the defects of the fractional-reserve banking system and describes how it provokes economic crises. According to Geyer, the banking system produces "artificial capital" (*künstliches Kapital*), which refers precisely to fiduciary media generated by banks and unbacked by real wealth from voluntary saving. Geyer explains why a boom follows and must inevitably reverse in the form of a bank crisis and an economic recession.[68] Finally, like Hübner, Otto Michaelis defended a

---

for the future would not also have been best in the past. We believe the advantages of the issuance of fiduciary media in the past were few compared with the severe damage it caused in the form of economic crises and recessions, and especially with the gross inadequacies of our current financial system, which is a result of those past errors.

[67]See Otto Hübner, *Die Banken*, published by the author in Leipzig in 1853 and 1854.

[68]Philip Geyer, *Theorie und Praxis des Zettelbankwesens nebst einer Charakteristik der Englischen, Französischen und Preussischen Bank* (Munich: Fleischmann's Buchhandlung, 1867). See also Geyer's book, *Banken und Krisen* (Leipzig: T.O. Weigel, 1865). Vera C. Smith criticizes Geyer and Tellkampf's proposal to abolish the issuance of fiduciary media and

free-banking system as a means to curb abuses and move toward the ideal of a 100-percent reserve requirement.[69]

The tradition of Modeste, Cernuschi, Hübner, and Michaelis was continued by Ludwig von Mises, who in 1912 conclusively upheld the tenets of the Currency School. He not only asserted that both banknotes and deposits were fiduciary media, but he also grounded monetary theory on that of marginal utility and Böhm-Bawerk's theory of capital. The result was, for the first time, a complete, coherent and integrated theory of economic cycles. Thus Mises realized that English Currency School theorists were mistaken in recommending a central bank and that the best, in fact the only, way to achieve the school's goals of monetary solvency was through the establishment of a free-banking system subject, without privileges, to private law (i.e., to a 100-percent reserve requirement). Furthermore Mises recognized that in the end most advocates of Banking School principles cheerfully accepted the establishment of a central bank which, as lender of last resort, would guarantee and perpetuate the expansionary privileges of private bankers. These individuals made an increasing effort to shirk their commitments and devote themselves to the lucrative "business" of creating fiduciary money via credit expansion, and central-bank support allowed them to do so without having to worry too much about liquidity problems. Not surprisingly, Mises is especially critical of the fact that Peel's Bank Charter Act of 1844, despite the excellent

---

establish a 100-percent reserve requirement. Smith claims such an action would involve a deflationary process, but she fails to take into account that, as we will see in the next chapter when we consider the process of transition toward a 100 percent-based system, it is not necessary to re-establish the relationship which existed between banknotes and specie prior to the issuance of fiduciary media. On the contrary, any healthy transition process demands the avoidance of deflation and the redefinition of the relationship between fiduciary media and specie in light of the total quantity of banknotes and deposits already issued by the banking system. Therefore the point is not to trigger a monetary contraction, but to prevent any subsequent credit expansion.

[69]Otto Michaelis, *Volkswirthschaftliche Schriften* (Berlin: Herbig, 1873), vols. 1 and 2.

intentions with which it was drafted, failed to ban the expansionary creation of fiduciary deposits as it did with banknotes. Mises also condemns the use of the law to constitute and reinforce a central-bank system which, as we know, was eventually used to justify and promote policies of monetary chaos and financial excess much more damaging than the ones it was designed to prevent.

Mises's essential contribution to the study of money and economic cycles appears in his work, *The Theory of Money and Credit*, first published in 1912.[70] It was not until eight years

---

[70]Mises, *Theorie des Geldes und der Umlaufsmittel*. H.E. Batson translated the work into English, and Jonathan Cape published the first English edition (in London) in 1934. Thus it may have influenced Vera Smith's doctoral thesis, which was published two years later. It is interesting to note that Smith includes Mises, along with Hübner, Michaelis, and Cernuschi, in the double-entry table on pp. 144–45 of her book. She lists them in the section corresponding to the strictest Currency School theorists, who nevertheless defend a free-banking system as the best route to a 100-percent reserve ratio, given the circumstances. Perhaps one of the most valuable aspects of Smith's book is that it reveals that the Banking School and Free-Banking School do not exactly and automatically coincide, nor do the Currency School and Central-Banking School. Instead theorists fall into four distinct groups which can be outlined in a double-entry table. Because Vera Smith's table is relevant and illuminating, we include a revised version here.

TABLE VIII-1

	Free-Banking School	*Central-Banking School*
Banking School *(fractional reserve)*	Most nineteenth-century Banking-School theorists. White, Selgin, Dowd and David Friedman in the twentieth century.	Keynesians and most twentieth-century monetarists.
	⇨ (Natural evolution of the Banking School)	
Currency School *(100 percent reserve ratio)*	Modeste Cernuschi Hübner Michaelis Mises, possibly Hayek in 1925 and 1937 Rothbard, Huerta de Soto Joseph Salerno, Hans-Hermann Hoppe and Jörg Guido Hülsmann	The proposal made by the Chicago School in the 1930s. Maurice Allais.
	⇦ (Natural evolution of the Currency School)	

later, in 1920, that he expounded his famous theorem of the impossibility of socialist economic calculation, initiating the important debate that would surround this topic in the following decades. No explicit evidence suggests Mises was aware that the fundamental arguments he raised in 1920 on the impossibility of socialism were also directly applicable to fractional-reserve banking, and especially to the establishment and operation of a central bank. However in the next section we will defend the thesis that our analysis on fractional-reserve banking and the central bank is simply a specific case which arises when the general theorem of the theoretical impossibility of socialism is applied to the financial sphere.[71]

The classification of theorists into four schools (Fractional-Reserve Free Banking, Fractional-Reserve Central Banking, Free Banking with a 100 percent reserve, and Central Banking with a 100 percent reserve) is much clearer and more accurate than the method chosen by (among others) Anna J. Schwartz and Lawrence H. White, who identify only three schools, the Currency School, the Banking School, and the Free-Banking School. (See Anna J. Schwartz, "Banking School, Currency School, Free Banking School," pp. 148–52.)

[71]On the development in Spain of the doctrine in favor of the central bank and on this doctrine's influence on the establishment of the Spanish bank of issue, see Luis Coronel de Palma, *La evolución de un banco central* (Madrid: Real Academia de Jurisprudencia y Legislación, 1976), and the references cited therein. See also the writings of Rafael Anes, "El Banco de España, 1874–1914: un banco nacional," and Pedro Tedde de Lorca, "La banca privada española durante la Restauración, 1874–1914." Both appear in volume 1 of *La banca española en la Restauración* (Madrid: Servicio de Estudios del Banco de España, 1974). Despite the valuable references included in these works, a history of Spanish economic thought on the debate between central- and free-banking supporters has yet to be written. The most important (fractional-reserve) free banking theorist in Spain was Luis María Pastor (1804–1872). See his book *Libertad de Bancos y Cola del de España* (Madrid: B. Carranza, 1865).

3

THE "THEOREM OF THE IMPOSSIBILITY OF SOCIALISM" AND ITS APPLICATION TO THE CENTRAL BANK

In chapter 2 we saw that throughout history central banks have emerged not as a result of the spontaneous, evolutionary free-market process, but as a consequence of deliberate government intervention in the banking sector. In fact the institution of the central bank is rooted in the failure of public authorities to adequately define and defend depositors' property rights; in other words, to put an end to bankers' misuse of the money their customers entrust to them on deposit. This failure gave rise to the development of fractional-reserve banking, a practice which, as we know, permits bankers to create new monetary instruments *ex nihilo*, and thus to generate large profits. We are already familiar with the harmful effects such banking activity exerts on the economic structure in the form of malinvestment, severe crises, and recessions which should, in principle, justify particularly diligent care on the part of governments to guarantee the fulfillment of traditional legal principles (a 100-percent reserve requirement on demand deposits). Nevertheless throughout history, far from increasing their zeal to ensure compliance with the law in banking, governments have been the first to take advantage of the banking business, granting bankers many privileges. In order to cope with the perpetual fiscal difficulties created by their financial carelessness, governments have not only legalized fractional-reserve banking via the corresponding privilege, but they have throughout history continually attempted to take advantage of this set-up, either by requiring that a large number of the loans created *ex nihilo* by the fractional-reserve banking system be given to the government itself, or by reserving all or part of the highly lucrative fractional-reserve banking business for themselves.

For their part, private bankers themselves did not fail to notice that their industry underwent recurrent panics and liquidity crises which regularly endangered the continuity of bankers' lucrative business. Hence private bankers have been the first to request the establishment of a central bank which, as lender of last resort, would guarantee their survival in times of trouble. In this way the interests of private bankers came to coincide with those of the state and its central bank, and a symbiosis formed between the two. The state obtains easy financing in the form of loans and inflation, the cost of which goes unnoticed by the citizens, who do not initially experience a heavier tax burden. Private bankers gladly accept the central bank's existence and the rules it imposes, since bankers realize the entire framework of their business would ultimately collapse without the support of an official institution to provide the necessary liquidity once the "inevitable" bank crises and economic recessions hit.

Therefore we can conclude with Vera Smith that the central bank is not a spontaneous result of the market process. Instead the state has coercively imposed it in order to achieve certain objectives (particularly easy financing and the orchestration of inflationary policies, which are always very popular), all with the acquiescence or support of private banks, which in this area have almost always acted as the government's accomplices in the past.[72]

---

[72]   A central bank is not a natural product of banking development. It is imposed from outside or comes into being as the result of Government favours. This factor is responsible for marked effects on the whole currency and credit structure which brings it into sharp contrast with what would happen under a system of free banking from which Government protection was absent. (Smith, *The Rationale of Central Banking and the Free Banking Alternative*, p. 169)

Thus we accept the hypothesis of Professor Charles Goodhart (see footnote 73), who believes the emergence of the central bank to be a necessary consequence of the shift from a system of commodity money to a system of fiduciary money. We accept this hypothesis as long as acknowledgment is made to the effect that such a shift is not a spontaneous result of the market, but on the contrary, an inevitable outcome of the violation of traditional legal principles (100-percent reserve ratio on demand deposits), which are essential to the correct functioning of any free market. The only serious flaw we see in Vera Smith's book lies in the author's failure to fully recognize that the central-bank system is simply the logical and unavoidable consequence of private bankers' gradual

The above explains the historical appearance of the central bank, which is founded on the complicity and community of interests which have traditionally united governments and bankers and which fully account for the intimate "understanding" and "cooperation" between these two types of institutions. Nowadays this relationship, with only slight variations, is evident in all western countries and in almost all situations. The survival of private banks is guaranteed by the central bank, and thus this institution, and ultimately the government itself, exercises close supervision and political and economic control over banks. Moreover the central bank is intended to direct the monetary and credit policy of every country, with the aim of achieving certain economic policy goals. In the next section we will see why it is theoretically impossible for a central bank to sustain a monetary and credit system which produces no severe economic maladjustments and disturbances.[73]

---

and surreptitious introduction (in historical complicity with governments) of the fractional-reserve banking system. It is unfortunate that Smith neglects to devote some attention to the proposals for a 100-percent reserve requirement which were already circulating at the time she wrote the book. If she had examined these proposals, she would have realized that a true system of free-banking requires the re-establishment of a 100-percent reserve ratio on demand deposits. As we will see, many present-day theorists who defend the free-banking system commit the same error.

[73]The classic work on the evolution of central banks is Charles Goodhart's *The Evolution of Central Banks,* 2nd ed. (Cambridge, Mass.: MIT Press, 1990), esp. pp. 85–103. A brief, helpful outline of the emergence and development of central banks appears on pp. 9ff. of Tedde de Lorca's book, *El Banco de San Carlos, 1782–1822.* Ramón Santillana provides a good illustration of the formation of the central bank in nineteenth-century Spain to cope with the financial difficulties of the state, which was continually forced to take advantage of the privileges of money creation (banknotes and deposits) enjoyed by the fractional-reserve banking industry. See Santillana's book, *Memoria histórica sobre los bancos Nacional de San Carlos, Español de San Fernando, Isabel II, Nuevo de San Fernando, y de España* (reprinted by the Banco de España [Madrid, 1982]), esp. pp. 1, 3, 132, 236 and 237.

THE THEORY OF THE IMPOSSIBILITY OF COORDINATING
SOCIETY BASED ON INSTITUTIONAL COERCION OR THE
VIOLATION OF TRADITIONAL LEGAL PRINCIPLES

Elsewhere we have defended the thesis that socialism should be redefined as any system of institutional aggression on the free exercise of entrepreneurship.[74] This aggression may take the form of direct physical violence (or the threat of it) perpetrated by government authorities or of privileges granted to certain social groups (unions, bankers, etc.) so that they may violate traditional legal principles with state support. To attempt to coordinate society via institutional coercion is an intellectual error, because it is theoretically impossible for an agency in charge of committing this type of aggression (a central planning board) to obtain the information it would need to establish social coordination with its decrees.[75] The above is true for the following four reasons: *first*, it is impossible for the agency to constantly assimilate the enormous volume of practical information stored in the minds of different human beings; *second*, the subjective, practical, tacit, and nonverbal nature of most of the necessary information precludes its transmission to the central organ; *third*, information which actors have not yet discovered or created and which simply arises from the free market process, itself a product of entrepreneurship subject to the law, cannot be transmitted; and *fourth*, coercion keeps entrepreneurs from discovering or creating the information necessary to coordinate society.

This is precisely the essence of the argument Mises originally raised in 1920 on the impossibility of socialism and, in general, of state intervention in the economy. The argument theoretically explains the failure of economies of the former Eastern bloc, as well as the growing tensions, maladjustments

---

[74]Huerta de Soto, *Socialismo, cálculo económico y función empresarial*, p. 87. See also Jesús Huerta de Soto, "The Economic Analysis of Socialism," in Gerrit Meijer, ed., *New Perspectives on Austrian Economics* (London and New York: Routledge, 1995), chap. 14.

[75]Huerta de Soto, *Socialismo, cálculo económico y función empresarial*, p. 95.

and inefficiency which stem from the interventionist welfare state characteristic of western economies.

Likewise, the granting of privileges which conflict with traditional legal principles prevents coordinated cooperation among the different agents in society. Indeed traditional legal principles are essential to the coordinated, peaceful exercise of entrepreneurship. Their systematic violation hinders the free creativity of entrepreneurs, as well as the creation and transmission of the information necessary to coordinate society. When these principles are disregarded, social maladjustments remain hidden and tend to worsen systematically.[76]

The inevitable outcome of states' systematic coercion of society and of the concession of privileges against traditional legal principles is widespread social disorder and lack of adjustment in all areas and at all levels of society which are affected by such coercion and privileges. In fact both coercion and privileges encourage inaccurate information and irresponsible acts, and both lead to the corruption of individual behavioral habits subject to the rule of law, favor the development of the underground economy and, in short, cause and sustain all sorts of social maladjustments and conflicts.

THE APPLICATION OF THE THEOREM OF THE IMPOSSIBILITY OF SOCIALISM TO THE CENTRAL BANK AND THE FRACTIONAL-RESERVE BANKING SYSTEM

One of the central theses of this book is that the theorem of the impossibility of socialism, and the Austrian analysis of the social discoordination which inevitably follows institutional coercion and the granting of privileges at variance with the law, are directly applicable to the financial and banking system which has evolved in our economies. This system is based on private fractional-reserve banking and is controlled by an official institution (the central bank) which has become the architect of monetary policy.

---

[76]A detailed analysis of all the theoretical conclusions outlined above appears in the first three chapters of Huerta de Soto, *Socialismo, cálculo económico y función empresarial*, pp. 21–155.

Indeed the modern financial and banking system of market economies is entirely based on systematic coercion against the free exercise of entrepreneurship in the financial sector and on the concession to private banks of privileges which conflict with traditional legal principles and allow banks to operate with a fractional reserve.

We need not dwell on the juridical nature of the "odious" privilege involved in fractional-reserve banking, since we studied this aspect in detail in the first three chapters. As to the systematic exercise of coercion in the field of banking and finance, it is easy to understand that such manipulation is carried out via the legal tender regulations which compel the acceptance, as a liberatory medium of exchange, of the monetary unit issued by the monopolistic central bank.[77] The institutional coercion the central bank applies also manifests itself in an entire network of administrative banking legislation designed to rigorously control the operations of banks and, on a macroeconomic level, to define and implement the monetary policy of each country.[78]

In short we can hardly avoid concluding that "the organization of the banking system is much closer to a socialist economy than to a market economy."[79] Therefore in banking

---

[77]For example, see article 15 of autonomy statute 13/1994 of the Bank of Spain, July 1. The statute reads:

> The Bank of Spain shall have *exclusive* authority to issue bills in pesetas, which, notwithstanding the status applied to coinage, *shall be the only legal tender with full, unlimited liberatory power in Spanish territory.* (Spain's *Official Gazette*, July 2, 1994, p. 15404; italics added)

Logically, with Spain's entrance into the European Monetary Union as of January 1, 2002, the euro and the European Central Bank have replaced the peseta and the Bank of Spain, respectively.

[78]See, for example, the general list of central-bank duties included in article 7 of the above autonomy statute of the Bank of Spain.

[79]See the paper written by our student Elena Sousmatzian Ventura, "¿Puede la intervención gubernamental evitar las crisis bancarias?" *Revista de la Superintendencia de bancos y otras instituciones financieras* 1 (April–June 1994): 66–87. In this paper Elena Sousmatzian adds that

and credit matters, our situation matches that which prevailed in the socialist countries of the former Eastern bloc, which attempted to coordinate their economic decisions and processes through a system of central planning. In other words "central planning" has become commonplace in the banking and credit sector of market economies, so it is natural that in this area we should see the same discoordination and inefficiency which plagues socialism. Let us now examine three separate instances of interventionism and/or privileges in the organization of banking. The theorem of the impossibility of socialism applies in each, namely: (a) the most widespread case of a central bank which oversees a fractional-reserve banking system; (b) the case of a central bank which manages a banking system that operates with a 100-percent reserve ratio; and finally, (c) the case of a free-banking system (with no regulation and no central bank) which nevertheless exercises the *privilege* of maintaining only a fractional reserve.

---

though the notion that the current banking system shares the characteristics of a socialist or controlled economy may initially surprise many, it is easy to understand when we remember that: (a) the entire system rests on the government monopoly on currency; (b) the system is based on the privilege which permits banks to create loans *ex nihilo* by holding only a fractional reserve on deposits; (c) the management of the whole system is performed by the central bank, as an independent monetary authority which acts as a true planning agency with respect to the financial system; (d) from a legal standpoint, the principle which applies to the government, i.e., that it may act only within its jurisdiction, also applies to banks, in contrast to the rule for other private entities, who may always do anything that is not prohibited; (e) banks are commonly excluded from the general bankruptcy proceedings stipulated in mercantile law and are instead subject to administrative law procedures such as intervention and the replacement of management; (f) bank failures are prevented by externalizing the effects of banks' liquidity crises, the costs of which are met by the citizenry through loans from the central bank at prime rates or non-recoverable contributions from a deposit guarantee fund; (g) a vast, inordinately complicated set of regulations applies to banking and closely resembles that which controls government; and (h) there is little or no supervision of government intervention in bank crises. In many cases such intervention is determined *ad hoc*, and principles of rationality, efficiency, and effectiveness are disregarded.

(a) A system based on a central bank which controls and oversees a network of private banks that operate with a fractional reserve

The system made up of a central bank and private banking with a fractional reserve is the most disruptive example of "central planning" in the financial sphere.[80] Indeed this system is founded upon a privilege which private bankers enjoy (the use of a fractional-reserve ratio) and which naturally causes distortions in the form of credit expansion, malinvestment and recurrent cycles of boom and recession. Moreover the entire system is orchestrated, managed, and supported by a central bank which acts as lender of last resort and exercises systematic, institutional coercion in the field of banking, finance and money.

In providing banks with the necessary liquidity in times of crisis, the central bank tends to counteract the mechanisms which work in a free market to spontaneously reverse the expansionary effects of banking. (Such mechanisms consist precisely of the rapid failure of the most expansionary and least solvent banks.) Consequently the process of deposit creation and credit expansion (i.e., without the backing of real, voluntary savings) may be prolonged indefinitely, thus aggravating its distortion of the productive structure and exacerbating the inevitable economic crises and recessions it creates.

The system of financial planning which rests on the central bank cannot possibly eliminate recurring economic cycles. The most it can do is to delay their appearance by creating new liquidity and providing support to endangered banks in times of crisis, at the cost of aggravating the inevitable economic recessions. Sooner or later, the market always tends to spontaneously react and to reverse the effects of monetary aggression unleashed on it, and therefore deliberate attempts to prevent such effects via coercion (or the granting of privileges) are condemned to failure. The most these attempts can achieve is the postponement, and consequent worsening, of the necessary reversion and recovery, or economic crisis. They

---

[80]We obviously exclude completely nationalized banking systems (China, Cuba, etc.), which at any rate are of little significance nowadays.

cannot prevent it. In a fractional-reserve free-banking system (with no central bank), the reversion tends to occur much earlier, due to spontaneous interbank clearing processes (though the productive structure is still somewhat distorted). The creation of a central bank to act as lender of last resort and supply the liquidity necessary in times of crisis tends to neutralize the market's spontaneous reversion and recovery processes, and as a result expansionary policies can become much more lasting and damaging.[81]

The central bank, as the "financial central-planning board," embodies an intrinsic contradiction. Indeed, as F.A. Hayek has revealed, *all central banks face a fundamental dilemma, since they invariably wield great discretionary power in the administration of their policies, yet they do not have all the information they need to reach their objectives.* The central bank exercises its power over private banks mainly by threatening to not provide them with the liquidity they need. And at the same time it is believed that the chief duty and purpose of the central bank consists precisely of not refusing to supply the liquidity necessary when bank crises hit.[82]

---

[81]Furthermore the central bank cannot guarantee all customers of private banks the recovery of their deposits in monetary units *of unaltered purchasing power*. The belief that central banks "guarantee" all citizens the return of their deposits, regardless of the actions of the private banks involved, is pure fiction, since the most central banks can do is to create new liquidity *ex nihilo* to meet all deposit demands private banks are confronted with. Nevertheless, by doing so they trigger an inflationary process which often significantly lowers the purchasing power of the monetary units withdrawn from the corresponding deposits.

[82] There is one basic dilemma, which all central banks face, which makes it inevitable that their policy must involve much discretion. A central bank can exercise only an indirect and therefore limited control over all the circulating media. Its power is based chiefly on the threat of not supplying cash when it is needed. Yet at the same time it is considered to be its duty never to refuse to supply this cash at a price when needed. It is this problem, rather than the general effects of policy on prices or the value of money, that necessarily preoccupies the central banker in his day-to-day actions. It is a task which makes it necessary for the central bank constantly

The above accounts for the great difficulty central bankers face in eliminating economic crises, despite their effort and dedication. It also explains the tight control the central bank maintains over private banking, through administrative legislation and direct coercion.[83]

Moreoever, like Gosplan, the most important economic-planning agency of the now extinct Soviet Union, the central bank is obliged to make an unceasing effort to collect an extremely vast quantity of statistical information on the banking business, the different components of the money supply, and the demand for money. This statistical information does not include the qualitative data the central bank would need to harmlessly intervene in banking affairs. For such information is not only extraordinarily profuse; but what is more important, it is also subjective, dynamic, constantly changing,

---

> to forestall or counteract developments in the realm of credit, for which no simple rules can provide sufficient guidance.
> (Hayek, *The Constitution of Liberty*, p. 336)

[83]The various systems and agencies designed to "insure" created deposits in many western countries tend to produce an effect which is the exact opposite of that intended when they were established. These "deposit guarantee funds" encourage less prudent and responsible policies in private banking, since they give citizens the false assurance that their deposits are "guaranteed" and thus that they need not take the effort to study and question the trust they place in each institution. These funds also convince bankers that ultimately their behavior cannot harm their direct customers very seriously. The leading role deposit guarantee or "insurance" systems played in the eruption of the American bank crisis of the 1990s is covered in, among other sources, *The Crisis in American Banking*, Lawrence H. White, ed. (New York: New York University Press, 1993). It is therefore disheartening that the process of harmonizing European banking law has included the approval of Directive 94/19 C. E. of May 30, 1994, with respect to deposit guarantee systems. This directive establishes that each member state must officially recognize a deposit guarantee system and requires each European credit institution to affiliate itself to one of the agencies created for this purpose in each country. The directive also establishes that guarantee systems will insure coverage of up to 24,000 ecus on all deposits made by any one depositor, and that the European Commission will revise this figure every five years.

and particularly difficult to obtain in the financial sector. Hence it is painfully obvious that the central bank cannot possibly acquire all the information it would need to act in a coordinated manner, and its inability to do so is one more illustration of the theorem of the impossibility of socialism, in this case applied to the financial realm.

Knowledge of the different components of the supply of and demand for money is never available for objective accumulation. On the contrary, it is of a practical, subjective, diffuse nature and is difficult to articulate. Such knowledge arises from economic agents' subjective desires, which change constantly and depend largely on the evolution of the money supply itself. We already know that any quantity of money is optimal. Once any changes in the money supply have exerted their effects on the relative-price structure, economic agents can take full advantage of the purchasing power of their money, regardless of its absolute volume. It is when the quantity and distribution of money *changes*, via the expansion of loans (unbacked by saving) or the direct spending of new monetary units in certain sectors of the economy, that a serious disturbance occurs and widespread maladjustments and discoordination appear in the behavior of the different economic agents.

Therefore it is unsurprising that the central-bank system of our analysis is marked by having triggered the most severe intertemporal discoordination in history. We have seen that the monetary policies adopted by central banks, especially that of England and the Federal Reserve of the United States, with the purpose of "stabilizing" the purchasing power of the monetary unit, encouraged a process of great credit and monetary expansion throughout the "roaring" twenties, a process which led to the most acute economic depression of the last century. Following World War II, economic cycles have been recurrent, and some have approached even the Great Depression in severity: for example, the recession of the late seventies and, to a lesser extent, that of the early nineties. These events have occurred despite many political declarations concerning the need for governments and central banks to conduct a stable monetary policy, and despite the massive efforts made, in terms of human, statistical, and material resources, to realize this objective. Nevertheless the failure of such efforts could not be more obvious.[84]

It is impossible for the central bank, as a financial central-planning agency, to somehow carry out the exact function private money would fulfill in a free market subject to legal principles. The central bank not only lacks the necessary information, but its mere existence tends to amplify the distorting, expansionary effects of fractional-reserve banking, giving rise in the market to severe intertemporal discoordination which, in most cases, not even the central bank is able to detect until it is too late. Even central-bank defenders, like Charles Goodhart, have been obliged to admit that, contrary to the implications of their equilibrium models, and despite all efforts made, in practice it is almost impossible for central-bank officials to adequately coordinate the supply of and demand for money, given the highly changeable, unpredictable, seasonal behavior of the multiple variables they work with. For it is exceedingly difficult, if not impossible, to manipulate the so-called "monetary base" and other aggregates and guides, such as the price index and rates of interest and exchange, without instigating erratic and destabilizing monetary policies. Furthermore Goodhart acknowledges that central banks are subject to the same pressures and forces that influence all other bureaucratic agencies, forces

---

[84]Thus the monetary-policy error which most contributed to the appearance of the Great Depression was that committed by European central banks and the American Federal Reserve during the 1920s. It was not, as Stephen Horwitz indicates and Milton Friedman and Anna Schwartz did before him, that the central bank, following the stock-market crash of 1929, failed to properly respond to a 30 percent decrease in the quantity of money in circulation. As we know, the crisis erupted because prior credit and monetary expansion caused distortions in the productive structure, not because the corresponding reversion process invariably brought deflation with it. Horwitz's error in interpretation, along with his defense of the arguments invoked by members of the modern Fractional-Reserve Free-Banking School, appear in his article, "Keynes' Special Theory," in *Critical Review: A Journal of Books and Ideas* 3, nos. 3 and 4 (Summer–Autumn, 1989): 411–34, esp. p. 425.

which have been studied by the Public Choice School. Indeed central-bank officials are human and are affected by the same incentives and restrictions as all other public officials. Therefore they may be somewhat swayed in their decision-making by groups with a vested interest in influencing the central bank's monetary policy. These include politicians eager to secure votes, private banks themselves, stock-market investors and numerous other special interest groups. Goodhart concludes:

> *There is a temptation* to err on the side of financial laxity. Raising interest rates is (politically) unpopular, and lowering them is popular. Even without political subservience, there will usually be a case for deferring interest rate increases until more information on current developments becomes available. Politicians do *not* generally see themselves as springing surprise inflation on the electorate. Instead, they suggest that an electorally inconvenient interest rate increase should be deferred, or a cut 'safely' accelerated. But it amounts to the same thing in the end. This political manipulation of interest rates, and hence of the monetary aggregates, leads to a loss of credibility and cynicism about whether the politicians' contra-inflation rhetoric should be believed.[85]

Acknowledgment of the harmful behavior (analyzed by the Public Choice School) of central-bank officials and of the "perverse" influence politicians and interest groups exert on

---

[85]Charles A.E. Goodhart has written an accurate summary of the insurmountable theoretical and practical difficulties the central bank encounters in implementing its monetary policy. See his article, "What Should Central Banks Do? What Should be their Macroeconomic Objectives and Operations?" published in *Economic Journal* 104 (November 1994): 1424–36. The above excerpt appears on pp. 1426–27. Other interesting works by Goodhart include: *The Business of Banking 1891–1914* (London: Weidenfeld and Nicholson, 1972), and *The Evolution of Central Banks*. Thomas Mayer also referred to the inevitable political influences exerted on the decisions of central banks, even those banks most independent of the executive branch from a legal standpoint. See Mayer's book, *Monetarism and Macroeconomic Policy* (Aldershot, U.K.: Edward Elgar, 1990), pp. 108–09.

them has led to the consensus that central banks should be as "independent" as possible of the political decisions of the moment and that this independence should even be incorporated into legislation.[86] This constitutes a small step forward in the reformation of the financial system. However, even if rhetoric for the independence of central banks finds its way into legislation or the constitution itself, and even if it is effective in practice (which is more than doubtful in most cases), many public-choice arguments regarding the behavior of central-bank officials would remain unrefuted. Moreover, and more importantly, the central bank would continue to generate massive, systematic intertemporal maladjustments even when appearing to pursue a more "stable" monetary policy.[87]

Oddly enough, the controversy over the independence of central banks has provided the context for the discussion on which structure of *incentives* would best motivate central-bank officials to develop the correct monetary policy. Thus, in connection with the "financial central-planning agency," the sterile debate about incentives has revived, a debate which in the 1960s and 1970s prompted theorists from the economies of the former Eastern bloc to expend a veritable river of ink. In fact the proposal of making the salary of central-bank officials conditional upon their performance with respect to set goals of price stability is strongly reminiscent of the incentive mechanisms which were introduced in socialist countries in an unsuccessful attempt to motivate the managers of state companies to act more "efficiently." Such proposals for reforming the incentive system failed, just as the latest, similar, well-intentioned

---

[86]A helpful overview of the different positions on this point and of the most recent related literature has been prepared by Antonio Erias Rey and José Manuel Sánchez Santos in "Independencia de los bancos centrales y política monetaria; una síntesis," *Hacienda Pública Española* 132 (1995): 63–79.

[87]On the positive effect which the independence of the central bank has on the financial system, see Geoffrey A. Wood et al., *Central Bank Independence: What is it and What Will it Do for Us?* (London: Institute for Economic Affairs, 1993). See also Otmar Issing's book, *Central Bank Independence and Monetary Stability* (London: Institute for Economic Affairs, 1993).

propositions regarding the central bank are bound to fail. They will be unsuccessful because from the start they ignore the essential fact that the officials responsible for government agencies, whether state-owned companies or central banks, cannot in their daily lives escape from the bureaucratic environment in which they work, *nor can they overcome the inherent ignorance of their situation.* János Kornai makes the following appropriate, critical comments concerning attempts to develop an artificial incentive system to make the behavior of functionaries more efficient:

> An artificial incentive scheme, supported by rewards and penalties, can be superimposed. A scheme may support some of the unavowed motives just mentioned. But if it gets into conflict with them, vacillation and ambiguity may follow. The organization's leaders will try to influence those who impose the incentive scheme or will try to evade the rules. . . . What emerges from this procedure is not a successfully simulated market, but the usual conflict between the regulator and the firms regulated by the bureaucracy. . . . Political bureaucracies have inner conflicts reflecting the divisions of society and the diverse pressures of various social groups. They pursue their own individual and group interests, including the interests of the particular specialized agency to which they belong. Power creates an irresistible temptation to make use of it. A bureaucrat must be interventionist because that is his role in society; it is dictated by his situation.[88]

(b) A banking system which operates with a 100-percent reserve ratio and is controlled by a central bank

In this system the distortion and discoordination which arise from the central bank's systematic attack on the financial market would be lessened, since private banks would no longer enjoy the privilege of functioning with a fractional reserve. In this sense bank loans would necessarily reflect

---

[88]János Kornai, "The Hungarian Reform Process," *Journal of Economic Literature* 24, no. 4 (December 1986): 1726–27.

economic agents' true desires with regard to saving, and the
distortion caused by credit expansion (i.e., unbacked by a
prior increase in real, voluntary saving) would be checked.
Nevertheless we cannot conclude that all discoordination generated by the central bank would disappear, since the mere
existence of the central bank and its reliance on systematic
coercion (the imposition of legal-tender regulations and a set
monetary policy) would still have a damaging effect on the
processes of social coordination.

In this example the most critical discoordination would be
intratemporal, rather than intertemporal,[89] because new money
created by the central bank and placed in the economic system
would tend to affect the relative-price structure "horizontally."
In other words it would tend to engender a productive structure
which, horizontally speaking, would not necessarily coincide
with the one consumers wish to sustain. A poor allocation of
resources would ensue, along with a need to reverse the effects
new injections of money would exert on the economic system.[90]

----

[89]Nonetheless we cannot completely rule out the possibility of intertemporal distortions in this case. Even if banks are required to maintain a
100 percent reserve, intertemporal distortions will inevitably occur if the
central bank injects new money into the economic system via massive
open-market purchases which directly affect securities markets, rates of
return, and hence, indirectly, the interest rate in the credit market.

[90]F.A. Hayek has explained that unemployment often stems from the
existence of intratemporal discrepancies between the distribution of the
demand for different consumer goods and services and the allocation of
labor and the other productive resources necessary to produce these
goods. The creation and injection of new money by the central bank at
different points in the economic system tends to produce and aggravate
such qualitative discoordination. This argument, which is illustrated
and reinforced by fractional-reserve banking to the extent that it combines intratemporal distortion with far more acute *intertemporal* discoordination, would still carry weight even if the central bank were to
direct a banking system which operated with a 100-percent reserve
ratio. In this case any increase in the money supply brought about by the
central bank to achieve its monetary-policy goals would always horizontally or intratemporally distort the productive structure, unless (and
this is inconceivable in real life) the new money were equally distributed among all economic agents. In this case the rise in the quantity of

Furthermore, although we cannot refer to any true instance in which a central bank has overseen a system of private banks which have operated with a 100 percent reserve, such a system would also be subject to the political influences and lobby pressures studied by the Public Choice School. It would be naive to believe that central bankers with the power to issue money would desire and be able to develop a stable, undistorted monetary policy, even if they supervised a private banking system which functioned with a 100-percent reserve requirement. The authority to issue money poses such an overwhelming temptation that governments and special interest groups would be unable to resist taking advantage of it. Therefore, even if the central bank did not compound its errors through a fractional-reserve banking system, it would still face the constant risk of succumbing to pressure from politicians and lobbyists eager to take advantage of the central bank's power in order to accomplish the political goals deemed most appropriate at any particular moment.

In short we must acknowledge that because the privilege of fractional-reserve banking is absent in the model covered in this section, most of the intertemporal discoordination behind economic cycles is absent there as well. Nevertheless multiple possibilities of intratemporal discoordination remain, owing to the injection into the economic system of new monetary units created by the central bank, and regardless of the specific method used to inject this new money into society (financing public spending, etc.). In addition, the effects examined by the Public Choice School would play a key role in these intratemporal maladjustments. Indeed it is almost inevitable that the central bank's power to issue money should be politically exploited by different social, economic, and political groups, with the resulting distortion of the productive structure. Though monetary policy would certainly be more predictable and less distorting if private banks maintained a 100 percent

money in circulation would exert no effect, except to proportionally boost the prices of all goods, services and factors of production. All real conditions which could initially be cited as justification for an increase in the money supply would remain unaltered.

reserve, theorists who defend the conservation of the central bank under these circumstances are naive in that they consider that the government and different social groups would desire and be able to develop a stable, and (as far as possible) "neutral," monetary policy. Even if banks kept a 100 percent reserve, the very existence of the central bank, with its tremendous power to issue money, would attract all sorts of perverse political influences like a powerful magnet.[91]

(c) A fractional-reserve free-banking system

The third and last system we will analyze in light of the theory of the impossibility of socialism is a *privileged* free-banking system, i.e., one with no central bank, but with permission to operate with a fractional reserve. The theory of the impossibility of socialism also explains that the concession of privileges which allow certain social groups to violate traditional legal principles produces the same widespread discoordination as socialism, understood as any system of regular, institutional aggression toward the free exercise of entrepreneurship. We have devoted a significant portion of this book (chapters 4–7) to examining how the infringement of traditional legal principles in connection with the monetary bank-deposit contract offers banks the possibility of expanding their credit base even when society's voluntary saving has not increased. We have also seen that as a consequence, discoordination arises between savers and investors and must reverse in the form of a bank crisis and economic recession.

The main clarification to be made concerning a fractional-reserve free-banking system is that the spontaneous market processes which reverse the distorting effects of credit expansion tend to begin sooner in this system than in the presence

----

[91]The principal defenders of a private banking system based on a 100-percent reserve requirement and managed by a central bank include the members of the Chicago School in the 1930s and, currently, Maurice Allais, a recipient of the Nobel Prize in Economics. In the next chapter we will analyze their proposals in detail.

of a central bank, and therefore abuses and distortions cannot become as severe as they often do when a lender of last resort exists and orchestrates the entire expansionary process.

Thus it is conceivable that in a free-banking system, isolated attempts to expand bank credit would be curbed relatively quickly and spontaneously by customers' vigilance toward banks' operations and solvency, the constant reassessment of the trust placed in banks, and, more than anything, the effect of interbank clearing houses. In fact any isolated bank expanding its credit faster than the sector average or issuing notes more rapidly than most would see the volume of its reserves drop quickly, due to interbank clearing mechanisms, and the banker would be forced to halt expansion to avoid a suspension of payments, and eventually, failure.[92]

Nonetheless, even though this definite market reaction tends to check the abuses and isolated expansionary schemes of certain banks, there is no doubt that the process only works *a posteriori* and cannot prevent the issuance of new fiduciary media. As we saw in chapter 2, the emergence of fractional-reserve banking (which in its early days was unaccompanied by a central bank) marked the beginning of substantial, sustained growth in fiduciary media, first in deposits and loans unbacked by saving, and later, in banknotes unbacked by reserves of specie. This process has continually distorted the productive structure and generated cycles of boom and recession which have been historically recorded and studied in many situations *in which private banks have functioned with a fractional reserve and without the existence and supervision of a central bank*. Some of the earliest of such studies can be traced back to the economic and bank crises which hit fourteenth-century Florence. Just as the theory of free banking indicates, the great majority of these expansionary banks did eventually fold, but only after issuing fiduciary media for a varying length of time, an activity which never failed to exert crippling

---

[92]It is precisely this process that Parnell originally described in 1826 and Ludwig von Mises later developed further in chapter 12 of *Human Action*: "The Limitation on the Issuance of Fiduciary Media," pp. 434–48.

effects on the real economy by provoking bank crises and economic recessions.[93]

Not only is fractional-reserve free-banking incapable of avoiding credit expansion and the appearance of cycles, but it actually tempts bankers in general to expand their loans, and the result is a policy in which all bankers, to one extent or another, are carried away by optimism in the granting of loans and in the creation of deposits.[94] It is a well-known fact that whenever property rights are not adequately defined—and this is the case with fractional-reserve banking, which by definition involves the violation of depositors' traditional property rights—the "tragedy of the commons" effect tends to appear.[95] Thus a banker who expands his loans brings in a handsome, and larger, profit (if his bank does not fail), while

---

[93]Charles A.E. Goodhart states: "There were plenty of banking crises and panics prior to the formation of central banks" and cites O.B.W. Sprague's book, *History of Crises and the National Banking System*, first published in 1910 and reprinted in New Jersey by Augustus M. Kelley in 1977. See Charles A.E. Goodhart, "What Should Central Banks Do? What Should be their Macroeconomic Objectives and Operations?" p. 1435. See also the article by the same author, "The Free Banking Challenge to Central Banks," published in *Critical Review* 8, no. 3 (Summer 1994): 411–25. A collection of the most important writings of Charles A.E. Goodhart has been published as *The Central Bank and the Financial System* (Cambridge, Mass.: MIT Press, 1995).

[94]On banks' optimism and the "passive inflationism" which arises from bankers' fear of aborting artificial expansion in time, see Mises, *Human Action*, pp. 572–73. Moreover Mises argues that benefits derived from privileges tend to run out (in the realm of banking this is due to an increase in branches, expenses, etc.), thus sparking demands for further doses of inflation (ibid., p. 749).

[95]The expression "tragedy of the commons" came into use following Garret Hardin's article, "The Tragedy of the Commons," *Science* (1968); reprinted on pp. 16–30 of *Managing the Commons*, Garret Hardin and John Baden, eds. (San Francisco: Freeman, 1970). However the process had already been fully described twenty-eight years earlier by Ludwig von Mises in his "Die Grenzen des Sondereigentums und das Problem der external costs und external economies," section 6 of chapter 10 of part 4 of *Nationalökonomie: Theorie des Handelns und Wirtschaftens* (Geneva: Editions Union, 1940; Munich: Philosophia Verlag, 1980), pp. 599–605.

the cost of his irresponsible act is shared by all other economic agents. It is for this reason that bankers face the almost irresistible temptation to be the first to initiate a policy of expansion, particularly if they expect all other banks to follow suit to one degree or another, which often occurs.[96]

The above example differs only slightly from Hardin's classic illustration of the "tragedy of the commons," in which he points to the effects an inadequate recognition of property rights may exert on the environment. Unlike in Hardin's example, in fractional-reserve free banking a spontaneous mechanism (interbank clearing houses) tends to limit the possibility that isolated expansionary schemes will reach a successful conclusion. Table VIII-2 outlines the dilemma banks encounter in such a system.

TABLE VIII-2

| | | *Bank A* | |
		Does not expand	*Expands*
	Does not expand	The survival of both (reduced profits)	The failure of A The survival of B
Bank B			
	Expands	The failure of B The survival of A	Large profits for both

[96]Selgin and White have criticized our application of the "tragedy of the commons" theory to fractional-reserve free banking. They claim that what occurs in this sector is a pecuniary externality (i.e., one derived from the price system), which has nothing to do with the technological externality on which the "tragedy of the commons" rests. See George A. Selgin and Lawrence H. White "In Defense of Fiduciary Media, or We are *Not* (Devo)lutionists, We are Misesians!" *Review of Austrian Economics* 9, no. 2 (1996): 92–93, footnote 12. Nevertheless Selgin and White do not seem to fully grasp that the issuance of fiduciary media stems from the violation of traditional property rights in connection with the monetary bank-deposit contract, and that hence fiduciary media are not a spontaneous phenomenon of a legally based free-market process. Hoppe, Hülsmann, and Block, for their part, have come to our defense with the following assertion:

This table reflects the existence of two banks, Bank A and Bank B, both of which have two options: either to refrain from expanding credit or to adopt a policy of credit expansion. If both banks simultaneously initiate credit expansion (assuming there are no other banks in the industry), the ability to issue new monetary units and fiduciary media will yield the same large profits to both. If either expands credit alone, its viability and solvency will be endangered by interbank clearing mechanisms, which will rapidly shift its reserves to the other bank if the first fails to suspend its credit expansion policy in time. Finally it is also possible that neither of the banks may expand and both may maintain a prudent policy of loan concession. In this case the survival of both is guaranteed, though their profits will be quite modest. *It is clear that given the choices above, the two banks will face a strong temptation to arrive at an agreement and, to avoid the adverse consequences of acting independently, initiate a joint policy of credit expansion which will protect both from insolvency and guarantee handsome profits.*[97]

> In lumping money and money substitutes together under the joint title of "money" as if they were somehow the same thing, Selgin and White fail to grasp that the issue of fiduciary media—an increase of property titles—is not the same thing as a larger supply of property and that relative price changes effected through the issue of fiduciary media are an entirely different "externality" matter than price changes effected through an increase in the supply of property. With this the fundamental distinction between property and a property title in mind, Huerta de Soto's analogy between fractional reserve banking and the tragedy of the commons makes perfect sense. (Hans-Hermann Hoppe, Jörg Guido Hülsmann and Walter Block, "Against Fiduciary Media," *The Quarterly Journal of Austrian Economics* 1, no. 1 (1998): 23, footnote 6)

Furthermore Mises emphasizes that the chief economic effect of negative external costs is to complicate economic calculation and discoordinate society, phenomena which clearly take place in the case of credit expansion in fractional-reserve banking. See Mises, *Human Action*, pp. 655ff.; and Philipp Bagus, "La tragedia de los bienes comunales y la escuela austriaca: Hardin, Hoppe, Huerta de Soto, y Mises," *Procesos de Mercado* 1, no. 2 (2004): 125–29.

[97]Table VIII-2 does not include any "weights" or values and is typically used to illustrate both cooperative games and "prisoner's dilemmas"

The above analysis extends to a large group of banks which operate in a free-banking system and maintain a fractional reserve. The analysis shows that under such circumstances, even if interbank clearing mechanisms limit *isolated* expansionary schemes, these spontaneous mechanisms actually encourage implicit or explicit agreements between the majority of banks to jointly initiate the process of expansion. Thus in a fractional-reserve free-banking system, banks tend to merge, bankers tend to arrive at implicit and explicit agreements among themselves, and ultimately, a central bank tends to emerge. Central banks generally appear as a result of requests from private bankers themselves, who wish to *institutionalize* joint credit expansion via a government agency

---

(as when a prudent and honest bank refuses to cooperate, or an irresponsible one wants to be the first one to expand). The reasoning behind our application of the "tragedy of the commons" to the fractional-reserve free-banking system parallels the argument originally offered by Longfield, though he attempts, without much justification, to apply his case even to isolated instances of expansion by a few banks, while in our analysis such instances are limited by the interbank clearing mechanism, a factor Longfield fails to consider. The tragedy of the commons also accounts for the forces which motivate banks in a fractional-reserve free-banking system to merge and to request the creation of a central bank, with the aim of establishing general, common policies of credit expansion. The first time we explained this typical "tragedy of the commons" process in this context was at the regional meeting of the Mont Pèlerin Society which took place in Rio de Janeiro September 5–8, 1993. At this meeting, Anna J. Schwartz also pointed out that modern fractional-reserve free-banking theorists cannot seem to grasp that the interbank clearing mechanism they refer to does not curb credit expansion if all banks decide to simultaneously expand their credit to one degree or another. See her article, "The Theory of Free Banking," presented at the above meeting, esp. p. 5. At any rate, the process of expansion obviously stems *from a privilege* which conflicts with property rights, and each bank clearly reserves for itself all the benefits of its credit expansion and allows the costs to be shared by the entire system. Moreover if most bankers implicitly or explicitly agree to "optimistically" join in the creation and granting of loans, the interbank clearing mechanism does not effectively curtail abuses.

designed to *orchestrate and organize* it. In this way, the "unco-operative" behavior of a significant number of relatively more prudent bankers is prevented from endangering the solvency of the rest (those who are more "cheerful" in granting loans).

Therefore our analysis enables us to conclude the following: (1) that the interbank clearing mechanism does not serve to limit credit expansion in a fractional-reserve free-banking system if most banks decide to simultaneously expand their loans in the absence of a prior rise in voluntary saving; (2) that the fractional-reserve banking system itself prompts bankers to initiate their expansionary policies in a combined, coordinated manner; and (3) that bankers in the system have a powerful incentive to demand and obtain the establishment of a central bank to institutionalize and orchestrate credit expansion for all banks, and to guarantee the creation of the necessary liquidity in the "troublesome" periods which, as bankers know from experience, inevitably reappear.[98]

The privilege which allows banks to use a significant portion of the money placed with them on demand deposit, i.e., to operate with a fractional reserve, cyclically can result in a dramatic discoordination of the economy. A similar effect appears when privileges are granted to other social groups in other areas (unions in the labor market, for example).

---

[98]Precisely for the reasons given I cannot agree with my friend Pascal Salin, who concludes that "the problem is [central bank] monetary monopoly, not fractional reserve." See Pascal Salin, "In Defense of Fractional Monetary Reserves." Even the most prominent defenders of fractional-reserve free banking have recognized that the interbank clearing system which would emerge in a free-banking environment would be incapable of checking a widespread expansion of loans. For example, see George Selgin's article, "Free Banking and Monetary Control," printed in *Economic Journal* 104, no. 427 (November 1994): 1449–59, esp. p. 1455. Selgin overlooks the fact that the fractional-reserve banking system he supports would create an irresistible trend not only toward mergers, associations and agreements, but also (and even more importantly) toward the establishment of a central bank designed to orchestrate joint credit expansion without compromising the solvency of individual banks, and to guarantee necessary liquidity as a lender of last resort with the power to assist any bank in times of financial difficulties.

Fractional-reserve banking distorts the productive structure and provokes widespread, intertemporal discoordination in the economy, a situation bound to spontaneously reverse in the form of an economic crisis and recession. Although in a fractional-reserve free-banking system independent reversion processes tend to curb abuses sooner than in a system controlled and directed by a central bank, *the most harmful effect of fractional-reserve free banking is that it provides banks with an immensely powerful incentive to expand loans jointly and, particularly, to urge authorities to create a central bank* aimed at offering support in times of economic trouble and organizing and orchestrating widespread, collective credit expansion.

CONCLUSION: THE FAILURE OF BANKING LEGISLATION

Society's market process is made possible by a set of customary rules of which it is also the source. These rules constitute the behavioral patterns embodied in criminal law and private contract law. No one has deliberately formulated them. Instead such rules are evolutionary institutions which emerge from practical information contributed by a huge number of actors over a very prolonged period of time. Substantive or material law, in this sense, comprises a series of *general, abstract rules or laws.* They are general because they apply equally to all people, and they are abstract because they establish only a broad scope of action for individuals and do not point to any concrete result of the social process. In contrast to this substantive conception of law, we find *legislation*, understood as a set of coercive, statutory, and *ad hoc* orders or commands which are the materialization of the illegitimate privileges and the systematic, institutional aggression with which the government attempts to dominate the processes of human interaction.[99] This concept of legislation implies the abandonment of the traditional notion of the law (explained above), and the replacement of it with "spurious law" composed of a conglomeration of administrative orders, regulations and

---

[99]Hayek, *The Constitution of Liberty* and *Law, Legislation and Liberty.* See also Huerta de Soto, *Socialismo, cálculo económico y función empresarial*, chap. 3.

commands which dictate exactly how the supervised economic agent should behave. Thus to the extent that privileges
and institutional coercion spread and develop, traditional
laws cease to act as standards of behavior for individuals, and
the role of these laws is taken over by the coercive orders and
commands of the regulatory agency, in our case, the central
bank. In this way the law gradually loses its scope of implementation, and as economic agents are robbed of the criteria
of substantive law, they begin to unconsciously alter their per-
sonalities and even lose the custom of adapting to general,
abstract rules. Under these conditions, to "elude" commands
is in many cases simply a matter of survival, and in others it
reflects the success of corrupt or perverse entrepreneurship.
Hence, from a general standpoint, people come to see deviation from the rules as an admirable expression of human
ingenuity, rather than a violation of a regulatory system which
seriously jeopardizes life in society.

The above considerations are fully applicable to banking
legislation. Indeed the fractional-reserve banking system,
which has spread to all countries with a market economy, primarily entails (as we saw in the first three chapters) the violation of an essential legal principle in relation to the monetary
bank-deposit contract and the granting of an *ius privilegium* to
certain economic agents: private banks. This privilege allows
banks to disregard legal principles and make self-interested
use of most of the money citizens have entrusted to them via
demand deposits. Banking legislation mainly constitutes the
abandonment of traditional legal principles in connection
with the monetary demand-deposit contract, the heart of
modern banking.

Furthermore banking legislation takes the form of a tangled web of administrative orders and commands which
emanate from the central bank and are intended to strictly
control the specific activities of private bankers. This welter of
injunctions has not only been incapable of preventing the
cyclical appearance of bank crises, but (and this is much more
significant) it has also fostered and aggravated recurrent
stages of great artificial boom and profound economic recession. Such stages have regularly seized western economies
and entailed a great economic and human cost. Thus:

Each time a new crisis hits, a complete set of new laws or amendments to prior ones is swiftly enacted under the naive assumption that the former laws were insufficient and that the new, more detailed and all-encompassing ones will better avoid future crises. This is how the government and the central bank excuse their unfortunate inability to avert crises, which nevertheless arise again and again, and the new regulations last only until the next bank crisis and economic recession.[100]

Therefore we can conclude that banking legislation is condemned to failure and will continue to be so unless the present form is thoroughly abolished and replaced by a few simple articles to be included in the commercial and penal codes. These articles would establish the regulation of the monetary bank-deposit contract according to traditional legal principles (a 100-percent reserve requirement) and would prohibit all contracts which mask fractional-reserve banking. In short, in

---

[100]See p. 2 of our student Elena Sousmatzian Ventura's article, "¿Puede la intervención gubernamental evitar las crisis bancarias?" Ms. Sousmatzian quotes the following description (offered by Tomás-Ramón Fernández) of the crisis-legislation cycle:

> Banking legislation has always developed in response to crises. When crises have hit, existing legislation has always been found inadequate and devoid of the necessary answers and solutions. Thus it has always been necessary to come up with hasty emergency solutions which, despite the context of their "invention," at the end of each crisis have been incorporated into a new general legal framework, which has lasted only until the following shock, when a similar cycle has begun. (Tomás-Ramón Fernández, *Comentarios a la ley de disciplina de intervención de las entidades de crédito* [Madrid: Serie de Estudios de la Fundación Fondo para la Investigación Económica y Social, 1989], p. 9)

Elena Sousmatzian expresses the problem in this way: if bank crises are preventable, government intervention has proven unequal to the task of preventing them; and if crises are inevitable, government intervention in this area is superfluous. Both positions have truth to them, since fractional-reserve banking makes crises inescapable, regardless of the banking legislation which governments insist on drafting and which often does more to further aggravate cyclical problems than it does to lessen them.

keeping with Mises's view, the above proposal entails the substitution of several clear, simple articles, to appear in the commercial and penal codes, for the current web of administrative
banking legislation, which has not achieved the objectives set
for it.[101]

It is interesting to note that modern defenders of fractional-reserve free banking wrongly believe, due in part to
their lack of legal preparation, that a 100-percent reserve
requirement would amount to an unfair *administrative*
restriction of individual freedom. Nevertheless, as the analysis of the first three chapters shows, nothing could be further
from the truth. For these theorists do not realize that such a
rule, far from being an example of systematic, administrative
government coercion, merely constitutes the recognition of
traditional *property rights* in the banking sector. In other
words, theorists who endorse a fractional-reserve free-banking system, which would infringe traditional legal principles,
fail to see that "free trade in banking is synonymous with free
trade in swindling," a famous phrase attributed to an anonymous American and reiterated by Tooke.[102] Moreover if a
free-banking system must ultimately be defended as a "lesser
evil" in comparison with central banking, the motive should

---

[101]Mises, *Human Action*, p. 443.

[102]To be specific, Tooke remarked:

> As to the free trade in banking in the sense which it is some-
> times contended for, I agree with a writer in one of the Amer-
> ican papers, who observes that free trade in banking is syn-
> onymous with free trade in swindling. Such claims do not
> rest in any manner on grounds analogous to the claims of
> freedom of competition in production. It is a matter of regu-
> lation by the State and comes within the province of police.
> (Thomas Tooke, *A History of Prices*, 3 vols. [London: Longman,
> 1840], vol. 3, p. 206)

We agree with Tooke in that if free banking implies freedom to operate
with a fractional reserve, then essential legal principles are violated and
the state, if it is to have any function at all, should diligently attempt to
prevent such violations and punish them when they occur. This appears
to be precisely what Ludwig von Mises had in mind when, in *Human
Action* (p. 666), he quoted this excerpt of Tooke's.

not be to permit the exploitation of the lucrative possibilities which always arise from credit expansion. Instead free banking should be seen as an *indirect route* to the ideal free-banking system, one subject to legal principles, i.e., a 100-percent reserve requirement. All legal means available in a constitutional state should be applied at all times in the *direct* pursuit of this goal.

4
A CRITICAL LOOK AT THE MODERN
FRACTIONAL-RESERVE FREE-BANKING SCHOOL

The last twenty years have seen a certain resurgence of the old economic Banking School doctrines. Defenders of these views claim that a fractional-reserve free-banking system would not only give rise to fewer distortions and economic crises than central banking, but would actually tend to eliminate such problems. Given that these theorists base their reasoning on different variations of the Old Banking School arguments, some more sophisticated than others, we will group the theorists under the heading, "Neo-Banking School," or "modern pro-Fractional-Reserve Free-Banking School." This school is composed of a curious alliance of scholars,[103] among

---

[103]As David Laidler accurately points out, recent interest in free banking and the development of the Neo-Banking School originated with Friedrich A. Hayek's book on the denationalization of money (F.A. Hayek, *Denationalization of Money: The Argument Refined*, 2nd ed. [London: Institute of Economic Affairs, 1978]). Prior to Hayek, Benjamin Klein offered a similar proposal in his article, "The Competitive Supply of Money," published in the *Journal of Money, Credit and Banking* 6 (November 1974): 423–53. Laidler's reference to the above two authors appears in his brief but stimulating article on banking theory, "Free Banking Theory," found in *The New Palgrave: A Dictionary of Money and Finance* (London and New York: Macmillan Press, 1992), vol. 2, pp. 196–97. According to Oskari Juurikkala, the current debate among free-banking theorists (pro-100-percent reserve requirement versus pro-fractional reserve) is strictly parallel to the nineteenth century French debate between Victor Modeste (and Henry Cernuschi) and J. Gustave Courcelle-Seneuil. See his article, "The 1866 False-Money Debate in the *Journal des Economistes*: Déjà Vu for Austrians?"

whom we could mention certain members of the Austrian School who, in our opinion, have missed some of Mises's and Hayek's teachings on monetary matters and the theory of capital and economic cycles, members like White,[104] Selgin[105] and, more recently, Horwitz;[106] members of the English Subjectivist School, like Dowd;[107] and finally, theorists with a monetarist background, like Glasner,[108] Yeager[109] and Timberlake.[110] Even

---

[104]Lawrence H. White, *Free Banking in Britain: Theory, Experience and Debate, 1800–1845* (London and New York: Cambridge University Press, 1984); *Competition and Currency: Essays on Free Banking and Money* (New York: New York University Press, 1989); and also the articles written jointly with George A. Selgin: "How Would the Invisible Hand Handle Money?" *Journal of Economic Literature* 32, no. 4 (December 1994): 1718–49, and more recently, "In Defense of Fiduciary Media—or, We are *Not* Devo(lutionists), We are Misesians!" *Review of Austrian Economics* 9, no. 2 (1996): 83–107. Finally, Lawrence H. White has compiled the most important writings from a Neo-Banking School standpoint in the following work: *Free Banking*, vol. 1: *19th Century Thought*; vol. 2: *History*; vol. 3: *Modern Theory and Policy* (Aldershot, U.K.: Edward Elgar, 1993).

[105]George A. Selgin, "The Stability and Efficiency of Money Supply under Free Banking," printed in the *Journal of Institutional and Theoretical Economics* 143 (1987): 435–56, and republished in *Free Banking*, vol. 3: *Modern Theory and Policy*, Lawrence H. White, ed., pp. 45–66; *The Theory of Free Banking: Money Supply under Competitive Note Issue* (Totowa, N.J.: Rowman and Littlefield, 1988); the articles written jointly with Lawrence H. White and cited in the preceding footnote; and "Free Banking and Monetary Control," pp. 1449–59. I am not very sure if Selgin does still consider himself a member of the Austrian School.

[106]Stephen Horwitz, "Keynes' Special Theory," pp. 411–34; "Misreading the 'Myth': Rothbard on the Theory and History of Free Banking," published as chapter 16 of *The Market Process: Essays in Contemporary Austrian Economics*, Peter J. Boettke and David L. Prychitko, eds. (Aldershot, U.K.: Edward Elgar, 1994), pp. 166–76; and also his books, *Monetary Evolution, Free Banking and Economic Order* and *Microfoundations and Macroeconomics* (London: Routledge, 2000).

[107]Kevin Dowd, *The State and the Monetary System* (New York: Saint Martin's Press, 1989); *The Experience of Free Banking* (London: Routledge, 1992); and *Laissez-Faire Banking* (London and New York, Routledge, 1993).

[108]David Glasner, *Free Banking and Monetary Reform* (Cambridge: Cambridge University Press, 1989); "The Real-Bills Doctrine in the Light of the Law of Reflux," *History of Political Economy* 24, no. 4 (Winter, 1992): 867–94.

Milton Friedman,[111] though he cannot be considered a member of this new school, has been gradually leaning toward it, especially following his failure to convince central bankers that they should put his famous monetary rule into practice.

Modern fractional-reserve free-banking theorists have developed an economic theory of "monetary equilibrium." They base their theory on certain typical elements of the monetarist and Keynesian analysis[112] and intend it to demonstrate that a fractional-reserve free-banking system would simply adjust the volume of fiduciary media created (banknotes and deposits) to public demand for them. In this way they argue that fractional-reserve free banking would not only preserve "monetary equilibrium" better than other, alternative systems but would also most effectively adjust the supply of money to the demand for it.

---

[109]Leland B. Yeager and Robert Greenfield, "A Laissez-Faire Approach to Monetary Stability," *Journal of Money, Credit and Banking* 15, no. 3 (August 1983): 302–15, reprinted as chapter 11 of volume 3 of *Free Banking*, Lawrence H. White, ed., pp. 180–95; Leland B. Yeager and Robert Greenfield, "Competitive Payments Systems: Comment," *American Economic Review* 76, no. 4 (September 1986): 848–49. And finally Yeager's book, *The Fluttering Veil: Essays on Monetary Disequilibrium.*

[110]Richard Timberlake, "The Central Banking Role of Clearinghouse Associations," *Journal of Money, Credit and Banking* 16 (February 1984): 1–15; "Private Production of Scrip-Money in the Isolated Community," *Journal of Money, Credit and Banking* 19, no. 4 (October 1987): 437–47; "The Government's Licence to Create Money," *The Cato Journal: An Interdisciplinary Journal of Public Policy Analysis* 9, no. 2 (Fall, 1989): 302–21.

[111]Milton Friedman and Anna J. Schwartz, "Has Government Any Role in Money?" *Journal of Monetary Economics* 17 (1986): 37–72, reprinted as chapter 26 of the book, *The Essence of Friedman*, Kurt R. Leube, ed. (Stanford University, Calif.: Hoover Institution Press, 1986), pp. 499–525.

[112]Thus Selgin himself states:

> Despite . . . important differences between Keynesian analysis and the views of other monetary-equilibrium theorists, many Keynesians might accept the prescription for monetary equilibrium. (Selgin, *The Theory of Free Banking*, p. 56; see also p. 59)

In a nutshell, this argument centers around the hypothetical results of an increase in economic agents' demand for fiduciary media, assuming reserves of specie in the banking system remain constant. In that event, theorists reason, the pace at which fiduciary media are exchanged for bank reserves would slacken. Reserves would increase and bankers, aware of this rise and eager to obtain larger profits, would expand credit and issue more banknotes and deposits, and the growth in fiduciary media would tend to match the *prior* increase in demand. The opposite would occur should the demand for fiduciary media decrease: Economic agents would withdraw greater quantities of reserves in order to rid themselves of fiduciary media. Banks would then see their solvency endangered and be obliged to tighten credit and issue fewer banknotes and deposits. In this way a decrease in the supply of fiduciary media would follow the *prior* decrease in the demand for them.[113]

The theory of "monetary equilibrium" obviously echoes Fullarton's law of reflux and, especially, the Old Banking School arguments concerning the "needs of trade." According to these arguments, private banks' creation of fiduciary media is not detrimental if it corresponds to an increase in the "needs" of businessmen. These arguments are repeated and crystallized in the "new" theory of "monetary equilibrium," which states that private banks' creation of fiduciary media in the form of notes and deposits does not generate economic cycles *if it follows a rise in public demand for such instruments.* Although Lawrence H. White does develop an embryonic version of this reformed "needs of trade" doctrine in his book on free banking in Scotland,[114] credit for theoretically formulating

---

[113]The detailed analysis appears, among other places, in Selgin's book, *The Theory of Free Banking,* chaps. 4, 5 and 6, esp. p. 34 and pp. 64–69.

[114]Stephen Horwitz maintains that Lawrence White

> explicitly rejects the real-bills doctrine and endorses a different version of the "needs of trade" idea. For him the "needs of trade" means *the demand to hold bank notes.* On this interpretation, the doctrine states that the supply of bank notes should vary in accordance with the demand to hold notes. As

the idea goes to one of White's most noted students, George A. Selgin. Let us now critically examine Selgin's theory of "monetary equilibrium," or in other words, his revised version of some of the Old Banking School doctrines.

THE ERRONEOUS BASIS OF THE ANALYSIS: THE DEMAND FOR FIDUCIARY MEDIA, REGARDED AS AN EXOGENOUS VARIABLE

Selgin's analysis rests on the notion that the demand for money in the form of fiduciary media is a variable exogenous to the system, that this variable changes with the desires of economic agents, and that the main purpose of the free-banking system is to reconcile the issuance of deposits and banknotes with shifts in the demand for them.[115] *Nevertheless such demand is not exogenous to the system, but endogenously determined by it.*

It is no coincidence that theorists of the Fractional-Reserve Free-Banking School begin their analysis by focusing on certain more or less mysterious variations in the demand for fiduciary media, and that they neglect to explain the origin or etiology of these variations.[116] It is as if these theorists realized

---

> I shall argue, this is just as acceptable as the view that the supply of shoes should vary to meet the demand for them. (Horwitz, "Misreading the 'Myth'," p. 169)

To be specific, White appears to defend the new version of the Old Banking School's "needs of trade" doctrine on pp. 123–24 of his book, *Free Banking in Britain*. In contrast to the thesis of Horwitz, Amasa Walker indicates, in connection with fiduciary media:

> The supply does not satisfy the demand: it excites it. Like an unnatural stimulus taken into the human system, it creates an increasing desire for more; and the more it is gratified, the more insatiable are its cravings. (Amasa Walker, *The Science of Wealth: A Manual of Political Economy*, 5th ed. [Boston: Little Brown and Company, 1869], p. 156)

[115]"Free banking thus works against short-run monetary disequilibrium and its business cycle consequences." Selgin and White, "In Defense of Fiduciary Media—or, We are *Not* Devo(lutionists), We are Misesians!" pp. 101–02.

[116]Joseph T. Salerno points out that for Mises, increases in the demand for money do not pose any coordination problem whatsoever, as long as the banking system does not attempt to adjust to them by creating new

that, on the side of the money supply, the Austrians have demonstrated that credit expansion seriously distorts the economy, a fact which in any case seems to warrant a rigid monetary system[117] capable of preventing the monetary expansions and contractions typical of any fractional-reserve banking system. Therefore on the side of supply, theoretical arguments appear to support the establishment of a relatively inelastic monetary system, such as a pure gold standard with a 100-percent reserve requirement for banknotes and deposits.[118] Hence if defenders of the Neo-Banking School

---

loans. Even a rise in saving (that is, a fall in consumption) expressed solely in increased cash balances (hoarding), and not in loans linked to spending on investment goods, would lead to the effective saving of consumer goods and services in the community and to a process by which the productive structure would become longer and more capital-intensive. In this case the rise in cash balances would simply boost the purchasing power of money by pushing down the nominal prices of the consumer goods and services of the different factors of production. Nonetheless, in relative terms, the price disparities characteristic of a period of rising saving and increasing capital intensity in the productive structure would arise among the different stages of factors of production. See Joseph T. Salerno, "Mises and Hayek Dehomogenized," printed in *Review of Austrian Economics* 6, no. 2 (1993): 113–46, esp. pp. 144ff. See also Mises, *Human Action*, pp. 520–21. In the same article, Salerno strongly criticizes White for maintaining that Mises was the forerunner of the modern free-banking theorists and for not realizing that Mises always challenged the essential premises of the Banking School and only defended free banking as a way to reach the final goal of a banking system with a 100-percent reserve requirement. See pp. 137ff. in the above article. See also upcoming footnote 119.

[117]Let us remember that Hayek's objective in *Prices and Production* was precisely

> to demonstrate that the cry for an "elastic" currency which expands or contracts with every fluctuation of "demand" is based on a serious error of reasoning. (See p. xiii of Hayek's preface to the first edition of *Prices and Production*)

[118]Mark Skousen states that a system based on a pure gold standard with a 100-percent reserve requirement in banking would be more elastic than the system Hayek proposes and would not have the defect of conforming to the "needs of trade": decreases in prices would stimulate the production of gold, thereby generating a moderate expansion of the money supply without producing cyclical effects. Skousen concludes:

wish to justify a fractional-reserve free-banking system in which there may be substantial increases and decreases in the money supply in the form of fiduciary media, they must independently look to the side of demand in the hope of being able to demonstrate that such modifications in the supply of fiduciary media (which are inevitable in a fractional-reserve system) correspond to *prior* variations in demand which are satisfied by the reestablishment of a hypothetical, preexistent state of "monetary equilibrium."

Growth in the money supply in the form of credit expansion distorts the productive structure and gives rise to an economic boom and subsequent recession, stages during which significant variations in the demand for money and fiduciary media take place. Hence the process is not triggered, as theorists of the modern Free-Banking School suppose, by independent, catalytic changes in the demand for fiduciary media, but by the manipulation of the supply of them. All fractional-reserve banking systems carry out such manipulation to one degree or another by expanding credit.

It is true that in a system composed of a multiplicity of free banks unsupported by a central bank, credit expansion would stop much sooner than in a system in which the central bank orchestrates widespread expansion and uses its liquidity to aid those banks in jeopardy. This is the pro-free-banking argument Parnell originally developed and Mises later identified as *second-best*.[119] However it is one thing to assert that in a

---

Based on historical evidence, the money supply (the stock of gold) under a pure gold standard would expand [annually] between 1 to 5 percent. And, most importantly, there would be virtually no chance of a monetary deflation under 100 percent gold backing of the currency. (Skousen, *The Structure of Production*, p. 359)

[119]Selgin himself recognizes that

Mises's support for free banking is based in part on his agreement with Cernuschi, who (along with Modeste) believed that freedom of note issue would automatically lead to 100 percent reserve banking;

and also that Mises "believed that free banking will somehow lead to the suppression of fractionally-based inside monies." See Selgin, *The*

completely free banking system credit expansion would be
curbed *sooner* than in the current system, and it is quite another
to claim that credit expansion brought about in a fractional-
reserve free-banking system would never distort the productive structure, since a state of supposed "monetary equilibrium" would always tend to return. In fact Mises himself very
clearly indicates that *all* credit expansion distorts the productive
system. Hence Mises rejects the essence of the modern theory of
monetary equilibrium. Indeed Mises affirms:

> The notion of "normal" credit expansion is absurd. *Issuance
> of additional fiduciary media, no matter what its quantity may be,
> always sets in motion those changes in the price structure the
> description of which is the task of the theory of the trade cycle.*[120]

The chief failing of Selgin's theory of "monetary equilibrium" is that it ignores the fact that *the supply of fiduciary media*

Theory of Free Banking, pp. 62 and 164. Lawrence H. White attempts to
place a different interpretation on Mises's position and presents Mises
as the forerunner of modern fractional-reserve free banking defenders.
See Lawrence H. White, "Mises on Free Banking and Fractional
Reserves," in *A Man of Principle: Essays in Honor of Hans F. Sennholz,* John
W. Robbins and Mark Spangler, eds. (Grove City, Penn.: Grove City College Press, 1992), pp. 517–33. Salerno, in agreement with Selgin, makes
the following response to White:

> To the extent that Mises advocated the freedom of banks to
> issue fiduciary media, he did so only because his analysis led
> him to the conclusion that this policy would result in a money
> supply strictly regulated according to the Currency principle.
> Mises's desideratum was . . . to completely eliminate the dis-
> tortive influences of fiduciary media on monetary calculation
> and the dynamic market process. (Salerno, "Mises and Hayek
> Dehomogenized," pp. 137ff. and p. 145)

[120]Mises, *Human Action,* p. 442, footnote 17; italics added. Mises adds:
"Free banking . . . would . . . not hinder a slow credit expansion" (*Human
Action,* p. 443). Here Mises conveys an excessively optimistic impression
of fractional-reserve free banking, particularly in light of this earlier passage from *Theory of Money and Credit* (1924): "[I]t is clear that banking
freedom *per se* cannot be said to make a return to gross inflationary policy impossible." Mises, *Theory of Money and Credit,* p. 436 (p. 408 in the
German edition).

largely creates its own demand. In other words, modern free-banking theory contains the Old Banking School's fundamental error, which, as Mises adeptly revealed, lies in a failure to reflect that public demand for credit depends precisely on banks' inclination to lend. Thus those bankers who, in the beginning, are not overly concerned about their future solvency are in a position to expand credit and place new fiduciary media in the market simply by reducing the interest rate they ask for the new money they create and easing their normal credit terms.[121] Therefore, in contrast with the assumptions of Selgin and the other theorists of his school, bankers can initiate credit expansion in a free-banking system if for some reason they disregard their own solvency, *whether or not a prior variation in the demand for fiduciary media has occurred*. Another factor explains why, during a prolonged period, the increase in the quantity of deposits (from credit expansion) *actually tends to stimulate demand for fiduciary media*. In fact all economic agents who are unaware that an inflationary process of expansion has begun, and that this process will ultimately cause a relative decrease in the purchasing power of money and a subsequent recession, will notice that certain goods and services begin to rise in price faster than others and will wait in vain for such prices to return to their "normal" level. Meanwhile they will most likely decide to increase their demand for fiduciary media. To again cite Mises:

----

[121] The Banking School failed entirely in dealing with these problems. It was confused by a spurious idea according to which the requirements of business rigidly limit the maximum amount of convertible banknotes that a bank can issue. They did not see that the demand of the public for credit is a magnitude dependent on the banks' readiness to lend, and that banks which do not bother about their own solvency are in a position to expand circulation credit by lowering the rate of interest below the market rate. (Mises, *Human Action*, pp. 439–40)

Moreover let us remember that the process spreads and feeds upon itself as debtors borrow more newly-created deposits to repay earlier loans.

This first stage of the inflationary process may last for many years. While it lasts, the prices of many goods and services are not yet adjusted to the altered money relation. There are still people in the country who have not yet become aware of the fact that they are confronted with a price revolution which will finally result in a considerable rise of all prices, although the extent of this rise will not be the same in the various commodities and services. These people still believe that prices one day will drop. Waiting for this day, they restrict their purchases and concomitantly *increase their cash holdings.*[122]

Not only are banks in a fractional-reserve free-banking system able to *unilaterally* instigate credit expansion, but during a prolonged period the resulting increase in the supply of fiduciary media (which can always be placed in the market through an opportune reduction in the interest rate) tends to create further demand. This increase in demand will last until the public loses some of its unrealistic optimism, begins to distrust the economic "bonanza," and foresees a widespread rise in prices, followed by a crisis and profound economic recession.

We have argued that the origin of monetary changes lies on the side of supply, that banks in a free-banking system are able to manipulate the money supply, and that the corresponding issuance of fiduciary media creates its own demand in the short and medium term. If the above assertions are true, then Selgin is utterly mistaken in claiming that the supply of fiduciary media merely adjusts to the demand for them. Indeed the demand for fiduciary media, at least during a considerable period of time, adjusts to the increased supply which banks create in the form of loans.[123]

---

[122]Mises, *Human Action,* pp. 427–28; italics added.

[123]Curiously, like Keynesians and monetarists, modern free-banking theorists are obsessed with supposed, sudden, unilateral changes in the demand for money. They fail to see that such changes tend to be endogenous and to occur throughout an economic cycle which is first triggered by shifts in the supply of new money the banking system creates in the form of loans. The only other situations capable of producing a sudden

THE POSSIBILITY THAT A FRACTIONAL-RESERVE FREE-BANKING SYSTEM MAY UNILATERALLY INITIATE CREDIT EXPANSION

Various circumstances make it possible for a fractional-reserve free-banking system to initiate credit expansion in the absence of a corresponding, prior increase in the demand for fiduciary media.

First, we must point out that the monetary equilibrium analysis of modern free-banking theorists contains many of the same limitations as the traditional neoclassical analysis, which, both in a micro- and macroeconomic context, merely deals with the *final* state of social processes (monetary equilibrium), a state to which the rational, maximizing behavior of economic agents (private bankers) supposedly leads. In contrast, the economic analysis of the Austrian School centers on dynamic entrepreneurial processes, rather than on equilibrium. Each entrepreneurial act coordinates and establishes a *tendency* toward equilibrium, which, nevertheless, is never reached, because during the process itself circumstances change and entrepreneurs create new information. Thus, from this dynamic point of view, we cannot accept a static model which, like that of monetary equilibrium, presupposes that immediate, perfect adjustments between the demand for and the supply of fiduciary media take place.

In real life, each banker, according to his insight and entrepreneurial creativity, subjectively interprets the information he receives from the outside world, both in terms of his level of optimism in evaluating the course of economic events, and in terms of the volume of reserves he considers "prudent" with a view to maintaining his solvency. Hence each banker, in an environment of uncertainty, decides each day what volume of fiduciary media he will issue. In the above entrepreneurial process, bankers will clearly commit many errors which will manifest themselves in the unilateral issuance of fiduciary media and will distort the productive structure.

---

rise in the demand for money are exceptional, like wars and natural disasters. Seasonal variations are comparatively less important and a free-banking system with a 100-percent reserve requirement could counteract them with a seasonal transfer of gold and slight price modifications.

Granted, the process itself will tend to reveal and eliminate the errors committed, but only following a period of varying length, and damage to the real productive structure will not be avoided. If we add that, as we saw in the last section, the supply of fiduciary media tends to create its own demand, we see it is highly unlikely that a fractional-reserve free-banking system (or any other market) could reach the "monetary equilibrium" that its theorists so desire. For in the best of cases, private bankers will attempt through a process of trial and error to adjust their supply of fiduciary media to the demand for them, which is unknown to bankers and tends to vary as a consequence of the very issuance of fiduciary media. Hence scholars may debate whether or not the entrepreneurial coordination process will bring the coveted state of "monetary equilibrium" within bankers' reach, but scholars cannot deny that throughout this process innumerable entrepreneurial errors will be committed in the form of the unjustified issuance of fiduciary media, and that these errors will inevitably tend to affect the productive structure by provoking economic crises and recessions, just as the Austrian theory of economic cycles explains.[124]

Second, a large or small group of bankers could also collectively orchestrate the expansion of fiduciary media or decide to merge in order to share and better "manage" their reserves, thus increasing their capacity to expand credit and improve profits.[125] Unless fractional-reserve free-banking theorists wish to prohibit this type of entrepreneurial strategy (which we doubt), it will obviously result in credit expansion and consequent economic recessions. It can be argued that in-concert expansion will tend to correct itself, since, as Selgin maintains, the total increase in interbank clearings will raise the variance in the clearing of debits and credits.[126] However, aside from Selgin's assumption that the total volume of metallic reserves in the banking system remains constant, and

---

[124]See Jörg Guido Hülsmann, "Free Banking and Free Bankers," *Review of Austrian Economics* 9, no. 1 (1996): 3–53, esp. pp. 40–41.

[125]Remember our analysis contained in pages 664–71. See Laidler, "Free Banking Theory," p. 197.

[126]Selgin, *The Theory of Free Banking*, p. 82.

despite the doubts of many authors regarding the effectiveness of Selgin's mechanism,[127] even if we allow for the sake of argument that Selgin is correct, it can still be argued that the adjustment will never be perfect nor immediate, and therefore in-concert expansion and mergers may provoke significant increases in the supply of fiduciary media, thus triggering the processes which set economic cycles in motion.

Third and last, with every increase in the overall stock of specie (gold) banks keep as a "prudent" reserve, a fractional-reserve free-banking system would stimulate growth in the issuance of fiduciary media which does *not* correspond to prior rises in demand. If we remember that the world stock of gold has been mounting at an annual rate of 1 to 5 percent[128] due to the increased world production of gold, it is clear that this factor alone will permit private bankers to issue fiduciary media at a rate of 1 to 5 percent per year, regardless of the demand for them. (Such creation of money will produce an expansion followed by a recession.)[129]

In conclusion, significant (fiduciary) inflationary processes[130] and severe economic recessions[131] may occur in any fractional-reserve free-banking system.

---

[127]See, for example, Schwartz, "The Theory of Free Banking," p. 3.

[128]Skousen, *The Structure of Production*, chap. 8, pp. 269 and 359.

[129]We cannot rule out even greater credit expansion in the event of shocks in the supply of gold, though Selgin tends to play down the importance of this possibility. Selgin, *The Theory of Free Banking*, pp. 129–33.

[130]Let us remember that for Mises (see footnote 120 above): "Banking freedom *per se* cannot be said to make a return to gross inflationary policy impossible," especially if an inflationary ideology prevails among economic agents:

> Many authors believe that the instigation of the banks' behavior comes from outside, that certain events induce them to pump more fiduciary media into circulation and that they would behave differently if these circumstances failed to appear. I was also inclined to this view in the first edition of my book on monetary theory. I could not understand why the banks didn't learn from experience. I thought they would certainly persist in a policy of caution and restraint, if they were not led by outside circumstances to abandon it. Only later did

The Theory of "Monetary Equilibrium" in Free Banking Rests on an Exclusively Macroeconomic Analysis

We must point out that the analysis of modern free-banking theorists ignores the *microeconomic* effects which arise from increases and decreases in the supply of and demand for fiduciary media instigated by the banking industry. In other words, even if we admit for the sake of argument that the origin of all evil lies, as these theorists suppose, in unexpected changes in economic agents' demand for fiduciary media, it is clear that the supply of fiduciary media which the banking system supposedly generates to adjust to changes in the demand for them does not instantaneously reach precisely those economic agents whose valuation of the possession of new fiduciary media has altered. Instead this supply flows into the market at certain specific points and in a particular manner: in the form of loans granted via a reduction in the interest rate and initially received by individual businessmen and investors who tend to use them to initiate new, more capital-intensive investment projects which distort the productive structure.

Therefore it is unsurprising that modern free-banking theorists overlook the Austrian theory of business cycles, since

---

> I become convinced that it was useless to look to an outside stimulus for the change in the conduct of the banks. . . . We can readily understand that the banks issuing fiduciary media, in order to improve their chances for profit, may be ready to expand the volume of credit granted and the number of notes issued. What calls for special explanation is why attempts are made again and again to improve general economic conditions by the expansion of circulation credit in spite of the spectacular failure of such efforts in the past. The answer must run as follows: According to the prevailing ideology of businessman and economist-politician, the reduction of the interest rate is considered an essential goal of economic policy. Moreover, the expansion of circulation credit is assumed to be the appropriate means to achieve this goal. (Mises, *On the Manipulation of Money and Credit*, pp. 135–36)

[131]"Crises have reappeared every few years since banks . . . began to play an important role in the economic life of people." Ibid., p. 134.

this theory does not fit in with their analysis of the issuance of fiduciary media in a fractional-reserve free-banking system. These theorists thus take refuge in an exclusively *macroeconomic* analysis (monetarist or Keynesian, depending on the case) and, at most, use instruments which, like the equation of exchange or the "general price level," actually tend to conceal the truly relevant microeconomic phenomena (variations in relative prices and intertemporal discoordination in the behavior of economic agents) which occur in an economy upon the expansion of credit and growth in the quantity of fiduciary media.

In normal market processes, the supply of consumer goods and services tends to vary along with the demand for them, and new goods generally reach precisely those consumers whose subjective valuation of them has improved. However where newly-created fiduciary media are concerned, the situation is radically different: an increased supply of fiduciary media never immediately and *directly* reaches the pockets of those economic agents whose demand for them may have risen. Instead, the money goes through a lengthy, cumbersome temporal process, or transition phase, during which it first passes through the hands of many other economic agents and distorts the entire productive structure.

When bankers create new fiduciary media, they do not deliver them directly to those economic agents who may desire more. On the contrary, bankers grant loans to entrepreneurs who receive the new money and invest the entire amount without a thought to the proportion in which the final holders of fiduciary media will wish to consume and save or invest. Hence it is certainly possible that a portion of the new fiduciary media (supposedly issued in response to increased demand) may ultimately be spent on consumer goods, and thereby push up their relative price. We know (chap. 7, p. 552) that according to Hayek:

> [S]o long as any part of the additional income thus created
> is spent on consumer's goods (*i.e.*, unless all of it is saved),
> the prices of consumer's goods must rise permanently in
> relation to those of various kinds of input. And this, as will
> by now be evident, cannot be lastingly without effect on the

relative prices of the various kinds of input and on the methods of production that will appear profitable.[132]

Hayek clarifies his position even further:

> All that is required to make our analysis applicable is that, when incomes are increased by investment, the share of the additional income spent on consumer's goods during any period of time should be larger than the proportion by which the new investment adds to the output of consumer's goods during the same period of time. And there is of course no reason to expect that more than a fraction of the new income [created by credit expansion], and certainly not as much as has been newly invested, will be saved, because this would mean that practically all the income earned from the new investment would have to be saved.[133]

As a graphic illustration of our argument, let us suppose that the demand for fiduciary media increases, while the proportion in which economic agents wish to consume and invest remains unchanged.[134] Under these conditions, economic agents must reduce their monetary demand for consumer goods, sell bonds and other financial assets and, especially, reinvest less money in the different stages of the productive process until they can accumulate the greater volume of bank deposits they wish to hold. Therefore if we suppose that the social rate of time preference has not altered, and we use a simplified version of the triangular diagrams from chapter 5 to represent society's real productive structure, we see that in

---

[132]Hayek, *The Pure Theory of Capital*, p. 378.

[133]Ibid., p. 394. This appears to be the extreme case of an increase in saving which manifests itself entirely as a rise in balances of fiduciary media, the case Selgin and White use to illustrate their theory. See Selgin and White, "In Defense of Fiduciary Media—or, We are *Not* Devo(lutionists), We are Misesians!" pp. 104–05.

[134]Such a situation is definitely possible, as Selgin and White themselves recognize when they affirm: "An increase in *savings* is neither necessary nor sufficient to warrant an increase in fiduciary media." Selgin and White, "In Defense of Fiduciary Media—or, We are *Not* Devo(lutionists), We are Misesians!" p. 104.

Chart VIII-1 the increase in the demand for fiduciary media shifts the hypotenuse of the triangle toward the left. This movement reflects a drop in the monetary demand for consumer and investment goods, since the proportion of one to the other (or time preference) has not varied. In this chart, surface "A" represents economic agents' new demand for (or "hoarding" of) fiduciary media (see Chart VIII-1).

The fundamental conclusion of the theory of monetary equilibrium in a fractional-reserve free-banking system is that banks would respond to this rise in the demand for fiduciary media by expanding their issuance by a volume equal to that of the new demand (represented by surface "A"), and the productive structure, as shown in Chart VIII-2, would remain intact (see Chart VIII-2).

Nonetheless we must remember that banks do not directly transfer the new fiduciary media they create to their final users (the economic agents whose demand for fiduciary media has increased by the volume represented by surface "A" in Chart VIII-1). Instead, the deposits are lent to entrepreneurs, who spend it on investment goods and thereby initially create a more capital-intensive structure, which we represent in Chart VIII-3.

Nevertheless this more capital-intensive productive structure cannot be maintained in the long term. For once the new fiduciary media reach their final recipients (who in the very beginning accumulated the bank money they needed, as surface "A" in Chart VIII-1 indicates), they will spend them, according to our postulate of unchanging time preference, on consumer and investment goods in a proportion equal to that shown in Charts VIII-1 and VIII-2. If we superimpose Chart VIII-3 on Chart VIII-2 (see Chart VIII-4), the distortion of the productive structure becomes clear. Shaded area "B" represents the investment projects entrepreneurs have launched in error, since all of the fiduciary media banks have issued to adjust to the increase in the demand for them have been channeled into investment loans.[135] Shaded area "C" (with a surface identical

---

[135]Selgin and White implicitly acknowledge this point when they assert:

> Benefits accrue . . . to bank borrowers who enjoy a more ample
> supply of intermediated credit, and to everyone who works

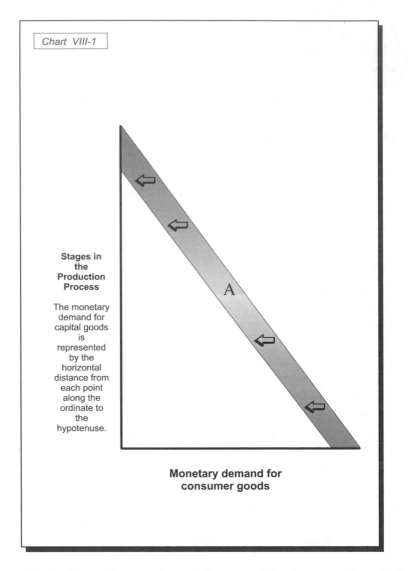

Chart VIII-1

**Stages in
the
Production
Process**

The monetary
demand for
capital goods
is
represented
by the
horizontal
distance from
each point
along the
ordinate to
the
hypotenuse.

A

**Monetary demand for
consumer goods**

to "B") reflects the portion of the new fiduciary media which
the final holders spend on the goods closest to consumption.
The productive structure regains the proportions shown in
Chart VIII-1, but only following the inevitable, painful readjustments which the Austrian theory of economic cycles

with the economy's consequently larger stock of capital equipment. (Selgin and White, "In Defense of Fiduciary Media—or,
We are *Not* Devo(lutionists), We are Misesians!" p. 94)

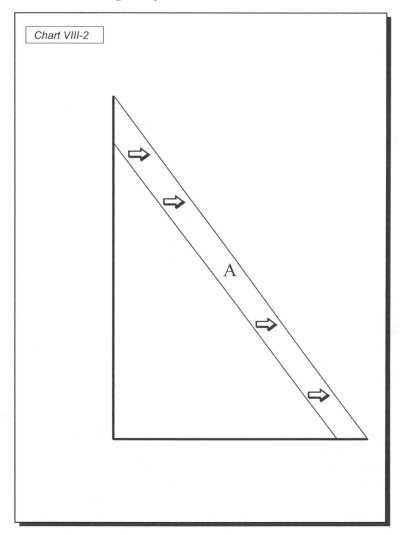

Chart VIII-2

explains and which a free-banking system, as we have just seen, would be incapable of preventing. Therefore we must conclude, in contrast to what Selgin and White suggest,[136] that even if the expansion of fiduciary media fully matches a prior increase in the demand for them, it will provoke the typical cyclical effects predicted by the theory of circulation credit.

---

[136] We deny that an increase in fiduciary media *matched by an increased demand to hold fiduciary media* is disequilibrating or sets in motion the Austrian business cycle. (Ibid., pp. 102–03)

THE CONFUSION BETWEEN THE CONCEPT OF SAVING
AND THAT OF THE DEMAND FOR MONEY

The attempt to recover at least the essence of the old "needs of trade" doctrine and to show that a fractional-reserve free-banking system would not trigger economic cycles has led George A. Selgin to defend a thesis similar to the one John Maynard Keynes presents in connection with bank deposits. Indeed let us remember that, according to Keynes, anyone who holds additional money from a loan is "saving":

> Moreover, the savings which result from this decision are just as genuine as any other savings. No one can be compelled to own the additional money corresponding to the new bank-credit, unless he deliberately prefers to hold more money rather than some other form of wealth.[137]

George Selgin's position resembles Keynes's. Selgin believes public demand for cash balances in the form of banknotes and deposit accounts reflects the desire to offer short-term loans for the same amount through the banking system. Indeed, Selgin states:

> To hold inside money is to engage in voluntary saving. . . . Whenever a bank expands its liabilities in the process of making new loans and investments, it is the holders of the liabilities who are the ultimate lenders of credit, and what they lend are the real resources they could acquire if, instead of holding money, they spent it. When the expansion or contraction of bank liabilities proceeds in such a way as to be at all times in agreement with changing demands for inside money, the quantity of real capital funds supplied to borrowers by the banks is equal to the quantity voluntarily offered to the banks by the public.

---

[137]Keynes, *The General Theory of Employment, Interest and Money*, p. 83. This thesis, which we covered in chapter 7, stems from the tautology of equating saving with investment, an error which underlies all of Keynes's work and which, according to Benjamin Anderson, is tantamount to equating inflation with saving.

Under these conditions, banks are simply intermediaries of loanable funds.[138]

Nonetheless it is entirely possible that the public may simultaneously increase their balances of fiduciary media and their demand for consumer goods and services, if they decide to cut back on their investments. For economic agents can employ their money balances in any of the following three ways: they can spend them on consumer goods and services; they can spend them on investments; or they can hold them as cash balances or fiduciary media. There are no other options. The decision on the proportion to spend on consumption or investment is distinct and independent from the decision on the amount of fiduciary media and cash to hold. Thus we cannot conclude, as Selgin does, that any money balance is equal to "savings," since a rise in the balance of fiduciary media may very well depend on a drop in investment spending (via the sale of securities on the stock market, for instance) which makes it possible to increase final monetary expenditure on consumer goods and services. Under these circumstances an individual's savings would drop, while his balance of fiduciary media would rise. Therefore it is incorrect to qualify as savings all increases in fiduciary media.

To maintain, as Selgin does, that "every holder of demand liabilities issued by a free bank grants that bank a loan for the value of his holdings"[139] is the same as asserting that any creation of money, in the form of deposits or notes, by a bank in a fractional-reserve free-banking system ultimately amounts to an *a posteriori* concession of a loan to the bank for the amount created. However the bank generates loans from nothing and offers additional purchasing power to entrepreneurs, who receive the loans without a thought to the true desires of all other economic agents regarding consumption and investment, when these other individuals will ultimately become the final holders of the fiduciary media the bank creates. Hence it is entirely possible, if the social time preference on

---

[138]Selgin, *The Theory of Free Banking*, pp. 54–55.

[139]Selgin, "The Stability and Efficiency of Money Supply under Free Banking," p. 440.

consumption and investment remains unchanged, that the new fiduciary media the bank creates may be used to step up spending on consumer goods, thus pushing up the relative prices of this type of good.

Fractional-reserve free-banking theorists generally consider any note or deposit a bank issues to be a "financial asset" which corresponds to a loan. From a legal standpoint, this notion involves serious problems, which we examined in the first three chapters. Economically speaking, the error of these theorists lies in their belief that money is a "financial asset" which represents the voluntary saving of an economic agent who "loans" present goods in exchange for future goods.[140] Nevertheless *money is itself a present good*,[141] and the possession of cash balances (or deposits) says nothing about the proportions in which the economic agent wishes to consume and invest. Thus increases and decreases in his

---

[140]How is it conceivable that banknotes and deposits, which are money in themselves, are also "financial assets" that signify that the bearer has turned over money to a third party today in exchange for a certain amount of money in the future? The idea that notes and deposits are "financial assets" exposes the fact that banks in a fractional-reserve banking system duplicate means of payment *ex nihilo*: there is the money lent to and enjoyed by a third party, and there is the financial asset which represents the operation and is *also* considered money. To put it another way, financial assets are titles or certificates which signify that someone has given up present money on handing it over to another in exchange for a larger quantity of future money. If, at the same time, financial assets are considered money (by the bearer), then an obvious, inflationary duplication of means of payment takes place in the market which originates in the granting of a new loan without anyone's having to save the same amount first.

[141]Money is a perfectly liquid present good. With respect to the banking system as a whole, fiduciary media are not "financial assets," since *they are never withdrawn from the system*, but circulate indefinitely and, hence, are money (or to be more precise, perfect money substitutes). In contrast, a financial asset represents the handing over of present goods (generally money) in exchange for future goods (also generally monetary units) on a specified date, and its creation corresponds to a rise in an economic agent's real saving. See Gerald P. O'Driscoll, "Money: Menger's Evolutionary Theory," *History of Political Economy* 4, no. 18 (1986): 601–16.

money balances are perfectly compatible with different combinations of simultaneous increases and decreases in the proportions in which he consumes or invests. In fact his balances of fiduciary media may rise simultaneously with his spending on consumer goods and services, if he only disinvests some of the resources saved and invested in the past. As Hans-Hermann Hoppe points out, the supply of and demand for money determine its price or purchasing power, while the supply of and demand for "present goods" in exchange for "future goods" determine the interest rate or social rate of time preference and the overall volume of saving and investment.[142]

Saving always requires that an economic agent reduce his consumption (i.e., sacrifice), thus freeing real goods. Saving does not arise from a simple increase in monetary units. That is, the mere fact that the new money is not immediately spent on consumer goods does not mean it is saved. Selgin defends

---

[142] First off, it is plainly false to say that the holding of money, i.e., the act of not spending it, is equivalent to saving. . . . In fact, saving is not-consuming, and the demand for money has nothing to do with saving *or* not-saving. The demand for money is the unwillingness to buy or rent non-money goods—and these include consumer goods (present goods) *and* capital goods (future goods). Not-spending money is to purchase *neither* consumer goods *nor* investment goods. Contrary to Selgin, then, matters are as follows: Individuals may employ their monetary assets in one of three ways. They can spend them on consumer goods; they can spend them on investment; or they can keep them in the form of cash. There are no other alternatives. . . . [U]nless time preference is assumed to have changed at the same time, *real* consumption and *real* investment will remain the same as before: the additional money demand is satisfied by reducing nominal consumption *and* investment spending in accordance with the same pre-existing consumption/investment proportion, driving the money prices of both consumer as well as producer goods down and leaving real consumption and investment at precisely their old levels. (Hans-Hermann Hoppe, "How is Fiat Money Possible?—or The Devolution of Money and Credit," in *Review of Austrian Economics* 7, no. 2 (1994): 72–73)

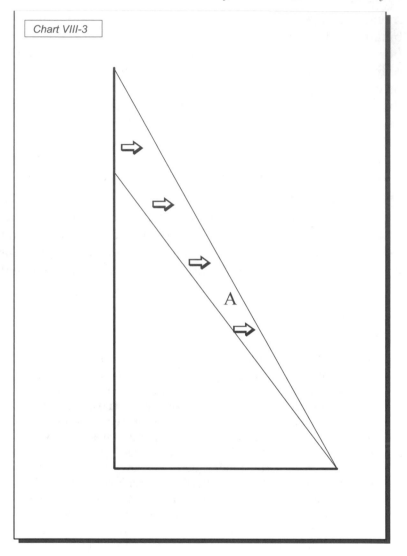

Chart VIII-3

this position when he criticizes Machlup's view[143] that the expansionary granting of loans creates purchasing power which no one has first withdrawn from consumption (i.e.,

---

[143]Selgin's unjustified criticism of Machlup appears in footnote 20 on p. 184 of his book, *The Theory of Free Banking*. Selgin would consider the entire volume of credit shown by surface "A" in our Chart VIII-2 "transfer credit," because it is "credit granted by banks in recognition of people's desire to abstain from spending by holding balances of inside

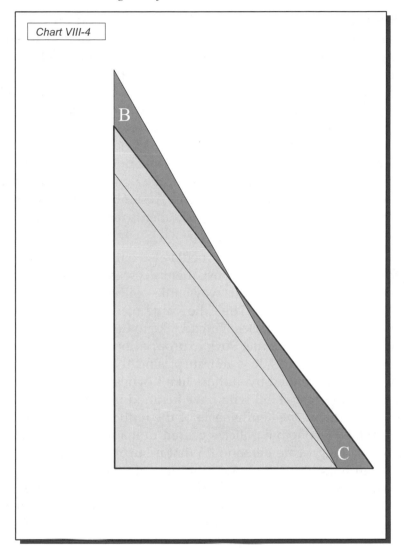

Chart VIII-4

saved). For credit to leave the productive structure undistorted, it logically must originate from *prior* saving, which
provides present goods an investor has truly saved. If such a

money" (ibid., p. 60). In contrast, for Machlup (and for us), at least surface "B" of Chart VIII-4 would represent "created credit" or credit
expansion, since economic agents do not restrict their consumption by
the volume shown by surface "C".

sacrifice in consumption has not taken place, and investment is financed by created credit, then the productive structure is invariably distorted, even if the newly-created fiduciary media correspond to a previous rise in the demand for them. Hence Selgin is obliged to redefine the concepts of saving and credit creation. He claims saving occurs *ipso facto* the moment new fiduciary media are created, provided their initial holder could spend them on consumer goods and does not. Selgin also maintains that credit expansion does not generate cycles if it tends to match a prior increase in the demand for fiduciary media. In short these arguments resemble those Keynes expresses in his *General Theory*, arguments refuted long ago, as we saw in chapter 7.

The creation of fiduciary media also entails an increase in the money supply and a consequent decrease in the purchasing power of money. In this way banks collectively and almost imperceptibly "expropriate" the value of citizens' monetary units. It certainly smacks of a bad joke to declare that the economic agents who suffer such expropriation are actually (voluntarily?) "saving." It is not surprising that these doctrines have been defended by authors like Keynes, Tobin, Pointdexter and, in general, all who have justified inflationism, credit expansion and the "euthanasia of the rentier" for the sake of aggressive economic policies geared to insure an "adequate" level of "aggregate demand." What *is* surprising, however, is that authors like Selgin and Horwitz, who belong (or at least belonged) to the Austrian School and thus should be more aware of the dangers involved, have had no alternative but to resort to this sort of argument in order to justify their "fractional-reserve free-banking" system.[144]

----

[144]As an additional advantage of the system he proposes, Selgin mentions that economic agents who maintain cash balances in the form of fiduciary media created in a free-banking system can obtain a financial yield on their money and use a series of banking facilities (payment, bookkeeping, cashier, etc.) "free of charge." However Selgin fails to mention certain costs of fractional-reserve free banking, such as artificial booms, malinvestment of resources, and economic crises. He also fails to touch on what we definitely consider the highest cost: the harmful effects of the violation of legal principles in a free-banking system give rise to a

THE PROBLEM WITH HISTORICAL ILLUSTRATIONS OF FREE-BANKING SYSTEMS

Neo-banking authors devote strong efforts to historical studies which they intend to support the thesis that a free-banking system would protect economies from cycles of boom and depression, owing to the "monetary equilibrium" mechanism. Nevertheless the empirical studies produced thus far have not focused on whether free-banking systems have prevented credit expansion, artificial booms and economic recessions. Instead they have centered on whether *bank crises and runs* have been more or less frequent and severe in this type of system than in a central-banking system (which is obviously quite a different issue).[145]

---

tendency toward the establishment of a central bank as a lender of last resort designed to support bankers and create the liquidity necessary to insure citizens the recovery of their deposits at any time. As for the supposed "advantage" of receiving interest on deposits and "free" cashier and bookkeeping services, there is no telling whether, in net terms, the interest economic agents would earn on funds truly saved and lent in a system with a 100-percent reserve requirement, less the cost of the corresponding deposit, cashier and bookkeeping services, would be equal to, higher than or lower than the real interest they currently receive on their demand checking accounts (minus the decline which chronically affects the purchasing power of money in the current banking system).

[145]To date, theorists have carefully examined around sixty free-banking systems from the past. The conclusion they have generally drawn follows:

> Bank failure rates were lower in systems free of restrictions on capital, branching and diversification (e.g., Scotland and Canada) than in systems restricted in these respects (England and the United States).

However this matter is irrelevant from the standpoint of our thesis, since the above studies do not specify whether cycles of expansion and economic recession were set in motion. See *The Experience of Free Banking*, Kevin Dowd, ed., pp. 39–46. See also Kurt Schuler and Lawrence H. White, "Free Banking History," *The New Palgrave Dictionary of Money and Finance*, Peter Newman, Murray Milgate and John Eatwell, eds. (London: Macmillan, 1992), vol. 2, pp. 198–200. The above excerpt appears on p. 108 of this last article.

In fact George A. Selgin looks at the occurrence of bank runs in different historical free-banking systems versus certain systems controlled by a central bank and reaches the conclusion that bank crises were more numerous and acute in the second case.[146] Moreover the main thesis of the main neo-banking book on free banking in Scotland consists entirely of the argument that the Scottish banking system, which was "freer" than the English one, was more "stable" and subject to fewer financial disturbances.[147]

However, as Murray N. Rothbard has indicated, the fact that, in relative terms, fewer banks failed in the Scottish free-banking system than in the English system does not necessarily mean the former was superior.[148] Indeed bank failures have been practically eliminated from current central-banking systems, and this does not make such systems better than a free-banking system subject to legal principles. It actually makes them worse. For bank failures in no way indicate that a system functions poorly, but rather that a healthy, spontaneous reversion process has begun to operate in response to fractional-reserve banking, which is a legal privilege and an attack on the market. Therefore whenever a fractional-reserve free-banking system is not regularly accompanied by bank failures and suspensions of payments, we must suspect the existence of *institutional factors which shield banks from the normal consequences of fractional-reserve banking and fulfill a role similar to the one the central bank currently fulfills as lender of last resort.* In the case of Scotland, banks had so encouraged the use of their notes in economic transactions that practically no one demanded payment of them in gold, and those who occasionally requested specie at the window of their banks met with general disapproval and enormous pressure from

---

[146]George A. Selgin, "Are Banking Crises a Free-Market Phenomenon?" a manuscript presented at the regional meeting of the Mont Pèlerin Society, Rio de Janeiro, September 5–8, 1993, pp. 26–27.

[147]White, *Free Banking in Britain.*

[148]Rothbard, "The Myth of Free Banking in Scotland," *Review of Austrian Economics* 2 (1988): 229–45, esp. p. 232.

their bankers, who accused them of "disloyalty" and threatened to make it difficult for them to obtain loans in the future. Furthermore, as Professor Sidney G. Checkland has shown,[149] the Scottish fractional-reserve free-banking system still went through frequent, successive stages of credit expansion and contraction, which gave rise to economic cycles of boom and recession in 1770, 1772, 1778, 1793, 1797, 1802–1803, 1809–1810, 1810–1811, 1818–1819, 1825–1826, 1836–1837, 1839, and 1845–1847. In other words, even though in relative terms fewer bank runs occurred in Scotland than in England, the successive stages of boom and depression were equally severe, and despite its highly praised free-banking system, Scotland was not free from credit expansion, artificial booms and the subsequent stages of serious economic recession.[150]

The nineteenth-century Chilean financial system provides another historical illustration of the inadequacy of fractional-reserve free-banking systems to prevent artificial expansion and economic recessions. In fact during the first half of the nineteenth century, Chile had no central bank and implemented a 100-percent reserve requirement in banking. For several decades its citizens firmly resisted attempts to introduce a fractional-reserve banking system, and during those years they enjoyed great economic and financial stability. The situation began to change in 1853, when the Chilean government hired Jean-Gustav Courcelle-Seneuil (1813–1892), one of the most prominent French fractional-reserve free-banking theorists, as professor of economics at the University of Santiago de Chile.

---

[149]Sidney G. Checkland, *Scottish Banking: A History, 1695–1973* (Glasgow: Collins, 1975). White himself recognizes in his book that Checkland's is the definitive work on the history of the Scottish banking system.

[150]Though much work remains to be done, historical studies on fractional-reserve free-banking systems with very few (if any) legal restrictions and no central bank appear to confirm that these systems were capable of triggering significant credit expansion and provoking economic recessions. This is what took place, for instance, in Italian and Spanish financial markets in the fourteenth and sixteenth centuries (see chapter 2, section 3), as Carlo M. Cipolla and others have revealed, as well as in Scotland and Chile, as we indicate in the text.

Courcelle-Seneuil's influence in Chile during the ten years he taught there was so great that in 1860 a law permitting the establishment of fractional-reserve free banking (with no central bank) was enacted. At this point the traditional financial stability of the Chilean system gave way to stages of artificial expansion (based on the concession of new loans), followed by bank failures and economic crises. The convertibility of the paper currency was suspended on several occasions (1865, 1867, and 1879), and a period of inflation and serious economic, financial and social maladjustment began. This period resides in the collective memory of Chileans and explains why they continue to mistakenly associate financial disturbances with the doctrinal economic liberalism of Courcelle-Seneuil.[151]

---

[151]Albert O. Hirschman, in his article, "Courcelle-Seneuil, Jean-Gustav," *The New Palgrave: A Dictionary of Economics,* John Eatwell, Murray Milgate, and Peter Newman (London: Macmillan, 1992), vol. 1, pp. 706–07, states that Chileans have even come to demonize Courcelle-Seneuil and to blame him for all the economic and financial evils which befell Chile in the nineteenth century. Murray N. Rothbard believes this demonization is unjust and stems from the fact that the poor functioning of the free-banking system Courcelle-Seneuil introduced in Chile also discredited the deregulating initiatives he launched in other areas (such as mining), when these efforts had a positive effect. See Murray N. Rothbard, "The Other Side of the Coin: Free Banking in Chile," *Austrian Economics Newsletter* (Winter, 1989): 1–4. George Selgin responds to Rothbard's article on free banking in Chile in his paper, "Short-Changed in Chile: The Truth about the Free-Banking Episode," *Austrian Economics Newsletter* (Spring–Winter, 1990): 5ff. Selgin himself acknowledges that the period of free banking in Chile from 1866 to 1874 was an "era of remarkable growth and progress," during which "Chile's railroad and telegraph systems were developed, the port of Valparaiso was enlarged and improved, and fiscal reserves increased by one-quarter." According to the Austrian theory, all of these phenomena are actually symptoms of the substantial credit expansion which took place during those years and was ultimately bound to reverse in the form of a recession (as, in fact, occurred). However Selgin attributes the subsequent bank crises (but not the recessions) to the Chilean government's maintenance of an artificial parity between gold and silver. When gold rose in value, this parity resulted in the massive outflow of gold reserves from the country (see Selgin, "Short-Changed in Chile," pp. 5, 6 and footnote 3 on p. 7).

Moreover the fact that various historical studies appear to indicate that fewer bank runs and crises arose in free-banking systems than in central-banking systems does not mean the former were completely free of such episodes. Selgin himself mentions at least three instances in which acute bank crises devastated free-banking systems: Scotland in 1797, Canada in 1837, and Australia in 1893.[152] If Rothbard is correct, and in the rest of the cases institutional restrictions played the role of central bank to at least some extent, then the number of bank crises might have been much larger in the absence of these restrictions.[153] At any rate we must not consider the elimination of bank crises to be the definitive criterion for determining which banking system is the best. If this were the case, even the most radical fractional-reserve free-banking theorists would be obliged to admit that the best banking system is that which requires the maintenance of a 100 percent reserve, since by definition this is the only system which in all circumstances prevents bank crises and runs.[154]

In short, historical experience does not appear to support the thesis of modern fractional-reserve free-banking theorists. Bank credit expansion gave rise to cycles of boom and depression in even the least controlled free-banking systems, which were not free from bank runs and failures. The recognition of this fact has led certain neo-banking authors, such as Stephen Horwitz, to insist that though historical evidence against their views is of some significance, it does not serve to refute the theory that fractional-reserve free banking produces only

---

[152]Selgin, "Are Banking Crises a Free-Market Phenomenon?" Table 1(b), p. 27.

[153]Raymond Bogaert appears to confirm Rothbard's thesis. According to Bogaert, we have documented proof that of 163 banks created in Venice starting at the end of the Middle Ages, at least 93 failed. Raymond Bogaert, *Banques et banquiers dans les cités grecques*, p. 392 footnote 513.

[154]Thus Selgin himself recognizes: "A 100-percent reserve banking crisis is an impossibility." See George A. Selgin, "Are Banking Crises a Free-Market Phenomenon?" p. 2.

benign effects, since strictly theoretical procedures must be used to refute this theory.[155]

IGNORANCE OF LEGAL ARGUMENTS

Theorists of fractional-reserve banking tend to exclude legal considerations from their analysis. They fail to see that the study of banking issues must be chiefly multidisciplinary, and they overlook the close theoretical and practical connection between the legal and economic aspects of all social processes.

Thus free-banking theorists lose sight of the fact that fractional-reserve banking involves a logical impossibility from a legal standpoint. Indeed at the beginning of this book we explained that any bank loan granted against demand-deposit funds results in the *dual availability* of the same quantity of money: the same money is accessible to the original depositor and to the borrower who receives the loan. Obviously the same thing cannot be available to two people simultaneously, and to grant the availability of something to a second person while it remains available to the first is to act fraudulently.[156]

---

[155]With respect to methodology, we fully concur with Horwitz's position (see his "Misreading the 'Myth', p. 167). However it is curious that an entire school which emerged with the analysis of the supposedly beneficial results of the Scottish free-banking system has been forced to stop relying on historical studies of the free-banking system. Stephen Horwitz, commenting on Rothbard's review of free-banking history, concludes:

> If Rothbard is correct about them, we should look more sceptically at Scotland as an example. But noting the existence of government interference cannot by itself defeat the theoretical argument. The Scottish banks were neither perfectly free nor a conclusive test case. The theory of free banking still stands, and its opponents need to tackle it on *both* the historical and the theoretical level to refute it. (p. 168)

This is precisely what we have attempted in this book.

[156]Hoppe, "How is Fiat Money Possible?—or, The Devolution of Money and Credit," p. 67.

Such an act clearly constitutes misappropriation and fraud, offenses committed during at least the early stages in the development of the modern banking system, as we saw in chapter 2.

Once bankers obtained from governments the privilege of operating with a fractional reserve, from the standpoint of positive law this banking method ceased to be a crime, and when citizens act in a system backed in this way by law, we must rule out the possibility of criminal fraud. Nevertheless, as we saw in chapters 1 through 3, this privilege in no way provides the monetary bank-deposit contract with an appropriate legal nature. Quite the opposite is true. In most cases this contract is null and void, due to a discrepancy concerning its *cause*: depositors view the transaction as a deposit, while bankers view it as a loan. According to general legal principles, whenever the parties involved in an exchange hold conflicting beliefs as to the nature of the contract entered into, the contract is null and void.

Moreover even if depositors and bankers agreed that their transaction amounts to a loan, the legal nature of the monetary bank-deposit contract would be no more appropriate. From an economic perspective, we have seen that it is theoretically impossible for banks to return, under all circumstances, the deposits entrusted to them beyond the amount of reserves they hold. Furthermore this impossibility is aggravated to the extent that fractional-reserve banking itself tends to provoke economic crises and recessions which repetitively endanger banks' solvency. According to general legal principles, contracts which are *impossible* to put into practice are also null and void. Only a 100-percent reserve requirement, which would guarantee the return of all deposits at any moment, or the support of a central bank, which would supply all necessary liquidity in times of difficulty, could make such "loan" contracts (with an agreement for the return of the face value at any time) *possible* and therefore valid.

The argument that monetary bank-deposit contracts are impossible to honor only periodically and under extreme circumstances cannot redeem the legal nature of the contract either, since fractional-reserve banking constitutes a breach of public order and harms third parties. In fact, because fractional-reserve banking expands loans without the support of real saving, it distorts the productive structure and therefore leads loan recipients, entrepreneurs deceived by the increased flexibility of credit terms, to make ultimately unprofitable investments. With the eruption of the inevitable economic crisis, businessmen are forced to halt and liquidate these investment projects. As a result, a high economic, social, and personal cost must be borne by not only the entrepreneurs "guilty" of the errors, but also all other economic agents involved in the production process (workers, suppliers, etc.).

Hence we may not argue, as White, Selgin, and others do, that in a free society bankers and their customers should be free to make whatever contractual agreements they deem most appropriate.[157] For even an agreement found satisfactory by both parties is invalid if it represents a misuse of law or harms third parties and therefore disrupts the public order. This applies to monetary bank deposits which are held with a fractional reserve and in which, contrary to the norm, both parties are fully aware of the true legal nature and implications of the agreement.

Hans-Hermann Hoppe[158] explains that this type of contract is detrimental to third parties in at least three different ways. *First*, credit expansion increases the money supply and thereby diminishes the purchasing power of the monetary units held by all others with cash balances, individuals whose monetary units thus drop in buying power in relation to the value they would have had in the absence of credit expansion. *Second*, depositors in general are harmed, since the credit expansion process reduces the probability that, in the absence of a central bank, they will be able to recover all of the monetary units originally deposited; if a central bank exists, depositors are wronged in that, even if they are guaranteed the

---

[157]See, for example, White, *Competition and Currency* (New York: New York University Press, 1989), pp. 55–56, and Selgin, "Short-Changed in Chile," p. 5.

[158]Hoppe, "How is Fiat Money Possible?—or, The Devolution of Money and Credit," pp. 70–71.

repayment of their deposits at any time, no one can guarantee they will be repaid in monetary units of undiminished purchasing power. *Third*, all other borrowers and economic agents are harmed, since the creation of fiduciary credit and its injection into the economic system jeopardizes the entire credit system and distorts the productive structure, thus increasing the risk that entrepreneurs will launch projects which will fail in the process of their completion and cause untold human suffering when credit expansion ushers in the stage of economic recession.[159]

In a free-banking system, when the purchasing power of money declines in relation to the value money would have were credit not expanded in a fractional-reserve environment, participants (depositors and, especially, bankers) act to the detriment of third parties. The very definition of money reveals that any manipulation of it, society's *universal* medium of exchange, will exert harmful effects on almost all third-party participants throughout the economic system. Therefore it does not matter whether or not depositors, bankers, and borrowers voluntarily reach specific agreements if, through fractional-reserve banking, such agreements influence money and harm the public in general (third parties). Such damage renders the contract null and void, due to its

---

[159]The multidisciplinary nature inherent in the critical analysis of the fractional-reserve banking system and the resulting importance of both legal and economic considerations in this analysis not only comprise the focal point of this book; Walter Block also highlights them in his article, "Fractional Reserve Banking: An Interdisciplinary Perspective," published as chapter 3 of *Man, Economy, and Liberty: Essays in Honor of Murray N. Rothbard*, Walter Block and Llewellyn H. Rockwell, Jr., eds. (Auburn, Ala.: Ludwig von Mises Institute, 1988), pp. 24–32. Block points out the curious fact that no theorist from the modern, Fractional-Reserve Free-Banking School has built a critical, systematic case against the proposal of a banking system with a 100-percent reserve requirement. In fact, except for a few comments from Horwitz, neo-banking theorists have yet to even attempt to show that a banking system with a 100-percent reserve requirement would fail to guarantee "monetary equilibrium" and an absence of economic cycles. See Horwitz, "Keynes' Special Theory," pp. 431–32, footnote 18.

disruption of the public order.[160] Economically speaking, the qualitative effects of credit expansion are identical to those of the criminal act of counterfeiting banknotes and coins, an offense covered, for instance, by articles 386–389 of the new Spanish Penal Code.[161] Both acts entail the creation of money, the redistribution of income in favor of a few citizens and to the detriment of all others, and the distortion of the productive structure. Nonetheless, from a quantitative standpoint, only credit expansion can increase the money supply at a fast enough pace and on a large enough scale to feed an artificial boom and provoke a recession. In comparison with the credit expansion of fractional-reserve banking and the manipulation of money by governments and central banks, the criminal act of counterfeiting currency is child's play with practically imperceptible social consequences.

The above legal considerations have not failed to influence White, Selgin, and other modern free-banking theorists, who have proposed, as a last line of defense to guarantee the stability of their system, that "free" banks establish a "safeguard" clause on their notes and deposits, a clause to inform customers that the bank may decide at any moment to suspend or postpone the return of deposits or the payment of notes in specie.[162] Clearly the introduction of this clause would mean

---

[160]Our position on this point is even more radical than the one Alberto Benegas Lynch takes in his book, *Poder y razón razonable* (Buenos Aires and Barcelona: Librería "El Ateneo" *Editorial*, 1992), pp. 313–14.

[161]   The following shall be punishable by a prison term of eight to
         twelve years and a fine of up to ten times the face value of the
         currency: 1. The creation of counterfeit currency. (Article 386
         of the new Spanish Penal Code)

It is important to note that credit expansion, like the counterfeiting of money, inflicts particularly diffuse damage on society, and therefore it would be exceedingly difficult, if not impossible, to fight this crime based on each injured party's demonstration of harm suffered. The crime of producing counterfeit currency is defined in terms of a perpetrator's act and not in terms of the specific personal damage caused by the act.

[162]Such "option clauses" were in force in Scottish banks from 1730 to 1765 and reserved the right to temporarily suspend payment in specie

eliminating from the corresponding instruments an important characteristic of money: perfect, i.e., immediate, complete, and never conditional, liquidity. Thus not only would depositors become forced lenders at the will of the banker, but a deposit would become a type of aleatory contract or lottery, in which the possibility of withdrawing the cash deposited would depend on the particular circumstances of each moment. There can be no objection to the voluntary decision of certain parties to enter into such an atypical aleatory contract as that mentioned above. However, even if a "safeguard" clause were introduced and participants (bankers and their customers)

---

of the notes banks had issued. Thus, in reference to bank runs, Selgin states:

> Banks in a free banking system might however avoid such a fate by issuing liabilities contractually subject to a 'restriction' of base money payments. By restricting payments banks can insulate the money stock and other nominal magnitudes from panic-related effects. (Selgin, "Free Banking and Monetary Control," p. 1455)

The fact that Selgin considers resorting to such clauses to avoid bank runs is as significant in terms of the "solvency" of his own theory as it is surprising from a legal perspective that the attempt is made to base a system on the expropriation, albeit partial and temporary, of the property rights of depositors and note holders, who, in a crisis, would be transformed into forced lenders and would no longer be considered true depositors and holders of monetary units, or more specifically, perfect money substitutes. Let us remember a comment from Adam Smith himself:

> The directors of some of those [Scottish] banks sometimes took advantage of this optional clause, and sometimes threatened those who demanded gold and silver in exchange for a considerable number of their notes, that they would take advantage of it, unless such demanders would content themselves with a part of what they demanded. (Smith, *An Inquiry into the Nature and Causes of the Wealth of Nations*, Book II, chap. 2, pp. 394–95)

On option clauses, see Parth J. Shah, "The Option Clause in Free Banking Theory and History: A Reappraisal," a manuscript presented at the 2nd Austrian Scholars Conference (Auburn, Ala.: Ludwig von Mises Institute, April 4–5, 1997), later printed in the *Review of Austrian Economics* 10, no. 2 (1997): 1–25.

were fully aware of it, to the extent that these individuals and all other economic agents subjectively considered demand deposits and notes to be perfect money substitutes, the clause referred to would only be capable of preventing the immediate suspension of payments or failure of banks in the event of a bank run. It would not prevent all of the recurrent processes of expansion, crisis and recession which are typical of fractional-reserve banking, seriously harm third parties and disrupt the public order. (It does not matter which "option clauses" are included in contracts, if the general public considers the above instruments to be perfect money substitutes.) Hence, at most, option clauses can protect banks, but not society nor the economic system, from successive stages of credit expansion, boom and recession. Therefore White and Selgin's last line of defense in no way abolishes the fact that fractional-reserve banking inflicts severe, systematic damage on third parties and disrupts the public order.[163]

---

[163]It is interesting to note that many free-banking theorists fail to see that fractional-reserve banking is illegitimate from the standpoint of general legal principles, and instead of proposing the eradication of fractional-reserve banking, they suggest the banking system be completely privatized and the central bank be eliminated. This measure would certainly tend to check the practically unlimited abuses authorities have committed in the financial field, but it would not prevent the possibility of abuses (on a smaller scale) in the private sphere. This situation resembles that which would arise if governments were allowed to systematically engage in murder, robbery, or any other crime. The harm to society would be tremendous, given the enormous power and the monopolistic nature of the state. The privatization of these criminal acts (an end to governments' systematic perpetration of them) would undoubtedly tend to "improve" the situation considerably, since the great criminal power of the state would disappear and private economic agents would be permitted to spontaneously develop methods to prevent and defend themselves against such crimes. Nevertheless the privatization of criminal activity is no definitive solution to the problems crime poses. We can only completely solve these problems by fighting crime by all possible means, even when private agents are the perpetrators. Thus we conclude with Murray N. Rothbard that in an ideal free-market economic system:

> [F]ractional-reserve bankers must be treated not as mere
> entrepreneurs who made unfortunate business decisions but

5

Conclusion: The False Debate Between Supporters of Central Banking and Defenders of Fractional-Reserve Free Banking

The traditional approach to the debate between advocates of central banking and those of fractional-reserve free banking is essentially flawed. First, this approach ignores the fact that the fractional-reserve free-banking system almost inevitably releases forces which lead to the emergence, development, and consolidation of a central bank. Fractional-reserve banking gives rise to credit expansion, which triggers reversion processes in the form of financial crises and economic recessions, which in turn inevitably prompt citizens to demand government intervention and state regulation of banking. Second, the very bankers involved in the system soon discover that they can reduce the risk of insolvency if they make agreements between themselves, merge or even demand the establishment of a lender of last resort to provide them with the liquidity necessary in times of difficulty or to institutionalize and officially direct the growth of credit expansion.

We can conclude that fractional-reserve banking has been the main historical cause of the appearance and development of the central bank. Hence we must not approach the theoretical and practical debate in traditional terms, but in terms of two radically different systems: a free-banking system subject to traditional legal principles (a 100-percent reserve requirement) and in which all fractional-reserve operations, whether voluntarily agreed upon or not, are cracked down on as illegal and a breach of public order; and a system which permits

---

as counterfeiters and embezzlers who should be cracked down on by the full majesty of the law. Forced repayment to all the victims plus substantial jail terms should serve as a deterrent as well as to meet punishment for this criminal activity. (Murray N. Rothbard, "The Present State of Austrian Economics," *Journal des Economistes et des Etudes Humaines* 6, no. 1 [March 1995]: 80–81; reprinted in Rothbard, *The Logic of Action I* [Cheltenham, U.K.: Edward Elgar, 1997], p. 165)

fractional-reserve banking and from which a central bank (lender of last resort) will inevitably emerge and control the entire financial system.

These are the only two theoretically and practically viable alternatives. Up to this point we have examined the economic effects of fractional-reserve banking, both orchestrated by a central bank and in a free-banking system. In the next and last chapter we will carefully analyze a free-banking system subject to traditional legal principles, i.e., a 100-percent reserve requirement.[164]

---

[164]Leland Yeager seems to have (at least tacitly) accepted my thesis on the unworkability of a fractional-reserve free-banking system, when he proposes a monetary system based only on bank money in which all bank reserve requirements are abolished and no outside or base money is used at all. Yeager's system would be prone, of course, to all the cyclical problems we have analyzed in detail in this book. See Yeager, "The Perils of Base Money."

9

A PROPOSAL FOR BANKING REFORM: THE THEORY OF A 100-PERCENT RESERVE REQUIREMENT

I n this last chapter, following a brief review of twentieth-century proposals for the establishment of a 100-percent reserve requirement in banking, we will present our recommendation for reforming the banking system, a proposal based on free-banking practices subject to the traditional legal principles which govern the monetary bank-deposit contract (a 100-percent reserve requirement). We will then compare the advantages of the proposed system with those of other possible systems, specifically the current banking and financial system and a fractional-reserve free-banking system. At that point we will review and answer the different objections made to proposals for a 100-percent reserve requirement. Then, after presenting a program of transitional stages which makes it feasible to move from the current banking and financial system to the model proposed, we will finish the chapter with a series of comments on the possible application of our recommendations to the specific cases of the European Monetary Union and the monetary and financial reconstruction under way in countries of the former Eastern bloc. The book ends with a summary of the most significant conclusions reached.

1

A HISTORY OF MODERN THEORIES IN SUPPORT OF A 100-PERCENT RESERVE REQUIREMENT

We know that distrust of fractional-reserve banking dates back at least as far as the Salamancan theorists of the sixteenth and seventeenth centuries, David Hume in the eighteenth century, theorists of the school of Jefferson and Jackson in the decades following the founding of the United States, and the important group of theorists from nineteenth-century continental Europe (Modeste and Cernuschi in France; Michaelis, Hübner, Geyer, and Tellkampf in Germany). Moreover, certain highly distinguished economists of the twentieth century, such as Ludwig von Mises and at least four recipients of the Nobel Prize for Economics (Friedrich A. Hayek, Milton Friedman, James Tobin, and Maurice Allais) have at some point defended the establishment of a 100-percent reserve requirement on demand deposits placed at banks.

THE PROPOSAL OF LUDWIG VON MISES

Ludwig von Mises was the first twentieth-century economist to propose the establishment of a banking system with a 100-percent reserve requirement on demand deposits. Mises made his recommendation in the first edition of his book, *The Theory of Money and Credit*, published in 1912. At the end of this first edition, in a section literally reproduced in the second, which was printed in 1924, Mises draws the following conclusion:

> Fiduciary media are scarcely different in nature from money; a supply of them affects the market in the same way as a supply of money proper; variations in their quantity influence the objective exchange value of money in just the same way as do variations in the quantity of money proper. Hence, they should logically be subjected to the same principles that have been established with regard to money proper; the same attempts should be made in their case as well to eliminate as far as possible human influence on the exchange ratio between money and other economic goods.

The possibility of causing temporary fluctuations in the exchange ratios between goods of higher and of lower orders by the issue of fiduciary media, and the pernicious consequences connected with a divergence between the natural and money rates of interest, are circumstances leading to the same conclusion. Now *it is obvious that the only way of eliminating human influence on the credit system is to suppress all further issue of fiduciary media. The basic conception of Peel's Act ought to be restated and more completely implemented than it was in the England of his time by including the issue of credit in the form of bank balances within the legislative prohibition.*

Mises adds:

It would be a mistake to assume that the modern organization of exchange is bound to continue to exist. *It carries within itself the germ of its own destruction;* the development of the fiduciary medium must necessarily lead to its breakdown.[1]

Mises again considers the model for an ideal banking system in his 1928 book, *Geldwertstabilisierung und Konjunkturpolitik* (Monetary stabilization and cyclical policy). There we read:

---

[1]Mises, *The Theory of Money and Credit*, pp. 446–48; italics added. This is the best and most recent English edition of Mises's book. The above excerpt, in Mises's exact words, follows:

Es leuchtet ein, dass menschlicher Einfluss aus dem Umlaufsmittelwesen nicht anders ausgeschaltet werden kann als durch die Unterdrückung der weiteren Ausgabe von Umlaufsmitteln. Der Grundgedanke der Peelschen Akte müsste wieder aufgenommen und durch Miteinbeziehung der in Form von Kassenführungsguthaben ausgegebenen Umlaufsmittel in das gesetzliche Verbot der Neuausgabe in vollkommenerer Weise durchgeführt werden als dies seinerzeit in England geschah. . . . Es wäre ein Irrtum, wollte man annehmen, dass der Bestand der modernen Organisation des Tauschverkehres für die Zukunft gesichert sei. Sie trägt in ihrem Innern bereits den Keim der Zerstörung. Die Entwicklung des Umlaufsmittels muss notwendigerweise zu ihrem Zusammenbruch führen. (Mises, *Theorie des Geldes und der Umlaufsmittel*, pp. 418–19)

The most important prerequisite of any cyclical policy, no
matter how modest its goal may be, is to renounce every
attempt to reduce the interest rate, by means of banking policy, below the rate which develops on the market. That
means a return to the theory of the Currency School, which
sought to suppress all future expansion of circulation credit
and thus all further creation of fiduciary media. However,
this does not mean a return to the old Currency School program, the application of which was limited to banknotes.
Rather it means the introduction of a new program based on
the old Currency School theory, but expanded in the light of
the present state of knowledge to include fiduciary media
issued in the form of bank deposits. *The banks would be
obliged at all times to maintain metallic backing for all notes—
except for the sum of those outstanding which are not now covered
by metal—equal to the total sum of the notes issued and bank
deposits opened. That would mean a complete reorganization of
central bank legislation. . . . By this act alone, cyclical policy
would be directed in earnest toward the elimination of crises.*[2]

Two years later, on October 10, 1930, before the Financial
Committee of the League of Nations in Geneva, Mises delivered a memorandum on "The Suitability of Methods of Ascer-
taining Changes in the Purchasing Power for the Guidance of

---

[2]Mises, *Geldwertstabilisierung und Konjunkturpolitik*, p. 81; English translation *On the Manipulation of Money and Credit*, pp. 57–173. The above
excerpt appears on pp. 167–68 and the italics have been added. The
exception Mises includes between dashes indicates that he, in keeping
with the spirit of Peel's Act, merely calls for a 100 percent reserve in relation to *newly-issued* fiduciary media (deposits and banknotes) which
would mean that the stock of these already issued at the time the reform
is launched would remain unbacked by specie. The implementation of
Mises's proposal would represent a large step forward and in practice
could be achieved quite easily without initially producing substantial
changes in the market value of gold. However the proposal is imperfect.
It would leave banks without backing on those bills and deposits *issued
in the past*, and banks would thus be particularly vulnerable to possible
crises of confidence. Therefore in this chapter we propose a more radical program consisting of a 100-percent reserve requirement on all fiduciary media (whether already issued or not). Bettina Bien Greaves has
developed Mises's proposal in detail in "How to Return to the Gold
Standard," *The Freeman: Ideas on Liberty* (November 1995): 703–07.

International Currency and Banking Policy." There, before the monetary and banking experts of his day, Mises expressed his ideas as follows:

> It is characteristic of the gold standard that the banks are not allowed to increase the amount of notes and bank balances without a gold backing, beyond the total which was in circulation at the time the system was introduced. Peel's Bank Act of 1844, and the various banking laws which are more or less based on it, represent attempts to create a pure gold standard of this kind. *The attempt was incomplete because its restrictions on circulation included only banknotes, leaving out of account bank balances on which cheques could be drawn.* The founders of the Currency School failed to recognize the essential similarity between payments by cheque and payments by banknote. As a result of this oversight, those responsible for this legislation never accomplished their aim.[3]

Mises would later explain that a banking system based on the gold standard and a 100-percent reserve requirement would tend to push prices down slightly, which would benefit most citizens, since it would raise their real income, not through a nominal increase in earnings but through a continual reduction in the prices of consumer goods and services and relative constancy in nominal income. Mises deems such a monetary and banking system far superior to the current system, which is beset with chronic inflation and recurrent cycles of expansion and recession. In reference to the economic depression then afflicting the world, Mises concludes:

> The root cause of the evil is not in the restrictions, but in the expansion which preceded them. *The policy of the banks does not deserve criticism for having at last called a halt to the expansion of credit, but, rather, for ever having allowed it to begin.*[4]

---

[3]This memorandum had been forgotten and was rediscovered in the League of Nations archives when Richard M. Ebeling was preparing materials for the book, *Money, Method, and the Market Process*, pp. 78–95. The above excerpt appears on p. 90; italics added.

[4]Ibid., p. 91; italics added.

Ten years after delivering this memo before the League of Nations, Mises once more defended a 100-percent reserve requirement, this time in the first German edition of his all-embracing economic treatise, published as *Nationalökonomie: Theorie des Handelns und Wirtschaftens* (*Economics: Theory of Action and Exchange*). Here Mises again presents his thesis that the ideas essential to the Currency School require the application of a 100-percent reserve requirement to all fiduciary media; that is, not only to banknotes, but also to bank deposits. Moreover, in this book Mises advocates the abolition of the central bank and indicates that while this institution continues to exist, even if the issuance of new fiduciary media (bills and deposits) is strictly prohibited, there will always be a danger that "emergency" budget difficulties will be cited as political justification for issuing new fiduciary media to help finance the needs of the state. Mises implicitly responds thus to theorists of the Chicago School who in the 1930s proposed that a 100-percent reserve requirement be set for banking, but that the monetary base remain fiduciary, and that the responsibility for issuing and controlling the stock of money continue to fall to the central bank. Mises does not consider this the best solution. In this case, even with a 100-percent reserve requirement, money would still ultimately depend on a central bank and would therefore be subject to all sorts of pressures and influences, particularly the danger that in a financial emergency the state would exercise its power to issue currency in order to finance itself. According to Mises, the ideal solution would thus be to establish a system of free banking (i.e., without a central bank) subject to traditional legal principles (and hence, a 100-percent reserve requirement).[5] In this book Mises accompanies his defense of

---

[5]Mises's exact words follow:

> Wenn heute, dem Grundgedanken der Currency-Lehre entsprechend, auch für das Kassenführungsguthaben volle—hundertprozentige—Deckung verlangt wird, damit die Erweiterung der Umlaufsmittelausgabe auch in dieser Gestalt unterbunden werde, dann ist das folgerichtiger Ausbau der Ideen, die jenem alten englischen Gesetz zugrundelagen. . . . Auch das schärfste Verbot der Erweiterung der

a 100-percent reserve requirement with his objection not only to the central bank, but also to a fractional-reserve free-banking system: although such a system would greatly limit the issuance of fiduciary media, it would be inadequate to completely eliminate credit expansion nor the recurrent booms and economic recessions which inevitably come with it.[6]

In 1949 Yale University Press published the first English edition of Ludwig von Mises's economic treatise, entitled *Human Action: A Treatise on Economics*. In this English edition Mises repeats the arguments from the German edition, but he expressly refers to Irving Fisher's plan for establishing a 100-percent reserve requirement for banking. Mises disapproves of Fisher's plan, not because it includes a proposal for a 100-percent reserve requirement, which Mises fully supports, but because Fisher seeks to combine this measure with

---

Umlaufsmittelausgabe versagt gegenüber einer Notstandsgesetzgebung. (Mises, *Nationalökonomie*, 2nd ed. [Munich: Philosophia Verlag, 1980, p. 403)

[6]In this sense, Mises's footnote on p. 402 of *Nationalökonomie* is particularly illustrative. It reads:

Für die Katallaktik ist der Begriff "normale Kreditausweitung" sinnlos. Jede Kreditausweitung wirkt auf die Gestaltung der Preise, Löhne und Zinssätze und löst den Prozess aus, den zu beschreiben die Aufgabe der Konjunkturtheorie ist.

This footnote was later translated into English on p. 442 of the 3rd rev. ed. of *Human Action*:

The notion of "normal" credit expansion is absurd. Issuance of additional fiduciary media, no matter what its quantity may be, always sets in motion those changes in the price structure the description of which is the task of the theory of the trade cycle. Of course, if the additional amount issued is not large, neither are the inevitable effects of the expansion.

This statement from Mises has generated substantial confusion among those members of the Austrian School who defend a fractional-reserve free-banking system (White, Selgin, Horwitz, etc.). The assertion reveals Mises's belief that such a system would not escape the phases of expansion and recession characteristic of the economic cycle (though they would be less severe than those which affect current banking systems backed by a central bank). Remember also what we said in footnote 120 of chapter 8.

the conservation of the central bank and the adoption of an indexed monetary unit. In fact, according to Mises, the suggestion to reestablish a 100-percent reserve requirement, yet preserve the central bank, is insufficient:

> [I]t would not entirely remove the drawbacks inherent in every kind of government interference with banking. What is needed to prevent any further credit expansion is to place the banking business under the general rules of commercial and civil laws compelling every individual and firm to fulfill all obligations in full compliance with the terms of the contract.[7]

Mises again expresses his ideas on a 100-percent reserve requirement in an appendix (on "Monetary reconstruction") to the 1953 English reissue of *The Theory of Money and Credit*, where he explicitly states:

> The main thing is that the government should no longer be in a position to increase the quantity of money in circulation and the amount of checkbook money not fully—that is, 100 percent—covered by deposits paid in by the public.

Furthermore, in this appendix Mises also proposes a process of transition to the ideal system, with the following goal:

> No bank must be permitted to expand the total amount of its deposits subject to check or the balance of such deposits of any individual customer, be he a private citizen or the U.S. Treasury, otherwise than by receiving cash deposits in legal-tender banknotes from the public or by receiving a check payable by another domestic bank subject to the same limitations. *This means a rigid 100 percent reserve for all future deposits; that is, all deposits not already in existence on the first day of the reform.*[8]

---

[7]Mises, *Human Action*, 3rd ed., p. 443. Here, for the first time, Mises indicates that the problems related to the banking system stem from the fact that its participants are not subject to traditional legal principles. This is the fundamental idea Murray N. Rothbard would later develop and which lies at the heart of our thesis.

[8]Mises, *The Theory of Money and Credit*, pp. 481 and 491; italics added.

Though further on we will again deal with the process of transition to the ideal banking system, we observe here that Mises, in keeping with his 1928 writings, proposes the same system of transition as the one applied to banknotes with Peel's Act (which required that only *newly-created* bills be backed 100 percent by specie).[9]

FRIEDRICH A. HAYEK AND THE PROPOSAL OF A 100-PERCENT RESERVE REQUIREMENT

Friedrich A. Hayek, undoubtedly Mises's most brilliant disciple, first wrote about a 100-percent reserve requirement when, at the age of twenty-five, he published the article, "The Monetary Policy of the United States after the Recovery from the 1920 Crisis," following his return from a study tour of the United States. Indeed, in this article, Hayek strongly criticizes the monetary policy the Federal Reserve had put into operation at the time. The Fed's policy was designed to maintain the stability of the dollar's purchasing power in a context of rapidly growing productivity, and it had already begun to generate the substantial credit expansion which would ultimately cause the Great Depression. For the first time in his life, Hayek

---

[9]Despite Mises's crystal clear statements in favor of a 100-percent reserve requirement, his defense of free banking as an indirect step toward the ideal of a 100 percent reserve (and thus toward a banking system subject to traditional legal principles) has prompted some Austrian theorists of the modern Neo-Banking School to make a self-interested interpretation of Mises's position. Thus these theorists view Mises as a defender of fractional-reserve free banking first, and of banking with a 100 percent reserve second. For instance, see White, "Mises on Free Banking and Fractional Reserves," pp. 517–33. In an interesting article, Joseph T. Salerno recently showed White's position to be untenable:

> because he overlooks important passages in the very works of Mises that he cites, and because he ignores significant developments in Mises's theory of money that occurred between the publication of the first German edition of *The Theory of Money and Credit* in 1912 and the publication of *Nationalökonomie* in 1940. (Salerno, "Mises and Hayek Dehomogenized," pp. 137–46)

refers to the 100-percent reserve requirement in a footnote of this seminal article. He states:

> As we have already emphasized, the older English theo-
> reticians of the currency school had a firmer grasp of this
> than the majority of economists who came after them. The
> currency school hoped also to prevent cyclical fluctuations
> by the regulation of the note issue they proposed. But since
> they took only the effects of the note issue into account and
> neglected those of deposit money, and the restrictions
> imposed upon bank credit could always be got round by
> an expansion of transfers through bank deposits, Peel's
> Bank Act and the central bank statute modelled upon it
> could not achieve this aim. *The problem of the prevention of*
> *crises would have received a radical solution if the basic concept*
> *of Peel's Act had been consistently developed into the prescrip-*
> *tion of 100 percent gold cover for bank deposits as well as*
> *notes.*[10]

In his remarkable work, *Monetary Nationalism and International Stability*, published twelve years later in 1937, F.A.
Hayek again speaks of establishing a banking system based
on a 100-percent reserve requirement. At that time, theorists
of the Chicago School had already made a similar proposal,
which they attempted to base on the central bank's paper
currency. In contrast Hayek asserts that the ideal solution
would be to combine a 100-percent reserve requirement for
banking with a return to a pure gold standard. In this way, all
bank-notes and deposits would be backed by gold 100 percent,
and a worldwide, sound monetary system effective at preventing government manipulation and "monetary nationalism"
would emerge. Hayek concludes:

---

[10]Hayek, "The Monetary Policy of the United States after the Recovery from the 1920 Crisis," chapter 1 of *Money, Capital and Fluctuations:*
Early Essays, p. 29; italics added. This article is the English translation
of the theoretical portion of the original, which was published in German with the title, "Die Währungspolitik der Vereinigten Staaten seit
der Überwindung der Krise von 1920," *Zeitschrift für Volkswirtschaft*
und Sozialpolitik, vols. 1–3, no. 5 (1925): 25–63 and vols. 4–6, pp.
254–317.

> The undeniable attractiveness of this proposal lies exactly in the feature which makes it appear somewhat impracticable, in the fact that in effect it amounts . . . to *an abolition of deposit banking as we know it*.[11]

Nearly forty years later, F.A. Hayek again took up the subject of money and banking in his famous work, *Denationalization of Money*. Although modern fractional-reserve free-banking theorists have used this book to justify their model, there is no doubt that Hayek proposes a system of free banking and private issuance of monetary units and that ultimately he wishes to see the banking model with a 100-percent reserve requirement prevail. In fact in the section he devotes to the change of policy in commercial banking, Hayek concludes that the vast majority of banks

> clearly would have to be content to do their business in other currencies. They would thus have to practise a kind of "100 percent banking," and keep a full reserve against all their obligations payable on demand.

Hayek adds a harsh criticism of the current banking system:

> An institution which has proved as harmful as fractional reserve banking without the responsibility of the individual bank for the money (i.e., cheque deposits) it created cannot complain if support by a government monopoly that has made its existence possible is withdrawn.[12]

---

[11]Hayek, *Monetary Nationalism and International Stability*, pp. 81–84, esp. p. 82; italics added. Hayek especially praises the proposal for a 100-percent reserve requirement "because it goes to the heart of the problem" (p. 81). Hayek sees only one disadvantage in this plan, apart from its being "somewhat impracticable": it seems unlikely that unbacked bank deposits would not appear in some other legal form, given that "banking is a pervasive phenomenon" (p. 82). Later we will deal with this objection.

[12]Hayek, *Denationalization of Money*, pp. 94–95 and p. 55. The above excerpts appear on p. 119 of the 2nd rev. expanded ed. (London: Institute of Economic Affairs, 1978). Hayek also calls for the drawing of a

Murray N. Rothbard and the Proposal of a Pure Gold Standard with a 100-Percent Reserve Requirement

In 1962 Professor Murray N. Rothbard's now classic article, "The Case for a 100-Percent Gold Dollar," appeared in the book, *In Search of a Monetary Constitution*[13] (which was edited by Leland B. Yeager and also contains articles by James M. Buchanan, Milton Friedman, Arthur Kemp, and others). In this article, Rothbard first develops his proposal for a pure gold standard based on a free-banking system with a 100-percent reserve requirement. In this paper, Rothbard criticizes all who support a return to the spurious gold standard rooted in a fractional-reserve banking system controlled by a central bank. Instead he suggests what he views as the only coherent, stable long-term solution: a free-banking system with a 100-percent reserve requirement, the abolition of the central bank, and the establishment of a pure gold standard. According to Rothbard, the result would be the prevention not only of the recurrent cycles of boom and recession caused by fractional-reserve banking, but also of the possibility, even with a 100-percent reserve requirement as defended by Chicago School theorists in the 1930s, that the conservation of the central bank should leave the entire system vulnerable to the political and financial needs of each moment.

---

definite distinction between simple deposit banking (to which a 100-percent reserve requirement would apply) and investment banking, which would be limited to the lending of those funds customers first lend their banks. Hayek concludes:

> I expect that it will soon be discovered that the business of creating money does not go along well with the control of large investment portfolios or even control of large parts of industry. (pp. 119–20, 2nd ed.)

Sharp, yet just criticism of Hayek's other proposals related to the denationalization of money and the establishment of a currency based on a commodities index (which are only *indirectly* related to our object of study) appears in Murray N. Rothbard, "The Case for a Genuine Gold Dollar," in *The Gold Standard*, Llewellyn H. Rockwell, Jr., ed. (Lexington, Mass.: Lexington Books), 1985, pp. 2–7.

[13]*In Search of a Monetary Constitution*, Leland B. Yeager, ed. (Cambridge, Mass.: Harvard University Press, 1962).

Nevertheless we deem Rothbard's main contribution to be the strong legal foundation on which he builds his proposal. In fact he accompanies his economic analysis with an essentially legal, though multidisciplinary, study aimed entirely at showing that banking with a 100 percent reserve is simply the logical result of applying traditional legal principles to the banking field. Hence, on this particular point, in the present book we merely try to develop and extend Rothbard's original thesis. Specifically, Rothbard compares the banker who operates with a fractional reserve with the criminal who commits the crime of misappropriation:

> [H]e takes money out of the company till to invest in some ventures of his own. Like the banker, he sees an opportunity to earn a profit on *someone else's assets*. The embezzler knows, let us say, that the auditor will come on June 1 to inspect the accounts; and he fully intends to repay the "loan" before then. Let us assume that he does; is it really true that no one has been the loser and everyone has gained? I dispute this; a theft has occurred, and that theft should be prosecuted and not condoned. Let us note that the banking advocate assumes that something has gone wrong only if everyone should decide to redeem his property, only to find that it isn't there. But I maintain that the wrong—the theft— occurs at the time the embezzler takes the money, not at the later time when his "borrowing" happens to be discovered.[14]

Although Rothbard has correctly presented the legal aspects of the issue, he has followed the Anglo-Saxon legal tradition without realizing that even stronger legal support for his thesis lies in the continental European legal tradition, based on Roman law, as we explained in the initial chapters.[15]

---

[14]Murray N. Rothbard, *The Case for a 100 Percent Gold Dollar* (Auburn, Ala.: Ludwig von Mises Institute, 1991), pp. 44–46.

[15]In September 1993, for the first time, we personally shared with Murray N. Rothbard the results of our research on the legal-Roman foundation of the bank deposit and the position of Salamancan theorists on the issue, and Rothbard was enthusiastic. He later encouraged us to publish a brief summary of our conclusions in an article for *Review of Austrian Economics*. Unfortunately he was unable to see the article published, as

MAURICE ALLAIS AND THE EUROPEAN DEFENSE
OF A 100-PERCENT RESERVE REQUIREMENT

In Europe, the Frenchman Maurice Allais, who received
the Nobel Prize for Economics in 1988, has championed the
proposal of a banking system subject to a 100-percent reserve
requirement. As Allais has stated:

> The credit mechanism *as it currently operates*, based on the
> fractional coverage of deposits, the *ex nihilo* creation of
> money, and the long-term lending of short-term-loan funds,
> substantially aggravates the disruptions mentioned. Indeed,
> all major crises in the nineteenth and twentieth centuries
> stemmed from an excessive expansion of credit, from prom-
> issory notes and their monetization, and from the specula-
> tion this expansion fueled and made possible.[16]

---

he passed away unexpectedly on January 7, 1995. Other important
works in which Rothbard deals with the topic include: *What Has Government Done to Our Money?*, 4th ed. (Auburn, Ala.: Ludwig von Mises
Institute, 1990); *The Mystery of Banking*; *Man, Economy, and State*, pp.
703–09; and the articles, "The Myth of Free Banking in Scotland," *pp.*
229–45, and "Aurophobia: or Free Banking on What Standard?"pp.
99–108. Besides Murray Rothbard, in the United States current advocates of a 100-percent reserve requirement for banking include: Hans-
Hermann Hoppe, *The Economics and Ethics of Private Property* (Dortrecht,
Holland: Kluwer Academic Publishers, 1993), pp. 61–93, and "How is
Fiat Money Possible?—or The Devolution of Money and Credit," pp.
49–74; Joseph T. Salerno, "Gold Standards: True and False," *Cato Journal:
An Interdisciplinary Journal of Public Policy Analysis* 3, no. 1 (Spring, 1983):
239–67, and also "Mises and Hayek Dehomogenized," pp. 137–46; Walter Block, "Fractional Reserve Banking: An Interdisciplinary Perspective," pp. 24–32; and Skousen, *The Economics of a Pure Gold Standard*. This
last work is a doctoral thesis on a 100-percent reserve requirement for
banking, and it contains an especially valuable, exhaustive review of all
related sources to date. Like Rothbard, the above theorists belong to the
long line of American thinkers (beginning with Jefferson and Jackson)
who assert that banking should be rigorously governed by legal principles and a 100-percent reserve requirement. The most important nineteenth-century theorist of this movement was Amasa Walker, *The Science
of Wealth*, pp. 138–68 and 184–232.

[16]Maurice Allais, "Les conditions monétaires d'une économie de
marchés: des enseignements du passé aux réformes de demain," *Revue*

Though Maurice Allais often quotes Ludwig von Mises and Murray N. Rothbard, and though Allais's economic analysis of the effects of fractional-reserve banking and its role in provoking economic crises is impeccable and heavily influenced by the Austrian theory of the economic cycle, in the end Allais does suggest the conservation of the central bank as the organization ultimately responsible for controlling the monetary base and overseeing its growth (at a fixed rate of 2 percent per year).[17] For Allais believes the state alone, and not

---

d'économie politique 3 (May–July 1993): 319–67. The above excerpt appears on p. 326, and the original text reads:

> Le mécanisme du crédit *tel qu'il fonctionne actuellement* et qui est fondé sur la couverture fractionnaire des dépôts, sur la création de monnaie *ex nihilo*, et sur le prêt à long terme de fonds empruntés à court terme, a pour effet une amplification considérable des désordres constatés. *En fait, toutes les grandes crises des dix-neuvième et vingtième siècles ont résulté du développement excessif du crédit, des promesses de payer et de leur monétisation, et de la spéculation que ce développement a suscitée et rendue possible.* (Italics added)

Maurice Allais introduced his theses to the general public in his well-known article, "Les faux monnayeurs," published in *Le Monde*, October 29, 1974. Allais also presents them in chapters 6–9 of the book, *L'impôt sur le capital et la réforme monétaire* (Paris: Hermann Éditeurs, 1989), pp. 155–257. In 1994 our critical evaluation of fractional-reserve banking was also published in France in Huerta de Soto, "Banque centrale ou banque libre," pp. 379–91.

[17]For example, see the quotations from Murray N. Rothbard's work on pp. 316, 317 and 320 of Allais's book, *L'impôt sur le capital et la réforme monétaire*. See also references to Amasa Walker on p. 317, and especially to Ludwig von Mises, whose book, *The Theory of Money and Credit*, Allais is perfectly familiar with and quotes on various occasions, among others, on pp. 355, 307 and 317. Moreover Maurice Allais pays warm tribute to Ludwig von Mises:

> Si une société libérale a pu être maintenue jusqu'à présent dans le monde occidental, c'est pour une grande part grâce à la courageuse action d'hommes comme Ludwig von Mises (1881–1973) qui toute leur vie ont constamment défendu des idées impopulaires à l'encontre des courants de pensée dominants de leur temps. Mises était un homme d'une intelligence exceptionnelle dont les contributions a la science économique ont été de tout premier ordre. Constamment en

bankers, should take advantage of the expropriation which comes with the possibility of creating money. Thus his proposal of a 100-percent reserve requirement is not the logical result of applying traditional legal principles to banking, as in the case of Murray N. Rothbard. Instead, it represents an attempt to assist governments in administering a stable monetary policy by preventing the elastic, distorting credit expansion which all fractional-reserve banking systems generate from nothing. In this sense, Maurice Allais simply follows the old tradition established by some members of the Chicago School, who proposed a 100-percent reserve requirement to make government monetary policy more effective and predictable.

---

butte à de puissantes oppositions, il a passé ses dernières années dans la gêne, et sans l'aide de quelques amis, il n'aurait guère pu disposer d'une vie décente. Une société qui n'est pas capable d'assurer à ses élites, et en fait à ses meilleurs défenseurs, des conditions de vie acceptables, est une société condamnée. (p. 307)

Although in practice Maurice Allais fully agrees with the analysis and prescriptions of the Austrian School on matters of money and cycles, he embraces the mathematical development of the general equilibrium model and thereby separates radically from the Austrians, as certain fundamental errors in his analysis attest (Huerta de Soto, *Socialismo, cálculo económico y función empresarial*, pp. 248–49). Pascal Salin has therefore concluded that rather than a liberal economist of the same type as Hayek, Maurice Allais is a "social engineer" with strong personal laissez-faire leanings, a theorist whose mathematical analysis often leads him to a pragmatic utilitarianism which Hayek and Austrian scholars in general would clearly label "constructivist" or "scientistic." See Pascal Salin, "Maurice Allais: Un économiste liberal?," manuscript pending publication, p. 12. Salin has also published a paper in which he analyzes the Austrian theory of economic cycles and the banking-policy prescriptions that derive from it. See Pascal Salin, "Macro-Stabilization Policies and the Market Process," *Economic Policy and the Market Process: Austrian and Mainstream Economics*, K. Groenveld, J.A.H. Maks, and J. Muysken, eds. (Amsterdam: North-Holland, 1990), pp. 201–21. In footnote 98 of chapter 8, we explain why we cannot agree with Salin's stance in favor of fractional-reserve free-banking.

THE OLD CHICAGO-SCHOOL TRADITION OF SUPPORT
FOR A 100-PERCENT RESERVE REQUIREMENT

The Chicago School prescription of a 100-percent reserve requirement dates back to March 16, 1933, when Henry C. Simons, Lloyd W. Mints, Aaron Director, Frank H. Knight, Henry Schultz, Paul H. Douglas, Albert G. Hart and others circulated an anonymous six-page document called "Banking and Currency Reform."[18] Albert G. Hart later expanded on this program in his article, "The 'Chicago Plan' of Banking Reform," published in 1935. Here Hart expressly recognizes Professor Ludwig von Mises as the ultimate father of the proposal.[19] Later, in November of 1935, James W. Angell published a comprehensive article in which he defends this position and analyzes its different aspects. His article is entitled "The 100-Percent Reserve Plan,"[20] and was followed by a paper by Henry C. Simons, "Rules *versus* Authorities in Monetary Policy," which appeared in 1936.[21]

Of the Chicago theorists, Henry C. Simons comes closest to the thesis that a 100-percent reserve requirement is not a mere economic-policy proposal, but an imperative of the institutional framework of rules which is vital for the correct functioning of a market economy. Indeed Simons asserts:

---

[18]See Ronnie J. Phillips, *The Chicago Plan and New Deal Banking Reform* (Armonk, N.Y.: M.E. Sharpe, 1995), pp. 191–98.

[19]Albert G. Hart, "The 'Chicago Plan' of Banking Reform," *Review of Economic Studies* 2 (1935): 104–16. The reference to professors Mises and Hayek appears at the foot of p. 104. Another interesting precedent for the Chicago Plan is found in a book by Frederick Soddy, a recipient of the Nobel Prize for Chemistry: *Wealth, Virtual Wealth and Debt* (New York: E.P. Dutton, 1927). Knight wrote a favorable review of Soddy's book that same year: "Review of Frederick Soddy's *Wealth, Virtual Wealth and Debt*," *Saturday Review of Literature* (April 16, 1927): 732.

[20]James W. Angell, "The 100 Percent Reserve Plan," *The Quarterly Journal of Economics* 50, no. 1 (November 1935): 1–35.

[21]Henry C. Simons, "Rules *versus* Authorities in Monetary Policy," *Journal of Political Economy* 44, no. 1 (February 1936): 1–30.

A democratic, free-enterprise system implies, and requires for its effective functioning and survival, a stable framework of definite rules, laid down in legislation and subject to change only gradually and with careful regard for the vested interests of participants in the economic game.[22]

Nevertheless Henry C. Simons defends a 100-percent reserve requirement with the basic purpose of restoring complete government control over the quantity of money in circulation and its value. He had announced his proposal one year earlier, in a pamphlet entitled "A Positive Program for Laissez-Faire: Some Proposals for a Liberal Economic Policy," published in 1934. As indicated in this pamphlet, at that time Simons already believed that deposit banks which maintained

100 per cent reserves, simply could not fail, so far as depositors were concerned, and could not create or destroy effective money. These institutions would accept deposits just as warehouses accept goods. Their income would be derived exclusively from service charges—perhaps merely from moderate charges for the transfer of funds by check or draft. . . . These banking proposals define means for eliminating the perverse elasticity of credit which obtains under a system of private, commercial banking and for restoring to the central government complete control over the quantity of effective money and its value.[23]

---

[22]Simons, "Rules *versus* Authorities in Monetary Policy," p. 181; reprinted as chapter 7, *Economic Policy for a Free Society* (Chicago: University of Chicago Press, 1948), pp. 181. It is highly significant that Simons makes this legal-institutional analysis in precisely the article in which he offers his proposal for banking reform based on a 100-percent reserve requirement.

[23]Henry C. Simons, "A Positive Program for Laissez-Faire: Some Proposals for a Liberal Economic Policy," originally published as "Public Policy Pamphlet," no. 15, Harry D. Gideonse, ed. (Chicago: University of Chicago Press, 1934). It was reprinted as chapter 2 of *Economic Policy for a Free Society*, pp. 64–65. On Henry Simons see Walter Block, "Henry Simons is Not a Supporter of Free Enterprise," *Journal of Libertarian Studies* 16, no. 4 (Fall, 2002): 3–36.

Simons's contributions[24] were followed by those Fritz Lehmann made in his article, "100 Percent Money"[25] and by the article Frank D. Graham published in September of 1936 with the title, "Partial Reserve Money and the 100 Percent Proposal."[26]

Irving Fisher compiled these proposals in book form in *100 Percent Money.*[27] Following World War II, they were taken up again by Henry C. Simons in his 1948 book, *Economic Policy for a Free Society*, and by Lloyd W. Mints in *Monetary Policy for a Competitive Society.*[28] This trend culminated in the publication of Milton Friedman's *A Program for Monetary Stability* in 1959.[29] Milton Friedman, like his predecessors, recommends the current system be replaced with one which includes a 100-percent reserve requirement.[30] The only difference is that Friedman suggests the payment of interest on such reserves,

---

[24]Henry C. Simons, in footnote 7 on p. 320 of his *Economic Policy for a Free Society*, adds:

> There is likely to be extreme economic instability under any financial system where *the same funds* are made to serve at once *as investment funds for industry and trade* and *as the liquid cash reserves of individuals.* Our financial structure has been built largely on the illusion that funds can at the same time be both available and invested—and this observation applies to our savings banks (and in lesser degree to many other financial institutions) as well as commercial, demand-deposit banking.

[25]Fritz Lehmann, "100 Percent Money," *Social Research* 3, no. 1: 37–56.

[26]Frank D. Graham, "Partial Reserve Money and the 100 Percent Proposal," *American Economic Review* 26 (1936): 428–40.

[27]Irving Fisher, *100 Percent Money* (New York: Adelphi Company, 1935).

[28]Lloyd W. Mints, *Monetary Policy for a Competitive Society* (New York, 1950), pp. 186–87.

[29]Milton Friedman, *A Program for Monetary Stability* (New York: Fordham University Press, 1959). Friedman first published his ideas on a 100-percent reserve requirement in 1953 in his article, "A Monetary and Fiscal Framework for Economic Stability," *American Economic Review* 38, no. 3 (1948): 245–64. Rothbard's criticism of Friedman is in his article, "Milton Friedman Unraveled," *Journal of Libertarian Studies* 16, no. 4 (Fall, 2002): 37–54.

[30]Friedman, *A Program for Monetary Stability.*

and in an interesting footnote he mentions the complete free-banking system, defended by Gary Becker, as one way to approach this objective.[31]

Henry C. Simons comes closest to recognizing the juridical-institutional demands for a 100-percent reserve requirement.[32] However, in general, Chicago theorists have defended

---

[31]Friedman does not mention Mises, who, nearly fifty years earlier in German and twenty-five years earlier in English, had already put forward a detailed version of the same theory. Milton Friedman, *A Program for Monetary Stability*, footnote 10. Gary Becker's proposal was many years later published: Gary S. Becker, "A Proposal for Free Banking," *Free Banking*, vol. 3: *Modern Theory and Policy*, White, ed., chap. 2, pp. 20–25. Though Gary Becker could easily be classified with modern neo-banking advocates of fractional-reserve free banking, he recognizes that, in any case, a system which includes a 100-percent reserve requirement would be a considerable improvement on the current financial and banking system (p. 24).

[32]Irving Fisher also dealt with the legal aspects of a 100-percent reserve requirement. He indicated that in this system

> demand deposits would literally be deposits, consisting of cash held in trust for the depositor . . . the check deposit department of the bank would become a mere storage warehouse for bearer money belonging to its depositors. (Irving Fisher, *100 Percent Money*, p. 10)

Unfortunately Fisher's underlying economic theory was monetarist, and hence he never understood how the credit expansion which results from fractional-reserve banking affects society's structure of productive stages. Moreover Fisher recommended an indexed standard be established and the government retain control over monetary policy, to which Ludwig von Mises responded with sharp criticism (*Human Action*, pp. 442–43). Specifically, Fisher's use of the monetarist equation of exchange led to important errors in his theoretical analysis and economic forecasting. Fisher failed to see that aside from the macroeconomic effects accounted for by his formula, growth in the money supply distorts the productive structure and inexorably feeds crises and recessions. Thus in the late 1920s Fisher thought economic expansion would continue "indefinitely" and did not realize that it rested on an artificial foundation which was condemned to failure. Indeed, the Great Depression of 1929 took him completely by surprise and nearly ruined him. On the intriguing personality of this American economist, see Irving N. Fisher's book, *My Father Irving Fisher* (New York: A Reflection Book, 1956), and the biography by Robert Loring Allen, *Irving Fisher: A Biography*.

a 100 percent-reserve banking system for exclusively practical reasons, believing this requirement would make government monetary policy easier and more predictable. Therefore the theorists of the Chicago School have been guilty of naiveté in ascribing to governments the desire and ability to administer a stable monetary policy under all circumstances.[33] This naiveté parallels that shown by modern neo-banking defenders of fractional-reserve free banking when they rely on spontaneous interbank liquidation and clearing mechanisms to halt under all circumstances planned, simultaneous expansion by most banks. These theorists fail to see that although a fractional-reserve free-banking system would have more limitations than the current system, it would not prevent the creation of fiduciary media, nor, logically, would it immunize the market against economic crises. Hence we must conclude that *the only effective way to rid society of special privileges and economic cycles is to establish a free-banking system governed by legal principles; that is, a 100-percent reserve requirement.*[34]

---

[33]As Pascal Salin states in his article on Maurice Allais, "Toute l'histoire monétaire montre que l'État a refusé de respecter les règles monétaires et que la source ultime de l'inflation provient de ce défaut institutionnel." Pascal Salin, "Maurice Allais: un économiste liberal?" p. 11. Thus we cannot trust that a central bank, which will always be influenced to some extent by the current political scene, will be able to maintain a monetary policy which immunizes society against the evils of economic cycles, even if the desire is present and a 100-percent reserve requirement is established for private banking. This is so because nothing bars the central bank from directly financing state expenditures or, via open-market operations, acquiring massive numbers of treasury bonds and other securities, and thus injecting liquidity into the system through the capital market and temporarily distorting the interest rate and society's structure of productive stages. This would set in motion the inexorable mechanisms of economic cycles, which would trigger a severe depression. This is the *prima facie* argument against the conservation of the central bank, and it shows the necessity of combining the re-establishment of legal principles in private banking with the complete deregulation of the sector and the abolition of the central bank. On the traditional strong leaning toward interventionism of the Chicago School, see "Symposium: Chicago versus the Free Market," *Journal of Libertarian Studies* 16, no. 4 (Fall, 2002).

[34]On the Keynesian side, James Tobin, who received the Nobel Prize for Economics in 1981, has proposed a "deposit currency" system which

2

Our Proposal for Banking Reform

Logical deduction based on this book's analysis points to a particular program of banking reform: on the one hand, the institutions related to the financial market should be made contingent on traditional legal principles; and on the other, the government agencies which until now have controlled and directed the financial system should be eliminated. We believe that in order to establish a truly stable financial and monetary system for the twenty-first century, a system which protects our economies as far as possible from crises and recessions, the following will be necessary: (1) complete freedom of choice in currency; (2) a system of free banking and the abolition of the central bank; and most importantly, (3) obligatory observance of traditional legal rules and principles by all agents involved in the free-banking system, particularly the important principle according to which no one may enjoy the privilege of loaning something entrusted to him on demand deposit. In short, it is necessary to maintain at all times a banking system which includes a 100-percent reserve requirement. We will now discuss in greater detail each component of our proposal.

Total Freedom of Choice in Currency

We recommend the privatization of currency and an end to state and central-bank intervention with respect to its issuance and control over its value. This goal requires the

incorporates many aspects of the Chicago Plan for a 100-percent reserve requirement. See his "Financial Innovation and Deregulation in Perspective," *Bank of Japan Monetary and Economic Studies* 3 (1985): 19–29. See also the comments Charles Goodhart makes on Tobin's proposal of a 100-percent reserve requirement in his *The Evolution of Central Banks*, pp. 87ff. Tobin seems to follow the tradition of Lauchlin Currie, *The Supply and Control of Money in the United States* (1934; New York: Russell & Russell, 1968). More recently Alex Hocker Pollock has again defended a similar banking system in his article, "Collateralized Money: An Idea Whose Time Has Come Again?" *Durrell Journal of Money and Banking* 5, no. 1 (March 1993): 34–38. The main disadvantage of Pollock's proposal is that it indicates reserves should be held not in money, but in assets with a market value that makes them easy to liquidate.

elimination of legal tender regulations which oblige all citizens, even against their will, to accept the state-issued monetary unit as a liberatory means of payment in all cases. The revocation of legal tender laws is therefore an essential part of any process of deregulation of the financial market. This "denationalization of money," in Hayek's words, would allow economic agents, who possess far more accurate, first-hand information on their specific circumstances of time and place, to decide in each case what type of monetary unit it would most benefit them to use in their contracts.

It is not possible to theorize *a priori* about the future evolution of money. Our theoretical analysis must be limited to the observation that money is an institution which emerges spontaneously, like law, language, and other legal and economic institutions which involve an enormous volume of information and appear in an evolutionary manner throughout a very prolonged period of time in which many generations of human beings participate. Moreover, as with language, certain institutions which in the social process of trial and error best fulfill their function tend to predominate. Trial alone, throughout the spontaneous, evolutionary market process, can lead to the predominance of those institutions most conducive to social cooperation, without the possession by any one person or group of the intelligence and information necessary to create these types of institutions *ex novo*.

These reflections are fully applicable to the emergence and evolution of money,[35] and hence in this field we must be

---

[35]On the theory of the emergence of institutions, specifically money, see Menger, *Untersuchungen über die Methode der Socialwissenschaften und der Politischen Ökonomie insbesondere* and "On the Origin of Money," pp. 239–55. We should also remember Mises's monetary regression theorem, according to which the price or purchasing power of money is determined by its supply and demand, which is in turn determined not by its purchasing power today, but by the knowledge the actor formed on its purchasing power yesterday. At the same time, the purchasing power of money yesterday was determined by the demand for money which developed based on the knowledge of its purchasing power the day before yesterday. We could trace this pattern back to the moment

particularly suspicious of proposals to create an artificial currency, no matter how many advantages such a plan may at first appear to have.[36]

---

when, for the first time in history, people began to demand a certain good as a medium of exchange. Therefore this theorem reflects Menger's theory on the spontaneous emergence and evolution of money, but in this case there is a retroactive effect. Mises's monetary regression theorem is of capital importance in any project for reforming the monetary system, and it explains why in this field there can be no "leaps in the dark," attempts to introduce *ex novo* monetary systems which are not the result of evolution and which, as in the case of Esperanto with respect to language, would inevitably be condemned to failure. On the monetary regression theorem, see Mises, *Human Action*, pp. 409–10, 425 and 610. The introduction in the market of new payment technologies (first paper, then plastic cards, and now electronic "money") does not affect at all the conclusion of our analysis. It is not possible nor convenient to try to introduce a constellation of private fiat electronic moneys competing among themselves in a chaotic world of flexible exchange rates, especially when we already know the final result of the secular and free monetary evolution of humankind: a single worldwide commodity (gold) that cannot be manipulated either by private individuals or public servants. For these reasons we cannot accept the proposal of Jean Pierre Centi, "Hayekian Perspectives on the Monetary System: Toward Fiat Private and Competitive Moneys," in *Austrian Economics Today I*, The International Library of Austrian Economics, Kurt R. Leube, ed. (Frankfurt: FAZ Buch, 2003), pp. 89–104. See also footnote 104.

[36]The best-known plan for the denationalization of money appears in Hayek's 1976 book, *Denationalisation of Money*. Nevertheless Hayek's follies in support of artificial monetary standards began thirty years earlier: "A Commodity Reserve Currency," *Economic Journal* 53, no. 210 (June–September 1943): 176–84 (included as chapter 10 of *Individualism and Economic Order*, pp. 209–19). While we consider Hayek's Mengerian analysis of the evolution of institutions to be correct, and we agree that it would be highly beneficial to permit in the monetary field as well the private experimentation characteristic of markets, we find it regrettable that Hayek ultimately proposed a completely artificial standard (comprised of a basket of various commodities) as a new monetary unit. Although one can interpret Hayek's proposal as a procedure for returning to traditional money (a pure gold standard and a 100-percent reserve requirement), Hayek clearly earned the criticism certain Austrian economists leveled against him. These economists judged his proposals quite severely and called them "scientistic" and "constructivist."

Therefore our proposal of free choice in currency is clear. In the transition process which we will examine further on, money in its current form is to be privatized via its replacement by that form of money which, in an evolutionary manner, generation after generation, has prevailed throughout history: gold.[37] In fact it is pointless to attempt to abruptly introduce a new, widespread monetary unit in the market while ignoring thousands of years of evolution in which gold has spontaneously predominated as money. According to the monetary regression theorem, such a feat is impossible, since no form of money can be used in society as a generally accepted medium of exchange if it does not rest on a very prolonged historical process which begins with the original industrial or commercial use of the commodity in question (as with gold and silver). Thus our proposal is based on *privatizing money in its current form by replacing it with its metallic equivalent in gold and allowing the market to resume its free development from the time of the transition, either by confirming gold as the generally accepted form of money, or by permitting the spontaneous and gradual entrance of other monetary standards.*[38]

Among the critics were Murray N. Rothbard, Hans-Hermann Hoppe and Joseph T. Salerno, "Mises and Hayek Dehomogenized." The same objections can be made to the very similar proposal of Leland B. Yeager, "The Perils of Base Money," p. 262.

[37]Silver could also be considered a secondary, parallel metallic standard which, if economic agents should wish, could coexist with gold at the fluctuating exchange rate determined by the market between the two at all times. Furthermore we must recognize that the decline in the use of silver as money was accelerated when nineteenth-century governments established fixed exchange rates between gold and silver which artificially undervalued the latter. See Rothbard, *Man, Economy, and State*, pp. 724–26.

[38]The gold standard we propose does not remotely resemble the spurious gold standard used until the 1930s, a standard based on the existence of central banks and a fractional-reserve banking system. As Milton Friedman indicates:

> A real honest-to-God gold standard . . . would be one in which gold was literally money and money literally gold, under which transactions would literally be made in terms either of the yellow metal itself, or of pieces of paper that

A SYSTEM OF COMPLETE BANKING FREEDOM

This second element of our proposal refers to the necessity of revoking banking legislation and eliminating central banks and in general any government agency devoted to controlling and intervening in the financial or banking market. It should be possible to set up any number of private banks with complete freedom, both in terms of corporate purpose and legal form. As the distinguished Laureano Figuerola y Ballester stated in 1869, it is necessary to leave "the choice of banking forms to each individual, who will know how to choose the best ones, according to particular circumstances of time and place."[39] Nevertheless the defense of free banking does not imply permission for banks to operate with a fractional reserve. At this point it should be perfectly clear that banking should be subject to traditional legal principles and that these demand the maintenance at all times of a 100 percent reserve with respect to demand deposits at banks. Hence free banking must not be viewed as a license to infringe this rule, since its infringement not only constitutes a violation of a traditional legal principle, but it also triggers a chain of consequences which are highly damaging to the economy. The legal and economic aspects of such affairs are intimately related, and it is impossible to violate legal and moral principles without causing grave, harmful consequences for the spontaneous

---

were 100-percent warehouse certificates for gold. (Milton Friedman, "Has Gold Lost its Monetary Role?" in *Milton Friedman in South Africa*, Meyer Feldberg, Kate Jowel, and Stephen Mulholland, eds. [Johannesburg: Graduate School of Business of the University of Cape Town, 1976])

On the economic theory of gold see chapter 8 ("The Theory of Commodity Money: Economics of a Pure Gold Standard") of Mark Skousen's book, *The Structure of Production*, pp. 265–81.

[39]Laureano Figuerola, *Escritos económicos*, preliminary study by Francisco Cabrillo Rodríguez, ed. (Madrid: Instituto de Estudios Fiscales, 1991), p. 268. This assertion, which even Mises and Hayek themselves could not have worded more accurately, appears in the report Laureano Figuerola delivered to the Spanish Constituent Assembly on February 22, 1869.

process of social cooperation. Thus free banking should have no other limit than that established by the framework of general legal principles. This brings us to the third essential element in our proposal; let us now consider it.[40]

---

[40]In short, we recommend replacing the current web of administrative legislation which regulates banks with a few simple articles to be established in the Penal and Commercial Codes. For instance, in Spain, the entire body of banking legislation could be eliminated and simply replaced with new Articles 180 and 182 of the Commercial Code. The text of these new articles might resemble the following (excerpts which differ from the current phrasing are shown in italics):

> Article 180: Banks will hold in their vaults an amount of cash equal to the *total* value of deposits, checking accounts and bills in circulation.

> Article 182: The sum of the bills in circulation, together with the amount corresponding to deposits and checking accounts, will in no case exceed the total of the cash reserves *held by each bank at any given moment.*

In our articles for the Commercial Code we need not make reference to operations carried out in evasion of the law in order to mask a true deposit contract (transactions with a repurchase agreement, or American put options, etc.), since the legal technique of the doctrine of law evasion would render such operations null and void. However, to avoid the possibility that a financial "innovation" might be converted into money prior to its legal annulment, it would be wise to add the following to Article 180: *"The same obligation must be fulfilled by all individuals and corporations which, in evasion of the law, conduct legal transactions which mask a true monetary-deposit contract."*

As to the Penal Code, in Spain the necessary reforms would be very few. Nevertheless in order to clarify even further the content of Article 252 of the new Penal Code and make it compatible with the phrasing we suggest for Articles 180 and 182 of the Commercial Code, it should be worded as follows:

> Article 252: The penalties specified will be applied to anyone who, to the detriment of another, appropriates or embezzles money, goods or any other movable property or patrimonial asset which he has received on deposit, *irregular deposit or monetary bank deposit*, on consignment or in trust, or by way of *any* other *similar* claim carrying the obligation to deliver or

THE OBLIGATION OF ALL AGENTS IN A FREE-BANKING SYSTEM
TO OBSERVE TRADITIONAL LEGAL RULES AND PRINCIPLES,
PARTICULARLY A 100-PERCENT RESERVE REQUIREMENT ON
DEMAND DEPOSITS

There remains little for us to add here on the recommendation of a 100-percent reserve requirement for banking. We
have devoted this book's entire analysis to justifying this third
element in our proposal, a point logically and intimately
linked to the other two. Indeed the only way to eradicate the
state central-planning agency related to money and the financial system (i.e., the central bank) is to permit society to resume
the use of that form of private money which in an evolutionary
manner has emerged throughout history (gold, and to a lesser
extent, silver). Moreover a free market economy can only operate based on the framework provided by the rules of substantive law. When applied to banking, these rules demand the
establishment of a completely free banking system, but one in
which bankers consistently observe the principle of maintaining a 100 percent reserve on demand-deposit contracts.

Combined, the three above elements comprise the core of
a proposal to definitively reform and privatize the modern
banking and monetary system, to free it from the obstacles
which now disrupt it, especially central-bank intervention
and state-granted privileges enjoyed by the most important
agents in the financial sector. This reform would permit the
development of banking institutions truly appropriate to a

---

return the property, or who denies having received it. . . .
These penalties will be increased by 50 percent in the case of
a necessary deposit, *an irregular or monetary bank deposit, or
any other operation which, in evasion of the law, masks a monetary
irregular deposit.*

These simple modifications to the Commercial and Penal Codes
would make it possible to abolish all current banking laws in Spain. It
would then fall to ordinary law courts to evaluate the behavior of
individuals who might be suspected of breaking any of the prohibitions
mentioned. (This process would logically include all the guarantees
characteristic of a constitutional state, guarantees conspicuously absent
today in many administrative actions of the central bank.)

market economy, institutions which would facilitate economic development and the accumulation of *wisely invested* capital, while preventing the maladjustments and crises which the current, rigorously controlled and centralized system causes.

WHAT WOULD THE FINANCIAL AND BANKING SYSTEM OF A TOTALLY FREE SOCIETY BE LIKE?

We agree with Israel M. Kirzner that it is impossible to know today what information and institutions entrepreneurs who participate in the financial and banking system of the future will freely and spontaneously create tomorrow, assuming they suffer no institutional state coercion and are subject merely to the legal framework of substantive rules required by the operation of any market. As we know, the most important of all such rules in banking is the principle of a 100 percent reserve.[41]

Despite the above, we can conjecture with F.A. Hayek[42] that under these circumstances a variety of mutual funds would spontaneously emerge,[43] in which people would invest

---

[41] We are not able to chart the future of capitalism in any specificity. Our reason for this incapability is precisely that which assures us . . . the economic future of capitalism will be one of progress and advance. The circumstance that precludes our viewing the future of capitalism as a determinate one is the very circumstance in which, with entrepreneurship at work, we are no longer confined by any scarcity framework. It is therefore the very absence of this element of determinacy and predictability that, paradoxically, permits us to feel confidence in the long-run vitality and progress of the economy under capitalism. (Israel M. Kirzner, *Discovery and the Capitalist Process* [Chicago and London: University of Chicago Press, 1985], p. 168)

[42]Hayek, *Denationalisation of Money*, pp. 119–20.

[43]On the development of this network of mutual funds, see the article by Joseph T. Salerno, "Gold Standards: True and False," pp. 257–58. The perception that shares in these mutual funds would eventually become money is incorrect, since such shares are merely titles to real investments and would not guarantee the recovery of the nominal value of such investments, which would always be subject to trends in the market

a portion of current "deposits." These mutual funds would be highly liquid, due to the existence of widespread secondary financial markets. However, as is logical, they would not guarantee their participants the recovery at any time of the nominal value of their investments. As with the value of any other security in the secondary market, this would be subject to changes in the market value of the corresponding shares. Thus a sudden change (albeit improbable) in the social rate of time preference would cause generalized fluctuations in the value of shares. Such oscillations in value would only affect the holders of the corresponding shares and not, as now occurs, all citizens, who, year after year, see a significant drop in the purchasing power of the state-issued monetary units they are obliged to use.

Quite possibly, this widespread system of mutual funds would be accompanied by an entire network of institutions devoted to providing their customers with such services as payments, transfers, bookkeeping, and cashier services in general. These companies would operate in an environment of free competition and would charge the corresponding market prices for their services.

Also conceivable is the appearance of a number of private firms *with no connection whatsoever to credit,* companies dedicated to the extraction, design, and supply of the different forms of private money. Such firms would also receive a profit (most likely a modest one) for their services. We say "extraction" because we have no doubt that in an environment of

---

prices of the corresponding capital goods, stocks and/or bonds. In other words, despite the high degree of liquidity these investments might reach, this liquidity would neither be immediate nor would it correspond to the nominal value attached to monetary units by definition. In fact any person with a need for liquidity would be obliged to find someone in the market willing to provide that liquidity by paying in gold the market value of the corresponding mutual-fund shares. Hence mutual funds can guarantee neither the value of the capital invested at the time the share is acquired, nor the interest rate of the investment. Any "guarantee" of liquidity simply refers to the relative ease with which the fund's shares can be sold on the market (though there is no legal guarantee that the sale will be possible under all circumstances nor much less at a set price).

complete freedom, the predominant form of money will always be a metallic one with at least those essential characteristics that until now gold alone has offered: immutability, great homogeneity, and above all, scarcity. For the scarcer money is, and the more unlikely significant increases or decreases in its volume within relatively short periods of time are, the better money fulfills its function.[44]

3

AN ANALYSIS OF THE ADVANTAGES OF THE PROPOSED SYSTEM

In this section we will consider the main advantages a free-banking system which adheres to legal principles, a 100-percent reserve requirement and a completely private form of money (gold) offers as opposed to the system of financial central planning (central bank) which currently controls the financial and banking spheres of all countries.

1. *The Proposed System Prevents Bank Crises.* Even the most prominent defenders of fractional-reserve free banking have recognized that the establishment of a 100-percent reserve requirement would put an end to bank crises.[45] Indeed bank crises stem from the inherent lack of liquidity of these institutions, which use in the form of loans most of the money deposited with them on demand. If, in keeping with traditional

---

[44]Therefore it is through no caprice of history that in a context of freedom gold has prevailed as generally accepted money, since it has the essential characteristics which, from the standpoint of general legal principles and economic theory, a widely accepted medium of exchange must have. In this area, as in many others (the family, property rights, etc.), economic theory has backed the spontaneous results of the process of social evolution.

[45]Among others, George A. Selgin, who confirms that "a 100-percent reserve banking crisis is an impossibility." Selgin, "Are Banking Crises a Free-Market Phenomenon?" p. 2.

legal principles in the irregular deposit, anyone who receives money on deposit is required to keep on hand at all times a *tantundem* equal to 100 percent of the money received, it is obvious that depositors will be able to withdraw the amount deposited at any time without placing any financial strain on the corresponding banks.

Of course banks, in the exercise of activities other than deposit banking, in their role as loan intermediaries for example, may certainly encounter economic problems as a result of entrepreneurial errors or poor management. However in these cases the simple application of the principles of bankruptcy law[46] would be sufficient to liquidate this type of bank operation in an orderly fashion *without affecting in any way* the guaranteed return of demand deposits. From a legal and economic point of view, this second type of bank "crisis" is completely unrelated, both qualitatively and quantitatively, with the traditional crises which have plagued banks since they began to operate with a fractional reserve. The only way to avoid these traditional crises is precisely to do away with fractional-reserve banking.

2. *The Proposed System Prevents Cyclical Economic Crises.* As we have seen based on both theory and history, successive cycles of artificial boom and economic recession have afflicted market economies since banks began to function with a fractional reserve. In addition, the damaging effects of these cycles became even stronger when governments granted banks the privilege of legally operating in this manner. The damage became most acute with the creation of the central bank as a lender of last resort designed to supply the system with the necessary liquidity in times of trouble. For while the central bank has reduced the frequency of bank crises, it has not been capable of ending economic recessions, which, in contrast, have in many cases become deeper and more severe.

A banking system in tune with traditional property-law principles (i.e., a 100 percent reserve) would immunize our

---

[46]See Cabrillo, *Quiebra y liquidación de empresas: un análisis económico del derecho español.*

societies against recurrent economic crises. In fact, under these circumstances, the volume of loans could not increase without a *prior*, parallel increase in society's real, voluntary saving. Under such conditions, it would be impossible to imagine that the productive structure could be distorted as a result of dis-coordination in the behavior of those economic agents who invest and those who save. The best guarantee against intertemporal maladjustments in the productive structure is observance of the traditional legal principles present in the innermost logic behind the legal institutions related to the irregular-deposit contract and property law.[47]

Contrary to the belief of the Chicago theorists (those who advocated a 100-percent reserve requirement for banking), the eradication of economic crises and recessions also clearly depends upon the total privatization of money (pure gold standard). For if the central bank continues to be responsible for the issuance of purely fiduciary money, there will never be any guarantee that this institution, via open-market operations on the stock exchange, could not temporarily and artificially reduce interest rates and inject capital markets with artificial liquidity which, in the end, would exert exactly the same discoordinating effects on the productive structure as credit expansion initiated by private banks without the backing of real savings.[48] The key Chicago defenders of a 100-percent

---

[47]An accurate definition of property rights with respect to the monetary bank-deposit contract (100 percent reserve) and a strong, effective defense of these rights is therefore the only prerequisite for a "stable monetary system," a goal Pope John Paul II views as one of the state's (few) key responsibilities in the economy. See John Paul II, *Centesimus Annus: Encyclical Letter on the Hundredth Anniversary of Rerum Novarum*, 1991, no. 48 (London: Catholic Truth Society, 1991), pp. 35–36. Here John Paul II states: "Economic activity, especially the activity of a market economy, cannot be conducted in an institutional, juridical or political vacuum." This assertion harmonizes perfectly with our support for the application of legal principles to the concrete case of the monetary bank-deposit contract.

[48]As we know, the government may also cause *horizontal* (intratemporal) discoordination in the productive structure by issuing new money to finance a portion of its expenditures.

reserve requirement (Simons, Mints, Fisher, Hart, and Friedman) primarily sought to facilitate monetary policy and prevent bank crises (point one above), but their macroeconomic-monetarist analytical tools kept them from seeing that even more harmful than bank crises are cyclical economic crises unleashed on the real productive structure by the fractional-reserve banking system. Only the complete abolition of legal-tender regulations and the total privatization of the state-issued money now in existence will prevent government institutions from triggering economic cycles even once a 100-percent reserve requirement is established for private banking.

Finally, we must recognize that the recommended system would not avoid *all* economic crises and recessions. It would only avert the recurrent cycles of boom and recession which we now suffer (and which constitute the vast majority and the most serious). It would not prevent those isolated crises provoked by wars, natural disasters, or similar phenomena which, due to their sudden attack on the confidence and time preference of economic agents, might cause shocks to the productive structure and thus demand considerable, painful readjustments. Nonetheless we must not be deceived, as a number of theorists are (mainly those adherents of "new classical economics"), by the notion that all economic crises stem from external shocks. These theorists fail to realize that most crises have an endogenous origin and are fueled by the very credit expansion which the banking sector brings about and central banks orchestrate. In the absence of this disruptive influence on credit, the number of shocks would fall to a minimum, not only because the prime cause of instability in our economies would disappear, but also, as we will explain later, because governments would adopt much more disciplined fiscal programs. With this increased restraint, the proposed system would act in time to abort many policies that would foster financial irresponsibility and even violence, conflicts, and wars, which without a doubt, are also ultimately responsible for the isolated appearance of external shocks which prove highly damaging to the economy.

3. *The Proposed System Is the Most in Tune with Private Property*. The establishment of a 100-percent reserve requirement

for demand-deposit bank contracts would stamp out the legal corruption which has plagued the institution of banking from its very beginning. As we saw in our historical study of the evolution of banking, governments first overlooked the fraudulent nature of fractional-reserve banking. Then, when the effects of the system became more evident, instead of adequately defining and defending the traditional principles of property law, they became accomplices and later the driving force behind the corresponding expansionary processes, always with the goal of obtaining an easier source of financing for their political projects. The evolution of banking on the fringe of legal principles has produced solely negative results: it has encouraged all sorts of fraudulent, irresponsible behaviors; it has triggered artificial credit expansion and highly damaging, recurrent economic recessions and social crises; and it has ultimately determined the inevitable appearance of the central bank and an entire web of administrative regulations on financial and banking activities, regulations which have not achieved the objectives set for them and which, surprisingly today, on the threshold of the twenty-first century, continue to destabilize the world's economies.

4. *The Proposed Model Promotes Stable, Sustainable Economic Growth, and Thus Drastically Reduces Market Transaction Costs and Specifically the Strains of Labor Negotiations.* Over ninety years of chronic worldwide inflation and continuous, and during many periods completely uncontrolled, credit expansion have corrupted the behavioral habits of economic agents, and hence today, most believe inflation and credit expansion are necessary to stimulate economic development. Furthermore the misconception that any economy not in an economic boom is therefore "stagnant" has become generalized. People fail to see that rapid, exaggerated economic expansion is always likely to have an artificial cause and must reverse in the form of a recession. In short, we have become accustomed to living in manic-depressive economies and have adjusted our behavior to an unstable, disturbing pattern of economic development.

However, following the proposed reform, this "manic-depressive" model of economic development would be replaced by another much more stable and sustained one. In fact, not only would artificial expansion be prevented, along with the *stress* it involves at all levels (economic, environmental, social, and personal), but the recessions which inevitably follow each period of expansion would be prevented as well. In the proposed model, the monetary system would be rigid and inelastic with respect to the money supply, both in terms of growth in the quantity of money in circulation and, especially, possible decreases or contractions in it. Indeed a 100-percent reserve requirement would preclude an expansionary increase in the money supply in the form of loans, and the quantity of money in circulation would simply grow naturally and would be tied to the annual rise in the worldwide stock of gold. The worldwide stock of gold has grown at an average of between 1 and 3 percent per year over the last 100 years.[49] Therefore, with a monetary system comprised of a pure gold standard and a 100-percent reserve requirement for banking, if we assume productivity mounts at an average rate of 3 percent per year, this model of economic growth would give rise to a *gradual, constant drop in the prices of consumer goods and services.*

---

[49]See Skousen, "The Theory of Commodity Money: Economics of a Pure Gold Standard," in *The Structure of Production*, pp. 269–71. Skousen also explains that, given the unchanging nature of gold, the worldwide stock of it accumulated throughout history only rises and does not decline. Therefore, other things being equal, if the volume of gold produced worldwide remains constant, the money supply will increase by less and less, in terms of percentage. However this circumstance is compensated for by technological improvements and innovations in the mining sector, which have determined that, on average, the worldwide stock of gold has risen from 1 to 3 percent per year since 1910. Mises, for his part, indicates that the annual increase in the worldwide stock of gold tends to match the gradual, enduring rise which population growth causes in the demand for money. Hence if demand mounts from 1 to 3 percent (a rate similar to that of the increase in gold), prices will drop by around 3 percent per year and nominal interest rates will fluctuate between 0.25 and 1 percent (assuming general economic productivity increases by 3 percent, on average). See *Human Action*, pp. 414–15. Mises does not mention that healthy, long-lasting deflation caused by growth in productivity tends, *ceteris paribus*, to reduce the demand for money, allowing for higher nominal rates of interest.

Not only is this drop perfectly compatible with sustainable economic development from a theoretical and practical standpoint, but it would also guarantee that the benefits of such growth would profit all citizens through a constant increase in the purchasing power of their monetary units.[50]

This model of rising productivity, economic development and a money supply which grows slowly (at a rate of around 1 percent) would generate, via a decrease in prices, an increase in the real income of the factors of production, especially labor, which in turn would result in an enormous fall in the negotiation costs currently associated with collective bargaining. (Assuming the demand for money is stable, productivity rises at a rate of 3 percent and the money supply grows at a rate of 1 percent, prices would tend to fall by approximately 2 percent per year.) In this model, the real income of all factors of production, especially labor, would be updated automatically, and hence collective bargaining, which presently creates so much tension and conflict in western economies, could be eliminated. Indeed this process would be relegated to those isolated cases in which, for example, a greater increase in productivity or in the market price of specific types of labor made it necessary to negotiate even greater rises than those automatically reflected each year in real income with the decline in the general price level. Moreover in these cases even the intervention of unions would be unnecessary (though the possibility is not excluded), since market forces themselves, guided by the entrepreneurial profit motive, would spontaneously provoke those income rises justified in relative terms. Therefore, in practice, collective bargaining would be limited to those isolated cases in which productivity rose less than average,

---

[50]George A. Selgin recently argued that the best monetary-policy rule is to allow the general price level to fall in accordance with growth in productivity. See his book, *Less Than Zero: The Case for a Falling Price Level in a Growing Economy*. We find this suggestion fundamentally sound. Nevertheless, for the reasons stated in chapter 8, we do not entirely support Selgin's theses. We particularly disagree with his view that the institutional measure most conducive to his suggestion would be to establish a fractional-reserve free-banking system.

making certain reductions in nominal wages necessary (in any case, these would generally be smaller than the drop in the general price level).[51]

Finally, we should point out that the chief virtue in the rigidity of the proposed monetary system is that it would *completely* prevent sudden contractions or decreases in the money supply such as inevitably occur now in the recession stage which in the economic cycle follows every expansion. Thus perhaps the greatest advantage of the reform we suggest is that it would totally eliminate the credit squeeze which succeeds every boom and is one of the clearest signs of the economic crises that repetitively grip our economies. The worldwide stock of gold is unchanging and has accumulated over the history of civilization. Hence it is inconceivable that its volume will suddenly plunge at some future point. One of the

---

[51]Mises, in the memorandum which he prepared for the League of Nations, and which we mentioned earlier in this chapter, expresses the above ideas brilliantly and concisely:

> [I]f all expansion of credit by the banks had been effectively precluded, the world would have had a monetary system in which—even apart from the discoveries of gold in California, Australia, and South Africa—prices would have shown a general tendency to fall. The majority of our contemporaries will find a sufficient ground for regarding such a monetary system as bad in itself, *since they are wedded to the belief that good business and high prices are one and the same thing. But that is prejudice.* If we had had slowly falling prices for eighty years or more, we would have become accustomed to look for improvements in the standard of living and increases in real income through falling prices with stable or falling money income, rather than through increases in money income. At any rate, a solution to the difficult problem of reforming our monetary and credit system must not be rejected offhand merely for the reason that it involves a continuous fall in the price level. Above all, we must not allow ourselves to be influenced by the evil consequences of the recent *rapid* fall in prices. *A slow and steady decline of prices cannot in any sense be compared with what is happening under the present system: namely, sudden and big rises in the price level, followed by equally sudden and sharp falls.* (Mises, *Money, Method, and the Market Process*, pp. 90–91; italics added)

most salient features of gold, and possibly the most influential in gold's evolutionary predominance as money par excellence, is its homogeneity and immutability throughout the centuries. Thus the main advantage of the proposed model is that it would preclude the sudden reductions in the volume of credit and, hence, in the quantity of money in circulation, which until now have been repetitive in the "elastic" monetary and credit systems which prevail in the world. In short, a pure gold standard with a 100-percent reserve requirement would prevent deflation, understood as any drop in the quantity of money or credit in circulation.[52]

5. *The Proposed System Would Put an End to Feverish Financial Speculation and its Damaging Effects.* We could liken banks' creation of money through credit expansion to the opening of Pandora's box. To close it again, we must eliminate the incentives that tempt individuals to indulge in all kinds of unscrupulous, fraudulent behaviors. Such incentives are extremely harmful, since they corrupt the established habit of saving and working conscientiously; that is, the habit of making a constant, honest, responsible, and long-term economic effort.[53] Furthermore

---

[52]We must remember that during the Great Depression of 1929, the money supply contracted by around 30 percent. A contraction of this sort would be impossible with a pure gold standard and a 100-percent reserve requirement, given that the monetary system we propose is inelastic with respect to contractions. Hence in our model, the monetary contraction which many mistakenly identify as the main cause of the Great Depression would not have occurred in any case. At the same time, it is highly improbable that the combination of a pure gold standard and a 100-percent reserve requirement has ever resulted in an inflationary rise in prices. See Mark Skousen, *Economics on Trial: Lies, Myths and Realities* (Homewood, Ill.: Business One Irwin, 1991), pp. 133–38. In fact, in no year from 1492 to the present has the total supply of gold increased by more than 5 percent, and the average increase, as we have already indicated, has been between 1 and 3 percent per year.

[53]In the exact words of Maurice Allais, "spéculation, frénétique et fébrile, est permise, alimentée et amplifiée par le crédit *tel qui fonctionne actuellement*." Maurice Allais, "Les conditions monétaires d'une économie de marchés," p. 326. Perhaps there is no more concise and elegant way to refer to what the Spanish have in recent years popularly

wild stock-market speculation would also be thwarted, and take-over bids, which are harmless in themselves, would only be made in the presence of true, objective, economic reasons for them. They would not be a mere result of great ease in obtaining external financing due to *ex nihilo* credit expansion in the banking sector. In other words, as Maurice Allais indicates:

> Take-over bids are *essentially useful,* but the legislation governing them should be revised. It should not be possible to finance them using means of payment created *ex nihilo* by the banking system or newly-issued junk bonds, as occurs in the United States.[54]

In the market, the expansionary supply of loans unbacked by saving creates its own demand, which is often embodied in unscrupulous economic agents whose only intention is to obtain a short-term benefit from the enormous advantages which, to the detriment of all other citizens, they derive from using newly-created means of payment before anyone else.

6. *The Proposed System Reduces the Economic Functions of the State to a Minimum and, in Particular, Permits the Eradication of the Central Bank.* The system we recommend would eliminate the need for the Federal Reserve, the European Central Bank, the Bank of England, the Bank of Japan, and in general any authority, central bank or official, public or government body with a monopoly on the issuance of money and, as a central

---

come to call "la cultura del pelotazo" [the culture of easy money], a trend which has undoubtedly been made possible and fed by the uncontrolled credit expansion brought about by the financial system. Alan Greenspan has popularized the expression "irrational exuberance" in reference to the typical behavior of investors in the recent financial bubble.

[54]Allais, "Les conditions monétaires d'une économie de marchés," p. 347. The original text reads:

> Les offres publiques d'achat sont *fondamentalement utiles*, mais la législation les concernant doit être réformée. Il n'est pas souhaitable qu'elles puissent être financées par des moyens de paiement créés *ex nihilo* par le système bancaire, ou par l'émission des *junk bonds*, comme c'est le cas aux États-Unis.

monetary-planning agency, on the control and management of the banking and financial system of any country. Even certain distinguished politicians, such as the nineteenth-century American President Andrew Jackson, understood this idea perfectly and, motivated by it, fiercely opposed the establishment of any central bank. Unfortunately their influence was not strong enough to prevent the creation of the current central-planning system in the sector of banking and finance, nor any of this system's harmful effects, past or present, on our economies.[55]

Moreover, as the Public Choice School indicates, privileged special interest groups and politicians will tend to exploit any fiduciary monetary system based on a state monopoly on the issuance of money. In fact, politicians face the irresistible temptation to try to *buy* votes with funds created from nothing, an enticement analyzed by theorists of the "political cycle," among others.[56] Furthermore the possibility of expanding money and credit allows politicians to finance their expenditures without resorting to taxes, which are always unpopular and painful. At the same time, with this course of action, the decrease in the purchasing power of money works in politicians' favor, since income taxes are generally progressive. For these reasons it is especially important that we find a monetary system which, like the one proposed

---

[55]Thus we should be especially critical of those authors who, such as Alan Reynolds, Arthur B. Laffer, Marc A. Miles and others, attempt to establish a pseudo-gold-standard in which the central bank continues to play the leading role in monetary and credit policy, but with a reference to gold. Friedman has appropriately characterized this pseudo-gold-standard as "a system in which, instead of gold being money, gold was a commodity whose price was fixed by governments." (See Friedman, "Has Gold Lost its Monetary Role?" p. 36). The proposals of Laffer and Miles appear in their book, *International Economics in an Integrated World* (Oakland, N.J.: Scott and Foresman, 1982). A brief, brilliant critique of these proposals can be found in Salerno, "Gold Standards: True and False," pp. 258–61.

[56]See, for example, chapter 5 ("Ciclo Político-Económico") of Juan Francisco Corona Ramón's book, *Una introducción a la teoría de la decisión pública* (*Public Choice*) (Alcalá de Henares; Madrid: Instituto Nacional de Administración Pública, 1987), pp. 116–42, and the bibliography provided therein. Remember also the references of footnote 57 of chapter 6.

here, permits the discontinuation of state intervention in the field of money and finance. Mises sums up this argument quite well:

> *The reason for using a commodity money is precisely to prevent political influence from affecting directly the value of the monetary unit.* Gold is the standard money . . . primarily because an increase or decrease in the available quantity is independent of the orders issued by political authorities. The distinctive feature of the gold standard is that it makes changes in the quantity of money dependent on the profitability of gold production.[57]

Therefore we see that the institution of a pure gold standard with a 100-percent reserve requirement has emerged from the choices made by millions and millions of economic agents in the market throughout a prolonged evolutionary process, and it provides the vital opportunity to check the tendency of all governments to meddle in and manipulate the monetary and credit system.[58]

7. *The Proposed System Is the Most Compatible with Democracy.* One of the key principles of democracy is that the financing of public activities must be the object of discussion and explicit decision-making on the part of political representatives. The current monopoly on the issuance of money, which is held by a public agency and a banking industry that

---

[57]Mises, *On the Manipulation of Money and Credit*, p. 22; italics added.

[58]Mises, *The Theory of Money and Credit*, p. 455. There we read:

> Thus the sound-money principle has two aspects. It is affirmative in approving the market's choice of a commonly used medium of exchange. It is negative in obstructing the government's propensity to meddle with the currency system.

Hence we consider our proposal vastly superior to that of the School of Monetary Constitutionalism, the adherents of which attempt to solve current issues via the establishment of constitutional rules on monetary growth and banking and financial markets. Monetary constitutionalism is not necessary in the context of a pure gold standard and a 100-percent reserve requirement, nor would it curb politicians' temptation to manipulate credit and money.

operates with a fractional reserve, permits the *ex nihilo* creation of purchasing power which benefits the state and certain individuals and companies, to the detriment of the rest of society. This possibility is exploited mainly by the government, which uses it as a mechanism for financing its expenditures without having to resort to the most obvious and politically costly route, an increase in taxes. Although governments try to conceal this financing mechanism by rhetorically demanding that budgets be financed in an "orthodox" manner, and that the deficit not be *directly* funded through the issuance of currency and credit, in practice the result is quite similar when a significant number of the treasury bonds governments issue to finance their deficit are later purchased by central and private banks with new money of their own creation (indirect process of monetization of the national debt). Furthermore we should emphasize that the hidden expropriation of citizens' wealth, an action permitted by the process of fiduciary inflation, profits not only governments, but also bankers themselves. Indeed, because bankers operate with a fractional reserve and governments do not oblige them to devote all credit expansion to financing the public sector (through the purchase of treasury bonds), banks also carry out a gradual, diffuse expropriation of a major portion of the purchasing power of citizens' monetary units, while banks' balance sheets reflect the amassment of considerable assets which are the cumulative result of this historical process of expropriation. In this sense, bankers' protests against the suggestion that they be required to devote such a large percentage of their assets to financing the public deficit must be understood as one side of an argument between the two "accomplices" in the socially detrimental credit-expansion process, accomplices who "negotiate" between themselves which share of the "profits" each will take.

In contrast to the above system, a pure gold standard with a 100-percent reserve requirement would oblige states to fully specify their expenditures and the sources of their income, which would prevent them from resorting to the covert financing available in inflation and credit expansion. Moreover, such a system would also preclude private bankers from profiting from a large portion of this "inflationary tax." Maurice Allais has given an abundantly clear assessment of this point. He states:

> Given that any creation of money exerts the same effects as would a true tax imposed on all whose income is diminished by the rise in prices which inevitably follows the issuance of new money, the profit derived from it, which is actually considerable, should return to the state and thus permit it to reduce the overall amount of its taxes.[59]

Nonetheless, we suggest a much more favorable option: that the state should relinquish its power to issue money and thus accept an obligation to rely on taxes in order to finance all of its expenditures, which it would be required to do with complete transparency. As a result of the above, citizens would directly perceive the entire cost involved and would hence be sufficiently motivated to subject all public agencies to the necessary monitoring.

8. *The Proposed System Fosters Peaceful, Harmonious Cooperation among Nations.* An analysis of the history of military conflicts over the last two centuries plainly reveals that many of the wars which have ravaged humanity could have been completely prevented or would have been much less virulent if it

---

[59]   Comme toute création monétaire équivaut par ses effets à un véritable impôt prélevé sur tous ceux dont les revenus se voient diminués par la hausse des prix qu'elle engendre inévitablement, le profit qui en résulte, *considérable à vrai dire*, devrait revenir à l'État en lui permettant ainsi de réduire d'autant le montant global de ses impôts. (Allais, "Les conditions monétaires d'une économie de marchés," p. 331)

In the same place, Allais identifies the following as one of the most striking paradoxes of our time: though the public has become more aware of the serious dangers involved in government use of the money press, *citizens remain completely ignorant of the identical dangers which the system of credit expansion unbacked by real saving poses in the form of fractional-reserve banking.* The Spaniard Juan Antonio Gimeno Ullastres has studied the tax effect of inflation, though unfortunately he fails to mention the consequences of the credit expansion fractional-reserve banking entails. See his article, "Un impuesto llamado inflación," published in *Homenaje a Lucas Beltrán* (Madrid: Editorial Moneda y Crédito, 1982), pp. 803–23.

had not been for states' mounting influence in monetary matters and, ultimately, their acquired control over credit expansion and the creation of money. Indeed, governments have concealed the true cost of military conflicts from their citizens by largely financing these costs using inflationary procedures which, under the pretext of each particular military emergency, states have employed with absolute impunity. Therefore we can confidently assert that inflation has fueled wars: if in each case the citizens of the nations engaged in battle had been aware of the true cost involved, either hostilities would have been averted in time by the corresponding democratic mechanisms, or citizens would have required governments to negotiate a solution long before the destruction and damage to humanity reached the immense degrees which, sadly, they have reached in history. Thus we conclude with Ludwig von Mises:

> One can say without exaggeration that inflation is an indispensable intellectual means of militarism. Without it, the repercussions of war on welfare would become obvious much more quickly and penetratingly; war-weariness would set in much earlier.[60]

At the same time, the establishment of a pure gold standard with a 100-percent reserve requirement would amount to a *de facto* adoption of a single, worldwide monetary standard. There would be no need for an international central bank, and

----

[60] Ludwig von Mises, *Nation, State and Economy: Contributions to the Politics and History of Our Time* (New York and London: New York University Press, 1983), p. 163; and also *Human Action*, p. 442. The former is Leland B. Yeager's translation of Mises's *Nation, Staat, und Wirtschaft*, which was originally published in 1919, in German (Vienna and Leipzig: Manzsche Verlags Buchhandlung, 1919). On this important topic, see also Joseph T. Salerno, "War and the Money Machine: Concealing the Costs of War Beneath the Veil of Inflation," chapter 17 of *The Costs of War: America's Pyrrhic Victories*, John V. Denson, ed. (New Brunswick and London: Transaction Publishers, 1997), pp. 367–87. Nevertheless the first to point out the close connection between militarism and inflation was, again, Father Juan de Mariana, in his book, *De Monetae Mutatione*, published in 1609. See *Tratado y discurso sobre la moneda de vellón*, p. 35 (English edition, *A Treatise on the Alteration of Money*).

thus no risk that such a bank would manipulate the worldwide supply of money and credit. In this way, we would enjoy all the advantages of a single, international monetary standard, yet suffer none of the disadvantages of intergovernmental agencies related to money. Furthermore this system would not provoke suspicion concerning a loss of sovereignty to the corresponding states, while all nations and social groups would benefit from the existence of a sole monetary unit which no one would govern nor manipulate. Therefore a pure gold standard and a 100-percent reserve requirement would promote international economic integration within a harmonious juridical framework of mutual satisfaction, a framework which would minimize social conflicts, thus encouraging peace and voluntary trade between all nations.

4

REPLIES TO POSSIBLE OBJECTIONS
TO OUR PROPOSAL FOR MONETARY REFORM

Although no integrated, coherent, systematic critique of our plan to reform the banking system has yet been produced,[61] there have been certain isolated, unsystematic objections to the proposal to establish a banking system with a 100-percent reserve requirement. We will now present and analyze these challenges one by one.

1. *"Banks would disappear, because they would lose their* raison d'être *and main source of income."* Such criticism is unfounded. All that banks would lose by adopting a 100-percent reserve requirement is the possibility of creating loans *ex nihilo*; i.e., loans unbacked by a rise in voluntary saving. The suggested reform would make it impossible for the banking system as a whole to expand credit artificially, and

---

[61]"Exhaustive research, however, fails to uncover any published critiques in this regard." Walter Block, "Fractional Reserve Banking," p. 31. Leland Yeager's brief critical comments on our proposal have already been answered in this section. See "The Perils of Base Money," pp. 256–57.

with it the money supply, and thereby trigger recurrent cycles of boom and recession.

A significant number of totally legitimate activities would remain to sustain the banking business, and bankers could continue to pursue these activities, thus fulfilling the needs of consumers. One such activity would be true credit intermediation, which consists of loaning, with a differential, funds previously lent banks by their customers (not demand deposits). In addition, as deposit banks (with a 100-percent reserve requirement), institutions could provide custody and safekeeping, while charging the corresponding market price for this service and even combining it with other peripheral ones (the making of payments, transfers, records of customers' operations, etc.). If to this we add the custody and management of securities, the rental of safe deposit boxes, etc., we get a reasonably good idea of the extensive range of legitimate functions banks could continue to perform.

Therefore the belief that the reestablishment of a 100-percent reserve requirement would mean the death of private banks is unjustified. There would simply be a modification, itself largely evolutionary and non-traumatic, to their structure and operations. We have already mentioned the strong probability of the spontaneous development of a banking system comprised of a network of mutual funds, deposit institutions that maintain a 100-percent reserve ratio, and companies that specialize in providing accounting and cashier services to their customers. Hence we conclude with Ludwig von Mises:

> It is clear that prohibition of fiduciary media would by no means imply a death sentence for the banking system, as is sometimes asserted. The banks would still retain the business of negotiating credit, of borrowing for the purpose of lending.[62]

In short, banks could continue to engage in a large number of activities, thus satisfying the needs of consumers and obtaining a legitimate profit in return.

---

[62]Mises, *The Theory of Money and Credit*, p. 361.

2. "*The proposed system would largely decrease the amount of available credit, thereby pushing up the interest rate and hindering economic development.*" This is the popular criticism most often expressed, and it mainly comes from those economic agents (businessmen, politicians, journalists, etc.) who allow themselves to be influenced chiefly by the external and most visible characteristics of the economic system. According to this objection, if we prevent banks from creating loans *ex nihilo*, many companies will meet significantly greater difficulties in obtaining financing, and hence, *ceteris paribus*, the interest rate will rise and obstacles to economic development will appear. This objection stems from the fact that presently, due to credit expansion, businessmen face little difficulty in securing financing for almost any investment project, no matter how outlandish, assuming the economy is in a phase in which bankers are not afraid to expand their loans. Credit expansion has altered the traditional habits associated with the "entrepreneurial culture," habits which rested on much more prudent, responsible, and careful consideration prior to a decision on whether or not to launch a particular investment project.

At any rate, it is a grave error to suppose credit would disappear in a banking system governed by a 100-percent reserve requirement. Quite the opposite is true. Banks would still loan funds, but *only* those funds previously and voluntarily saved by economic agents. In short, the proposed system would guarantee that only that which has been saved would be lent. The new arrangement would thus ensure coordination between the supply and demand of present and future goods in the market and, consequently, prevent the profound maladjustments which the current banking system produces and which ultimately generate economic crises and recessions.

Moreover the notion that the loan funds devoted to investment in the current system can ultimately exceed society's voluntary saving is a fallacy. As we know, *ex post*, saving is always equal to investment, and if, *ex ante*, banks grant loans (through a process of credit expansion) at a faster pace than that of voluntary saving, entrepreneurs will simply tend to err en masse and allot the scarce, real resources saved by society to *disproportionate* investment projects which they will never be able to successfully complete.

Therefore this second objection is unfounded: with a 100-percent reserve requirement, banks would continue to loan what is saved, yet entrepreneurs would tend to invest saved funds in a much more prudent, realistic manner. If, from the start, businessmen were to encounter greater obstacles to financing certain entrepreneurial projects, such difficulties would be the logical manifestation of the healthy functioning of the only market mechanism capable of halting the initiation of unprofitable investment projects in time, and thus avoiding their unwise and discoordinated execution, which the current system promotes during credit booms.

As to the interest rate, there is no indication that in the long term it would be higher in the proposed system than in the current one. Indeed the interest rate ultimately depends on economic agents' subjective valuations of time preference. In our model, economic agents would not be affected by the massive squandering of capital goods which accompanies recurrent economic recessions. Furthermore it is clear that, other things being equal, in a system like the one we recommend, the interest rate would tend to be quite low in nominal terms, since the corresponding premium for the expected evolution of the purchasing power of money would in most cases be negative. Also, the component of risk would depend on the precariousness of each specific investment project undertaken and, following a period without economic recessions, would tend to fall as well. Hence we conclude that there is absolutely no theoretical basis for the assumption that the interest rate would be higher in the proposed system than it is now. Quite the reverse would be true. There are very powerful reasons to believe that in both real and nominal terms, the market rates of interest would be lower than those we are presently accustomed to.[63]

---

[63]For example, let us suppose the economy grows at an average rate of around 3 percent per year, and the money supply (the world stock of gold) rises by 1.5 percent. Under these circumstances, we will see very slight deflation of 1.5 percent per year. If the real market rate of interest is 4 percent (a natural rate of 3 percent and a risk component of 1

Therefore a system composed of a pure gold standard and a 100-percent reserve requirement would not weaken economic development. In fact, such a system would give rise to a model of stable, continuous development, free from the *manic-depressive* reactions which we have, with difficulty, become used to and which, unfortunately, involve the regular malinvestment of a huge quantity of society's scarce resources, to the serious detriment of sustainable economic growth and harmony in society.

3. *"The proposed model would penalize those who profit from the current banking and financial system."* It has at times been argued that the recommended system would unjustly penalize all those who profit from the present financial and banking system. Among its chief beneficiaries we must first list the government, which, as we know, manages to finance its expenditures (directly and indirectly) via credit expansion, without having to resort to the politically painful measure of raising taxes. Next we could mention bankers themselves (who line their pockets by the same procedures as the government, yet directly and privately), and also depositors, if they receive interest on their deposits and "do not pay" for the set of peripheral services banks perform.[64]

Nevertheless those who voice this objection do not take into account that many of the supposed "profits" individuals obtain from the banking system are not truly profits. Indeed it is inaccurate to argue that depositors currently enjoy substantial benefits (in the form of cashier, payment and bookkeeping services) without paying for them, since depositors

---

percent), the nominal market interest rate will be approximately 2.5 *percent per year*. In footnote 48 we supposed nominal interest rates would be even lower, due to population growth and a consequent, perennial low increase in the demand for money.

[64]   Under competitive conditions the benefits are partly enjoyed by the holders of fractionally-backed bank liabilities themselves, whose gain takes the form of explicit interest payments or lowered bank service charges or a combination of these. (Selgin, "Are Banking Crises a Free-Market Phenomenon?" p. 3).

themselves actually bear the full cost (explicitly or implicitly) of these benefits.

As to the explicit interest often available on deposits, such payments are usually compensated for by the continual decline in the purchasing power of depositors' monetary units. In the proposed system, which includes a 100-percent reserve requirement, the purchasing power of deposited monetary units would not only not decline, but, as we have seen, would grow gradually and constantly. This enormous benefit to *all* citizens would be remarkably superior to the supposed "advantage" of receiving explicit interest which hardly compensates for the devaluation of money. Hence today in most cases the real interest rate on deposits (after deducting the drop in the purchasing power of money) is almost null or even negative.

In a society with a pure gold standard and a 100-percent reserve requirement, *all* citizens would gain from the gradual, continuous increase in the purchasing power of their monetary units. They would receive interest on effective savings and be openly and explicitly obliged to pay the market price for those legitimate banking services they chose to use. The proposed system would thus be much more coherent and almost certainly more advantageous to the people in general than the present financial and banking system.[65]

As to the argument that governments and bankers would be unable to continue profiting from the current system, more than a defect and motive for criticizing our proposal, this would be a positive result which would offer *prima facie* justification for it. Indeed, above we emphasized the great

---

[65] *Il n'y a pas lieu de rendre gratuitement des services qui en tout état de cause ont un coût qu'il faut bien supporter.* Si un déposant est affranchi des frais relatifs à la tenue de son compte, la banque doit les supporter. Dans la situation actuelle elle peut le faire, car elle bénéficie des profits correspondants à la création de monnaie par le mécanisme du crédit. *Qui en supporte réellement le coût?*: l'ensemble des consommateurs pénalisés par la hausse des prix entraînée par l'accroissement de la masse monétaire. (Allais, "Les conditions monétaires d'une économie de marchés," p. 351)

importance of preventing governments from using inflation
and credit expansion to finance their expenditures in a concealed manner. Moreover we need not reiterate the details of
the obscure legal basis and harmful effects of private banks'
power to issue loans and deposits.

4. *"A 100-percent reserve requirement is an example of state
intervention and jeopardizes the contractual freedom of the parties."*
Modern neo-banking advocates of fractional-reserve free
banking often argue that it is "inadmissible" from a "libertarian" standpoint to limit the contractual freedom of the parties,
specifically, the ability of depositors to freely enter into pacts
with their bankers by which the former agree to open
demand-deposit accounts on which only a fractional reserve is
to be maintained. In the first three chapters we saw that a 100-
percent reserve requirement on demand deposits would not at
all constitute intolerable government interference ("legislation
through commands," in Hayekian terminology). Instead, it
would merely represent the natural application of traditional
property-law principles to the monetary irregular-deposit
contract ("substantive or material law," in Hayekian terminology).[66] Furthermore a voluntary decision by two parties to
enter into a contract and full knowledge of its *cause* (which,
incidentally, is not usually the case in the present financial and
banking system) are necessary conditions for the legitimacy of
an operation, but they alone are in no way sufficient to grant

---

[66]   [T]he free market does not mean freedom to commit fraud or
        any other form of theft. Quite the contrary. The criticism may
        be obviated by imposing a 100% reserve requirement, not as
        an arbitrary administrative fiat of the government, but as a
        part of the general legal defense of property against fraud.
        (Rothbard, *Man, Economy, and State*, p. 709)

As Jevons stated:

        "It used to be held as a general rule of law, that any present
        grant or assignment of goods not in existence is without
        operation," and this general rule need only be revived and
        enforced to outlaw fictitious money-substitutes. Then bank-
        ing could be left perfectly free and yet be without departure
        from 100% reserves. (Jevons, *Money and the Mechanism of
        Exchange*, pp. 211–12)

this legitimacy in keeping with traditional legal principles. In fact if third parties suffer harm as a result of such a contract, the contract is illegitimate, null, and void, because it disrupts the public order.[67] According to the analysis we present in this book, it is precisely this lack of legitimacy which pertains to fractional-reserve banking. This practice not only gives rise to the creation of additional means of payment to the detriment of all citizens, who watch as their monetary units decline in purchasing power;[68] it also deceives entrepreneurs on a broad scale, leading them to invest where and when they should not, and triggering recurrent cycles of boom and recession with a very heavy cost in human, economic and social terms.

Finally, we must counter the oft-heard argument[69] which centers around the claim that economic agents are unwilling

---

[67]By the same token, a free, voluntary "contract" by which two parties agree that one will pay the other to murder a third party would be invalid, since it would disturb the public order and be detrimental to third parties. The contract would be null and void even in the absence of deception or fraud, and even if both parties entered into it willfully and with full knowledge of its nature.

[68]We are not referring to a drop in purchasing power in absolute terms, but in relative terms, with respect to the growth which could be expected in the purchasing power of money in a banking system with a 100-percent reserve ratio. In addition, the economic consequences of current banking practices are, in this respect, identical to those of counterfeiting, an activity everyone agrees should be punished as a breach of public order, even if it is impossible to individually identify its victims.

[69]Juan José Toribio Dávila offers this critical argument, among others, in his paper, "Problemas Éticos en los Mercados Financieros," which he presented at the *Encuentros sobre la dimensión ética de las instituciones y mercados financieros*, which took place in Madrid under the auspices of the Fundación BBV in June 1994. Moreover Toribio Dávila argues that a stable monetary policy could be achieved with any reserve ratio, while he fails to consider the factors behind the theoretical impossibility of central planning in general, and of its application to the financial sector in particular. These factors account for central bankers' lack of ability and desire to adequately calculate the demand for money and to control the supply which, supposedly, should match the demand. Furthermore Toribio Dávila overlooks the profound discoordinating effects which any growth in the money supply in the form of credit expansion (i.e.,

to *voluntarily* establish a banking system based on a 100-percent reserve requirement and that their unwillingness is evidenced by the fact that nowadays they could freely agree to a similar arrangement (but do not) by using the safe deposit boxes banks rent out in the market. In contrast to this argument, we must point out that safe-deposit-box services are in no way associated with the contract governing the irregular-deposit of a fungible good such as money (rather, they are connected with a typical regular-deposit contract concerning specific goods). In addition, the safe-deposit-box business (which entails a cost to customers, and in their subjective view, does not provide the same services as a monetary bank-deposit contract) could never really compete on equal terms with the current fractional-reserve deposit system. In fact banks commonly pay interest on deposits nowadays (which suggests improper use is made of them). Also, banks offer valuable services at no explicit cost, which makes it impossible for voluntary deposit contracts that include a 100 percent reserve to compete and prosper, especially in an inflation-ridden environment in which the purchasing power of money declines continuously. A very similar counter-argument is called for concerning the public goods the state provides at no apparent direct cost to the consumer. It is notoriously difficult in a free-market environment for any private company with plans to offer the same services at market prices to thrive, due to this unfair, privileged competition from government agencies. These agencies supply "free" benefits to citizens and generate heavy losses which we all ultimately cover with our taxes via the national budget (inflationary tax).[70]

---

that unbacked by real saving) exerts on the productive structure. Finally, there is a clear connection between a 100-percent reserve requirement and ethics in the operations of financial institutions. In fact the link is evident not only in the host of ethically irresponsible behaviors characteristic of the feverish speculation credit expansion provokes, but also in the unquestionable fact that economic crises and recessions stem from the violation of an ethical principle which demands the maintenance of a 100 percent reserve on monetary demand-deposit contracts.

[70]Furthermore, Hülsmann has explained that

> [T]he confusion between monetary titles and fractional-reserve IOUs brings into operation what is commonly known

5. *"Financial 'innovations' will inevitably trigger the resurgence of fractional-reserve banking."* According to this argument, any legal precautions taken to prohibit fractional-reserve banking and, thus, to establish a 100-percent reserve requirement on demand deposits will be insufficient; such measures will always, ultimately be circumvented via new forms of business and financial "innovations" which, in evasion of the law or not, in one way or another, will tend to achieve the same end as fractional-reserve banking. Hence as early as 1937 even Hayek affirmed:

> It has been well remarked by the most critical among the originators of the scheme that banking is a *pervasive* phenomenon and the question is whether, when we prevent it from appearing in its traditional form, we will not just drive it into other and less easily controllable forms.[71]

Hayek cited Peel's Act of 1844 as the most notable precedent. Because those who introduced this act neglected to impose a 100-percent reserve requirement on deposits, from that point on, monetary expansion mainly took the form of deposits, rather than banknotes.[72]

---

as Gresham's Law. Imagine a potential bank customer who is offered two types of deposits with a bank. He believes that both deposits deliver exactly the same services. The only difference is that he has to pay for the first type of deposit, whereas he does not have to pay—or even receives payment—for the second type of deposit. Clearly he will choose not to be charitable to his banker and will subscribe to a deposit of the second type. When genuine money titles and fractional-reserve IOUs are confused, therefore, the latter will drive the former out of the market. (Hülsmann, "Has Fractional-Reserve Banking Really Passed the Market Test?" pp. 399–422; quotation is from pp. 408–09)

[71]Hayek, *Monetary Nationalism and International Stability*, p. 82. On the same topic, see Simons, "Rules *versus* Authority in Monetary Policy," p. 17.

[72]However, we can imagine how different the economic history of the last 150 years would have been had Peel's Act not neglected to impose a 100-percent reserve requirement on deposits as well! Incidentally, Hayek has argued that it is impossible to radically separate the different

To begin with, even if this objection were justified, it would not constitute even a hint of an argument against the attempt to reach the ideal goal: a proper definition and defense of traditional private-property-law principles in connection with demand deposits. In fact in many other contexts, for example that of criminal activities, we see that, although from a technical standpoint it is often very difficult to correctly apply and defend the corresponding traditional legal principles, an all-out effort should still be made to appropriately define and defend the legal framework.[73]

Furthermore, contrary to the view of some, fractional-reserve banking is not so "omnipresent" that it is impossible to fight in practice. It is true that throughout this book we have considered different legal forms of business which, in evasion of the law, have been devised in an attempt to disguise monetary, irregular bank deposits as other contracts. We

---

instruments which could represent money as a generally accepted medium of exchange, and thus there would only be a "continuum" of different degrees of liquidity, which would further complicate the challenge of determining when the traditional legal principles we defend here are upheld and when they are not. We do not find this a solid argument. As Menger maintains, it is always possible in practice to adequately distinguish between money and all other highly liquid instruments which, nevertheless, do not constitute immediate, generally accepted mediums of exchange. The distinction between these two types of goods lies in the fact that money is not only a highly liquid instrument; *it is the only perfectly liquid good*. Therefore people are willing to demand it even if they receive no interest for keeping it, while the holders of other, borderline instruments which lack *perfect* liquidity demand interest for possessing them. The essential difference between money and other peripheral "mediums" hinges on the existence of perfect liquidity (i.e., a loss of perfect, immediate availability). Gerald P. O'Driscoll elaborates on this point in his article, "Money: Menger's Evolutionary Theory," pp. 601–16.

[73]For example, it is certainly possible to commit murder using increasingly sophisticated poisons which leave no trace and seriously hinder the collection of evidence concerning the true source and nature of the homicide. However no one has any doubt that murder is a violation of fundamental legal principles, and that all efforts necessary to prevent and punish this sort of conduct should be made.

have touched on operations with an agreement of repurchase at their nominal value; different transactions with "American" put options; so-called time "deposits," which in practice act as true demand deposits; and demand deposits carried out through the completely unrelated institution of life insurance. The specific combinations of these legal forms of business, and any other similar form or combination which might be developed in the future, are easily identifiable and classifiable under civil and criminal law, just as we proposed in the second section (footnote 40) of this chapter. For it is relatively easy for any impartial judge or observer to ascertain whether the essence of an operation permits the withdrawal at any time of the funds initially deposited and whether, from a subjective viewpoint, human behavior shows that people regard certain claims as money, i.e., a generally accepted medium of exchange which is perfectly available (i.e., liquid) at all times.

Moreover the creation of new businesses and "contracts" in an effort to circumvent the basic legal principles which should govern banking has taken place in an environment in which economic agents have been unable to identify the extent to which such "novelties" are illegitimate and cause great harm to the economy and society. If from now on judicial and public authorities clearly identify the issues we analyze in this book, it will be much easier to combat the deviant behaviors which may arise in the financial sector. It is unsurprising that Peel's Act of 1844 was followed by a disproportionate expansion of bank deposits, since at that time economic theorists had not yet established the absolute equivalence between bank deposits and banknotes, in terms of their nature and effects. Peel's Act did not fall short of its objective due to the "omnipresent" nature of fractional-reserve banking, but precisely to humans' failure to realize that banknotes and deposits have the same nature and produce the same economic effects. In contrast, today economic theory has provided judges with analytical tools of incalculable value to guide them toward the correct identification of criminal behaviors and the pronouncement of fair, studied jurisprudential rulings with respect to all "doubtful" cases which may arise in practice.

Finally, we must make a few important clarifications regarding the concept of "innovation" in the financial market and the essential difference between so-called "financial innovations" and the technological and entrepreneurial innovations introduced in the sectors of industry and commerce. While any technological and entrepreneurial innovation adopted successfully in commerce and industry should be welcome from the beginning, since such changes tend to increase productivity and better satisfy the desires of consumers, *in the financial sector, where activities should always take place within an unchanging framework of stable, predictable legal principles, "innovations" should initially be viewed with suspicion.* Indeed, in the sphere of banking and finance, innovations may be considered positive when, for example, they consist of new computer equipment and software, channels of distribution, etc. However when "innovations" directly influence the role essential legal principles must play in providing the inviolable framework for the functioning of the entire market, these changes will tend to inflict serious harm on society, which should reject and crack down on them. Hence it is a bad joke to term a "financial innovation" that which is ultimately designed to hide frauds and to circumvent general legal principles vital for the healthy functioning and maintenance of a market economy.[74]

Financial products conform to the different contract types which have traditionally developed within the law, and the

---

[74]There are also financial innovations which, like takeover bids, fulfill a legitimate function in the market and do not in themselves violate any traditional legal principle, but which become corrupted in the presence of fractional-reserve banking and credit expansion unbacked by real saving. A concise, yet exhaustive analysis of the financial "innovations" which have emerged as a result of the poorly named process of "financial deregulation" (which has largely consisted of reducing the compliance of the financial sector with traditional legal principles) appears in Luis Barrallat's book, *La banca española en el año 2000: un sector en transición* (Madrid: Ediciones de las Ciencias Sociales, 1992), pp. 172–205. We should point out that many of these financial "innovations" arise within the fertile environment of feverish speculation ("irrational exuberance"), a consequence of the credit expansion fractional-reserve banking fuels.

fundamental structure of these types cannot be modified without distorting and violating the most basic legal principles. Therefore the only conceivable way to introduce "new" financial products is to make different combinations of legitimate, existing legal contracts, though innovation possibilities in this field are quite limited. We must also remember that on many occasions "innovations" are forced into existence by the fiscal voracity of governments and the welter of fiscal legislation they introduce in all historical periods. In many cases, such "innovations" are aimed at diminishing as far as possible the payment of taxes, and they lead to the strangest and most forced, complicated and juridically unnatural forms of business. At this point the direct violation of traditional legal principles is only one step away,[75] and experience shows that the temptation to cash in on the large profits fractional-reserve banking generates prompts many to take this step without hesitation. Therefore it is essential in this field to maintain an attitude of constant, rigorous vigilance and prevention with respect to the infringement of traditional legal principles.

6. *"The proposed system would not allow the money supply to grow at the same rate as economic development."* Economic agents have become accustomed to the current inflationary environment and believe economic development is impossible without a certain amount of credit expansion and inflation. Moreover various schools of economic thought have praised increases in effective demand and tend to reinforce ever popular inflationary appeals. Nevertheless, just as economic agents have adapted to an inflationary environment, they would adjust to one in which the purchasing power of the monetary unit rose gradually and continuously.

Here again it is important to distinguish between two different meanings of the term "deflation" (and "inflation")

---

[75]Hence this is another example which perfectly illustrates the acute corruptive effects which the fiscal and economic interventionism of the state exerts on the concept of substantive or material law, related social habits, and the sense of justice. We have dealt with this topic extensively in Huerta de Soto, *Socialismo, cálculo económico y función empresarial*, pp. 126–33.

which are often confused in theoretical discussion and analysis. Deflation refers to either an absolute decrease or contraction in the money supply or to the result such a contraction generally (but not always) tends to produce, i.e., a rise in the purchasing power of the monetary unit, or in other words, a fall in the general price "level." The proposed system of a pure gold standard and a 100-percent reserve requirement would obviously be completely inelastic with respect to contractions, and therefore *would prevent any deflation understood as a decrease in the money supply, something the present "flexible monetary system" cannot guarantee, as economic crises repeatedly remind us.*[76]

If by "deflation" we understand a drop in the general price level or a rise in the purchasing power of the monetary unit, it is clear that to the extent that general economic productivity increased faster than the money supply, such "deflation" would be present in the monetary system we recommend. We described this model of economic development above, and it offers the great advantage of not only preventing economic crises and recessions, but also spreading the benefits of economic development to all citizens by stimulating gradual, continuous growth in the purchasing power of each person's monetary units and a parallel decrease in each person's demand for money.

We must recognize that the proposed system would not guarantee a monetary unit of unchanging purchasing power. This is an unattainable goal, and even if it were achieved, it would present no other advantage than to eliminate the premium which is included in the interest rate depending on the

---

[76]After the stock market crash of October 1987, a credit squeeze was kept at bay only momentarily by the massive doses of liquidity all central banks injected into the system. Even so, in the economic recession that followed (1990–1991), central bankers were helpless to convince economic agents to borrow new money, even when interest rates were set at historically low levels (2–3 percent in the United States). More recently (2001), Japanese monetary authorities lowered the interest rate in that country to 0.15 percent, without provoking the expansionary effects predicted. Later, history repeated itself again after the stock market crash of 2001–2002 and the fixing of the rate of interest at 1 percent by the Federal Reserve. And again it was fixed as the historical low level of 0–0.25 percent at the end of 2008 as a desperate reaction to the worldwide financial crisis.

expected future evolution of the purchasing power of money. However in this respect it is only important that in practice economic agents be able to easily predict the evolution of the purchasing power of money and to take it into account when making decisions. This would be sufficient to avert the sudden, unjustified redistribution of income between creditors and debtors which in the past has always accompanied the expansionary credit or monetary shocks economic agents have failed to foresee in time.

It has been argued that if the supply of specie grows less rapidly than economic productivity, the consequent rise in the purchasing power of the monetary unit (or decrease in the general price level) may, under certain circumstances, even exceed the social rate of time preference incorporated in the market rate of interest.[77] Although the social rate of time preference depends on humans' subjective valuations, and thus its evolution cannot be theoretically ascertained in advance, we must recognize that if it drops to very low levels, due to a substantial rise in society's tendency to save, the above effect could actually appear on occasion. However market rates of interest would under no circumstances reach zero, much less a negative number. To begin with, the well-known Pigou effect would become evident: the increase in the purchasing power of the monetary unit would boost the value of the real cash balances held by economic agents, whose wealth would grow in real terms and who would increase their consumption, thus pushing the social rate of time preference back up.[78] In addition, entrepreneurs would always find financing, via a positive interest rate, for all investment projects which generated the expected accounting profits in excess of the rate prevailing in the market at any given moment, no matter how low. We should keep in mind that gradual reductions in the

---

[77]This is the argument C. Maling presents in his article, "The Austrian Business Cycle Theory and its Implications for Economic Stability under Laissez-Faire," chapter 48 of J.C. Wood and R.N. Woods, *Friedrich A. Hayek: Critical Assessments* (London: Routledge, 1991), vol. 2, p. 267.

[78]On the Pigou effect, see Don Patinkin's article, "Real Balances," *The New Palgrave: A Dictionary of Economics*, vol. 4, pp. 98–101.

market rate of interest tend to drive up the present value of
capital goods and investment projects: a decrease from 1 to 0.5
percent will double the present value of durable capital goods,
and this value will double again if rates fall from 0.5 to 0.25
percent. Therefore it is inconceivable that nominal interest
rates should reach zero: as they approach that limit, growth in
the present value of capital goods will give rise to fantastic
opportunities to earn considerable entrepreneurial profits,
which will always guarantee an inexhaustible flow of entrepreneurial profits and investment opportunities.

Consequently one aspect we can foresee is that in the proposed model, nominal interest rates would reach historically
low levels. Indeed, if on average we can predict an increase in
productivity of around 3 percent and growth in the world's
gold reserves of 1 percent each year, there would be slight
annual "deflation" of approximately 2 percent. If we consider
a reasonable real interest rate, including the risk component,
to be between 3 and 4 percent, then we could expect the market rate of interest to be between 1 and 2 percent per year and
to oscillate within a very narrow margin of around one-eighth
of a point. Economic agents who have only lived in environ-
ments of inflation based on monetary and credit expansion may
feel we have just described a panorama from outer space, but it
would be a highly favorable situation, and economic agents
would become accustomed to it with no major problem.[79]

----

[79] In a world of a rising purchasing power of the monetary unit
everybody's mode of thinking would have adjusted itself to
this state of affairs, just as in our actual world it has adjusted
itself to a falling purchasing power of the monetary unit.
Today everybody is prepared to consider a rise in his nominal
or monetary income as an improvement to his material well-
being. People's attention is directed more toward the rise in
nominal wage rates and the money equivalent of wealth than
to the increase in the supply of commodities. In a world of rising purchasing power for the monetary unit they would concern themselves more with the fall in living costs. This would
bring into clearer relief the fact that economic progress consists
primarily in making the amenities of life more easily accessible.
(Mises, *Human Action*, p. 469)

Even various members of the Neo-Banking School of fractional-reserve free banking have exaggerated the supposed dangers of "deflation." For example, Stephen Horwitz questions the gradual, continuous decline in prices in our model and states that just as sudden changes affect growth in prices today, abrupt decreases in prices would be inevitable in the system we propose (!). Horwitz fails to see that a monetary standard inflexible to contractions would render such abrupt decreases practically impossible, except under the extraordinary circumstances of natural disasters, wars and other similar phenomena. Under normal conditions, there would be no reason for the demand for money to ever increase traumatically; in fact it would gradually decrease as the rise in the purchasing power of the monetary unit made it unnecessary for economic agents to hold such high real cash balances.[80]

The model of slight, gradual, and continuous "deflation" which would appear in a system that rests on a pure gold standard and a 100-percent reserve requirement would not only not prevent sustained, harmonious economic development, but would actively foster it. Furthermore this has taken place

---

[80]Horwitz, "Keynes' Special Theory," footnote 18 on pp. 431–32. Moreover Horwitz asserts that the Austrians who defend a 100-percent reserve requirement have been unable to explain why a drop in the demand for money would necessarily be different, in terms of favoring the appearance of economic crises, than a rise in the supply of money. Horwitz overlooks the fact that it is the granting of fiduciary media unbacked by real saving, i.e., credit expansion, rather than a generalized decrease in the demand for money, which distorts the productive structure and causes crises. Other things being equal, a fall in the demand for money could only cause a decline in the purchasing power of the monetary unit and would not necessarily influence the creation of loans unbacked by real saving and thus, society's productive structure. Hence we must reject Horwitz's conclusion that "100-percent reserve banking is insufficiently flexible to maintain monetary equilibrium," since this notion is based on a misleading theoretical analysis which fails to adequately deal with the mechanisms of discoordination set in motion in the economic cycle.

in the past on various occasions. For example, we have already mentioned the case of the United States during the period from 1867, following the Civil War, until 1879. Even Milton Friedman and Anna J. Schwartz have had to admit that this period

> was a vigorous stage in the continued economic expansion that was destined to raise the United States to a first rank among the nations of the world. *And their coincidence casts serious doubts on the validity of the now widely held view that secular price deflation and rapid economic growth are incompatible.*[81]

7. "*The maintenance of a pure gold standard and a 100-percent reserve requirement would be very costly in terms of economic resources and would therefore inhibit economic development.*" The argument that a pure gold standard would be quite expensive in terms of economic resources was raised by John Maynard Keynes, who viewed such a standard as no more than a "barbarous relic" of the past. This argument then found its way into the most commonly used textbooks. For instance, Paul A. Samuelson indicates: "(It) is absurd to waste resources digging gold out of the bowels of the earth, only to inter it back again in the vaults of Fort Knox."[82] It is obvious that a pure gold standard, with slight "deflation," i.e., a constant, gradual increase in the purchasing power of the monetary unit, would offer a continuous incentive to find and mine larger quantities of gold, thus employing valuable, scarce economic resources in the search for, extraction and distribution of the yellow metal. Although there is no unanimous estimate of the economic cost of this monetary standard, for the sake of argument we might even admit, as Leland B. Yeager does, that

---

[81]Friedman and Schwartz, *A Monetary History of the United States, 1867–1960*, p. 15; italics added. Mises expresses an identical conclusion in *Money, Method, and the Market Process*, pp. 90–91, and he conveyed the same idea in the previously cited 1930 memorandum to the specialists of the financial committee of the League of Nations. See also the detailed economic study of the period from 1873 to 1896 which Selgin includes in his book, *Less Than Zero*, pp. 49–53.

[82]Samuelson, *Economics*, 8th ed. (New York: Macmillan, 1970).

it would be equal to about 1 percent of the gross domestic product of each nation.[83] It is obviously much "cheaper" to issue paper money than to mine the earth for gold at a cost of around 1 percent of the gross domestic product of all countries throughout the world.

Nevertheless to reject this monetary system based on the supposed cost of the gold standard, as Keynes and Samuelson do, is to be deceived. It is not correct to merely compare the costs of gold production with those of issuing paper money; instead, it is necessary to compare the overall (direct and indirect) costs involved in both monetary systems. In doing so, we must weigh not only the serious harm cyclical economic recessions inflict on the economy and society, but also the range of costs associated with a monetary standard that is elastic, entirely fiduciary, and controlled by the state. Required reading on this topic includes Roger W. Garrison's "The Costs of a Gold Standard."[84] In this article, Professor Garrison estimates the *opportunity costs* of a purely fiduciary monetary standard and compares them with those of a pure gold standard and a 100-percent reserve requirement. Garrison states:

> The true costs of the paper standard would have to take into account (1) the costs imposed on society by different political factions in their attempts to gain control of the printing press, (2) the costs imposed by special-interest groups in their attempts to persuade the controller of the printing press to misuse its authority (print more money) for the benefit of special interests, (3) the costs in the form of inflation-induced misallocation of resources that occur throughout the economy as a result of the monetary authority succumbing to the political pressures of the special interests, and (4) the costs incurred by businesses in their attempts to predict what the monetary authority will do in the future and to hedge against likely, but uncertain, consequences of monetary irresponsibility. With these considerations in mind, it is not

---

[83]Leland B. Yeager, "Introduction," *The Gold Standard: An Austrian Perspective*, p. x.

[84]Roger W. Garrison, "The Costs of a Gold Standard," chapter 4 of the book, *The Gold Standard: An Austrian Perspective*, pp. 61–79.

difficult to believe that a gold standard costs less than a paper standard.[85]

In addition, we would add the high cost of maintaining the entire worldwide network of central banks and their well-paid employees, and the substantial economic resources used in gathering statistics and financing "research" projects, international conferences and meetings (the International Monetary Fund, World Bank, etc.). We should also bear in mind the significant cost involved in the excessive provision of banking services; specifically, the exaggerated proliferation of new branches and the sheer squandering of human and economic resources it entails.[86] Therefore it comes as no surprise that even Milton Friedman, who for many years agreed with the majority that the cost of a pure gold standard was too high, has changed his mind and now feels that economically speaking, a pure gold standard poses no problem of opportunity cost.[87]

In short, we conclude that a monetary and banking system based on a pure gold standard and a 100-percent reserve requirement for banking is a "social institution" essential to the correct functioning of any market economy. A social institution can be defined as any set of behavior patterns which

---

[85]Ibid., p. 68.

[86]Furthermore, Roger W. Garrison reminds us that the cost in terms of real resources allocated for the production and distribution of gold is to a great extent inevitable, since people continue to devote a considerable volume of economic resources to the extraction, refining, distribution and storage of the yellow metal, regardless of whether it forms the basis of the monetary standard. Ibid., p. 70.

[87]See Friedman and Schwartz, "Has Government any Role in Money?" pp. 37–62. Therefore it is clear that a pure gold standard and a 100-percent reserve requirement should strongly appeal to monetarists, since this arrangement would mean the equivalent of a relatively stable monetary rule, and given the indestructible nature of the gold stock, it would preclude sudden contractions in the money supply while at the same time totally eliminating the government's discretionary use of authority in the monetary field. From this standpoint, for reasons of strict coherence, it is unsurprising that monetarists like Friedman have increasingly been leaning toward a pure gold standard, a system they had always categorically disregarded in the past.

has spontaneously evolved over a very prolonged period of time, as a result of the contributions multiple generations of people have made to social processes through their participation in them. Thus such institutions, like the pure gold standard, private-property law, and the family, carry with them an enormous volume of information and have been successfully proven in the most varied historical contexts and circumstances of time and place. That is why we cannot innocuously dispense with these institutions, nor can we sacrifice moral principles without incurring inordinate social costs. For behavior patterns, traditions, and moral principles, far from being "repressive or inhibitory social traditions" (as authors like Rousseau and, in general, "scientistic" theorists have irresponsibly called them), have made the development of civilization possible. When human beings deify reason and come to believe they can modify and "improve" social institutions or even reconstruct them *ex novo* (Keynesians and monetarists have most fostered this attitude among economic theorists), they lose sight of vital guidelines and points of reference and invariably rationalize their most atavistic and primitive passions, thus jeopardizing society's spontaneous processes of cooperation and coordination. The gold standard and the principle of a 100-percent reserve ratio constitute an integral part of those vital social institutions which must act as an autopilot or guide for practical human behavior in the processes of social cooperation. The irresponsible elimination of these institutions generates excessive, unpredictable costs in the form of social tensions and maladjustments which endanger the peaceful, harmonious progress of civilization and humanity.

8. *"The establishment of a system like the one proposed would leave the world too dependent on countries which, like South Africa and the former Soviet Union, have always been the largest producers of gold."* The danger that a pure gold standard might come to rely too heavily on the gold production of South Africa and the nations which today make up the former Soviet Union has been highly exaggerated. Furthermore such warnings are based on a mistaken disregard for the fact that though these countries mine a substantial proportion of the *new* gold

extracted each year (South Africa with 34 percent and the former Soviet Union with 18 percent of the annual production of new gold),[88] the relative importance of the volumes they produce, in comparison with the existing stock of gold in the world (which has accumulated throughout the history of civilization because gold is immutable and indestructible), is practically insignificant (no more than 0.5 percent per year). In fact most of the worldwide stock of gold is spread among the countries of the European Union, America, and Southern Asia. Moreover now that the Cold War has ended, it is unclear how nations like South Africa and the former Soviet Union, whose annual gold production amounts to only a tiny fraction of the world's total, could play a disruptive role, especially when they would be the first nations to suffer from the effects of any policy aimed at artificially reducing the production of gold.

In any case we must recognize, as we will see in the next section, that the transition toward a monetary system such as the one we recommend would inevitably raise by several times (maybe more than twenty) the market value of gold today in terms of current monetary units. This increase in value would initially and inevitably lead to a significant, one-time capital gain for the current holders of gold and in particular, companies which mine and distribute it. However the desire to prevent certain third parties from profiting (perhaps) undeservedly from the reestablishment of a monetary system with so many benefits for society as the one proposed constitutes no prima facie argument whatsoever against such a system.[89]

---

[88]Skousen, *Economics on Trial*, p. 142.

[89]Rothbard states:

> Depending on how we define the money supply—and I would define it very broadly as all claims to dollars at fixed par value—a rise in gold price sufficient to bring the gold stock to 100 per cent of total dollars would require a ten- to twenty-fold increase. This of course would bring an enormous windfall gain to the gold miners, but this does not concern us. *I do not believe that we should refuse an offer of a mass entry into Heaven simply because the manufacturers of harps and angels' wings would enjoy a windfall gain.* (Rothbard, "The Case for a 100-Percent Gold Dollar," p. 68; italics added)

9. *"The supposed failure of a 100-percent reserve requirement in Argentina during the regime of General Perón."* The twentieth century provides one historic attempt, at least in a *rhetorical* sense, to establish a 100-percent reserve requirement for banking. However in this case, the reform was not accompanied by an overall privatization of the monetary system and the elimination of the central bank. Instead, credit was completely nationalized, a step which drove inflation to a high level and caused profound credit distortions which devastated the Argentinian economy. Therefore this example does not illustrate any disadvantage of the reform we have proposed. On the contrary, it offers a perfect historical confirmation of the harmful effects public-sector intervention exerts on the financial, monetary and credit sector. Let us analyze the history of the Argentinian "experiment" in greater detail.

The reform was introduced shortly after General Perón took office in Argentina in 1946; it was implemented via decree-law number 11554, which was ratified by law 12962. These legal provisions nationalized bank deposits, as they contained the official declaration that the nation of Argentina would guarantee all deposits from that point on. The explanatory statement of these texts included, among other considerations, the following:

> Indeed, now that all deposits remain in the banks at the expense of the central bank, which defrays the financial and

---

At any rate, we must admit, as Rothbard does, that such growth in the value of gold would, mainly during the first years following the transition, give an enormous push to the industry of gold mining and distribution, and consequently would somewhat modify the present structure of international trade, migratory flows and capital. Murray Rothbard later changed his mind, and in order to prevent banks from profiting illegitimately, he suggested that bank bills form the sole basis for gold conversion. This measure would force a deflation of the monetary stock corresponding to deposits. Despite this change in Rothbard's position, we find our proposal (to be presented further on) quite superior, since it would avoid the unnecessary deflation which would result from his. See Murray N. Rothbard, "The Solution," *The Freeman: Ideas on Liberty* (November 1995): 697–702.

administrative expenses, and now that recipient banks can no longer use deposits in the absence of an agreement with the central bank, those deposits have ceased to "weigh on" banks, so to speak, and they have stopped impelling banks to expand loans beyond useful limits. This is the road to healthy credit, credit geared more to long-term economic goals than to banks' accomplishment of purely financial purposes.[90]

Nevertheless despite this apparently sound *rhetoric*, Perón's banking reform was condemned to failure from the start. In fact, the reform was based on a complete nationalization of the monetary and banking sector, such that the responsibility for granting new loans fell on the central bank, and central bank officials depended directly on the government. In other words, not only did the state not completely privatize financial and monetary institutions and permit credit to spontaneously coincide with the country's rate of saving; but the central bank actually embarked on a reckless campaign of expansionary loans to privileged recipients. These loans reached the economic system through open-market operations on the stock exchange, and especially through the discount rate offered those banks most in tune with the administration.

The reform gave the central bank the power to carry out open-market operations each year for an amount of up to 15 percent of the total money supply. It also entirely divested the Argentinian currency of its gold backing and abolished the preexisting relationship between this currency and gold. In 1949, law 13571 modified the constitution of the central bank's council of directors and designated the finance minister himself president of this council, thus converting the institution into a mere appendage of the government. Finally, the reform established that from that point on, credit would be granted

---

[90]A brief, clear description of the banking system General Perón established appears in José Heriberto Martínez's article, "El sistema monetario y bancario argentino," in *Homenaje a Lucas Beltrán* (Madrid: Editorial Moneda y Crédito, 1982), pp. 435–60. We find the above excerpt on pp. 447–48.

by the central bank in the form of a discount to the different banks, with no limit on volume or expansionary capacity. Hence this enormous power would be used to favor those institutions most sympathetic to the current political regime. Consequently, and despite its initial rhetoric, Perón's reform fostered unprecedented growth in the volume of credit, a tremendous expansion of means of payment, and severe inflation which grossly distorted the country's productive structure and gave rise to a profound economic recession from which Argentina has taken many years to recover. For example, during the nine years of Perón's first period in office (from 1946 to 1955), the money supply increased by more than 970 percent, and the gold and foreign exchange backing of bills issued fell from 137 percent in 1946 to slightly over 3.5 percent in 1955.

The reform was abolished by the revolutionaries who ousted General Perón in 1956 and again privatized deposits. Nonetheless this measure was inadequate to end financial chaos, and private banks resumed their expansionary policies with new enthusiasm, thus following the example set by the central bank under Perón. As a result, Argentinian hyperinflation became chronic and infamous all over the world.[91]

We may conclude that the designers of the Argentinian experiment sought merely to reserve the advantages of credit

---

[91]Curiously, bank deposits were again brought under government control during the new, brief Peronist period which began in 1973. This decision to nationalize deposits was reversed when a military junta overthrew the regime and seized power on March 24, 1976. What happened next has gone down in economic history and revealed that the system of banking "freedom" and irresponsibility which followed was almost as disruptive as the system previously instituted by Perón. Again, in December 2001, Argentina had the dubious honor of illustrating economic theory. In this case, its fractional-reserve currency board failed upon an evaporation of public confidence and a subsequent, corresponding run to withdraw dollars from bank deposits. This led Minister Cavallo to limit the amount people could withdraw weekly from banks to 250 dollars (limit popularly known as the "corralito") and clearly demonstrates one of the essential theoretical principles highlighted in this book: that a fractional-reserve banking system without a lender of last resort is an impossibility.

expansion for the government, and hence to prevent private banks from profiting from a substantial portion of this expansion, as had been the norm until then. In any case, the intention was never to privatize the monetary system and do away with the central bank. The Peronist reform confirms a fact we have acknowledged here, i.e., that a 100-percent reserve ratio combined with a central-bank monopoly on the issuance of currency and loans can distort the economy just as seriously if monetary authorities decide for political reasons to embark on a policy of credit expansion (either by directly creating and granting loans or by making open-market purchases on the stock exchange). Therefore the failure of Argentina's experiment under General Perón does not constitute any historical illustration of the disadvantages of a 100-percent reserve ratio. Rather, it confirms the need to consistently couple such a reform with a complete privatization of money and the elimination of the central bank.

In short, Perón's system was aimed at precluding the expansionary creation of loans by private banks. However, it replaced this activity with an even greater expansion of unbacked loans at the hands of central bankers and the government itself, and thus it ultimately harmed the country's monetary, financial, and economic system even more seriously. Therefore nothing is gained by eliminating one process of credit expansion (that of private fractional-reserve banking) if the very state applies another directly and on an even larger scale.[92]

10. *"The proposed reform could not be accomplished by any single country, but would require a difficult and costly international*

---

[92]Perón's experiment revealed the failure not of a 100-percent reserve ratio, but of the nationalization of credit, and it produced all the adverse effects Ludwig von Mises had predicted in his 1929 article on the topic: *Die Verstaatlichung des Kredits: Mutalisierung des Kredits* (Bern, Munich, and Leipzig: Travers-Borgstroem Foundation, 1929). This paper was later translated into English with the title, "The Nationalization of Credit?" It appeared in *A Critique of Interventionism: Inquiries into the Economic Policy and the Economic Ideology of the Present* (New York: Arlington House, 1977), pp. 153–64.

agreement." Although the most advantageous course of action would be to establish a pure gold standard and 100-percent reserve requirement on an international level, and though an agreement to do so would tremendously facilitate a transition to the new system, there is no reason the different states should not work separately toward the ideal monetary system until such an international agreement is possible. This is precisely what Maurice Allais recommended for France (before that country decided to be included in the European Monetary Union).[93] Allais indicates that the establishment of a 100-percent reserve requirement and the maintenance of a highly rigorous monetary policy on the part of the central bank (a policy which would permit the monetary base to grow by no more than 2 percent per year) would be an initial step in the right direction, and the United States, the European Union, Japan, Russia, or any other country could take it alone. Moreover we must keep this idea in mind when evaluating the different programs for monetary unification which have been established in certain prominent economic areas, specifically the European Monetary Union. We will consider again this matter in the following section.

Furthermore the establishment of fixed, yet revisable exchange rates between the different countries might oblige the nations of an economic area to follow the leadership of those states which most clearly and steadily advance in the ideal direction. Thus an irresistible trend toward the achievement of the proposed goal may arise.[94]

---

[93]See Allais, "Une objection générale: la construction européenne," pp. 359–60 of his article, "Les conditions monétaires d'une économie de marchés."

[94]At any rate, if strong economies, like the United States and the European Union, were to establish a gold standard and 100-percent reserve requirement, they would be setting an immensely powerful example in the monetary field, an example other countries would be compelled to heed.

5
An Economic Analysis of the Process of Reform and Transition Toward the Proposed Monetary and Banking System

To begin this section, we will briefly consider the major issues involved in any political strategy for bringing about economic reform in any area, including that of finance, credit, and money.

A Few Basic Strategic Principles

The most serious danger to all reform strategies looms in the *political pragmatism of daily affairs,* which often causes authorities to abandon their ultimate goals on the grounds that they are politically "impossible" to reach in the short term. This is a grave danger which in the past has sabotaged different programs for reform. Indeed, pragmatism has systematically prompted politicians to reach joint, *ad hoc* decisions in order to acquire or retain political power, and these decisions have often been fundamentally incoherent and counter-productive with respect to the most desirable long-term objectives. Furthermore, as discussion has centered exclusively on what is politically feasible in the immediate short term, and final goals have been postponed or forgotten entirely, authorities have not completed the necessary, detailed study of these goals nor the process of spreading them to the people. As a result, the possibility of creating a coalition of interests in support of the reform is continually undermined, since other programs and objectives considered more urgent in the short term weaken and overshadow such an effort.

The most appropriate strategy for the reform we propose must therefore rest on a *dual* principle. The first part consists of constantly studying and *educating* the public about the substantial benefits they would derive from the achievement of the final medium- and long-term objectives. The second part involves the adoption of a short-term policy of gradual progress toward these objectives, a policy which must always be *coherent* with them. This strategy alone will make politically possible in the medium- and long-term what today may seem particularly difficult to accomplish.[95]

Let us now return to our topic: banking reform in market economies. In the following sections, we will suggest a process for reforming the current system. In formulating our recommendation, we have taken into account the above strategy and the essential principles theoretically analyzed in this book.

STAGES IN THE REFORM OF THE FINANCIAL AND BANKING SYSTEM

Chart IX-1 reflects the five basic stages in a reform process involving the financial and banking system. In our outline the stages progress naturally from right to left; that is, from the most controlled systems (those with central planning in the banking and financial sector) to the least controlled ones (those in which the central bank has been abolished and complete freedom prevails, yet the banking industry is subject to legal principles—including a 100-percent reserve requirement).

The *first stage* corresponds to "central planning" for financial and banking matters; in other words, a system strictly controlled and regulated by the central bank. This type of arrangement has predominated in most western countries up

---

[95]See William H. Hutt's now classic work, *Politically Impossible...?* (London: Institute of Economic Affairs, 1971). A very similar analysis to that presented in the text, but in relation to the reform of the Spanish social security system, appears in Huerta de Soto, "The Crisis and Reform of Social Security: An Economic Analysis from the Austrian Perspective," *Journal des Economistes et des Etudes Humaines* 5, no. 1 (March 1994): 127–55. Finally, we have updated, developed and presented our ideas on the best political steps to take to deregulate the economy in Jesús Huerta de Soto, "El economista liberal y la política," *Manuel Fraga: homenaje académico* (Madrid: Fundación Cánovas del Castillo, 1997), vol. 1, pp. 763–88. English version entitled, "A Hayekian Strategy to Implement Free Market Reforms," included in *Economic Policy in an Orderly Framework: Liber Amicorum for Gerrit Meijer,* J.G. Backhaus, W. Heijmann, A. Nentjes, and J. van Ophem, eds. (Münster: LIT Verlag, 2003), pp. 231–54.

to the present time. The central bank holds a monopoly on the issuance of currency and at any given time determines the total amount of the monetary base and the rediscount rates which apply to private banks. Private banks operate with a fractional reserve and expand credit without the backing of real saving. They do so based on a bank multiplier which regulates growth in fiduciary media and is established by the central bank. Thus the central bank orchestrates credit expansion and increases the money supply via open-market purchases (which go toward the partial or complete monetization of the national debt). In addition it instructs banks as to the strictness of the credit terms they should offer. This stage is characterized by the independence of the different countries with respect to monetary policy (monetary nationalism), in a more or less chaotic international environment of flexible exchange rates which are often used as a powerful competitive weapon in international trade. This system gives rise to great, inflationary credit expansion which distorts the productive structure and repeatedly provokes stock-market booms and unsustainable economic growth, followed by severe economic crises and recessions that tend to spread to the rest of the world.

In the *second stage* the reform process advances a bit in the right direction. The central bank is legally made "independent" of the government, and an attempt is made to come up with a monetary rule (generally an intermediate one) to reflect the monetary-policy goal of the central bank. This goal is usually expressed in terms of a rate of monetary growth exceeding the rise in productivity (between 4 and 6 percent). This model was developed by the *Bundesbank* of the Federal Republic of Germany and has influenced the rule followed by the European Central Bank and other central banks throughout the world. This system fosters an increase in international cooperation among different central banks and promotes, even in large geographical areas, where economic and trading uniformity is greater, the establishment of a system of fixed (but in some cases revisable) exchange rates to end the competitive anarchy typical of the chaotic environment of flexible exchange rates. As a result, credit expansion becomes more moderate, though it does not completely disappear, and hence stock-market crises and economic recessions continue to hit, though they are less serious than in the first stage.[96]

In the *third stage*, the central bank would remain independent, and a radical step would be taken in the reform: a 100-percent reserve requirement would be established for private banks. As we pointed out at the beginning of this chapter, this step would necessitate certain legislative modifications to the commercial and penal codes. These changes would allow us to eradicate most of the current administrative legislation issued by central bankers to control deposit and credit institutions. The sole, remaining function of the central bank would be to guarantee that the monetary supply grows at a rate equal to or slightly lower than the increase in productivity in the economic system. (As we know, Maurice Allais proposes a growth rate of around 2 percent per year.)

THE IMPORTANCE OF THE THIRD AND SUBSEQUENT STAGES IN THE REFORM: THE POSSIBILITY THEY OFFER OF PAYING OFF THE NATIONAL DEBT OR SOCIAL SECURITY PENSION LIABILITIES

In the banking industry, reform would revolve around the concept of converting today's private bankers into mere managers of mutual funds. Specifically, once authorities have announced and explained the reform to citizens, they should give the holders of current demand deposits (or their equivalent) the opportunity to manifest their desire, within a prudent time period, to replace these deposits with mutual-fund shares. (People would receive the warning that if they should accept this option, they would no longer be guaranteed the nominal value of their deposits, and a need for liquidity would oblige them to sell their shares on the stock market and take the current price for them at the moment they sell

---

[96]José Antonio de Aguirre, in his appendix to the Spanish edition of Vera C. Smith's book, *The Rationale of Central Banking and the Free Banking Alternative* (Indianapolis, Ind.: Liberty Press, 1990), explains why a broad consensus has arisen in favor of the independence of monetary authorities.

them).[97] Each depositor to select this option would receive a number of shares strictly proportional to the sum of his deposits with respect to the total deposits at each bank. Each bank would transfer its assets to a mutual fund which would encompass all of the bank's wealth and claims (except for, basically, the portion corresponding to its net worth).

After the period during which deposit holders may express a wish to continue as such or instead to acquire shares in the mutual funds to be constituted following the reform, the central bank, as Frank H. Knight recommends,[98] should print legal bills for an overall amount equal to the aggregate of all demand deposits and equivalents recorded on the balance sheets of all the banks under its control (excluding the sum represented by the above exchange option). Clearly the central

---

[97]A depositor at a bank is a holder of "money" inasmuch as he would be willing to keep his deposits at the bank even if they bore no interest. The fact that in fractional-reserve banking systems deposits have been confused with loans makes it advisable, in our view, to give depositors the chance to exchange deposits, within a reasonable time period, for shares in the mutual funds to be constituted with the bank's assets. In this way it would become clear which deposits are subjectively regarded as money and which are seen as true loans to banks (involving a temporary loss of availability). Also, massive, disturbing and unnecessary transfers of investments from deposits to mutual fund shares once the reform is complete would be prevented. As Ludwig von Mises points out,

> The deposits subject to cheques have a different purpose [than the credits loaned to banks]. They are the business man's cash like coins and bank notes. The depositor intends to dispose of them day by day. *He does not demand interest,* or at least he would entrust the money to the bank even without interest. (Mises, *Money, Method and the Market Process,* p. 108; italics added)

[98] The necessary reserve funds will be created by printing paper money and putting it in the hands of the banks which need reserves by simple gift. Even so, of course, the printing of this paper would be non-inflationary, since it would be immobilized by the increased reserve requirements. (Hart, "'The Chicago Plan' of Banking Reform," pp. 105–06, and footnote 1 on p. 106, where Hart attributes this proposal to Frank H. Knight)

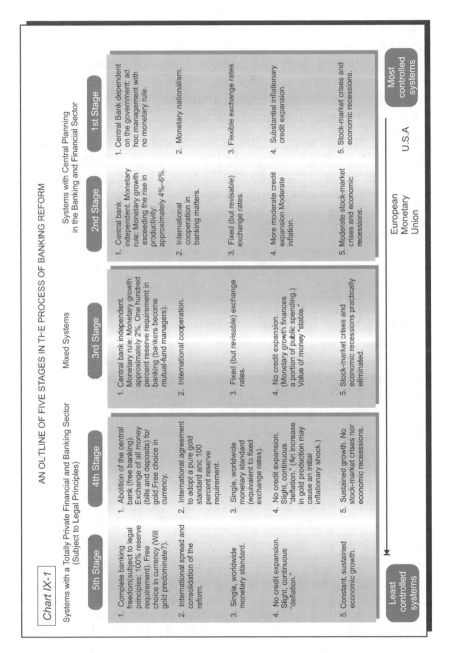

Chart IX-1

AN OUTLINE OF FIVE STAGES IN THE PROCESS OF BANKING REFORM

Systems with a Totally Private Financial and Banking Sector (Subject to Legal Principles) — Mixed Systems — Systems with Central Planning in the Banking and Financial Sector

5th Stage — 4th Stage — 3rd Stage — 2nd Stage — 1st Stage

5th Stage

1. Complete banking freedom (subject to legal principles): 100% reserve requirement). Free choice in currency (Will gold predominate?).

2. International spread and consolidation of the reform.

3. Single, worldwide monetary standard.

4. No credit expansion. Slight, continuous "deflation."

5. Constant, sustained economic growth.

4th Stage

1. Abolition of the central bank (free banking). Exchange of all money (bills and deposits) for gold. Free choice in currency.

2. International agreement to adopt a pure gold standard and 100 percent reserve requirement.

3. Single, worldwide monetary standard (equivalent to fixed exchange rates).

4. No credit expansion. Slight, continuous "deflation." (An increase in gold production may cause an initial inflationary shock.)

5. Sustained growth. No stock-market crises nor economic recessions.

3rd Stage

1. Central bank independent. Monetary rule: Monetary growth: approximately 2%. One hundred percent reserve requirement in banking (bankers become mutual-fund managers).

2. International cooperation.

3. Fixed (but revisable) exchange rates.

4. No credit expansion. (Monetary growth finances a portion of public spending.) Value of money "stable."

5. Stock-market crises and economic recessions practically eliminated.

2nd Stage

1. Central bank independent. Monetary rule: Monetary growth exceeding the rise in productivity: approximately 4%–6%.

2. International cooperation in banking matters.

3. Fixed (but revisable) exchange rates.

4. More moderate credit expansion. Moderate inflation.

5. Moderate stock-market crises and economic recessions.

1st Stage

1. Central Bank dependent on the government: ad hoc management with no monetary rule.

2. Monetary nationalism.

3. Flexible exchange rates.

4. Substantial inflationary credit expansion.

5. Stock-market crises and economic recessions.

Least controlled systems — Most controlled systems

European Monetary Union — U.S.A

bank's issuance of these legal bills would not be inflationary in any way, since the sole purpose of this action would be to back the total amount of demand deposits (and equivalents), and each and every bank would receive banknotes for a sum identical to its corresponding deposits. In this way a 100-percent reserve requirement could be established immediately, and banks should be prohibited from granting further loans against demand deposits. In any case, such deposits would always have to remain perfectly balanced with a reserve (in the form of bills held by banks) absolutely equal to the total of demand deposits or equivalents.

We must point out that Hart suggests the new paper money the central bank prints to back deposits be handed over to banks as a *gift*. If this occurs, it is obvious that banks' balance sheets will reflect an enormous surplus, one precisely equal to the sum of demand deposits backed 100 percent by a reserve.

We might ask ourselves who should own the total of banks' accounting assets which exceed their net worth. For the operation we have just described reveals that by functioning with a fractional reserve, private banks have historically created means of payment in the form of loans produced *ex nihilo*, and these loans have permitted banks to gradually expropriate wealth from the whole of the rest of society. Once we take into account the difference between banks' income and expenditures each year, the aggregate wealth the banking system has expropriated in this way (by a process that produces the effects of a tax, just as inflation does for the government) is precisely equal to the assets banks possess in the form of real estate, branch offices, equipment and especially, the sum of their investments in loans to industry and trade, in securities acquired on the stock market and elsewhere, and in treasury bonds issued by the government.[99]

---

[99]Mises first pointed out that banknotes and deposits created from nothing through the fractional-reserve banking system generate wealth that could be considered the profit of banks themselves, and we explained this idea in chapter 4, when we indicated that such deposits provide an indefinite source of financing. The fact that in account

Hart's proposal that the basis of the reform consist of simply *giving* banks the sum of the bills they need to reach a 100-percent reserve ratio is a bitter pill to swallow. This method would make the total of private banks' current assets unnecessary in the account books as backing for deposits, and hence, from an accounting viewpoint, they would automatically come to be considered the property of banks' stockholders. Murray N. Rothbard has also advocated this solution,[100]

---

books, loans created *ex nihilo* square with deposits also created *ex nihilo* conceals a fundamental economic reality from the general public: deposits are ultimately money which is never withdrawn from the bank, and banks' assets constitute a body of great wealth expropriated from all of the rest of society, from which banking institutions and their stockholders exclusively profit. Curiously, bankers themselves have come to recognize this fact implicitly or explicitly, as Karl Marx states:

> So far as the Bank issues notes, which are not covered by the metal reserve in its vaults, *it creates symbols of value, that form not only currency, but also additional, even if fictitious, capital* for it to the nominal amount of these unprotected notes. And this additional *capital* yields an additional profit for it.—In B.A. 1857, Wilson asks Newmarch, No. 1563: "The circulation of a bank's own notes, that is, on an average the amount remaining in the hands of the public, forms an addition to the effective capital of that bank, does it not?"—"Assuredly."—1564. "All profits, then, which the bank derives from this circulation, is a profit arising from credit, not from a capital actually owned by it?"—"Assuredly." (p. 637; italics added)

Thus Marx concludes:

> [B]anks create credit and capital, 1) by the issue of their own notes, 2) by writing out drafts on London running as long as 21 days but paid to them in cash immediately on being written, and 3) by paying out discounted bills of exchange, which are endowed with credit primarily and essentially by endorsement through the bank, at least for the local district. (Karl Marx, *Capital: A Critique of Political Economy*, vol. 3, p. 638; italics added)

[100]On the transition to a 100-percent reserve requirement, see Rothbard, *The Mystery of Banking*, pp. 249–69. In general we agree with the transition program formulated by Rothbard. However we object to the *gift* he plans for banks, a contribution which would allow them to keep the assets they have historically expropriated from society. In our opinion, it would be perfectly justifiable to use these assets toward the other ends

which does not seem equitable. For if any group of economic agents has historically taken advantage of the privilege of granting expansionary loans unbacked by real saving, it has precisely been the stockholders of banks (to the extent that the government has not at the same time partially expropriated the profits of this extremely lucrative activity, thus obliging banks to devote a portion of their created monetary stock to financing the very state).

The sum of private banks' assets can and should be transferred to a series of security mutual funds, the management of which would become the main activity of private banking institutions following the reform. Who should be the holders of the shares in these mutual funds, which at the time of their conversion would have a value equal to the total value of all of the banking system's assets (except those corresponding to the equity of its stockholders)? *We propose that these shares in the new mutual funds to be created with the assets of the banking system be exchanged for the outstanding treasury bonds issued in all countries overwhelmed by a sizeable national debt.* The idea is simple enough: the holders of treasury bonds would, in exchange for them, receive the corresponding shares in the mutual funds to be established with the assets of the banking system.[101] This

_____

we discuss in the text. Rothbard himself recognizes this weak point in his reasoning when he states:

> The most cogent criticism of this plan is simply this: Why should the banks receive a gift, even a gift in the process of privatizing the nationalized hoard of gold? The banks, as fractional reserve institutions are and have been responsible for inflation and unsound banking. (p. 268)

Rothbard appears to lean toward the solution from his book because he wishes to ensure that both bills and deposits receive 100 percent backing, and not merely bills, which would obviously be deflationary. Nevertheless he does not seem to have thought of the idea we suggest in the text. Moreover we should remember that, as we indicated at the end of footnote 89, just before his death, Rothbard changed his mind and proposed that only bills in circulation be exchanged for gold (leaving out bank deposits).

[101]Ideally, the exchange would take place at the respective market prices of both the treasury bonds and the shares in the corresponding mutual

move would eliminate a large number (or even all) of the bonds issued by the government, which would benefit all citizens, since from that point on they would no longer have to pay taxes to finance the interest payments on the debt. Furthermore the current holders of treasury bonds would not be adversely affected, since their fixed-income securities would be replaced by mutual-fund shares which, from the time of the reform, would have a recognized market value and a rate of return.[102] Moreover there are other government liabilities (for example, in the area of state social-security pensions) which could be converted into bonds and might also be exchanged for shares in the new mutual funds, either instead of or in addition to treasury bonds, and with highly beneficial economic effects.

Chart IX-2 shows a breakdown of the different accounting assets and liabilities which would appear on the consolidated balance sheet for the banking system once all bank deposits

---

funds. This goal would require that these funds be created and placed on the market some time before the exchange occurs (especially considering the number of depositors who may first opt to become shareholders and cease to be depositors).

[102]For example, in Spain, in 1997, demand deposits and equivalents totaled sixty trillion pesetas (around 60 percent of GNP), and outstanding treasury bonds in the hands of individuals added up to approximately forty trillion. Therefore the exchange we propose could be carried out with no major trauma, and it would permit the repayment of all treasury bonds at one time without placing the holders of them at a disadvantage nor producing unnecessary inflationary tensions. At the same time, we must remember that banks hold a large percentage of all live treasury bonds, and hence in their case, instead of an exchange, a simple cancellation would be made in the account books. The difference between the sixty trillion pesetas in demand deposits and equivalents which would be backed by a 100 percent reserve and the forty trillion pesetas in treasury bonds could be used for a similar, partial exchange involving other financial, government liabilities (in the area of state social-security pensions, for example). In any case, the sum available for this type of exchange would be that remaining after subtracting the amounts corresponding to those deposit-holders who had freely decided to convert their deposits into shares of equal value in the above mutual funds.

had been backed by a 100 percent reserve and mutual funds had been created with the system's assets. From that point on, banks' activities would simply consist of *managing* the mutual funds created with their assets, and bankers could obtain new loans (in the form of new shares in these funds) and invest them, while charging a small percentage as a fee for the management of this type of operation. Bankers could also continue to engage in the other (legitimate) activities they had always pursued in the past (the performance of payment, cashier and bookkeeping services, transfers, etc.), and they could charge the corresponding market prices for these services.

In any case, international cooperation (and fixed, but revisable exchange rates) would continue in this third stage, and once deposits were backed with a 100 percent reserve, credit expansion would completely disappear. As we have indicated, the central bank would be limited to increasing the size of the money supply by a small percentage and using this increase to finance a portion of state expenditures, as Maurice Allais proposes.[103] In no case would this new money be used to make open-market purchases or directly expand credit, activities rampant in Argentina's failed attempt at banking reform under General Perón. The reforms described above would lead to the almost complete elimination of stock-market crises and economic recessions. Beginning at that point, the behavior of savers and investors in the market would be very closely coordinated.

The establishment of a 100-percent reserve requirement is a necessary condition for the definitive abolition of the central

---

[103]Maurice Allais demands not only that monetary growth be used to finance the current expenditures of the state (which would reduce direct taxes; specifically, income taxes), but also that deposit banking (with a 100-percent reserve ratio) be radically separated from investment banking, which involves loaning to third parties money the bank has first been loaned by its customers. See Allais, "Les conditions monétaires d'une économie de marchés." A detailed examination of the transition measures Maurice Allais suggests appears on pp. 319–20 of the book, *L'Impôt sur le capital et la réforme monétaire*. The separation between deposit banking and investment banking is also defended by Hayek in his work, *Denationalisation of Money*.

bank, which would occur in the *fourth stage*. Indeed, once private banking is made subordinate to legal principles, complete banking freedom should be demanded, and remaining central-bank legislation could be eliminated, as could the central bank itself. This would require the replacement of today's fiduciary money, which the central bank alone has the power to issue, with a form of private money. It is impossible to take a leap in the dark and establish an artificial monetary standard which has not emerged through an evolutionary process. Hence the new form of money should consist of the substance humanity has historically considered money par excellence: gold.[104]

---

[104]The impossibility of replacing today's fiduciary money with artificial, private monetary standards follows from the monetary regression theorem, explained in footnote 35. This is why Murray N. Rothbard is especially critical of authors who, like Hayek, Greenfield, and Yeager, have at times recommended the creation of an artificial monetary system based on a basket of commodities. Rothbard states:

> It is precisely because economic history is path-dependent that we don't want to foist upon the future a system that will not work, and that will not work largely because such indices and media cannot emerge "organically" from individual actions on the market. Surely, the idea in dismantling the government and returning (or advancing) to a free market is to be as consonant with the market as possible, and to eliminate government intervention with the greatest possible dispatch. Foisting upon the public a bizarre scheme at variance with the nature and functions of money and of the market, is precisely the kind of technocratic social engineering from which the world has suffered far too much in the twentieth century. (Rothbard, "Aurophobia: or Free Banking on What Standard?" p. 107, footnote 14)

Rothbard chose this curious title for his article in order to call attention to the obstinate efforts of many theorists to dispense with gold (historically the quintessential form of money) in their mental lucubrations on the ideal form of private money. On Richard H. Timberlake's critique of the monetary regression theorem ("A Critique of Monetarist and Austrian Doctrines on the Utility and Value of Money," *Review of Austrian Economics* 1 [1987]: 81–96), see Murray N. Rothbard's article, "Timberlake on the Austrian Theory of Money: A Comment," printed in *Review of Austrian Economics* 2 (1988): 179–87. As Rothbard discerningly points

Murray N. Rothbard has devoted considerable thought to the process of exchanging for gold all bills already issued by the Federal Reserve, a step which would follow the establishment of a 100-percent reserve requirement on all bank deposits. Based on data from 1981, Rothbard reaches the conclusion that this exchange would be contingent on a gold price of $1,696 per ounce. Over the past fifteen years the price of the exchange has risen noticeably. Therefore, if we take into account that the current [1997] price of gold is around $350 an ounce, it is clear that in a country with an economy as large as that of the United States, the complete privatization of fiduciary money and its replacement with gold would require a nearly twenty-fold increase in the present market value of gold.[105] This sharp rise in the price of gold would initially drive up its supply and perhaps cause an inflationary shock which we could hardly quantify, but which would be felt only once and would not exert any acute distorting effects on the real productive structure.[106]

----

out, Timberlake resolutely claims that money has a direct, subjective utility, just like any other good, yet he fails to realize that money only generates utility as a medium of exchange, unlike consumer and intermediate goods, and thus the absolute volume of it is irrelevant with respect to the fulfillment of its function. Therefore one must turn to the "monetary regression theorem" (which is simply a retrospective version of Menger's theory on the evolutionary emergence of money) to explain how economic agents estimate money's purchasing power today based on that which it had in the past. This is the key to avoiding the vices of circular reasoning in this matter.

[105]Rothbard, "The Case for a Genuine Gold Dollar," chapter 1 of *The Gold Standard: An Austrian Perspective*, p. 14; see also "The Solution," p. 700.

[106] Thus it would be unnecessary and damaging to implement the proposal F.A. Hayek made in 1937, when, in reference to the establishment of a 100-percent reserve requirement for banking in a context of a pure gold standard, he concluded:

> [I]t would clearly require as an essential complement an international control of the production of gold, since the increase in the value of gold would otherwise bring about an enormous increase in the supply of gold. But this would only provide a safety valve probably necessary in any case to prevent

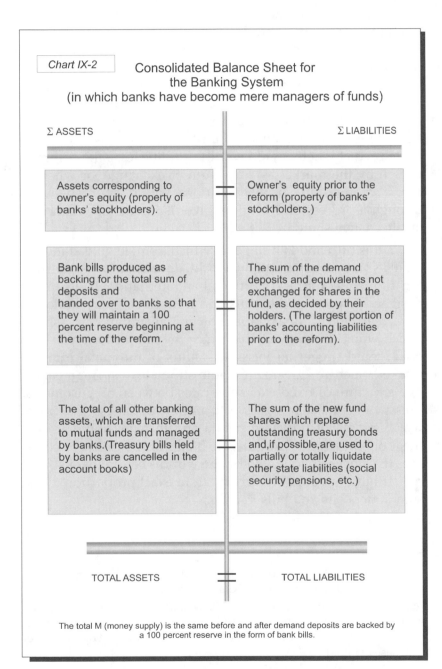

Chart IX-2 — Consolidated Balance Sheet for the Banking System (in which banks have become mere managers of funds)

Σ ASSETS

Σ LIABILITIES

Assets corresponding to owner's equity (property of banks' stockholders).

Owner's equity prior to the reform (property of banks' stockholders.)

Bank bills produced as backing for the total sum of deposits and handed over to banks so that they will maintain a 100 percent reserve beginning at the time of the reform.

The sum of the demand deposits and equivalents not exchanged for shares in the fund, as decided by their holders. (The largest portion of banks' accounting liabilities prior to the reform).

The total of all other banking assets, which are transferred to mutual funds and managed by banks.(Treasury bills held by banks are cancelled in the account books)

The sum of the new fund shares which replace outstanding treasury bonds and,if possible,are used to partially or totally liquidate other state liabilities (social security pensions, etc.)

TOTAL ASSETS

TOTAL LIABILITIES

The total M (money supply) is the same before and after demand deposits are backed by a 100 percent reserve in the form of bank bills.

The *fifth and last stage* in the privatization of the financial and banking system would begin when the conditions of gold production and distribution had stabilized. This last stage would be characterized by absolute freedom in banking (though the system would be subject to legal principles, and hence, a 100-percent reserve requirement on demand deposits) and the existence of a single, worldwide gold standard with a 100-percent reserve ratio in an environment of slight, gradual "deflation" and sustained economic growth. At any rate, the evolutionary process of experimentation in the field of money and finance would continue, and it is impossible to predict whether gold would continue to be the currency chosen by the market as a medium of exchange, or whether future changes in social conditions would spontaneously, through a process of evolution, give rise to the emergence of an alternative standard.

In this fifth and last stage, in which a single gold standard would spread throughout the world, it would be advisable for the different countries to arrive at an international agreement designed to prevent the transition from having any unnecessary, real effects (apart from the initial, inflationary shock which would be unavoidable, since the jump in the value of gold would trigger an increased influx of the metal into the market). Such an agreement would stipulate the prior creation of a structure of fixed exchange rates between all currencies. This would make it possible to uniformly assess the entire world supply of fiduciary media and to redistribute among the economic agents and private banks of the different countries the stocks of gold held by the world's central banks. This redistribution would be carried out in exact proportion to the sum of deposits and bills in each.

----

the system from becoming all too rigid. (Hayek, *Monetary Nationalism and International Stability*, p. 82)

In any case, the initial inflationary shock could be reduced if, during the years prior to the transition to the fifth stage, central banks were to inject their 2 percent increase in the money supply in the form of open-market purchases of gold.

Thus would be the end of the final stage in the privatization of the banking and financial sector, and economic agents would reinitiate the spontaneous market process of experimentation in the field of money and finance, a process which was historically interrupted by the nationalization of money and the creation and fortification of central banks.

THE APPLICATION OF THE THEORY OF BANKING AND FINANCIAL REFORM TO THE EUROPEAN MONETARY UNION AND THE BUILDING OF THE FINANCIAL SECTOR IN ECONOMIES OF THE FORMER EASTERN BLOC

The above remarks on the reform of the western banking and financial system might be helpful in the design and management of the European Monetary Union, a topic that is currently sparking great interest among specialists in the field.[107] These considerations provide at least an indication of the direction European monetary reform should take at all times and of the dangers to avoid. It is evident we should steer clear of a system of monopolistic national currencies which compete with each other in a chaotic environment of flexible exchange rates. Moreover we should avoid maintaining a European central bank which prevents competition between currencies in a broad economic area, fails to meet the challenges of banking reform (100-percent reserve requirement), fails to guarantee a level of monetary stability at least as high as that of the most stable national currency at any given point in history and, in short, represents an insurmountable obstacle to subsequent reforms, i.e., the elimination of the central financial planning agency (the central bank). Therefore perhaps the most workable and appropriate model in the short

---

[107]For example, see the book, *España y la unificación monetaria europea: una reflexión crítica*, Ramón Febrero, ed. (Madrid: Editorial Abacus, 1994). Other relevant works on this debate include: Pascal Salin, *L'unité monétaire européene: au profit de qui?* (Paris: Economica, 1980); and Robin Leigh Pemberton, *The Future of Monetary Arrangements in Europe* (London: Institute of Economic Affairs, 1989). On the different ideas of Europe and the role of its nations, see Jesús Huerta de Soto, "A Theory of Liberal Nationalism," *Il Politico* LX, no. 4 (1995): 583–98.

and medium term would consist of the introduction through-out Europe of complete freedom of choice in currencies, both public and private and from both inside and outside the Union. The national currencies still in use due to tradition would be placed in a system of fixed exchange rates[108] which would adjust the monetary policy of each country to the most solvent and stable policy among all the countries at any point in time. Thus the door would at least remain open to the pos-sibility that nation-states in the European Union might in the future advance in the three fundamental areas of monetary and banking reform (freedom of choice in currency, free bank-ing, and a 100-percent reserve requirement on demand deposits). In doing so, states would oblige the other Union members to follow their strong monetary leadership, as Mau-rice Allais maintains.

Once the European Central Bank was created on June 1, 1998, it became important that criticism of it and the single European currency center around the distance between this system and the ideal of a pure gold standard and 100-percent reserve requirement. Many libertarian theorists (mainly those of the Chicago School) mistakenly focus their criticism on the fact that the new arrangement does away with the former sys-tem of monetary nationalism and flexible exchange rates. However, a single European monetary standard which is as rigid as possible would represent a healthy step toward a pure gold standard. Furthermore it would complete the institu-tional framework of the European free-trade system, since it

---

[108]The prescription of fixed exchange rates is traditional among Aus-trian theorists who consider it second best in the pursuit of the ideal monetary system, which would consist of a pure gold standard and in which economic flows would be free of unnecessary monetary distur-bances. The most exhaustive Austrian analysis of fixed exchange rates appears in Hayek's book, *Monetary Nationalism and International Stabil-ity*. Mises also defends fixed exchange rates (see his book, *Omnipotent Government: The Rise of the Total State and Total War* [New York: Arlington House, 1969], p. 252, and also *Human Action*, pp. 750–91). A valuable analysis, from an Austrian point of view, of the economic theory behind fixed exchange rates can be found in José Antonio de Aguirre's book, *La moneda única europea* (Madrid: Unión Editorial, 1990), pp. 35ff.

would preclude monetary interference and manipulation on the part of each member country and oblige those countries with more rigid economic structures (Germany and France, for example) to introduce the flexibility they need to compete in an environment in which resorting to inflationary national monetary policies to compensate for structural rigidities is no longer an option.

Some very similar thoughts could be applied to the necessary establishment of a financial and banking system in the economies of the former Eastern bloc. While we must recognize that these economies start from a highly unfavorable position after decades of central planning, the present transition toward a market economy offers a unique and crucially important opportunity to avoid the major errors committed in the West up to now and to advance directly to at least the third or fourth stage in our reform plan. At the same time, a jump straight to the fourth stage would be quite feasible in the former Soviet Union, where abundant gold reserves would permit the establishment of a pure gold standard, a measure which would benefit the nation a great deal. At any rate, if these countries fail to learn from the experience of others and attempt, in awkward imitation of the West, to set up a fractional-reserve banking system directed by a central bank, the financial pressures of each moment will lead to policies of rampant credit expansion and enormous harm to the productive structure. Such policies will foster feverish speculation and create a climate of social unrest which might even endanger the overall transition of these societies to a full-fledged market economy.[109]

---

[109]In chapter 6 (footnote 110), we referred to the severe banking crises which have already erupted in Russia, the Czech Republic, Romania, Albania, Latvia, and Lithuania due to the disregard shown by these countries for recommendations like the ones we make in the text. See Richard Layard and Andrea Richter, "Who Gains and Who Loses from Russian Credit Expansion?" *Communist Economies and Economic Transformation* 6, no. 4 (1994): 459–72. On the different issues which interfere with plans for monetary reform in ex-communist countries, see, among other sources, *The Cato Journal* 12, no. 3 (Winter, 1993). See also the work

6

CONCLUSION: THE BANKING SYSTEM OF A FREE SOCIETY

The theory of money, bank credit, and financial markets represents the greatest theoretical challenge confronting economists as we enter the twenty-first century. In fact it is no stretch to claim that once the theoretical gap embodied by the analysis of socialism was filled, perhaps the most important, yet least-understood field was that of money. For, as we have attempted to reveal in detail throughout this book, this area is fraught with methodological errors, theoretical confusion and, as a result, systematic government coercion. The social relationships in which money is involved are by far the most abstract and obscure, and the knowledge generated through them is the most vast, complex, and difficult to grasp. Consequently the systematic coercion of governments and central banks in this field is by far the most damaging. In any case the intellectual delay in the theory of money and banking has severely affected the development of the world economy, as we see from the acute, recurrent cycles of boom and recession which continue to grip market economies at the dawn of the new millennium.

Nevertheless economic thought on banking issues is quite long-standing, and as we have seen, can be traced back even to the scholars of the School of Salamanca. Closer to our time, we find the controversy between the Banking and Currency Schools, a debate which laid the foundation for the development of subsequent doctrine. We have made an effort to demonstrate the absence of complete agreement between the Free-Banking School and the Banking School, on the one hand, and between the Central-Banking School and

---

by Stephen H. Hanke, Lars Jonung, and Kurt Schuler, *Russian Currency and Finance* (London: Routledge, 1993). The authors of this book propose the establishment of a currency-board system as the ideal model for monetary transition in the former Soviet Union. For reasons given in footnote 91, we deem this reform plan much less adequate than our proposal to institute a pure gold standard and 100-percent reserve requirement using Russia's substantial gold reserves.

the Currency School, on the other. Many free-banking advocates did base their position on the fallacious, unsound inflationary arguments of the Banking School, and most Currency School theorists did plan to reach their objectives of financial solvency and economic stability via the inception of a central bank to curb abuses. However, from the very beginning, certain able Currency School theorists found it impossible and utopian to believe the central bank would do anything but further aggravate the problems that had emerged. These scholars were aware that the best way to limit the creation of fiduciary media and to achieve monetary stability was through a free-banking system governed, like all other economic agents, by the traditional principles of civil and commercial law (i.e., a 100-percent reserve requirement on demand deposits). Paradoxically, nearly all Banking School defenders ended up cheerfully accepting the establishment of a central bank which, as lender of last resort, would guarantee and perpetuate the expansionary privileges of the private banking system. Meanwhile private bankers sought with increasing determination to participate in the lucrative "business" of generating fiduciary media by credit expansion without having to give too much thought to problems of liquidity, due to the support offered at all times by the central bank, the lender of last resort.

Furthermore, although Currency School theorists were correct in almost all of their theoretical contributions, they were unable to see that every one of the drawbacks they rightly perceived in the freedom of private banks to issue fiduciary media in the form of banknotes were also inherent in the "business" of granting expansionary loans against demand deposits at banks, though in this case the drawbacks were more concealed and surreptitious, and hence much more dangerous. These theorists also committed an error when they claimed the most appropriate policy would be to introduce legislation to abolish merely the freedom to issue banknotes unbacked by gold and to set up a central bank to defend the most fundamental monetary principles. Only Ludwig von Mises, who followed the tradition of Modeste, Cernuschi, Hübner, and Michaelis, was capable of realizing that the Currency School's prescription of a central bank was a mistake, and that the best and only way to uphold the school's sound monetary principles was through a free-banking system subject without privileges to private law (i.e., with a 100-percent reserve requirement).

The failure of most Currency School theorists was fatal. These theorists were responsible for the fact that Peel's Act of 1844, despite the honorable intentions behind it, failed to eliminate the creation of fiduciary deposits, though it prohibited the issuance of unbacked banknotes. Moreover members of the Currency School also defended the institution of a central-banking system which, mainly due to the negative influence of Banking School theorists, would eventually be used to justify and promote policies of monetary recklessness and financial excess, policies much more foolish than those theorists originally sought to remedy.

Therefore the central bank, understood as a central planning agency in the field of money and banking, cannot be considered a natural product of the evolution of the free market. On the contrary, it has been dictatorially imposed from the outside as a result of governments' attempts to profit from the highly lucrative possibilities of fractional-reserve banking. In fact governments have deviated from their essential role, as they have ceased to adequately define and defend the property rights of bank depositors, and they have taken advantage of the practically unlimited possibilities of money and credit creation which the establishment of a fractional-reserve ratio (on bills and deposits) has opened up for them. Thus in the violation of the private-property-law principles which apply to demand deposits, governments have largely found their longed-for philosopher's stone, which has provided them with unlimited financing without requiring them to resort to taxes.

The construction of a true free-banking system must coincide with the reestablishment of a 100-percent reserve requirement on amounts received as demand deposits. The original neglect of this obligation led to all the banking and monetary issues which have given rise to the current financial system, with its high level of government intervention.

The idea is ultimately to apply a seminal idea of Hayek's to the field of money and banking. According to this idea, whenever a traditional rule of conduct is broken, either through institutional government coercion or the granting of special privileges by the state to certain people or organizations, sooner or later grave, undesirable consequences always ensue and cause serious damage to the spontaneous process of social cooperation.

As we saw in the first three chapters, the traditional rule of conduct transgressed in the banking business is the legal principle that the *safekeeping* obligation, an essential element in a non-fungible deposit, manifests itself, in the contract governing the deposit of a fungible good (for example money), in the requirement that a reserve of 100 percent of the fungible good (money) received on deposit be maintained constantly. Hence any use of such money, specifically the granting of loans against it, implies a violation of this principle and thus, an illegitimate act of misappropriation.

At each stage in history, bankers have promptly become tempted to breach this traditional rule of conduct and make self-interested use of their depositors' money. At first they did so secretively and with a sense of shame, since they were still aware of the dishonest nature of their behavior. Only later did bankers manage to make the violation of the traditional legal principle an open and legal practice, when they obtained from the government the *privilege* of using their depositors' money, almost always in the form of loans, which initially were often granted to the government itself. Thus arose the relationship of complicity and the coalition of interests which have become customary between governments and banks and explain the current "understanding" and "cooperation" between these two types of institutions. Such a climate of collaboration is evident, with only subtle differences, in all western countries under almost all circumstances. For bankers soon realized that the violation of the above traditional legal principle led to a financial activity which earned them fat profits, but which in any case required the existence of a lender of last resort, the central bank, to provide the necessary liquidity in the moments of crisis which experience taught would always reappear sooner or later. The central bank would also be responsible for orchestrating increases in joint, coordinated credit expansion and for imposing on all citizens the legal tender regulations of its own monopolistic currency.

Nevertheless the unfortunate social consequences of this *privilege* granted to bankers (yet to no other institution or individual) were not entirely understood until Mises and Hayek developed the Austrian theory of economic cycles, which they based on the theory of money and capital and we analyzed in chapters 5 through 7. In short, Austrian theorists have demonstrated that the pursuit of the theoretically impossible (from a legal-contractual and technical-economic standpoint) goal of offering a contract comprised of fundamentally incompatible elements, a contract which combines ingredients typical of mutual funds (particularly the possibility of earning interest on "deposits") with those typical of a traditional deposit contract (which by definition must permit the withdrawal of the nominal value at any time) will always, sooner or later, trigger certain spontaneous readjustments. Initially these readjustments take the form of the uncontrolled expansion of the money supply, inflation, and generalized poor allocation of productive resources on a microeconomic level. Eventually they manifest themselves in a recession, the elimination of the errors exerted on the productive structure by credit expansion, and massive unemployment.

It is important to understand that the privilege which allows banks to operate with a fractional reserve represents an obvious attack by government authorities on the correct definition and defense of depositors' private-property rights, when respect for these rights is essential to the proper functioning of any market economy. As a result, a typical "tragedy of the commons" effect invariably appears, as it does whenever property rights are not adequately defined and defended. This effect consists of an increased inclination on the part of bankers to try to get ahead of their competitors by expanding their own credit base sooner and more than their rivals. Consequently the fractional-reserve banking system always tends toward more or less rampant expansion, even when it is "monitored" by central bankers who, contrary to what has normally occurred in the past, seriously (and not just rhetorically) concern themselves with setting limits.

In short, the essential goal of monetary policy should be to subject banks to the traditional principles of civil and commercial law, according to which each individual and company must fulfill certain obligations (100-percent reserve requirement) in strict keeping with the terms agreed to in each contract.

At the same time, we should be strongly critical of most of the literature which, following the publication in the late seventies of Hayek's book, *Denationalization of Money*, has defended a model of fractional-reserve free banking. The most important conclusion to draw from all of this literature is that its authors too often fail to realize that they frequently commit the old errors of the Banking School. As we explained in chapter 8, this is true of the works of White, Selgin, and Dowd. There is nothing wrong with their attention to the advantages of an interbank clearing system in terms of self-control in credit expansion, and in this sense their system would produce better results than the current central-banking system, as Ludwig von Mises originally pointed out. However fractional-reserve free banking is still a second best which would not keep a wave of excessive optimism in loan concession from triggering the joint action of different banks. At any rate, these authors fail to see that as long as the fractional-reserve privilege remains, it will be impossible in practice to dispense with the central bank. In brief, as we have argued in this book, the only way to eliminate the central planning agency in the field of banking and credit (the central bank) is to do away with the fractional-reserve privilege private bankers currently enjoy. This is a necessary measure, though it is not sufficient: the central bank must still be completely abolished and the fiduciary money it has created up to now must be privatized.

In conclusion, if we wish to build a truly stable financial and monetary system for the twenty-first century, a system which will protect our economies as far as humanly possible from crises and recessions, we will have to: (1) ensure complete freedom of choice in currency, based on a metallic standard (gold) which would replace all fiduciary media issued in the past; (2) establish a free-banking system; and, most importantly, (3) insist that all agents involved in the free-banking system be subject to and comply with traditional legal rules and principles, especially the principle that no one, not even a banker, can enjoy the privilege of loaning something entrusted to him on demand deposit (i.e., a free-banking system with a 100-percent reserve requirement).

Until specialists and society in general fully grasp the essential theoretical and legal principles associated with money, bank credit, and economic cycles, we may realistically expect further suffering in the world due to damaging economic recessions which will inevitably and perpetually reappear until central banks lose their power to issue paper money with legal tender and bankers lose their government-granted privilege of operating with a fractional reserve. We now wrap up the book as we began it, with this opinion: Now that we have seen the historic fall of socialism, both in theory and in practice, the main challenge to face both professional economists and lovers of freedom in this new century will be to use all of their intellectual might to oppose the institution of the central bank and the privilege private bankers now enjoy.

BIBLIOGRAPHY

Abrams, M.A., *Money in a Changing Civilisation* (London: John Lain, 1934).

Aguirre, J.A. de, *El poder de emitir dinero: De J. Law a J.M. Keynes* (Madrid: Unión Editorial, 1985).

——, *La moneda única europea* (Madrid: Unión Editorial, 1990).

——, Appendix to the Spanish edition of V.C. Smith's, *The Rationale of Central Banking and the Free Banking Alternative* (Indianapolis, Ind.: Liberty Press, 1990).

——, "Introducción" to the Spanish edition of Böhm-Bawerk's book, *Capital and Interest*, vol. 2, *Positive Theory of Capital* (*Teoría positiva del capital*) (Madrid: Ediciones Aosta/Unión Editorial, 1998).

Albácar López, J.L., and J. Santos Briz, *Código Civil: doctrina y jurisprudencia* (Madrid: Editorial Trivium, 1991), vol. 6.

Albaladejo, M., *Derecho Civil*, vol. 2, *Derecho de las obligaciones: los contratos en particular y las obligaciones no contractuales* (Barcelona: Librería Bosch, 1975).

——, ed., *Comentarios al Código Civil y compilaciones forales* (Madrid: Editorial Revista del Derecho Privado EDERSA, 1982).

Alchian, A.A., and W.R. Allen, *University Economics* (Belmont, Calif.: Wadsworth Publishing, 1964).

Alderfer, E.B., and H.E. Michel, *Economics of American Industry*, 3rd ed. (New York: McGraw-Hill, 1957).

Allais, M., "Les Faux Monnayeurs," *Le Monde* (October 29, 1974).

——, *L'Impôt sur le capital et la réforme monétaire* (Paris: Hermann Éditeurs, 1989).

——, "Les conditions monétaires d'une économie de marchés: des enseignements du passé aux réformes de demain," *Revue d'économie politique* 3 (May–July 1993): 319–67.

Allen, R.L., *Irving Fisher: A Biography* (Oxford: Blackwell, 1993).

Alonso Neira, M.A., "Hayek's Triangle," *An Eponimous Dictionary of Economics: A Guide to Laws and Theorems Named after Economists* (Cheltenham, U.K.: Edward Elgar, 2004)

Anderson, B.M., *Economics and the Public Welfare: A Financial and Economic History of the United States, 1914–1946* (Indianapolis, Ind.: Liberty Press, 1979).

Andreu García, J.M., "El coeficiente de caja óptimo y su posible vinculación con el déficit público," *Boletín económico de Información Comercial Española* (June 29–July 5, 1987): 24–25.

——, "En torno a la neutralidad del coeficiente de caja: el caso español," *Revista de economía* 9.

Anes, R., "El Banco de España, 1874–1914: un banco nacional," in *La banca española en la Restauración* (Madrid: Servicio de Estudios del Banco de España, 1974), vol. 1.

Angell, J.W., "The 100 Percent Reserve Plan," *Quarterly Journal of Economics* L, no. 1 (November 1935): 1–35.

Aranson, P.H., "Bruno Leoni in Retrospect," *Harvard Journal of Law and Public Policy* (Summer, 1988).

Arena, R., "Hayek and Modern Business Cycle Theory," in *Money and Business Cycles: The Economics of F.A. Hayek*, M. Colonna and H. Hagemann, eds., vol. 1, chap. 10, pp. 203–17.

Arrow, K.J., "The Economics of Moral Hazard: Further Comments," *American Economic Review* 58 (1968): 537–53.

——, "Uncertainty in the Welfare Economics of Medical Care," *American Economic Review* 53 (1963): 941–73.

Azpilcueta, M. de, *Comentario resolutorio de cambios* (Madrid: Consejo Superior de Investigaciones Científicas, 1965); original Spanish edition (Salamanca: Andrés de Portonarijs, 1556); Portuguese ed., *Comentario resolutorio de onzenas* (Coimbra: Ioam de Barreyra, 1560).

Backhaus, J., W. Heijmann, A. Nantjes, and J. van Ophem, eds., *Economic Policy in an Orderly Framework: Liber Amicorum for Gerrit Meijer* (Münster: LIT Verlag, 2003).

Bagus, P. "La tragedia de los bienes comunales y la escuela austriaca: Hardin, Hoppe, Huerta de Soto, y Mises." *Procesos de Mercado* 1, no. 2 (2004): 125–34.

Bajo Fernández, M., M. Pérez Manzano, and C. Suárez González, *Manual de derecho penal*, Special section, "Delitos Patrimoniales y

Económicos" (Madrid: Editorial Centro de Estudios Ramón Areces, 1993).

"Banco de España," *Boletín estadístico* (August 1994): 17.

Barnes, H.E., *An Economic History of the Western World* (New York: Harcourt, Brace, 1940).

Barnett, W., and W. Block, "On Hayekian Triangles," *Procesos de Mercado* 3, no. 2 (Autumn 2006): 39–142.

Barrallat, L., *La banca española en el año 2000: un sector en transición* (Madrid: Ediciones de las Ciencias Sociales, 1992).

Becker, G.S., "A Proposal for Free Banking," Chapter 2 in *Free Banking, Modern Theory and Policy*, L.H. White, ed., vol. 3, pp. 20–25.

Belda, F., "Ética de la creación de créditos según la doctrina de Molina, Lessio y Lugo," *Pensamiento* 73, no. 19 (1963): 53–89.

Bell, D., and I. Kristol, eds., *The Crisis in Economic Theory* (New York: Basic Books, 1981).

Beltrán, L., "Sobre los orígenes hispanos de la economía de mercado," in *Ensayos de economía política* (Madrid: Unión Editorial, 1996), pp. 234–54.

Benegas Lynch, A., *Poder y razón razonable* (Buenos Aires and Barcelona: Librería "El Ateneo" Editorial, 1992).

Benham, F., *British Monetary Policy* (London: P.S. King and Shaw, 1932).

Bérenger, J., *A History of the Habsburg Empire, 1273–1700*, C.A. Simpson, trans. (London and New York: Longman, 1994).

Birner, J., and R. Van Zijp, *Hayek Co-ordination and Evolution: His Legacy in Philosophy, Politics, Economics, and the History of Ideas* (London: Routledge, 1994).

Biblia Sacra vulgatam versionem, R. Weber, ed. (Stuttgart, 1969).

Blanchard, O.J., and S. Fischer, *Lectures on Macroeconomics* (Cambridge, Mass.: The MIT Press, 1990).

Blaug, M., *Economic Theory in Retrospect* (Cambridge: Cambridge University Press, 1978).

——, "Hayek Revisited," *Critical Review* 7, no. 1 (Winter, 1993): 51–60.

Block, W., "Fractional Reserve Banking: An Interdisciplinary Perspective," Chapter 3 in *Man, Economy, and Liberty: Essays in Honor of*

Murray N. Rothbard, W. Block and L.H. Rockwell, Jr., eds. (Auburn, Ala.: Ludwig von Mises Institute, 1988), pp. 24–32.

——, "Henry Simons is Not a Supporter of Free Enterprise," *Journal of Libertarian Studies* 6, no. 4 (Fall, 2002).

Block, W., and K.M. Garschina, "Hayek, Business Cycles and Fractional Reserve Banking: Continuing the De-Homogenization Process," *Review of Austrian Economics* 9, no. 1 (1996): 77–94.

Block, W., and L.H. Rockwell, Jr., eds., *Man, Economy, and Liberty: Essays in Honor of Murray N. Rothbard* (Auburn, Ala.: Ludwig von Mises Institute, 1988).

Boettke, P., "Where Did Economics Go Wrong? Modern Economics as a Flight from Reality," *Critical Review* 1 (Winter, 1997): 11–64.

Boettke, P., and Prychitko, D.L., eds. *The Market Process: Essays in Contemporary Austrian Economics*, 2 vols. (Aldershot, England: Edward Elgar, 1998).

Bogaert, R., *Banques et Banquiers dans les Cités Grecques* (Leyden, Holland: A.W. Sijthoff, 1968).

Böhm-Bawerk, E.v., "Capital and Interest Once More," *Quarterly Journal of Economics* (November 1906 and February 1907).

——, *Kapital und Kapitalzins: Geschichte und Kritik der Kapitalzins—theorieen* (Innsbruck: Verlag der Wagner'schen Universitäts-Buchhandlung, 1884); English translation by Hans F. Sennholz, *Capital and Interest: History and Critique of Interest Theories* (South Holland, Ill.: Libertarian Press, 1959); Spanish translation by Carlos Silva, *Capital e interés: historia y crítica de las teorías sobre el interés* (Mexico: Fondo de Cultura Económica, 1986).

——, "The Nature of Capital: A Rejoinder," *Quarterly Journal of Economics* (November 1907).

——, "Professor Clark's Views on the Genesis of Capital," *Quarterly Journal of Economics* 9 (1895): 113–31; reprinted in *Classics in Austrian Economics*, I.M. Kirzner, ed., vol. 1, pp. 131–43.

——, *Kapital und Kapitalzins: Positive Theorie des Kapitales* (Innsbruck: Verlag der Wagner'schen Universitäts-Buchhandlung, 1889); English translation by Hans F. Sennholz, *Capital and Interest: Positive Theory of Capital* (South Holland, Ill.: Libertarian Press, 1959). Spanish translation by J.A. de Aguirre, *Teoría positiva del capital* (Madrid: Ediciones Aosta/Unión Editorial, 1998).

Boorman, J.D., and T.M. Havrilesky, *Money Supply, Money Demand and Macroeconomic Models* (Boston, Mass.: Allyn and Bacon, 1972).

Borch, K.H., *Economics of Insurance* (Amsterdam and New York: North-Holland, 1990).

Bresciani-Turroni, C., *Curso de economía política*, vol. 2, *Problemas de economía política* (Mexico: Fondo de Cultura Económica, 1961).

——, *Le vicende del marco tedesco* (Milan: Università Bocconi Editrice, 1931); English translation by Millicent E. Savers, *The Economics of Inflation: A Study of Currency Depreciation in Post-War Germany* (London: Routledge, 1937 and London and New York: Augustus M. Kelley, 1968).

Butos, W.N., "The Recession and Austrian Business Cycle Theory: An Empirical Perspective," *Critical Review* 7, nos. 2–3 (Spring and Summer, 1993).

Cabrillo, F., ed., *Lecturas de economía política* (Madrid: Minerva Ediciones, 1991).

——, *Quiebra y liquidación de empresas: un análisis económico del derecho español* (Madrid: Unión Editorial, 1989).

Cagan, P., *Determinance and Effects of Changes in the Stock of Money, 1875–1960* (New York: Columbia University Press, 1965).

Caldwell, B., *Beyond Positivism: Economic Methodology in the Twentieth Century* (London: George Allen and Unwin, 1982; 2nd ed., London: Routledge, 1994).

Cantillon, R., *Essai sur la nature du commerce en général* (Holborn, London: Fletcher Gyles, 1755).

Carande, R., *Carlos V y sus banqueros*, 3 vols. (Barcelona and Madrid: Editorial Crítica, 1987).

Casas Pardo, J., *Curso de economía*, 5th ed. (Madrid, 1985).

Castañeda Chornet, J., *Lecciones de teoría económica* (Madrid: Editorial Aguilar, 1972).

Centi, J.P., "Hayekian Perspectives on the Monetary System: Toward Fiat Private and Competitive Moneys," *Austrian Economics Today I*, The International Library of Austrian Economics, K.R. Leube, ed. (Frankfurt: FAZ Buch, 2003), vol. 7, pp. 89–104.

Cernuschi, H., *Contre le billet de banque* (Paris: Guillaumin, 1866).

——, *Mécanique de l'échange* (Paris: A. Lacroix, 1865).

Cicero, M.T., *De re publica* (Cambridge, Mass.: The Loeb Classical Library, 1961).

Chafuen, A.A., *Christians for Freedom: Late-Scholastic Economics* (San Francisco, Calif.: Ignatius Press, 1986).

Checkland, S.G., *Scottish Banking: A History, 1695–1973* (Glasgow: Collins, 1975).

Churruca, J. de, "La quiebra de la banca del cristiano Calisto (c.a. 185–90)," *Seminarios Complutenses de Derecho Romano* (February–May 1991; Madrid, 1992), pp. 61–86.

Cipolla, C.M., *The Monetary Policy of Fourteenth-Century Florence* (Berkeley: University of California Press, 1982).

——, *Money in Sixteenth-Century Florence* (Berkeley.: University of California Press, 1989).

Clark, J.B., "Concerning the Nature of Capital: A Reply," *Quarterly Journal of Economics* (May 1907).

——, *The Distribution of Wealth* (New York: Macmillan, 1899; New York: Augustus M. Kelley, 1965).

——, "The Genesis of Capital," *Yale Review* (November 1893): 302–15.

——, "The Origin of Interest," *Quarterly Journal of Economics* 9 (April 1895): 257–78.

Clough, S.B., *The Economic Development of Western Civilization* (New York: McGraw-Hill, 1959).

Cochin, H., *Memoire pour Richard Cantillon, intimé & appellant. Contre Jean & Rémi Carol, Appellans & intimez* (Paris: Andre Knapen, 1730).

Cohen, E.E., *Athenian Economy and Society: A Banking Perspective* (Princeton, N.J.: Princeton University Press, 1992).

Colmeiro, M., *Historia de la economía política española* (1863; Madrid: Fundación Banco Exterior, 1988), vol. 2.

Colonna, M., and H. Hagemann, eds., *Money and Business Cycles: The Economics of F.A. Hayek,* 2 vols. (Aldershot, England: Edward Elgar, 1994).

Colunga, A., and L. Turrado, eds., *Biblia Sacra Iuxta Vulgatam Clementinam* (Madrid: Biblioteca de Autores Cristianos, 1994).

Coppa-Zuccari, P., *Il deposito irregolare*, Biblioteca dell "Archivio Giuridico Filippo Serafini" (Modena, 1901), vol. 6.

———, "La natura giuridica del deposito bancario," *Archivio Giuridico "Filippo Serafini,"* n.s. 9 (Modena, 1902): 441–72.

Corona Ramón, J.F., *Una introducción a la teoría de la decisión pública ("Public Choice")* (Alcalá de Henares and Madrid: Instituto Nacional de Administración Pública, 1987).

Coronel de Palma, L., *La evolución de un banco central* (Madrid: Real Academia de Jurisprudencia y Legislación, 1976).

Corpus Juris Civilis, Dionysius Gottfried edition (Geneva 1583).

Costouros, G.J., "Development of Banking and Related Book-Keeping Techniques in Ancient Greece," *International Journal of Accounting 7*, no. 2 (1973): 75–81.

Courcelle-Seneuil, J.G., *La banque libre: exposé des fonctions du commerce de banque et de son application à l'agriculture suivi de divers écrits de controverse sur la liberté des banques* (Paris: Guillaumin, 1867).

Covarrubias y Leyva, D., *Veterum collatio numismatum,* in *Omnia opera* (Salamanca, 1577). Partial Spanish translation by Atilano Rico Seco in *Textos jurídico-políticos,* compiled by Manuel Fraga Iribarne (Madrid: Instituto de Estudios Políticos, 1957).

Cowen, T., *Risk and Business Cycles: New and Old Austrian Perspectives* (London: Routledge, 1998).

Crick, W.F., "The Genesis of Bank Deposits," *Economica* (June 1927).

Cuello Calón, E., *Derecho penal*, 13th ed. (Barcelona: Editorial Bosch, 1972), tome 2, special section, vol. 2.

Cuenta corriente de efectos o valores de un sector de la banca catalana: su repercusión en el crédito y en la economía, su calificación jurídica en el ámbito del derecho penal, civil y mercantil positivos españoles según los dictámenes emitidos por los letrados señores Rodríguez Sastre, Garrigues, Sánchez Román, Goicoechea, Miñana y Clemente de Diego, seguidos de un estudio sobre la cuenta de efectos y el Mercado Libre de Valores de Barcelona por D. Agustín Peláez, Síndico Presidente de la Bolsa de Madrid, La (Madrid: Delgado Sáez, 1936).

Currie, L., *The Supply and Control of Money in the United States,* together with *A Proposed Revision of the Monetary System of the United States,* submitted to the Secretary of the Treasury (September 1934), with a paper by Karl Brunner "On Lauchlin Currie's Contribution to Monetary Theory" (New York: Russell & Russell, 1968).

Dabin, J., *La teoría de la causa: estudio histórico y jurisprudencial*, F. de Pels-maeker, trans. and adapted by F. Bonet Ramón, 2nd ed. (Madrid: Editorial Revista de Derecho Privado, 1955).

Davanzati, B., *A Discourse upon Coins* (London: J.D. and J. Churchill, 1696).

Davenport, H.J., *The Economics of Enterprise*, 1913 (New York: Augustus M. Kelley, Reprints of Economic Classics, 1968).

Davenport, N., "Keynes in the City," in *Essays on John Maynard Keynes*, Milo Keynes, ed. (Cambridge: Cambridge University Press, 1975).

Davies, J.R., "Chicago Economists, Deficit Budgets and the Early 1930's," *American Economic Review* (June 1968).

De Roover, R., *The Rise and Decline of the Medici Bank, 1397–1494* (Cambridge, Mass.: Harvard University Press, 1963).

Delvaux, T., and M.E. Magnee, *Les nouveaux produits d'assurance-vie* (Brussels, Belgium: Editions de L'Université de Bruxelles, 1991).

Demosthenes, *Discursos privados I* (Madrid: Editorial Gredos, Biblioteca Clásica Gredos, 1983).

——, *Discursos privados II* (Madrid: Editorial Gredos, Biblioteca Clásica Gredos, 1983).

Dempsey, B.W., *Interest and Usury*, Introduction by Joseph A. Schumpeter (Washington, D.C.: American Council of Public Affairs, 1943).

Diamond, D.W., and P.H. Dybvig, "Bank Runs, Deposit Insurance, and Liquidity," *Journal of Political Economy* 91, no. 3 (1983): 401–19.

Díez-Picazo, L., and A. Gullón, *Sistema de derecho civil*, 6th ed. (Madrid: Editorial Tecnos, 1989).

Dimand, R.W., "Irving Fisher and Modern Macroeconomics," *American Economic Review* 87, no. 2 (May 1997): 442–44.

——, "Hawtrey and the Multiplier," *History of Political Economy* 29, no. 3 (Fall, 1997): 549–56.

Dolan, E.G., ed., *The Foundations of Modern Austrian Economics* (Kansas City, Mo.: Sheed and Ward, 1976).

Dorn, J.A., ed., *The Future of Money in the Information Age* (Washington, D.C.: Cato Institute, 1997).

Dowd, K., *The State and the Monetary System* (New York: Saint Martin's Press, 1989).

———, *The Experience of Free Banking* (London and New York: Routledge, 1992).

———, *Laissez-Faire Banking* (London and New York: Routledge, 1993).

Drucker, P.F., "Toward the Next Economics," in *The Crisis in Economic Theory*, D.Bell and I. Kristol, eds. (New York: Basic Books, 1981).

Durbin, E.F.M., *The Problem of Credit Policy* (London: Chapman and Hall, 1935).

———, *Purchasing Power and Trade Depression: A Critique of Under-Consumption Theories* (London and Toronto: Jonathan Cape, 1933).

Eatwell, J., M. Milgate, and P. Newman, *The New Palgrave: A Dictionary of Economics*, 4 vols. (London: Macmillan, 1987). Second edition in 8 vols., Steven N. Durlauf and Lawrence E. Blume, eds. (London: Palgrave Macmillan, 2008).

Ebeling, R., "The Great Austrian Inflation," *The Freeman* (April 2006).

Enciclopedia práctica de la banca (Barcelona: Editorial Planeta, 1989), vol. 6.

Enciclopedia universal ilustrada europeo-americana (Madrid: Editorial Espasa-Calpe, 1979).

Erias Rey, A., and J.M. Sánchez Santos, "Independencia de los bancos centrales y política monetaria: una síntesis," *Hacienda pública española* 132 (1995): 63–79.

Escarra, J., E. Escarra, and J. Rault, *Principes de droit commercial* (Paris: Recueil Sirey, 1947).

Estey, J.A., *Business Cycles: Their Nature, Cause, and Control*, 3rd ed. (Englewood Cliffs, N.J.: Prentice Hall, 1956); Spanish edition *Tratado sobre los ciclos económicos* (Mexico: Fondo de Cultura Económica, 1948).

Estapé, F., Introduction to the third Spanish edition of Joseph A. Schumpeter's book, *The History of Economic Analysis* [*Historia del análisis económico*] (Barcelona: Editorial Ariel, 1994).

Febrero, R., ed., *España y la unificación monetaria europea: una reflexión crítica* (Madrid: Editorial Abacus, 1994).

———, ed., *Qué es la economía* (Madrid: Ediciones Pirámide, 1997).

Feldberg, M., K. Jowel, and S. Mulholland, eds., *Milton Friedman in South Africa* (Johannesburg, South Africa: Graduate School of Business of the University of Capetown, 1976).

Fernández, T.R., *Comentarios a la ley de disciplina e intervención de las entidades de crédito,* Serie de Estudios de la Fundación Fondo para la Investigación Económica y Social (Madrid, 1989).

Ferrer Sama, A., *El delito de apropiación indebida.* Publicaciones del Seminario de Derecho Penal de la Universidad de Murcia (Murcia: Editorial Sucesores de Nogués, 1945).

Fetter, F.A., *Capital, Interest, and Rent* (Kansas City, Mo.: Sheed Andrews and McMeel, 1977).

——, "Interest Theory and Price Movements," *American Economic Review* 17, no. 1 (1926): 72.

Figueroa, E., *Teoría de los ciclos económicos* (Madrid: CSIC, 1947).

Figuerola, L., *Escritos económicos,* edited with a preliminary study by Francisco Cabrillo Rodríguez (Madrid: Instituto de Estudios Fiscales, 1991).

Fisher, I., *The Nature of Capital and Income* (New York: Macmillan, 1906).

——, *100 Percent Money* (New York: Adelphi Company, 1935).

——, *The Purchasing Power of Money: Its Determination and Relation to Credit Interest and Crises* (New York: Macmillan, [1911] 1925; New York: Augustus M. Kelley, 1963).

——, "What is Capital?" *Economic Journal* 6 (December 1896): 509–34.

Fisher, I.N., *My Father Irving Fisher* (New York: A Reflection Book, 1956).

Fraser, H.F., *Great Britain and the Gold Standard* (London: Macmillan, 1933).

Friedman, M., "Comment on the Critics," in *Milton Friedman, Monetary Framework,* Robert J. Gordon, ed. (Chicago: Chicago University Press, 1974).

——, *Dollars and Deficits* (Englewood Cliffs, N.J.: Prentice Hall, 1968).

——, "Has Gold Lost its Monetary Role?" in *Milton Friedman in South Africa,* M. Feldberg, K. Jowel, and S. Mulholland, eds. (Johannesburg, South Africa: Graduate School of Business of the University of Capetown, 1976).

——, *The Optimum Quantity of Money and Other Essays* (Chicago: Aldine, 1979).

——, "The 'Plucking Model' of Business Fluctuations Revisited," *Economic Inquiry* 30 (April 1993): 171–77.

——, *A Program for Monetary Stability* (New York: Fordham University Press, 1959).

——, "Quantity Theory of Money," in *The New Palgrave: A Dictionary of Economics*, J. Eatwell, M. Milgate, and P. Newman, eds. (London: Macmillan, 1987), vol. 4, pp. 3–20.

——, *A Theory of the Consumption Function* (Princeton, N.J.: Princeton University Press, 1957).

Friedman, M., and A.J. Schwartz, "Has Government Any Role in Money?," *Journal of Monetary Economics* 17 (1986): 37–72; reprinted as Chapter 26 in *The Essence of Friedman*, Kurt R. Leube, ed. (Palo Alto, Calif.: Hoover Institution Press, Stanford University, 1986) pp. 499–525.

——, *A Monetary History of the United States, 1867–1960* (Princeton, N.J.: Princeton University Press, 1971).

——, *Monetary Trends in the United States and United Kingdom: Their Relation to Income, Prices and Interest Rates, 1867–1975* (Chicago: University of Chicago Press, 1982).

Fullarton, J., *On the Regulation of Currencies, being an examination of the principles on which it is proposed to restrict, within certain fixed limits, the future issues on credit of the Bank of England and of the other banking establishments throughout the country* (London: John Murray, 1844. 2nd rev. ed., 1845).

Galiani, F., *Della moneta* (Naples: Giuseppe Raimondi, 1750).

Gallatin, A., *Considerations on the Currency and Banking System of the United States* (Philadelphia, Penn.: Carey and Lea, 1831).

García del Corral, I.L., ed., *Cuerpo de derecho civil romano: a doble texto, traducido al castellano del latino,* translated into Spanish by Ildefonso L. García del Corral; reprint, 6 vols. (Valladolid: Editorial Lex Nova, 1988).

García-Garrido, M.J., "La Sociedad de los Banqueros (Societas Argentaria)," in *Studi in Honore di Arnaldo Biscardi* (Milan, 1988), vol. 3.

García-Pita y Lastres, J.L., "Depósitos bancarios y protección del depositante," in *Contratos Bancarios* (Madrid: Colegios Notariales de España, 1996), pp. 119–266.

——, "Los depósitos bancarios de dinero y su documentación," *La Revista de Derecho Bancario y Bursátil*, Centro de Documentación Bancaria y Bursátil (October–December 1993): 919–1008.

Garrigues, J., *Contratos bancarios* (Madrid: Published by the author, 1975).

Garrison, R.W., "Austrian Macroeconomics: A Diagrammatical Exposition," originally published in *New Directions in Austrian Economics,* L.M. Spadaro, ed. (Kansas City, Mo.: Sheed Andrews and McMeel, 1978, pp. 167–201; reprinted as an independent book by the Institute for Humane Studies, 1978).

——, "The Austrian-Neoclassical Relation: A Study in Monetary Dynamics" (Doctoral thesis, University of Virginia, 1981).

——, "The Costs of a Gold Standard," in *The Gold Standard: An Austrian Perspective,* L.H. Rockwell, Jr., ed. (Lexington, Mass.: Lexington Books, 1985).

——, "The Limits of Macroeconomics," *Cato Journal: An Interdisciplinary Journal of Public Policy Analysis* 12, no. 1 (1993).

——, "Is Milton Friedman a Keynesian?" in *Dissent on Keynes: A Critical Appraisal of Keynesian Economics,* M. Skousen, ed. (New York and London: Praeger, 1992), chap. 8.

——, "The Roaring Twenties and the Bullish Eighties: The Role of Government in Boom and Bust," *Critical Review* 7, nos. 2–3 (Spring–Summer, 1993): 259–76.

——, *Time and Money: The Macroeconomics of Capital Structure* (London and New York: Routledge, 2001).

——, "Time and Money: The Universals of Macroeconomic Theorizing," *Journal of Macroeconomics* 6, no. 2 (Spring, 1984).

——, "What about Expectations?: A Challenge to the Austrian Theory," presented at the 2nd Austrian Scholars Conference, Auburn University, April 4–5, 1997.

Gellert, W., H. Kustner, M. Hellwich, and H. Kastner, eds., *The Concise Encyclopedia of Mathematics* (New York: Van Nostrand, 1975).

Geyer, P., *Theorie und Praxis des Zettelbankwesens nebst einer Charakteristik der Englischen, Französischen und Preussischen Bank* (Munich: Fleischmann's Buchhandlung, 1867).

——, *Banken und Krisen* (Leipzig: T.O. Weigel, 1865).

Gherity, J.A., "The Evolution of Adam Smith's Theory of Banking," *History of Political Economy* 26, no. 3 (Fall, 1994): 423–41.

Gil Peláez, L., *Tablas financieras, estadísticas y actuariales,* 6th revised, enlarged edition (Madrid: Editorial Dossat, 1977).

Gimeno Ullastres, Juan A., "Un impuesto llamado inflación," *Homenaje a Lucas Beltrán* (Madrid: Editorial Moneda y Crédito, 1982), pp. 803–23.

Glasner, D., *Free Banking and Monetary Reform* (Cambridge: Cambridge University Press, 1989).

——, "The Real-Bills Doctrine in the Light of the Law of Reflux," *History of Political Economy* 24, no. 4 (Winter, 1992): 867–94.

Gómez Camacho, F., Introduction to *La teoría del justo precio*, by Luis de Molina (Madrid: Editora Nacional, 1981).

Goldstein, I., and A. Pauzner, "Demand-Deposit Contracts and the Probability of Bank Runs," *Journal of Finance* 60, no. 3 (June 2005): 1293–1327.

Goodhart, C.A.E., *The Business of Banking, 1891–1914* (London: Weidenfeld and Nicholson, 1972).

——, *The Central Bank and the Financial System* (Cambridge, Mass.: The MIT Press, 1995).

——, *The Evolution of Central Banks*, 2nd ed. (Cambridge, Mass.: The MIT Press, 1990).

——, "The Free Banking Challenge to Central Banks," *Critical Review* 8, no. 3 (Summer, 1994): 411–25.

——, "What Should Central Banks Do? What Should be their Macroeconomic Objectives and Operations?" *Economic Journal* 104 (November 1994): 1424–36.

Gordon, R.J., ed., *Milton Friedman's Monetary Framework* (Chicago: Chicago University Press, 1974).

——, "What is New-Keynesian Economics?" *Journal of Economic Literature* 28 (September 1990).

Gottfried, D., ed., *Corpus iuris civilis* (Geneva, 1583).

Graham, F.D., "Partial Reserve Money and the 100 Percent Proposal," *American Economic Review* 26 (1936): 428–40.

Granger, C.W.J., "Investigating Causal Relations by Econometric Models and Cross-Spectral Methods," *Econometrica* 37, no. 3 (1969): 428.

——, "Testing for Causality: A Personal Viewpoint," *Journal of Economic Dynamics and Control* 2, no. 4 (November 1980): 330.

Grassl, W., and B. Smith, *Austrian Economics: History and Philosophical Background* (London and Sydney: Croom Helm, 1986).

Graziani, A., "Book Review of Stephen Kresge and Leif Wenar, eds., *"Hayek on Hayek: An Autobiographical Dialogue,"* European Journal of the History of Economic Thought* 2, no. 1 (Spring, 1995): 230–32.

Graziani, A., "Sofismi sul risparmio," *Rivista Bancaria* (December 1932); reprinted in Graziani, A., *Studi di Critica Economica* (Milan: Società Anonima Editrice Dante Alighieri, 1935), pp. 253–63.

Greaves, B.B., "How to Return to the Gold Standard," *The Freeman: Ideas on Liberty* (November 1995): 703–07.

Gregory, T.E., *Gold, Unemployment and Capitalism* (London: P.S. King and Shaw, 1933).

Grice-Hutchinson, M., *Early Economic Thought in Spain, 1177–1740* (London: George Allen and Unwin, 1978).

——, *Economic Thought in Spain: Selected Essays of Marjorie Grice-Hutchinson*, L.S. Moss and C.K. Ryan, eds. (Aldershot, England: Edward Elgar, 1993).

——, "The Concept of the School of Salamanca: Its Origins and Development," Chapter 2 in *Economic Thought in Spain: Selected Essays of Marjorie Grice-Hutchinson*, p. 25.

——, *The School of Salamanca: Readings in Spanish Monetary Theory, 1544–1605* (Oxford: Clarendon Press, 1952).

Groenveld, K., J.A.M. Maks, and J. Muysken, eds., *Economic Policy and the Market Process: Austrian and Mainstream Economics* (Amsterdam: North-Holland, 1990).

Gullón, A., and L. Díez-Picazo, *Sistema de derecho civil*, 6th ed. (Madrid: Editorial Tecnos, 1989).

Guzmán Hermida, J.M., "Introducción General" to *Discursos de Isocrates* (Madrid: Biblioteca Clásica Gredos, 1979), vol. 1.

Haberler, G., *Der Sinn der Indexzahlen: Eine Untersuchung über den Begriff des Preisniveaus und die Methoden seiner Messung* (Tübingen: Verlag von J.C.B. Mohr [Paul Siebeck], 1927).

——, *The Liberal Economic Order*, vol. 2, *Money and Cycles and Related Things*, A.Y.C. Koo, ed. (Aldershot, England: Edward Elgar, 1993).

——, "Mr. Keynes' Theory of the 'Multiplier': A Methodological Criticism," *Zeitschrift für Nationalökonomie* 7 (1936): 299–305; reprinted as Chapter 23 of *Selected Essays of Gottfried Haberler*, Anthony Y. Koo, ed. (Cambridge, Mass.: The MIT Press, 1985).

——, "Monetary Equilibrium and the Price Level in a Progressive Economy," *Economica* (February 1935): 75–81; reprinted in Gottfried Haberler, *The Liberal Economic Order*, vol. 2, *Money and Cycles and Related Things*, A.Y.C. Koo, ed. (Aldershot, England: Edward Elgar, 1993), pp. 118–25.

——, "Money and the Business Cycle," 1932; reprinted in *The Austrian Theory of the Trade Cycle and Other Essays* (Washington, D.C.: Ludwig von Mises Institute, 1978), pp. 7–20.

——, *Prosperity and Depression* (Geneva: League of Nations, 1937); Spanish translation by G. Franco and J. Márquez (Mexico: FCE, 1942).

——, "Reviewing A Book Without Reading It," *Austrian Economics Newsletter* 8 (Winter, 1995); reference in *Journal of Economic Perspectives* 10, no. 3 (Summer, 1996): 188.

Hagemann, H., and M. Colonna, eds., *Money and Business Cycles: The Economics of F.A. Hayek* (Aldershot, England: Edward Elgar, 1994).

Hahn, L.A., *Common Sense Economics* (New York: Abelard-Schumann, 1956).

Hall, R.E. "Macrotheory and the Recession of 1990–1991," *American Economic Review* (May 1993): 275–79.

Hanke, S.H., L. Jonung, and K. Schuler, *Russian Currency and Finance* (London: Routledge, 1993).

Harcourt, G.C., *Some Cambridge Controversies in the Theory of Capital* (Cambridge: Cambridge University Press, 1972).

Hardin, G., and J. Baden, eds., *Managing the Commons* (San Francisco, Calif.: Freeman, 1970).

Hart, A.G., "The 'Chicago Plan' of Banking Reform," *Review of Economic Studies* 2 (1935): 104–16.

Hawtrey, R.G., *Capital and Employment* (London: Longmans Green, 1937).

——, "Review of Hayek's *Prices and Production*," *Economica* 12 (1932): 119–25.

——, *The Art of Central Banking* (London: Longman, 1932).

Hayek, F.A., *The Counter-Revolution of Science* (Glencoe, Ill.: Free Press, 1952; Indianapolis, Ind.: Liberty Press, 1979).

——, *Contra Keynes and Cambridge: Essays, Correspondence, The Collected Works of F.A. Hayek*, vol. 9, B.J. Caldwell, ed. (London: Routledge,

1995); Spanish edition, J. Huerta de Soto, ed., F. Basáñez, and J.A. de Aguirre, trans., *Contra Keynes y Cambridge: ensayos, correspondencia* (Madrid: Unión Editorial, 1996).

——, *Prices and Production,* with a foreword by Lionel Robbins (London: Routledge, 1931; 2nd revised, enlarged edition, London: Routledge, 1935); later reprinted over ten times in England and the United States (Clifton, N.J.: Augustus M. Kelley); Spanish translation by C.R. Braun, *Precios y produccion* (Madrid: Unión Editorial, 1996).

——, "Price Expectations, Monetary Disturbances and Malinvestment," 1933; reprinted in *Profits, Interest and Investment* (London: Routledge, 1939; Clifton, N.J.: Augustus M. Kelley, 1975), pp. 135–56.

——, "Reflections on The Pure Theory of Money of Mr. J.M. Keynes (1)," *Economica* 11, no. 33 (August 1931): 270–95; reprinted in *Friedrich A. Hayek: Critical Assessments,* J.C. Wood and R.N. Woods, eds. (London: Routledge, 1991); also in *Contra Keynes and Cambridge: Essays, Correspondence, The Collected Works of F.A. Hayek,* B. Caldwell, ed. (London: Routledge, 1995), vol. 9.

——, "Reflections on The Pure Theory of Money of Mr. J.M. Keynes (continued)(2)," *Economica* 12, no. 35 (February 1932): 22–44; reprinted in *Friedrich A. Hayek: Critical Assessments,* J.C. Wood and R.N. Woods, eds. (London: Routledge, 1991); also in *Contra Keynes and Cambridge: Essays, Correspondence.*

——, "Das intertemporale Gleichgewichtssystem der Preise und die Bewegungen des 'Geldwertes,'" *Weltwirtschaftliches Archiv* 2 (1928): 36–76; English translation, "Intertemporal Price Equilibrium and Movements in the Value of Money," in *Money, Capital and Fluctuations: Early Essays,* R. McCloughry, ed. (Chicago: University of Chicago Press, 1984), pp. 71–118; English translation, "The System of Intertemporal Price Equilibrium and Movements in the 'Value of Money,'" in *Classics in Austrian Economics: A Sampling in the History of a Tradition,* vol. 3, *The Age of Mises and Hayek,* Israel M. Kirzner, ed. (London: William Pickering, 1994), pp. 161–98.

——, *Hayek on Hayek: An Autobiographical Dialogue,* S. Kresge and L. Wenar, eds. (London: Routledge, 1994).

——, *The Collected Works of F.A. Hayek,* vol. 3, *The Trend of Economic Thinking: Essays on Political Economists and Economic History,* W. W. Bartley III and S. Kresge, eds. (London and New York: Routledge, 1991).

——, "A Rejoinder to Mr. Keynes," *Economica* 11, no. 34 (November 1931): 398–404; reprint, Chapter 5 in *Friedrich A. Hayek: Critical Assessments,* J.C. Wood and R.N. Woods, eds., vol. 1 (London and

New York: Routledge, 1991), pp. 82–83; also in *Contra Keynes and Cambridge*.

——, *Monetary Theory and the Trade Cycle* (Clifton, N.J.: Augustus M. Kelley, [1933] 1975).

——, *The Constitution of Liberty* (London: Routledge, [1960] 1990).

——, *The Fatal Conceit: The Errors of Socialism* (Chicago: University of Chicago Press, 1989).

——, "The Pretence of Knowledge," Nobel Memorial Lecture, delivered December 11, 1974; reprinted in *American Economic Review* (December 1989): 3–7.

——, "Die Währungspolitik der Vereinigten Staaten seit der Überwindung der Krise von 1920," *Zeitschrift für Volkswirtschaft und Socialpolitik,* n.s. 5 (1925), vols. 1–3, pp. 25–63; vols. 4–6, pp. 254–317; English translation, "The Monetary Policy of the United States after the Recovery from the 1920 Crisis," Chapter 1 in *Money, Capital and Fluctuations: Early Essays,* R. McCloughry, ed. (Chicago: University of Chicago Press, 1984).

——, "Kapitalaufzehrung," *Weltwirtschaftliches Archiv* 2, no. 36 (1932): 86–108; English translation, "Capital Consumption," Chapter 6 in *Money, Capital and Fluctuations: Early Essays,* R. McCloughry, ed. (Chicago: University of Chicago Press, 1984).

——, *1980s Unemployment and the Unions: The Distortion of Relative Prices by Monopoly in the Labour Markets,* 2nd ed. (London: Institute of Economic Affairs, 1984).

——, *Money, Capital, and Fluctuations: Early Essays,* R. McCloughry, ed. (Chicago: University of Chicago Press, 1984).

——, "The Keynes Centenary: The Austrian Critic," *Economist* 7293 (June 11, 1983).

——, "Three Elucidations of the Ricardo Effect," *Journal of Political Economy* 77, no. 2 (1979); reprinted as Chapter 11 in *New Studies in Philosophy, Politics, Economics and the History of Ideas* (London: Routledge and Kegan Paul, 1978), pp. 165–78.

——, *Law, Legislation and Liberty* (Chicago: University of Chicago Press, 1978).

——, ed. *An Inquiry into the Nature and Effects of the Paper Credit of Great Britain,* by H. Thornton (Fairfield, N.J.: Augustus M. Kelley, 1978).

——, *Denationalisation of Money—The Argument Refined,* 2nd extended ed. (London: Institute of Economic Affairs, 1978).

——, *New Studies in Philosophy, Politics, Economics and the History of Ideas* (London: Routledge and Kegan Paul, 1978).

——, *¿Inflación o Pleno Empleo?* (Madrid: Unión Editorial, 1976).

——, *"Profits, Interest and Investment" and Other Essays on the Theory of Industrial Fluctuations* (London: Routledge, 1939; Clifton, N.J.: Augustus M. Kelley, 1969 and 1975).

——, *Geldtheorie und Konjunkturtheorie*. Beitrage zur Konjunktur-forschung, herausgegeben vom Österreischischen Institut für Konjunkturforschung (Vienna and Leipzig: Hölder-Pichler-Tempski, A.G., 1929), no. 1; English translation by N. Kaldor, *Monetary Theory and the Trade Cycle* (London: Routledge, 1933; Fairfield, N.J.: Augustus M. Kelley, 1975); Spanish translation by L. Olariaga, *La teoría monetaria y el ciclo económico* (Madrid: Espasa Calpe, 1936).

——, "The Maintenance of Capital," *Economica* 2 (August 1935); also Chapter 3 in *Profits, Interest and Investment* (London: Routledge, 1939; Clifton, N.J.: Augustus M. Kelley, 1975), pp. 83–134.

——, "Gibt es einen 'Widersinn des Sparens'?" *Zeitschrift für Nationalökonomie* 1, no. 3 (1929); English translation, "The 'Paradox' of Saving," *Economica* (May 1931); and appendix to *"Profits, Interest and Investment" and Other Essays on the Theory of Industrial Fluctuations* (London: George Routledge and Sons, 1939; Clifton, N.J.: Augustus M. Kelley, 1975), pp. 199–263.

——, *A Tiger by the Tail: 40-Years Running Commentary on Keynesianism by Hayek,* S.R. Shenoy, ed. (London: Institute of Economic Affairs, 1972).

——, *Monetary Nationalism and International Stability* (London: Longman, 1937; New York: Augustus M. Kelley, 1971).

——, "The Ricardo Effect," *Economica* 34, no. 9 (May 1942): 127–52; reprinted as Chapter 11 in *Individualism and Economic Order* (Chicago: University of Chicago Press, 1948), pp. 220–54.

——, *Individualism and Economic Order* (Chicago: University of Chicago Press, 1948).

——, *The Pure Theory of Capital* (1941; London: Routledge and Kegan Paul, 1976); Spanish translation, *La teoría pura del capital* (Madrid: Aguilar, 1946). New edition by Lawrence H. White, as vol. XII of *The Collected Works of F.A. Hayek* (Chicago: University of Chicago Press, 2007).

——, "A Commodity Reserve Currency," *Economic Journal* 53, no. 210 (June–September 1943): 176–84; also Chapter 10 in *Individualism and Economic Order*, pp. 209–19.

——, "Investment that Raises the Demand for Capital," *Review of Economics and Statistics* 19, no. 4 (November 1937); reprinted in *Profits, Interest and Investment*, pp. 73–82.

——, "The Mythology of Capital," *Quarterly Journal of Economics* (February 1936): 199–228.

——, "Saving," originally published in the *Encyclopedia of the Social Sciences*, 1933; reprinted as Chapter 5 in *Profits, Interest and Investment*.

——, "Über 'Neutrales Geld.'" *Zeitschrift für Nationalökonomie* 4 (1933): 659–61; subsequent English translation, "On Neutral Money," Chapter 7 in *Money, Capital and Fluctuations*, pp. 159–62.

——, "Das Schicksal der Goldwährung," *Deutsche Volkswirt* 20 (February 1932): 642–45 and no. 21, pp. 677–81; English translation, "The Fate of the Gold Standard," Chapter 5 in *Money, Capital and Fluctuations*, pp. 118–35.

Hazlitt, H., ed., *The Critics of Keynesian Economics* (New York: Arlington House, 1977).

Herbener, J.M., "The Myths of the Multiplier and the Accelerator," Chapter 4 in *Dissent on Keynes, A Critical Appraisal of Keynesian Economics*, M. Skousen, ed. (New York and London: Praeger, 1992).

——, *The Meaning of Ludwig von Mises* (Amsterdam: Kluwer Academic Publishers, 1993).

Hernández-Tejero Jorge, F., *Lecciones de derecho romano* (Madrid: Ediciones Darro, 1972).

Hey, J.D., "The Bayesian approach rules out the possibility of surprise," *Economics in Disequilibrium* (New York: New York University Press, 1981).

Hicks, J.R., "Is Interest the Price of a Factor of Production?" in *Time, Uncertainty, and Disequilibrium: Exploration of Austrian Themes*, M.J. Rizzo, ed. (Norwell, Mass.: Lexington Books, 1979).

——, *Capital and Time: A Neo-Austrian Theory* (Oxford: Clarendon Press, 1973).

——, *The Theory of Wages* (London: Macmillan, 1932).

Hicks, J.R., and A.G. Hart, *The Social Framework of the American Economy* (New York: Oxford University Press, 1945).

Higgs, H., ed., *Palgrave's Dictionary of Political Economy*, 3 vols. (London: Macmillan, 1926).

——, "Richard Cantillon," *Economic Journal* 1 (June 1891): 276–84.

Hippolytus, *Hippolytus Wercke*, vol. 2, *Refutatio Omnium Haeresium* (Leipzig: P. Wendland, 1916).

Hirschman, A.O., "Courcelle-Seneuil, Jean-Gustav," *The New Palgrave: A Dictionary of Economics*, vol. 1, pp. 706–07.

Holden, Milnes J., *The Law and Practice of Banking*, vol. 1, *Banker and Customer* (London: Pitman Publishing, 1970).

Homenaje a Lucas Beltrán (Madrid: Editorial Moneda y Crédito, 1982).

Hoppe, H.H., "How is Fiat Money Possible?—Or The Devolution of Money and Credit," *Review of Austrian Economics* 7, no. 2 (1994): 72–73.

——, *The Economics and Ethics of Private Property* (Dortrecht, Holland: Kluwer Academic Publishers, 1993).

Hoppe, H.H., J.G. Hülsmann, and W. Block, "Against Fiduciary Media," *Quarterly Journal of Austrian Economics* 1, no. 1 (1998): 19–50.

Horwitz, S., *Monetary Evolution, Free Banking, and Economic Order* (Oxford and San Francisco: Westview Press, 1992).

——, "Keynes' Special Theory," *Critical Review* 3, nos. 3 and 4 (Summer–Fall, 1989): 411–34.

——, *Microfoundations and Macroeconomics* (London: Routledge, 2000).

Hübner, O., *Die Banken* (Leipzig: Published by the author, 1853 and 1854).

Huerta Ballester, J., *A Brief Comparison Between the Ordinary Life Contracts of Ten Insurance Companies* (Madrid, 1954).

Huerta de Soto, J., "Conjectural History and Beyond," *Humane Studies Review* 6, no. 2 (Winter, 1988–1989): 10. Reprinted as chapter 3 in *The Theory of Dynamic Efficiency* (London and New York: Routledge, 2009).

——, "The Ongoing Methodenstreit of the Austrian School," *Journal des Économistes et des Études Humaines* 8, no. 1 (March 1998): 75–113. Reprinted as chapter 2 in *The Theory of Dynamic Efficiency* (London and New York: Routledge, 2009).

——, "Banque centrale ou banque libre: le débat théorique sur les réserves fractionnaires," *Journal des Économistes et des Études Humaines* 5, nos. 2 and 3 (June–September 1994): 379–91; Spanish version, "La teoría del banco central y de la banca libre" Chapter 11 in J. Huerta de Soto, *Estudios de economía política*, pp. 129–43; English translation, "A Critical Analysis of Central Banks and Fractional Reserve Free Banking from the Austrian School Perspective," *Review of Austrian Economics* 8, no. 2 (Summer, 1995): 117–29; Romanian translation by O. Vasilescu, "Banci centrale si sistemul de free-banking cu rezerve fractionare: O analizá criticá din perspectiva Scolii Austriece," *Polis: Revista de stiinte politice* (Bucharest) 4, no. 1 (1997): 145–57. Reprinted as chapter 10 in *The Theory of Dynamic Efficiency* (London and New York: Routledge, 2009).

——, "New Light on the Prehistory of the Theory of Banking and the School of Salamanca," *Review of Austrian Economics* 9, no. 2 (1996): 59–81. Reprinted as chapter 16 in *The Theory of Dynamic Efficiency* (London and New York: Routledge, 2009).

——, "A Theory of Liberal Nationalism," *Il Politico* IX, no. 4 (University of Pavia, Italy, 1995): 583–98. Reprinted as chapter 7 in *The Theory of Dynamic Efficiency* (London and New York: Routledge, 2009).

——, "The Economic Analysis of Socialism," Chapter 14 of *New Perspectives on Austrian Economics*, G. Meijer, ed. (London and New York: Routledge, 1995). Reprinted as chapter 4 in *The Theory of Dynamic Efficiency* (London and New York: Routledge, 2009).

——, "A Critical Note on Fractional-Reserve Free Banking," *Quarterly Journal of Austrian Economics* 1, no. 4 (Winter, 1998): 25–49. Reprinted as chapter 11 in *The Theory of Dynamic Efficiency* (London and New York: Routledge, 2009).

——, *Estudios de economía política* (Madrid: Unión Editorial, 1994).

——, *Nuevos estudios de economía política* (Madrid: Unión Editorial, 2002).

——, "La teoría austriaca del ciclo económico," *Moneda y Crédito* 152 (March 1980): 37–55; reprint, Chapter 13 in J. Huerta de Soto, *Estudios de economía política* (Madrid: Unión Editorial, 1994), pp. 160–76.

——, "Método y crisis en la ciencia económica," *Hacienda pública española* 74 (1982): 33–48; reprint, Chapter 3 in J. Huerta de Soto, *Estudios de economía política* (Madrid: Unión Editorial, 1994), pp. 59–82.

——, "Interés, ciclos económicos y planes de pensiones," Annals of the *Congreso Internacional de Fondos de Pensiones* (Madrid, April 1984), pp. 458–68; reprint, Chapter 23 in J. Huerta de Soto, *Estudios de economía política* (Madrid: Unión Editorial, 1994), pp. 285–94.

——, "Génesis, esencia y evolución de la Escuela Austriaca de Economía," Chapter 1 in J. Huerta de Soto, *Estudios de economía política* (Madrid: Unión Editorial, 1994), pp. 17–55.

——, "Historia, ciencia económica y ética social," Chapter 7 in Jesús Huerta de Soto, *Estudios de economía política* (Madrid: Unión Editorial, 1994), pp. 105–09; English version, "Conjectural History and Beyond," in "'The Fatal Conceit,' by F.A. Hayek, A Special Symposium,"*Humane Studies Review* 6, no. 2 (Winter, 1988–1999): 10. Reprinted as chapter 3 in *The Theory of Dynamic Efficiency* (London and New York: Routledge, 2009).

——, "The Crisis and Reform of Social Security: An Economic Analysis from the Austrian Perspective," *Journal des Économistes et des Études Humaines* 5, no. 1 (March 1994): 127–55. Reprinted as chapter 9 in *The Theory of Dynamic Efficiency* (London and New York: Routledge, 2009).

——, *Socialismo, cálculo económico y función empresarial* (Madrid: Unión Editorial, 1992 and 2001). Russian edition by Alexander Kouryaev, *Sotsialism, ekonomicheski raschet i predprenimatelskaya funktsiya* (Moscow: Irisen, 2008).

——, *Lecturas de economía política* (Madrid: Unión Editorial, 1986–1987), vols. 1–3.

——, *The Austrian School: Market Order and Entrepreneurial Creativity* (London and New York: Edward Elgar, 2008). Spanish edition *La Escuela Austriaca: Mercado y creatividad empresarial* (Madrid: Editorial Síntesis, 2000 and 2001); Italian translation by Paolo Zanotto, *La Scuola Austriaca: Mercato e creatività impreditoriale* (Soveria Mannelli, Catanzaro, Italy: Rubbetino, 2003). Portuguese translation by A. Azevedo Alves, *Escola Austríaca: Mercado e Criatividade Empresarial* (Lisbon: Espírito das Leis, 2005). German translation by Ingolf Günter Krumm, *Die Österreichische Schule der Nationalökomonie: Markt und Unternehmerische Kreativität* (Vienna: Hayek Institut, 2007). French translation by Rosine Létinier, *L'ecole autrichienne: marché et créativité entrepreneuriale* (Paris: Institut Charles Coquelin, 2008). Russian edition by Alexander Kouryaev, *Austriskaya ekonomicheskaya shkola: rynok i predprenimatelskoye tvorchestvo* (Moscow: Sotsium, 2007 and 2008).

——, "A Hayekian Strategy to Implement Free Market Reforms," in *Economic Analysis in an Orderly Framework: Liber Amicorum for Gerrit Meijer*, J. Backhaus, W. Heijmann, A. Nantjes, and J. van Ophem, eds. (Münster: LIT Verlag, 2003), pp. 231–54. Reprinted as chapter 13 in *The Theory of Dynamic Efficiency* (London and New York: Routledge, 2009).

——, "Hayek's Best Test of a Good Economist," *Procesos de Mercado* 1, no. 2 (Autumn, 2004): 121–24. Reprinted as chapter 19 in *The Theory of Dynamic Efficiency* (London and New York: Routledge, 2009).

——, "Ricardo Effect," *An Eponymous Dictionary of Economics: A Guide to Laws and Theorems Named after Economists*, J. Segura and C. Rodriques Braun, eds. (Cheltenham, U.K.: Edward Elgar, 2004). Reprinted as chapter 20 in *The Theory of Dynamic Efficiency* (London and New York: Routledge, 2009).

——, *The Theory of Dynamic Efficiency* (London and New York: Routledge, 2009).

Huerta Peña, J., *La estabilidad financiera de las empresas de seguros* (Madrid, 1954).

Hughes, A. Middleton, "The Recession of 1990: An Austrian Explanation," *Review of Austrian Economics* 10, no. 1 (1997): 107–23.

Hülsmann, J.G., "Review of *Dinero, Crédito Bancario y Ciclos Económicos*," *Review of Austrian Economics* 3, no. 2 (2000): 85–88.

——, "Free Banking and Free Bankers," *Review of Austrian Economics* 9, no. 1 (1996): 3–53.

——, "Has Fractional-Reserve Banking Really Passed the Market Test?," *Independent Review* vii, no. 3 (Winter, 2003): 399–422.

Hume, D., *Essays: Moral, Political and Literary*, E.F. Miller, ed. (Indianapolis, Ind.: Liberty Classics, 1985).

Hutt, W.H., *The Keynesian Episode: A Reassessment* (Indianapolis, Ind.: Liberty Press, 1979).

——, *Politically Impossible...?* (London: Institute of Economic Affairs, 1971).

Ibn Abí Zayd (Al-Qayrawâní), *Compendio de derecho islámico (Risála, Fí-l-Fiqh)*, J. Riosalido, ed. (Madrid: Editorial Trotta, 1993).

Ihering, R.v., *El espíritu del derecho romano*, F. Vela, ed. (Madrid: Marcial Pons, 1997). Original German edition, Geist des Römischen Rechts (Aalen, 1968).

Iglesias, J., *Derecho romano: instituciones de derecho privado*, 6th revised, enlarged ed. (Barcelona: Ediciones Ariel, 1972).

Imbert, J., *Historia económica (de los orígenes a 1789)*; Spanish translation by Armando Sáez (Barcelona: Editorial Vicens-Vives, 1971). Original French edition *Historie Economique (Des Origines a 1783)* (Paris: Presses Universitaires de France [P.U.F], 1965).

Ingram, J.K., "Banks, Early European," in *Palgrave's Dictionary of Political Economy*, H. Higgs, ed. (London: Macmillan, 1927), vol. 1, pp. 103–06.

Isocrates, *Discursos*, general introduction by J.M. Guzmán Hermida (Madrid: Biblioteca Clásica Gredos, 1979).

Issing, O., *Central Bank Independence and Monetary Stability* (London: Institute of Economic Affairs, 1993).

Jevons, W.S., *The Theory of Political Economy* (1871; reprint, 5th ed., New York: Kelley and Millman, 1957).

——, *Money and the Mechanism of Exchange* (New York: D. Appleton, 1875; London: Kegan Paul, 1905).

John Paul II, *Centesimus Annus: Encyclical Letter on the Hundredth Anniversary of Rerum Novarum*, 1991, no. 48 (London: Catholic Truth Society, 1991).

Jouvenel, B. de, "The European Intellectuals and Capitalism," in *Capitalism and the Historians*, F.A. Hayek, ed. (Chicago: University of Chicago Press, 1954).

Junankar, P.N., "Acceleration Principle," in *The New Palgrave: A Dictionary of Economics*, vol. 1, pp. 10–11.

Justinian, *Digest*, Spanish translation by Ildefonso L. García del Corral, *Cuerpo de derecho civil romano: a doble texto, traducido al castellano del latino*, reprint, 6 vols. (Valladolid: Editorial Lex Nova, 1988); alternate translation by A. D'Ors, F. Hernández-Tejero, B. Fuentes Aca, M. García-Garrido, and J. Murillo (Pamplona: Editorial Aranzadi, 1968).

Juurikkala, O., "The False Money Debate in the *Journal des Économistes*: Déjà Vu for Austrians?," *Quarterly Journal of Austrian Economics* 5, no. 4 (Winter, 2002): 43–55.

Kaldor, N., "Capital Intensity and the Trade Cycle," *Economica* (February 1939): 40–66.

——, "Professor Hayek and the Concertina Effect," *Economica* (November 1942): 359–82.

Katz, J.N., "An Austrian Perspective on the History and Future of Money and Banking," *Erasmus Programme in Law and Economics* (Summer, 1997).

Keynes, J.M., *The General Theory of Employment, Interest and Money* (London: Macmillan, 1936); German translation by F. Waeger, *Allgemeine Theorie der Beschäftigung, des Zinses und des Geldes*, with a special prologue written by Keynes on September 7, 1936 (Berlin: Duncker and Humblot, 1936 and 1994).

——, *The Collected Writings of John Maynard Keynes*, vol. 13, *The General Theory and After*, Part 1, *Preparation*, Donald Moggridge, ed. (London: Macmillan, 1973).

——, *The Collected Writings of John Maynard Keynes*, vol. 29, *The General Theory and After: A Supplement* (London: Macmillan, 1979).

——, *The Collected Writings of John Maynard Keynes*, Part 2, *The General Theory and After*, vol. 14, *Defence and Development* (London: Macmillan, 1973).

——, *The Collected Writings of John Maynard Keynes*, vol. 7, *The General Theory of Employment, Interest and Money* (London: Macmillan, 1973).

——, *The Collected Writings of John Maynard Keynes*, vol. 1, *A Treatise on Money* (London: Macmillan, 1971).

——, *The Collected Writings of John Maynard Keynes*, vol. 5, *The Pure Theory of Money* (London: Macmillan, 1971).

——, *The Collected Writings of John Maynard Keynes*, vol. 12, *Economic Articles and Correspondence: Investment and Editorial*, Donald Moggridge, ed. (Cambridge: Cambridge Univesity Press, 1983).

——, "The Pure Theory of Money: A Reply to Dr. Hayek," *Economica* 11, no. 34 (November 1931): 394.

——, "Review of Ludwig von Mises' *Theorie des Geldes und der Umlaufsmittel*," *Economic Journal* (September 1914); reprinted in *Collected Writings*, vol. 11, pp. 400–03.

Keynes, M., ed., *Essays on John Maynard Keynes* (Cambridge: Cambridge University Press, 1975).

Kindleberger, C.A., *A Financial History of Western Europe*, 2nd ed. (New York: Oxford University Press, 1993).

Kirzner, I.M., *Essays on Capital and Interest: An Austrian Perspective* (Cheltenham, England: Edward Elgar, 1996).

——, ed., *Classics in Austrian Economics: A Sampling in the History of a Tradition*, 3 vols. (London: William Pickering, 1994).

——, "The Pure Time-Preference Theory of Interest: An Attempt at Clarification," Chapter 4 in *The Meaning of Ludwig von Mises: Contributions in Economics, Sociology, Epistemology, and Political Philosophy*, J.M. Herbener, ed. (Dordrecht, Holland: Kluwer Academic Publishers, 1993), pp. 166–92.

——, *Discovery and the Capitalist Process* (Chicago and London: University of Chicago Press, 1985).

——, "Economics and Error," Chapter 8 in *Perception, Opportunity and Profit* (Chicago: University of Chicago Press, 1979), pp. 120–36.

——, *An Essay on Capital* (New York: Augustus M. Kelley, 1966).

Klein, B., "The Competitive Supply of Money," *Journal of Money, Credit and Banking* 6 (November 1974): 423–53.

Knight, F.H., "Capitalist Production, Time and the Rate of Return," in *Economic Essays in Honour of Gustav Cassel* (London: George Allen and Unwin, 1933).

——, "Review of Frederick Soddy's *Wealth, Virtual Wealth and Debt*," *Saturday Review of Literature* (April 16, 1927): 732.

Kornai, J., "The Hungarian Reform Process," *Journal of Economic Literature* 24, no. 4 (December 1986): 1726.

Kretzmer, P.E., "The Cross-Industry Effects of Unanticipated Money in an Equilibrium Business Cycle Model," *Journal of Monetary Economics* 2, no. 23 (March 1989): 275–96.

Kydland, F.E., and E.C. Prescott, "Business Cycles: Real Facts and a Monetary Myth," *Federal Reserve Bank of Minneapolis Quarterly Review* 14 (1990): 3–18.

——, and E.C. Prescott, "Time to Build and Aggregate Fluctuations," *Econometrica* 50 (November 1982): 1345–70.

Lachmann, L.M., "Austrian Economics under Fire: The Hayek-Sraffa Duel in Retrospect," in *Austrian Economics: History and Philosophical Background*, W. Grassl and B. Smith, eds. (London and Sydney: Croom Helm, 1986), pp. 225–42.

——, "John Maynard Keynes: A View from an Austrian Window," *South African Journal of Economics* 3, no. 51 (1983): 368–79.

——, *Capital and its Structure* (Kansas City, Mo.: Sheed Andrews and McMeel, 1978).

——, "A Reconsideration of the Austrian Theory of Industrial Fluctuations," *Economica* 7 (May 1940); reprinted in Ludwig M. Lachmann, *Capital, Expectations and the Market Process: Essays on the Theory of the Market Economy* (Kansas City, Mo.: Sheed Andrews and McMeel, 1977), pp. 267–84.

——, *Capital, Expectations and the Market Process: Essays on the Theory of the Market Economy* (Kansas City, Mo.: Sheed Andrews and McMeel, 1977).

——, "On Austrian Capital Theory," *The Foundations of Modern Austrian Economics,* Edwin E. Dolan, ed. (Kansas City, Mo.: Sheed and Ward, 1976).

——, "On Crisis and Adjustment," *Review of Economics and Statistics* (May 1939).

——, *Macroeconomic Thinking and the Market Economy* (London: Institute of Economic Affairs, 1973).

Lacruz Berdejo, J.L., *Elementos de derecho civil,* 3rd ed. (Barcelona: José María Bosch, 1995), vol. 2.

Laidler, D., "Free Banking Theory," *The New Palgrave: Dictionary of Money and Finance* (London and New York: Macmillan Press, 1992), vol. 2, pp. 196–97.

——, *The Golden Age of the Quantity Theory* (New York: Philip Allan, 1991).

——, "Hayek on Neutral Money and the Cycle," in *Money and Business Cycles: The Economics of F.A. Hayek,* M. Colonna and H. Hagemann, eds., vol. 1, pp. 3–26.

Lavoie, D.C., "Economic Calculation and Monetary Stability," *Cato Journal* 3, no. 1 (Spring, 1983): 163–70.

Law, J., *John Law's "Essay on a Land Bank,"* A.E. Murphy, ed. (Dublin: Aeon Publishing, 1994).

——, *Money and Trade Considered with a Proposal for Supplying the Nation with Money* (Edinburgh: A. Anderson, 1705; New York: Augustus M. Kelley, 1966).

Layard, R., and A. Richter, "Who Gains and Who Loses from Russian Credit Expansion?" *Communist Economies and Economic Transformation* 6, no. 4 (1994): 459–72.

Lee, G.A., "The Oldest European Account Book: A Florentine Bank Ledger of 1211," in *Accounting History: Some British Contributions,* R.H. Parker and B.S. Yamey, eds. (Oxford: Clarendon Press, 1994), pp. 160–96.

Lehmann, F., "100 Percent Money," *Social Research* 3, no. 1: 37–56.

Leijonhufvud, A., "What Would Keynes Have Thought of Rational Expectations?," *UCLA Department of Economics Discussion Paper* No. 299 (Los Angeles, Calif.: University of California, Los Angeles, 1983).

Leoni, B., *Freedom and the Law* (Princeton, N.J.: D. Van Nostrand, [1961] 1972; Indianapolis, Ind.: Liberty Fund, 1991).

——, *Scritti di Scienza Politica e Teoria del Diritto* (Milan: A. Giuffrè, 1980).

Lessines, A., *De usuris in communi et de usurarum contractibus* (1285).

Leube, K.R., ed., *The Essence of Friedman* (Palo Alto, Calif.: Hoover Institution Press, Stanford University, 1986).

——, ed., *Austrian Economics Today I*, The International Library of Austrian Economics (Frankfurt: FAZ Buch, 2003), vol. 7.

Lewin, P., "Capital in Disequilibrium: A Reexamination of the Capital Theory of Ludwig M. Lachmann," *History of Political Economy* 29, no. 3 (Fall, 1997): 523–48.

Lipsey, R.G., *An Introduction to Positive Economics*, 2nd ed. (London: Weidenfeld and Nicolson, 1966), pp. 682–83.

Lloyd, Jones S. (Lord Overstone), *Reflections Suggested by a Perusal of Mr. J. Horseley Palmer's Pamphlet on the Causes and Consequences of the Pressure on the Money Market* (London: P. Richardson, 1837); reprinted in *Tracts and Other Publications on Metallic and Paper Currency*, by the Rt. Hon. Lord Overstone, by J.R. McCulloch (London: Harrison and Sons, 1857).

Locke, J., *Some Considerations of the Consequences of the Lowering of Interest, and Raising the Value of Money (In a Letter to a Member of Parliament)* (London: Awnsham and John Churchill, Black-Swan in Pater-Noster-Row, 1692).

——, *Further Considerations Concerning Raising the Value of Money* (London: Awnsham and John Churchill, Black-Swan in Pater-Noster-Row, 1695).

——, *The Works of John Locke*, 12th ed. (London: C. and J. Rivington, 1824), vol. 4.

——, *Several Papers Relating to Money, Interest, and Trade, etc.* (New York: Augustus M. Kelley, 1968).

Longfield, S.M., "Banking and Currency," 4 articles, *Dublin University Magazine* 15: 3–15, 218–33; 16: 371–89, 611–20, 1840.

López, G., *Las siete Partidas de Alfonso X "El Sabio,"* annotated by G. López, facsimile ed. (Madrid: Boletín Oficial del Estado, 1985).

López-Amor y García, M., "Observaciones sobre el depósito irregular romano," *Revista de la Facultad de Derecho de la Universidad Complutense* 74 (1988–1989): 341–59.

Lucas, R.E., "Nobel Lecture: Monetary Neutrality," *Journal of Political Economy* 104, no. 4 (August 1996): 661–82.

Lugo Hispalensis, J. de, *Disputationum de iustitia et iure, Tomus Secundus* (Lyon: Sumptibus Petri Prost, 1642).

Machlup, F., *Economic Semantics* (London: Transaction Publishers, 1991).

——, "Forced or Induced Saving: An Exploration into its Synonyms and Homonyms," *Review of Economics and Statistics* 25, no. 1 (February 1943); reprinted in *Economic Semantics,* by Fritz Machlup (London: Transaction Publishers, 1991), pp. 213–40.

——, "Professor Knight and the 'Period of Production,'" *Journal of Political Economy* 43, no. 5 (October 1935); reprinted in *Classics in Austrian Economics,* I.M. Kirzner, ed., vol. 2, pp. 275–15.

——, "The Consumption of Capital in Austria," *Review of Economics and Statistics* 17, no. 1 (1935): 13–19.

——, *The Stock Market, Credit and Capital Formation* (London: William Hodge, 1940); original German edition, *Börsenkredit, Industriekredit und Kapital-Bildund.* Beiträge zur Konjunkturforschung 2 (Vienna: Verlag von Julius Springer, 1931).

Macrae, Duncan C., "A Political Model of the Business Cycle," *Journal of Political Economy* 85 (1977): 239–63.

Maling, C., "The Austrian Business Cycle Theory and its Implications for Economic Stability under Laissez-Faire," vol. 2, *Friedrich A. Hayek: Critical Assessments,* J.C. Wood and R.N. Woods, eds. (London: Routledge, 1991), chap. 48.

Mant, L., "Origen y desenvolvimiento histórico de los bancos," *Enciclopedia Universal Ilustrada Europeo-Americana* (Madrid: Editorial Espasa Calpe, 1979), vol. 7, p. 477.

Mariana, J. de, *Tratado y discurso sobre la moneda de vellón que al presente se labra en Castilla y de algunos desórdenes y abusos;* original ed., *De monetae mutatione,* 1609; reprint with a preliminary study by Lucas Beltrán (Madrid: Instituto de Estudios Fiscales, Ministerio de Economía y Hacienda, 1987); English translation by P.T. Brannan, S.J., Introduction by A. Chafuen, "A Treatise on the Alteration of Money," *Journal of Markets and Morality* 5, no. 2 (Fall, 2002): 523–93.

Marshall, A., *Official Papers by Alfred Marshall* (London: Royal Economic Society and Macmillan, 1926).

——, *Money Credit and Commerce* (London: Macmillan, 1924).

——, *Principles of Economics*, 8th ed. (London: Macmillan, 1920).

Martínez, J.H., "El Sistema monetario y bancario argentino," *Homenaje a Lucas Beltrán* (Madrid: Editorial Moneda y Crédito, 1982), pp. 435–60.

Marx, K., *Capital: A Critique of Political Economy*, F. Engels, ed., E. Untermann, trans., vol. 3, *The Process of Capitalist Production as a Whole* (Chicago: Charles H. Kerr and Company, 1909; England: Penguin Books, 1981); German edition, *Das Kapital: Kritik der politischen Ökonomie* (Berlin: Dietz Verlag, 1964).

Mata Barranco, N.J. de La, *Tutela penal de la propiedad y delitos de apropiación: el dinero como objeto material de los delitos de hurto y apropiación indebida* (Barcelona: Promociones y Publicaciones Universitarias [PPU, S. A.], 1994).

Mayer, H., "Der Erkenntniswert der funktionellen Preistheorien," *Die Wirtschaftheorie der Gegenwart* (Vienna: Verlag von Julius Springer, 1932), vol. 2, pp. 147–239b; English translation, "The Cognitive Value of Functional Theories of Price: Critical and Positive Investigations Concerning the Price Problem," Chapter 16 in *Classics in Austrian Economics: A Sampling in the History of a Tradition*, vol. 2, *The Interwar Period*, I.M. Kirzner, ed. (London: William Pickering, 1994), pp. 55–168; revised, enlarged Italian ed., "Il concetto de equilibrio nella teoria economica," in *Economia Pura*, G. del Vecchio, ed., Nuova Collana di Economisti Stranieri e Italiani (Turin: Unione Tipografico-Editrice Torinese, 1937), pp. 645–799.

Mayer, T., *Monetarism and Macroeconomic Policy* (Aldershot, England: Edward Elgar, 1990).

McCulloch, J.R., *Historical Sketch of the Bank of England with an Examination of the Question as to the Prolongation of the Exclusive Privileges of that Establishment* (London: Longman, Rees, Orme, Brown and Green, 1831).

——, *A Treatise on Metallic and Paper Money and Banks* (Edinburgh: A. and C. Black, 1858).

Meltzer, A., "Comments on Centi and O'Driscoll," presented at the general meeting of the Mont Pèlerin Society, Cannes, France, September 25–30, 1994.

Menger, C., *Grundsätze der Volkswirthschaftslehre* (Vienna: Wilhelm Braumüller, 1871). English edition, *Principles of Economics,* trans. by J. Dingwall and B. Hoselitz, (Glencoe, Ill.: Free Press, 1950; New York: New York University Press, 1981).

——, "On the Origin of Money," *Economic Journal* (June 1892): 239–55; reprinted in *Classics in Austrian Economics: A Sampling in the History of a Tradition,* I.M. Kirzner, ed., vol. 1, pp. 91–106.

——, *Untersuchungen über die Methode der Socialwissenschaften und der Politischen Ökonomie insbesondere* (Leipzig: Duncker and Humblot, 1883). English edition, *Investigations into the Method of the Social Sciences with Special Reference to Economics* (New York: New York University Press, 1985).

Mercado, T. de, *Suma de tratos y contratos,* Nicolás Sánchez Albornoz, ed. (Madrid: Instituto de Estudios Fiscales, 1977); original edition (Seville: Hernando Díaz, 1571; Restituto Sierra Bravo, ed. Madrid: Editora Nacional, 1975).

Michaelis, O., *Volkswirthschaftliche Schriften* (Berlin: Herbig, 1873), vols. 1 and 2.

Mill, J.S., *Principles of Political Economy* (1848; reprint, Fairfield, N.J.: Augustus M. Kelley, 1976).

Mill, M.A., and A.B. Laffer, *International Economics in an Integrated World* (Oakland, N.J.: Scott Foresman, 1982).

Miller, H.E., *Banking Theory in the United States Before 1860* (1927; reprint, New York: Augustus M. Kelley, 1972).

Mills, F.C., *Prices in Recession and Recovery* (New York: National Bureau of Economic Research, 1936).

Mints, L.W., *Monetary Policy for a Competitive Society* (New York, 1950).

Mises, Ludwig von, *Human Action: A Treatise on Economics,* 3rd ed. (Chicago: Henry Regnery, 1966); 4th ed. by B.B. Greaves (New York: Foundation for Economic Education, 1996); Scholar's Edition (Auburn, Ala.: Ludwig von Mises Institute, 1998); Spanish translation from the English by J. Reig Albiol, *La acción humana: tratado de economía;* 7th ed., with a preliminary study by J. Huerta de Soto (Madrid: Unión Editorial, 2004).

——, "The Position of Money Among Economic Goods," originally published in *Die Wirtschaftstheorie der Gegenwart,* H. Mayer, ed. (Vienna: Julius Springer, 1932), vol. 2; English translation by A.H. Zlabinger, in *Money, Method and the Market Process: Essays by Ludwig von Mises,*

R.M. Ebeling, ed. (Dordrecht, Holland: Kluwer Academic Publishers, 1990), p. 55.

——, *Money, Method and the Market Process: Essays by Ludwig von Mises*, R.M. Ebeling, ed. (Dordrecht, Holland: Kluwer Academic Publishers, 1990).

——, *Nation, State and Economy: Contributions to the Politics and History of Our Time*, translated from the original German by L.B. Yeager (New York and London: New York University Press, 1983); original German ed., *Nation, Staat und Wirtschaft* (Vienna and Leipzig: Manzsche Verlags Buchhandlung, 1919).

——, *Nationalökonomie: Theorie des Handelns und Wirtschaftens* (Geneva: Editions Union, 1940; Munich: Philosophia Verlag, 1980).

——, *Theorie des Geldes und der Umlaufsmittel* (Munich and Leipzig: Duncker and Humblot, 1912), 2nd ed., 1924; English translation by H.E. Batson, *The Theory of Money and Credit* (Indianapolis, Ind.: Liberty Classics, 1980); Spanish translation by J. Marcos de la Fuente (Madrid: Unión Editorial, 1997).

——, *On the Manipulation of Money and Credit*, trans. from the German by B.B. Greaves (Dobbs Ferry, N.Y.: Freemarket Books, 1978), German ed., *Geldwertstabilisierung und Konjunkturpolitik* (Jena: Gustav Fischer, 1928).

——, "Die Stellung und der nächste Zukunft der Konjunkturforschung," in *Festschrift in honor of Arthur Spiethoff* (Munich: Duncker and Humblot, 1933), pp. 175–80; English translation, "The Current Status of Business Cycle Research and its Prospects for the Immediate Future," in *On the Manipulation of Money and Credit* (New York: Freemarket Books, 1978), pp. 207–13.

——, *Die Verstaatlichung des Kredits: Mutalisierung des Kredits* (Bern, Munich and Leipzig: Travers-Borgstroem Foundation, 1929); English translation, "The Nationalization of Credit?" in *A Critique of Interventionism: Inquiries into the Economic Policy and the Economic Ideology of the Present* (New York: Arlington House, 1977), pp. 153–64.

——, "Pensions, the Purchasing Power of the Dollar and the New Economics," in *Planning for Freedom and Twelve Other Addresses* (South Holland, Ill.: Libertarian Press, 1974), pp. 86–93.

——, *Omnipotent Government: The Rise of the Total State and Total War* (New York: Arlington House, 1969).

——, "Elastic Expectations in the Austrian Theory of the Trade Cycle," *Economica* (August 1943): 251–52.

——, "La causa de las crisis económicas," *Revista de Occidente* (February 1932).

——, *Theory and History* (New Haven, Conn.: Yale University Press, 1957).

Modeste, V., "Le billet des banques d'émisión et la fausse monnaie," *Le Journal des Économistes*, n.s., 3 (August 15, 1866).

Moggridge, D.E., *Maynard Keynes: An Economist's Biography* (London: Routledge, 1992).

Molina, L. de, *Tratado sobre los cambios* (Cuenca, 1597); Francisco Gómez Camacho, ed. (Madrid: Instituto de Estudios Fiscales, 1991).

——, *Tratado sobre los préstamos y la usura* (Cuenca, 1597); Francisco Gómez Camacho, ed. (Madrid: Instituto de Estudios Fiscales, 1989).

——, *La teoría del justo precio* with an introduction by F. Gómez Camacho (Madrid: Editora Nacional, 1981).

Montanari, G., *La zecca in consulta di stato.*, reprinted as *La moneta*, in *Scrittori classici italiani di economía Política* (Milan: G. Destefanis, 1804), vol. 3.

Moss, L.S., and K.I. Vaughn, "Hayek's Ricardo Effect: A Second Look," *History of Political Economy* 18, no. 4 (Winter, 1986): 545–65.

Mueller, R.C., "The Role of Bank Money in Venice, 1300–1500" in *Studi Veneziani*, n.s. 3 (Pisa: Giardini Editori, 1979), pp. 47–96.

——, *The Venetian Money Market: Banks Panics, and the Public Debt, 1200–1500* (Baltimore, Maryland: Johns Hopkins University Press, 1997).

Murphy, A.E., *Richard Cantillon: Entrepreneur and Economist* (Oxford: Clarendon Press, 1986).

——, *John Law: Economic Theorist and Policy Maker* (Oxford: Clarendon Press, 1997).

Neira, Alonzo, M.A., "Hayek's Triangle," *An Eponymous Dictionary of Economics: A Guide to Laws and Theorems Named after Economists* (Cheltenham, U.K.: Edward Elgar, 2004).

Newman, P., M. Milgate, and J. Eatwell, *The New Palgrave Dictionary of Money and Finance*, 3 vols. (London: Macmillan, 1992).

Nichols, D.M., *Modern Money Mechanics: A Workbook on Deposits, Currency and Bank Reserves* (Chicago: Federal Reserve Bank of Chicago, 1970).

Niveau, M., *Historia de los hechos económicos contemporáneos,* Spanish translation by A. Bosch Doménech (Barcelona: Editorial Ariel, 1971). Original French edition, *Historie des Faits Economiques Contemporains* (Paris: Presses Universitaires de France [P.U.F.], 1966).

Nordhaus, W.E., "The Political Business Cycle," *Review of Economic Studies* 42, no. 130 (April 1975): 169–90.

Norman, Warde G., *Remarks upon some Prevalent Errors with respect to Currency and Banking, and Suggestions to the Legislature and the Public as to the Improvement in the Monetary System* (London: P. Richardson, 1838).

Nove, A., "Tugan-Baranovsky, M.," in *The New Palgrave: A Dictionary of Economics,* J. Eatwell, M. Milgate, and P. Newman, eds., vol. 4, pp. 705–06.

O'Brien, D.P., *The Classical Economists* (Oxford: Oxford University Press, 1975).

O'Driscoll, G.P., "Rational Expectations, Politics and Stagflation," Chapter 7 in *Time, Uncertainty and Disequilibrium: Exploration of Austrian Themes,* M.J. Rizzo, ed. (Mass.: Lexington Books, 1979).

——, "The Specialization Gap and the Ricardo Effect: Comment on Ferguson," *History of Political Economy* 7 (Summer, 1975): 261–69.

——, "Money: Menger's Evolutionary Theory," *History of Political Economy* 4, no. 18 (1986): 601–16.

——, "An Evolutionary Approach to Banking and Money," Chapter 6 of *Hayek, Co-ordination and Evolution: His Legacy in Philosophy, Politics, Economics and the History of Ideas,* J. Birner and R. van Zijp, eds. (London: Routledge, 1994).

O'Driscoll, G.P., and M.J. Rizzo, *The Economics of Time and Ignorance* (Oxford: Basil Blackwell, 1985; London: Routledge, 1996).

Oscáriz Marco, F., *El contrato de depósito: estudio de la obligación de guarda* (Barcelona: J.M. Bosch Editor, 1997).

Parnell, H., *Observations on Paper Money, Banking and Other Trading, including those parts of the evidence taken before the Committee of the House of Commons which explained the Scotch system of banking* (London: James Ridgway, 1827).

Parker, R.H., and B.S. Yamey, *Accounting History: Some British Contributions* (Oxford: Clarendon Press, 1994).

Pastor, L.M., *Libertad de Bancos y Colas del de España* (Madrid: B. Carranza, 1865).

Patinkin, D., "Real Balances," in *The New Palgrave: A Dictionary of Economics,* vol. 4, pp. 98–101.

Pauly, M.V., "The Economics of Moral Hazard," *American Economic Review* 58 (1968): 531–37.

Pedraja García, P., *Contabilidad y análisis de balances de la banca,* vol. 1, *Principios generales y contabilización de operaciones* (Madrid: Centro de Formación del Banco de España, 1992).

Pemberton, R.L., *The Future of Monetary Arrangements in Europe* (London: Institute of Economic Affairs, 1989).

Pennington, J., "On the Private Banking Establishments of the Metropolis," February 13, 1826; published as an appendix to the works of Thomas Tooke, *A letter to Lord Grenville; On the Effects Ascribed to the Resumption of Cash Payments on the Value of the Currency* (London: John Murray, 1826) and *A History of Prices and of the State of Circulation from 1793–1837* (London: Longman, 1838), vol. 2, p. 369.

Petty, W., *The Economic Writings of Sir William Petty* (New York: Augustus M. Kelley, 1964), vol. 1.

Philbin, J.P., "An Austrian Perspective on Some Leading Jacksonian Monetary Theorists," *Journal of Libertarian Studies: An Interdisciplinary Review* 10, no. 1 (Fall, 1991): 83–95.

Phillips, C.A., *Bank Credit: A Study of the Principles and Factors Underlying Advances Made by Banks to Borrowers* (New York: Macmillan, [1920] 1931).

Phillips, C.A., T.F. McManus, and R.W. Nelson, *Banking and the Business Cycle* (New York: Arno Press, 1937).

Phillips, R.J., *The Chicago Plan and New Deal Banking Reform* (Armonk, N.Y.: M.E. Sharpe, 1995).

Piquet, J., *Des banquiers au Moyen Age: les Templiers, étude de leurs opérations financières* (Paris, 1939).

Pirenne, H., *Economic and Social History of Medieval Europe* (London: Kegan Paul, Trench, Trubner and Co., 1947).

——, *Histoire Économique et Sociale du Moyen Age* (Paris: Presses Universitaires de France, 1969).

Pollock, A.H., "Collateralized Money: An Idea Whose Time Has Come Again?" *Durrell Journal of Money and Banking* 5, no. 1 (March 1993): 34–38.

Powell, E.T., *Evolution of Money Markets* (London: Cass, 1966).

Principe, A., *La responsabilità della banca nei contratti di custodia* (Milan: Editorial Giuffrè, 1983).

Raguet, C., "Report on Bank Charters," *Journal of the Senate, 1820–1921* (Pennsylvania Legislature), pp. 252–68.

Ramey, V.A., "Inventories as Factors of Production and Economic Fluctuations," *American Economic Review* (June 1989): 338–54.

Rappaport, A., "Prisoners' Dilemma," *The New Palgrave: A Dictionary of Economics*, J. Eatwell, M. Milgate, and P. Newman, eds. (London: Macmillan, 1987), vol. 3, pp. 973–76.

Real Cédula de S.M. y, *Señores del Consejo, por la qual se crea, erige y autoriza un Banco nacional y general para facilitar las operaciones del comercio y el beneficio público de estos Reynos y los de Indias, con la denominación de Banco de San Carlos baxo las reglas que se expresan* (Madrid: Imprenta de D. Pedro Marín, 1782).

Reisman, George, "The Value of Final Products Counts Only Itself," *American Journal of Economics and Sociology* 63, no. 3 (July 2004): 609–25.

——, *Capitalism* (Ottawa, Ill.: Jameson Books, 1996).

Ricardo, D., *The Works and Correspondence of David Ricardo*, vol. 1, *On the Principles of Political Economy and Taxation*, 1817, P. Sraffa and M.H. Dobb, eds. (Cambridge: Cambridge University Press, 1982).

——, *The Works and Correspondence of David Ricardo*, vol. 4, *Absolute Value and Exchange Value*, P. Sraffa and M.H Dobb, eds. (Cambridge: Cambridge University Press, 1951).

——, *The Works and Correspondence of David Ricardo*, Piero Sraffa, ed. (Cambridge: Cambridge University Press, 1951–1973).

——, *Minor Papers on the Currency Question, 1805–1823*, J. Hollander, ed. (Baltimore, Maryland: Johns Hopkins University Press, 1932), pp. 199–201.

Ritter, L.S., and W.L. Silber, *Principles of Money, Banking and Financial Markets*, 3rd revised, enlarged ed. (New York: Basic Books, 1980).

Rizzo, M., ed., *Time, Uncertainty, and Disequilibrium: Exploration of Austrian Themes* (Lexington, Mass.: Lexington Books, 1979).

Robbins, L., *The Great Depression* (New York: Macmillan, 1934).

Robinson, J., *Collected Economic Papers* (London: Blackwell, 1960).

Roca Juan, J., "El depósito del dinero," *Comentarios al Código Civil y compilaciones forales,* Manuel Albaladejo, ed. (Madrid: Editorial Revista del Derecho Privado EDERSA, 1982), tome 22, vol. 1, pp. 246–55.

Rockwell, Jr., L.H. ed., *The Gold Standard: An Austrian Perspective,* introduction by L.B. Yeager (Lexington, Mass.: Lexington Books, 1985).

Rojo, L.A., *Keynes: su tiempo y el nuestro* (Madrid: Alianza Editorial, 1984).

——, *Renta, precios y balanza de pagos* (Madrid: Alianza Universidad, 1976).

——, *Teoría Económica III: Apuntes basados en las explicaciones de clase, Curso 70–71* (Madrid: Published by the author, 1973).

Romer, D., *Advanced Macroeconomics* (New York: McGraw Hill, 1996).

Röpke, W., *Economics of the Free Society,* P.M. Boarman, trans. (Grove City, Penn.: Libertarian Press, 1994; Chicago: Henry Regnery Co., 1963).

——, *Crises and Cycles* (London: William Hodge, 1936).

Rostovtzeff, M., *The Social and Economic History of the Roman Empire,* 2nd ed. (Oxford: Clarendon Press, 1957), vol. 2.

——, *The Social and Economic History of the Hellenistic World* (Oxford: Clarendon Press, 1953), vol. 1.

Rothbard, M.N., *America's Great Depression,* 5th ed. (Auburn, Ala.: Ludwig von Mises Institute, 2000).

——, "The Present State of Austrian Economics," *Journal des Économistes et des Études Humaines* 6, no. 1 (March 1995): 43–89; reprinted in *The Logic of Action I* (Cheltenham, England: Edward Elgar, 1997), p. 165.

——, *Wall Street, Banks, and American Foreign Policy* (Burlingame, Calif.: Center for Libertarian Studies, 1995).

——, *Economic Thought before Adam Smith,* vol. 1 of *An Austrian Perspective on the History of Economic Thought* (Aldershot, England: Edward Elgar, 1995).

——, *Classical Economics,* vol. 2 of *An Austrian Perspective on the History of Economic Thought* (Aldershot, England: Edward Elgar, 1995).

——, "The Solution," *The Freeman: Ideas on Liberty* (November 1995): 697–702.

——, *The Case Against the Fed* (Auburn, Ala.: Ludwig von Mises Institute, 1994).

——, *Man, Economy, and State: A Treatise on Economic Principles*, 3rd ed. (Auburn, Ala.: Ludwig von Mises Institute, 1993). The Scholar's Edition, *Man, Economy, and State with Power and Market* (Auburn, Ala.: Ludwig von Mises Institute, 2004).

——, "Aurophobia: or Free Banking on What Standard?" *Review of Austrian Economics* 6, no. 1 (1992): 98–108.

——, *The Case for a 100 Percent Gold Dollar* (Auburn, Ala.: Ludwig von Mises Institute, 1991).

——, *What Has Government Done to Our Money?* (Santa Ana, Calif.: Rampart College, 1974; Auburn Ala.: Ludwig von Mises Institute, 1990).

——, "The Other Side of the Coin: Free Banking in Chile," *Austrian Economics Newsletter* (Winter, 1989): 1–4.

——, "The Myth of Free Banking in Scotland," *Review of Austrian Economics* 2 (1988): 229–45.

——, "Timberlake on the Austrian Theory of Money: A Comment," *Review of Austrian Economics* 2 (1988): 179–87.

——, "The Case for a Genuine Gold Dollar," in *The Gold Standard*, L.H. Rockwell, Jr., ed. (Lexington, Mass.: Lexington Books, 1985), pp. 2–7.

——, "The Federal Reserve as a Cartelization Device: The Early Years: 1913–1930," Chapter 4 in *Money in Crisis: The Federal Reserve, The Economy and Monetary Reform*, B.N. Siegel, ed. (San Francisco, Calif.: Pacific Institute, 1984), pp. 89–136.

——, *The Mystery of Banking* (New York: Richardson and Snyder, 1983).

——, "Austrian Definitions of the Supply of Money," in *New Directions in Austrian Economics*, L.M. Spadaro, ed. (Kansas City, Mo.: Sheed Andrews and McMeel, 1978), pp. 143–56.

——, "New Light on the Prehistory of the Austrian School," in *The Foundations of Modern Austrian Economics*, E.G. Dolan, ed. (Kansas City, Mo.: Sheed and Ward, 1976), pp. 52–74.

——, "Inflation and the Creation of Paper Money," Chapter 26 in *Conceived in Liberty*, vol. 2, *"Salutary Neglect": The American Colonies in the First Half of the 18th Century* (New York: Arlington House, 1975).

——, *The Panic of 1819: Reactions and Policies* (New York and London: Columbia University Press, 1962).

——, "Milton Friedman Unraveled," *Journal of Libertarian Studies* 16, no. 4 (Fall, 2002): 37–54.

Rubio Sacristán, J.A., "La fundación del Banco de Amsterdam (1609) y la banca de Sevilla," *Moneda y crédito* (March 1948).

Rueff, J., "The Fallacies of Lord Keynes' General Theory," in *The Critics of Keynesian Economics*, H. Hazlitt, ed. (New York: Arlington House, 1977), pp. 239–63.

Ruiz Martín, F., *Pequeño capitalismo, gran capitalismo: Simón Ruiz y sus negocios en Florencia* (Barcelona: Editorial Crítica, 1990).

Salerno, J., "War and the Money Machine: Concealing the Costs of War Beneath the Veil of Inflation," Chapter 17 in *The Costs of War: America's Pyrrhic Victories*, J.V. Denson, ed. (New Brunswick, N.J. and London: Transaction Publishers, 1997), pp. 367–87.

——, "Mises and Hayek Dehomogenized," *Review of Austrian Economics* 6, no. 2 (1993): 113–46.

——, "Gold Standards: True and False," *Cato Journal: An Interdisciplinary Journal of Public Policy Analysis* 3, no. 1 (Spring, 1983): 239–67.

Salerno, J.T., and R.M. Ebeling, "An Interview with Professor Fritz Machlup," *Austrian Economics Newsletter* 3, no. 1 (Summer, 1980): 12.

Salin, P., "Macro-Stabilization Policies and the Market Process," in *Economic Policy and the Market Process: Austrian and Mainstream Economics*, K. Groenveld, J.A.M. Maks, and J. Muysken, eds. (Amsterdam: North-Holland, 1990), pp. 201–21.

——, *L'unité monétaire européene: au profit de qui?* (Paris: Economica, 1980).

——, "In Defense of Fractional Monetary Reserves," 7th Austrian Scholars Conference, Auburn, Alabama, March 30–31, 2001.

——, "Maurice Allais: un économiste liberal?" Forthcoming.

Samuelson, P.A., *Economics*, 8th ed. (New York: Macmillan, 1970; 11th ed., McGraw-Hill, 1980; 13th ed., 1989; 14th ed., 1992; 15th ed., 1995).

——, "Paradoxes in Capital Theory: A Summing Up," *Quarterly Journal of Economics* 80 (1966): 568–83.

Santillana, R., *Memoria histórica sobre los bancos nacional de San Carlos, Español de San Fernando, Isabel II, Nuevo de San Fernando, y de España* (Madrid: Banco de España, 1982).

Saravia de la Calle, L., *Instrucción de mercaderes* (Medina del Campo: Pedro de Castro, 1544; Madrid: Colección de Joyas Bibliográficas, 1949).

Sardá, J., *La política monetaria y las fluctuaciones de la economía española en el siglo XIX* (Barcelona: Ediciones Ariel, 1970; Madrid: Consejo Superior de Investigaciones Científicas, Instituto de Economía "Sancho de Moncada," 1948).

Scaramozzino, P., *Omaggio a Bruno Leoni* (Milan: A. Guiffré, 1969).

Schubert, A. *The Credit-Anstalt Crisis of 1931* (Cambridge: Cambridge University Press, 1991).

Schuler, K., and L. White, "Free Banking History," in *The New Palgrave Dictionary of Money and Finance* (London: Macmillan, 1992), vol. 2, pp. 198–200.

Schumpeter, J.A., *The Theory of Economic Development* (Cambridge, Massachusetts: Harvard University Press, 1968); original German edition, *Theorie der Wirtschaftlichen Entwicklung: Eine Untersuchung über Unternehmergewinn, Kapital, Kredit, Zins und den Konjukturzyklus* (Munich and Leipzig: Verlag von Duncker Humblot, 1911).

——, *History of Economic Analysis* (Oxford and New York: Oxford University Press, 1954); Spanish edition (Barcelona: Editorial Ariel, 1994).

Schwartz, A.J., "The Theory of Free Banking," presented at the regional meeting of the Mont Pèlerin Society, Rio de Janeiro, September 5–8, 1993.

——, "Banking School, Currency School, Free Banking School," in *The New Palgrave: Dictionary of Money and Finance* (London: Macmillan, 1992), vol. 1, pp. 148–51.

Schwartz, P., "Macro y Micro," *Cinco Días* (Madrid, April 12, 1993): 3.

——, "El monopolio del banco central en la historia del pensamiento económico: un siglo de miopía en Inglaterra," in *Homenaje a Lucas Beltrán* (Madrid: Editorial Moneda y Crédito, 1982).

Selgin, G.A., "The Stability and Efficiency of Money Supply under Free Banking," *Journal of Institutional and Theoretical Economics* 143 (1987): 435–56; reprinted in *Free Banking*, vol. 3, *Modern Theory and Policy*, L.H. White, ed. (Aldershot, England: Edward Elgar, 1993), pp. 45–66.

——, *Less Than Zero: The Case for a Falling Price Level in a Growing Economy*, Hobart Paper 132 (London: Institute of Economic Affairs [I.E.A.], 1997).

——, "Free Banking and Monetary Control," *Economic Journal* 104, no. 427 (November 1994): 1449–59.

——, "Are Banking Crises a Free-Market Phenomenon?" presented at the regional meeting of the Mont Pèlerin Society, Rio de Janeiro, September 5–8, 1993.

——, "Short-Changed in Chile: The Truth about the Free-Banking Episode," *Austrian Economics Newsletter* (Spring–Winter, 1990).

——, *The Theory of Free Banking: Money Supply under Competitive Note Issue* (Totowa, N.J.: Rowman and Littlefield, 1988).

Selgin, G.A., and L.H. White, "In Defense of Fiduciary Media or, We are *Not* Devo(lutionists), We are Misesians!" *Review of Austrian Economics* 9, no. 2 (1996): 83–107.

——, "How Would the Invisible Hand Handle Money?" *Journal of Economic Literature* 32, no. 4 (December 1994): 1718–49.

Sennholz, H.F., *Money and Freedom* (Spring Mills, Penn.: Libertarian Press, 1985).

Serrera Contreras, P.L., *El contrato de deposito mercantil* (Madrid: Marcial Pons, 2001).

Shah, P.J., "The Option Clause in Free Banking Theory and History: A Reappraisal," *Review of Austrian Economics* 10, no. 2 (1997): 1–25.

Sherman, H.J., *Introduction to the Economics of Growth, Unemployment and Inflation* (New York: Appleton, 1964).

Shorter Oxford English Dictionary, 3rd ed., 2 vols. (Oxford: Oxford University Press, 1973).

Siegel, B.N., ed., *Money in Crisis: The Federal Reserve, the Economy and Monetary Reform* (San Francisco, Calif.: Pacific Institute for Public Policy Research, 1984).

Sierra Bravo, R., *El pensamiento social y económico de la Escolástica desde sus orígenes al comienzo del catolicismo social* (Madrid: Consejo Superior de Investigaciones Científicas, Instituto de Sociología "Balmes," 1975).

Simons, H.C., *Economic Policy for a Free Society* (Chicago: University of Chicago Press, 1948).

——, "Rules versus Authorities in Monetary Policy," *Journal of Political Economy* 44, no. 1 (February 1936): 1–30; reprinted as Chapter 7 in *Economic Policy for a Free Society*, pp. 160–83.

——, "A Positive Program for Laissez-Faire: Some Proposals for a Liberal Economic Policy," original version, "Public Policy Pamphlet" no. 15, H.D. Gideonse (Chicago: University of Chicago Press, 1934); reprinted as Chapter 2 in *Economic Policy for a Free Society*.

Skidelsky, R., *John Maynard Keynes: The Economist as Saviour, 1920–1937* (London: Macmillan, 1992).

Skousen, M., *The Economics of a Pure Gold Standard* (Auburn, Ala.: Praxeology Press, [1977] 1988; New York: Foundation for Economic Education, 1996).

——, "I Like Hayek: How I Use His Model as a Forecasting Tool," presented at the general meeting of the Mont Pèlerin Society, Cannes, France, September 25–30, 1994.

——, "Who Predicted the 1929 Crash?" in *The Meaning of Ludwig von Mises*, J.M. Herbener, ed. (Amsterdam: Kluwer Academic Publishers, 1993), pp. 247–84.

——, ed., *Dissent on Keynes: A Critical Appraisal of Keynesian Economics* (New York and London: Praeger, 1992).

——, *Economics on Trial: Lies, Myths and Realities* (Homewood, Ill.: Business One Irwin, 1991).

——, *The Structure of Production* (London and New York: New York University Press, 1990).

——, "The Free Market Response to Keynesian Economics," in *Dissent on Keynes*.

——, "The Perseverance of Paul Samuelson's *Economics*," *Journal of Economic Perspectives* 2, no. 2 (Spring, 1997).

——, *Vienna and Chicago: Friends or Foes* (Washington, D.C.: Capital Press, 2005).

Smith, A., *An Inquiry into the Nature and Causes of the Wealth of Nations* (London: W. Strahan and T. Cadell in the Strand, 1776); E. Cannan, ed. (New York: Modern Library, [1937] 1965); The Glasgow Ed. (Oxford: Oxford University Press, 1976).

Smith, V.C., *The Rationale of Central Banking and the Free Banking Alternative* (Indianapolis, Ind.: Liberty Press, 1990).

Soddy, F., *Wealth, Virtual Wealth and Debt* (New York: E.P. Dutton, 1927).

Soto, D. de, *De iustitia et iure*. (Salamanca: Andreas Portonarijs, 1556); bilingual Latin/Spanish ed., 5 vols. (Madrid: Instituto de Estudios Políticos, 1968).

Sousmatzian Ventura, E., "¿Puede la intervención gubernamental evitar las crisis bancarias?" *Revista de la Superintendencia de bancos y otras instituciones financieras* (Caracas, Venezuela), no. 1 (April–June 1994): 66–87.

Spadaro, L.M., ed., *New Directions in Austrian Economics* (Kansas City, Mo.: Sheed Andrews and McMeel, 1978).

Sprague, O.B.W., *History of Crises and the National Banking System* (1910; Fairfield, N.J.: Augustus M. Kelley, 1977).

Sraffa, P., "Doctor Hayek on Money and Capital," *Economic Journal* 42 (1932): 42–53.

——, *Production of Commodities by Means of Commodities: Prelude to a Critique of Economic Theory* (Cambridge: Cambridge University Press, 1960).

Stankiewicz, T., "Investment under Socialism," *Communist Economies* 1, no. 2 (1989): 123–30.

Steuart, J., *An Enquiry into the Principles of Political Oeconomy: Being an Essay on the Science of Domestic Policy in Free Nations* (London: A. Miller and T. Cadell in the Strand, 1767).

Stigler, G.J., *Production and Distribution Theories* (London: Transaction Publishers, 1994).

Stiglitz, J.E., "Risk, Incentives and Insurance: The Pure Theory of Moral Hazard," *The Geneva Papers on Risk and Insurance* 26 (1983): 4–33.

Strigl, R.v., *Kapital und Produktion* (Munich and Vienna: Philosophia Verlag, [1934] 1982); English translation *Capital and Production*, M.R. and H.H. Hoppe, trans., J.G. Hülsmann, ed. (Auburn, Ala.: Mises Institute, 2000).

——, *Curso medio de economía*, Spanish translation by M. Sánchez Sarto (Mexico: Fondo de Cultura Económica, 1941).

Summers, L., *Understanding Unemployment* (Cambridge, Mass.: The MIT Press, 1990).

Tamames, R., *Fundamentos de estructura económica*, 10th rev. ed. (Madrid: Alianza Universidad, 1992).

Taussig, F.W., *Principles of Economics*, 3rd ed. (New York: Macmillan, 1939), vol. 1.

Tavlas, G.S., "Chicago, Harvard and the Doctrinal Foundations of Monetary Economics," *Journal of Political Economy* 105, no. 1 (February 1997): 153–77.

Taylor, J., *Construction Construed and Constitutions Vindicated* (Richmond, Va.: Shepherd and Polland, 1820; New York: Da Capa Press, 1970).

Tedde de Lorca, P., *El banco de San Carlos, 1782–1829* (Madrid: Banco de España y Alianza Editorial, 1988).

——, "La banca privada española durante la Restauración, 1874–1914," in *La banca española en la Restauración* (Madrid: Servicio de Estudios del Banco de España, 1974), vol. 1.

Tellkampf, J.L., *Die Prinzipien des Geld- und Bankwesens* (Berlin: Puttkammer and Mühlbrecht, 1867).

——, *Essays on Law Reform, Commercial Policies, Banks, Penitentiaries, etc., in Great Britain and the United States of America* (London: Williams and Norgate, 1859).

Temin, P., and H.-J. Voth, "Riding the South Sea Bubble," *American Economic Review* 94, no. 5 (December 2004): 1654–68.

Termes Carreró, R., *Carlos V y uno de sus banqueros: Jacobo Fugger* (Madrid: Asociación de Caballeros del Monasterio de Yuste, 1993).

Thatcher, M., *The Downing Street Years* (New York: HarperCollins, 1993).

Thies, C.F., "The Paradox of Thrift: RIP," *Cato Journal* 16, no. 1 (Spring–Summer, 1996): 119–27.

Thorbecke, W., "The Distributional Effects of Disinflationary Monetary Policy" (George Mason University, 1995).

Thornton, H., "Evidence given before the Lords' Committee of Secrecy appointed to inquire into causes on which produced the Order of Council of the 27th February 1797"; reprinted in *An Inquiry into the Nature and Effects of the Paper Credit of Great Britain,* F.A. Hayek, ed. (Fairfield, N.J.: Augustus M. Kelley, 1978), p. 303.

——, *An Inquiry into the Nature and Effects of the Paper Credit of Great Britain,* 1802; reprinted with an introduction by F.A. Hayek (Fairfield, N.J.: Augustus M. Kelley, 1978).

Timberlake, R., "The Government's Licence to Create Money," *Cato Journal: An Interdisciplinary Journal of Public Policy Analysis* 9, no. 2 (Fall, 1989): 302–21.

———, "A Reassessment of C.A. Phillips' Theory of Bank Credit," *History of Political Economy* 20, no. 2 (1988): 299–308.

———, "A Critique of Monetarist and Austrian Doctrines on the Utility and Value of Money," *Review of Austrian Economics* 1 (1987): 81–86.

———, "Private Production of Scrip-Money in the Isolated Community," *Journal of Money, Credit and Banking* 19 (October 4, 1987): 437–47.

———, "The Central Banking Role of Clearinghouse Associations," *Journal of Money, Credit and Banking* 16 (February 1984): 1–15.

Tobin, J., "Financial Innovation and Deregulation in Perspective," *Bank of Japan Monetary and Economic Studies* 3 (1985): 19–29.

Todd, S.C., *The Shape of Athenian Law* (Oxford: Clarendon Press, 1993).

Tooke, T., *A History of Prices and of the State of the Circulation from 1793–1837*, with an appendix by J. Pennington (London: Longman, 1838), vol. 2.

———. *An Inquiry into the Currency Principle* (London 1844).

Toribio Dávila, J.J., "Problemas éticos en los mercados financieros," presented at the *Encuentros sobre la dimensión ética de las instituciones y mercados financieros*, Fundación BBV, Madrid, June 1994.

Torre Saavedra, E. de la, R. García Villaverde, and R. Bornardell Lenzano, eds., *Contratos Bancarios* (Madrid: Editorial Cívitas, 1992).

Torrens, R., *A Letter to the Right Hon. Lord Viscount Melbourne, on the Causes of the Recent Derangement in the Money Market, and on Bank Reform* (London: Longman, Rees, Orme, Brown and Green, 1837).

Torrero Mañas, A., *La crisis del sistema bancario: lecciones de la experiencia de Estados Unidos* (Madrid: Editorial Cívitas, 1993).

Torres López, J., *Introducción a la economía política* (Madrid: Editorial Cívitas, 1992).

Tortella-Casares, G., *Banking, Railroads, and Industry in Spain, 1829–1874* (New York: Arno Press, 1977).

Trautwein, H-M., "Money, Equilibrium, and the Business Cycle: Hayek's Wicksellian Dichotomy," *History of Political Economy* 28, no. 1 (Spring, 1996): 27–55.

———, "Hayek's Double Failure in Business Cycle Theory: A Note," in *Money and Business Cycles: The Economics of F.A. Hayek*, M. Colonna and H. Hagemann, eds. (Aldershot, England: Edward Elgar, 1994), vol. 1, chap. 4, pp. 74–81.

Trigo Portela, J., "Historia de la Banca," in *Enciclopedia práctica de la banca* (Barcelona: Editorial Planeta, 1989), vol. 6, chap. 3.

Tufte, E.R., *Political Control of the Economy* (Princeton, N.J.: Princeton University Press, 1978).

Tugan-Baranovsky, M., *Industrial Crises in Contemporary Britain* (St. Petersburg, 1894). Second Russian edition translated into French by Joseph Schapiro, *Les crises industrielles en Angleterre* (Paris: M. Giard & E. Briere, 1913).

——, *Las crisis industriales en Inglaterra* (Madrid: La España Moderna, 1912).

Usabiaga Ibáñez, C., and J.M. O'Kean Alonso, *La nueva macroeconomía clásica: una aproximación metodológica al pensamiento económico* (Madrid: Ediciones Pirámide, 1994).

Usher, A.P., *The Early History of Deposit Banking in Mediterranean Europe* (Cambridge, Mass.: Harvard University Press, 1943).

Valpuesta Gastaminza, E.M., "Depósitos bancarios de dinero: libretas de ahorro," in *Contratos bancarios*, E. de la Torre Saavedra, R. García Villaverde, and R. Bonardell Lenzano, eds. (Madrid: Editorial Cívitas, 1992).

Valmaña Ochaita, A., *El depósito irregular en la jurisprudencia romana* (Madrid: Edisofer, 1996).

Van Zijp, R., *Austrian and New Classical Business Cycle Theory* (Aldershot, England: Edward Elgar, 1994).

Viaña Remis, E., *Lecciones de contabilidad nacional* (Madrid: Editorial Cívitas, 1993).

Vilar, P.A., *History of Gold and Money, 1450–1920* (London: NLB, 1976).

Wainhouse, C.E., "Empirical Evidence for Hayek's Theory of Economic Fluctuations," Chapter 2 in *Money in Crisis: the Federal Reserve, the Economy and Monetary Reform*, B.N. Siegel, ed. (San Francisco, Calif.: Pacific Institute for Public Policy Research, 1984).

——, "Hayek's Theory of the Trade Cycle: The Evidence from the Time Series" (Ph.D. dissertation, New York University, 1982).

Walker, A., *The Science of Wealth: A Manual of Political Economy Embracing the Laws of Trade, Currency and Finance* (Boston, Mass.: Little Brown, [1867] 1869).

West, E.G., *Adam Smith and Modern Economics: From Market Behaviour to Public Choice* (Aldershot, England: Edward Elgar, 1990).

White, L.H., "What Has Been Breaking U.S. Banks?" *Critical Review* 7, nos. 2–3 (Spring–Summer, 1993): 321–34.

——, ed., *Free Banking*, vol. 1, *19th Century Thought;* vol. 2, *History;* vol. 3, *Modern Theory and Policy* (Aldershot, England: Edward Elgar, 1993).

——, ed., *The Crisis in American Banking* (New York: New York University Press, 1993).

——, "Mises on Free Banking and Fractional Reserves," Chapter 35 in *A Man of Principle: Essays in Honour of Hans F. Sennholz* (Grove City, Penn.: Grove City College Press, 1992), pp. 517–33.

——, *Competition and Currency: Essays on Free Banking and Money* (New York: New York University Press, 1989).

——, *Free Banking in Britain: Theory, Experience and Debate, 1800–1845* (London and New York: Cambridge University Press, 1984).

Wicker, E., *The Banking Panics of the Great Depression* (Cambridge: Cambridge University Press, 1996 and 2000).

Wicksell, K., *Geldzins und Güterpreise: Eine Studie über die den Tauschwert des Geldes bestimmenden Ursachen* (Jena: Verlag von Gustav Fischer, 1898); English translation by R.F. Kahn, *Interest and Prices: A Study of the Causes Regulating the Value of Money* (London: Macmillan, 1936; New York: Augustus M. Kelley, 1965).

——, *Lectures on Political Economy* (London: Routledge and Kegan Paul, 1935 and 1950), vols. 1 and 2.

Wilson, J., *Capital, Currency and Banking* (London: *The Economist*, 1847).

Winiecki, J., *The Distorted World of Soviet-Type Economies* (London: Routledge, [1988] 1991).

Wood, C.J., and R.N. Woods, eds., *Friedrich A. Hayek: Critical Assessments* (London and New York: Routledge, 1991).

Wood, G.A., et al., *Central Bank Independence: What is it and What Will it Do for Us?* (London: Institute of Economic Affairs, 1993).

Wubben, E.F.M., "Austrian Economics and Uncertainty," presented at the First European Conference on Austrian Economics (Maastricht, April 1992).

Yeager, L.B., ed., *In Search of a Monetary Constitution* (Cambridge, Mass.: Harvard University Press, 1962).

——, "The Perils of Base Money," *Review of Austrian Economics* 14, no. 4 (2001): 251–66.

——, *The Fluttering Veil: Essays on Monetary Disequilibrium*, G. Selgin, ed. (Indianapolis, Ind.: Liberty Fund, 1997).

Yeager, L.B., and R. Greenfield, "Competitive Payments Systems: Comment," *American Economic Review* 4, no. 76 (September 1986): 848–49.

——, "A Laissez-Faire Approach to Monetary Stability," *Journal of Money, Credit, and Banking* 3, no. 15 (August 1983): 302–15; reprinted in *Free Banking*, L.H. White, ed., vol. 3, chap. 11, pp. 180–95.

Zahka, W.J., *The Nobel Prize Economics Lectures* (Aldershot, England: Avebury, 1992).

INDEX OF SUBJECTS

INDEX OF NAMES